AF352732

The Life and Work of John C. Campbell

THE LIFE AND WORK OF
JOHN C. CAMPBELL

OLIVE DAME CAMPBELL

EDITED BY
ELIZABETH MCCUTCHEN WILLIAMS

UNIVERSITY PRESS OF KENTUCKY

Editorial and Sales Offices: The University Press of Kentucky
663 South Limestone Street, Lexington, Kentucky 40508-4008
www.kentuckypress.com

Cataloging-in-Publication data available from the Library of Congress

ISBN 978-0-8131-6854-8 (hardcover : alk. paper)
ISBN 978-0-8131-6855-5 (pdf)
ISBN 978-0-8131-6856-2 (epub)

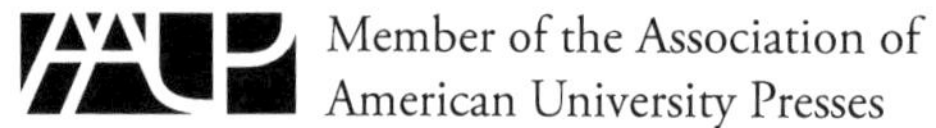

This edition of John C. Campbell's biography

is dedicated to those who still write letters.

Contents

Foreword

The following piece was included in the typescript copy of the biography in the Campbell Papers at the Southern Historical Collection at the University of North Carolina at Chapel Hill. It is assumed to have been written by Lois Bacon.

On her death in 1954, Olive Dame Campbell left a partly completed biography of her husband, John Charles Campbell, based for the most part on his correspondence and her diaries. Her family wished to complete a working version, reproduce it, and place copies in certain libraries so that students of the Southern Highlands could use the source material therein. Edith R. Canterbury, Mr. Campbell's secretary in the last months of his life, a close friend of Mrs. Campbell's thereafter, [who] was informally named literary executor, devoted herself to the manuscript. She completed the first draft, agreed on suggested revisions with the other literary executors, Louise Pitman and Lois Bacon, and had begun editing the final version when she died in 1963. For that editing, Lois Bacon had responsibility.

Mrs. Campbell was unusually well equipped to write of her husband's work in the southern mountains, for she shared in it from the time they were married, assisting in all its phases and making her own special contribution through her interest in and collection of folk ballads then still sung in the mountains, an interest that led directly to the saving of these ballads for future generations. When her husband died, she continued his work, carrying out some of his most cherished plans, notably the completion of a study in depth of the mountain people, unsentimental and unsensational, by editing his manuscript *The Southern Highlander and His Homeland,* which was published by the Russell Sage Foundation in 1921; an investigation of the folk schools of Denmark as a type of education which would help build up the rural sections of the mountains, by making an on-the-spot study and publishing her findings for general use in *The Danish Folk School,* which appeared in 1928; and establishing in 1925 the John C. Campbell Folk School in Brasstown, North Carolina, that aimed at developing individuals and inspiring a community life and social order that might be found satisfying to the young people in the mountains.

She not only established the John C. Campbell Folk School, but, as its director until 1947, she applied on a pilot basis many of the plans and ideas that Mr. Campbell had advocated for adoption by mountain schools. How his approach and hers succeeded was well expressed by the directors of the John C. Campbell Folk School after her death when they said:

We are mindful of the unique and far-reaching pioneer work of her husband, John C. Campbell in the mountain region . . . to which she gave her full interest and large gifts to carry on after his death in 1919. Her vision for this work was the outgrowth of his own, but her endorsement of mind, of heart, and of courage enabled her to become a creative builder and a leading spirit throughout the Highland region as well as in this School. Her vision designed the building of the School in order to build thereby better rural living. Her wisdom enabled it to develop a program for young adults, not only in the classroom but in many aspects of living. Her broad knowledge gained here and in Scandinavia gave impetus to community cooperatives and organization for sound economic growth. Her spirit set alight new thinking and new motives in young people who have come to the school year by year. She strengthened the local Church by her constant help. Her imagination and skill promoted handicraft in carving, weaving, woodworking, and iron-work which has brought satisfaction in the achievement of high artistic standards to our people, and distinction to our school. Her strength of character has carried the School through many problems and difficulties. Her generous spirit has shared with all who could use them her ideas and her experience. She built herself into the fabric of this community in a way that has spread her influence far beyond the bounds of Brasstown, and beyond the Southern Highland region.

The biography of her husband was Mrs. Campbell's last tribute to him and her last service to the Southern Highlands. While recognizing that work on the biography after her death was done out of devotion to her and respect for her wishes, her family cannot but feel inexpressibly grateful to Miss Canterbury for her efforts to bring the working version to completion. In the final editing, no attempt was made to check all the documents quoted back to the originals; those that remained are now with the Southern Historical Collection of the University of North Carolina at Chapel Hill. Nor was an attempt made to eliminate all duplication and inconsistency. Rough as it is, this working version nevertheless presents in readily accessible form the fruits of Mr. Campbell's long experience of mountains, his philosophy, ideals, ideas, and methods of work in seeking the goal he set himself—helping the mountain people to help themselves to a better, fuller life. Much of it has a modern sound and could well be applied to present-day plans and programs for Appalachia and other underdeveloped areas at home and abroad.

November 1967

Note on Editorial Method

The biography of John C. Campbell by Olive Dame Campbell is reproduced in this volume in a form as near as possible to the original copy housed in the John C. Campbell and Olive D. Campbell Papers in the Southern Historical Collection in the Wilson Library at the University of North Carolina at Chapel Hill. The text has been authenticated and is presented by the editor with minimal alterations for clarity.

This work is a companion to *Appalachian Travels: The Diary of Olive Dame Campbell.* It chronicles the effort made by the Campbells and other mountain workers to improve the lives of the mountaineers, among whom they lived and worked. The *Diary* includes considerably more notations than the biography. For the biography, already quite long, the editor added notes only where needed to clarify the content; the reader may consult the *Diary* for more information. The editor's summaries at the beginnings of the chapters have been added to help the reader quickly find discussions of the people and events of personal interest.

True to the writing style of her day, Olive Campbell often failed to provide full names; personal names were sometimes omitted or given in various forms. When the correct spelling of a name is known, errors are silently corrected; for partial names, the full name, if known, is supplied in brackets: [ ]. The index includes the full names and variations, if known. The initials JCC, ODC, and EMW are used in the text by the author and by the editor as abbreviations.

Edits are minimal and in accordance with *The Chicago Manual of Style,* 16th edition, and the house style of the University Press of Kentucky. Some punctuation, grammatical, and typographical errors are silently corrected as needed. Spelling, hyphenation, capitalization, and number style are modernized for clarity and ease of reading. The foreword and certain extracts were edited more lightly. The formatting of the text and the annotations follows *The Chicago Manual of Style,* 16th edition; and *Editing Historical Documents,* by Michael E. Stevens and Steven E. Burg (Walnut Creek, CA: Altamira Press, 1997), served as a guide to customary methods for reproducing historical documents.

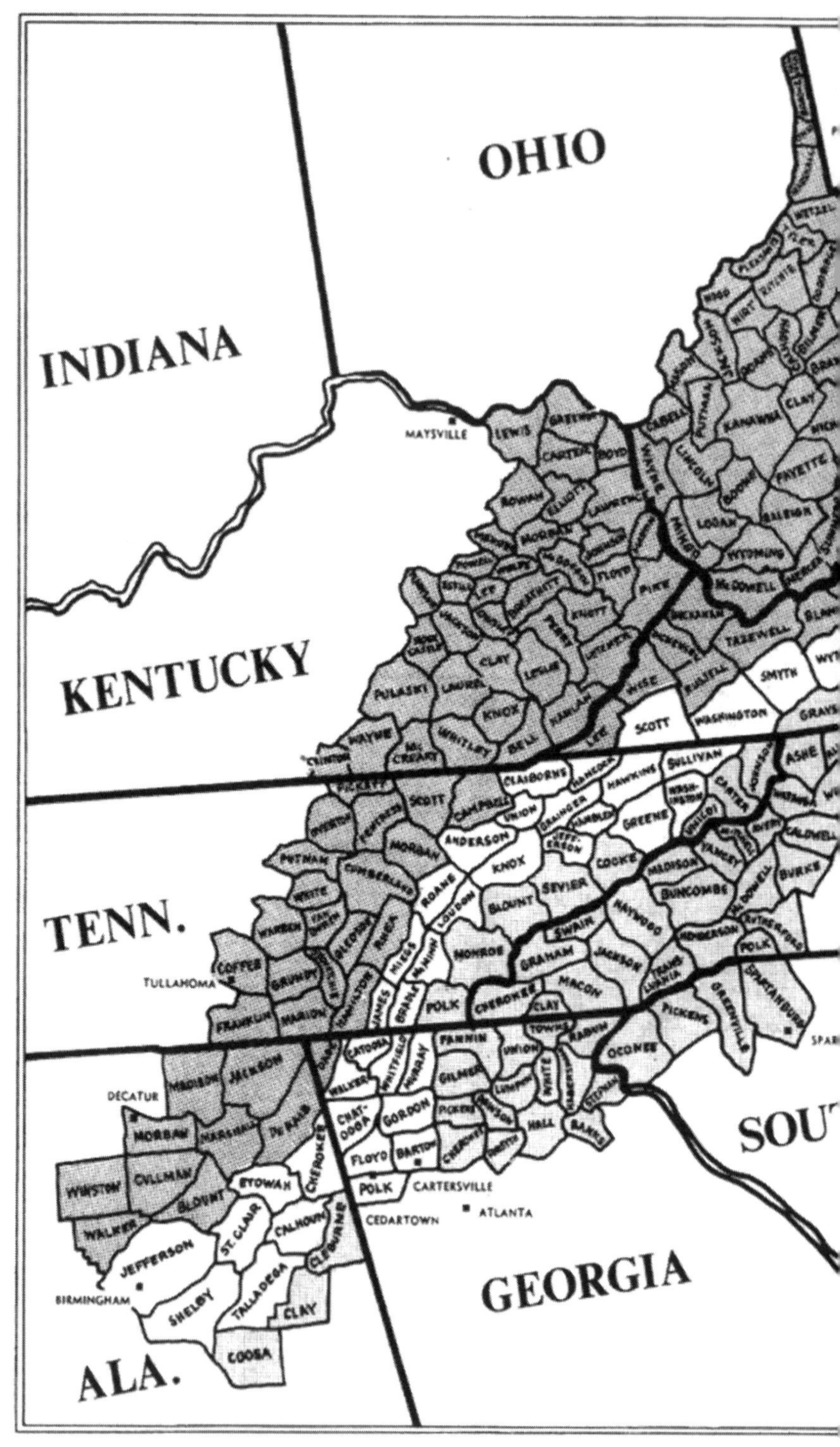
OHIO
INDIANA
KENTUCKY
TENN.
ALA.
GEORGIA
SOUT
MAYSVILLE
TULLAHOMA
DECATUR
CARTERSVILLE
ATLANTA
CEDARTOWN
BIRMINGHAM
SPAR
LEWIS
GREENUP
CARTER
BOYD
WAYNE
CABELL
LINCOLN
KANAWHA
CLAY
FAYETTE
ROWAN
ELLIOTT
LAWRENCE
MINGO
LOGAN
BOONE
RALEIGH
WYOMING
MORGAN
JOHNSON
MARTIN
FLOYD
PIKE
MCDOWELL
MERCER
BLUEFIELD
MAGOFFIN
KNOTT
BUCHANAN
TAZEWELL
LETCHER
DICKENSON
SMYTH
WYT
CLAY
LESLIE
WISE
RUSSELL
GRAYSON
PULASKI
LAUREL
KNOX
BELL
LEE
SCOTT
WASHINGTON
GRAYS
WAYNE
MCCREARY
WHITLEY
CLAIBORNE
HAWKINS
SULLIVAN
ASHE
CLINTON
PICKETT
SCOTT
CAMPBELL
UNION
GRAINGER
HAMBLEN
GREENE
UNICOI
CARTER
JOHNSON
WATAUGA
FENTRESS
ANDERSON
JEFFERSON
COCKE
MADISON
YANCEY
CALDWELL
OVERTON
MORGAN
KNOX
PUTNAM
ROANE
SEVIER
BUNCOMBE
BURKE
WHITE
CUMBERLAND
LOUDON
BLOUNT
HAYWOOD
MCDOWELL
WARREN
VAN BUREN
BLEDSOE
RHEA
MONROE
SWAIN
GRAHAM
JACKSON
TRANSYLVANIA
RUTHERFORD
COFFEE
GRUNDY
MEIGS
MARION
GRAHAM
MACON
POLK
SPARTANBURG
FRANKLIN
MARION
SEQUATCHIE
HAMILTON
BRADLEY
POLK
CHEROKEE
CLAY
TOWNS
RABUN
PICKENS
GREENVILLE
OCONEE
MADISON
JACKSON
DEKALB
DADE
CATOOSA
WHITFIELD
MURRAY
FANNIN
UNION
WHITE
HABERSHAM
WALKER
GILMER
LUMPKIN
DECATUR
MADISON
JACKSON
CHATTOOGA
GORDON
PICKENS
HALL
DEKALB
MORGAN
MARSHALL
FLOYD
BARTOW
CHEROKEE
FORSYTH
CULLMAN
ETOWAH
CHEROKEE
POLK
WINSTON
BLOUNT
WALKER
ST. CLAIR
CALHOUN
CLEBURNE
JEFFERSON
TALLADEGA
SHELBY
CLAY
COOSA

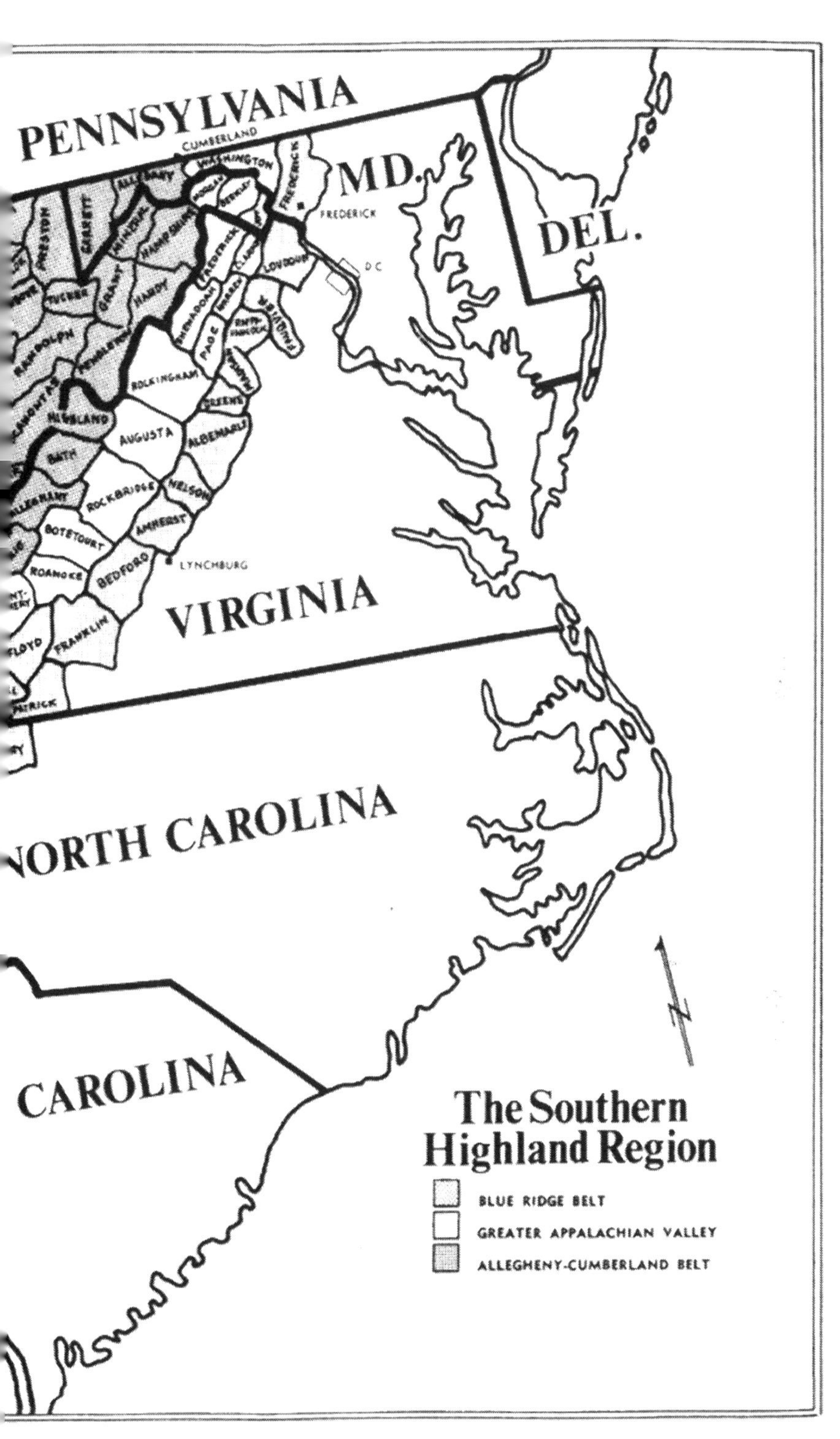

PENNSYLVANIA
MD.
DEL.
VIRGINIA
NORTH CAROLINA
CAROLINA
CUMBERLAND
WASHINGTON
ALLEGANY
GARRETT
PRESTON
MINERAL
GRANT
HAMPSHIRE
MORGAN
BERKELEY
FREDERICK
FREDERICK
TUCKER
HARDY
SHENANDOAH
FREDERICK
CLARKE
LOUDOUN
RANDOLPH
PENDLETON
PAGE
WARREN
RAPP.
FAUQUIER
POCAHONTAS
HIGHLAND
ROCKINGHAM
GREENE
BATH
AUGUSTA
ALBEMARLE
ALLEGHANY
ROCKBRIDGE
NELSON
BOTETOURT
AMHERST
ROANOKE
BEDFORD
FLOYD
FRANKLIN
PATRICK
LYNCHBURG
FREDERICK
DC
The Southern
Highland Region
BLUE RIDGE BELT
GREATER APPALACHIAN VALLEY
ALLEGHENY-CUMBERLAND BELT

Introduction

The Progressive Era barely made it into the Southern Highlands of Appalachia at the turn of the twentieth century. John Charles Campbell and the Russell Sage Foundation deserve much of the credit for the progress that was made, along with the other individuals, organizations, and government officials chronicled in this biography. Never before widely published, *The Life and Work of John C. Campbell* includes much of Campbell's correspondence with the Russell Sage Foundation and with denominational and educational co-workers in the region. Compiled by his wife, Olive Dame Campbell, it is a significant historical source. Her narrative, along with letters, details their work and life and the efforts made to enlist the support of educators, ministers, and government for the improvement of conditions in the Appalachian region—social, educational, religious, and economic. Indeed, the letters tell the story, which gives the text an immediacy it would not otherwise have.

After the Civil War, Protestant missionaries and social workers descended upon the mountain region to save the mountaineers. But those who came to minister to the mountaineers knew little about their real needs. Benevolent work in Appalachia was seen as an effort to establish a sense of community, like the settlement houses, to alter the social, cultural, and economic environment, and to encourage ways to live a "normal" life, justifying the move toward industrialization. Settlement houses, in both North and South, were providing careers for women who had attended northern colleges. Although many came to convert the heathens, they increasingly saw their role as social workers, proponents of progress, and sought "the alteration of mountain values." This approach implied that mountaineers might be better served by joining the new industrial movement and going to work in the factories and mills. There was a major clash between the cultures of the paternalistic reformers and the mountain people. Reformers believed that the culture and life in the hills was not moving with the progress of civilization and must be "uplifted" into the new century. But the social reforms of the Progressive Era came with a price that many mountaineers did not want to pay: the loss of their treasured independence and local culture.[1]

Born in Indiana in 1868 and raised in Wisconsin, John Campbell attended Phillip's Academy in Andover, Massachusetts, from 1886 to 1888.[2] There he discovered that many of the people in the Southern Appalachians were descendants of the Highland Scots, as he was. He then went to Williams College and realized that he wanted to do service work, so in 1892 he went back to the seminary in Andover. He did not want to go into the ministry, but, well trained, he taught for three years in Joppa, a small community in northern Alabama. He became concerned about the ways that many of the mountain missionaries were conducting their missions and schools and was convinced that mountain workers needed a venue where the various denominations could get together to discuss their work and to pursue a mutual goal, rather than competing with each other. Fortunately, he was also blessed with remarkable tact and diplomacy. As the correspondence in the biography demonstrates, his most persistent roadblock was denominationalism: disagreement and jealousies between the denominations represented in the communities, the churches, and the schools.

Campbell worked in the mountains for more than ten years, the first three (1895–1898) in the mountain school in Joppa, Alabama. Then, disillusioned by teaching in a school operated by the American Missionary Association, as there was never enough money to support the school, he went back to Wisconsin to teach for a year. He and his wife Grace missed the mountains, so in the spring of 1899, he took a job as principal of Pleasant Hill Academy in Tennessee. Pleasant Hill was a larger community and even had a doctor, but it was also an AMA school, and by 1900 he was looking for another place in the mountains. In 1902 he was asked to assume the presidency of J. S. Green College, soon to be renamed Piedmont College, in Demorest, Georgia. The college had local support but was still dependent on the fifteen hundred dollars a year it received from the AMA. As president, Campbell had the responsibility of raising the rest of the operating expenses and a permanent endowment fund.

After four years of extensive traveling, he was sent away by the college to try to recover from overwork and the recent death of his wife. A long ocean voyage was suggested, so he decided to visit his Scottish relatives in June of 1906. On this trip he met the lively, young Olive Campbell, who was from Massachusetts. She was on a long-anticipated trip with her mother and sister. He eventually joined the Dame family as they traveled around Scotland and England. By the end of the summer, Olive and John were nearly engaged; he was almost forty years old and she was twenty-four. They married the following March and set off for a honeymoon in Italy. He wanted to get back into mountain work and was hoping to find an organization to sponsor him, when he learned of the establishment in 1907 of the Russell Sage Foundation in New York, a group that sponsored benevolent projects. He thought it might be interested in his plan to do a systematic study, "a social survey," of the living conditions in the mountains of the South.[3]

The Russell Sage Foundation's role in the social survey movement was significant. Russell Sage was one of the richest men in America, and when he died in 1906, his wife, Olivia, quickly began investigating ways to spend the $65 million he had left her. Sage himself had been opposed to philanthropy, so it was ironic that his wife would spend her inheritance to support philanthropic endeavors. Educated at the famous Troy Female Seminary, she found an outlet for her charitable inclinations during her marriage by service in Christian women's societies, which offered opportunities for women to use their skills in raising and handling money and organizing and running their own organizations.[4] Foundations were then still a novelty in the United States, with only eight such organizations existing in 1907; only two of them held as much money as the Sage Foundation, and none were as active in the field.[5] A major player in the national movement, the Sage Foundation sought "to alleviate poverty through the professionalism of social work, the study of social problems, the shaping of legislation, and the creation of private agencies designed to meet specific social needs."[6]

Mrs. Sage planned to create a center for the study of social problems and for promoting cooperation among charitable organizations. "Every member of the Board of Trustees was selected for his or her ability to contribute to the broad purpose of defining and studying social problems."[7] John Glenn, the Foundation's first general director, was a dedicated reformer. He had served as president of the National Conference of Charities and Corrections in 1901. At the time of his election as general director of the Foundation, he was president of the Board of Supervisors of City Charities of Baltimore, chairman of the executive committee of the Baltimore Charity Organization Society, and a lecturer at Johns Hopkins University.[8] Earlier, he had been active in Protestant home missions work in West Virginia, exemplifying the Foundation's predilection for linking reform movements with religious faith and other philanthropic traditions, combining material aid and the raising of the standard of living. His wife, Mary Willcox Glenn, shared his dedication; she considered social work a natural part of religion.[9]

In 1908 Theodore Roosevelt's Country Life movement and the Progressive movement, both supported by the Russell Sage Foundation, were closely allied with the social survey movement. But instead of trying to better social conditions in the cities, as the social surveys tried to do, their surveys were designed to keep people from leaving rural areas. The surveys were conducted by a group appointed by Roosevelt, "two dozen men who mirrored his own image: endlessly energetic, confident, self-proclaimed Progressives."[10] Trying to prevent the exit of the younger, more adaptable rural dwellers to the cities, the Country Life movement intended to increase the efficiency and appeal of farming by bringing in electricity and running water and improving rural roads. Its surveys collected data on farm production, farm life, housing, health, sanitation, and the preferences and opinions of rural residents. This volume contains copious correspondence between Campbell and leaders of the movement, notably Dr. Warren Wilson, the controversial superintendent of the Country Life Department of the Presbyterian Church, USA (Northern).

In May 1908, the National Conference of Charities and Correction met in Richmond, Virginia. Mrs. John M. Glenn was chairman of the section on needy families. The program included a discussion of social and economic conditions in the Southern Appalachian region, and Mrs. Glenn invited several workers in the field, including John C. Campbell. At the time, Campbell had been involved in educational work across Appalachia for thirteen years and was greatly concerned about conditions in the area. In a letter to Mrs. Glenn, Campbell outlined his plan to "prepare maps, routes, and gather data" to compile a comprehensive study of the needs of the Appalachian people. He wanted to outfit a wagon for himself and his wife, a primitive kind of Winnebago, and use it to travel around the region, get to know the people in their homes, and talk to the school superintendents, teachers, missionaries, and doctors who were working among them. Campbell asked for money solely to cover expenses. Eventually, John Glenn and the Executive Committee of the Foundation agreed to provide a grant of three thousand dollars to study the "Southern Mountain communities."[11]

Under the auspices of the Russell Sage Foundation, John Campbell set out in 1908 to travel across the entire region to determine the true state of the living conditions of the people and to collect factual data to discover what their needs were and the best ways to fulfill them. Seventeen separate denominations, both northern and southern, were operating church-related mission schools; there were public schools in certain sections; but there was little or no cooperation or communication between them. As Campbell saw it, the question was what would be "the best and most speedy way" to provide "educational opportunities for the people in the rural highlands."[12] He had learned from experience about the best way to educate mountaineers and help them adapt to their surroundings.

Campbell's designation of the Southern Highlands effectively recognized the independent existence of the region and, furthermore, implied that the disparity between mountain life and life in the rest of America was merely another instance of the normal disparity between life among highlanders and lowlanders.[13] To constructively help the people, Campbell believed that the native culture of Appalachia must be accepted as an immutable fact of life; the most serious mistake that social workers and missionaries made was assuming that what was good for the city was good for the highlands. Mountaineers, for instance, were insulted when mission workers considered them "heathens." Their way of expressing their faith was simply different. Deborah McCauley observed, "Like other sensitive observers, Campbell picked up on the central place of the 'heart' in mountain religion and the pronounced role of intuitive discernment and non-rational religious experience."[14]

For personal or professional reasons, people were often encouraged to think of Appalachia as a place of "otherness," or as a "land apart." William Goodall Frost, inaugurated as president of Berea College in 1893, was one who emphasized the homogeneity of conditions rather than acknowledging patterns of real diversity in the region. Frost began his work in the mountains of Kentucky to bring opportunities for education to the mountaineers. He considered himself a "principal spokesman for the 'misunderstood' mountain people" and wanted Berea to be the foremost exponent of mountain work.[15] This biography includes much of the correspondence between Frost and Campbell, tracing their debate over the best course for the benefit of the people. Campbell and John Glenn of the Sage Foundation wondered at Frost's motives in wanting a more active part in the Conference of the Southern Mountains. From the beginning Frost felt the conference should take place in Berea, where, incidentally, it finally went, after Campbell's death in 1919, when the office of the Southern Highland Division closed.[16]

Campbell wanted his survey to be comprehensive, to collect empirical data about the demographic, economic, educational, and occupational characteristics of the geographical area as a whole. He was the first to define the region and drew what some consider the quintessential map, with three separate areas—the Blue Ridge, the Greater Appalachian Valley, and the Allegheny-Cumberland belts—each with its own characteristics (see map). Campbell saw the differences between the various parts and peoples of Appalachia, the mountains and the valleys, the rural and the urban, the farmers and the factory or mine workers. It was obvious to him that programs to improve the conditions in the region would have to be customized to meet the needs of a population that was neither coherent nor homogeneous.[17] After several years of investigation, the Southern Highlands Division was established and headquarters were set up in Asheville, North Carolina, in March 1913, with Campbell as director.[18] Campbell and the Southern Highlands Division were virtually synonymous, working to increase social cooperation while trying to improve the quality of life in the mountains.

The establishment of the Southern Highlands Division brought many requests for information about the Southern Highlands. An editor of the Sage Foundation tried to prepare Campbell's report for publication in 1913 and presented suggestions, some of which "seemed to indicate a desire for more picturesque and extreme, if not sensational, treatment of his theme." Campbell replied, expressing his point of view on the publication of his research: "There are certain things that I must not do and other things that I cannot do. It is necessary for me to keep always before me the fact that my work is now to be of a constructive kind. . . . When I am asked to address mountain audiences, I speak very frankly and do not hesitate to strike from the shoulder on moon-shining, selling votes, impurity and other failings. . . . They welcome me back always, but if I should go out of the mountains and publish those things, I could never work again with them."[19] The Southern Highlands Division published only one report written by Campbell, *The Future of the Church and Independent Schools in Our Southern Highlands.* At the annual meeting of the National Child Labor Committee in 1913, Campbell delivered an address on the relative merits of life in the mountains and in mill villages, and for the Conference of Southern Mountain Workers, he wrote a pamphlet, *The Southern Highlands,* describing the needs evident in the region and the qualifications one should have to take on mountain work.[20]

In *The Southern Highlander and His Homeland,* Campbell wrote: "The Highland country is in truth a land of paradoxes and contradictions, because here in a restricted area are taking place all the changes that are going on in the world elsewhere. . . . Constant qualification is necessary." John Alexander Williams agreed in *Appalachia: A History,* "In contrast to most other writers, Campbell emphasized the diversity of Appalachia, both in its class structure and its geographic features." Further, Williams suggested that if Campbell had lived longer, he might have been able to further dispel the prevalent misconceptions of the period. "Had scholars followed up his observations on the differences between town and country . . . or the class differences between bottomland, cove, and branchwater farmers, the social dimensions of Appalachian history would not have remained unexplored for the next fifty years."[21]

In the pamphlet for the Russell Sage Foundation, Campbell outlined some of his dreams for the improvement of conditions in the highlands. He wrote that he wished more church and independent schools in the region would adapt their programs to a mountain environment. As noted in his letters, he agreed with the General Education Board that public schools should be introduced in as many locations as possible, and he hoped that they would "work toward the ideal of a better rural life through church and other community activities, rather than purely academic activities." He admired the principles and purpose of folk schools. The worst mistakes that schools made, Campbell thought, had "arisen from the assumption that what was good for the city school, or the school in the lowland rural sections . . . was, without change, good for the highlands."[22]

Olive Campbell was herself a notable figure in Appalachian history. In her husband's memory, she established the John C. Campbell Folk School in Brasstown, North Carolina, to fulfill his dream of a school in the mountains that would support and educate mountaineers to be productive citizens in the community. Allen Eaton of the Sage Foundation, in his *Handicrafts of the Southern Highlands* (1937), said he saw her as instrumental in the promotion of crafts in Appalachia, and Philis Alvic also documented her central role in the craft revival in Appalachia in her 2003 book *Weavers of the Southern Highlands.* In addition to her other interests, Mrs. Campbell was an accomplished writer. She authored books and articles about education and folk schools in the mountains and cofounded the journal of the Council of the Southern Mountains, *Mountain Life and Work.* Moreover, after her husband's death, she assembled his notes and finished his book *The Southern Highlander and His Homeland,* the most thorough survey of the Appalachian region. First published in 1921, two years after Campbell's death, by the Russell Sage Foundation, it was reprinted in 1969 by the University Press of Kentucky and in 1973 by the Reprint Company in Spartanburg, South Carolina.

But Olive Campbell was best known as a ballad collector. In 1908, on the Campbells' first trip through the mountains, she was mesmerized when she heard a ballad sung by a local girl at Hindman Settlement School. She began to collect Appalachian folk songs and eventually persuaded Cecil Sharp, the eminent English scholar, that the Appalachian region was a storehouse of uncollected and undocumented songs; she and Sharp were two of the few collectors who noted the music of the songs as well as the words. Sharp was excited to see her work and made plans to come to Appalachia to follow up on her discovery. The story of Sharp's collecting in Appalachia is recorded in this biography, partly by means of the multitude of letters that were exchanged, across an ocean as well as across America. Sharp and his secretary Maud Karpeles became friends and collaborators of the Campbells, and in 1917 Olive Campbell and Sharp jointly published the first edition of *English Folk Songs from the Southern Appalachians: Comprising 122 Songs and Ballads, and 323 Tunes.*

John C. Campbell's impact on Appalachian history is seen in virtually every book published on the social, educational, or religious history of the region; his study *The Southern Highlander and His Homeland* is a classic in Appalachian history. The suppositions of earlier historians who implied that Appalachian poverty and backwardness were due to poor genetic strains were refuted by compiling a record of the true origins of the mountain people and by describing the conditions that propagated false notions about them. John C. Inscoe wrote, "Campbell's characterization of the region was both more sophisticated and more balanced than those that preceded it. An odd but often effective mix of social science data and literary descriptions . . . his book recognizes and readily acknowledges both the region's geographical variables and how they shaped a far more diverse socioeconomic structure among southern Appalachians."[23]

In 1928, after Campbell's death, *Mountain Life and Work* devoted an issue to the celebration of his life and work. One of the articles was written by John F. Smith, a professor at Berea College, and entitled "This Was a Man." Smith wrote, "Often his good sense and sound judgment came into conflict with the petty sectarianism . . . of some mediocre theologian, but on such occasions his calmness never deserted him. . . . His love for his people amounted to a dominant passion in his life." Campbell knew that mountain people needed ways to help themselves more than they needed outsiders to help them: "He had a profound understanding of human nature. . . . For some workers in the mountains he had great respect. . . . For others he had a sort of benevolent disgust, for he knew that their methods were wrong and that their labors would be in vain." Knowing that the mountain people had often been misrepresented by self-serving or misdirected missionaries, educators, fiction writers, and journalists, Campbell wanted to correct the impressions they had made so that the rest of the country would know the truth.[24]

John C. Campbell was an extraordinary individual, an intelligent, perceptive, thoughtful man, whose convictions and ideas were ahead of his time and are still being discussed in the ongoing saga of Appalachian cultural, economic, social, and educational history. Olive Campbell also made significant contributions to the history of Appalachia, not the least of which is her biography of her husband, presented here. With literary skill and a flair for plot development, she tells an intriguing story: a personal, moving account of their work in the mountains, with recollections of the mountain country and the life they lived and the friends they made, as well as Campbell's correspondence with prominent educators, social workers, and religious leaders in Appalachia in the early part of the twentieth century. By creating the folk school in his memory, she applied his philosophy of education to a real-life situation. *The Life and Work of John C. Campbell,* the personal account of their work and life, flows effortlessly and is, in its entirety, an unofficial history of the important educational, religious, and social changes that were occurring in the Southern Highlands during the Progressive Era in the United States.

1

Family Background and Early Life, 1868–1895

John Charles Campbell was born in LaPorte, Indiana, but spent most of his boyhood in Wisconsin, where his father was master mechanic and division superintendent of the Wisconsin Central Railway. His mother was born in Germany, and the Campbells were originally from Scotland. Letters in this chapter from members of the family to each other describe the society of the Midwest at the end of the nineteenth century.

John attended Phillip's Academy in Andover, Massachusetts, where he was introduced to what became his life's work. He learned about Pleasant Hill Academy in the Cumberland Mountains of Tennessee and discovered that many of the people in the Southern Appalachians were descendants of the Highland Scots and therefore kin to him.

He then went to Williams College, and while there he realized that he wanted to go into some sort of service work rather than business, so he attended the seminary in Andover. After graduation he applied to the Presbyterian Church for a job as a minister and also applied for a position as principal at a new school that the American Missionary Association was opening in Joppa, Alabama. He was married in September of 1895 to Grace Buckingham before he left to begin his great adventure.

It was my intention to write, in this record of John C. Campbell's life, nothing which could not be substantiated by the written word. If I have not quite reached this legal consideration, I have, at least in the early chapters, come very close to it. The facts were outside my personal knowledge. A not-too-reliable memory of what he told me has had to be reinforced by letters, clippings, and, where possible, the memories of those who knew the Campbell family in former days.

The early years, however, set the stage for later happenings. One can hardly understand what has grown out of John Campbell's personality and influence unless he knows something of the man—his home and upbringing, his environment and education. Many times I have wished that I had set down the things he told me, in casual fashion, of his people and his boyhood surroundings. He was born in LaPorte, Indiana, on September 15, 1868; but all his stories were of Wisconsin, where his father, Gavin Campbell, moved in 1871 as master mechanic and division superintendent of the Wisconsin Central Railway. Temporarily situated at

Menasha, Mr. Campbell worked with the construction company which was building the railroad, while his wife waited impatiently at LaPorte with their three children: John, Gavin Junior, and Maggie. In 1873 he again moved, to Stevens Point, the geographical center of Wisconsin and the appointed seat of the Wisconsin Central Railway shops. Here he brought his family. Thus, from five years of age, John was brought up on the waning edge of the pioneer period in Wisconsin.

Certain facts of family history have been hard to establish. John told me, for example, that his mother, Barbara (Kipp) Campbell, was born in Germany near the Black Forest region—as I remember it, not far from Stuttgart. Mrs. Eda Nebelthau Gilpatrick, one of Barbara Campbell's nieces and daughter of her sister Anna (Kipp) Nebelthau, wrote me in 1947, not long before her death:

In answer to your questions, I am sorry that we can give you so little information about Aunt Campbell. The Kipp family came over (from Germany) to this country in about 1851 or 1852. Mother was about eleven or twelve, and Aunt Campbell three or four years younger. They settled in LaPorte. I don't know just where they were born, but I've heard mother speak of Sulz on the Neckar, a town on that stream or river, in Wurttemberg.

They lived in LaPorte and were both married there. Mother married in 1857. I don't know when Aunt Barbara was married. . . . Aunt Emma (an unmarried sister of Barbara and Anna) wants me to say that their father's father was president of the Cabinet and adviser to the King in Germany.

An old chest, strapped with iron and said by tradition to have been Barbara Kipp's wedding chest, bears on the front the legend:

Johan George Klei
Reist uber Flavn nach
1854.

As Barbara was married at LaPorte on April 28, 1864, the place of the chest in her history would seem a little blurred, but at least it appears to have come from Germany and to have been treasured enough in the Campbell family to descend finally to me, who, by blood, am neither Kipp nor Campbell.

John did not leave me a clear impression of his mother, nor have I been able to find any letters written by her, although there are a number written to her by her sister Anna (Kipp) Nebelthau, Eda's mother. These are all in fine German script and concerned almost exclusively, in good hausfrau fashion, with matters of home and children. I conclude that Barbara, like her sister, learned German script first—perhaps not too well—and never wrote. Or else she was one of those people who do not express themselves easily on paper. As a child, John learned German—even wrote it—but apparently did not keep it up in his very American surroundings.

Barbara, we might surmise, was self-effacing and perhaps a little melancholy by temperament. Forest Grant, a contemporary of John and Gavin, who lived next door to the Campbells during most of their life in Stevens Point, Wisconsin, has told me that "the Campbell children owed very much that made them patient, gentle, and friendly to a most kindhearted, lovable, and deeply concerned mother."[1] He added that she "nobly filled a most difficult position. It would have to be a most unusual woman that would not be forced into the background by a husband whose business required so much aggressive action and thought."[2]

Gavin Campbell, John's father, was indeed an outstanding man. He not only expressed himself fluently on paper but also in so many other ways that he remains a vivid, living personality to all who knew him. He was born in Glasgow on April 16, 1836, of the Breadalbane branch of the Campbell family, the third of five brothers and sisters. His father, Charles Campbell, was a stone mason, who died when Gavin was still a young boy. His mother, Margaret Campbell, from Perthshire, was left to bring up the five children, of whom the two youngest (girls) were mere babies. She also brought up an adopted boy, Andrew.

Margaret Campbell must have been a woman of ability and character. I have a picture of her, a distinguished old lady in [a] black silk dress with a muslin kerchief and cap, an open Bible on her knee. It is said that so great was her piety she would use tongs to remove a newspaper should one stray into the house on the Sabbath. She was a strict disciplinarian as well. Her son Gavin, so John told me, in later years could recite whole chapters of the Bible which he had been obliged to learn as punishment for his boyish misdeeds. "Oh, Gavvy, Gavvy, what shall I do with you?" she used to sigh over the spirited boy, who—among his many diversions—went wassailing in good old Scottish fashion on New Year's Eve.

Many years later—in March 1914—John himself wrote to Isabel Rawn, a young friend who had just produced a Christmas play:

> My father, as a little lad in Scotland, used to take part in the street plays that the youngsters in Scotland indulge in about New Year's time. He had a large scar on one of his fingers which was received in a knightly fray on one of these occasions. He was Sir Somebody, and Sir Somebody-else, with whom he was battling, got his sword, made of a piece of iron barrel hoop, under his father's shield, which was made of the head of the barrel.

I remember father's singing to us children some of the songs they used to sing on New Year's Eve:

> Rise up guid' wife and shak' your feathers,
> But dinna' think that we are beggars.
> We're but bairns come out to play
> Rise up and gie us your Hogmanay.

And another one—and this is the one I think that you used:

> Bless the Master of this house,
> And the Mistress also.
> And all the little children
> That round the table go.
> With your pockets full of money
> And your bottles full of beer,
> Ye ne'er can miss a ha'penny
> To begin the glad New Year.[3]

"You used to be a great mimic," wrote Gavin's sister Mary Smith from Glasgow in 1866 to her brother in the States. "Do you ever sing anything to earn a crust now?"[4] He did sing and also recited from memory long poems by Bobbie Burns, with the strong Scottish burr which, to the end of his life, crept onto his tongue when he was moved or excited—as he often was. Quick of movement, quick of temper, warm-hearted, generous, and affectionate, he passed these qualities on to his oldest son, along with the strict integrity which was an outstanding characteristic of all the Campbell children.

Apprenticed to John Napier and Son, he served six years on the Clyde (working on several Cunarders) with the intention of becoming a marine engineer. He came to America at twenty-three, in June 1859, a skilled mechanic with a reputation for ability, honesty, and industry, which soon found him a place in the rapidly expanding railroad industry of the period. His brother John and his adopted brother Andrew followed him. The affection was great among them. From Chicago, on October 9, 1865, his brother John wrote to Gavin: "I am glad you are now better, but like me you will have to be careful of your health. We are weak in the upper story; I don't mean the head. I hardly like to ask you to come up again; Barbara might think me too hoggish. Still, if nobody has objections, I should like very well to see you. I will take care of you and see you returned safe, barring railway accidents." He died in 1866, and I have a long, sad letter from Gavin describing the event to the family in Scotland.

The death of this brother evidently sharpened Gavin's longing to see his home people. Among his papers appears the following:

Michigan Southern and Northern Indiana R.R. Co.
LaPorte, Indiana
June 5, 1868

To Railroad Officers,
The bearer, Mr G. Campbell, is Foreman of the Machine Shops of the Division. He has been in the employ of the Company for several years and has leave of absence to visit Scotland. Any favors shown him will be thankfully received and will be reciprocated by me.
C. Hains, Supt. Western Div.

Doubtless Barbara would have liked to go to Scotland to visit his family with him, but by this time there was a first child, Maggie Anna, and another expected in September (John Charles). Gavin Junior was to follow in 1870. It was no time for her to be traveling, and we may assume she accepted the situation philosophically, glad that her husband could go where he so longed to go. It is more than likely that he missed her quite as much as she missed him, for he was devotedly attached to her.

Our information relative to the journey is from Mrs. Mary Campbell Smith, Gavin's sister, in a letter written after his return to Wisconsin:

Glasgow, Scotland
October 13, 1868

My Dear Barbara,
Mother received Gavin's letter and was glad to see he had arrived safe home and got all his goods safe. We were just thinking it would have been very bad if it had been all black losses. We were all so sorry to hear of your house being broken into. However, as Gavin says, it can't be helped, and it was only a good thing that none of you were hurt.

Dear Barbara, Mother, Jeanie, and I cannot express to you how we feel in regard to you for your kindness in allowing Gavin to come home and see us. If you only knew the pleasure it gave us all it would more than repay you for your kindness and above all to hear him say how comfortable he was both with you and your mother. We were all quite delighted to see him looking so well and in such good spirits. My opinion is that the jaunt will do him a great deal of good, so if you have lost on the one hand, if it does his health good on the other, you see it is not all loss.

I really wish, Barbara, you had been here to see us all. I think you would have thought we were crazy, we had so much to talk of—so much to laugh at and so much to be sad about; and, Barbara, if you only knew how much we as a family thought of one another you would not wonder at my saying we were sad no little when we thought of the pleasure we had been awanting when Jack was absent, and the reflection we all had together about his trouble. However, these are sorrows we all have to encounter in the world, and therefore we must submit.

. . . Tell Maggie Anna that our baby takes all the children about to see her hanging on the wall. "That is Maddie Anna, and wee Jonny is in the book." When we were at Kilwinning, little Bobbie Scott and our Bobbie and Charlie had great talks about "Uncle Gavin being far, far away over the sea gone to see wee Maddie Anna and wee Jonny."

Happy as his visit to Scotland had been, it cured Gavin of any looking backward. From that time America was his home; his life was wrapped up with the fortunes of his adopted country. His son John was no less American, but when many years later he drew near to the coast of Scotland, on his first visit to those familiar yet never-seen aunts and uncles and cousins, he could not keep the tears from his eyes. This was Scotia, the home of his Highland ancestors, where his father had been born and learned his trade—on this very Clyde which his son was now ascending. "But," with the Scottish twinkle which always kept sentiment in its place, "it's not safe to try to go too far back with one's ancestry. I might find one strung up for stealing cattle in the Lowlands."

That Gavin Campbell's rise in the railroad world was not swift or easy is indicated in his letters to his wife Barbara, who continued to stay at LaPorte with the three children—Maggie, Johnnie, and baby Gavin Junior—when he took what appeared to be a good opening at Buffalo in 1870 as foreman of the Lake Shore and Michigan Shops. His slightly formal letters during this trying period are written in a clear, flowing hand, well-spelled and expressed, and seem to carry with them some of the vitality that distinguished the writer. They usually begin with "My Dear Barbara" and end with "Hoping to hear from you soon, I remain, my dear Barbara, your affectionate Husband." Messages to the children are always included, and often promises to bring them something when he comes home.

Lake Shore and Michigan Southern R.R.
Buffalo
December 5, 1870

My Dear Barbara,

I received your welcome letter and was extremely glad to hear from you. I was very sorry to learn that Baby was so sick. I trust that both you and he will get all right before long. You don't know how anxious I feel about you all. I trust that you will see and take good care of yourself and not fret or worry about my absence, as I am getting along first rate and never was in better health in my life.

I enclose your papers to Chicago and return. You can purchase whatever you wish, but see and pay strict attention to yourself. Tell Maggie and Johnnie that papa will bring them something from Buffalo if they are good children. Baby, too.

Yesterday I had a drive all over the City, and I must say that it is a very nice and beautiful City, but down where the shops are it is not as good. . . .

I don't think I can get home on Saturday but will do so as soon as I can. We are very busy. You can pay the rent when it falls due, and use your own judgment about any other matters. You must not go to Chicago alone. Can Annie not go with you? Write soon, as I long to hear from you. I won't find fault with anything you do, only you must try and keep your spirits up till I come and see you. . . . And now with my love to you all and with a kiss for the children, I remain, my dear Barbara . . .

December 1870

I am glad to learn that the children are no worse, and I do hope they will be better soon, as I am getting extremely anxious to have you here. Every day seems a week. I'll bet if I ever move again I shall take you right along with me. I am extremely tired of boarding. I have not succeeded yet in getting a house.

Houses are very scarce at present. I have got some folks looking out for one, however, and I hope to have one by the time you are able to move. . . . I got the present of a very splendid plug hat from a gentleman in town here. I forgot to mention it in my last letter. I bought some clothes which cost me over twenty dollars so appear more respectable than I did on Sundays. . . .

You can have no idea how much I feel your absence. I think if you were here, I would enjoy your society now more than ever I did, as I do not require to go to the shop nights here as I did at LaPorte, and we could have pleasant walks evenings, which we could not do there. Hurry up and get all well, as I shall want you here as soon as I get a house.

Buffalo, New York
December 20, 1870

I cannot get home before Saturday week. My health is first rate. If you and the children were here, I would feel quite at home.

I am boarding with a widow lady. There are about ten boarders in the house. The meals are first rate, but the accommodations are not so very good. However, I can put up with it first rate, as you know. I am not very hard to please.

Have you bought any furs for Maggie? If not, if I can get a good bargain here, I will bring her some. I do not know what to bring Johnnie and the baby. Please let me know. I will bring some little thing anyway, as coming from Buffalo they will appreciate it more.

Lake Shore and Michigan Southern R.R.
Buffalo, New York
April 18, 1871

I was sorry to learn that Johnnie was sick. I hope he will be better soon. I am also sorry to learn that Anne [his wife's sister's child] is so sick. I trust it is not so bad as you imagine. I hope your next letter will be more cheery. . . .

I saw Mr. Sedgley, but there is nothing definite about Elkhart yet. Mr. Taylor has the promise, if he don't like the job he has gone to, to return in three months. After that we shall see what they will do.

I do not think Hill is so big a man as they say he is. Of course, he is temporarily looking after things, but getting the appointment as master mechanic is a different thing. However, there is no telling what sweet talking will bring about. Should they throw me out in the cold on this occasion, it can't be helped. I can console myself with the fact that my reputation as a mechanic among men who know is second to none on this road and, unfortunately for me, I may not have the influence to get me positions that other men have. But I do not despair. I feel confident that I shall yet attain the position I am entitled to, although it may be some time yet. We will see how things go. If I do not go home this week, I will send you money this week. I have made up my mind to bring you here about the middle of next month, as I cannot bear the idea of being separated any longer.

L.S. & M.S. R.R.
Buffalo, New York
April 19, 1871

The next time I come I will probably move you all down here. I have been promised by Kidder that he will do all he can to get me $1,500 per year, $125 per month, which will suit me first rate.

L.S. & M.S. R.R.
Buffalo, New York
May 5, 1871

So Mr. Hill has got the appointment as master mechanic at Elkhart. I have thereby been thrown out in the cold. Well, it can't be helped. I have tried by all honorable means to get promoted, but it has been of no effect. My services evidently are not appreciated by Mr. Sedgley, notwithstanding the zeal I displayed and the attention to business that characterized me. They have forgotten, evidently, the way I worked when they had their trouble five years ago. If they ever get into another scrape, they need not count on me to do anything for them. If I had another situation somewhere, I do not think I would stay long with this company, but as I am fixed I have to grin and bear it. I hope, dear Barbara, that the day is not far distant when I may be rewarded for my labors, but I have been too straightforward to get along always as I ought to.

L.S. & M.S. R.R.
Buffalo, New York
June 29, 1871

I have been on the keen jump these last three weeks to find a house, but unfortunately I have not succeeded. I never saw houses so scarce in all my life as I find them here. I could get a house where other people live in, but that would not suit. I am still keeping parties looking out for me, and whenever I succeed I shall duly let you know. If I do not succeed in getting one to suit, I shall take anything for the present so that I can have you here. What do you think about it? This is a very bad time of the year to get one. I will write you immediately on my success. You must not get discouraged, as it will come all right yet. I do wish you were here. I feel quite downhearted when I consider the position we have been placed in by my coming to Buffalo, but I am in hopes it will be all right yet. Kiss the children for me and tell them that pa will come for them as soon as he possibly can.

Following this, a gap of several weeks in the letters I have leaves us ignorant of the conditions which led to his next move—transfer to the Wisconsin Central Railroad, with the coveted position of master mechanic and division superintendent, at Menasha, Wisconsin.

However the change had come, it could not have been better suited to one of his temperament, training, and abilities. These were the latter years of the era in which the cutting of the great stand of pine covering northern Wisconsin was in progress and the huge rafts of lumber were piloted down the rivers.[5] This was soon to change, in part to railroad transit. Wisconsin was a rapidly changing frontier. Even Gavin's young sons must have seen many a "Wisconsin-raft" taking its old, difficult, and dangerous way through the rapids, and have witnessed the phenomenal growth of Stevens Point, though I do not remember that John ever mentioned these things to me. His mind, as a boy, like that of the people about him, had been caught up in the throbbing, expanding life of which the railroad was the center and his own vivid, virile father the immediate presiding genius.

It seems likely that before beginning his work at Menasha, Gavin was able to visit Barbara and the children in LaPorte. His next letter, written in November, came from Menasha and seems to breathe his exuberant spirit:

Wisconsin Central Railroad
Phillips and Colby Construction Co.
Superintendent's Office
Menasha, Wisconsin
November 2, 1871

My Dear Barbara,

   I arrived here all safe this morning and found snow on the ground. Still, the weather is very pleasant. I am going to the end of the road tomorrow. We will get through to Stevens Point and stop overnight and return here next day.

If the house suits me, I shall move up right away, as it will be better for both of us. I cannot say how I will like it, but I am of the opinion this will be one of the best railroads in the West.

Menasha, Wisconsin
November 17, 1871

I have been waiting to see how things were going to turn up so that I could let you know when I could bring you up here. I am still located here, as they won't have the engine house finished for some time yet at Stevens Point.

I have been making inquiries to see if I could not get a house to board in, you and our children, until we could get up to the Point, but so far I have not found one that will suit. I wish very much to have you here, as it will make considerable difference in expenses to live together; besides, I will feel much better to have the pleasure of your and the children's company. I am very sorry, indeed, that you should be knocked around so. I feel it as bad as you do; but I am determined to stop stationary in the next place, if I succeed, for some long time.

No one feels it more than I do to have you put to such annoyance and trouble as you have been subjected to this last year, but I could not help it. . . . I trust you will not feel put about any by this unsettled state of affairs, as I am considerably worried myself.

If the round house at the Point were finished, I would have you here right away. . . . I am getting along here easily, not much to do but probably will have plenty after a while. The round house is but a short distance from the house, so that I won't require to be out nights except in case of any emergency.

W. C. R. R.
P. & C. Construction Co.
Menasha, Wisconsin
December 11, 1871

I duly received your letter and was extremely sorry to hear that you and Johnnie had been sick. I am sure your health would be better here, as there is not such a thing known as chills and fever or ague. I have increased in weight since I came here; and if you were here, I should feel perfectly contented. I am boarding at a hotel where Mr. Harris boards. The board is quite high, but I could not better myself much. I am not out on the road at nights as we do not do any night running. In fact, I have not run but very little, and it is not likely

I shall require to do any running hereafter except for my own amusement. . . . Hoping your next letter will be more cheery than the last. . . .

The weather for the last few days has been delightful, very clear atmosphere; but last week it was fearful cold—twenty degrees below zero. I tell you it was stinging, but you still don't seem to feel it much, the air being so dry.

Menasha, Wisconsin
February 13, 1872

I am very glad to inform you that I am thoroughly recovered and feel better than I have for a long time, and I have no doubt I will be in a number one condition. I have more vitality about me than I have had for years. . . .

I have a man looking for a house for me at Stevens Point, and I am in hopes that he will be successful. I think I shall buy some land and build a house there. Mr. Harris and a few more are going to invest there, and they wish I should do so. I think it will be very valuable before long. I would like to have a nice residence, with barn attached so that I could keep a horse and be somebody. . . .

Enclosed please find check for forty dollars. I have sent forty dollars to McKenzie and paid my doctor's bill, and I am unable to send any more money to you this month.

Menasha, Wisconsin
February 26, 1872

I went to Stevens Point yesterday to see after a house, but I am sorry to say I was not successful in finding one. Houses are extremely scarce there. I am heartily sick of being separate. I am sorry now we didn't move right up here at first. I am going to come down to LaPorte to see you when I get my passes. I will let you know when in my next . . .

I received a handsome present from the men of this road last Thursday. Mr. Hains presented it. It was a case of drafting instruments. I feel very proud over it, considering that I have been such a short time here. It shows good feeling on their part, and I hope that the same feelings will always exist. I will send you a paper with an account of it in the beginning of the week.

The weather is magnificent here now. Probably we will have some cold weather next month.

Barbara might well be excused for not always being quite "cheery." It is hard to carry on alone with three small children and all responsibility for home affairs, especially if one has a husband as lively and devoted as hers, eager always to meet her wishes. But at last a house was found, and the family was united in Stevens Point in 1873—a year in which one Eric Baker is reported as having "killed a large lynx on the outskirts of the village, it being the third one he had killed that year."

What kind of a house Gavin secured we do not know. A description of the old Jacobs House, built about 1872, suggests that housing in Stevens Point was simple at that time:

> In early days this old hotel sported no modern conveniences. The rooms were large, with four or five beds in each room; and it was no uncommon occurrence to find guests doubled up, two in a bed, and sometimes they were lucky to get even that accommodation. In the large hall on the second floor, a large stand was located, and on it was an array of candlesticks filled with long tapering candles that were used to light the guests to bed. Each room had a small box stove for heating purposes, and it was the duty of the P. J. to rouse the guests each morning and build the fires in the rooms. No utensils were furnished for the ablutions, but each guest came downstairs and used the sink in the office and dried himself on the long roller towel. The hotel used about two hundred cords of good hard maple wood per annum. You would often see a couple of hundred cords of wood piled up in the back yard, seasoning for the next year.[6]

Probably the Campbells lived near the railroad yards, so that Gavin could reach his work quickly. One of John's earliest remembrances was of some boys named Kelly who lived just across the high board fence which separated Kelly and Campbell backyards. John and little Gavin took a fearsome delight in issuing forth and shouting at the top of their lungs:

> Kelly, Kelly, with the cast-iron belly
> Full of sticks and full of stones
> And full of old grand-daddy bones Yah!

Pang! came the retaliatory rocks against the fence, but Johnnie and Gavvy had already retired to a safer vantage point.

Wherever the house was situated, we may be sure that it was enough for Barbara that the family was together under one roof. She could generally count on Gavin's being home at night to tell of his day's adventures, to laugh and sing old

Scottish songs and play with the children. He was essentially a social being, and the house was a lively place when he was there. "I am sure there wasn't a happier family anywhere than the Campbells," wrote Forest Grant. "I wish more could be told of John's life at that particular time. It must be remembered that the events that were recorded at that time very naturally were centered around Mr. Campbell, and rightly so because he was a very forceful and able man, and his progress and that of the railroads were of great interest to all." "A History of the Wisconsin Central," Bulletin 54 of the Railroad and Locomotive History Society, giving the following data under Gavin Campbell, indicates his progress in the railroad world:

master mechanic and division supt.	1871–1878
assistant to gen'l. supt.	1878–1881
general supt.	1881–1882
purchasing agent	1882–1883
supt. of Penokee Division of W.C.	1883–1885
general supt. of Green Bay and Western R.R.	1885–1890
general supt. of Wisconsin Central	1890–1893

When Gavin was established in the confidence and respect of the railroad officials and did not need to be so near the shops, the family seems to have moved to a more residential section. John used to tell how he and Gavin would go down to meet their father at the train and how they would see the locomotive engineer–aristocrat of the railroad leap from cab to buggy, snatch the reins from a waiting boy, whip up his blooded team, and whirl off in a cloud of dust. Walking home, a small boy by each hand, the superintendent-father would thus admonish his sons: "Never forget that your father wore overalls!" And the boys never forgot.

John remembered, too, how, after they all were in bed, he could hear his father and mother talking—often about some employee whom Gavin had been obliged to dismiss for drinking in defiance of the strict railroad edict. Barbara would plead for him, telling how the wife had been to her, crying and promising that her husband would never break the rule again. "But dammit, Barbara!"—"Hush, Gavin! Remember the children." Gavin himself gave up his Scotch whiskey and all liquors when the railroad put this regulation into practice for the men—this despite the fact that the other officials went out with the official car well stocked.

By the time the three children had really begun to grow up, Stevens Point had developed into an ordinary prosperous small town, proud of its schools, its churches, its business activity, and its railroad. The colorful pioneer period had passed into legend. Maggie Campbell might have tied the old days and the new together, for she was to marry young Fred Hawn, son of "Sailor Jack Hawn," one of the well-known pilots who had run rafts down to St. Louis. Dr. Galen Rood, a famous old doctor in the region, used to recall seeing the Hawn children rolling twenty-dollar gold pieces on the floor when their father returned from a river run. None of this wealth remained with the children, however. Fred, a clever, hard-working young fellow, had to work his way up in the railroad. Maggie herself was a pretty, fair girl, domestic by nature, an expert in fine embroidery, loving good clothes and knowing how to wear them. "Sister was a fine dresser," John often said, and well she might be—her father, and his boys after him, liked good clothes and wore them well. Many years after Gavin's death (January 31, 1894), Forest Grant recalled:

> His forceful personality commanded the greatest respect at all times. His splendid straight figure, always clothed in perfectly fitted garments of the finest materials, naturally increased the respect of everyone with whom he came in contact. Doubtless it was this careful attention to his personal appearance and his good taste, as well as his ability to present his point of view in a colorful manner that impressed not only his immediate friends but also the businessmen of the railroad world. He was, of course, by far the most polished and able man in Stevens Point. It would be very difficult even today to find a man with higher ideals, or that could equal him in brilliance of conversation.

If John was not his father's favorite, as I have often been told, he was the oldest and stronger of the boys, and probably better able to take part in Gavin's strenuous and exciting life. Perhaps, too, he was more like his father in temperament. Gavin Junior was never physically robust, though he loved athletics, took a deep interest in baseball, and developed into an unusually strong tennis player. The boys owned a lively western pony and a big Newfoundland dog which accompanied them everywhere, sometimes proving[providing] effective aid when the hot-headed little brother became involved in fights he could not handle. John came to be a fine horseman. He was also a skillful driver, able to take his team safely over many a rough and difficult mountain road, as I was to witness myself many years later, under very different conditions.

The boys went to public school and both did well—John exceptionally so, to his father's great satisfaction. Neither father nor mother were strong church people. Perhaps Gavvy was glad to escape from the strict Scottish Presbyterianism of his boyhood. John found his own way in matters of religious observance. He used to tell how he imbibed his first doctrine sitting on a nail-keg in a little Baptist Sunday school over a store in Stevens Point. As the family grew better acquainted, the boys joined a popular Sunday school class in the Presbyterian church, attended by most of their young friends. It was taught by Waite Buckingham, one of the oldest businessmen of Stevens Point and one of its best citizens. The Buckinghams were early settlers and strong Presbyterians. It is probably due to them that the boys joined the Presbyterian church, although the Reverend Walter Frame had a strong influence on all the young people. He, in particular, encouraged them to go on with their education and may well have had a hand in John's preparing for college. Gavin senior needed no urging there, however.

In 1881, when John was thirteen, a great adventure fell to his lot. His father had a railroad acquaintance, a German ex–army officer and engineer, who was connected with the Northern Pacific Railroad. Colonel Bausenhausen asked if the boy would like to go out with him that summer to North Dakota and Montana, where he was laying tracks for the railroad. Johnnie would be errand boy, carrying messages from where the track ended one day to the immediate operations of the next day. He would have his own pony—which, it turned out, had belonged to Sitting Bull, just defeated though not captured until 1890.

Of course Johnnie wanted to go! What boy could have resisted such an opportunity, and with such a romantic companion—handsome and commanding, with long mustachios twisted at the ends, sealskin cap, and fur coat with a beaver collar.

A tintype taken of John that summer shows a slim, serious-faced boy in a fur cap, short jacket, and high leather boots. In his gauntleted hand he holds a riding whip. Little did the father realize to what company he was committing his beloved older son! The camp was of the roughest, with gamblers, drinkers, camp followers, and violence of all kinds. Passing the tents clustered along the tracks, the boy came to understand the sights uncovered by gaping curtains. The colonel himself played heavily—often into the small hours. Many a night the boy was left alone in the car staked down on the prairie. During the daytime he usually had leisure to mount his pony and go exploring over the country, hunting petrified rock, arrowheads, buffalo horns, and other relics. He was puzzled one day by constant whirrings and whizzings about his head. Not until later did he realize that he had been a target for the Indians still hovering about.

We have two of John's letters home:

Northern Pacific Railroad
Engineering Department
End Track Division

June 26, 1881

Did you see the comet the night of the 24th and 25th?

Dear Maggie,

I received your letter yesterday evening. Was glad to hear from you. I answered Pa's letter a few days ago. Why does Johnnie Hill not answer my letter? I wrote him one the same time as I wrote Ma's German letter. Tell Ma I have my clothes washed as often as I have enough to send to the laundry. Why do you not write Colonel? He says you cannot have the L. picture until you write him a long letter.[7] Col. wrote and sent you your passes wants you to come right away he will probably not stay here over two or three weeks. He says you should start to be here before the 10 of July as our passes run out then. Tell Pa he had better come along with you. I must close now as I have to write Ma and Gavin a letter. I remain

Your affect. Bro.
J.C.

Northern Pacific Railroad
Engineering Department
End Track Division
June 26, 1881

Dear Gavin,

I received your letter yesterday was very glad to hear from you. I have not received the July utensil yet expect them every day you will probably be here to help me fire them off we will have a great time they have put up the flag staff in Glendive will be there about next Saturday the bridges held us or we would have been there this week. Is Bert getting ready for the 4th tell him to be careful not to burn his fingers. Colonel and Ed Donavan his teamster are going to Glendive this morning. I sent Maggie some plants called needle cushions hope she received them. I found an Indian spear head day before yesterday. The hunter gave me an arrow head the same day bring your old clothes when you come we will have lots of fun. I must close now I am going out riding. I remain

Your affect. bro.
J.C.

It was too bad that Gavin could not have been at that great Glendive 4th of July celebration, where the railroad crew put up Johnnie, the only little white boy for miles around, to run a one-legged race in competition with a little Negro and [a] little Indian. He was a good runner, as well as a favorite with the men, and all the bets were on him. How the men roared as he forged ahead, and he kept the lead almost to the line—*almost*—for just as the victory seemed secure, he tripped and fell! No one ever knew how much money was lost on him that day.

The great experience came to an end at last, and father and mother came out to take their boy home. They sat that first morning in their private car, detached from the train, enjoying a leisurely breakfast, when suddenly yells, shots, and curses rose about them! A gambler trying to escape his debts dodged in and out of the protection of the car, while his fierce pursuer took potshots at him at every opportunity. Gavin and Barbara, crouched down out of range, looked aghast at the scene. A later walk revealed to the horrified parents some of the things that their Johnnie had been taking as part of his daily fare. "It didn't hurt me," John used to say, "but it did make me old before my time."

Perhaps the experience affected him more than he realized. I find the following letter from his father, written about one and a half years later from Milwaukee, where he had been sent as purchasing agent of the railroad. It would seem to suggest that Johnnie suffered a natural reaction from the limelight of his exciting adventures.

Wisconsin Central Railroad
Office of G. Campbell, Purchasing Agent

My Dear Johnnie,

I do not want you to feel bad or despondent at what I am going to say to you, but rather glad that your Father takes so much interest in you to point out some of your defects, which, if not checked now while you are young, may grow upon you to such an extent as will prevent your getting along in the world as well as we all wish you. No boy ever had a father who felt more pride in his son and loved him more than I do you, and would indulge him in his tastes and desires any more, and it is with no small amount of pleasure that I hear of your progress in your studies. I have often pictured in my mind a position of eminence which I hope you will attain.

I know you are a very good boy and that you have no bad habits and that you wish to become a prominent man, and anything I can do to help you along you know I would be only too glad to do it, but I am somewhat pained at the seeming want of affection which ought to exist between your sister and brother and you. You know that frequently I have seen a display of temper which ought not to exist, in fact a want of a spirit of accommodation, which is not pleasant to see, and which I know you do not realize. I wish to impress upon you the necessity of curbing this disposition. It will grow upon you, then it will be harder to get rid of. In order to make your Mother happy and me feel glad, you should not show this disposition, but rather be obliging and willing to do everything you can for Maggie and Gavin, and they should do the same with you. This would make you feel happy yourself and all of us glad.

I trust, my dear Johnnie, you will think this over and change your way in this respect. I assure you, Johnnie, I am not displeased with you, only in this respect, as I feel an intense pride in you and would sacrifice everything almost for your good. I know you are a sensible boy and that you will accept of my cautioning in the spirit in which it is written. I shall be very glad to hear from you, and now with my warmest love to you, and hoping you will guard against these things I have hinted at. Believe me to be

Your affectionate Father,

G. Campbell

Gavin's transfer to Milwaukee brought forth many expressions of regard and regret from his old employees and business associates. The men knew him not only as a fair and generous boss, but they had reason to respect his ability and skill. Many a time the train crew had called him from his berth in the middle of the night, when they were unable to make the necessary repairs. He would crawl under the engine himself and get the train started on its way. A superb mechanic, he had no patience with bad work. "Damn freight engineer!" he would explode when cars bumped and jolted.

Nor could he abide dishonesty. In his new position as purchasing agent for the Railroad (1882–1883), he had just concluded a contract and his pen was poised to sign when the salesman asked the significant question, "How much for the Boy?" In a rage, Gavin tore up the contract and kicked the salesman downstairs. "Not exactly fair," his son commented, "for it was a common enough practice; the salesman was undoubtedly doing what he thought was expected." Gavin, however, would countenance no such practices.

Wisconsin Central

J. A. Stewart & E. H. Abbot

Milwaukee Northern and

Wisconsin & Minnesota

R. M. Griswold, Agent

Christmas

Stevens Point, Wis.
December 25, 1882

Mr. Campbell:

Biblical history records the fact that this is Christ's birthday. Since the time of His birth, this day has been celebrated in various ways among all Christian nations. One feature is the presentation of Christian gifts to honor one's friends and relatives.

We—your friends and late employees—have assembled on this occasion for the purpose of presenting you with a slight testimonial of our esteem and affection. The intrinsic value of which must not at all be compared with feelings which prompt our action.

We hope that you will accept it with our kind regards for your future welfare. We hope that its machinery is so perfect that with this and a timecard of the latest date you will at all times be able to make the pay car on time without other assistance.

Because life is uncertain and switch engines are not always on hand for one's convenience, this gift is from your old boys, as the roll of names will indicate, who were only too glad to have an opportunity of leaving in your hands (or pocket) a memento of their pleasant associations with you. We anticipate the new situation you have accepted will be a pleasant one. You will be pleasantly located in the city of Milwaukee, away from the howling blasts you have previously encountered in winter and the no-see-ems of summer.

But do not forget your friends up on the Middle Northern and Southern divisions of the W. C.

We will be glad to see you at any time and our latch string will be on the outside. Take the gift and may its pleasant face ever be a pleasant reminder of highest esteem and good wishes for your future welfare. We all join in best wishes to you and family and wish you a Merry Christmas.

Employees

How often I have seen John pull out the handsome gold watch—for such it was—and turn to the inscription on the inner cover. A large silver service was presented the following year, "To Mrs. Gavin Campbell by the Mill Owners on the line of the Wisconsin Central R. R., May 1, 1883."

"I met him first," said old Dr. Rood, a famous pioneer doctor of the regions, "when, as my train was just pulling out of the station, a man came running down the platform, his hand pressed to his jaw—just too late. 'That man is looking for me,' I said to a gentleman sitting opposite me. 'He needs a doctor.' 'Are you a doctor?' and in a flash his hand went to the signal rope." The train backed into the station, a tooth was extracted on the platform, the patient went off wiping his mouth, and the superintendent and the doctor continued on their way—to be friends for many years. What tales the doctor might have told!

It was, in fact, a tremendous period of birth, growth, and development. Gavin loved the activity and excitement and gave himself without reserve to his work and the interests of the company he was with. His strict integrity allowed of no relaxing, although fortunes were being made all around him. "It belongs to the railroad," he would say when other men asked him why he did not take advantage of his chances to make money. "They will take care of me when the time comes." Perhaps the company had no understanding of a man so honest that he would not provide for his own future—even at their expense. When he needed their help, their indifference was a deep blow to the man who had served and trusted them. It might well have made his sons cynical. To them, however, descended the strict honesty, the humor, the kindness, the democracy, which had made the father the idol of his men wherever he worked.

Milwaukee, Wisconsin
January 26, 1883

My Dear Barbara,

I have been to Dayton, Ohio, and got back all right. I am feeling first rate and hope you are much better than when I left home. I trust you will keep your health and also keep up your spirits; do not worry about me. I am all right. . . . Say to Maggie that I am much pleased with the way she kept house when I was home. If she will only help you right along as she has done, I won't forget her. I hope the boys are doing right and obeying you in every particular. They can help both you and Maggie a great deal if they try. Tell them I shall be pleased to hear of their doing so. WRITE SOON.

Milwaukee, Wisconsin
January 27, 1883

I hope you are getting on well and that your health is improving. When you are able, you might take a run down here and I shall endeavor to make your visit very pleasant. I feel very much on account of your sickness and I assure you, Barbara, that you and the children are my only comfort. If I could place you all where you could enjoy all of the pleasures and comforts of life, I would be happy. . . . I realize daily what a good wife and mother you are. Now I want you to keep up your spirits and be cheerful. Do not let anything worry or annoy you. Take things easy and look on the bright side of things, then all will be well. I have got a room on the first floor now, quite convenient to get out in case of danger.

Milwaukee, Wisconsin
February 12, 1883

My Dear Maggie,

I received your very welcome letter and was very glad indeed that Ma was still improving in her health and that you are all well. Johnnie and Gavin must be getting to be fashionable, attending fancy dress parties with white "chokers" on. I do not expect that this will interfere with their other duties at home and in their studies. Recreation and pleasure of this sort is all right enough provided we keep it within due bounds. I hope they will show their appreciation of Ma's kindness by doing everything pleasantly for her and making her happy. This I wish to impress on you all. You have no idea how happy I felt when I was last at home to see how feeling you all were for her. How much better it all is to be that way than to have jarring contention all the time. This you can avoid by being obedient, loving and faithful. The inward satisfaction it gives one compensates for all extra efforts we may make to bear each other's burdens. I will see what I can do about the napkins and tablecloths. . . . I would be glad if Johnnie or Gavin would write me.

Wisconsin Central Railroad
Milwaukee, Wisconsin
March 16, 1883

My Dear Johnnie,

I duly received your letter and was glad to hear from you. You can go another term to the Dancing School if you wish. Tell Gavin I shall let him know all about the Colorado when I come home. . . . I will when I get home see about your staying at Stevens Point until school dismisses.

These references to the Colorado and John's staying at Stevens Point have to do with the management of a mining property in Colorado which Gavin Senior about this time was greatly tempted to undertake. Many letters passed to and fro weighing the advantages and disadvantages of the proposed move. Gavin Senior even went out to Silver Cliff to look into the matter and described to Barbara the "beautiful climate" and the "splendid military school where all the boys are in uniforms of gray with brass buttons."

Milwaukee, Wisconsin
March 20, 1883

Everyone out there [in Silver Cliff] feels good with the prospects and says there is no doubt it will be a grand success. I only hope so. If it is, we will be fixed comfortably the balance of our days. I sincerely hope it will prove so. If [so] you can be paid back for the many years of hard work and the great help you have been to me in the past. If I can only attain this, I shall feel satisfied. I will have a family talk as Gavin [junior] suggested when I get home about our future intentions. My business relations here are very pleasant and probably I can arrange to stay here and draw my profits. In that case I shall move down as soon as the weather is favorable.

Milwaukee, Wisconsin
April 16, 1883

My Dear Barbara,
Mr. Cook and Mr. Smith are here today and are talking the mining matter over. (Mr. Smith, the president, I mean.) They are very urgent I should go out and manage matters. Mr. Cook will put in five thousand dollars if I go. I am in a quandary what is best to do. I shall not go out there without I have a thorough understanding in regard to my duties, salary, etc. and how I am to be paid, and what guarantee I shall have for my salary. Mr. Cook says there is no doubt but there is a fortune for all if properly managed and they seem to think I am the only man who can manage things. I will decide what I will do when I see Mr. Colby. He will be home Wednesday. I shall lay the whole matter before him and decide after I hear what he says.

Apparently what Mr. Colby said was unsatisfactory, since he did not go. The next we hear of Gavin, he is superintendent of the Penokee Division of the Wisconsin Central (1883–1885), with offices at Ashland, Wisconsin. It seems to have been a wise decision, for among his papers after his death was worthless Silver Cliff stock, and we know that others lost heavily in the venture. Naturally, we do not know how things would have come out if Gavin had been manager.

Ashland, Lake Superior, Wis.
May 21, 1883

My Dear Barbara,

I leave here tomorrow morning either to go to the work from Penokee, or by boat to Montreal River. The weather has been stormy, so probably we shall not go by boat. It will take a little longer time to go from Penokee, but I prefer that to taking any chances. I shall be going about in the woods. I eat hearty and sleep well and have not felt any better for a long time. . . . I shall run down to Stevens Point when I come out of the woods. I shall have to buy a pair of shoes. The boots will be too heavy for tramping through the woods.

Kirby House, Milwaukee
Sunday night

I telegraphed you yesterday that I was not going to New York. I go to Marquette tonight and will return in two or three days. Passes were sent to you to go to Chicago. I will telegraph you when to come down so you can meet me and we shall go to Chicago together to the exposition. . . . Would Johnnie like to go on the surveying party? If so, I can give him Nathan Finney's job. I am afraid he might not be able to stand tramping through the woods. I shall see about this when I get home.

Ashland, Wisconsin
August 28, 1883

On account of fogs and bad weather, we have been unable to get away from here but will leave tomorrow morning. Will try and get back in time so Johnnie can get to school Monday, but if I am detained, you can tell Maggie to see the principal and explain how it is and not allow his not being there to interfere with any of his rights in the school. I am desirous he should go with me and learn something he may not have an opportunity of seeing again. We are going with a steamboat, so you need not worry. I am getting along all right. My eyes are better, so I get along without the glasses. Mr. Abbot has straightened my financial matters all right and has got a guarantee. I shall not be bothered any more with it. I have also got a statement in full of my car shock, which I shall show you when I come home. I feel better now.

Office of the Penokee and Gogebic Development Company
Bessemer, Michigan
January 4, 1884

. . . I received the German socks, which please me very much; they are very comfortable. We have shut down all work with the exception of keeping four or five men to work. I expect there will not be much done this winter. The snow is very deep in the woods, and work cannot be done to any advantage. We expect Mr. L. J. Colby and party up Wednesday night, when they may possibly make other arrangements and possibly may go ahead with some work. The weather has been very cold. Last Friday was an exceedingly cold day. I understand one of our men has got his feet and hands very badly frozen; probably will lose them. He undertook to walk from the W.C.R. to our Camp and I presume got so fatigued that he could go no further than where he was found. Some parties on their way here discovered him laying in the snow. He is now at a camp about eight miles away, where he was taken to. About twenty of our men go out tomorrow morning to Ashland, but the weather is comparatively mild now. I have been quite comfortable, but it is rather monotonous in the woods. Every day seems alike. It is quiet all the time. I hope the company will conclude to do something before long, as it will make it a little livelier. . . .

Did Johnnie find out how much the trunk cost for express, and has he got the check for the other? If so, keep it until I come home.

Fragment, undated, to his son John:

P. & G., Bessemer, Michigan
March 1884

. . . number of prominent men here who expressed themselves well satisfied with the property. I expect we shall start up again in the spring.

I have no objections to once in a great while that Ma should let you go to the roller rink, but she is right upon general principles when she says you got five dollars for the Ice Rink. While I wish to encourage you all I can, still self-denial is a commendable virtue which you ought to practice. Ma is the best judge of what you should do and I wish you to be governed entirely by her wishes on all matters. This, as dutiful children, you ought to submit to.

I am glad you enjoyed yourselves at the German Theatre and that Mrs. Bujlet performed her part so well. I will be glad to hear from you as often as you can. Have Gavin write also. You have no idea how pleasing it is to me to hear from you, no matter what you write.

Tremont House
Oshkosh, Wisconsin
January 15, 1885

My dear Barbara,

I will leave here at 5:00 a.m., and when I get to Bessemer, I will write you. I would like to have stayed a day longer at home, but I thought it best to go. You must not feel bad at my having to be away so much. I would like to stay at home all of the time myself, but we have to provide means to live; consequently, we cannot always have things as we might wish. I hope, however, we shall be able to be more together in the future than in the past. I have no desire to be anywhere now but with you and the children. My only pleasure is to have you all around me, and I feel the home ties more binding as I become older. I must say that I am proud of how Maggie and the boys behave. My thoughts are with them constantly. It is a great source of pleasure to us to know that they are good. This must certainly be a great pleasure to themselves. . . . As it is now about twelve o'clock, and the train leaves at 5:00 a.m., I must draw to a close and go to bed.

The next letter finds him general superintendent of the Green Bay, Winona & St. Paul Railroad—the railroad which opened the iron mines on Lake Superior. Of this period (1885–1889) the *Stevens Point Gazette* wrote after his death, January 31, 1894, "To his untiring energy and recognized ability is due a great portion of the prosperity that that road has since enjoyed, he having built it up on a solid paying foundation."

Green Bay, Wisconsin
May 28, 1885

My Dear Children,

I have received your notes this evening, and as I am going off in the morning, I thought I would answer you. I sent Mr. Frame the passes.

I am glad Johnnie's Valedictory pleased Mr. Cooley. Glad to learn Maggie's work pleased so well, and as for Gavin, I shall, if I don't forget it, bring him a baseball.

I will be in Green Bay Sunday morning and possibly Saturday night. If John will come over, he can go to the Cook House, and the landlord will take care of him until I get there. I will arrange with the landlord to fix him a room, etc., etc. Love to all, Ma and the rest of you.

Kirby House, Milwaukee, Wisconsin
May 29, 1885

My Dear Maggie,

In my hurry last night I forgot to say how pleased I was that your work has given satisfaction so much that you were engaged still further. I believe it was a good thing to do as you did. It shows you could earn your living, and work is honorable.

I had an interview of a very pleasant nature with Mr. Colby, who told me the New York folks were well pleased with me. He was very much elated over it. He has endorsed fully my plan of operations and assures me of his continued confidence in my judgment.

I will go to Milwaukee in the a.m., and hope I will be as successful with the Northwestern manager as I have been with Mr. Colby. I hope to see Johnnie at the hotel Sunday morning in Green Bay when I arrive. I arranged with the proprietor of the hotel to give him a room and take care of him until I get there. Mr. Fox will be the conductor. He will take him to the Hotel.

I will try and not forget Gavin's baseball. Mr. Clifford was in Green Bay yesterday. His daughter Mrs. Fox wishes you to make her a visit there when you get through with your work.

As Gavin's previous letter indicated, John graduated from high school Friday evening, June 19, 1885, valedictorian of his class. The graduating class, fifth in the history of the Stevens Point Free High School, was small, to be sure—fourteen students and two teachers. John loved to retell how he delivered his weighty address on the platform of McCullough Hall "amid potted plants and the respectful attention of the town notables."

"The course of study a student pursues," reads his clear boyish handwriting,

molds his character and lays the foundation for a higher structure. The discipline we have derived and the habits we have formed from our studies will probably be among the direct causes of our success or failure. . . . The goal for which we have so long been striving has been reached, and tonight some take our leave of school forever. . . . As a man is known by the company he keeps, so the standing of a city is known by its schools. . . . The friends of Stevens Point cannot fail to rally to the support of popular education. . . . Encouragement, influence, and money are the three necessary aids. . . .

Teachers, the end has come. From this point our paths diverge. The high standing to which our school has attained reflects great credit upon you and shows that we have been highly favored in having you as our instructors. You will continue to bring others to this point, while we are to carve out our own future. It is sincerely hoped that the training we have received will be of lasting benefit, and though we no longer meet as classmates, let us so act that we may be able to do our part in the battle of life with honor and become active and worthy citizens. We must now bid farewell to our school associations, but while memory lasts, the name of the high school of Stevens Point and our worthy principal, Mr. Cooley, and his able assistant, Miss Shipman, will be remembered by us with the warmest feelings. And now, classmates, teachers, friends, one and all, farewell.

"I hear you made a fine talk up there at the high school." So the oldest citizen greeted him on the street the next day. John, as modestly as he could, allowed he had. "I suppose you know a great deal," continued the old man. "And when you go east to that academy I hear about, I suppose you'll know a great deal more. And when you get through college, I suppose you'll know about all there is to know." He paused to emphasize his final words. "And when you get to be an old man like me," John always smiled at this point, "you'll find you are nothing but an old fool after all."

Nothing short of an eastern college for a boy like this! The Scottish father arranged at once for John to go to Andover Academy to complete the preparation which could not be furnished by the Stevens Point High School in spite of its local reputation. The father went east to Massachusetts with his son and entered him in the academy in 1886. Dr. Bancroft was then principal, and he and the breezy railroad superintendent took an immediate liking to each other. Probably John said little while they talked, but those clear, observing eyes undoubtedly took in all the details of the principal's person and room as he lent, at the same time, an attentive ear to the conversation. I have heard him describe the meeting many times. The father was anxious to make it clear that his son was to behave himself and do his work. If he failed in these respects, he was to be reprimanded without hesitation, and sent home if necessary. The principal was frankly delighted with the sincerity, humor, and directness of the father, whose pride and confidence in his boy could not be concealed by his firm words. He answered in November an anxious inquiry as to how things were going.

Phillips Academy, Andover
Principal's Office
Andover, Massachusetts
November 17, 1886
G. Campbell, Esq.
Green Bay, Wisconsin

Dear Sir,
Your Nov. 17 came duly to hand. Your son is almost a model of industry, courtesy, and all exemplary conduct, and is doing good, honest, and successful work in his studies. We could carry a thousand such boys without friction.
Faithfully yours,
C. F. F. Bancroft, Prin.

John studied hard at Andover and got a college preparation which gave him easy going in his first years at Williams. He was, of course, a little older than most of the boys, which did not keep him from having an extremely good time. He lived at Cheever House, opposite the Old Academy Building at the juncture of School and Main streets, and many were the pranks in which he took part, at the expense of the long-suffering Cheever sisters. One which he used to tell with considerable relish had to do with pantryraiding, evidently a long-established custom. Every Sunday night two boys were detailed to slip down into the pantry and rifle the icebox of its Sunday remains. If they were successful in bringing up the loot, the boys had a great feast. This particular Sunday night, the elected two made the icebox transaction without trouble, but as they started up the back stairs with the remains of the turkey and a large pan of milk set out to raise cream, one and then the other began to giggle uncontrollably. Down went the milk pan with a splash, heard by the waiting accomplices above, and down went the turkey, waking the sleeping dragons below. "Of course, there was no excuse," John used to say. "We had good food and plenty of it always—turkey and ice cream, once a week."

It was at Andover that John was first introduced to what was to prove his life interest. Mrs. Frederick W. Whittemore, a widow and a staunch Congregationalist, had a famous Sunday school class attended by many of the academy boys. Her daughter Margaret, then a child of nine or ten, has told me that she remembered John "only as one of the many boys in my mother's Sunday school class who came on Sunday evenings to sing hymns and talk after our eight o'clock bedtime, and who dropped in occasionally between times."

"Hundreds of boys," says Forest Grant, who himself went to Andover for a year or two, "can testify that class did much for them, not only while in Andover but especially in their work afterward. Of course, I haven't forgotten how wonderful it was to belong to the splendid group of fellows of all classes and to enjoy the home that was open every Tuesday evening at eight o'clock for a drop-in call. The faculty gave standing permission." Sherwood Eddy was one of the active members of John's time, Harry McCormick another.

Margaret Whittemore declared that her mother "never competed with the theological seminary professors," but she recalled that "at one time the theologs had quite a fad of coming to our house and playing marbles, fishing them out from under the piano with a poker, or crawling under the table to make a short when the marble strayed that way." John may have been in this group in his seminary days. In any case, his first interest in the southern mountains began when Mrs. Whittemore talked to her class about Pleasant Hill Academy in the Cumberlands of Tennessee and showed them pictures and pamphlets. Like many others, John believed at that time that the people living in the Southern Appalachians were descendants of the Highland Scottish and, as such, akin to him. His Scottish sentiment was aroused, and a sort of clan loyalty which was to last him long after he found that Highland Scottish blood was by no means predominant in the mountains.

I am not clear why he chose to go to Williams College, when he had planned from the beginning to go to Harvard. Probably he was influenced by some of his academy friends who were going to Williams. The blessings of Dr. Bancroft ushered him into this new adventure.

September 15, 1888

> Best congratulations on your twenty-first birthday—your freedom day. I hope your manhood will be strong and happy and useful like your boyhood, and fruitful unto the end.
> Faithfully yours,
> C. F. F. Bancroft

The years of 1888 to 1892 saw the end of an era at Williams. Some of the famous old professors who had made the reputation of the college were in the last years of their teaching. John's recollections of them would have filled a popular Williams book. There was Professor Cyrus Morris Dodd (mathematics), who could concentrate so intensely that one might bounce tennis balls on the blackboard where he was working. It was Truman Henry Safford (professor of astronomy), affectionately known by his students as "Saffy," who, I think, would not teach in a cold classroom and who examined the thermometer as soon as he came to class. The boys, recognizing his peculiarity, would thrust the thermometer out on the snowy window ledge until the lookout announced that the professor was coming. Then they all pulled up their coat collars and sat shivering conspicuously. The professor would examine the registered figure with concern. It was very low. "Young gentlemen," he would say, "learning is good, but health is better. The class is dismissed. We will take the same lesson for tomorrow."

It was "Saffy" too, I think, whose room was under that of perhaps the best known of the professors, Arthur Latham Perry (political economy). He was then almost beyond teaching and retired while John was still in college. "Peri," as the boys knew him, was fond of making jokes, of which the boys showed their appreciation by giving out a tremendous yell known as the "Peri" yell. In his last years, the coming of his joke was recognized afar off, and the yell had become a first-rate nuisance. The class leader would throw back his head, snap his fingers, and the class would burst into a roar which often brought poor "Saffy" pattering upstairs in protest.

One of John's favorite stories concerned Vanderzee (Newton Briggs), later to become a judge on the New York bench. A group of bright fellows gathered about the bulletin board one morning [and] beheld Vanderzee streaking down late from his hall. Immediately a plan took form: at Peri's first joke, Bartlett, the leader, was to throw back his head, snap his fingers in signal, and then everyone was to keep still. "But don't tell Vanderzee!" The first joke came soon. Bartlett threw back his head, snapped his fingers, and Vanderzee, who had a large mouth and tremendous lung capacity, came out alone with a terrific war-whoop. This time Peri was not pleased at the demonstration. Planting his feet firmly in front of the offender, the old professor issued his dictum: "Vanderzee, Vanderzee, if you ever make a noise like that in my classroom again, I'll kick you downstairs quicker than chain lightning." As the deafening roar which followed died down, "Saffy's foot was heard on the stair. Peri received his visitor at the door, and in response to his mild protestations answered with dignity that he knew how to conduct his own classes. Upon which, the roar burst forth again, accompanying "Saffy" down the stair.

That John enjoyed his college thoroughly there is no doubt; his tales were too full of reminiscent joy. He was also a good student, missing Phi Beta Kappa by a bare fraction of a point. He played tennis and baseball exceptionally well, although he was never on the college team. Forest Grant wrote me in 1947:

> I feel I want to say a lot about John as an athlete. I knew him only as an extremely healthy young man with no trace of any physical disability. He was not, however, with great strength or weight, but was one of the most skillful players in tennis and baseball that I ever knew. He relied on his brains and careful work to win and was generally successful. By nature he was a leader, and under his leadership it was a pleasure to work. His quiet but firm manner appealed to all and downed the usual blatant opposition offered by so many players on the field. He was a most enthusiastic player and I am sure greatly enjoyed every minute he spent in athletics.

He joined Delta Upsilon Fraternity, but he was never much of a fraternity man. When one realizes that his father was a Scottish Rites Mason, and his brother Gavin a Mason too, as well as his revered Sunday school teacher Mr. Buckingham, it seems strange how little interest John had in Masonry or in any other secret organizations. At college some of his closest friends belonged to different fraternities, and many were nonfraternity. He liked people in general and found friends wherever his interests led him—sports, out-of-door activities (including study of birds and flowers), books, literary work, college papers, public speaking. In his '92 Class Book, John H. Hewitt—professor of ancient languages—is named as his favorite professor.

In spite of his boyhood dancing lessons, a naturally quick and graceful figure, and a dancing foot, he gave up dancing, probably because it did not have the approval of the Presbyterian group at home, especially perhaps because of Grace Buckingham, in whom he was becoming increasingly interested. She was behind him in school but followed him east and, after three years in Gannett Institute in Boston, went through Smith College. Pictures show her a sweet-faced, dark-eyed girl, sedately dressed in the fashion of the nineties. We may be sure she played her part in John's interest in matters of religion at Williams, where he belonged to the not-too-popular Young Men's Christian Association. In fact, he gave up cards because a YMCA friend was profoundly shocked to find him playing whist (taught him by his father) and felt it would hurt his influence. He kept his pledge for years. On the '92 Commencement Program his choice for the Graves Prize Contest in Public Speaking was "Elements of Christianity in Seneca." I believe it brought him the prize. Public speaking all through his student life brought him prizes. At the commencement exercises, however, on Wednesday, June 22, 1892, his subject was more worldly: "A Plea for the Collegian."

Like his father, he was always interested in history. How pleased his father would have been to read in *The Southern Highlander and His Homeland,* written many years later, John's memories of his college days linked with his southern mountain experiences and study:

Associated in memory with these experiences are others of college days in the Berkshire Hills of far-away Massachusetts. On a "mountain day" expedition to the top of Greylock, the return trail had been lost in a gathering storm. Forced to seek shelter, we finally made our way to the door of a log cabin, such a cabin as one may see today at the foot of Graybeard or Grandfather in the Carolina Blue Ridge. Given a cordial welcome by the young mother within, we sought to establish friendly relations with the little daughter cuddled, in fear of the storm and in shyness of strangers, in her mother's arms. The fire lighted up the room furnished with a simplicity which might duplicate many a mountain cabin of the South. With the passing of the storm came a halloo from the stalwart young husband, as he returned from the clearing with axe gleaming over his shoulder. We lingered at the bend to wave them goodbye—mother, babe now in father's arms, with the rainbow over all.

The beauty of the picture lives fresh in the writer's memory, but in later years there has come to him more than the memory of its beauty. To the haunting, half-asked question of the connection between this family group and the straggling train through the mountain hamlet, between the cabin on the slope of the Berkshires and the cabins in the southern mountains, an answer has at last been given. What he saw in the Berkshires, and what one still sees occasionally in the Green Mountains and White Mountains, the Catskills and Adirondacks, are, as it were, reenacted scenes of the great drama of settlement once lived from New England to Georgia along the frontier line moving ever toward the West. Physiographic and other natural causes will explain why in our Southern Highlands these scenes persist along lingering segments of that frontier line; and why they are found only at isolated points in the highlands of the North.[8]

One more letter we have from John's father, written during the years John and Gavin junior were at Williams College:

Green Bay, Winona & St. Paul Railroad Company
G. Campbell, General Manager
Green Bay, Wisconsin
June 6, 1889

My Dear Gavin,

I received your letter, also one from John. I was pleased to learn that John's team is doing so well. Enclosed find passes from Boston to Chicago. I do not think I can get east before you leave, as it is quite likely I may be with the Central by that time. Do not say anything about this to Forest or anyone. As soon as it is definitely arranged, will notify you.

Please let me know soon how much money you need to square up all your bills, so I can send it. The weather is now pleasant after a long wet spell. The month of May and the first of June has been very unpleasant, but it seems to be all right now. I saw the Chicagoes play Cleveland two games yesterday in Chicago. The Chicagoes are not the players they used to be. I think the foreign trip demoralized them. The Clevelands play well and is the better club.

I expect a visit from Mr. Cooley and Maggie tomorrow to stay over Friday night and go home Saturday p.m. I will drive them around the city. Mr. C. L. Colby is again president of the Wisconsin Central.

Hoping to hear from you soon, I am your aff. Father.

This is the last letter I have from Gavin Campbell, and I lay it down with regret. Though I never saw him, or—outside of John—any of the family to whom he wrote with such affection, I feel I knew him and am loath to let him slip into the past—big, warm-hearted, generous, honest, impulsive Scotsman, adored by his children and by all the men who worked with him. The appointment to which he referred in the letter came through: general superintendent of the Wisconsin central. In 1891 his jurisdiction extended to the Chicago and Northern Pacific and the Chicago and Calumet Terminal. The family moved to Milwaukee and then to Oak Park to be with him.

Meanwhile John, in his last year of college, had been wrestling with the problem of what to do next. He did not particularly want to be a minister, but he knew he wanted some kind of service work rather than a business career. Divinity school offered him a chance to think things through; perhaps he would find what he wanted to do. If his father was disappointed, he did not show it. He had begun to fail in health, and a trip to California in the spring of '92 seemed to aggravate rather than improve his condition. John returned to Andover and seminary life with some serious misgivings, despite Dr. Bancroft's warm letter of encouragement.

Phillips Academy
Andover, Mass.
C. F. F. Bancroft, Principal
August 22, 1892

Dear Campbell,

I am delighted to know you are coming to the seminary. I think there is no doubt the instruction here is the most inviting and stimulating there is. I send you a catalogue showing that the term begins Sept. 21st.

The academy begins 14th. I sent you an academy catalogue for your friend the last mail Saturday.

I recall your life here and your brother's with much pleasure. Your father's first visit here is perfectly vivid in my memory. I can see us three sitting about the round table now! Best regards to you all.

Faithfully yours,

Cecil F. F. Bancroft

The seminary proved as inviting and stimulating as Dr. Bancroft had represented. For John it was more than that; it was what he had unconsciously been wanting. He enjoyed the life, which was by no means too serious, the comradeship of congenial minds, the stirring classes, and the serenity and beauty of the great campus. Dr. William J. Long, a fellow-classman of John's, wrote in an article in the *Boston Evening Transcript* on Saturday, May 16, 1893:

Andover's first object has never been to make preachers. That is beyond the power of any institution. . . . her mission was first of all to educate men in the truth. . . .

I must confess at the outset that Andover seemed a bit old-fashioned and conservative. The seminary had the idea—borrowed from Christ and St. Paul, and all the great preachers of the church—that before a man goes out on a mission, he ought to "live apart" for a while and fast and pray, and get acquainted with truth and be certain of God and himself. . . . Andover stuck to her old mission of educating men in the truth, and led them apart to Andover Hill, a beautiful, peaceful place, with its wide outlook, its immense campus, its noble trees and lawns, and, crowning the hilltop, its simple, dignified old buildings without sham or pretense in their architecture. The rooms were bare, it is true, but it does not take much to make an altar—a table, a white cloth, a couple of candles, and an unseen God to worship. And if they were not merry with banjos and redolent with cigarette smoke, most of us bore the loss with resignation and made shift to be happy with the sunshine that streamed into our windows, and with the unutterable glory that transformed our old studies when the sun dropped low behind the western trees. I have never known but two places where one was reasonably sure of a sunset that would stir by its beauty and splendor all that is deepest and most inexpressible in a man's soul. One was the Roman Campagna; the other was Andover Hill. Moreover, those sunny old rooms were consecrated by generations of plain living and high thinking, and by the memories of good men who had lived and worked and prayed in them and who are now doing the Master's work out in the big world.

Across the big campus were the professors' houses; and there we found men, and also women, worthy of the beautiful place and of the high call-ing to which they had given themselves. . . . To be with these men, to share their noble life and thought was in itself an education. I have been in many schools and universities, but I never found their like gathered together in one place again.

As for the students, we were a varied lot, rich and poor, talented and simple—one of the most varied lot of men that ever gathered in a lecture room. As I think of them now, some eighty men, nearly every one college bred, my impression is one of single strength and uniformity. These men hated shams; and to them, spiritual dishonesty was the one unpardonable sin. From the seminary they demanded truth, and from one another sin-cerity. So, if a misguided youth began in a holy tone to speak glibly of infi-nite things, he was promptly chaffed and jollied into a more humble and reverent spirit. . . . I got my own share, scripture measure, of sand paper-ing; but if I am ever mentally hazed again, or my sermons are ever criti-cized, may it be done by men as honest of purpose and as kind of heart as they were.

John lived in one of the two brick buildings flanking the Bartlett Chapel, the classroom building with an assembly hall in it. Winters were cold and windy and stoves the prevailing method of heating. Rollin Lynde Hartt, who had—with Mor-ris Ellsworth Merriam and Ernest Clark Bartlett—continued on with John from

Williams, possessed a famous stove appropriately named "Exit." As he lay in bed and meditated on how to warm up his cold room without freezing in the process, Hartt contrived means whereby he could reset the damper without crawling out from under his billowing comforters. Many of the students lived on a narrow financial margin. At one time Hartt and his roommate seem to have boarded themselves for economy's sake. At the end of the year they claimed they could have "a very-well-seasoned and nourishing stew" made by boiling the rug underneath the stove—probably not "Exit."

Andover was kind to the young theologues. John used to get a good deal of amusement out of what he was pleased to call the "Underwear Fund." The fact seemed to be that some fund for needy or sick students had long been untouched, so that the authorities gave two or three sets of underwear to all who wished to accept. Doubtless some greatly appreciated the help, but John always objected to special financial concessions because men were, or were planning to be, ministers. "I remember," writes Merriam, "that in a students' assembly, Campbell denounced the practice of giving clergymen cut rates."

Andover at this time had passed through its great crisis, but the echoes were still rumbling.[9] Students were called upon to pass from classes in extreme German rationalism to those strictly orthodox in view, with all degrees between. There was room for hard thinking and some real mental struggle. John loved the honest presentation of the professors; he always enjoyed a good argument where people kept their tempers. "It was hard sometimes," he used to say, "but when you came through, what you had was your own."

The summer of 1893 found Gavin Campbell so much worse in health that the family decided to take him from Stevens Point to Montello, in the hope the change would help him. He was in great pain much of the time but kept up his cheerful manner and his interest in life as well as he was able. Forest Grant was with the family most of the summer. He says:

It so happened that the baseball team in Montello had always been beaten by the teams of the surrounding country and had grown tired of it. Under the advice of John and Gavin Jr., they decided to get some help and retrieve their reputation. So two of us who were playing on college teams and a couple other good players accepted an invitation from the Baseball Association to spend a month at the Montello Hotel and do something about that reputation. And we did, much to their satisfaction. John and Gavin, Arthur Week and I, with at least two others, drove a team of mustangs all over that part of the state. We as a group were being left behind very rapidly until I, who was driving, discovered that my team of mustangs didn't know how to trot. They either had to gallop or walk. So gallop we did—carriage and all—and soon led the procession. I mention this because that summer meant so much to the Campbell family, with their great concern over the health of their very wonderful father. Baseball was a diversion to us all, and it came into John's life that summer with a welcome, I am sure.

John returned to the Seminary in the fall, while young Gavin, who was not well himself, stayed at home to be near his father and mother—Maggie being married at this time. Both boys were at home when their father died on January 31, 1894.

A sheaf of letters and telegrams lies before me. They say all the things one might expect. I note one from Rollin Hartt, written from Andover: "Hard as the trial is, you have surely had much to thank God for. It is not every boy that grows into manhood under the constant influence of a father as good and wise as yours. I think I know the losses that attend fatherless boyhood, for you know I lost my own father so long ago that I have little memory of him to live with me for comfort."

Another to John, among the many letters received from officials of the railroad, was from Charles A. Lamareux, formerly Mr. Campbell's secretary and a "most unusually efficient man":

Office of General Superintendent
Milwaukee, Wisconsin
February 6, 1894

My Dear Friend:

How many times I have thought of you all since returning from Stevens Point. When I recall the five years association I had with your father, who seemed like a father to me, who gave me my first promotion, who advanced me numerous positions, who always trusted me with his private as well as business matters, who had unbounded confidence in my integrity, a man who was loved by everyone, who has been faithful and loyal to his employers, a man whose every characteristic was founded on the noblest principle, unselfish, manifestly fair and just to all, of the most tender dealings.

Indeed, when I say he seemed like a father to me, it but faintly expresses the regard and affection I had for him.

C. A. Lamareux

And the superintendent of motive power, James McNaughton, writing to Barbara from Waukesha, adds: "I wish it were possible for me to fully express the feelings of regret and sympathy prevailing among our employees generally, as there must be some consolation in the fact that your husband was loved by all who knew him."

The last months at Andover were naturally filled with anxious consideration of what the coming year would bring to the men now almost ready to face the world. It seems that a group in John's class—he among them—had made a pact to go to the Southern Highlands after graduation if an opportunity should present itself. Merriam explains, May 1947, in a somewhat distant fashion: "Some missionary who had had Kentucky, or at least mountain, experience, spoke to the Andover men about going into the mountains in pairs, one man and wife, making four, in each county seat, who were supposed to carry on a mountain *school* and *church* à la mode. It was assumed that county after county would fall for the plan. At that time the character or type of these progressive institutions was not (at least in public) discussed. Presumably Campbell was influenced by this scheme. For some reason (money perhaps), nothing came of this plan."

Who influenced him, Merriam does not say. Perhaps he had forgotten that he himself was one of the first to go to the mountains, while Rollin Hartt, who had also come from Williams to the seminary with John, was another. Carl Kelsey, later professor of economics at the Wharton School, University of Pennsylvania, was still another. There may have been more who tried the mountains but eventually found congenial work elsewhere. John seems to be the only one who held to his first interest. The following letter would indicate that he sent a letter of inquiry to [the] assistant corresponding secretary of the American Missionary Association, who was brother to Professor William H. Ryder of Andover Seminary:

American Missionary Association
New York
March 22, 1895
Rev. John C. Campbell
Andover Theological Seminary
Andover, Massachusetts

My Dear Friend:
    Your kind and very interesting letter of March 5th did not reach me till the 18th. It may be possible that you learned from my brother the reason. . . .
    I read your letter with great appreciation. We are just now getting the schedule in shape for appointments for the new year. I shall take great pleasure

in bringing your name before the proper authorities, and I have great hope that even in this time of curtailment and limitation they will be able to offer you appointment. I will write you just as soon as the matter is settled by the board. The school and work at Joppa have not yet been settled, as no action has been taken authorizing the secretaries to open that work next year. There seems little doubt but the committee will adopt the work there. I will let you know as soon as possible.

I cannot tell you how thoroughly I appreciate this interest on the part of the students at Andover and some of our other seminaries, in this great mountain field. It means hard work for you brethren, but at the same time it means great things for the Kingdom, in my judgment, if we can only hold that mountain field for the Lord and introduce among them intelligent Christianity.

I enclose you a blank form of application as this gets before the committee such facts as they desire to know. Would you kindly fill it out and return to me that I may have it to present with the other papers?

Thanking you again for your most satisfactory letter, and with most cordial Christian greetings, I remain,

Very sincerely yours,

C. J. Ryder

John often said that the theological course he had taken helped him to understand the point of view of the people among whom he had made his home—predominantly Southern Baptists and Methodists of varying shades of belief. What appeared to be deep doctrinal differences were so often, he found, a matter of phraseology which covered ideas and human feelings not so far apart. We may assume it helped him, too, to understand what lay behind the formal phraseology of church boards and officials.

Evidently he wrote, too, about openings to the Presbyterian board, for when the hoped-for opportunity came, he had a choice between a pastorate at Marshall, North Carolina, under the Presbyterian Church, and a teaching position under the American Missionary Association at Joppa, Cullman County, Alabama. He chose to go to Joppa as principal of a new school which the AMA was opening on Sand Mountain. As the years had gone on, he had come to feel that he could not conscientiously subscribe to all that the Presbyterian minister must accept when ordained. What was more, he felt he could work more freely and effectively as layman than as minister. He was destined to "preach" much in the years that followed; he was even licensed to do so at Joppa, but he was never ordained.

In September 1895, he and Grace Buckingham were married and set forth on their great adventure.

Appendix 1: Lumber Rafting in the Mid-Nineteenth Century

Mr. Forest Grant, a boyhood friend of John in Stevens Point, sent me in 1948 an account of lumbering during these early days in Wisconsin. In this account he quoted from contributions to the *Stevens Point Journal* in 1928, made by one Pat Collins (or Tap Snilloc, as he signed himself), who wrote from personal recollection of the rafting of timber down the Wisconsin River. The following is briefed from a letter of Mr. Grant to me and clippings from the *Journal* articles by Mr. Collins:

Wisconsin in early days was covered with a heavy forest of pine. As late as 1840, Indian trails were the only thoroughfares through the dense pineries. The "old Pinery Road" in the forties from Fort Winnebago north to the trading post of the American Fur Company passed through monotonous forest, broken only by occasional bluffs and rocky cliffs along the river. While a number of sawmills, loosely connected by the Great Pinery Road, were established in the upper waters of the river in the first half of the nineteenth century, real logging, as it came to be practiced on the Wisconsin, did not begin until around 1836.

The same year the government extinguished Indian rights for three miles on each side of the river from Point Bas, forty miles up the stream, and a careful survey of the stream itself was made from Point Bas to Big Bull Falls. Occupation and claiming of the most eligible sites quickly followed.

The forty-mile strip taken over by the government from the Indians coincided with an area of rough water on the upper Wisconsin River. From Merrill to Point Bas is a

succession of rapids and eddies, most of which surge over rocky bottoms with a wild current of ten to twenty miles an hour, the channel broken and divided, offering almost insurmountable obstacles to anything like navigation, yet over all of these the lumber has to pass.

Its passing, attended with great labor and extreme peril, called for the utmost vigilance, knowledge of the river, skill, and courage.

It produced a class of men known as "pilots" who "became both masters of the rapids and capitalists in the lumber trade, as nothing could be done without them, at least to get the product to market after it had been cut in the mills.

"Wages paid in those days were from $20 to $30 per month. Logs were selling from $5.00 to $7.50 per thousand. . . . These pilots, when engaged by the day, make their own terms at from $5.00 to $15.00. Those of better character, with a little means ahead, are accustomed to job the business, entering into contract with the producer to take the boards in the pile at the mills, and furnishing all the necessary men and outlays at their own costs and charges to deliver the lumber at Dubuque or St. Louis at a stipulated price per thousand feet."

It was the custom for mill owners to locate a good stand of timber on the river and the many small streams that empty into it and hire lumber jackers to cut logs in the winter and drive them to the mill, where they were sawed into lumber.

These men worked for their employers 365 days in the year, were always ready night or day to respond to the appeal of their bosses, and they were experts in their line. They could swing a four-pound axe on a four-foot handle from morning until night and miss the mark but once in a thousand strokes. They could walk on a round saw-log floating in the swift water of a great rapids with the ease of a squirrel, where one misstep meant sure death either from drowning or from being crushed among the floating logs. They were expert with a team in snow or on rough roads and could fell a pine tree with uncanny accuracy.

They went into the northern woods in the early fall and built their shanties for the winter's work. There was no lumber to build the cabins. They split the logs and hewed them for the floors, doors, and tables. The sleeping bunks were built on the sides of the camp, one tier above the other. These bunks were filled with hay, and a blanket spread on the mattress; several blankets were used for covering.

It was in camps similar to these, I infer, that Gavin Campbell's men were housed and where he stayed for stretches of time when, as superintendent of the

Penokee Division of the Wisconsin Railroad, he was working with the Penokee and Gogebic Development Company to put the tracks into Ashland. I have today, still strong and in good condition, some double red and gray blankets, almost like homespun, which he used in the woods at that time. In the national museums in Washington are similar red blankets, displayed with an Indian figure and from that general region.

Once cut, the lumber was assembled into "cribs" containing each thirty-five hundred feet of lumber and "rapids pieces"—several cribs coupled end to end.

Two to eight men were necessary to manage a rapids piece, according to the difficulties and dangers of the various rapids. Twenty of these rapids pieces constituted a "fleet" managed by one pilot and his gang hands.

If the channel is missed, a wrong one taken, and the fleet runs into a slough, it is little better than lost, as the expense of breaking up, hauling out, moving across islands to the channel, reconstructing the raft, would in all probability be more than the lumber would be worth. It is difficult to back out, or run the raft upstream, to get out of such a dilemma.

On the pilot rested the responsibility.

Partaking somewhat of the rigorous, wild character of the river and its whirlpools, they are nevertheless for the most part men of generous impulses, honest and trustworthy; being entrusted frequently not only with the custody of a year's earnings of a large establishment in its transit to market, but with the sale of the rafts, the disbursement of large amounts of the proceeds to hand, and the rendition of final accounts to the owners.

One must remember that there were no banks for many years. The barter and trade between the merchants and lumbermen was of a cash nature, or an even swap. When a fleet of lumber was taken to the southern markets in the spring of the year, the sale was for cash; the men received their wages at the place of sale, and the balance of the payment was brought back in currency and put into local circulation.

Four miles north of Point Bas, all rapids in the Wisconsin River came to an end, with the passing of Jennie Bull Falls, Big Bull Falls, Little Bull Falls, Shaurette and Conant Rapids, Grand Rapids, Clint's Dam, and Whitney Rapids.

The cribs were warily examined and the Rapids Pieces securely coupled into rafts—usually two Rapids Pieces, side by side, making a "Wisconsin-raft." The long oar at either end [was] manned, balanced, and dropped onto the pin in the head block. The great fleet containing thousands of feet of choicest lumber swung out into the current headed for the final goal, the world's market on the Mississippi River.

In this was the material furnished for the immense prairies of Illinois, Iowa, and Missouri. The run from Wausau to Saint Louis was done sometimes in twenty-four days but usually took several weeks.

From Point Bas down the river, it was smooth running with the joy of living in the open as the rafts nosed their way around curves and between wooded banks, leisurely moving with the current "down the old Wesconce." These were the days when men afforded to make the river run dressed in broadcloth, and occasionally lighted a cigar with a ten-dollar-bill for lighter. Many made their return trip on foot, bringing their treasure with them. Others wasted and rioted, and there was many a king among the lumberjacks who allowed the twenty- and fifty-dollar gold pieces to roll away, leaving him to want in old age.

In 1873, two years after Gavin Campbell went to Stevens Point, the reported cut of pine on the Wisconsin River just above Stevens Point was over 13 million. Much of this must still have come down by raft, but so swift was the change that by 1875, according to Pat Collins, rafting was almost at an end. Logs could be moved with so much less time and labor by rail. Rafts continued to run the rapids some fifteen years longer; the last went down in 1888.

2

First Mountain Teaching

Joppa, Alabama, 1895–1898

No letters survive indicating John Campbell's first impressions of Joppa, Alabama, where he began his teaching career as a missionary. Joppa was on the southern end of Sand Mountain, about two thousand feet above sea level. The town had about twelve houses and a few stores, where trade was conducted by bartering, a school, and a "church minus everything a church should have—even windows." He and his bride Grace stayed with neighbors until they could get into their own home.

The schoolhouse was a source of pride to the town, but it was far different from what the Campbells expected. They found it bare, dirty, and lacking heat and other equipment. John found the ignorance appalling, but it was tempered by a great deal of common sense. After one prayer meeting, a student remarked that Mr. Campbell might get into a lot of trouble speaking so plainly: "Truth and Liberty have ever been prisoners, and Ignorance and Tyranny their turnkeys."

Grace Campbell's letters to her mother and father in Stevens Point, Wisconsin, describe a young couple trying to make a home and a place for themselves in a small mountain community more than twenty miles away from a store that had "ordinary supplies." She writes of the scarcity of meat: "I would not have believed that people could eat as many eggs as we do and not turn into chickens." Of sickness, she wrote in one letter: "O, the sick people whom we visit in dirty rooms, surrounded by dirty children!"

Restrictions imposed by the American Missionary Association (AMA) Board in New York as to the use of funds added difficulties in terms of purchasing equipment and supplies. There was an obligation to have a teacher for every fifty pupils, but in spite of a great deal of interest, there was never enough money or teachers. The school expected 250 pupils the following year, but the AMA Board could only make the same appropriation for Joppa as the year before. For family reasons, the Campbells had to return to Stevens Point the next year. Appendix 2 consists of letters from Joppa pupils expressing their appreciation.

Dear Friend John,

I am just out of school work for the day, and feel little like doing anything heavier than writing a letter. I am teaching in an independent school in the mountains, the western end of old Virginia. There is quite a town here on a new railroad, with a number of stores, one Methodist Church, a "city drug store," some mills, shops, etc., an "academy" with a new "professor." I shall have been here a week tomorrow morning.

Had a very pleasant ride through the Bluegrass region of Kentucky. Near Berea College, in a town where I stopped a few hours, I met my first mountaineer. He was a "right smart good-natured human." (I have already learned a little of their brogue; it is by no means so bad as we have supposed—so I think, at least.)

I have a school of one hundred scholars with one native assistant. Have not taken my public examination yet and am afraid of not passing—arithmetic especially comes hard.

My pupils are very much brighter than I supposed. I think you will be pleasantly disappointed in this respect. Some of the most insignificant-looking boys are very bright. The scholars I taught in Maine were not so good. One little cuss who dresses very negligee (shirt, pants, and suspenders) is better in arithmetic than I am; and you would find it very difficult to fool him in anything. Please write me when you get south and give me your impressions.

Morrison E. Merriam

This letter from his friend of Andover Seminary and Williams College days, who had also committed himself to work under the AMA in the southern mountains, was perhaps some preparation for what John was to find when he at last reached his journey's end in Joppa. No letters have survived describing his first impressions, but among his papers are penciled notes and various drafts of material he evidently intended to use in some speaking appointment or, it may be, in some later published form. I have tried to arrange such material in a sequence which will give some idea of his early observations and reflections. We will begin at the beginning and use his own words:

There were unusual signs of life about Culpepper station for a summer afternoon. It had been noised abroad that the *Planters' Vestibule* was to stop that day. The crowd of Negroes taking their usual nap in the shade of the cotton bale on the platform were roused from their happy dreams by the whistle of the express rounding the curve.

When court was in session, it was customary for Culpepper to take its siesta after the passing of the Up-Accommodation. All business was then suspended. Silence and heat brooded over the village until the echoes from the valley below announced the approach of the Down Local with night and the mail. The entire male population flocked to the station to welcome the stranger within its gates and to accompany the postmaster and mailbags to the office.

Courtesy as well as curiosity took them today through red dust and heat, in answer to the whistle of the *Vestibule*. Some months before, it had become known that an educational society from the North proposed opening a school at Smyrna Mountain, the part of the county to the northwest; and word had been brought today by the mail carrier that the professor was to arrive on the *Vestibule*. Unwonted excitement reigned as groaning brakes confirmed the whistle's promise that the *Vestibule* was going to stop, sure enough.

As the heavy train of coaches came to a standstill, a young man and woman alighted from the rear platform and looked about them with an air of expectancy. They were the only passengers, and the effusiveness of the porter, increased by a generous tip (for one breveted "colonel" must rise to his rank if he would deserve the respect of those who serve him), added to the impressive unscheduled stop, was all [that] was needed to assure the waiting crowd that the notables had arrived in its midst. By common and unspoken consent, the judge and the editor of the *Peoples' Advocate* stepped forward to greet the newcomers and to welcome them. To these two the mail carrier, as representative of the population of Smyrna, joined himself.

At a peremptory signal from the judge, a half score of darkies lolling on the cotton bales sprang forward in eager rivalry to carry the bags. Escorted by the judge and editor and followed by a body of their retainers, the "colonel" and his lady were presented as friends of the judge to the urbane host of the Traveller's Rest, over whose dingy portals was emblazoned the Latin motto Hic Requiescamus. With innate courtesy the travelers were left to rest, and after a period of refreshment were waited upon by the judge and editor and a group of their friends who called to pay their compliments. Under the genial warmth of their southern welcome, Northern reserve melted; and motives, purposes, plans, and hopes were revealed to sympathetic hearts.

Now, long years ago a beloved father—then a lad from the highlands of Scotland—had come to the South to seek his fortune. Stricken by pestilence, which had marked the lintel of many a southern house, he, though a stranger in a strange land, was taken into a southern home, nursed to health, and sent to a brother in a northern city, who had preceded him in his quest for fortune. War had brought many changes, and all trace of benefactors was lost; but the son had long cherished the hope of coming south to repay in some slight measure the debt of gratitude that was his. Perhaps it was the call of the blood that prompted him eagerly to accept the offer of a principalship in the Highland Industrial, Normal and Collegiate Institute, which the National Educational Association, with the faith of a good-sized grain of mustard seed, had first named and then built in this remote section of Appalachia County.

The judge, whose name testified to his Scottish forebears, furtively brushed aside a tear, grasped the stranger's hand in both of his, and, with a profound bow to the lady, pledged the united support of the county to this notable and commendable educational enterprise. Nay, he would go even further and pledge the support of his state and the entire southland to this stupendous undertaking so pregnant with possibilities. The South welcomed such cooperation from the North. When he and his comrades, in response to the mandates of duty and the compulsion of the love of their native states, took up arms in fratricidal strife, it was with the profoundest sorrow. When they at Appomatox laid down their rifles, it was not with smouldering animosities. "We who wore the gray, Sir," said he, "know that those of the blue who met us in battle array, face to face, responded to the mandates of duty and the summons of a love no less profound than ours. We and our children cherish no hatred toward them nor their children. Our hatred—or may I say rather our contempt—is for those damned rascals (craving the pardon of the lady for this impetuous utterance, forced by warm southern blood) of reconstruction days, who arrayed race against race to further their own nefarious ends."

"As for myself,' continued the judge, "I entertain the deepest respect and admiration for all who trim and burnish the lamp of learning and teach the youth of our reunited country to drink deeply at the Pierian Spring. My joy is profound, Sir, in that I cherish the hope that I may number you, Sir, and your fair companion, among my warm personal friends, and I here give you my hand, professor, in token of my unwavering allegiance."

It had come. With his beloved Lee, I too must seek the quiet walks and academic shades, no more to be known as "colonel," but as "professor."

It is many years since "taps" were sounded for the judge to join his worthy comrades of the gray and of the blue, and the complimentary copy of the *Appalachian Herald and Tribune* sent to the professor by the editor has yellowed with age, but still distinct stands out the spirit of the judge, the editor, and their friends, as evidenced in their heartfelt welcome: "These illustrious and learned educators are altogether welcome to our sunny southland."

The mail carrier was a man of important business. It was therefore early next morning that the professor and his lady made ready to start for Smyrna. The trunk was strapped to the mail hack—a task in which all Culpepper fought to assist. Though the sun had hardly dispelled the morning mists, judge, editor, joined by banker and other town notables, were on hand to give a last parting clasp of the hand. The mail carrier cracked his whip over his dozing mules, and the professor and his bride were on their way to Smyrna.

As they ascended the hill which was to shut Culpepper from view, the professor caught a final glimpse of the judge, the editor, and the banker waving a farewell with hats in hand; behind them the rank and file of Culpepper, and at a respectful distance in the background the sleepy smiles of the Negroes who had not already dropped in the shade to catch a few minutes before the coming of the Up-Accommodation and the noon siesta.

The professor could not speak. The welcome of strangers had touched the young man deeply. He had expected his mission to be misunderstood; and now, as the kind offices of the judge and his associates came before him in review, there was kindled in his heart a flame that the experiences of years increased. A hand slipped into his. "Aren't they dear," Grace said, with just the suspicion of quaver in her voice, "and aren't you glad we came!"

The road wound slowly upward, to the grunt of the straining mules and the rattle and creak of the brake. Smyrna, or Joppa, let us say, lay on the southern end of Sand Mountain, several hundred feet above Cullman, the county seat, and nearly a thousand feet above Guntersville.[1]

Rocks and cedars (characteristic of the Great Valley); the sound of an axe and rolling logs; the indignant gobble of a turkey cock; distant tinkling bells mingled with woodland calls of jay, wren, chickadee, cardinal, bright against the cedar green.

So John pictured the country; but his own coming that day

was distinguished by such a welcome as summer gives at its height. It had been planned for Smyrna to have a preliminary term during laying-by time, which lies between plantin' and gatherin'—when the corn is laid by, the punkins are ripening, and all the world seems to pause before the coming harvest.

The new teacher turned to the mail carrier, who now had the honor and responsibility of answering questions until the young brother had wearied of asking them, and the mules had settled into the steady jog which experience had taught was sufficient to finish the twenty-mile journey by early candle-lighting time.

John was silent, but his mind went on with questions:

Nature has done her best in prodigality of beauty to conceal from us the dreadful poverty of man. The pink and white azalea charm us with their fragrance. Avenues of bending trees welcome us to their cooling shade; rich roses before the cabin doors give promise of cheer and comfort within. To the south of us iron and coal; miles and miles of pine; cotton in abundance. Surely we are in a land of promise; but years of patient effort must pass before the poor citizen of the mountains can realize even in part what this wonderful southland has for those who understand how to make the promise of nature real. Our meditation is broken into now by a woman with sallow, careworn face, who takes her snuff stick from her mouth long enough to ask our driver to exchange the few eggs she gives for snuff and coffee. We pass cabins with stick chimneys, men riding mules, one oxcart, and now a family all drinking "wild-cat" whiskey—even the baby, scarcely more than a year, having his share. There is another baby with snuff stick in his mouth to keep him quiet while the tired mother helps to get the ox team down the steep hill in safety.

At last we reach Joppa, the site of our school. We take a look about town, and it takes but one look to see it all. A dozen houses; a few stores carried on by barter, a fairly good school building, and a church minus everything that a church should have—even windows.

John and Grace were to stay, until they could get settled in their own home, with neighbors. They sat, that first night, at one of those round tables not too common in the mountains, with a revolving upper deck for the food. As he bowed his head to give the blessing, he caught, out of the corner of his eye, a glimpse of the host rolling up his long gray beard preparatory to tucking it inside his shirt—an operation which he completed at the end of the meal by pulling it out in three strong jerks. Before the guest could quite recover himself, he was called upon to give his attention to the capture of eatables as they were whirled by on the revolving deck. "Bread," he soon discovered, was corn bread made without eggs or sugar. White bread was "light bread"; biscuits were plentifully yellowed with soda. Accepting with enthusiasm the "milk" offered, he found it was not the "sweet milk" he had expected, but buttermilk considerably past its prime. His discomforture as he tried to swallow this and keep it down was quickly marked by his host, who observed, "We're mighty clever if we are homely. (We are very open-hearted, if we do live plainly). We'll give you the best we have."

While Grace began to assemble the small belongings they had brought into a home, John turned his first attention to the school. The schoolhouse may have been the "most important of all the buildings in Joppa," but it was a long way from what John expected of a schoolhouse—bare, open to the elements, dirty, and without provision for heating or equipment of any kind. John enjoyed telling in later years how the razor-backed hogs slipped in from the surrounding woods and stole the lunch boxes from among the rows of little sunbonnets and tattered straw hats. Once he even found a big fellow pattering down the stairs, a lunch bucket in its mouth. To get the place in reasonable order for speedy use was a task which occupied days, even weeks, and called for the combined labors of himself and his assistant, Miss Fairchild. Grace, too, was drafted away from her housesettling to help. When the doors were finally opened, the principal and his assistant were faced with 185 pupils ranging in age from five to twenty-five, poorly clothed and not all too clean but by no means lacking in intelligence.

Let us enter, and those of us who have not been born great or achieved greatness must be ready to have greatness thrust upon us. The boy who just told us that the poles of the earth stick out as an axle for the world to turn on is George Washington. That bright little fellow over there is Byron. Next is Cleveland and next to him Noah, who gives evidence of having passed through the deluge without a drop of water touching him. The tall boy with trousers above his ankles is David, brother of Napoleon, whose mule might well take the last name of the historic Napoleon. There is Isaac Elisha, and there is little Joseph, his brother, helping history to repeat itself by wearing a polka-dot waist of various colors, which was brought from the depth of a mission barrel.

Robert Lee is absent—sick with the measles—and Martin Bird has taken his flight for a similar reason. That empty seat was once occupied by the Greek bard Homer, who left to make a crop; and the vacant seat beyond was once graced by the presence of the sweet Latin Virgil, a truant of many days and afraid to take the examination awaiting him. Cyrus is still with us. Alexander's pride kept him from returning after being obliged to stand on the platform for trying to conquer the primary world in fist combat. Luther ran away from home, but we expect him back next fall. John Wesley, Luther's brother, may be seen at his headquarters in the road-bed, plus dirt and minus pocket handkerchief, making mud pies and fighting imaginary battles from a sand fort. Jesse is not in school at present, and Ezekiel has been prevented from entering; but Daniel Malachi is in regular attendance.

There are the girls: Doshy, Luler, Leler, Odor, Jimmie, Willie, Larkanelia, Saraleira, and Parthenia—poor, poor girls struggling toward the goal of enlightened womanhood in a place where woman counts for little, walking miles to school, even in winter clad only in their calico, the little ones barefooted, their bodies shivering, their lips blue with cold. Parthenia gives up the struggle, for she must cut and pile brush. Her sister must plow. There is Odor, whose parents are religious fanatics, while Odor is groping for the light. "I believe in the Bible," she says, "so far as it has been correctly translated." Our suppressed smile of amusement and wonderment at the statement is lost in her next statement, which reveals her humility and her yearning: "If I have religion, it is the religion of Jesus Christ." I learned that a week's absence was due to her traveling through the mountains with a band of her father's friends—so-called Saints—and when I remonstrated with her, she replied, "I didn't want to leave school, but father wanted me to and, Mr. Campbell, I am doing what seems to be best with the light I have." She is one of our brightest girls, and yet she lives on nothing but cornmeal; and she, with many others too poor to buy oil, studies her lessons at night by the light from a pine-knot fire.

A total disregard for sex is evident in the names. Jesse, the patriarch, spells his name Jessie; and Jimmie and Willie are girls. Willie is a beautiful girl even in her hideous sunbonnet, the universal headgear of women. She is one of a family of thirteen. "I want to make something of myself. I don't want to marry anyone about here and become just what all the women become here." She has an inborn sense of the fitness of things, and how hard must be the depressing influence of her environment. Most of the girls are striving for better things; and their efforts to follow out the directions for conduct and dress, given in our *Ladies' Home Journal,* afford us the amusement which has more of tears than laughter in it.

Two girls who came to our house but cannot come to school have moved our hearts greatly. Their father is dead, and to support an invalid mother, they have cleaned their acres of trees and stumps and raised a crop from year to year, and they are but sixteen and fourteen years of age.

You wonder, perhaps, regarding the conduct of these children in school, and their ability. We are surprised as often at their intelligence as at their ignorance. I have in mind a young man of twenty-four, formerly in our primary department. Drink is his greatest fault, but he has that genial spirit of companionship which so often is seen in those who have a like failing. My attention was first drawn to him in listening to a political discussion at the post office. Charley's father lived on this mountain during the war, was a Union spy, and had been hunted by the soldiers of the Confederacy. His son has inherited some of the bitterness of those former times. He is what the people of Joppa call a war Republican, and his opponent was a war Democrat, his audience populists. It is perhaps a little unfair for one of Republican training to give Charley's definition of democracy without giving our friends who differ from us a chance to reply. I do it merely to give more idea of the intensely political feeling, and not to take unfair advantage.

"Yes," he said, "Democracy used to mean a government of the people by the people; but now it means God bless me and my wife, my son John and his wife, us four and no more; and whom we cannot rule, we'll destroy." We smile, but may I say in passing that those of us who hold the political doctrines of Republicanism need a large charity for the enlightened democracy of the South which must meet face to face an illiterate black vote of large proportions and a large white vote needing much enlightenment.

To my surprise, this same young man, who knows nothing of arithmetic or grammar, has read all of Josephus and characterizes him as a fine old fellow. Napoleon Bonaparte is his hero, and when I expressed the hope that he would come to school regularly, he replied, "Professor, I aim to become one of the old guard to the emperor." After prayer meeting one evening, he said, jokingly, that I might get into trouble by speaking so plainly to the people; and when I replied that it was only the truth, he said, "Yes, but Truth and Liberty have ever been prisoners, and Ignorance and Tyranny their turnkeys."

I knew he loved books, so I took him into my study. As he entered, he trembled, grasped the chair near him, and said, while a look of indescribable yearning swept over his face, "O, I never saw so many books before. How I wish I had them!" I lent him a number and felt that at last I had started him in the right direction. The next morning, Christmas Day, I saw him stagger by, drunk, going with the pillars of the church to a cockfight.

The ignorance of many is appalling. One little boy of ten, the son of a minister, didn't know who Christ was; and the extent of another's knowledge of Christ was given in her statement that Christ was a Baptist. Their religion is largely a matter of temporary feeling and of rigid adherence to what they believe is orthodox. This adherence is more in theory and statement than in practice, but it is nonetheless orthodox.

But despite the fact that they lack so much that is essential to truest life, they have a sense of honor that would surprise many of us. I may leave my room for any length of time, placing the pupils on their honor, and with one or two exceptions there will not be any disturbance, any whispering—a statement, I venture to say, that few teachers here or elsewhere can make. I shall not enter into the details of our schoolwork save to say that the highest branches we are teaching at present are geometry, algebra, history, and civil government. We strive to follow in our teaching the motto "For God, Home, and Native Land." Our enrollment for the year has been 199. Sometimes 186 have been in attendance; and we have been trying, my assistant and myself, to do justice to this number—an impossible task. The average number of children to a family is eight; and there are hundreds within sound of the school bell.

The patter of little bare feet coming down the schoolhouse steps is heard. The joyous laugh of children comes to our ears. They linger about the playground they love as if unwilling to return to their cheerless homes. That little figure hurrying away as if to escape the merry laugh and joyous shout is hurrying to conceal her tears. This is her last day at school. Tomorrow she must go to the field. Twilight begins to fall, and the long line of faded sunbonnets and little dirty legs forms reluctantly. We watch them from our view as the yearning for help to give them all they need sweeps over us.

A group of letters which Grace wrote to her mother in Stevens Point that first winter, between December 1895 and February 1896, are full of the problems and details of everyday living in a region where many ordinary supplies could not be had at the local store, or even in the county seat twenty miles away. The first were written during the holidays.

Joppa, Alabama
December 1895

John read me your letter this morning while I was getting breakfast. We get up so late during vacation that he often gets the mail before breakfast. . . .

As I understand it, the mail route which passes through here is from Cullman to Guntersville and is divided into three stages: Cullman to Baileyton, Baileyton to Warrenton, and Warrenton to Guntersville. We are on the second stage. The mail leaves Cullman about three in the afternoon and gets to Baileyton in the evening. The next carrier does not start till morning, and gets here about half-past eight. Going back, he's overnight at Baileyton again. The quickest way to get a telegram to us would be to telegraph right to the agent in Cullman and ask him to send it right out by the livery. If it were not so very urgent, and reached Cullman before three o'clock, of course it would be cheaper to send it out by the carrier; and in case of a telegram, he would bring it right over on that night for extra pay. But the quick way is by the livery, and they would come out for two dollars and a half.

We have been taking a vacation on house-furnishing this week, and have been working on school matters. Posting books, for one thing, and grading the school and deciding on new books to be introduced. It is almost maddening to try to grade a school where some have been allowed to go through the fourth reader without knowing a thing about numbers, and where a knowledge of grammar is almost entirely lacking, even among the older ones. Parents send their children to school with fourth readers when they ought to be in the second because they had a chance to get the fourth readers cheap. And then they do not like it because the children cannot go into the fourth reader class. There are a thousand and one perplexities that never come to a teacher in a graded school at home, and sometimes it seems like pretty hard work to bring order out of chaos. Prof. Sherrill added to the confusion by pushing scholars ahead in certain branches so that they would bring in higher tuition. That is, the parents think so, and they are generally ready enough to believe that their children get ahead because they are smart. But John is beginning to see his way out, I think, and I am glad. He does not sleep at nights, and he wears wrinkles by day when matters are unusually perplexing.

Beautifully warm. I have been on the back porch in a calico dress most of the morning.

Joppa, Alabama
December 1895

I have about given up writing on Sunday. The day is very short, and it is about the only time John and I have to read together, so neither of us gets much writing done. Preaching, when we have it, is now at three in the afternoon, so we have Sunday school at two. Our Sundays are something like this: breakfast, dishwashing, house straightening, dressing, Sunday school lesson, Sunday school, preaching, reading, dinner, more reading, bed. On the Sundays when there is no preaching, there is a prayer meeting at half past six. . . . It was suggested at one of the prayer meetings that with Mr. Campbell and Mr. Cooley, the Baptist minister here in Joppa, we might have preaching once a month from each. John is to preach next Sunday, and if Mr. Cooley agrees, I daresay it will be kept up. I hope they will get a stove in the church; outdoor preaching is not very comfortable or safe in wintertime, and that is about what it is in the church, except that you do not have the sun to warm you.

The neglected buildings and the uncertain winter attendance might have led one to conclude that the church was of little concern to the people. The contrary was true. It might not hold first place in their life, but it certainly did in their interest, which manifested itself too often in heated doctrinal discussions and uncompromising theological pronouncements. Methodist and Baptist were the prevailing denominations, but many other sects were represented—their only common bond being a belief in eternal punishment. "We enter the church on some Sabbath," says John in his notes, "and hear only the dreadful recital of the condemned sinner's torture. Hell with its lurid flames and the worm that never dies are essential parts of most sermons." "The religious tendencies are shown," he continues,

in the names of places as well as in the names of the children. Thus Joppa; not far away are Ruth and Boaz; and yonder Hebron and Mt. Pisgah; but with this range in choice, a community of Saints has settled at Hogs Jaw. We have not as yet been able to learn what the Saints believe, but they have a practice, all too common among more educated people, of finding Scriptural sanction for almost anything they wish to do. This they do, I am told, by taking verses without reference to their context or to what intervenes. A shrewd neighbor of mine thinks they all ought to commit suicide in following out this doctrine, for in one place the scripture says, "And Judas went and hanged himself," and in another, "Go thou and do likewise."

Grace wrote her mother again during the holidays:

Joppa, Alabama
December 1895

Today I have been a carpenter. I have made two tables: one small round one of a barrel head and three saplings, the other a larger square one out of a box cover and three more saplings. The little round one I covered with my mahogany muffler, and it holds my pink-lined work basket that Beth gave me. It stands in the dining room window. The larger one I have covered with the cretonne spread that you sent down, and it stands in the study beside John's desk, to relieve the desk of books and papers. . . . At last a letter has come from New York with regard to the new teacher. It seemed that John's letter, written three or four weeks ago, did not reach them until shortly before they wrote. Secretary Ryder says that he will send the new teacher as soon as possible, so we look for her now the last of this week.

It has been cloudy and dark for a good many days, and we shall be very glad to see the sun shine again. The house is very dark when it is cloudy, especially in the dining room. There is only one small window in it, with a very wide veranda roof outside. Nothing goes very well when it is cloudy, for no one can tell what time it is. The boy that builds the fires and rings the bell at school is almost always late. The children who come from a distance get to school late—sometimes not before recess.

We have word today of a box for us in Cullman, and we suppose it is the melodeon. We shall have it brought out as soon as possible, of course. . . . Here I stopped to sell two pairs of shoes to two little boys. To be sure, one pair was for girls and one for men, but they were suited, so it was all right.

What the Cullman box contained is not told us—perhaps Christmas presents for the young couple—but about this time John's mother, sister, and a friend sent gifts which he, after much consideration, decided to expend in Bibles for the Sunday school. One of his appointed or elected duties was to teach every Sunday the Men's Union Bible Class, attended by Methodist, Baptist, Campbellite, Old-School Presbyterian, Cumberland Presbyterian, Universalist, and Perfectionist. Grace taught the girls, and Miss Fairchild the infants.

When the books came, John found that by some mistake he had ordered an extra copy. I have already referred to the young man whose father had been a Union scout, or spy. A private in the Confederate ranks, he had been handcuffed for some offense by a cousin who was captain. The handcuffs were too small, and the sufferer, out of his torture, vowed that if he ever got loose he would kill the one responsible for it. This vow he proceeded to carry out as soon as it was possible. He shot the captain with buckshot, escaped, and became a spy in the Union Army. After the war, he returned to Joppa and killed six or eight men before people would let him alone. A great reader and a heavy drinker, he lived a life to himself, and his boys became the black sheep of the community. He, too, liked to read and borrowed from the school library, but took no part in school activities. Sometimes he came to John's Bible class—not so much for information as to wait for a girl. John meditated on Rad. Would he like a Bible? He decided to take a chance on him.

The Christmas Eve tree was a great success. The Bibles were joyfully received by all, including Rad; and John retired to rest, well pleased with his evening. It was around one o'clock Christmas morning when he was aroused by a fusillade of shots in the business center. He got up, dressed, and went out to investigate. The moon was shining bright on the crossroads, and as he approached he could see two large, dark figures, accompanied by a smaller one, shooting into the air as fast as they could pull the trigger. Coming nearer, he recognized a neighbor named McCutcheon, his little boy, and Rad Berry. They lowered their guns and stopped firing as he spoke to them. "Mr. McCutcheon, do you think this is a proper way to celebrate the birthday of the Prince of Peace—to get drunk and fire a pistol— before your own son, too? You send him to school to me to make a man of him, and there you set an example like this and undo all my teaching." McCutcheon began to cry. He turned to Rad: "The perfessor is right. This ain't no way for us to be a-doin'"—celebratin' the birthday of the Prince of Peace by gettin' drunk and firin' guns, and me a-settin' an example like this ter my little boy, Newton here, when I send him ter school ter the perfessor ter make a man of him. You go home with the perfessor, Rad, and me and Newton'll go home; and the perfessor'll see ye get home."

John saw father and son on their uncertain way; then, taking Rad by the arm, started down the Big Road. At his own gate he halted. "Do you think you can make the rest of the way yourself, Rad?" Rad thought he could. "Can you cross the foot log? You remember it hasn't any rail." "I reckon I can, Perfessor. I've straddled her many a time." Not entirely reassured by the response, the professor stood at the gate watching the dark figure zigzagging back and forth across the moonlit road. Suddenly it stopped and came staggering back. Throwing his arms around the professor's neck, Rad rested his head on John's shoulder and began to sob aloud: "Perfessor, Charlie told me I was drunk, but I'm worse than that—I'm damn drunk. I'm damn drunk, but I want you to know I sure appreciated that Bible you gave me, and I want you to know that henceforth I'm going to read it every day and be a better man."

The professor finally succeeded in detaching the moist head from his shoulder and started its owner on his way straddling the foot log. He reflected with rueful humor on his evening adventure and his experiment with Christmas gifts. What was there he could do, he wondered.

Again Grace wrote home:

Joppa, Alabama
January 1896

School opened with very small numbers this morning because of the measles. I think neither of us will take them. We do not go where they are, and I guess we have both had them. I had them when I was little, didn't I?

The new teacher has not put in an appearance, and we have heard nothing about when she will be here. Secretary Ryder wrote John that he was in correspondence with a Boston teacher but would not engage her until he heard from her. John wrote over two weeks ago but has heard nothing. It is quite a disappointment not to have her here for the opening of the term, as they are all ready to grade the school, introduce new books, and so on. I hope she will come this week. I am rather glad to have school open again. John gets along better when he is real busy than he does when he has more time to think. He has fallen into the habit of waking three or four o'clock and not going to sleep again, and it tells on him. I think when the work is well started again he will not worry so much over it. Do not say anything about what I have said when you write. I do not want him to think I have been making out a bad case.

The new stove is set up in our bedroom, and we had our baths beside it Saturday night. It is a treasure—a little piece of the good old North in this miserable poor country. We have sent for another zinc and a thimble for the roof, and then we shall set up the little stove in the dining room and defy cold weather.

I went up to lead the singing for morning exercises this morning. I had just begun on the breakfast dishes when three men came to look at the shoes that came in the barrels and boxes. I had not finished the dishes when another man came to get a coat for his little girl. One day I stopped my work no less than six times to distribute clothing. I like to do it, but it takes lots of time. We have disposed of four children's dresses, six pairs of shoes, four shirtwaists, a pair of pants, a flannel blouse, three pairs of gloves, and eleven coats. There is a greater call for coats and shoes than anything else, for they get along as much as possible without shoes, and they wear thin little capes that are no protection at all. We sell the best coats for seventy-five cents, and the shoes at ten cents a pair, so that anyone can have one that can find a fit. They are paid for mostly in work, eggs, chickens, or whatnot; only two have paid cash thus far.

We have had some of the nicest sausage I ever ate. Mrs. Corde sent us enough for Sunday dinner a week ago, and Friday I said to Miss Fairchild that I did not know what we should have to eat over Sunday if someone did not come to the rescue. "If someone would only bring us some more sausage!" she said. And before the day was over, Mrs. Ogletree brought some. I never ate such sausage in my life—it was elegant; and we had enough for Saturday and Sunday. This morning Mrs. Ogletree sent me some head cheese, but it is not half so good as Mrs. Campbell's.

You don't know how good the things looked that you sent in the box with the stove. The kitchen aprons I captured for myself and was pretty glad, too, to get them. I never had time to finish the one I have that is partly made, so I have been rather short of aprons. . . . And so the melodeon has started! If it comes through as the last box did, it will be here the last of this week. But that was unusually quick time. Speaking of not sending anything with the melodeon, if anything happens that should bring about another shipment to Joppa, please put in a small can of furniture polish. . . .

Well, dearie, I certainly thought I should get a good letter written to you, but just let me tell you: When I was ready to sit down and write, Mrs. Scidmore came with eggs and butter and had a good deal to tell me about all the people who have measles. Then she wanted a coat, and before she went, Mrs. Lively came. She wanted old pasteboard boxes to make bark-covered baskets of, and I spent some time with her. I got time to start my letter after she left, and then John came from school, and close upon his heels, four boys to look at shoes. So it goes.

Joppa, Alabama
January 24, 1896

My Dear, Dear Papa

If I had written yesterday, my letter would have gone to Mama. But as I had to put it off until today, and as your letter came this morning, you shall have it instead. Miss Fairchild brought the mail up at noon and handed your letter to John, thinking it was addressed to him. When he said it was for me from you, I fairly grabbed it. But while I was opening it I said very likely you just directed it. The first thing I saw was Mama's writing, and I said, "Yes, that is all." Then I saw your writing and gave three cheers, but on unfolding it I read "Directions for setting up the melodeon" and my hopes fell again. At last I came to the letter, and I held it fast in both hands while John asked the blessing, and then read it aloud between mouthfuls. *Please* write to me again sometime, won't you?

I hope we can manage the melodeon all right. We shall try very hard. Of course, it will be some help; even a tuning fork would be some help after pitching everything at random for four months. We are very impatient to have it come, but we can hardly expect it before the middle of next week.

How your letter did bring up our wedding again! It seems like a dream of beauty, now that we look back upon it from among the very plain realities that surround us now. It certainly was beautiful; there was nothing to be regretted, nothing that I would have changed in the least particular if I had it to live over again. I wish marriage could seem as beautiful a thing to every girl as it seems to me. . . .

Oh, my! but it will be elegant to come home. Why, just think of having someone to get breakfast for you in the morning. To me that seems the height and perfection of luxury. And we can have meat every day, probably twice a day and sometimes three times! It hardly seems possible. I would not have believed that people could eat as many eggs as we do and not turn into chickens. But I am learning that people can do a great many things when they have to.

Fifteen years later John was to answer a minister who had written him of his privations in the mountains:

Your letter of October 13th has just come to the office, and I appreciate deeply the situation in which you are placed. I have received letters from other sections of the mountains which are almost exact duplicates of yours in their appeal, and I know how true they are, for I myself have been in the same situation—even as to the furniture. My first home in the mountains, twenty miles from a railroad, was furnished with furniture which I myself made out of dry-goods boxes, and fresh meat was so scarce that I could get none for the first three months, and after that at uncertain intervals—and they were generally long. I, too, have had teachers who have given up good salaries elsewhere and have come to the mountains to live on a mere pittance.

Grace's series of letters home continues:

Joppa, Alabama
January 1896

The sun is shining for the first time in many days, and it makes us feel good just to look out of doors. I promised John I would go for a walk after school, so my letter may be short. I do not like to refuse to go, for he will not go without me, and he gets very nervous if he stays in all the time. It does me good to get away from the house for a while, too.

Before I was through with my dinner dishes, two women and a baby came to look at clothing. I sold them three dress waists and a skirt, pair of shoes, two children's flannel skirts, and one child's jacket. And they did not go until nearly three, and then my kitchen fire was out and my dishwater cold, and that was the end of the dishes. I am the most erratic housekeeper that I ever heard anything about. Most of the work gets done sometime somehow, but some does not get done at all. John is without doubt the easiest man to live with that ever walked the face of the earth. But even he said the other day that when the warm weather came he guessed I would have to sweep under the bed or we should have a good many fleas. Even then he added that he did not want me to think he was finding fault.

Yesterday was even more discouraging than the average Sunday, and they are always the worst days we have. I had a headache all day Saturday, so I did not get up to school to write the songs on the board. We went up before Sunday school to put them on, and it came time for the first bell, and none was there to ring it. John rang the bell and watched for the boy to come to build the fires. Finally he had to build them himself. That is, he built one. We had two matches, and one went out. . . . Miss Fairchild had to keep the infant class in the big room, and by the time Sunday school was over, the room was quite warm. The spiritual interest of the people seemed to be as cold as the room, and we came home wishing that we might take the next train for the North. Such times will come, but we get over them, and by another Sunday we are ready to try just as hard to accomplish something as we did the week before. Not that it is all left for Sunday, of course, but the effort is greater on Sunday than on weekdays.

Measles patients are beginning to come back to school. Elisha started in today, after being out three weeks.

I have been interrupted twice since I started this—once to sell a coat and once to receive the money for a coat that I sold this morning.

January 1896

We had a great time yesterday. Just before dinner a man came to put a new back in our fireplace. As soon as dinner was over, John went up to school to put up stoves, and we thought we would let the dishes go until it was finished. But it was just done when Mr. Ogletree came from town, bringing us a cupboard for the kitchen, a box of new schoolbooks, and the box from home. That was the end of the dishes, for we had to open the box and see the new stove. Oh, how good it looked! It is so black and shiny! We have not seen any shiny sheet iron since we left home. It was dark before we began to wash dishes, and we were still at it when John came home. Then he had to see everything that came in the box, and we did not get any supper until after seven o'clock.

Today I have been working at the kitchen and woodshed. The new cupboard is a great relief. There are three shelves with screen doors and sides, a drawer, and a cupboard with two shelves underneath. My silver and kitchen cutlery have gone into the drawer, my eatables into the screen part, and my sugar, eggs, molasses, vinegar, etc. into the cupboard. Now I have nothing under the kitchen table but my flour barrel, my bread box, and a basket of apples; and it is a great relief! Also, I can bring my tins and cooking dishes in from the wood house and keep them on my kitchen shelves. I have put up a high corner shelf in one corner of the kitchen, and from it have hung a curtain made of half of my blue and white bed tick, with stripes of blue denim across the top and bottom. Behind the curtain hang John's work clothes, Brownie pants, sweater, mackintosh, and so on. And on the shelf above are stored my extra supplies of oatmeal, coffee, and the like. This morning I hinged my molding board to the wall just above John's trunk. When not in use, it is fastened up to the wall with a button; and when I want it, I just turn it down onto the trunk.

January 1896

Still the new teacher does not come, and the "fessor" is a little bit more discouraged about it every day, and quite a little more provoked with the New York office for doing nothing and writing nothing. He has given her until tonight to get here, and then if she does not come he is going to write a very dignified letter to New York demanding an explanation. You should read these dignified letters of his! They are the most gentlemanly, mild, friendly, respectful epistles imaginable. And I suppose in his position and at his age, that is what they should be. But it always makes me laugh to read them after he has told how fierce he is going to be.

(January or February 1896)

We are having beautiful weather just now, warm and sunny. But it looks like rain, and when it rains it will be colder. Gavin says we are to have another stove.[2] When that comes we shall have a hole cut in the roof above the dining room and have our little stove in there. Then the stove upstairs can open into the same pipe, and it will draw much better than it does now. It seems queer enough to think of running four stoves without a single chimney, but that is what we are doing. And I guess we are safe. We keep watch of our stovepipes and the holes they go through, and they seem to be all right. We shall be as warm as toast when the new stove comes. We have not really suffered since the new door was cut through and the kitchen stove was moved. But the dining room is still pretty cold sometimes.

You do not say anything about your cold. Does it still keep you in evenings? And do you cough this winter as you did last? I have had a hard cough ever since Gavin left, but it is about well now. . . .

I have achieved quite a triumph in the cooking line. We thought we had better pay our social debts before school began, and so on Friday night we had Mr. and Mrs. Ogletree and Mr. and Mrs. Cordell to supper. We had pork and beans, fresh bread, baking powder biscuits, coffee, chopped pickle, jelly, applesauce with sliced lemons in it, and fig cake. Mrs. Ogletree is a woman who has grandchildren almost grown up and who has the reputation around here of being a pretty good cook. She is a great deal like Mrs. Leadbeeter in some ways—a great talker and very outspoken. I felt that when she came here to a meal I should be under examination, so I did my level best. She kept still for quite a while, but finally she said, "Well, Mistress Campbell, I shall never know unless I ask. Do you make your biscuits with sweet milk or buttermilk?" I said, "With sweet milk"; and she said she and Mrs. Cordell would have to get me to give them some lessons; and Mrs. Cordell, who is very mild and deliberate, said, "Yes, indeed, they are the best biscuits I ever ate." "And I like your light bread, too," said Mrs. Ogletree. White bread is always light bread down here, and corn bread is bread. So I was quite delighted.

They stayed and stayed after supper. Both the men are old soldiers, and they got started on the war. Finally Mrs. Ogletree said, "Well, I guess we'd better go; I reckon it must be nearly night. Have you the time, Professor?" John laughed and told her it was half past nine. "Why, John Ogletree," she said, "we must go this very minute. I promised those children I would be home by eight o'clock." If you read this part to Gav, he will know just how it all sounded. Tell Gav that Hoe Ogletree and Homer McClusky and Tom Holder have the measles, and Elisha thinks he is coming down with them. Both the storekeepers are sick with them. They say there are between twenty and thirty cases of them right in "Joppy," and that is quite a good many in a dozen families.

If I say the least thing about our wanting to come home, John is afraid you will think we are discouraged and homesick. He has been reading the first part of my letter, and he seems to be worried about the impression it will make. I am not afraid, for I think you know what I mean. We are comfortable and well, and contented and happy. But we do want to see you, and it will be nice to get home again, and you know it as well as we do.

February 3, 1896

I meant to write you Saturday as much as I meant to cook the meals and wash the dishes, and put the house in order. But where, O where, do the days go, especially Saturdays and Sundays?

Saturday was full of the things which leave nothing to show for the work that has been done. I still drive a flourishing trade in old clothes, especially in shoes, cloaks, and men's clothes. It is really a great help to us, for so many pay in work, eggs, butter, chickens, and so forth, that it helps us out a great deal. The money we get goes into the school fund, but the provisions come to us. I took in a dozen and a half eggs this afternoon for three pairs of shoes, and a boy has just cleaned up our barnyard for another pair. Your black coat went to one of the prettiest girls in the settlement—Mary Ann Humphries. Mrs. Henderson would have taken it if it had been warmer. The Hendersons have had a very sad experience. Mr. Henderson's younger brother fell thirty feet from a hickory tree and was paralyzed from his shoulders down. He lived as much as a week or ten days in that helpless condition and then died. He was his mother's "main stick," as Mr. Henderson told me, and she felt his death very much. It was sad but amusing to hear him talk about the boy before he died. He said to me one morning, "'Pears to me like if his spinal 'colume' was hurt anyway, he would be frenzied; but as it is, he is plumb rational."

John preached on Sunday on indebtedness from the text, "I am debtor to the Greek and the barbarian, to the wise and the unwise." The line of thought was our indebtedness to all that is higher than ourselves, for what it has done for us, and our obligation to extend what we have received to those less fortunate than ourselves. It seemed good to hear a real sermon once more.

I must stop now, for I am going up to school to put some songs on the board. We are teaching the school songs of God, country, and home. Just now they are learning "The Old Oaken Bucket," and tomorrow I am going to begin on "From Greenland's Icy Mountains." We sing one sacred song and one secular song every morning that I go up.

February 5, 1896

Miss Irene Baker, of Boston, will be here soon to take the intermediate classes. So we hear from New York, so we have begun to look for her again. I think she must surely come this week.

I made Saratoga potatoes for supper the other night, and they were pretty good. We ate two vegetable dishfuls. Things are made to come about so that we get along all right in some way. The mail carrier now comes from Cullman in a sulky instead of a wagon, and so he cannot bring things out as he used to. But now we have two merchants who go to Cullman—one twice a week and one once a week.

We have not succeeded in getting the melodeon out here yet. We thought a Mr. Powell was going to bring it out last week, but something interfered. Then we thought Mr. Ogletree would bring it out today, or later in the week, but he is obliged to go to Guntersville, so he cannot bring it until next week. I hope it is not hurting it to stand so long as it is. It cannot be helped anyway. It is very slow work getting anything out here in such bad weather as we have had. My wheel came out only today, and now I cannot do anything with it because the working wrench is missing and there is not one in Joppa.

Today I have sold two dress skirts, one dress waist, and three pairs of stockings. I do not like to let that gingham dress of yours go. Do you care if I keep it?

The measles still rage. John has eighteen in his room out of seventy. It is very discouraging, but of course it cannot be helped.

February 16, 1896

We have word that the flags are in Cullman, and we shall get them as soon as we can. Many, many thanks to you. About that gingham dress, the reason we sell things instead of giving them is that we do not want to encourage laziness. It had not seemed to me that I had been very much beset with that sin of late, but if you think I have, I will willingly work out the pay for the dress when I come home.

The day is very windy, but bright and not very cold. I had a small Sunday school class, but it is always much more interesting than a large class. I have three girls who are very delightful to teach, and none who are really disagreeable. It is hard to do good work except with a very few of them, because the others are so very irregular in their attendance.

Miss Fairchild is hard at work getting ready for Washington's birthday, and I am helping her with the music. She does not sing very much, and she thinks she cannot sing at all, so she does not get very much music out of the children. So I came to the rescue with my large amount of "nerve" and limited musical ability, and at least they sing louder than they did for her. I hope the exercises will be good. Some of the little pieces are very funny. One is:

> If all the trees were cherry trees,
> And every little boy
> Should have like young George Washington
> A hatchet for a toy,
> And use it in a way unwise,
> What should we do for cherry pies?

Your letter came this morning, and you must not worry about me. John has talked "girl" off and on to me ever since we came down here, but I do not want a girl. If I get a little tired, or have a headache, he thinks I ought to get a girl. But there is no one around here whom I could get who is not in school, and it is during school hours that I should want help, if at all. If I had a girl, it would have to be a German girl from Cullman, and she would have to have the only spare room in the house and go through the sitting room to get to it. There is not a hired girl in the community, and she would have no companions, so she would have to be more or less one of the family, or suffer from being always alone. It is not because we have not the money to hire help that I do not have it, but because under the circumstances I do not want it. And, dearie, I wish you could see me. I am the healthiest specimen of an overworked woman that you ever saw, I am sure. Why, I put on one of my blouse waists the other morning and split it from the neck to the waist in the back, I was so large for it. I never have been better since I grew to be a woman than I am at this very minute. At least do not worry about me for this year, and if at the end of it those who love me best think that I am overworked and running down, we will make some other arrangement for next year.

February 20, 1896

My Dear Mother:

Cold? O, yes indeed, it is very cold in February. But having a stove in the dining room makes a great difference with our comfort. With a big fire in every room, we manage to keep pretty comfortable. The only trouble is having everything freeze up at night.

Probably the little minister and his wife are as sober as they have been since they came down to "Joppy." A letter from New York tells us that Miss Irene Baker, who applied very enthusiastically for a needy field, writes that she cannot accept the position offered her at Joppa. A Miss Flora Crane of Washington, DC, has been offered the position and has written John for information about the school, the people, the quality, price of board, etc. He answered her questions down to the matter of board, and told her that she would probably board with us, and he did not consider himself qualified to give an unbiased opinion on my cooking. We have waited four weeks for Miss Baker, and now it will be two weeks, probably, before Miss Crane comes, if she comes at all. Her letter amused me a little. She said, "Kindly tell me whether I shall be able to secure good board, and at what price. If it is the Master's will, I should like to enter the work in the mountains." I did not suppose that the Lord's will depended so much upon one's personal comfort.

All this does not cheer us very much, and then for the first time John has been obliged to use a little discipline in the school, and one of the fathers wrote him rather a disagreeable letter this morning. He said the boy told him that John talked pretty rough to him; if you can imagine such a thing, you can do more than I can. John wrote Mr. Holder a letter putting the facts just as they are and telling just what he said to Ambrose, and in all probability it will come out all right. But such things are hard, especially in a school like this. I wish they could know how it affects John when he has to scold them. He came home just about used up yesterday and could think and talk of nothing else but those poor boys whom he had been obliged to reprimand.

I have been at school every day this week since Monday, sometimes twice a day, singing with the children, and how they enjoy it! Their smiles are so broad that they can hardly sing.

Do you know of any Sunday school singing book that you consider better than *Winnowed Songs?* We want to get some books as soon as we can, and I think we can do it before very long.

February 26, 1896

We are very much worried about Mr. Cordell today. He is very ill, and the only good doctor is drunk. They do not think he will live, and it seems terrible to let a man die because the only man who can help him is not in condition to do it. Of course, we still hope that he will come out all right, but it looks very doubtful. We are more and more impressed with what a forlorn thing sickness is when one is poor. O, the sick people whom we visit in dirty rooms, surrounded by dirty children! Night clothes they have none. When they are sick in bed they wear their old calico dresses and shirts. . . . It is pretty hard to know how to help them except by example, and I believe that the most is to be accomplished with the children who are growing up.

Grace's letters come to an end here, but we know that Brother Cordell did not get well. John recorded in his notes:

He died because the only skilled doctor we have was drunk when we needed him most. We drove four miles in a jolt wagon, the coffin home-made, placed high up on two wagon seats. The widow and daughters, dressed in black with black sunbonnets, wailed all the way in a strange monotone. At last we reached the graveyard, and when all was ready I was asked, without any previous knowledge on my part, to conduct the service. It was my first funeral, but a kind Providence helped me out. Either by foreordination or special Providence—I know not which—I had slipped in my pocket a little Bible. A kindly old neighbor, knowing that I had not expected to take charge of the services, tried to help me out by whispering in a loud tone, "Give us anything; we don't know the difference."

Just before I began to read the fifteenth chapter of Corinthians, the widow ceased her wailing and called me to her side, and with triumph in her eye said, "These people always said that Universalism was good enough to live by but it would not hold out to die by. Tell 'em he died a Universalist."

After I had concluded my brief remarks, the coffin was opened, the cotton which kept the head in position during the long drive removed, the winding sheet thrown back; and while the lonely widow and orphans wept and wailed over the dear one, an impromptu choir sang "Hark from the Tombs a Doleful Cry" to an old Scottish tune. Then the coffin was lowered. The men took turns in shoveling in the earth, and when rocks and rocks had been placed over the grave to keep the animals away, we drove back to the desolate home. Later I went over to see if I could help the widow in any way. Just to start conversation, I asked how old Brother Cordell was. She cheered up at once. "It was funny about Brother Cordell; his birthday never came the same time a year." A further inquiry revealed that he was born on Easter, and the movable feast was celebrated regularly instead of the calendar date.

One of John's most puzzling problems was a gang of boys who would respond to none of his overtures. The only real interest they showed was in beating neighboring gangs at baseball. John happened to ask one of the team one day if he knew how to pitch a curved ball. Would he like to learn? He "didn't care," which, being interpreted, meant he would like it very much. Thereupon the professor volunteered to instruct him in the fine art of pitching curved balls, if he in return would help to split wood for the ravening stoves. John's notes continue:

It was a happy exchange. The pupil was apt with the ball as well as powerful with the axe, and the team, impressed and hopeful, urged the teacher to play with them in the coming big game at Holly Pond. It was a little difficult to find a way to get to the game on time and at the same time carry through the school session, but that problem was solved by commandeering an old two-wheeled racing sulky, in which [the] pupil personally drove instructor to the rendezvous.

Never would the professor have imagined that baseball would prove one of his most valuable college assets. Down to ignominious defeat went the Holly Pond team, while glorious victory crowned the heroes of Joppa. The Joppa team was beside itself with joy, and the heart of the pitcher was warm with gratitude as he and the professor jogged the long miles homeward through the starlit night. They talked little. The new moon faded; a great planet hung low before them. It was Jupiter, the professor said; and in answering the questions which followed, he found himself, all unintending, enlarging on the order and beauty of the universe. He checked his enthusiasm with the final comment, "Don't you reckon if there is such order up there, we down here ought to try and order our lives?" There was no answer, but some time later, when he had almost forgotten his question, he received a call one night from his curved-ball pupil. What church should he join was his problem. Pappy was a Baptist and Mammy a Methodist. If he committed himself to either church, there would be hard feeling at home. What would the professor advise? Sad at heart, the professor pondered on the evils of denominationalism.

A few weeks later, he was conducting the usual Sunday night service, when he became aware of a disturbance in the back of the building—scuffling and audible talking. A rough gang from a neighboring community had come into the house with the obvious intention of breaking up the meeting. John had been reading aloud from the Bible. Before he thought what he was doing, he slammed the covers shut, culled out his watch, and issued his challenge: "There is a time to pray and a time to fight! I'll give that crowd in the back of the house just three minutes to get out!" In the dead silence which followed, he realized the significance of what he had done: he must make his warning good or the place he was beginning to fill in the community would be lost forever. Did minutes ever pass more slowly? One, two, three—time up! There was nothing to do but to start. Closing his watch with a click, he put it in his pocket and started down the steps.

Fortune was with him. The disturbing group, as he neared them, rose and quietly moved out of the house. Encouraged by his success, John thought he might as well go a step further. He followed the retreating figures out into the darkness. The gang were untying and mounting their horses. He approached them. Didn't they know it was against the state law to interrupt a meeting opened by prayer? The young men had been drinking but had begun to sober up a little. The leader allowed they hadn't meant any harm and, promising not to disturb again, put spurs to his horse and galloped off, followed by his companions.

The professor stood looking after them a moment, then turned to reenter the church. Dim forms slowly took shape out of the darkness and closed in about him. The ball team! "Why, boys, I didn't know you were here!" Half-shamefacedly the pitcher responded, "Well, perfessor, we know them fellows. They are a bad lot. We thought if there was going to be any trouble, we'd like to be there."

Troubles near at hand may be more immediately disturbing than those arising from a distance, but at least they are more tangible, and one can do something about them. More difficult are those arising from distant control, as John's letters addressed to one of the New York AMA Board secretaries reveal. We do not have those written from the board to him. John was troubled about restrictions as to use of funds in hand—both the board allowance and the public funds paid as tuition for pupils. These made for problems in the businesslike running of the school, the securing of equipment and supplies, and the use of funds sent him for the school by personal friends; also problems as to the obligation to employ a teacher for every fifty pupils, with no limitation as to total number of pupils under the state school contract if public funds were to be accepted for tuition. He spent long hours in writing details of the situation and in pleading for permission to proceed with the many plans—and modest they seemed—that he felt he must carry through, as well as for an additional qualified teacher.

The board was not entirely indifferent, but it was far away and absorbed in many problems. Mountain work was new, and the New York secretaries were not too familiar themselves with its special conditions. One member of the board did not even know where Joppa was, or whether the pupils were black or white.

His friend Merriam wrote John again, this time from North Carolina:

Whittier, North Carolina
December 27, 1897

The AMA treat these mountains too superficially. They are fooled by the natives all the time; they are led too much by stories about Cindy and John, and they do not get at the conditions and study how to meet them.

The fact is, both from conversation in New York and by correspondence (a great deal of the latter), I am persuaded that the officers are ignorant of their missionary work. I do not know what your conclusion is, but I have never met a mountain AMA man but who said the same thing, and of his own choice. The result will be that both you and I are going to resign from this work. I am in a sense selfish, just as you are and just as every man is. The society must allow me to do all I can, you the same; otherwise we must go elsewhere. I should like to spend my life in the mountains, provided I can find a suitable work; but I do not propose to teach primary classes year by year with no growth and no increase of pay.

In spite of this prophecy and a lack of understanding by no means peculiar to this particular board or situation, John found advantages as well as disadvantages in being so far from headquarters and undisturbed by visits from his superiors. He was, on the whole, especially as he established himself in the confidence of the board, able to make his own decisions and to act quickly on his own judgment. If he lacked experience, he had plenty of opportunity to acquire it firsthand, and some of the wisdom that comes with it.

There is something intoxicating about being used to one's full capacity—about being heard, depended upon, wanted by one's neighbors. John threw himself into the life of the community and loved it as he never loved any other. Out of his closeness and his love, he slowly began to see that life as something not "peculiar" but merely an expression of the intensely rural character of the section. How deeply that rural character had shaped the life he did not realize fully until long after he had left Joppa, but he recognized that "cabins were, after all, homes," even if they were more picturesque than comfortable; that so-called mountain dialect expressed ordinary human emotions, for all [that] the phrases might be pithy and some of the words forgotten since the days of Shakespeare. The native humor and individuality of the people were something to enjoy and cherish even in the midst of poverty, [along with] lack of comforts, conveniences, and medical aid.

Poverty! What was the cause? What could he do about it? The existing conditions were so hard, his own efforts so pitifully inadequate! As he looked down, day by day, into the young faces before him—so hopeful and some so full of promise—his heart ached for them. He taught them, one may be sure, out of his heart as well as his acquired knowledge. Such teaching seldom shows tangible results. Letters written to him years later by some of these Joppa students indicate something of what it had meant.[3] One of these students, David Davis, John helped to get into his old school, Andover Academy; another, Walter McClusky, to board with his mother, Mrs. Gavin Campbell, in Stevens Point, while he completed high school there. Both boys he lost track of during the troubled and strenuous years which followed his own leaving Joppa.

As it happened, he was speaking one night to a New England audience in an effort to raise an endowment for Piedmont College, when he happened to get to talking about the courageous struggles that some of his boys had made to get an education. For the first time he mentioned David. After he had finished, a man came up to him. "I was interested in what you had to say," he volunteered. "I am working in the Yale Law Library, and there is a boy there whose name is Davis. His speech makes me think he is a southerner, and something you said made me wonder if he could be your David Davis." And so it happened. John had a happy letter from David, delighted to be in touch again, for he too had lost track of his former teacher. He spoke briefly of his past experiences and explained that he was helping in the library to put himself through law school.

That John had been thinking seriously, while still at Joppa, about rural education is indicated by his notes written in 1897, very possibly for the eye of board officials:

> There is great interest in education throughout these regions. A committee rode thirty miles to visit the school. We expect 250 pupils next year. We must have more teachers, more money; and yet the present difficulties compel the board to make only the same appropriation for Joppa as last year. This work which we are trying to do is but a fraction of what should be done. We need an industrial department where boys may learn to do what they may be called to do with the simple tools at their command, and one where the girls may practice the cooking and home-keeping sorely needed and possible under the conditions in which they live. We should have, too, a department for instructing the many mountain teachers who come to us. We hold a strategic point, and money is needed to bring to this land the enlightenment it needs, the help it craves.

How great was the contrast between his hopes and reality was brought home sharply one day:

> The complacency with which we viewed our work for several years was destined to receive a severe jolt. It was at the noon hour, after a busy morning, that one of the girls came to the desk. She was a little older than the average of her class and had shown some hesitancy about entering school at all. On looking up, the professor noticed that she had been weeping, and in reply to his inquiry she said:
> "I've come to tell you goodbye, for I'm aimin' to quit school."
> "But why, Myrtle?"
> "What's the use of educating me? I'm only a girl, and they's eight young ones at home. You know where we live."
> "But you will be a more helpful girl with an education, and you will have a much wider influence through your own home later."
> "That ain't fer me," she said; and in answer to a surprised look, for she was winsome, "Don't you see what's happening: The best boys, the only kind I would want to marry, don't stay here when they finish school. There's nothing ahead fer me but to stay home and let my menfolks support me, or to marry someone I don't want now I been to school. I'm wanting things I can't have. I'd better be left in my ignorance."

The conversation sank deep. At the time John did not feel its full significance, but it lingered on in his mind and was, he used to say, the beginning of his real thinking on rural education.

The Williams Class of 1892 circular letter dated January 26, 1898, under the name of John Campbell, contains the following:

Am still in this field. Money and help greatly needed. . . . I have a school of two hundred; have two teachers and need two more, and larger buildings.

My address from September to May is Joppa, Cullman County, Alabama—simply John Campbell—no Rev., Prof., or other to go to the name, please. From May to September I am north. Letters addressed to me at 640 Clark St., Stevens Point, Wisconsin, will reach me.

Was married in September 1895 to Miss Grace Buckingham at Stevens Point, Wisconsin. We have had a little boy, but he died when two months old.

The year had been a hard one. Grace had almost died when the baby was born, and continued very delicate. She was never really strong again, and remained with her father and mother that winter, while John boarded with a neighbor at Joppa and continued his teaching. Everyone was exceedingly kind to him, but work and worry combined poorly with fried "meet," fried eggs, and biscuits heavy with soda. He came out in the spring yellow as saffron. Pictures taken about this time show a thin, youthful face, distinguished by large and shining eyes, and a full sensitive mouth quick to quiver in sympathy or curl in humor. He left, as usual, for his summer in Wisconsin and did not receive, until he reached home, Dr. Ryder's notification that the Joppa school was open to him again the coming year.

John was not ready to leave Joppa, but conditions in Stevens Point made him realize he could not return, for the present anyway. Not only was Grace unequal to pioneering, but her mother, too, was seriously ill and needed her. With real sorrow he wrote Dr. Ryder that he had decided to stay in Stevens Point for the coming year.

Appendix 2: Letters from Joppa Pupils

Birmingham, Alabama
October 9, 1904
Mr. and Mrs. Campbell
Demorest, Georgia

Dear Friends:

Through the kindness of Mr. Buckingham I have finally located you all. And it is with great pleasure that I write you all this afternoon.[4]

It was with great sorrow that I heard of Mrs. Campbell's death [John's mother]. At losing your mother you have my regrets and deepest sympathies. The entire family join me in condoling with you.

My stepfather is dead also, having died in May, last. He was sick for eighteen months with cancer. We spent everything for his treatment, but to no avail. I owe thirty dollars on his burial expenses yet, to be paid November 10; then I will be practically out of debt.

I am with the St. Louis Car and Foundry Co. of this city and have been for about twenty-seven months. I make on an average of seventy-five dollars per month now.

If we can have health another year, I hope to save some money.

Mother and the girls are here with me—and my youngest brother, Plenn, also. Plenn is with the St. Louis Company too and works in the department with me. He makes twenty-five dollars per month now and will be promoted as fast as he becomes eligible to promotion.

I hope to hear from you all real soon, and a long letter. I would have written you all much sooner, but had lost all trace of you.

Very sincerely yours,
Walter McClusky

Water Canyon via Socorro, New Mexico
August 25, 1908
Mr. J. C. Campbell
Stevens Point, Wisconsin

Dear Professor,

Doubtless you will be surprised to hear from one of your old school boys that has been quiet so long.

I have not been to Joppa since 1901. Went to Mississippi in the Pine Belt and started a little mercantile business. Did extremely well for five years, when my health completely broke down and I was advised by my physician to come out west. I did so and rambled in the Rockies a year—in Wyoming, Colorado, and New Mexico. Am glad to say that I now am in fine health. Weight 180.

I am living outdoor life. Have position with the Forest Service as Ranger. Haven't heard from any of the Joppa people in a long time.

Would be glad to hear from you. Regards to Mrs. Campbell.
Yours as ever,
R. F. Rhinehart

Rosedale, New Mexico
April 19, 1909
Mr. John C. Campbell
Demorest, Georgia

Dear Professor Campbell,

I received your letter today, and to say that I was pleased to hear from you does not in the least express my feelings.

It has been so long since I wrote you that I do not remember much that was in my letter and probably may repeat some of it in this.

I came west on account of my health over three years ago. My weight was not over 145 for several years before my health broke down, and since I came west I am weighing 175 and feel as though I had never been sick.

I think there is no place like the Rockies. Las Cruces and Carlsbad are rather warm in summer, and the water is not so good as up in the mountains.

I have been away from Alabama ten years and have not heard from any of my schoolmates for several years.

I suppose that they are badly scattered.

I have been in the Forest Service over a year as forest ranger and am riding a great deal of the time, which is ideal for one in my physical condition.

My father died last May. My mother is in good health, and I shall be pleased to advise her that I have heard from you.

I shall always feel grateful to you for what you did for me at Joppa and have endeavored to follow your teachings. I have been very successful up to my sickness, and as I am apparently over that now I hope to accomplish something yet.

Sincerely yours,
R. F. Rhinehart

Fort Wayne, Michigan
December 1, 1909
Mr. John C. Campbell

Dear Friend,
I suppose you will be surprised to hear from me.

I got a letter from home telling me about you visiting Joppa. I wish you had come while I was at home; I would like to have seen you very much.

I was very sorry to hear of your bad health.

I have had my ups and downs since I last saw you. Say, do you remember the letter you wrote to me when you was away in December 1897? I have got it yet.

That shows you how much I thought of you; and if you had stayed at Joppa, I would have never left.

So you see luck was against me.

Say, what do you think of my little Katherine! Well I lost out when young but, by the help of God, if she will listen to me, she will never lose.

I guess you have been in Detroit, have you not? It is a very nice place, and the people are very kind to us. How do you like my old state, Georgia?

I had my picture taken the other day; will send you one tomorrow if nothing happens.

I hope your health is better; health is a great thing to have. My health has been bad ever since I got back from the Island.

But I feel fine now. Well, I will have to ring off; got to study some. We have school three times a week—that is, the Noncommission officers. So good bye for this time.

Your friend,
Sergt. J. N. Bryan
Col "M" 26 Inf.

Fort Wayne, Michigan
Joppa, Alabama
November 29, 1909
Mr. John C. Campbell
Demorest, Georgia

Dear Mr. Campbell:

It seems that I had just a glimpse of you while you were here, but just a glimpse of you did me a great deal of good. I think you know, though, that no one at Joppa thinks more of Mr. Campbell than I do, but I had given up the hope of ever seeing you again. And now since you made that flying trip to Joppa I feel the loss more than ever. It seems such a short time since we were all so happy in school together, and now they are all gone except Eldgar, John, and myself. It seems rather hard, but such is life.

Elisha thought that the social we had while you were here was for the young people, but he went over and thought he might get a peep at you through the window but the shades were down. So he came back the next morning thinking that he would get to see you, and was very sorry that he did not get there in time.

School is very small at present (only twenty). But I suppose I will have quite a large school after Christmas.

Pardon me if I am asking too much, but I would like so much to have a picture of Mr. and Mrs. Campbell.

Perhaps I can write a more interesting letter next time. Write me sometimes.
Sincerely your friend,
Willie A. Bryan

The following from David Davis was written in response to John's request for an account of his doings since he left Joppa for Andover:

Birmingham, Alabama
September 17, 1913
Mr. John C. Campbell
412 Legal Building
Asheville, N. C.

Dear Mr. Campbell:

I was very pleasantly surprised when I received your letter today, and will say that I will be very glad to give you any data that you think will be of benefit to young people in their work.

In giving you the information you asked me to give, I want to say in the outset that the inspiration and help received from you contributed more toward my reaching whatever success I have attained than anything else, and I take a great deal of pleasure when I am asked how came me to go to Andover in relating the story of your influence. . . .

While at Joppa I had planned to go to Andover in the fall of 1897, as well as I remember, but was taken down with typhoid fever in July of that year, and when the time came for school I was not strong enough to undertake it. As soon as I regained my strength, I went to Texas, landing in Cooper, Texas, with ten dollars and no job. I spent all but a few cents of this munificent sum hunting for a position in Cooper, but failed. I then invested fifteen cents in a railroad ticket to Ennis, Texas, where I met a farmer who, as he related to me afterward, employed me as a cotton picker with many misgivings. I worked at this for about a month, earning fairly good money. At that time, as a result of my efforts in Cooper, I was offered a position in a grocery store, which I accepted and stayed with until sometime in July 1898, when I was again stricken with fever. This was of short duration but depleted my treasury so much that I did not have enough money to get to Andover. A friend loaned me fifty dollars, which enabled me to make the trip, leaving me $4.95 cents upon my arrival. With this, a letter of introduction from you, and a very limited supply of clothing—none too stylish, all securely packed in a telescope bag—I wended my way up Main Street in Andover. As well as I can remember, Mrs. Whittemore gave me meals for a day or two, for which I gathered some apples, cut the lawn, and sawed some wood. Then I obtained a place to wait on table for meals, which I held for the entire three years I was in Andover.

On the day of my arrival, I went to see Dr. Bancroft but found that he was in Europe, and met Mr. Pettee, registrar. During my conversation with him— or rather his conversation with me—I told him that I expected to work my way through school. He stated that a great many boys did that but that I should have one hundred and fifty or two hundred dollars to start with, "until I got the ropes." When I told him that I only had $4.95, he smiled—not an unkindly smile but rather encouragingly—and said, "I like your nerve, and if you have come this far under that condition, you will no doubt get through." He assigned me to a room in the commons, where they furnished a bedstead and a table. I purchased a mattress, two sheets, pillow, and pillow case, which cost me, I think, $2.50. Mrs. Whittemore presented me with a comforter. My first night was spent in this room and on this improvised bed. With a place to eat and a place to sleep, I started out to get money with which to buy my books, fuel, clothing, and meet my other expenses. Most of my tuition was rebated, although I had to pay thirty-six dollars a year, as well as I can remember. Dr. Bancroft gave me a job tending to his furnace at $1.50 a week. Several other people paid me fifteen and twenty cents an hour for cutting wood, mowing lawns, gathering fruit, waxing floors, washing windows, and so on. These jobs I did after school was out and Saturday half holiday days. I was kept pretty busy earning enough money to pay my necessary current expenses. Everything went pretty well until spring, when I had chills. I had these every other day for the most of the time during April, May, and June. They took a great deal of my strength, and I was not able to do as much work as I had prior to that time, but did enough to pay most of my expenses. The doctor prescribed that I take a sea trip for them when school was out. The condition of my finances was such that it was impossible for me to pay my way, so I packed all my belongings in my trunk and locked them in my room, except the suit I had on and a change of underclothing, and went to Boston. There I tried to get a job on a fruit steamer to Cuba, but failed. Finally I got a job on a cattle steamer going to Glasgow, Scotland, which gave me a pass back from Scotland for feeding the cattle. I had borrowed some money from a friend so that I wouldn't be stranded in Scotland. I stayed on the Isles for about fifteen days, then came back to Boston. The trip was a novel one, and I enjoyed it. I think it worth every man's while to take it if he cannot go otherwise.

I landed in Boston, bought me a shirt and collar, got a haircut and shave, bought a ticket to Andover, and had five cents left. On arriving at Andover, I learned that the dormitory in which I had left my trunk had burned, together with all my earthly belongings. The suit I had on was ruined on the trip, so I had five cents and no clothing, and owed the money I had borrowed with which to take the trip. I borrowed money to buy me some clothes and to pay my fare to Block Island, where I got a position to wait on table. I waited on table the rest of the summer, making a few dollars; but this did not pay my indebtedness, so I had no money to buy books. I managed to defer my indebtedness and worked just as I had the year before, except I did not do so much cutting lawns and such as that. I got the job of marking out the football field and did some tutoring. In this way; by the end of the year I had pulled myself out of debt, except the fifty dollars I borrowed before starting to school.

I again waited on table at Block Island during the summer and had this money to start on my third year. The third year I did not do any cutting of lawns or work of that kind except for Mrs. Whittemore, for whom I worked all the time I was there. I did more tutoring. In February of the third year I received news that my father was seriously ill, and went home. His illness lasted until in June, when he died. The affairs were in such condition at home that I stayed out of school the next year and taught a country school, trying to get things in such shape that my brothers and sisters could make a living and I could go to school. What time I wasn't teaching, I was making a crop.

The following year I entered Yale Law School. Had seventy dollars when I got there. I tended furnace for my room the first year and waited on table for my board. I got a job as assistant superintendent of a boys club and did some little tutoring of parties who expected to enter Yale the following year. My tuition was $150 per year, $55 of which I paid and the balance was extended through the summer upon my making notes.

I got a job as motorman on a streetcar in New Haven and worked at this during the summer months. This netted me fairly good money and enabled me to pay my back tuition, get some clothes and books. The following year I tended a furnace for two dollars a week and paid six dollars a month for a room. This year I tutored the first-year men in law some, but at the end of the year owed one hundred dollars tuition. Through that summer I got a place as head-waiter at a summer hotel, which paid me sixty dollars a month and board. This enabled me to pay my back tuition and left me a little money for clothing and books.

The next year I kept my same room at the same place, tending the furnace at two dollars a week, and had a place in the Law Library as Assistant Librarian, which paid my entire tuition. I did some tutoring.

The last two years I got my board by getting up a club of ten men, including myself—in other words, the landlady gave me board to keep a table filled with nine other men. After graduating, I again went to the summer hotel until the season was over, when I came to Birmingham. I arrived here with twenty dollars.

This is a detailed history of my doings from Joppa to Birmingham as well as I remember them, and some of the facts were particularly impressed upon me. I have not attempted to give my feeling at the different times—how at times I felt discouraged, how at times I felt encouraged, and so on.

I have seldom related this story, not because I am ashamed of it, for I feel rather proud of it, but for fear, when I relate same and in that way assert that I am a self-made man, someone—like a little urchin—will ask, "Why did you do it that way?" I have told the story to a few boys who I thought would be interested, and as a result two or three of them have gone through school and are making good. For this you can claim the credit.

I feel that you will be interested in knowing what my brothers and sisters have done. Napoleon is married, has a little girl about seven years old, and is farming near home. Lorrimer went through dental college, recently married, and is now practicing his profession. Lona, my eldest sister, is married, has two little girls and a boy, and lives on a place next to our home place. Lula and Dosia both graduated from Albertville last year, have first grade certificates, and are now teaching. T. V., the youngest, graduated from high school in Birmingham a year ago, took a business course, and is going to work in the city presently.

Mrs. Davis and I are the proud possessors of a fine daughter seven months old, who we—like all other parents—think is "the girl." Should you ever come to Birmingham, we do not want you to fail to let us know so that we can have you out at the house.

With best wishes to you and yours, I am

Sincerely yours,

David J. Davis

3

Teaching Years

Pleasant Hill and Demorest

Grant for Study of Mountain Region, 1898–1908

Teaching in Stevens Point, Wisconsin, in the winter of 1898, John Campbell knew that his heart was not there. In spring of 1899, the American Missionary Association asked if he would return to Joppa to teach. He didn't want to teach again in an AMA school, but Grace wanted to go back to the mountains, so when he was offered a job as principal of Pleasant Hill Academy in Tennessee, he accepted. Pleasant Hill was a larger community (with a doctor) on the Cumberland Plateau. He liked the work there, in spite of some "gun-toting" in the school. But by February of 1900, he was looking for another place, partly because of the problems AMA was having in overseeing their remote schools.

He went back to Stevens Point until he got a letter in 1902 about the establishment of Piedmont College, formerly J. S. Green College, in Demorest, Georgia, encouraging him to take the job of President. The college was on the eastern side of the Greater Appalachian Valley and had been founded in 1881 by northern prohibitionists, leaning toward Methodism. The school had local support, but it would not have gotten off the ground without funds from the AMA. There is a great deal about denominationalism in this chapter. Campbell, a Presbyterian, was leading three Congregationalist schools, and his pupils were mostly Methodist or Baptist. Grace Campbell, never well, became an invalid in Demorest and died in 1904. John was not well himself and was burdened with problems involved in financing the school. Many letters in this chapter are about his efforts to raise money; he was haunted by visions of failure. Finally a doctor ordered him to take a sea voyage to Scotland, his father's homeland. "A pleasant group of fellow-travelers diverted his mind and cheered his spirits." One was the lively young Olive Dame. They were married the following year.

On their honeymoon trip, Campbell read an account of a newly formed organization, the Russell Sage Foundation. "Wouldn't it be wonderful if we could get them to make a study of the whole mountain region? That is something I would really like to do," he exclaimed. Correspondence follows between Campbell and the Foundation's general *director, John Glenn, about conditions in the mountains and how the Foundation could support the workers in the region. Campbell proposed a study of the needs of the mountaineers and sent an outline to the Foundation in May 1908. In June 1908, a resolution by the Executive Committee of the Foundation was passed: "A grant of $3,000 was made for a study of the Southern Mountain communities."*

Notes from Forrest Grant:

> I often have had occasion to refer to John as the best-equipped and by far the finest college man I ever knew. I mention it again in this letter because, after meeting hundreds of young college men, I still have not met his superior. He was always happy and good-natured and had a well-developed sense of humor; and by inheritance he was sincere, unselfish, gentle and friendly, patient and considerate. . . .
>
> It happened that from September 1898 to June 1899, John and I taught in the public schools of Stevens Point, Wisconsin. We were the principals of the seventh and eighth grades, respectively; and Mrs. Grant, then Annette Bandow, was John's assistant. The year was a break in the career he and Grace had planned, and as I recall it, it was caused by Grace's health. At any rate, during that year, we had abundant opportunities to observe a practical demonstration of how he used this long list of qualities I have mentioned, in giving the pupils of that seventh-grade school the best he had. With his wonderful mental equipment, it became very clear why he was always able to successfully meet the requirements of the situation at hand in a delightful and pleasing manner.

John may have been a successful teacher in Stevens Point, but his winter could not be said to have been entirely happy, nor did he lose his intention of going south again. "His heart is in that work," wrote his brother Gavin, who was at that time—December 1898—teaching in Mankato, Wisconsin, where most definitely *his* heart was not. Two months later this much-loved brother, "the best boy I ever knew," came home to die of "galloping consumption." His death, entirely unexpected, and some of the conditions attending it, blinded John, perhaps, to similar danger signals in Mrs. Buckingham's illness. Neither he nor Grace seemed to have been conscious of the risk she was running in taking care of her mother. His sister Maggie, too, was not well, nor was she happy. She and her little boy Gavin had come home to live with her mother while her husband took new work in another part of the state. John could not but be troubled by the situation, carrying the family responsibilities as he did, but at that time no mention of tuberculosis was made. When one realizes how recently the infectious nature of tuberculosis had been recognized, this is perhaps not surprising. "You know," says a friend's letter, written to Gavin a month before his death in an effort to persuade him to go to a Christian Science healer, "a positive cure is hardly thought possible by regular physicians."

The spring of 1899 brought another letter from the AMA, asking John if he would not return to Joppa. This he knew was out of the question, and he hesitated to accept an opening in another AMA school. Grace, however, in spite of her health, was as eager as he to go back to the mountains. When the following letter appeared, they decided to take the chance.

Pleasant Hill, Tennessee
June 26, 1899

Professor John C. Campbell

Dear Bro:—I wrote you a word the other day in reference to our work here, but I did not tell all. It seemed unnecessary; now I wish to say more. . . .

It has occurred to Mrs. Wheeler and myself that as our climate is considerably different from Joppa, your wife might come here [and] you and she occupy our cottage while we assume charge of Dodge Hall.

We have a good doctor here every Monday and he is connected by phone with his branch office here in charge of a student. We also have telephone connection with the outside world. I believe our railroad will be completed by Christmas so that your wife could come within four or five miles of Pleasant Hill by that time. We should be glad to make things easy for you as we could if you thought it any way safe for you to come here and assume the duties of principal of our academy. At the best, of course it would be somewhat hard, but I think you would enjoy the work here and I believe we could work together amicably.

Mr. McClusky [John's Joppa boy of that name] reached our place last Thursday and went on home the next day. We were favorably impressed and hope we shall be able to help him some.

Truly yours,
W. E. Wheeler

P.S. Coming to Bon Air, you can get within eleven miles of Pleasant Hill over a very comfortable road.

Mr. Wheeler wrote again July 20th, on receipt of a letter from John telling of his acceptance of the appointment as principal of Pleasant Hill Academy:

Pleasant Hill, Tennessee
July 20, 1899

Your good letter reached me yesterday. . . .

I cannot express my satisfaction in your appointment to Pleasant Hill. I had not heard from New York, and Prof. Burnell had only intimated the possibility of his not returning. . . . I hope that you may not have reason to feel that I am over-critical, and still I am heart and soul interested in the prosperity of our academy. . . . Perhaps you remember that our school received the public money of the school district in which it is situated. Last fall I did not teach any. In the winter I taught physics, bookkeeping, and political economy. Prof. Burnell taught two classes in arithmetic, geometry, spelling, and a small Greek class in winter and spring.

We are badly off in [the] way of [a] reference library, and during last year there was not much use made of what we had. Our dictionaries are worn out. We have no up-to-date encyclopedias and no gazetteer. There [have] been so many calls for those who were getting beyond the chance of any education that *my* efforts have been more in the line of support, though we greatly need these things and I hope you may be as successful in getting them for us here as you were in Joppa. We are better off for wall maps. I will write you just what we have when I go home.

I judge you have arrangements at New York for keeping house all together, in which case if you need to board at the Hall temporarily, we should only charge our usual table rates of $1.50 per week. I suppose, however, that matter properly refers to New York, though I am willing to take responsibility myself.

We have no cellar at the cottage. Things could be kept in the large cellar at Girls' Hall, though it is a little distance away. We have a splendid bored well in our cottage yard, cold and pleasant to drink. Many consider it the best in town, though all is good. . . .

I have written all that I can think of now. We shall welcome you to Pleasant Hill with open hearts and hands, speaking for Mrs. Wheeler and myself; and if the old teachers return, I believe they will welcome you as cordially.

We want to do all we can to make it pleasant for yourself and wife here.

The Cumberland Plateau, on which Pleasant Hill was situated, was farther north than Joppa but in general features not dissimilar—a true plateau surface, thin-soiled and with scattered population. The school itself was a boarding school; some 263 pupils are listed in the 1899–1900 catalog, which states: "Too much emphasis cannot be put on the unsurpassed location of the Academy. It is a spot in which young people can study amid the healthful, educating, and inspiring influences of nature, free from the distracting and demoralizing influences of town, there being no saloon within a radius of seventeen miles. The object of the school is the Christian education of its pupils and to furnish them with a thorough preparation for teaching according to advanced methods."

Few details have come down from this brief interlude in John's life. He liked the work and people, and his students were as interesting as ever. He used to tell amusing stories of his experiences, especially, I remember, of his efforts to do away with "gun-toting" in the school. Many of the boys carried pistols, which was quite against the rule of the institution. He was finally able to stop the practice, but not until the boys had tried him out with various nerve-racking devices.

His students kept him on his toes. I recall an encounter he had with one bright youth who seemed unable or unwilling to define the word *extremity*. John, in desperation after many attempts, made the fatal mistake of thrusting out his always neat foot to illustrate extremity of the body. "What would you call that?" he demanded. The pupil took his time. He examined the outstretched shoe with deliberate care, first from one side and then from the other, while the professor balanced with what dignity he could. At last the answer came: "I reckon, Perfesser, I'll have to call that a hoof."

I remember, too, how one boy stated in class: "Niggers are like mules. Ain't got no souls." John was unable to change his mind at the time, but when, not long after, they were reading the story of Philip and the eunuch, he asked the same boy what kind of man the eunuch was: "Why, I reckon he was a nigger, Perfessor." "Do you suppose," responded the professor, "Philip would have baptized him if he didn't have a soul?"

It would not be worthwhile, after all these years, to go into details of the reasons, if all of them had been peculiar to Pleasant Hill, why John did not stay there longer. That he was considering leaving as early as the last of February is indicated by the fact that he was in correspondence with Dr. McAfee of the Presbyterian Board:

Pleasant Hill, Tennessee
February 23, 1900
Rev. George F. McAfee
New York City

My Dear Sir:

Your kind letter of recent date received, and I am grateful to you for your continued thought of me for the work at Marshall [North Carolina], and for your frankness in regard to it.

I receive $700 a year here and pay my house rent, which amounts to $50 a year. I boarded the teachers in Alabama, receiving $10 per month, but did not clear expenses. I inquired of Mr. Hedenburgh as to price he charged the teachers, and if my memory serves me aright, he charged about the same amount, and he did not think he cleared expenses. The teachers could not be expected to pay more. I think that living is higher at Marshall than here or in Alabama, but I am not positive of that.

Mrs. Campbell would be unable to teach but could board the teachers and make a home for them.

My interest in the mountain people has kept me in the field, and I would not expect a large salary, only sufficient to meet the demands upon me.

There followed, during July 1900, correspondence between the New York office of the AMA and John, and between him and the business manager at Pleasant Hill, whom John liked and respected in spite of strong differences, which reveal John's reasons for his making up his mind at this time not to continue there. His wife's frail health, the problems of poor housing and poor food for both staff and students, essential disagreement with the thinking and practice of the business manager, the remoteness in every sense from the AMA Board in New York; all these figured in his decision. Most of these difficulties were probably typical of much of the home mission work of church boards during the closing years of the nineteenth century.

John did not go back to Pleasant Hill, and the next word we have of him—in the decennial report of the Williams College Class of 1892—is headed "Stevens Point, Wisconsin, February 5, 1902": "Now what about myself since graduation? Much of joy and sorrow. . . . Spent four very happy years teaching in Alabama and Tennessee, and since then have been somewhat of a wanderer, accompanying those near to me in a vain search for health. We go south in a few days for the winter and hope again to take up work in dear old Dixie."

Perhaps they were eager to get away from Stevens Point, where the last years had been so full of sickness and sorrow. Mrs. Buckingham died of tuberculosis on December 11, 1901, after a long illness. Maggie, too, died of tuberculosis the following January, leaving little Gavin—a handsome, brilliant boy of four indulged by a sick, unhappy mother and a doting grandmother—to John's guardianship at a time when Grace was ill able to care for him. Legal and painful personal problems had complicated the situation. They might well lift their eyes to the hills.

The immediate reason for turning south was a letter from Dr. Frank E. Jenkins, at that time pastor of the Central Congregational Church in Atlanta and superintendent of the Congregational Home Missionary Society in Georgia. It opened a new possibility—the J. S. Green College, soon to become Piedmont College, Demorest, Habersham County, Georgia.[1]

Atlanta, Georgia
March 31, 1902

Dear Brother Campbell:

Mr. [Charles C.] Spence, president of J. S. Green Institute, has been down here and spoken to our people and interested them even more than they were in the Demorest institution. Our people have made a subscription of $902 for the college, and this comes [on] top of a $10,000 subscription for the new church. We are a small people and not wealthy. Both Mr. Spence and I are convinced that you must come to the institution. We must make some arrangement for it. Have you decided definitely when you will be in Demorest?

Yours cordially,
Frank E. Jenkins

The suggested arrangement was indefinite, but April found John at Demorest eagerly studying the new work to see how it might develop and whether there was a real place for him. Demorest, Georgia, was situated on the eastern side of the Greater Appalachian Valley, across from Joppa and Pleasant Hill. Technically, it lies at the end of the Blue Ridge Plateau, where the mountains begin to roll down into the red Piedmont country and cornfields give way to cotton.[2] Atlanta was only forty miles away, and the main line of the Southern Railway passed within a few miles; in fact, a spur was being built through Demorest to Franklin, North Carolina.

Here, in antebellum days, rich planters had come with coach and Negroes from Charleston to escape the summer heat. Here, too, smaller farmers found an escape from plantation competition in the lowlands, or from the limitations of the rough upper country. Small industrialists following water power discovered opportunity for independent business in a climate cooler than the lowlands and milder than the higher regions to the north. One of these small factories—Flor's Saddle-Tree Factory—making use of water power and forest resources still flourishes at Demorest.

The "city" of Demorest was founded in 1881 by a group of Prohibitionists from the North and Northwest who were looking for a healthful location for a town in which there would be no saloons. "Saloons and gambling are forever excluded by a provision of the title deeds," says a statement in the first catalogue of the Demorest Seminary, which was chartered March 11, 1890, as a high school for the county. An antislavery sentiment also existed, though it couldn't have been too strong. Negroes were not allowed to own or occupy property, a ruling which had its inconveniences when domestic help was needed.

The interest of the founders in education seems to have been strongly tinged with Methodism. At the beginning, the town turned over its school tax funds to the Northern Methodist Church and stipulated that a majority of the sixteen trustees of the new institution should be members of that denomination. Displeased at the way the money was used, the authorities withdrew their support and set up a "Normal" school, which was also unsatisfactory. In 1897 an appeal was made to the trustees of Young Harris College, a Southern Methodist institution in Towns County, Georgia, and, through this, to the North Georgia Conference of the Methodist Church South, to open a similar work at Demorest, from the first grade through college. Reverend C. C. Spence, for several years president of Young Harris, was sent to organize the new venture, which opened its doors in September. When the Church Board of Education voted, in November 1897, not to support it, for fear it would interfere with the older school, Spence remained as president of what was first called J. S. Green Institute, then J. S. Green College in 1898, and in 1903 Piedmont College.

The local people rallied to his support with enthusiasm, pupils, and what money they could raise. Unfortunately, these assets were not enough, and in 1901 an appeal was made to the American Missionary Association for help, with the agreement that the AMA be represented on the Board of Trustees. Dr. Spence, in the *American Missionary* in 1903, explains: "Suffice it to say—it [the college] came near perishing until the AMA came to its rescue." The *American Missionary* lists J. S. Green College in 1901 for the first time among its other schools, with a total of 504 students. "This was the original agreement," writes Dr. [J. W.] Cooper of the AMA on February 11, 1904, to Reverend G. S. Butler, treasurer of the Board of Trustees. "The Association pledged $1,500, and the balance for current expenses was to be raised by the college through its financial agent and other friends."

John knew little, when he came, about Green College (now Piedmont), which, indeed, was perhaps not too thoroughly understood by all the officials of the AMA; but he could not have chosen a better place to study and gain experience in the problems of cooperation between public and private, local and centralized, denominational and secular agencies. He was able some years later to answer Katherine Pettit, of the Hindman Settlement School, out of his own experience when she wrote him that two different organizations wished to sponsor the new school she wished to start at Pine Mountain:

Hindman, Kentucky
September 27, 1911

I would much rather have it quite independent—incorporate with a good board, six men and six women who will be really interested and will work for it, who will keep a financial secretary in the field all the time.
Which would you prefer?
I would not like a sectarian board. Please tell me just what you think of all this.

John replied, writing to her at Hindman:

October 4, 1911

Dear Miss Pettit:
I have your letter of September 27th and feel grateful for the confidence you have in my judgment, although I feel it is not entirely deserved. I would like nothing better than to . . . talk over the whole matter thoroughly with you.
I recognize from my own experience the appeal the independent school has for one, but there are many difficulties in the way of bringing about the ideal necessary for the on-carrying of independent work. Local trustees too often do not see the work in the proper perspective. "Foreigners" view the situation at long run, or, coming for a hasty visit to the field, make up their minds as to what should be done from conceptions formed in their home environments, which are entirely different; and unless they are broad-minded enough to give full confidence to the person in charge to have full control, there is liability of obstruction based upon the conscientious difference of views. It is hard, too, to get trustees to do more than trust. They are willing to give the sanction that their names carry but generally are too busy with other interests to take any active part in the raising of funds. If one chooses trustees financially able to support the school, if such trustees have ideas and hobbies as to the running of a remote rural school, there may fol-

low necessarily the development of a kind of school not adapted to mountain conditions. . . .

Another objection to independent work is that so much depends upon the head of the school. All would go very well, I am sure, while you live and remain at the head, but unless you were successful in training up a successor imbued with the same splendid spirit which has characterized your work and Miss Stone's, the foundation which you have laid might be overturned.[3]

Do not take this, however, as opposition to independent work; sometimes it is necessary, and there is ample return in the intangible influences for good set in motion during the brief period of an individual life.

In the *Piedmont Bulletin* of October 1905, John tried to express his feeling about Demorest:

There is a charm about this little village hard to define. In springtime we are wont to think that it is due to the song of the birds, the beauty of dogwood and laurel; in summer, to the softness of the moonlight. When the forests have put off their gorgeous robes of autumn and we see the peaceful green of holly, cedar and pine against the rich blues and purples of the mountains, we exclaim, "Here, at last, we have it!"

These are, after all, a part. The people themselves contribute much to the charm of the place. To be real honest, we are all interesting, and each is different from his neighbor. On any public occasion, the scene to the initiated is intensely interesting. Yonder is one whose father held many slaves, in friendly conversation with a man of abolitionist extraction. That breezy laugh comes from a man of the prairies who is expressing his appreciation of the quiet humor of a lady who traces her ancestry to one of the traditional three brothers of Mayflower fame. And that courteous visitor from a neighboring village represents in his person a Virginia abolitionist who, though a Quaker, was an officer in the Union Army. The chances are that if you approach any of these persons, you will soon hear that our school has prospects, for each one has the interests of the school at heart. Its interests are his, whether his crest be badger, bear, palmetto, sword, or pine.

The mixture of elements, backgrounds, and loyalties, stimulating though it might be, called for tact and understanding. As always, John was greatly interested in the history of those who settled the region, although at this time he did not know much about the great Scotch-Irish, German, and English migrations up the Valley of Virginia from Pennsylvania, and from the coast along the rivers and Indian trails, into and through the Appalachian barrier. He noted, however, the covered wagons still trekking down from the blue ranges to the northeast, with their apples, chestnuts, and their strong young people. Who were these lean, rugged men? What was their race? Where did they come from? How far did their backcountry extend, and what was its part and place in our national life? He read Fiske but could not entirely accept his theories; they needed, he felt, more study, more data.[4] He came to recognize, too, the growing tentacles of the cotton mills reaching up from below into the depressed agricultural life of this border country—whether for better or for worse, he could not say.

It was all absorbing, challenging—full of pathos, too, and humor. The little town would make a good story, he thought, but he would not exploit his neighbors, not even to raise the money the college so needed.

The church affiliations were also interesting, although the denominational factor does not seem to have played too important a part in the conduct of the college. The AMA did not demand that teachers or students—or, for that matter, the trustees, except for the stipulation that the AMA be represented on the board—should be Congregationalists, nor were they. As a matter of fact, John was technically a Presbyterian while heading three Congregational schools, and his pupils were predominantly Methodists and Baptists of one kind or another. It was not until the local church at Demorest lost its pastor and combined with the Presbyterian minister, who had lost his congregation, that he took his letter from his old home church in Stevens Point and became a member of the Union Congregational Church thus formed. Whether the teaching of seminary days or the liberal policy of the AMA was responsible, he never felt that denominational differences in theology were important. The various local church organizations at Demorest—some with buildings and resident ministers, and some without—all had their strong doctrinal disagreements, but their ideas of what conduct *became* a Christian were more or less similar. Dancing, for instance, was frowned upon in general, in part because the old square dances, usually accompanied by drinking and disorder, had gained the thorough disapprobation of church members over the whole mountain area. John had been surprised in Joppa to find that the church did not approve of his playing dominoes with his boys; dominoes were used in that section for gambling. Cards were especially banned in Demorest—cards with the "naughty red and black spots." You might play whist, or a similar game, as much as you liked, provided especially designed pasteboards were issued under a new name. In fact, staid church members were known to have been "taken up" with such suspicious entertainment—much to the amusement of a few unregenerate youngsters.

Just when John acquired the title of dean is not clear. He seems to have been deep in problems of policy and finance almost at once. His old friend Carl Kelsey, of Andover Seminary days and now in social work, stopped by to see him when south at a conference. He wrote following his visit:

September 16, 1902

I suggest that Mr. Spence write a letter to Dr. [Wallace] Buttrick (General Education Board) asking if Mr. D. E. Cloyd can't visit Demorest in the near future. Mr. Cloyd is the school inspector of the board. Better get this letter off at once, as Mr. Cloyd is to be in Georgia for a time. I suppose the attention of the board has already been called to your needs. If not, this should be done, showing what you plan to do in the way of industrial and normal training. You understand, of course, that these suggestions are to be yours and in no way mine.

That they talked about the use of public money for a private school is suggested by Kelsey's further comment: "I should like to know, and you should know, just what the law of Georgia is regarding the turning over of public school money to private or denominational schools. Look this up sometime and let me know."

The legal aspect of the use of public school money was for a while an academic question, as was the question of turning over the grade school to the city. John found plenty of immediate practical problems to engage his energies, in his work as principal of the "Hill" or grade school. One of his most able teachers, a hot-tempered little "Rebel" as he always referred to her later, had no use for her Yankee principal or his ways. Many explosions and adjustments had to take place before the two became fast friends and worked harmoniously for a better school.

He used to talk much of his experiences at Demorest. He discovered one of his boys in a piece of flagrant dishonesty, and the angry father threatened to horsewhip him [Campbell] at their first meeting. The meeting took place without incident, and in time friendly relations were established.

Starting out on a drive himself, he casually inquired of a man who was selling vegetables off his wagon, what he had there under the straw. The bootlegger—for so he was—swore at him and whipped up his mules. With a flash of the temper which would come out occasionally, John whipped up his own horse and followed. Away went the vegetable wagon and its owner, still whipping and cursing. Away went the professor down the main street into country byways and winding ruts till a sudden fork brought the pursuer to a halt and left the pursued, more familiar with the vicinity, to escape into the woods.

The moonshiners as a group, however, respected his open challenge when he discovered they were getting liquor to his boys. "When our business interferes with your business," they sent him word, "we expect you to get after us." The fathers, too, were generally on his side.

Prof Campbell

My Dear Sir:
Your kind letter received and I am very sorry to hear about my son doing the way he did and will certainly see if the law can't do something with Mr. Church; he ought not to let young boys have any kind of drinks. And Prof, I wish you would keep him there until commencement. I would hate for him to come home before then; and pin right down on him. I have written him a long letter. I want you to punish him for everything wrong he does. Willie has allways been a good obedient child at home. I guess he has been led off by keeping company he ought not to keep. Thanking you for your kindness,
I remain
Yours Truly,
. . . .

Prof J. C. Campbell
Demorest, Ga.
January 19, 1904

Dear Sir:
My Bro . . . asks my consent to take bookkeeping. He don't know what he wants to study. In fact he don't much care to go to school. I wish you would put him in such books as best for him; take charge of him as if he was twelve years old. I want him to have a better education before starting out in life. Don't give away to his notions because of his age. Dictate to him and I will pay expenses and Oblige.
Please tell him I wrote you.
. . . .

The individual students made a constant appeal. So many had so little. As at Joppa, he helped them all he could financially, though he could not pretend to keep up with the need. Anyone who has taught in a mountain school can quote letters similar to the following and knows how almost impossible it is to refuse them:

Tenn., August 9, 1904

My dear Mr. Campbell:

A few days ago I wrote you regarding your school. I wish to inform you that I am very much interested. If you can possibly arrange any way for me to work my way, I shall be very grateful to you. I cannot see now how I can come to school unless some work is furnished. I worked a part of my way at Pleasant Hill.

Regarding my capabilities of doing work, I can do anything reasonable.

Some other schools have offered me free tuition, but I was so much impressed with the work at Pleasant Hill, that I think I can do better and can do more good in a school carried on as it is.

Possibly you cannot give me work enough to pay all my way at first. If not, I shall be willing to execute my note for a part.

I am in earnest. I mean business.

Now, Mr. Campbell, please consider my application, and consider seriously before you turn me away.

Thanking you in advance for any kindness you may show me,

Yours very truly,

. . . .

Sixteen years later came the acknowledgment to me, after John's death:

Stillwater, Oklahoma
January 19, 1920

My dear Mrs. Campbell:

You cannot know, I think, what Mr. Campbell has meant to me, and I wanted to say just a word, as one for whom it was made possible to get an education. He helped me by securing the work that enabled me to pay my way. I knew him very intimately during those first years at college. I took care of the furnace and was in the house nearly every day. When I was discouraged, he often took the time to cheer me; when I was out of money, he gave it to me. He taught me many things an awkward country boy needed to know.

I had lost touch with him for about ten years, but knew he was in the mountain work. I thought the greeting might bring his address and I wanted to write him telling him some of the things he did for me. But as often, we wait too long and then plant flowers on graves. I used to tell him at times what I thought of him, but I wanted him to know my regard had increased during the years. (I was at Piedmont from 1904–1908.)

The years have brought many experiences, pastorates in several states, some happy home life for nearly six years, then when I was a chaplain in the army, my wife was taken from me by influenza. I am this year starting the whole experiment of life over, much where I was when I left the seminary. I have spent about ten years in frontier work in Arizona, Oregon, and Washington. I am now in what is still frontier work, though we have here a great state college, Oklahoma A. and M., and I have a splendid church.

I should rather have some boys say of me what I can say of Mr. Campbell than to have all the oil in Oklahoma. Though he has gone, his life still remains in us.

Very sincerely,

. . . .

P.S.: I shall treasure the little clipping and picture. It is all I have of him.

Would he have said, if John could have talked with him, that the greatest thing he got from his years of working for an education was the influence of a personality? What would he have said about the college? Its academic standing was good, better than many a wealthier, better-equipped school, but what was its purpose? Did it meet the need of the great majority of the students? Such thoughts, usually buried under the pressure of work, worry, and money-raising, sometimes raised themselves in John's mind, especially when he sent a boy or girl out to get a better preparation for life elsewhere. He found himself wondering about those who were left. Was the college making life better for them where they lived? Or perhaps the question was, Did it help them to make life better where they lived.

We see the direction of his thinking in the *Piedmont Bulletin* of May 1905:

We have already an elementary course of seven years, an academic of three, and a collegiate of four. This year marks the enlargement of the domestic science department and a Model Home. We are praying for help to increase our other departments. We desire it not alone for the support it gives to pupils while here. We are coming to see that the excellent training given to pupils of another race will but intensify race prejudice unless our own youth are fitted to take a worthy part in the industrial development of the near future. We need a department of manual work to show that there are aesthetic and spiritual values in common things well done.

Unfortunately, many of the girls—especially those from areas where Negroes had always done the manual work—did not wish to learn to cook and clean; that was no work for white girls. The new "Model Home," the title "domestic science," and an attractive young teacher, Mary Sheak, helped to solve this difficulty. It was less easy to translate wood-chopping and stoking furnaces into "Industrial Work." If there was to be a real industrial department, there had to be equipment and qualified teachers, and for this, money was necessary.

J. W. Cooper, corresponding secretary of the AMA, refers in a letter (February 11, 1904) to G. S. Butler, treasurer of Piedmont, to a request from the Executive Committee of the College for a grant of $6,265, the "probable deficit of the college at the end of this present fiscal year." This "could not of course be granted. Instead of having resources to draw on in our treasury here, we are heavily in debt." The man engaged to raise money had failed to do this, and in addition he must be paid for salary and expenses something between five and six hundred dollars. "This is indeed a bad failure. Professor Campbell should go into the collecting field at the earliest possible moment. . . . The college is too prosperous and the work too vital to be allowed to fail."

"Professor Campbell" was having his own personal difficulties and sorrows. For some months it had been clear that Grace was dying of tuberculosis. She was his only thought now, to make her as comfortable as possible, and free from worry. The house must be serene. The restless, strong-willed little nephew must not disturb her. College problems must not enter in, even if they grew heavier with waiting, and they were growing heavier, he knew. President Spence was resigning; full responsibility was already on his own shoulders. Money must be raised; the work must go on. But this was no time for the "collecting field."

Grace died in March 1904. She had been an invalid almost ever since she had come to Demorest, but she was generally beloved. John had the sympathy of the whole little town. He was not well himself. The long strain, and what was pronounced "bilious remittent fever" (probably typhoid) the year before had left him nervous and debilitated. He could not sleep, and his tired mind went over and over again the problem of financing the college.

At the end of May, Dr. Jenkins wrote Dr. W. L. Tenney, DD, in Chicago, Secretary of the AMA:

Dear Dr. Tenney:

This will introduce President John C. Campbell of Piedmont College, who was enthusiastically elected to his office at the recent meeting of the Board of Trustees. President Campbell has been well tried in our AMA fields, and has so proved his efficiency as to win the hearty commendation of the New York secretaries. Piedmont College has a splendid beginning and a promising future. I am expecting President Campbell's administration to add greatly to the strength of the college. I bespeak for him your hearty cooperation in enabling him to carry out the plans of the trustees, which have the unqualified approval of the AMA representatives on the Board.

Wishing you great success in your work,

Yours very cordially,

Frank E. Jenkins

By July, John was back in Stevens Point. His mother had died, the last of the family except little Gavin and himself. When he returned to Demorest, it was to the center of his life and work—the center of which he was always thinking, for which he was always planning. He slept badly, both when at home and while he was out on "collecting campaigns." His sense of humor and his friendly spirit were as active as ever, but his health was failing.

It was while he and his dean, Henry C. Newell, were on their way back from a money-raising trip in New England the following spring, that he happened to read in the *Tribune* that Dr. D. K. Pearsons of Chicago was about to give some money to southern colleges. He passed the clipping to Mr. Newell with instructions that when they reached New York he was to take the first train for Chicago. An article by Mr. Newell in the *Piedmont Bulletin,* October 1905, gives the next news on this shot into the blue:

> The greatest need of the institution is an endowment large enough to pay all running expenses, in order that its officers may devote their energies entirely to the development of the local field. A fund of at least three hundred thousand dollars will be necessary to guarantee this result. Of this amount, seventy-five thousand dollars must be raised before July 1, 1906, in order to meet a conditional gift from Dr. D. K. Pearsons of Chicago. Dr. Pearsons, after a careful survey of the southern field, has deemed the institution worthy of his assistance, and the officials of the college are making a strenuous effort to meet the conditions which he has thought best to require.

I am well aware that there are good points in a conditional money offer. It was, too, John's opportunity as well as the result of his own initiative. I find myself, nevertheless, questioning always whether the giver in such a case realizes the almost unendurable strain he puts on the one who accepts the challenge, for he cannot well afford to refuse it. A person who has never tried to raise a large sum of money, against time, in the interest of an inconspicuous and little-known institution, can never know what it means in nervous strain, weariness, discouragement. He puts out his best efforts, sometimes three times a day, to interest: a women's sewing circle so deep in good works that the members cannot stop their sewing-machines to listen, a Sunday school where the infant class fidgets on the front seats and the older ones listen only if there are many "bright and lively stories," a church supper where latecomers are still trying to fill their plates and the harassed committee to clean up, to the more-or-less subdued clatter of dishes. Or maybe the speaker—more fortunate—is offered three to five minutes after some other speaker, or—still more fortunate—he is asked to occupy the sermon time or to address the Men's Bible Class. Of course, he must not ask directly for money; all must go to the board, which will apportion as it thinks best whatever comes in.

Not everything is black. Cheering episodes can happen. A quiet man asks some questions and makes an appointment to hear more, which usually means he is going to give, later. A woman slips a bill or check into his hand and thanks him for what he has said. Those occasions give him courage to go on, but he sometimes feels that nothing which he himself considers important has value in the eyes of the moneyed world. Contacts he has cultivated carefully are closed; no new avenues open. The days are long and the nights still longer, haunted by visions of what will happen or not happen if he does not succeed.

In September 1906, the *Piedmont Bulletin* was able to announce:

Since the issue of the *Bulletin* in May a substantial addition to our endowment pledges has been made by Mr. Carnegie. This, together with what Dr. Pearsons and other generous friends have pledged, makes the outlook encouraging.

The president and dean of the college are doing their best to complete the necessary amount before June, which will ensure the first one hundred thousand dollars toward an endowment. The seven thousand dollars on current expenses must be raised by these officers as well. Any amount sent to the college to meet its regular expenses will help and will allow more time and effort to be expended in securing the permanent fund so much desired.

It did not say that in the intervening months the president had been twice sent away by the doctor to rest. The time came when the doctor put him to bed, with a nurse to care for him, and he talked solemnly to him. At last the sympathetic nurse packed his bag, bought him a ticket to Glasgow, and put him on shipboard, bound as a last resort to his father's people. He sailed, June 1906, on a small Scottish steamer, not caring much whether he ever reached his destination or not.

It is wonderful what a long sea voyage, free from responsibilities, can do for a tired man. John was a good sailor; he loved the keen northern air; a pleasant group of fellow travelers diverted his mind and cheered his spirits. Among them was a handsome white-haired matron, Mrs. Lorin Dame, and two lively daughters, Ruth and Olive—the latter of whom is the author of this biography—ready for any fun or new experience. John is first seen through the eyes of Ruth, the elder. "There is a Mr. Campbell," she wrote July 2, 1906, to the college classmate whom she was later to marry, "president of Piedmont College, Georgia, a young man and a terrible wag, but tremendously interesting. He is really inspiring in his devotion to the cause of spiritual uplift among those mountain districts of Georgia, and full of such humorous experiences, yet up to the scratch in jollying and in compliments." Both girls had been teaching three to four years, saving money for the trip, but found great amusement in posing as undergraduates.

Ruth continued her letter: "'What are you going to do after graduation' says Mr. Palmer, a graduate of Syracuse, wedded to a coed. 'Teach?' Olive and I smile consciously. 'Aha! Get married!' he cries gleefully, and we let our experience of several years' teaching pass in a conscience-smitten blush. Our profession has leaked out among a few, and they play dangerously near the question and tease us unmercifully." "Mr. Campbell" is among the initiated, and Ruth's writing continues, "Just as the cliffs of Newfoundland faded blue in the distance, a great white iceberg came drifting by, with white seabirds screaming above, and white waves dashing against its sides. The next day, the thermometer being, by the way, at 34°, a whole school of whales ('Sssh,' cries Mr. Campbell) came at various hours, puffing and blowing along."

It was natural that travelers so congenial on shipboard should plan to continue on together after landing at Glasgow, through the Trossachs to Stirling, and by "fair Melrose," which my mother, Ruth, John, and I saw from the top of a surrounding fence by the poet's "pale moonlight," and on to Edinburgh, where we delighted in the castle, the plaids, and the bagpipes, the romance of Holyrood with its memories of Mary, Queen of Scots. Later in the summer the party joined again for a coaching trip through Cornwall and Devonshire and a boat trip down the Thames to London.

John confided to his sympathetic kinfolk in Glasgow, whom he had deserted for these expeditions, that he was getting interested in one of these fellow travelers, and they encouraged this interest all they could. There was time, too, for them to inspect and approve, for the party came together at Glasgow to sail home on the same ship. So richly were they feasted on "typical" Scottish dainties that John was the only one to escape the dire effects of the rough seas which began the homeward voyage. He arrived in Boston practically engaged to me, and physically so much better that he could face the waiting endowment campaign with energy and hope. Unfortunately, however, he was not yet equal to the strain, and by spring he had lost so much ground that the doctor advised him to give up his work entirely—to resign—and try what marriage and a complete rest abroad for a year would do. He followed the advice.

Looking back over the more than forty years that have passed since that time, I see that the treatment prescribed was far more drastic than I realized. One does not cut off a man of John's intensity, in his late thirties, from a life work as absorbing as his had been. Sicily, where we went first, was an ideal spot to rest, with plenty to divert one's mind from the problems of the southern mountains. Its history was full of interest; its ancient monuments of fascination; and Taormina, where we made our headquarters, was beautiful beyond words, with snowy Aetna above and the blue Ionian Sea below. We rented a little apartment in a modern pink villa in the midst of an orchard of almonds, grapes, and lemons—the seat of an old Greek cemetery where the gardener still dug up remnants of tear vases. Shepherds piped their pipes on the hills about us; the harvesters sang their folk melodies in the heavy clover-laden air. Sometimes, in the freshness of early morning, we rode diminutive donkeys down to the tideless Mediterranean for a swim; sometimes we joined friends at some little sidewalk café and breakfasted on "granite"—snow from Aetna mixed with coffee. He searched out every nearby ruin and by no means neglected the hidden treasures of antique shops. Under the stimulus of Douglas Sladen's *Sicily,* we ventured further afield: Castrogiovanni, Syracuse, Girgenti, Modica, Ragusa, Palermo, Monreale.

It was an idyllic life, but once John relaxed in the quiet of our little apartment looking off across the Adriatic to the hills of Calabria, he was back again at the old questions: How was Newell getting on with the endowment? And, after all, what was the endowment for—for what kind of education? For what kind of life? Where?

He looked forward eagerly to letters and rolls of forwarded papers. It was from one of the latter—I remember well when he found the item—that he read aloud an account of the organization of the Russell Sage Foundation, its purpose, and the appointment of John M. Glenn as first general director. "Wouldn't it be wonderful," he said, "if we could get them to make a study of the whole mountain region. That is something I would really like to do."[5]

Such ideas sometimes do work out. We came home a little earlier than we had planned, partly because of John's lurking restlessness, partly because he was really better and eager to be at work again. "Work" to him was, of course, the mountains; but just what would open to him? In Demorest he seemed so well that the citizens circulated a petition to the college trustees, urging that he be recalled to the presidency:

I. What we as citizens wish to testify to the high esteem in which Mr. Jno. C. Campbell is held in this community. What we know personally of his many deeds of kindness and charity; of his unfailing loyalty to the school under all circumstances; of his efficiency as president of Piedmont College; of the effective manner in which he has ever governed the students for the upbuilding of character, moral, spiritual, and intellectual.

II. That we do most earnestly petition Mr. Campbell's reelection as president of Piedmont College; not because of any prejudice or ill feeling toward any other nominee, but because the welfare of the college depends upon the perfect harmony of students, faculty and citizens. That understanding and loving us, as he does, we are convinced of the fact that Mr. Campbell can carry on in the work of this school with less friction, with greater ease and more success than an entire stranger could do.

III. We understand that some of the nonresident trustees labor under the impression that Mr. Campbell is unpopular in the community. To the utter incorrectness of any such impression the undersigned names will bear full testimony.

IV. That the petition signed and sent to the board last summer in which the name of Dr. C. C. Spence was offered for president of Piedmont, was signed by citizens who were and are now loyal to Mr. Campbell, but who were of the impression that said Mr. Campbell was permanently disabled for the work on account of poor health.

This obstacle has now been entirely removed by his restoration to health.

G. S. Hunt, mayor
E. D. Hendrickson, councilman
W. W. Sosebee
Pink Carpenter
W. H. Van Hise
Lutie L. Van Hise
George H. Van Hise
Jno. P. Brown, justice of peace

G. W. Sears
S. C. Fletcher
G. H. Lamb, MD, college physician
Paul Carpenter, merchant
Homer Sears
O. J. Addition
L. B. Addition
Ruth Hamilton

Several tentative opportunities, outside the desired area, offered themselves. One from Mr. C. C. Carstens of the Child Labor Committee was especially tempting. The letter was so understanding, and the work he suggested so interesting that he [John] was almost ready to apply. Still he hesitated, clinging in his heart to the hope that he might continue in his own mountain field, even make that study, which grew increasingly important in his mind.

"When you next see Mr. Glenn, head of the Russell Sage Foundation," he wrote to Carl Kelsey, who had been helping him in his search for the right place, "tell him, if you get a chance, that you know a fellow who could make a good study of the mountains."

Kelsey was a staunch friend, with excellent social work standing. He had the opportunity, and he spoke. Mr. and Mrs. Glenn were from Baltimore, with some personal knowledge of the mountain South, where Mrs. Glenn's grandparents had spent their summers. What was more, the Sage Foundation was new, its course not fixed, and its entire resources as yet not mortgaged. If Mr. Campbell would come to the Conference of Charities at Richmond on May 6, they would be glad to meet him. Eager and uncertain, John responded to both Carstens's and Kelsey's letters. To Carstens he explained, on March 31, 1908, the possibility of meeting Mr. Glenn, adding, "I thank you for mentioning my name tentatively for the possibility in Boston. I appreciate fully the wisdom of your decision of silence in detail. I myself feel it wise that my name should be mentioned only tentatively, for I do not wish to give the impression that I am playing one position against another; nor would I at this time feel justified in committing myself unreservedly."

To Kelsey, on April 3, 1908, he says:

I was much interested in what you told me about Mr. Glenn. Will you please write me soon, giving me in detail, so far as you can remember, your conversation with him regarding the mountaineers and my connection with them, and whether you think a conference with him at Richmond would lead to something definite in that line, or whether I could do anything for the college here through him? I am a trustee of Piedmont and also of Atlanta Theological Seminary, and our annual meetings are on the 6th and 7th of May respectively; but if you regard it as highly important, and if I can manage it without detriment here, I shall try to come. Of course, I do not wish to go to the expense unless there seems to be a warrant for it. . . .

Do you think, from your knowledge of Mr. Glenn's interest, whether an investigation department could be connected with an institution of this sort? If so, an endowment for that purpose might be accepted by Dr. Pearsons as a part of the general sum which would ensure his conditional gift and that of Mr. Carnegie.

Now that the time for a decision was at hand, John began to realize how hard it would be to break away from Demorest, its red roads, green pines, and blue hills, the friendly people who cared for him and whom he had come to love. He was torn by inner conflict—between the desire to come back, as he was being urged, and the consciousness that he could not take the presidency from his former dean and friend Henry Newell, who was the likely candidate for that office.

Just how deep was the warm devotion of the people I began to realize when my sister Ruth came down to recuperate from an illness. My Line-a-Day, April 18, 1908, records: "Aroused by a note from R., first mail, that she would be on hand in the p.m. Galloped cooking and housecleaning while John foraged for flowers. Everyone contributed—roses, narcissus, and tulips; and John added fresh dogwood in spite of pouring rain. Mrs. Boutelle sent jelly and hermits, and Mrs. Sosebee, pickled peaches and pickles. Miss Sheak came down to get supper, and J. and I drove over to Cornelia to meet the train."

Ruth's letters to her fiancé Richard B. Coolidge bring back the suspense of the moment, while they make vivid again the flavor of the Demorest life:

Demorest
April 20, 1908

You would love this frontier life—chickens running through all the yards, mules drawing down the mountaineers from church in the long wagons filled with cane-bottomed chairs, cows lowing in the next yard. Everyone is neighborly and interested, and around all is the warm, fresh windy air of the South.

You know how I love to pick flowers, and here the violets just call to me and the birds send my head into the air until I feel like a wise robin with my head cocked aside.

I hope that business of John's will amount to something. He is much touched at your interest.

Demorest
April 23, 1908

You would laugh at John's garden. It has about ten shoots of lettuce and some radishes set in a plot about as large as a bread board, in the midst of the back yard, which is a paradise of dock. (Olive says this is poetic license.) Here in Georgia it seems cheaper to fence in gardens rather than hens. So our yard is a rendezvous of neighbors' hens, chickens, ducks, and turkeys, who are always fighting. The ducks scrape among the dock in the early morning in search of dew, and one hen is promenading with two small ducklings in hot pursuit. There are two or three peach trees loaded with small fruit, while in the front yard two hollies are slowly putting out fresh green leaves among the old winter ones.

The woods are much like the Fells, although really not so varied, as almost all the trees are oak and pine; but the shrubbery and flowers are more varied. John knows a lot about flowers and birds, and we wander along, stopping every few steps to study and question. . . . The air is delicious, cool, and fresh at morning and night, and clear and dry all the time. . . .

In one way the life is crude, narrow, and petty; in another it is alert, progressive, and open to a hundred new influences. More than anything else, it draws upon all the resources of the man who wants to help, and appeals as an unlimited possibility in proportion to its poverty. I wonder sometimes if my opportunities of service will be nearly as broad in the North.

John returned from the Richmond meeting full of hope and enthusiasm. He had found Mr. and Mrs. Glenn not only most friendly, but genuinely concerned over some of the conditions they knew personally existed in the mountains. They knew how little real knowledge there was of the region and saw the value of a careful study. "Would Mr. Campbell send Mr. Glenn a full statement of his proposed investigation, with reasons for it?"

How he labored over that statement! It was finished on May 15, 1908, and should have been in New York by the 18th at the latest. Ruth wrote on the 27th:

Don't tell the family, as I don't want to worry them, but the carefully prepared report which was to be presented at the Sage Committee meeting
last Thursday was delayed by some awful chance, in the mails and, by the
date on the return receipt, didn't get there until Saturday. It took over a
week to get to Baltimore from here! John had registered it and put on a
special delivery stamp. He had been about to telegraph that he had sent
it, but the operator here couldn't reach Cornelia that morning, and Olive
and I a little ridiculed his excessive caution. So, perhaps they'll think John
was too indifferent to get the work through on time and he lose the entire
chance. . . . If ever I try to influence you in such a way, just remind me of
this!

It was a painful interim. I ache today when I think about it. But all's well that
ends well. The delay was not fatal, although after we heard that the report had
arrived, we had to endure another soul-trying wait before we could hear that a decision had been reached. Letter and plan called for consideration and approval by an
executive committee, which was not quickly assembled, as one realizes on rereading them:

Demorest, Georgia
May 15, 1908
Mrs. John M. Glenn,
Baltimore, Maryland.

My dear Mrs. Glenn,
    I take much pleasure in sending herewith a statement of what I had pur-
posed to do. It seems to me that it can be carried out. There are many details
which I did not think best to incorporate in the statement. It was my purpose,
had I been able to carry out the plan myself, to prepare maps, routes, and
gather data during the summer, perhaps to spend a few weeks at the Amherst
Agricultural Summer School, where they are making a very wise beginning in
the study of rural conditions. With this preliminary work done, I had intended
to start in with a conveyance in the mountains of Virginia and work southward visiting schools, and during the brief winter rainy season to settle down
in some center such as Asheville, in whose environs are many schools that can
be easily reached. Then when the spring opened, to continue the journey, and
during the early summer to visit the conferences and religious gatherings that
are held.

It is perhaps needless to say that Mrs. Campbell and I would welcome the opportunity of doing this work, which we had planned to do ourselves but which our financial situation forbids at present. We should be glad to do it without any remuneration except the expenses which, as I have indicated, ought not to exceed $2,500. The kindly interest shown by you and Mr. Glenn prompts me to bespeak your recommendation toward that end if you can consistently do so. I appreciate deeply the confidence implied by your interest in the work of one who is a stranger to you. As I have asked your recommendation, it seems but fair that you should know more about us, and I therefore make free to speak of ourselves personally.

Mrs. Campbell is the daughter of the late L. L. Dame, for many years head of the high school in Medford, Mass. She is a graduate of Tufts College and for three years after graduation was a teacher of literature in the high school at Medford. Should some wish references, I feel sure that Mr. Morss, superintendent of schools at Medford, would respond to any inquiry.

My father was Gavin Campbell, general superintendent of the Wisconsin Central Railroad and general manager of the Green Bay, Winona and St. Paul Railroad. I spent ten years studying at Phillips Academy, Andover, Mass.; Williams College; and Andover Theological Seminary. After graduation, I went into educational work for the mountaineer and have been in that work in Alabama, Tennessee, and Georgia ever since, with the exception of two years spent in the Far West and abroad. I have made a number of trips through the mountains doing some of the work indicated, and I feel the need of carrying it out thoroughly and systematically. Should anyone wish to inquire regarding me, inquiries might be directed to any of these institutions, or to Mr. Clark Williams, superintendent of banking, New York state, or Mr. Arthur B. Chapin, state treasurer of Massachusetts. I have not asked these gentlemen or institutions to vouch for me, so I think it would be an impartial response.

I understand from one of Mr. Glenn's remarks that this report might be presented next Thursday. May I presume to ask that if there is any thought on the part of the committee of offering us the opportunity, I may know of it soon, as I am holding off a consideration of other offers to which I must reply soon. I sincerely hope that the committee will undertake it, for I know great good would come from it.

In my haste on leaving, I neglected to get from you the list of schools you so kindly offered. May I trouble you to send them at your convenience. Let me assure you again of my deep appreciation of the kindness extended by you and Mr. Glenn, an appreciation which Mrs. Campbell shares fully.

Very sincerely yours,

John C. Campbell

P.S. Should the plan carry, I hope to visit the Maryville Conference on my way north.

Statement Outlining Proposed Study (enclosed with foregoing letter)
May 15, 1908

An experience of ten years in the Southern Highlands has convinced me of the splendid possibilities dormant in the American Highlander. These possibilities are dormant because of his environment, and would be the more readily awakened to realities if the many efforts in his behalf were carefully and sympathetically studied and then coordinated.

There is much good work being done, and some perhaps that is ill-advised. It is my thought that a careful, independent study might result in some plan of cooperation whereby good work already under way might be made more effective, other work begun, and work which is already established, but ineffective, be corrected or allied with other work if there should prove to be any overlapping of effort. The agencies in the field for the betterment of Highland conditions are the church boards of the South and of the North, other philanthropic organizations, and independent institutions.

The great need that I as a worker have felt, and I know that I am not alone in my feeling, is for a touch with other workers in like fields and for data based on a comprehensive understanding of the entire field. Much of our knowledge, if such it may be called, arises from opinions formed by those at a distance from the field, who view the situation academically, or from those in the field in isolated sections, who are so near the problems of their own section that they do not see them in proper perspective.

Different methods have been proposed to bring about the desired result. The workers of a certain church board purposed publishing a paper which the principals and pastors might send the results of their experience and investigation, but it was found that such a course would defeat itself because of the extreme sensitiveness of the mountaineer.

A second method suggested, and in some cases carried out in part, was a conference of all the workers under a particular board. A handicap to this plan is the fact that the communities are isolated, roads are poor, and generally the salaries of the workers so low as not to warrant such a conference at the expense of the individual, even were other conditions favorable.

A third attempt within denominational lines is through visitations by agents, superintendents, and secretaries of the denomination. In many instances these officers are so burdened with duties of administration and money-raising that visits to the field are cursory and infrequent and generally are made, of necessity, only to those settlements near the railroads, where the prevailing conditions of the mountain section do not always exist.

To those desiring information, the question often arises as to whether data based upon such investigation, and also by conferences of workers within denominational lines, are not colored unconsciously by the denominational preferences of those giving information. The question also arises whether the pressing need for money to carry on such work does not also lead to emphasis upon the abnormal picturesque and pathetic phases of mountain life. These queries may not perhaps always be warranted, but may suggest themselves to careful inquirers.

It has seemed to me that the time has come for an impartial but sympathetic study to find out what needs are common to these isolated sections, and what needs are peculiar to each, in the hope that when the diagnosis is made, a remedy may be found. I would emphasize the necessity of an investigation made with appreciative sympathy for the mountaineer and his environment. I reiterate the word *sympathy.*

First—A sympathy deep enough to view the mountaineer as a man necessary to us and not simply as a picturesque type for journalistic exploitation, and an insight keen enough to see the truth behind its somewhat crude expression. He has qualities that we need in our national character.

Second—A sympathy wide enough to comprehend what is fundamental in the religious and educational efforts put forth by the various boards from the North and from the South.

Third—A sympathy thoughtful enough to understand the necessity of allying all educational effort with the efforts furthered by the state. Such an understanding will enable the investigator to meet on common ground with the county and state officials of education, upon whom he ought to call.

It has been in my thought to make such a study with my wife, for a woman may often learn many essential facts from the women teachers and from the women of the mountains which would not otherwise be available. The following is the plan which I had outlined for myself:

To fit out a wagon in which to dwell; to travel through the country in this way and come into intimate touch with the people, learn their needs, and see what they themselves are doing to meet those needs. Such a method seems necessary.

To avoid appearing in the light of investigators, I purpose carrying a stereopticon to give helpful lectures; in fact, I have done something in this line before. To obtain necessary pictures to illustrate later such conditions as can be illustrated through photography, I had purposed combining with my duties as lecturer those of a photographer. The photographer has entrance to the mountain home. I have often been called upon as a teacher and as an amateur photographer to take pictures of the mountain people and have even been urged to enter the home where death had entered previously to take a picture of some departed dear one, that some likeness might be left to the sorrowing ones.

Sketching as an artist is one of the ways my wife would employ; and preaching, which I have often done before for the mountaineer, gives abundant opportunity for helpfulness, study, and entrance to the mountain home and to their religious meetings.

I had planned also to interview the various county school commissioners of the mountain section, who are ever ready to talk with teachers, that I might get their point of view as to the needs, what is being done, and their expression as to how much the church schools are doing to further the public school interests. I had planned also to study carefully the work done in different schools throughout the mountains to get firsthand information, and to learn from the teachers themselves what they are doing.

With these data at hand, I planned further to visit the superintendents of secondary education in the mountain states for their views, as well as for the views of any field superintendents or missionaries who might have oversight of particular work in particular fields.

If such an investigation could be made, when the facts are at hand, an invitation might be sent by your committee, or some other responsible body, to the higher-up secretaries and officials who guide the policies of the various boards to meet in conference. It might be possible to have some connection with the rural development section of the United Charities. The mountain section of the South is different from its Lowland and Piedmont rural sections, but no doubt there are some needs in common.

It is my impression that an exchange of experience with workers in the New England hill sections might be of mutual advantage, though the hill town people of New England live under different climatic conditions and are of a different stock.

The plan as indicated will doubtless need much modification, but to me it has seemed in the main to be the most feasible. It is not an easy task; the situation is a delicate one for many reasons, and I would respectfully suggest that it be carried out very quietly. It is a task that ought to be done, and can be done, and it is well worth the doing.

The question of cost will doubtless suggest itself. It is impossible to give an accurate estimate, but I feel very sure that the outside cost for equipment, including horses and conveyance, living expenses, and necessary incidentals for a year's study, as outlined, will not exceed $2,500 for two persons for twelve months.

I take pleasure in submitting this outline, which is inadequate, but which I trust may be of some service.

Respectfully,

John C. Campbell

In early June the final decision had not been made. "I am deferring any decisions," wrote John to Mr. Glenn, "until later when I may, perhaps, know what in your judgment is the outlook in the matter in which we are interested. I trust it may go through." Nor had it come when we left for Nantucket on June 9th. On the 20th, the following resolutions recommended by Mr. Glenn were signed by four members of the Executive Committee and forwarded:

[Signed] Recommended, John M. Glenn, Director

RUSSELL SAGE FOUNDATION

Resolutions for Executive Committee

June 20, 1908

RESOLVED: That a grant of $3,000 be made for a study of the southern mountain communities.

The object of this grant is to secure a report on what is being done in the mountains and what the needs are for other work, and how cooperation among the various agencies now working in the mountains can be secured.

Such a report will provide information which is now greatly needed to standardize work in the mountains and lead to more intelligent giving.

This study and report will be made by Mr. John C. Campbell of Demorest, Ga., formerly president of Piedmont College. He and his wife will take a wagon and spend six months to a year in traveling through the mountains. Mr. Campbell is an able man of good judgment and is familiar with the mountain districts and people.

Mr. Campbell offered to do the work without any compensation for services.

Approved: [Signed] Margaret Olivia Sage
Robert W. de Forest
Gertrude S. Rice
Helen Miller Gould[6]

John received within a week a personal letter from Mr. Glenn:

June 26, 1908

Dear Mr. Campbell:

I have not yet gotten formal authority to make a definite arrangement with you about your mountain trip, but I feel little doubt about its being authorized.

I am leaving for Europe tomorrow by the steamer *Kroonland* and will be back by the first of September. Will not this be time enough for you to make definite arrangements about your expedition?

But the next day our suspense was relieved by another letter stating that enough members of the Executive Committee had agreed with the suggestion to make it sure. Mr. Glenn went on to say: "I would rather talk with you before you incur any serious expense, and confer with you about best plans. We can do this early in September. . . . I will leave word with my secretary to let you know when the other members of our Executive Committee have been communicated with. If you then think it important to incur expenses for preparation before my return, you may feel at liberty to do so, on the basis of your suggestions in your letter to Mrs. Glenn and outline of plans contained therein."

Almost a month passed. It was July 21st when a message from Miss Forbes, Mr. Glenn's secretary, confirmed the full approval of the Executive Committee, and we could settle down to a merry month, relieved of tensions and full of anticipations. When action came, on August 27th, it came rapidly.

[Mr. Glenn to JCC]
August 27, 1908

I have just returned from Europe. Can you come down to see me Monday or Tuesday next? We can then make arrangements for your undertaking. This, of course, will be at our expense. Please write me as soon as you can.

One does not need to be told that John was on the way to New York Monday, and, in accordance with further directions, was at the headquarters of the Russell Sage Foundation, 105 East 22nd Street, at 9:45 Tuesday morning, September 1st. I remained in Medford, but I can see the interview almost as if I had been there: Mr. Glenn friendly and businesslike, his seemingly casual gray glance keenly sizing up his new worker; John all concentrated attention, his shining eyes taking in every detail. Whatever each may have thought to himself—and I remember John was impressed with Mr. Glenn's dry humor as well as his courteous consideration— the interview was evidently satisfactory. And so began the second great adventure!

4

Travel in the Mountains

The Study, 1908–1909

With the grant from the Russell Sage Foundation, the Campbells set out in 1908 to traverse the region, to get to know the inhabitants, and to discover what their needs were. They were planning to gather data for the Foundation about the true social, religious, and economic conditions in the Southern Highlands. Visiting the eastern parts of Kentucky, eastern Tennessee, and western North Carolina, they interviewed missionaries, teachers, settlement school workers, and residents, going to out-of-the-way villages and towns on roads that were often nothing more than creek beds. They were trying to find ways to coordinate the missionary and educational work in the region, often by disparate institutions.

Much of the chapter is from the "Day-by-Day" diary that Olive wrote at John's request. On this trip she began to pursue her interest in folk songs, which she chronicles in the diary. She heard a mountain version of the ballad "Barbra Allen" at a program at Hindman Settlement School. Fascinated by Appalachian culture and the craftsmanship of mountain people, the Campbells hoped to encourage them to value their work and make their talents known. The entire diary, edited by the current editor, was published in 2012 by the University Press of Kentucky as Appalachian Travels: The Diary of Olive Dame Campbell.

John Campbell's study of the mountain region was the first comprehensive investigation of conditions in the Southern Highlands in the early decades of the twentieth century. His wife's diary makes informative observations throughout, about Campbell and his mission, about the individuals with whom and organizations with which he worked, and about life in the mountains during this period. In its entirety, it is an unofficial history of the important educational, religious, and social events that were occurring in Appalachia.

The beginning could hardly have been made under more favorable conditions. Mr. Glenn, head of a new organization with untraveled ways to chart, was ready for experiment. Conscious of the full weight of his responsibility, he yet placed great reliance on the personality of the worker. Mrs. Glenn stood closely behind him, adding her balanced judgment of people and causes to his decisions. Though not always agreeing, they made a remarkably wise and happy combination. I remember how lovely I thought her when we were first invited to their home on East 19th Street—one of those tall, narrow houses which are so hard to make seem home-like. It *was* homelike, and it was beautiful, with family heirlooms which formed a fitting background for her gracious dignity. Her naturalness and sincerity made her a perfect hostess, and we were always happily aware of her deep personal interest in our venture. We felt ourselves fortunate in having the field of our work so far away from the rest of the Foundation. Being in New York rather seldom, we were somewhat in the nature of guests of Mr. and Mr. Glenn while there and often stayed at their house when they had room. Thus we came to know them in a social as well as a business relation. They had many influential friends, largely in the low-land South, and knew almost everyone prominent in social work. To these they introduced us when they thought it might be of help. A little typed sheet, signed and explaining who we were, helped to vouch for us whenever we needed such an introduction.

Russell Sage Foundation
September 22, 1908

This will introduce Mr. John C. Campbell, who is to make an expedition through the southern mountains with a view to studying conditions there for the Russell Sage Foundation.

Any attention shown him will be greatly appreciated by the Foundation and by

[Signed] John M. Glenn
Director

I find a number of letters in the files similar to the following from Mr. Glenn to John:

October 21, 1908

I was anxious for you to see Mr. James H. Dillard, the president of the Jeanes' Fund, before you started out on your trip. Unfortunately he has been kept at Saluda, North Carolina, where he and his family were spending the summer, by the illness of several of his children. I think he is still there.[1]

His special function at present is in connection with the development of Negro schools, but he has a good knowledge of the South and is very much interested in any problems looking to its social development. His advice would be valuable; so it will be well for you to write to him. . . .

Please do not consider this as a suggestion that you interrupt your course especially to see Mr. Dillard. I only suggest that you be on the lookout for an opportunity to meet him. It is quite possible that he can give you better facts after you have followed your investigations some distance than he can at the present stage. His acquaintance of mountain conditions is limited.

My kind regards to Mrs. Campbell, and hoping you are enjoying your expedition, I remain . . .

Such letters, evidencing interest and a desire to help, and at the same time careful not to interfere with the free action of the investigator, were to be characteristic of our whole relation with Mr. Glenn. John kept him and Mrs. Glenn informed of our main steps and experiences and asked advice from time to time. In this way the study went forward to the best advantage and, I believe, to mutual satisfaction. I have here the detailed diary which John asked me to keep, that first year of the study, as an aid to his memory.[2] I had made a short record in my Line-a-Day the previous spring at Demorest, but now, with most of the South new to me and everything of interest, I recorded experiences faithfully, in detail as requested—from weather and character of the terrain to persons and personalities, what was said and how it all seemed to me personally.[3] I am impressed, as I read it over, by our almost constant activity day after day for months at a time; traveling by train, by wagon, surrey, "hack," buckboard or buggy, horse or mule—even on foot—absorbing new sights, new information, making planned and chance contacts, gathering material of all sorts. We called on well-known state and federal officials such as President [Edwin] Alderman of the University of Virginia and Bruce Payne, then state superintendent of rural education. We interviewed Archdeacon [Frederick] Neve, who lived at Ivy, not far from Charlottesville, and who had charge of the missions of the Protestant Episcopal Church in that part of Virginia. We talked with Jerry M. Pound, superintendent of state education in Atlanta; with R. E. Wright, assistant commissioner of agriculture; and with Reverend John E. White, Second Baptist Church, Atlanta, formerly of Mars Hill College, North Carolina.[4]

Interviews were generally rewarding, some especially so. I remember the first one with Dr. P. P. Claxton on October 7, 1906, at that time superintendent of secondary education in Tennessee, in Knoxville:[5]

He emphasizes the good stock of the mountain people; thinks their education should be of a nature to keep them in the mountains to develop the natural resources of East Tennessee and North Carolina with which he is familiar; has great faith in the industrial future of the mountains—coal, iron, marble, timber. . . . He feels that the time for the church work is almost past, on its present basis; perhaps some work along the present lines in the remote sections. Church schools and the secondary departments of the colleges hinder the growth of country high schools and a healthy local atmosphere of self-support. They are tending to pauperize the poor and are patronized very largely by well-to-do farmers with a false pride, which leads them to send their children to a "pay private school" rather than to the public school provided by the state. . . . Three ideas to emphasize:

1st. Adapt the school's curriculum to the life of the people.

2nd. Let all effort from outside tend to build up a spirit of self-support; not to be antagonistic, even unconsciously.

3rd. Establish schools for grown-ups. Cites grown-up schools of Denmark and Sweden. Sage Fund [could be] a mediator or go-between to bring about these things.

In the next weeks, months, and even years, these points were to come to mind constantly. The larger private and denominational schools were our first goals. They were not primarily, most of them, denominational in the aggressive sense but had been established by different boards and philanthropic groups to meet the great poverty of public education throughout the rural areas. Beginning with "day schools" and elementary boarding schools, they had gradually broadened their scope until the larger ones offered an "academy" or full high school course, often the only such course to be secured in the county. "Colleges" had naturally followed, not always standard in equipment and curriculum, but certainly institutions of higher learning, and important out of proportion to their size and equipment. They were, too, very hospitable and, whatever their academic standing, could give us information which it would have taken us long to have gathered elsewhere. More important still were the friends we made—friends who were to become the foundation of later work.

From larger and more accessible schools, we reached out to the smaller and more remote, public and private, and stopped by little one- and two-roomed public schools and high schools, where there were any. We talked with teachers, county superintendents, doctors, ministers of all sorts, where John was almost invariably called on to speak. We asked about resources, farm practices, and income, and if there was an established industry besides farming, we tried to get data on it and knowledge of conditions associated with it. We took many pictures and bought or were given many more. We inquired into local history, ancestry, travel routes. Later we checked carefully with Geological Survey folios and delved into the census of 1790 and *A Century of Population Growth.*

John was insatiable. He pushed travel as fast as he could and let no opportunity slide for gathering new information. From my diary one may pick almost at random a characteristic series of days. For example, from November 7 to November 11 we were traveling by buggy—John driving—over the Cumberland Plateau in Tennessee to Pleasant Hill, Grassy Cove, Jewett, Grandview, Ozone, and so to the train which would take us to Knoxville for the opening meeting of President Roosevelt's Rural Commission. We started from Chattanooga, on November 3, 1908. My diary reads:

Arose at 3:45 a.m. for the 5:05 train. It was absolutely dark when we left, and we could not see much before six. It seemed odd enough to rattle along in that dark, silent city behind a fat old Negro, our lantern beaming as if it were early in the evening.

We had to wait five hours at Rockwood for our Tennessee Central train, most of which time we spent at Hotel Mourfield—a neat-looking structure without, but cold and dark within. My first picture, as the door opened on "the best hotel in town," was a dusty room with a stove in the center surrounded by seven chairs (all rockers but two, and these were well tilted). . . .

. . . John went out to look for the pastor of the Christian Church and presently returned with him to the hotel, having picked him out by his wife's description: "A little, short, chunky man with black eyes; looks like a preacher . . ." After he left, a Jewish drummer from Austria fell into animated discussion on biblical subjects. . . . Said he did not meet much prejudice.

At the station we talked with a man who was starting out shooting. He said there were plenty of wild turkey, a few deer, and even bear on Caney Creek. . . .

. . . Mr. Stanley met us at Pomona Road with a buggy and a horse (to ride himself). Then we drove six miles of a fierce road—trail, rather—of rocks and stumps, which brought us into Pleasant Hill about 2:00–3:00 p.m. Mrs. Wheeler met us and put us into a comfortable room, while all the boys hung out of the dormitory windows to watch our movements.

After a careful description of personalities, classes, and handicraft, the diary continues:

In the afternoon [of November 4 or 5] John and I each gave the geography class a little spiel on Sicilian and Italian life. . . . The country seems different [from Georgia]—more oaks here to the exclusion of pine, more grass and more rock. Rock creeps through everywhere—in fact, bursts through, as one finds in the roads.

November 6th. I never saw such roads as those from Pleasant Hill to Grassy Cove, especially the last few miles near Grassy Cove. The horses fairly jump to clear a gully. It seems they had been hauling lumber from Grassy Cove to Crab Orchard. Also, they were cutting limestone and hauling that. In places we fairly bounced down rocky stairs. I enjoyed the ride immensely, however.

. . . Further along we asked the way. . . . "Eight miles to Grassy Cove, and an awful road!" Just beyond . . . we ran into a little forest fire, partially under control. A number of men were fighting it. It seems that it has been fearfully dry in this region for weeks and weeks. All the water is very low, woods dry, and roads very dusty. John drove the horses right through, though we found it pretty smoky for a bit. . . .

Grassy Cove itself is one of the prettiest little valleys I have ever seen . . . very green and level, and shut in close by high, blue hills or mountains. The first houses we came to were all log cabins, with roofs of hand-made shingles. . . . The land, most of it, seems to be used for meadows and hay. Some corn, which seems to be shocked in this country, and [a] number of good orchards.

We drove by Kimmer's store and found a note from Mr. Beecham, who had been called to Crossville and advised us to make Jewett. Decided to look up teachers. Found man had gone home, as it was Friday night; and the woman, Miss R[edding], was staying one and a half miles up the road at Mr. H[anby]'s. So we rode up there and had a short conversation with her—a pretty girl, with her shirtwaist pinned with common pins in front. She said they had about fifty-eight pupils, but school was not up to the old standard.

Mrs. H—— said she could not take us in for the night, and as it was nearing four, we decided it was too late to try for Jewett, so drove back to Mr. Kimmer's. There we found an open fire (at his house) and a table of magazines—mostly *Cosmopolitans* and *Woman's Home Journals*. . . . Mr.

Kimmer called out for Frank to take care of us, and as we went to the porch, a boy came out—"Frank," as we supposed. John called him Frank, told him to grease the axles and feed the horses so much roughness—they had had no dinner—then corn later. In the morning he asked Frank to harness up, and it then appeared that Frank was the nice grown-up daughter, and John the boy—they were both much amused.

It was growing dark when we arrived, and quite dark by five—smoky, too. By 5:30 it seemed seven o'clock. A wonderful moonlight night, with mountains dimly to be seen. We had a very nice and bountiful supper and retired to a clean room, with two beds, at 7:15. All was very nice, though my bed was a feather one, and both had but one sheet. However, we slept hard—to awake before light at five, for a 5:30 breakfast, another bountiful meal—fried chicken, scrambled eggs, coffee, biscuits, blackberry jam, and fried potatoes. . . .

We were off at six thirty—the horses very lively and gay, particularly the crabbed sorrel, who was full of interest in everything. A few rods down the street, we were stopped by a fine-looking old man on horseback, who wanted a word. He proved to be Mr. H——, much concerned that his wife had not taken us in the night previous—particularly when we were on the business (school) that he supposed we were. Said he did not like that way of doing. Yes, they did have company (the school teacher was there, his daughter and son-in-law, five of them, and I don't believe there were that number of rooms in the little house), but he thought they could have found a peg to hang us on. "You see my wife is a Baptist!" (as if that explained all!) "I told her the next time, whether it was a Baptist preacher or not, to take him in." He told us the school was not doing very well; that they hadn't appreciated the Presbyterian school until it was too late; now they would like it back.

A few rods beyond a nice white house, we turned to the left down into an insignificant little lane, bordered closely by Virginia rail fence and trees, backed by the blue mountains, behind which the sun had not risen. There were plenty of stumps and rough places, but we did not strike roads until we began to climb Walden's Ridge. I am sorry I have left no words to describe that ride.[6]

The road (over which they told us there was travel perhaps once in two months) was hardly a trail, beset with rock and so covered with fallen leaves that it was hardly distinguishable. We wound round and round and up, even the big bay beginning to sweat, while I hung over the wheel both in interest and to keep the buggy balanced from the edge. The woods were wonderfully pretty—oaks and some chestnuts . . . with great ropes of grapevine climbing high up in the branches. We kept getting glimpses through, but the smoky air and morning mist kept us from getting distant views. We reached the top of the first ridge in about thirty-five minutes. . . .

About nine o'clock at last [after a rugged descent leading into a dry creek bed], we sighted the store on the main Spring City road and were rejoiced to hear that our worst was over, our left-hand road—the right one—and that Jewett was hardly three-quarters of a mile on.

We swung to the left and before long sighted a little white building on the edge of the road. The house, a nice-looking one, was set a little back—a cornfield around, and a little deserted log cabin. I held the horses while John went up the plank walk to the house. He returned saying the teachers were there—then drove the horses back a half mile to get in through a gate. . . .

These two girls [the teachers] lived alone up there in the house, doing their own work. They got their mail once a week, had no telephone connection, and could get no horses to drive themselves. In her one and one-half years, Miss [Vickery] said they [had] had horses once, and a week before; the minister and his wife, Mr. and Mrs. Beecham, had ridden up on horseback and had let them use the horses for awhile. Mr. Beecham preached there once a month—otherwise they saw no one from the outside world. Were glad to see us. . . .

They had fifty-three scholars enrolled from a vicinity of five miles, some of these coming almost that distance to school. The community people were all proud of the school and well-disposed, and the children eager to come, but the winter presented great difficulties—mountain torrents, mud, etc. The children would come if possible, and were often soaking wet when they arrived, and would be more or less so all day. Also, as soon as it began to be decent in spring, they must help on the farm. Little girls six or seven must dig potatoes, plant, etc. . . .[7]

The diary then reports a long discussion on the health problem—especially the prevalence of tuberculosis, and the difficulty of getting a doctor. He "would come only when pay was guaranteed, and he charged twenty-five dollars—a prohibitive price, of course, though as [Miss V——] said, he had to start at dawn and arrive home late, after a drive of thirty miles, and his rig cost him five dollars."

On November 8th (Sunday), we overtook Mr. Beecham at Meridian, on the way to Crab Orchard, and stopped in at the little one-roomed schoolhouse where he was preaching.

He guessed who we were and stopped to invite us in. The place was full—women in sunbonnets, men, boys, and children, mostly nice-looking. He was exhorting them to take thought of the boys and girls, stop jealousies, and have a regular church. He was a good-looking man, slim and dark, with beard and moustache—thirty to forty, I should say. He looked to me like a Scottish Presbyterian. After he closed, he asked John to speak, which John did, along the same line, asking them to join in making Christians, not put stones in the way.

Mr. Beecham's district is all through these mountains—Ozone, Crab Orchard (where he lives), Meridian, Grassy Cove, Jewett, and another mountain. He has no horse and sometimes walks twenty-five miles a day or more. Said he had a horse once, but feed was too expensive to pay him to keep it. He was full of perplexity as to the situation and felt himself so helpless, his duties scattered over so wide an area. The people, fearfully poor, with crops mortgaged ahead, were afraid to be seen in church by their creditors. The lack of medical treatment was a constant source of distress to him. He told how one night he had tramped eighteen miles over the mountain to the call of a dying woman, and when he came, he could do nothing. He felt strongly that the first help must be material, and that would lead to spiritual uplift. . . . The tears stood in his eyes as he talked of his helplessness. He had almost planned to leave but felt the course cowardly.

. . . To the Melrose house for supper and for the night. . . . After supper we went to bed, and on looking at watch discovered it to be 6:00 p.m. Dead tired, and slept directly.

[November 9th] Up again for 6:30 breakfast. . . . We then went to call on Mr. [Klein], the county superintendent, . . . [who], it appears, has a farm on Crab Orchard Mountain, runs a saw-mill, teaches county school, is county superintendent, and is building a new house—"the busiest man in the county." . . . Seemed quite vague as to ideas. . . . Agreed it would be a good thing if the church schools would supplement the county schools by industrial work.

. . . We then went to the county school, which was a sight. Mr. K——had senior grades. . . . His costume bore evidence of hurry, and his black dangling tie was up under one ear. He snapped boys and girls up in good shape: "Stand up there! Don't you hear what I say?" etc., etc. There was discipline at least in the room, if not order of the housewife kind. Below, where the young assistant was struggling, conditions were worse. . . .

We were back at Pleasant Hill by November 10, a glorious, crisp morning—white frost heavy on the walks after a night of thundershowers. We had time there to pack and mend and write letters between meeting classes and delivering talks. In the evening at prayer meeting, John gave an address on Europe, and the next day he gave a good talk at chapel. Between packing (three of us sat on the trunk lid to close it) and final calls, John even wrote his communication for the "Fifteenth Year Report, Class of 1892" at Williams College.

Pleasant Hill, Tennessee
November 11, 1908
James C. Rogerson
84 Wall Street, New York

My dear Jimmy:

I have been a wanderer in the mountain section of the South for some time, and before I get farther from the railroad I must send you a line, inasmuch as you are so anxious to hear from me. Really, I have been moving around so much for the last two years that I have not received all the letters written me, and doubtless you and Peabody are thinking all sorts of hard things of me because I did not answer all the letters I did not receive.

Two years ago I broke down from overwork in an effort to secure an endowment for Piedmont College, gave up my work, was married to Olive A. Dame of West Medford, Massachusetts, and spent a year in Sicily and Italy. This year Mrs. Campbell and I are making an extensive study of the whole mountain situation in the South for the Russell Sage Foundation.

My home is still in Demorest, Georgia, where I shall be glad to see any of the fellows who come that way. Address any communication to me at Demorest. It will be forwarded by my secretary.

With best wishes,

Sincerely yours,

[Signed] John C. Campbell

Early on the morning of November 12 we made the long drive over to Pomona, in very cold weather, to the railroad which would get us to Knoxville. In the combination station and store, I spent the hour we had to wait sitting with my feet on the stove rail getting warm, while John talked with a mountaineer of humorous turn outside on the track. Flagging the train consisted of putting our trunk near the track and waving arms to the engineer.

November 13th was a long day spent listening to the "Hearing of the President's Rural Research Committee" in Knoxville. The points were all interesting and thought-provoking; major ones, as noted in my diary, included the following:

> Farming must be made to pay on economic and human side. . . . Compulsory education must carry with it provisions for better and more teachers and schools. . . . Corn robs land of fertility year by year, [land] decreases steadily in fertility unless there is rotation of crops. But even this poor land increases in price when roads and railroads come near. Rotation in crops should be one of the provisions in contracts for tenancy. Too much tenancy . . . mountain and rural people are drawn to cotton mills not only by better wages but by better home and sanitary conditions provided by company. . . . Lack of ambition in mountain people and mill operatives is result of disease, hookworm, anemia, etc.

The conclusion was especially good: "Citizenship we are after, not merely raising more crops, and good citizenship is making the best man one can be in the place one is. Agricultural and industrial training should not be taught as something separate on a money basis, but through all studies. Beauty of the common things—the aesthetic and spiritual values of common things—should be shown. Help toward doing these things must come from outside. One of the great things is to teach the country man who wants better things that a local tax to get them is not robbery."

Where schools lay along the Louisville and Nashville Railroad, as they did to the north of Knoxville, we were able to cover much ground in a few days: Lincoln Memorial Episcopal at Barbourville; Episcopal School at Corbin; Congregational School at Williamsburg; Sue Bennett Memorial (Methodist Episcopal South) at London. We also visited a Swiss colony near London and found a sturdy people who had succeeded in surviving land exploitation, though not by agriculture alone. Everywhere we met with a kind reception, were shown over the various plants, and our questions were answered. The teachers seemed very much in earnest, and most of them expressed a desire for more vocational work, but we could not see that any understanding effort was being made to adapt education to existing conditions—perhaps because no one had a real knowledge of what conditions were. "A study of denominationalism rather than mountaineers," John said as we moved on toward Berea. Indeed, evidences of friction, rivalry, and overlapping too often outweighed happier impressions of good work being done.[8]

What was to be the future of these schools, and what was the way to a better public school system? Not long before this, the Honorable J. G. Crabbe, superintendent of public instruction in Kentucky, had succeeded in putting through a bill in the 1908 legislature providing for a county board of education system. It also provided for the creation of a county high school in every county of the state—not later than two years after the measure became law. Protests were loud. The law was "impossible to carry out; premature; there were not enough qualified graduates of the elementary grades to justify the expense," etc., etc., etc. The private and denominational schools had their own special arguments, which they voiced with great conviction. The quality of what public schools could offer, supposing they were able to furnish adequate secondary education—which obviously they could not— would not be what they themselves were furnishing. Besides, they gave "Christian education," which the public schools would never be able to do.

We found Berea College, where we arrived November 20, greatly disturbed. President Frost was a strong believer in adapting their work to existing conditions. Berea's peculiar mission was to the mountains, regardless of what curricula and standards might prevail elsewhere. Students should be helped where they needed it, which meant they should be helped to earn their way as well as learn it. As we did not have long this time to study their plan, we were taken immediately on our arrival to a number of classes, among which were elementary classes for grown-ups, sewing, painting, forestry, botany, practical carpentry, and so many others that my head spun. We were also given a glimpse into a collection of old homespun "covers," a peep into the big laundry, and a brief glance into the way the Union Church was working out the "mission barrel" problem.[9]

The next day, Saturday, November 21, Mrs. Frost (the president's wife), a very delightful woman, and Mr. [Will C.] Gamble, the secretary, drove us out to visit in a neighboring community.

My diary reads:

Berea is really the "gateway to the mountains," being literally in the bluegrass on one side and the sandstone mountain region on the other. It also lies on the only thoroughfare there from Cumberland Gap. The hills, though not high, still are jagged and imposing. The forests are pretty well cut off on many, and ploughing has been done where the sides are very steep and washing cannot be prevented. The school owns a whole line of hills, which forms its watershed and wood supply. These are being carefully forested and ought eventually to make a fine forest. On the way out, Mrs. Frost and I stopped at a two-roomed log cabin (climbing over the stile) where an old lady was doing some spinning. Her wheel was out of gear then, but she had fixed it up on our return, and we saw her spinning goats' wool. . . .

[November 22] I rested Sunday morning, though John visited Sunday schools. . . . In the p.m. Pres. Frost drove us to the Narrow Gap Sunday school. A Miss Fox, who had been one of their teachers and had started a Sunday school in this district, which was one of the worst near Berea, had gone up there to live and teach. They say the community has been revolutionized since her coming, though she has had to live down all kinds of slander and opposition. It seems there is great suspicion of a woman working alone in a community. Mountain people do not understand it. . . . The district seemed to be rough still, for she told of some trouble the night before at their social; also of several stills in the region and much drunkenness.

[November 23] In the morning John made a *fine* talk at chapel. . . . Then we started off to McKee, at 11:00 a.m., with Mr. Gamble. Had rough roads the first half, especially over Big Hill, which is the steepest drive we have had. It is fearfully rocky—an unsteady crunch and jolt continuously. . . .

. . . It was dark long before we reached McKee, though fortunately the road here was good. It was picturesque enough to see the night settle on the mountains—till finally we could see only the high mountainside on our left and a Virginia rail fence so close to the right I could almost touch it. Occasionally a light would glimmer at the foot of a distant hill, or we could see door or window chinks outlined in the flickering light of an open fire. Suddenly we heard hoofs, and a horseman galloped down the hill ahead, drew rein, and wheeled, waiting. I was all expecting a highwayman when he spoke—and it proved to be Mr. [Isaac] Messler, the head of the McKee School. He had come out to make sure we should stay with them instead of at the hotel. . . .[10]

We found a very pleasant home [at the school]. Mr. Messler proved to be a young man of perhaps forty, with hair prematurely gray and a fine, rather worn face. He was a minister of the Dutch Reformed Church, a New Yorker by birth and of old Dutch parentage. They had a tall clock which had been in his family for over two hundred years. Mrs. Messler was buxom and rosy, and they have two children, the younger a boy of one–two and a fine little fellow. They gave up big northern chances to settle here and have been in McKee three years. Have had much to contend against in prejudice. . . . They have no regular church but are building one (to be union) at Grayhawk, five miles beyond. [Mr. Messler] felt very much the need of industrial work and is to start some soon several miles distant from McKee, which, as the county seat, is not so desirable.

[November 24] We visited the school [at McKee] in the morning and found it well kept up and attractive. Good work was very evidently being done. John spoke and Mr. Gamble sang. Then we got five horses: Mr. Messler has three himself; Mr. Gamble rode Rex, one of our horses, a fine saddler; John was lent a beautiful Kentucky thoroughbred of pale buff with cream mane and tail—a beauty with his arched neck and pawing feet. We then rode over to Grayhawk (my first experience side-saddle), where there is a sort of mission social settlement, in a small way, with Sunday school work. I certainly enjoyed my gallop, and my fine little horse Captain loped like a rocking chair. I never enjoyed myself more.

The two ladies in charge of the work at Grayhawk welcomed us. During our visit, two mountain women walked in from homes some two miles away, one of them to ask about work, the other—expecting a baby soon—to "buy mission barrel stuff." There was nothing for either. The workers told us of the prevalence of tuberculosis, typhoid, measles, and, last year, smallpox. The mountaineers, they said, had no idea of contagion and resented and opposed any fumigation or isolation process. There was much superstition in "doctoring," seen especially in the case of babies.

We had a beautiful ride back to McKee in the afternoon, after showers had let up. . . .

Got home about five, just as darkness had set in. After supper there was a meeting, when John spoke again most successfully and Mr. Gamble sang. When over, a number lingered and we talked. . . . Mr. M. spoke of difficulties of this mission field. Also believed in not hurrying forces, but in slow growth.

[November 25] Started to Berea early in morning—a glorious morning when hills were golden and purple. Stopped again for John to speak and Mr. G. to sing at the little one-room school in Clover Bottom. We heard part of their Thanksgiving exercises and much lusty singing.

Had an uneventful and pleasant return, arriving about 2:00 p.m. Mrs. Frost greeted us most cordially. . . .

After ordination of a young minister, we went over to a convocation of teachers which President Frost had called to discuss with us. Had an interesting time—various speakers. The substance of their talks was as follows:

Mountains about as well inhabited now as possible with support from crops. Some counties too few—and some too many—people. Many leaving and buying bluegrass farms, though wish to live in sight of the mountains. Natural affection for mountains. Most of Berea students go back, especially those in shorter courses. Where they make their own homes, these are better than their old ones. . . . Berea does not encourage boys to go away for education—north, etc.—unless they are coming back to teach at Berea. Feel that shorter courses and lower grades are most helpful now. College for the next generation.

Some disagreement as to a tenant class in mountains, but strong evidence for it for renters (two or three) to one man's estate. Perhaps they should each own a plot of their own, then help out by renting more on shares. . . .

Berea has found it successful to return educated mountaineers to teach in own section. Does not believe (so Mrs. Frost says) in "foreigners." They have just so many new points of view and adjustments to make, while the mountaineer starts in even. She thinks it best, then, not to start social settlement work by outside (church) schools. People, however, to be reached best by schools. . . .

Dr. [Robert H.] Cowley spoke of the amount of tuberculosis, typhoid, and trachoma in the mountains, due, he thought, to lack of water. Hard, at times almost impossible, to get water. All family use one towel. Barn used as privy, and swarming flies bred contagion. No idea of contagion in mountains, or what it meant. Many deaths from measles. Told of women who walked three miles to Berea and brought water buckets with her. Said yes she could get water one and a half miles on other side, but she was coming to Berea and thought she'd bring her buckets along.

Nice custom at Berea on Sunday matter: All required to go to morning Sunday school, and then might go during the rest of the day to any service. At evening, must be at students' chapel. No trouble on sentimental side. Calling allowed twice a week and socials several times where boys and girls could go together. Very sad when boy went back and married uneducated girl. Dragged him down to the same level. Some difficulty here as to getting girls—needed at home, or did not need education, etc., etc. Boys and girls eat together. Student waiters. Have red tablecloths.

To go from Berea into the mountains by train, one had to bear north through Winchester, where the Lexington and Eastern Railroad struck eastward. The so-called Kentucky mountains are really a deeply dissected plateau with steep hillsides and very narrow, winding valleys. At that time they afforded the largest area in the entire mountain region, unbroken by railroads and only lightly affected by modern influences. The Hindman Settlement School, toward which we were now on our way, lay in about the center of this area. To reach it we were to take a wagon, but first we had to take the train to Jackson, where there was a Southern Presbyterian school.[11]

[November 27] The ride to Jackson was quite impressive—great sandstone ridges and bluffs. A woman behind me punched me with her forefinger and wanted to know my county seat. She proved to be a widow, a mountain girl. Husband died three months ago with tuberculosis. She did not wish to be a drain on family, but to pay her way. Had met two old people (who sat behind, at snuff and tobacco—he had been drinking) who wished her to go to Cannel City as postmistress and she was on the way, knowing no more than that. Said she was green about some things, but hard to fool. Always watched—had been taught to "work, watch, and pray." Didn't like the old man's looks, but reckoned she could go back if it wasn't a good place. Had never heard of a timetable.

It was dark when we arrived in Jackson, but [the head of the school] met us and piloted us over the worst streets, a half mile to the dormitory. We found it pleasant and his family nice.

As they came from the bluegrass and had been there only six months, they could not give us a great deal of seasoned information. The school had about 150 pupils, drawn practically entirely from the town—a few boarders. There was a public school, very short in term, and poor. There were no water works in town, and they had great difficulty in drawing all the water for the dormitory. No one in the town could fix pumps for them. The three or four churches were fairly well attended.

[November 28] Had a very interesting ride from Jackson to Helechawa—in a mangy little car, discolored and patched and smelly, but with a nice young conductor who had been "raised" in Jackson. Said he couldn't see much difference in it from twenty years ago—as mean and meaner than ever. Hargis-Cockerell feud was responsible for much; thought feud would end now, with the death of Judge Hargis (shot by his own drunken son) and Cockerells also pretty well shot out.[12] We heard also from other sources that old judge controlled state elections by same means, and simply assassinated everyone in his way. Saw bullet-hole in his own store, where one bullet, shot by his son, had lodged. Conductor, Mr. Back, also said he bet there were twenty blind tigers in Jackson—moonshine and otherwise.[13] Possible to shut them out if strong man would push it. Afraid of antagonizing. Said his superintendent would spend one thousand dollars to prevent liquor getting into Morgan County. All conductors had government warrant to search baggage and arrest men carrying more than one gallon of liquor with them. Told of one man who had seventy-eight bottles of beer in his trunk. Another, half drunk, slashed him with his knife—but on another occasion gave him his pistol to keep until he got off. Lots of drinking. Said superintendent had tried to get Express [Company] to promise not to bring in liquor. They refused and he took out all Express offices on L & E line.[14] Express reshipped at Jackson under company care at express rates.

At Helechawa President [M. O.] Carter of Hazel Green Academy, a pleasant young man, met us with a team and drove us out to the school. All the country is suffering with fearful drought. We saw small boys hauling water, and at the school they are having an expensive time hauling water for electric lights. The country (Wolfe County) is not so rough as that around and on the way to Jackson. The hills are lower and more rolling; soil looks better. The school itself, at Hazel Green, is situated in a long valley, though on a little plateau-like rise in it. It is quite surrounded by hills, with the little town at its foot. It has a fine new boys' dormitory of concrete, a brick recitation building, wooden girls' hall, and an industrial building, of wood and new, and two or three student cottages. . . . They have from thirty-two to thirty-three acres. We were given a pleasant room in the Girls' Dormitory, where Professor and Mrs. Carter live, and a little luncheon in our room. We rested awhile, then walked over a swinging bridge (made me seasick) between boys' dormitory and us, to make a call on the former minister's wife, Mrs. [H. J.] Derthick.[15] He is out getting help, preaching, etc. . . . In the evening we went to a production of one of the literary societies—boys and girls. . . . The children did well and showed a pleasant spirit throughout the faculty jokes, which, I was told, were uncontrolled from headquarters. There is a fine auditorium, with circular seats.

Professor Carter personally is much interested in industrial work and anxious to push it, especially to give work to the needy boys from whom he is constantly hearing. His desire was to teach that side, but when Mr. Derthick withdrew, he was obliged to take up, against his will, the principalship. Believed thoroughly in secondary education, and said few boys graduated. At last he had realized that perhaps this was best at present, as these further advanced boys did not go back to the mountains.

In the morning [Sunday, November 29] we went to Christian Sunday school and then to a Revival Methodist preaching. I was much pleased with the liberal spirit. It was Communion, and "all who truly repent" were invited to the rail—of whatever denomination and even if they had not joined a church. The minister then invited the ministers present of other denominations to assist him in dispensing the elements. . . . [Talked] with Mrs. Carter in the evening (while others had gone to hear John speak).

The town has a neat, rather progressive look—houses painted, etc. Most of the women in sunbonnets, though the well-to-do wear elaborate ones. Mrs. [Niles] had on a beautiful black silk one with white ruffling inside. She also has a beautiful white one, Mrs. Carter says. . . . Mr. N—— says this is a fine country—raises splendid small vegetables, especially tomatoes, but need to know how. . . .

[November 30] Mr. Carter drove us to the station (at Helechawa) the following morning, where we met Mr. Derthick, who turned out to be a young man. . . . Spoke liberally of all denominations. Said they never asked a boy wishing help to what church he belonged, etc. Need of union among churches and education based on strong Christian foundation—no other would succeed. County schools would need twenty years in this county before successful. Failed in teachers, Christian training, etc. Told of one town near by (about five hundred inhabitants); only four men were not drunk at election time. Complete lack of religious life. Liked people, however. Hated to give up [the principalship of] the school.

We were greeted in Jackson with a letter from Miss Katherine Pettit, one of the two joint directors of the Hindman Settlement School, which we were to visit. Her boy, with wagon, who would take and guide us to Hindman, would not arrive until Tuesday noon. The trip would be a matter of forty-five hard miles, and we had better make our start early Wednesday morning in order to have a good stopping place for that night. We gladly turned in early.

[December 1] Had quite a furious talk at breakfast with a Mr. ——, who believed that the railroads were the only salvation of the mountain people, at least in this section. Said the conditions were not paralleled in any section of the United States—marriage and intermarriage, degeneracy, lack of ambition, etc.—was didactic and severely hopeless. Insinuated that he could prove the point if I were not present. Mr. K——, another young man present, differed from him. Said he had seen improvement in the time he had been there. . . .

A lovely sunny day after a pouring night. . . . We took a little stroll during the morning up to a coal mine, where the young engineer was not enthusiastic over the country. Jackson is not a progressive place. . . . It is small, too, streets fearfully irregular, houses at all angles. No pigs loose, but sties are in evidence, and sad-looking cows trip and lumber along the narrow, irregular plank walks or lie dejectedly on the bare, damp earth. I don't see why they range—there is nothing to eat but paper.

The evening was spent in talk with Mr. [Vaughan], the superintendent of the Kentucky Sabbath School Society, who had spent years traveling through the country, and also with Mr. [Kelly], a young Presbyterian minister who told us some of his adventures. The latter was particularly distressed over health conditions, accidents, etc. He was eager for a hospital at Jackson; was full of interest and not afraid of work and obstacles; "intended to stay by until the place is whacked into better shape."[16]

[December 2] A clear but very cold morning. Grover C. Perkins, a handsome dark boy of nineteen, came about seven, and we got off by 7:45. The road began early to be rough, the mud being frozen in heavy ruts. We wound out through peaked hills bared to timber—houses painted and frame. At noon we stopped before a cabin and fed horses and selves. . . . The road by this time had begun to run in the creek bed and continued to do this, with occasional short lapses to the bank, the rest of the day. Of course, there was little water, the season being so dry, but how we jolted and rattled among rocks and stones, crashing into frozen pools and out! Although the sun was bright and high, the air continued so cold all day that my hands were stiff and tingling when I tried to eat lunch. John and I got out and walked about five miles to get warm. The houses grew more and more far apart, their vicinity being heralded by flocks of ducks and geese in the creek and a few hogs rooting on the hillsides. More timber on the hills. It began to get dark by 3:00–3:30; indeed the sun first dropped out of sight before two and only reappeared at intervals. Fortunately there was a half moon, bright and very cold, which reflected in the creek. I couldn't help thinking of what the family would say if they could see us crashing through the ice of the creek bed that cold moonlit night—

the dark hills high on either side and dark hemlocks close at hand—no houses in sight.

Finally, about 5:00 p.m., Grover pulled out of the creek and we stopped at a faint light on the left bank. Here proved to be a dark barn and a two-story house, faintly lighted. Someone hailed us—and there was old Mr. Hayes (a former Confederate soldier), who was to take us in for the night.

We introduced ourselves and were ushered into the room, where there was a brisk soft coal fire. Two girls were sitting by it, pretty, big-eyed and shy, "hired girls," Mr. Hayes said, and a small boy of two–three whom Mr. Hayes explained laconically as "said to be my grandson. Hardly think so; but I've got him and mean to keep him." . . .

The girls then went out, and after we were warmed up, we were ushered into the cold dining room—set with a long table, low homemade chairs, oilcloth, and slim crockery. Had black coffee without sugar or cream, fried fat pork, corn bread, white butter, and sorghum. The girls waited and the men ate.

After supper we returned to the fire and the older girl (surname, Fugit) put the small boy into one of the two beds in the room. Then they retired to get our room ready. Presently Mr. Hayes told us we could go up when we were ready, and asked if we minded having Grover sleep with us. I bit my lip, and John answered with overdone cordiality, "Of course not. Be glad to have him. I'm used to sleeping with the whole family."

We then retired to our room, which was chilly in spite of a fire. I pulled off my boots, dress, and petticoat and crawled between the one sheet and pile of homespun covers. John followed suit, after putting out the light and spreading my coat over us. Then we waited. There was a good deal of moving about, but no Grover—nor did he turn up all night. He had been to the school and was evidently embarrassed. I don't know where he slept. We had a chilly night and were glad to get up at 4:00 a.m. in spite of the cold. Had a good breakfast of fried chicken and biscuit; and for all three, and horses' feed, paid $2.30. Mr. [Vaughn], by the bye, in Jackson, declared that the old mountain hospitality is a thing of the past. Once, a minister or educator could not have paid a cent keep from Lexington on, but commercial spirit had come in. Money made the people mad. . . .

Got off at 6:30 [December 3] into the creek bed again, and we continued in it all day practically. Troublesome, Town Creek, —— Fork [full name not given], crashing, grinding in and out. We had two mountains to cross, and John and I must have walked a good seven miles. All the cabins

. . . were log, except a few box cabins. Some of the chimneys were below the roof of the house. I saw many spinning wheels, and one loom on a porch. All cabins roofed with hand-split shingles. All creek and valley land seems pretty thickly settled. Hillsides are ploughed high up. Most of the corn is in shocks, however. Creeks lined with marked and stranded logs.

At one we drew into Hindman, which we found remarkably neat and prosperous in appearance. It has practically no bottomland, just a rift in the hills by the creek, so that the school itself, a little beyond the town, has to be crowded close to the road. It has a big log house where the girls and teachers live, a small cottage for the boys, a power house and water tank, though no water to use in this dry season. They haul all their water, and boil that for drinking.

Miss Pettit and Miss Stone ran out to meet us and took us into a fine big room to warm up over a roaring open fire while dinner was put on the table for us. The house is not sealed inside, just finished carefully with plaster between the chinks. It has quite a charming effect. All the furniture in the house, except the "mission" in that one room, has been made by the students. It is quite charming, too, of black walnut, finished dull, and on simple old lines.[17]

Our guest room is a big one with two white iron beds covered with natural color linen spreads and blue "kivers," woven rugs on the oiled floors. Electric lights throughout, run by steam. The school furnishes them to town for a small sum, which goes to support of a man to run them and watch the buildings. They have had two fires (one incendiary) and now keep watch. House is steam heated.

Hindman was probably the first mountain school to appreciate fully the native culture of the mountains, to use the old handmade things, and to try to preserve the crafts themselves. They also used native shrubs and "pretties," such as gourds, hornets' nests, vines and berries. The "Big House" made a great impression on us, as indeed did the fund of information passed on to us by Miss Pettit and Miss Stone. They were remarkable women with experience and wisdom—Miss Pettit quick and sparkling, Miss Stone balanced and serene. I shall never cease to be grateful to Miss Pettit for opening to me what was to become an absorbing and illuminating interest as the years went on. She asked, that first night, as we sat after supper in the living-room before a huge open fire, if I would like to hear an old ballad. When I politely assented, without too much real enthusiasm, she called on one of the girls—Ada B. Smith, her name was—to sing me "Barbry Allen."

Shall I ever forget it? The blazing fire, the young girl on her low stool before it, the soft strange strumming of the banjo—different from anything I had heard before—and then the song! I had been used to sing "Barbara Allen" as a child, but how far from that gentle tune was this—so strange, so remote, so thrilling. I was lost almost from the first note, and the pleasant room faded from sight; the singer only a voice. I saw again the long road over which we had come, the dark hills, the rocky streams bordered by tall hemlocks and hollies, the lonely cabins distinguishable at night only by the firelight flaring from their chimneys. Then these, too, faded, and I seemed to be borne along into a still more dim and distant past, of which I myself was a part.

Of course, I would not rest until I had learned this new, fascinating "Barbara Allen"—quite an undertaking, I found, for the new intervals were subtle. Later I was to learn much about "gapped scales" and "modal tunes" and the special characteristics of these "old-timey song-ballets or love-songs," the ballet or ballad being the words, the "song," the melody. I was attracted by both words and songs, but it was the melodies that especially intrigued me, and I began at once to pursue them whenever I had an opportunity. The search, continued over the years, has proved one of the most illuminating and rewarding experiences of my life, leading, as it has, into the realms of pure and lasting beauty and opening the way into many related and inexhaustible fields—folk hymns, folk games, folk dances, folk tales, folk arts, folk material in general, here and abroad. At the beginning, however, I merely watched for "song-ballets," learned the tunes, and wrote down the words, thus adding a new subject to our expanding and deepening inquiry.[18]

Remote as we felt, we found letters awaiting us, and more kept coming—several from Mr. and Mrs. Glenn, who followed our adventures with great interest:

[Mr. Glenn to JCC]
November 25, 1908

I am very glad to get your letter of November 22, and the book on Congregationalism. Please accept my thanks for the latter.

I enclosed you yesterday copies of the telegram from Mr. Desha Breckinridge and of my answer to him, for your information. I do not think it desirable to switch off to side issues when one has as important a task as yours in hand, unless his work on the side is going to help the main work.[19]

At the same time, I think you can judge better about the advisability of doing such a piece of work as that suggested by Mr. Breckinridge and of its value to your main work, better than I can.

I wish I could be with you at Hindman. Please give my kindest regards to Mrs. Campbell and Miss Pettit.

[Mrs. Glenn to JCC]
December 2, 1908

Thank you very much for *Anglo-Saxon Congregationalism in the South.* I have read it with much interest. I was especially interested in seeing on page 266 that there is a colony of Russian Jews within half a mile of Greene Academy, and also on page 224 that there are a number of Swedish and Norwegian families settled near Thorsby Institute, Thorsby.[20] In connection with the general study that is being made of rural conditions, especially in the South, it would be interesting to know how far these stranger people fit into the life of the mountaineers, and whether there will be some results to learn from their settlement that will be of value in considering the emigration of some of our immigrants from the city to country communities. . . .

Hoping that you and Mrs. Campbell are enjoying your trips through the mountains, I am, with kind regards . . .

[Mr. Glenn to JCC]
December 8, 1908

There is one question about mountain conditions which my knowledge of the Virginia mountains brings up, and which was impressed upon me still more by a conversation with some educators the other day. It is whether there is enough in the mountains themselves to support the mountain people. A further question arises, whether, supposing the mountain people can live comfortably and decently in the mountains, [. . .] they [are] likely, without outside aid, to keep up standards if they continue to live in the mountains more or less in isolation. These questions seem to me to be fundamental in your investigation. I have no doubt that you already had them in mind.

I am glad that you seem to be enjoying yourselves. I am sure that your study is going to be of great value.

I would like to linger over the many things we saw, heard, and did at Hindman—the talks on health conditions with Harriet Butler, the wise nurse; with Ann Cobb, who wrote poetry and loved carols and folk songs; with Hilliard Smith, a lawyer and neighbor and trustee of the school, who knew much local history and sang ballads, too. We took many longer and shorter expeditions by foot and by horseback up little branches and trails closely set between hills, gray beeches, and mossy green rocks. They were thickly populated—mostly double log houses with a fireplace between. One branch visited on a horseback trip with Miss Pettit had, she said, 150 to 200 children in two miles. We stopped to call in a number of homes where there were ten to twelve children. Along the way we talked at length of the needs of secondary and industrial education and the lack of understanding on the part of people away from the field.

There was always something to do, diverting and enlightening, at the Hindman School. Best of all, we had the companionship and wisdom of Miss Pettit and Miss Stone, who had started the school and lived through many exciting and trying experiences. They were remarkable women and complemented each other in an astonishing way. There could not have been a more alive, progressive, and stimulating hostess than Miss Pettit. I did not wonder that a wealthy Lexington friend used to beg her to come, on her winter vacation, on a cruise with him and help him entertain his friends. She was the life of the party. Miss Stone was the quiet balance wheel, who kept finances in order and was so loved in the country about that dozens of babies were named "May" in her honor. Both were to remain our good friends as long as they lived, and strong supporters of the Mountain Workers' Conference when it was organized.

From Hindman as a center, John and I made our first long trip on horseback. The school people asked me to ride side-saddle, explaining that cross-saddle for women was new to the mountains and they thought I might meet with some unpleasant experiences. Also, it might reflect on the school. Good saddles were not easy to get, at best—horse or mule—and owners objected to renting them for sidesaddle use, which was apt to result in sore backs. At last, however, I got a mount, and John had little trouble in securing another for himself, such as it was. It seemed as if we would never get through adjusting bridles, tightening girths, straightening saddle bags; and this was only the beginning, as I found. Limps must be investigated, horseshoes replaced, pressure eased on sore backs. John worried, too, over my fashion of becoming absorbed in the scenery and not, he feared, on the alert for a bad stumble or an unexpected shy. I was not a practiced rider, but, happily, I came through with only a few minor tumbles. My diary records:

[December 8] Splendid bracing morning—which called for my flannel shirt, vest, sweater and Pontiac coat, tights, and woolen stockings. . . . At seven the horses were brought up—two blacks. The younger, livelier one was saddled for John, and the other (Mr. Napier's) for me. It proved to have a bad limp and in addition would hardly crawl along the road. We stopped in town to get a pair of woolen socks to draw over my boots, then went to see Mr. Napier. By that time the boy's saddle which John was riding was already becoming pretty uncomfortable, and we felt quite a sorry pair—with saddle bags agape and uneven under my saddle. Mr. Napier said the horse had just been shod and probably the shoe pinched; also he was to meet his brother partway, and this brother, Callaway, would bring an extra saddle which John could take. So we hied up to the blacksmith's and had the horse's shoe fixed—also changed horses, giving John the old boy to hike along with a spur, as Mr. Napier said he wouldn't go for ladies. Then we waited for Mr. Napier to catch up. . . . After a good half hour he appeared, galloping along on a white steed. We rode cheerfully some miles. . . . After meeting numerous men and mules, none of which had seen Callaway, at length a man hove in view who turned out to be the same. By good luck, he had not forgotten the saddle, and at length we were fixed. Off rode the Napiers (Napper, pronounced) through to Morgan County to help their brother get nominated for sheriff, and we took our way along Troublesome at about 10:30. We rode along this a piece and turned up Mill Creek, then over the mountain to the head of Lot's Creek.

We stopped twice on Lot's Creek, first at Reese Young's to feed our horses. A woman "welcomed us cordially" and took us in, where an old man of eighty-six was sitting warming up over a coal grate fire (recently put in by his son to replace [a] big wood fireplace). He had been husking corn all the morning and felt stiff. He chatted along amiably—said he had never traveled much; born four miles from there eighty-six years before; son was up on the mountain getting wood. . . .

From there we rode a mile further, by log cabins on Lot's Creek, to Mrs. Alec Young's. . . . She welcomed us in to the usual coal grate fire and told us about the processes of weaving, while two tame gray squirrels climbed all over us. . . . She brought in a hackle for us to see and took us out behind the house, where her loom was in the sun (under a roof) with quilts pinned up on either side to keep out the wind.[21] She was weaving some linen curtains for Miss Pettit. . . .

We then rode on to the mouth of Lot's Creek. By that time it was quite dark and we were all (people and horses) tired and cold. My saddle had a fearful tilt forward so that my feet were way up and all the strain was thrown on my back. It was bent like a bow, and I couldn't sit up straight. We were glad to be at the mouth of Lot, for it empties into the North Fork of the Kentucky three miles from Hazard. We met several groups of people but rode on in the darkness through what appeared to be exceptionally pretty scenery—a full river and peaked hills beyond.

It was fully 5:30 before we dragged into Hazard—my pony sadly relinquishing his proud morning's lead and slowly plodding up the hill behind John's slow, but steady, old nag. We asked for Mr. [Asbel S.] Petrey, head of the Baptist school, and rode out to his house, up a steep hill some quarter of a mile out of town. My poor pony moved most reluctantly, and I was too cold and tired to talk. Arrived at the house—a woman was outlined in the doorway—Mrs. Petrey: "Mr. Petrey wasn't home. Wished he was. He didn't expect us till Friday." I was almost ready to cry, but we turned our horses and plodded back to town to D. Y. Combs's hotel. Had a very decent room, and I fairly fell off the pony in John's arms and crawled up to the grate fire where I could bake arms and legs and aching back. The bed was hard and none too clean as to its pillow cases and single sheet, but we turned the former inside out, heaped clothes from the second bed over us, and, clad in cambrics and stockings, crawled gladly into bed. . . .

[December 9] Up at 6:30 feeling more encouraged in spirit, though I, at least, felt pretty stiff and lame. Made ready for a prompt start, feeling none too enthusiastic toward Mr. Petrey, but about 7:30 he showed up—a pleasant man of forty with clean-cut features and English cut of hair and whiskers. Had not known we were in town until too late, and evidently was cut up at our reception. He insisted on paying our bill and urged us to stay over. Then he took us up over the buildings (two), which had a truly beautiful site on a knoll overlooking the town and surrounded by cedars. The morning was perfect—warmer, a white frostlike snow on the ground and on beeches, cedars outlined against them, hills above. The buildings were of brick and good, but very dirty inside, as the school building is leased to town up to Christmas (keeping teachers, employed by board, and paying enough to pay janitor—but no good janitor now—hence dirt). . . . Mr. Petrey does not expect county high schools to amount to anything for ten–twenty years. County too poor to support them. Besides, politics will be bad for them. State was setting premium for them by granting graduate teacher's license without examination. Idea that county high school is to be only a school for graduates of the grammar department of public school—not to include common public school grades. These students will be few in number for years to come. Did not think magistrates would want to vote or put before people plans for raising money to put up buildings and supply teachers for the few—especially when there were good buildings and good church schools. . . .

Took us up to his house . . . then to hotel to pack up. Also got another saddle pad to fix my saddle, which proved comfortable. . . . Mr. Petrey appeared at eleven with nice box of crackers and fried chicken, and we started off in good spirits, our saddle bags pinned up and strapped on. . . . Forded North Fork of the Kentucky and went over the mountain and down the Curly Fork of Brown's Fork—got off the road up Brown's Fork—then followed it down through two gates to where it unites with Big Creek. Up Big Creek, after luncheon on Right Fork of Big Creek, and across mountain and down to Makintosh Creek, up Makintosh and over the mountain to Wooten's (pronounced Ooten) Creek to Felix Farmer's, where we had most comfortable quarters. A pleasant ride all day with fine scenery . . . twelve miles.

[December 10] Wooten, Leslie County. . . . Up about 6:40. Colored boy had made the fire and we dressed in luxury. Had a fine breakfast—chicken, sweet potatoes, oatmeal and real cream, coffee, corn flapjacks, and hot biscuit—also eggs, jam, and sorghum. House was clean and family up. . . . While we waited for the sun to rise over mountains and thaw road, we talked to Mrs. Farmer and Mrs. Napier and took pictures.

Mrs. Napier, who was Mrs. Farmer's mother, her face buried in a big ruffled black sunbonnet, was full of dreams and visions and stories of the great French-Eversole feud.[22] She had just had her son's funeral preached—"died of pure corruption"—by a Campbellite preacher who said in his sermon that the boy had prayed and had been a mighty good boy all his life, but it was too late. He had not been baptized or joined the church. About two weeks ago the boy spoke in a dream, "just as clear as you-all," and said that his death was "due to catching cold while waggonin' in the rain." He also told her in the dream that he wasn't "goin' to have nary preacher standing over his grave and saying such things when his soul was shining bright as any star; but to get young minister and tell him to tell his mother's experience at the preaching." Circumstantial directions to the local storekeeper, Eversole, followed, in which a new cloak for herself figured, and political support for her dead boy's half brother. If the storekeeper did not respect these charges, "his heart dropsy will wear him away, drap by drap, drap by drap till he's all gone."[23]

Got off about 10:00. A heavenly morning again—quite warm and springlike with brooks flowing and wrens singing. Had the roughest road yet of our travel—and the mountain was really quite a stiff one. Even I got off, while John's old blacky wheezed and crackled and his poor old nose ran. These beech woods of this country are wonderfully pretty with their fawn-colored leaves and pale trunks shaded with black and set with green moss. The steep hill slopes are covered with the fallen leaves, and the fallen trunks of old trees lie among them heavy with rich green moss. Above, the sky is an intense blue, and the sparkling air makes it a joy to be alive and riding along.

Just below Hyden we had to cross the Middle Fork—quite a deep ford, at least in part—and we started straight across to some old wheel tracks instead of zigzagging up to the more beaten track. Got up to the bottom of the saddlebags in water—and then had to follow up the bank. Got to Hyden 12:00–12:15 and found Mr. Lowrie expecting us—our room at the Oakland Hotel and dinner waiting.

Mr. Lowrie [the young Presbyterian minister and school principal] only last year graduated from Green-Tusculum [College]. He appeared much astonished and worried at the indifference of people to school matters . . . believed it had been arranged [last year] for county and Presbyterian Board to build and run the public and board school together. . . . Now new school law, and the whole thing had fallen through.[24] Teaching two together, however, this year on same plan.

We walked up to the schoolhouse (which had been closed for two or three weeks on account of scarlet fever). Met two young women teachers . . . then John went down town with Mr. Lowrie and I came back to hotel in time to be earwitness, at least, to a hog.

In the evening met at table Judge Brown from London, Kentucky, and also the county superintendent of Leslie County. . . . Neither thought the high school law possible to enforce, though believed it would work out in a modified form eventually. Judge Brown said wonderful change over county in his time, because of schools.

. . . specific directions next morning, which we followed: Go down big road and ford Middle Fork below Roberts—a deep ford. Several miles on, ford again. Next ford is at mouth of Cutshin and Bull's Creek—dangerous because of shifting quicksand bottom brought in by these creeks. Better to remain on left bank of Middle Ford past mouth of Bull's Creek and ford at shoals one-half mile below. Then keep on right bank of Middle Fork two miles past mouth of Hell-for-Certain [pronounced Sartain] to Adam Huff's store. Follow up Wilder Creek one mile or more—then take main wagon road across the mountain—down Elkhorn Creek to its mouth. Ford Middle Fork again and go upstream (instead of down) through a lane with two gates to Robert Bowling's house. Then turn up through Bowling's Holler and down Bowling's Branch to Middle Fork (near Possum Bend and Judas Hill). Ford again at Buckhorn, and follow up Squabble Creek to village and college.

We followed directions above except that we forded quicksand ford at Cutshin, as it seemed safe. Squabble Creek is so called from a squabble or quarrel years ago over a deer. It heads at Whoop-for-Larrie Hill—so called from a man who used to get loaded with moonshine and whoop it up. Most of the names around here have significance. . . . Hell-for-Certain gets its name from two hunters who got lost in rough country around creek. One said, "This is sure Hell," which, being interpreted, is Hell-for-Certain.

Left Hyden at 6:45 [probably December 11]—horses in fine fettle, especially John's, with saddlebags rearranged. A gentle rain when we started, settling into heavy pour. Our oilskins stood well, however. The best road in the county along the river, and pretty scenery. White, ghostly sycamores (with mistletoe, some) on banks or outlined against hill back. A regular bridle path in places—getting squashy as the morning wore on. Wonderfully pretty over the mountain. . . . Bigger trees than before—chestnuts and oaks—arbutus all along the banks. Passed a house where Mr. [Harvey S.] Murdoch says a Democrat (few here) painted high on new white house "Corner Stone of Democracy."[25] He has changed now to Republican . . . natural aptitude for politics. No interest in election of president. All peaceful, but a week later, on county judge election, great excitement, drinking, etc.

At Bowling's Hollow (or just beyond) we climbed over a high hill and asked at a typical one-roomed cabin how far to Buckhorn. A worn woman with a crowd of children came to the door and said she "reckoned three miles." John asked if she were sure—and she said she had never been there, but she had "heerd tell it was three miles." It was seven. She asked us to come by, and I should have liked to, but we pushed on, and as we went up the hill we could hear the thump of her loom.

Forded Middle Fork and got to Buckhorn about 1:15. Mr. and Mrs. Murdoch ran out and brought us in out of the rain, and we had a fine luncheon of fried chicken, potatoes, baked apples, tea, and biscuit.

The school has a beautiful situation on the slope of a hill, with a broad flat ground immediately at its foot for campus, baseball diamond, etc. The buildings are all of logs. Girls' dormitory, boys' dormitory (where a few boys live and Mr. and Mrs. Murdoch keep house with three girls), a refectory, a school building, a new and exceedingly pretty hospital, a primary building. They have been here only six years.

We had a delightful and restful time [December 11–13] with the Murdochs at Buckhorn and, among other things, learned much of the difficulties of cooperating with the public school, both locally and in surrounding county seats.

Mr. Murdoch explained workings of the new law, which does not allow church and public school to run together. Here, for instance, money for next year voted this year, but cannot be collected until next November. Public school has no house, no fuel, no books, maps, etc. Result will probably be that some scalawag will open old log building for a few days, close up and draw salary; or they will want to rent a room of Mr. Murdoch, which he will not do—as that would bring on the campus boys (perhaps bad) over whom he has no control at all. This is the case at Hazard. . . . Conditions in Hyden also unsatisfactory. . . . Manchester man, Mr. M——, a Christian gentleman but overworked and unequal to the situation. Great mistake of Presbyterian boards to draw out now. County unable to handle situation. Need of church schools for years yet. . . .

[Mrs. Murdoch] says Mr. M—— runs the town—has a powerful way with him. No trouble with discipline. Trouble, however, with drinking. . . . Told of one unusual and charming girl twelve years old at school one year, devoted to a young sister who died when Mrs. M—— was away. She wrote Mrs. M—— of her sorrow, how she wandered round trying to find comfort and some remembrance of her sister. Remembered they had buried some apples and went to find them. Her sister was dead—but there were the apples and near them the little print of her sister's bare foot. Said, "I never knowed what trouble was 'till Mandy died." . . . She put her foot in the print and found a certain peace at the tangible evidence. . . .

. . . Sunday . . . went to church, which was held today in school building as the "window-lights" were out of church on the hill. The hall was full—many young children. John preached. . . . In the afternoon . . . made a short call on the two young teachers, Miss Taylor and Miss Lanier. Went to bed pretty early.

[December 15] Up early, and off about eight o'clock—very sorry to leave the Murdochs. My pony was gay as a lark and cantered off merrily across the campus, with the black horse pounding behind. The air was fresh and mild and the sun dimmed slightly by thin clouds—roads pretty rough where the mud had stiffened.

We forded the Middle Fork and followed up the river for a mile or more on our Friday's route, then at the fork of the telephone wires followed up Gay's [?] Creek to Chavis, about seven miles. Had to climb a mountain and stop several times to fix the saddles, but found it pleasant riding. Chavis is only a cluster of houses with a church house and schoolhouse and store. We stopped at the store to get directions and had some trouble rousing anyone. . . . Finally a half-drunken man told us to keep to the right across a bridge and ford the river. We "followed directions," but could find no ford and the river was running deep and swift. So we turned up toward Hazard instead of fording and going up Grapevine Creek. The river was full and sycamores with mistletoe and the hemlocks were fine. Still, we worried a little as to where we were.

We rode two–three miles up and down dale till at last we heard a shout and found a small boy driving a yoke of steers. At every question of John's, he roared "Hey?" . . . but we finally discovered that he had a grandfather up a little piece, and, avoiding the steers, we hurried on. Found the old man, Mr. Napier, and his son outside a neat house. Proved to be son of a Campbell and uncle of Mrs. Napier of Wooten Branch. Directed us to a ford at about one-half mile and told us to follow the river down to Jim Campbell's—"Black Jim's"—and get directions there. The ford was deep, but we crossed safely and followed up the river about seven miles looking for Black Jim. The road was good but very hilly. It was up and down continually, so we could not make good time. River scenery very pretty. . . .

At last arrived at Black Jim's on Sam Campbell's Creek. The old lady, round and pretty face and smoking a pipe, invited us in, where we drew chairs round the grate fire (black kettle boiling on it), took out our lunch, and ate (though she offered to feed us), sharing oranges, cookies, and candy. Then Black Jim came in, and we all claimed kinship. Said his great-great-grandmother came from Scotland. Lived to see five generations and (400?) grandchildren. Said there were 500–600 Campbells in Perry County (and as many in Breathitt), and no one had ever been "penitentiaried"—only one indicted for false swearing, and he got off. (Didn't know whether he did it or not. Rather thought he did.) Said father was still living, one hundred years old, and came when nine years from North Carolina. Forty-odd families of Campbells in that bend, and none had less than six children, running up to twelve-plus. In giving account of good Campbells, he neglected to say that John Campbell was leader in French-Eversole "war" (feud) on Eversole side, was killed in feud. Also neglected to say how many died with their boots on.[26]

John gave them a good list of old Scottish names for boys and girls, which the daughter wrote down. They refused to let us pay for corn. Said they had plenty and couldn't let kin pay. Then we rode up Campbell's Creek and over one mountain to second creek, over another mountain to first creek. Not very thickly populated right here. Saw one entirely isolated and lonely cabin near top of mountain. Many children, but not remote possibility that I could see for education. Followed first creek for about three hundred yards, then turned to left on main wagon road over small mountain, down to North Fork, about two miles from the bridge at the mouth of Lot's Creek. Passed first house on river, Cranfords' (good place to stay). Went up Lot's Creek past Joe Feltner's (place to stay) and landed at dusk on Trace Fork of Lot's Creek at old man Holliday's.

Two wagons had just come from Jackson, and stable was full, but they took us in and gave us a good room, iron bed and two sheets. . . .

Got off again about 8:00, December 15. Fair again but promising rain, and in fact spattered a bit toward twelve o'clock. Followed up Trace's Fork and over several mountains to Dwarf (three miles), then down an excellent road along Troublesome, twelve miles to Hindman.

We stayed at Hindman over Christmas; indeed, we would not have been willing to leave before, for Christmas, celebrated as it was by the settlement school, was a thing to be remembered always: the lavish decorating with holly and ivy, which grew all about (I myself strung yards of holly berries); the old carols sung outside our windows in the cold, gray Christmas dawn and fading in the distance as the carol group made its way about the town; the towering spruce-pine, covered with little cones, which served as a Christmas tree; the joy of the children climaxing all! How sorry we were to leave! And we could have kept right on learning. But after all, this was only part of the mountains. We packed our trunk, sadly [on New Year's Eve], and said farewell to all our friends.

Whatever its drawbacks, riding horseback over rough mountain country was usually to be preferred to going by jolt wagon, especially in winter. We had a trunk to transport, however, and so by wagon on a cold but brilliant January 1, 1909, we left Hindman via the regular eastern route to Beaver Creek on the Chesapeake and Ohio Railroad.

Our departure was to be at 11:00 a.m., but no team appeared until after 12:00. Then it appeared in front of the schoolhouse—John's old black horse and the white horse harnessed to our Jackson wagon. The black horse was balking, and no amount of coaxing or whipping did any good. Evidently the driver—a big rough man, [Bray] by name—had started them wrong, and the black finally ended by kicking the harness to pieces. At length he was replaced by a mule. We said our farewells for the third and fourth time and rolled off in triumph. It was then after one.

The team went fairly well during the afternoon, with some balking on the part of the white and a resultant seesaw, but the mule was steady. It grew very cold and gray, and the roads were fearful—muddy out of the creek, and rocky and beset with logs in the creek. The houses all along seemed very forlorn to me. . . . We passed a government distillery, the most prosperous-looking place around. About 4:30 we came to a stop in a mud-hole that swallowed the wheels above the hubs. The horses would not pull together, and I danced on a log to keep warm while first the man tried to combine the seesaw, then John took the reins and the man pried. Finally I took the reins, John the whip, the man pried, and with a rope to mend a broken bolt, we came out. By this time it was quite dark and the moon was shining. The roads were in such fearful condition that we determined to stop at [Frederick] Webb's instead of pushing on to Allen's.[27]

We found a very comfortable place—warmed our toes before the open grate, had supper, and piled into bed early, to be up again at 4:30 [January 2]—a chill morning. A little girl brought us a fresh towel, and we were electrified next (we in bed) by the entrance of Mr. B——, who came to wipe his hands. John was dressed first, and while I was finishing, Mrs. Webb entered and talked and watched me complete my toilette. Had a good breakfast on fried chicken and went out to find the old gray [i.e., the white] in a balky mood. He was finally started, but stopped at every rise of ground so that our progress was slow. What with bucking and whipping and seesawing, the harness, in addition, was soon reduced to smithers, and we stopped at every few houses to get a bolt, rope, chain—and finally, a grand climax, the singletree broke. That was three miles from Beaver. There were two boys watering mules across the creek, and we called to them to take us to town. This they agreed to after some dickering, or rather, hesitation. So we transferred luggage, said farewell to Mr. B——, and gaily trotted off to Beaver behind two willing curly brown mules. Arrived about four.

Went to Combs Hotel, where a stream of people seemed to be circulating—many on their way to State Normal School [Eastern State Teacher's College] at Richmond. We had an interesting talk with [a man who had been teaching public school]. He spoke frankly of bad conditions existing in the schools: lack of good teachers . . . lowness and vulgarity in very little children; necessity of educating parents; old feud feeling which prevented one set of families from sending children where the other set was sending; no papers except a few low-class ones subscribed for; no farm papers. . . . Was discouraged at the outlook, with dwindling farms, no mineral rights, lumber gone. He thought mountain people would be pushed to the wall.

We left at about 8:45—a mild night. Walked the platform awhile waiting for train, and talked with boy who had been at Hindman and had much to say in praise. Got to Pikeville at ten plus. . . .

[January 3–9] Our first stop was at the Presbyterian School in Pikeville, quite strictly a literary affair, with teacher training. From there we moved on up the Big Sandy Valley, visiting private and public schools in Paintsville, Louisa, Catlettsburg, Ashland, and Morehead. Sometimes we stayed at little local hotels—not too cheerful—and again with church people, who were glad to show us their equipment, or lack of it, and to discuss conditions. A variety of opinions were expressed about the new school law, some thinking it would hold and some not, but all agreeing it was not feasible at this time.

We also heard much of feuds, which were dying out slowly. It was in this region that the famous and brutal Hatfield-McCoy war raged across state lines.[28] The following is one of a number of episodes vividly described to us:

Hatfields surrounded McCoy house having in it 4–5 women and 3 men. Set fire to house and shot women who tried to put it out. Knocked old woman's head on ground till she was senseless. One man escaped, one was shot through the door, and an old man, taking revolver in either pocket and loading pans of old breech loader with powder, opened door, and amid smoke of explosion run through enemies firing revolvers—escaping thus through "big old cornfield" to woods. Is alive yet. Two McCoys on one side of river and old Hatfield on other. If either should cross boundary, other would kill him. So feud stands.

In Ashland, Dr. [W. C.] Condit, a fine old Presbyterian, added more stories, equally brutal, of Frank Phillips, leader on the Hatfield side, who had once been sheriff and became the worst man in the county.[29] Dr. Condit did not believe feuds were a result of war bushwhacking. They were in existence before the war. It was frontier country, and men took justice into their own hands. Gradually lawlessness followed; there was no outside control. He discussed the friction between denominations, particularly between Northern and Southern Presbyterians, and expressed great hope of church union. "Perhaps when some of us old fellows get out of the way, the younger ones will fix it up between them."

At the station in Morehead, we were ceremoniously received by Professor [J. M.] Robinson of the Morehead School and seven students, who marched in front and carried our cases. President [F. C.] Button came on the afternoon train, and we looked over the plant, a good one, and talked over general conditions.

Country here is more like Demorest—lower rounded hills—pines—rhododendron and laurel. Very pretty. Soil is thin, they say, though valley has been a famous one in its day. They used to drive through it to market one thousand hogs in the early days. These could not get enough corn here now. Soil exhausted with continuous corn crop. Believed there were, however, great fruit possibilities, peaches especially, and small vegetables. Most of their advanced boys leave the mountains. Town population is shifting, men moving here from the interior, making a little more and moving on. . . . Have about 360 pupils now. John addressed them with great applause at chapel.

Morehead had been the seat of the Martin-Tolliver feud, the Martins being Republicans and the Tollivers Democrats—"both families equally bad." President Button told us of his first experience some years ago. He was talking to a friend when he was suddenly pulled aside, and Tollivers and Martins came rushing through, shooting at each other. Not all his stories were of feuds. We gathered many amusing ones to add to those we had heard from Dr. Condit and Dr. [James F.] Record at Pikeville. One was of an old Baptist preacher who sold brandied peach stones for one dollar apiece, under promise to give five dollars for every shoot. The same man sold yellow jackets for queen bees at one dollar apiece. Another old Baptist preacher is said to have electioneered at funerals in contest with a dentist who could not speak but who pulled teeth on the same occasions. At one funeral-preaching, the dentist saw a man suffering and told him he could relieve him: ". . . pulled out forceps while Baptist preached on, and gave a yank. The sufferer cried ouch and jumped up. Tooth came out and preaching kept right on. He ran to branch and washed out mouth then came back and said, 'Friend,

I've never voted the Democratic ticket in my life—but I'm going to vote for you.' Dentist won out."

A student, asked to give in his own words the lesson of the ten foolish virgins, responded, "Lesson is always to be on the watch for a bridegroom and any other necessary thing." Asked to speak of a Hatfield feud leader, another boy said, "He was a pretty old feller, but had two no-account sons."

Such trips were always harder on John than on me, for everywhere he had to speak, and often, while I snatched a little rest or wrote up my notes, he was interviewing someone, taking outside trips with some eager principal, superintendent, or teacher, or roaming about the community in conversation with whomever he might meet. We were glad to move on to Lexington (January 9) and relax a bit in a comfortable hotel—the old Phoenix. A mountain of mail was awaiting us, and we were soon deep in it, interrupted only by the telephone, which began to ring as soon as we arrived.

One letter was from John's old college and seminary friend Morrison Merriam, who had started his teaching experiences in a mountain school on the border of Virginia and Kentucky and was at this time teaching in California. John had asked his opinion on a number of questions, and this was his reply:

I. "The future of the mountain people?" Do not believe that ultimately or in comparatively few years there can properly any distinction be made between the "mountain people" and any other. Least of all, they should not themselves from any source be made to feel that they are a peculiar people, set apart from other groups or from the American people in their entirety. The several means of communication with the outside world must have had, must increasingly continue to have, great influence in breaking down the identity of this heretofore isolated people. Of course, it is an idea which only the future can answer, but it would seem that our increasing population all around this limited section would ultimately break through the more or less artificial foothill and mountain barriers and modify the existing population with a considerable infusion of new blood—hence a change in customs, industry, conceptions of life in general; for the most part such change would be for the better. To be sure, the entire region has already been "raked fore and aft" by outsiders, but rather by those who have "exploited" rather than settled to make their permanent homes in this region. From an industrial standpoint, the leading purpose seems to have been to get all possible from the region and then get out. Undoubtedly, though, the people have at first gained something through the capital and business force of these northern exploiters; in the end they are in most every way damaged.

II. "Can the mountains support them?" Do you mean can the country support the present population in the future when they begin to *want* a great deal more than they do now? Unquestionably, it seems to me. There is a great deal of waste land in that region. All it wants is more intensive cultivation, more muscle and more brain, an improved cultivation, better seed, better fruit trees, etc. As the country is now, it may not be able to support the few ambitious young people who get ahead of their people in education, capacity, and ambition. Many will migrate, as they have in the past. That is one real or apparent loss in establishing schools for the mountain youth. All that are good for much of anything seek better fields in which to live. No matter what is done, even though the general level is raised, as of course it has been and will be still more, the inefficient and more worthless of the population must necessarily be forced back into the worst regions of any country (here as elsewhere). This particular region can be nothing but agricultural for the most part, and the best farmers will buy the best locations. When new blood comes in, sometime in the future, under pressure of increasing population, the average of the mountain people must be greatly improved.

III. So far as schoolwork is concerned, I have for some time thought that the several missionary associations ought to give more attention as to just what sort of an education the mountain people ought to have. I think they copy the curricula of northern schools too much, which only in part are adaptable to the needs of this region. Will you permit me to suggest that you look into this matter particularly. I made, myself, mistakes along this line when I was in that work. I have since learned better.

The points of view expressed in this letter John was glad to have an opportunity to talk over with several people in Lexington, especially with Miss Pettit, who was at home for her winter vacation.

Callers began to arrive the next morning—Sunday (January 10)—after church and trod on each other's heels so fast that we missed dinner almost by necessity. All had their own ideas as to mountain problems, including ancestry and what might be done to improve conditions. Miss Pettit came later, and we had much to talk over. She wished to introduce us to many friends— interesting socially, as well as for their information and connections. One of them, Mrs. Desha Breckinridge, great-granddaughter of Henry Clay, came the next day with a team to take us to see a public charity in which she was interested and to discuss a social center. She then drove out to Ashland, Henry Clay's old home, where her mother still lives. She and a friend took me another day to the State University—Transylvania College—and a number of fine old houses. Transylvania, "the oldest college west of the mountains," had made a specialty of historical records, and I noted a variety of material to be consulted later. A trip to Frankfort occupied another day for John, who wished to see Mr. [J. G] Crabbe. He also met the governor, the commissioner of education, and several others. Mr. Crabbe was very optimistic about the law; he felt there would be no backward step and that the effect on the denominational schools would not be serious. Commissioner [M. E.] Rankin believed that intensive agriculture would solve many difficulties.

Our visitors included several denominational officials, state secretary of the YMCA, and the head of the Women's Christian Temperance Union, which sponsors the settlement school at Hindman. One of our last callers was Mr. Walker, the postmaster, who brought up Mr. [James Anderson] Burns of Oneida [January 12]. We had a most interesting talk. My diary records:

> Mr. B. is of Kentucky parentage and leanings (Clay County) though born in West Virginia, where his father took the family when feud conditions seemed imminent. Has a rugged Scottish face and slow manner, with humorous reserve. Persuaded us quite easily to go to Oneida with him— as his personality is strong and interesting. . . .[30]
>
> [January 13] A heavy snowy day changing into rain. I was busy packing all day, and we were only just ready when Mr. Walker sent the carriage at 4:00 p.m. Found his house pleasant—Mr. Burns there and a jovial Mr. [Josh] Carnahan, a mountain man (originally from Oneida) who was to go with us. . . . We had pleasant dinner and got off about 8:30 p.m.
>
> Mr. Carnahan was amusing. Told us of his efforts to start first store— annoyed by pistol shots. Mr. Burns tried to act as mediator, but Carnahan was furious and would have killed the man if he hadn't apologized (Mr. B.'s influence) and stayed across the river. Bullets came through doors and windows, once right above his and wife's bed. Said he wouldn't have drunken man in store. Told them to get out and if they didn't, he knocked them out. Said every man was his own protector in the mountains. Had to fight his own way. Said man who didn't drink, didn't need pistols—or wear them. Whiskey and pistols went together. Told of hearing drummers talking in train of every mountaineer carrying pistols. He himself was in splendid physical trim—and as a joke, jumped out in aisle (L & E—near Jackson), announced he was mountaineer and had no gun nor knife and would fight any man singly in train and knock him down—as lie to drummers' story. Had low opinion of mountain cooking. Is a lumberman.

. . . Got into London at 2:15 a.m. [January 14]. Electric lights off on account of sleet storm damaging wires. Crawled into bed by a feeble Christmas candle of red. Up early to start off—only to find roads flooded and that Mr. Carnahan's team had not come through. A heavy rainy morn with a "tide" which took Mr. C. back to the river to superintend his logs. We waited all day for team, only to find late in p.m. that it was not coming. Decided to go horseback in the morning. . . .

Left London at 7:00 a.m. [January 15] after a wait for breakfast and horses. The latter were good, however—and we made good time. (The mail caught up to us on the way and looked very amusing—a man on a mule laden with mail bags and driving another mule who bulged all over with sacks, quite a terrifying object. We made way for the "US Mail." Roads were fearfully muddy, always over horses' hoofs, often over hocks, and at times above the knees. A fascinating day, however, warm, gray, and still— black trunks rising from flooded meadows—branches interlaced against the gray sky. We were constantly splashing through water, but my little horse was willing and comfortable, and I enjoyed every inch of the way.

Laurel County is part of Cumberland Plateau—not mountainous in appearance, though one goes downhill all the way to Manchester and Oneida. Many grassy fields and meadows—open country, and the woods, oddly enough, do not seem to be cut as much as around Knott. Mr. B. says the road is good in summer. We made the twenty-four miles in six hours, getting into Manchester about 1:30. Went to Mrs. Lucas's, where we had dinner and waited for Mr. Miller, the minister in charge of the Presbyterian work. . . . Left Mr. B. and went out to dormitory to spend the night. . . .

. . . In the evening we went over to call on Mr. and Mrs. Walker, some fine young married people near by. She was educated in Pennsylvania. Her father, Dr. Manning, came from North and married a White (one of feud families). All vitally interested in school matter. Clay County is in good shape financially—ten thousand dollars in the bank—but cannot support a good school. Need not only of high school, but a school which will carry all grades. Manchester School has a work [program?], but has never been effective, as Presbyterian Board has either sent worn-out preachers to school, or young ones to practice—not equal to some of the inhabitants.

. . . Great corruption in the county schools, some districts having none at all. According to new law, sheriff collects all taxes—getting 10 percent on school. . . . (Mr. W. said, however, that even with twenty-five hundred dollars net, the sheriff was not paid for his job.) District no longer managed own fund, which was in hands of county superintendent and board. County superintendent was more powerful than ever and was very often a corrupt man. Good roads a great necessity. Had tried to get cooperation of Barbourville for half of pike, and Barbourville had gone back on it. This would be one of education solutions. Also needed new life. Thought the good summer visitors who were coming in of late at Oneida had done as much as school for that place.

An old aristocracy in the county—former slave owners who had big tracts of land, ten thousand acres, and almost a feudal tenantry. Tenants worked lands and lumber, traded at owner's store, and either came even or fell short. Often were in debt to start with. Never made anything. Emigrated in every direction. People round Manchester were selling coal rights for from fifty cents to five dollars an acre. This included rights to what timber would be needed to work mines. Had been talking railroad before Mr. W.'s father's time, but lately had had new boom. Southern expected to come from Knoxville. . . .

[Mr. Walker also said that] Mr. Miller was employed by board to preach and oversee—not teach. Could be hired by town to teach public schools. Said Mr. M. got $50 a month—and two other teachers $28.50 a month. Could not expect decent work on such a pittance. Only two or three Presbyterian families in town. All Baptists. Much liquor brought—especially at election time, and Mrs. W. told me that with the new Judge [Lewis], many thought more liquor would come in, resulting in the outbreak again of feud. Mr. Burns said this feud began in 1806 (families had come with hard feeling from Virginia). Included best men in county. Did not mean to get in but were drawn in. Young ones always were ones to start it afresh. Pistols and moonshine—"white lightning," as Mr. B. called it.

[Saturday, January 16] Mr. Miller drove us down to the hotel—raining again, pouring rather. Spent the morning there mending John's oilskins, where his horse rubbed him against the barbed wire, and talking to Mr. Walker and Dr. Manning. The latter seemed vague about sickness in the mountains—a little typhoid—a little smallpox—some tuberculosis and granulated lids. . . .

I dropped my thread on the floor and in hunting looked under bed. There was a nice long rifle. Mr. B. says you generally find them. One of his great troubles has been to keep his boys from wearing pistols. It is part of their manhood creed.

We got off about 1:30 to 2:00 p.m. Still raining but not quite so hard. I am always much amused at men's (and women's, too) wonder and admiration of my daring. "Not many women could ride that twenty-four miles in six hours"—"Mr. Campbell wants to get rid of his wife to take her out on such a day—over such roads," etc., etc. Very amusing.

This part of the country is the prettiest and most fertile we have seen in Kentucky. Valleys are quite broad and grassy, timber left on the hilltops— brooks from every quarter (of course, these must dry up in summer).

Our course lay along Big Goose Creek—Big and Little Wildcat—Pinhook Branch, etc. Part of the way Mr. Burns rode ahead looking like some old Covenanter with his black coat and derby hat and leggings—sitting very erect in his saddle and looking straight ahead. Part of the time he and John talked while my little black trotted me nimbly ahead. Passed J. D. Rockefeller's pipeline, which carried oil in a straight line over hills and valleys from Somerset, Kentucky, to Parkersville, West Virginia, four hundred (?) miles. It was dark when we got in, and had begun to sprinkle again, though most of the way the rain had ceased to fall. Mr. B. went home, and we went to the dormitory for a good supper, cheerful room, and bed.[31]

[January 17] Breakfast at 7:30. We did not go to Sunday school but went over to church at 11:00, where John made a fine talk—much to the enthusiasm of the people. Talked in p.m. to Mr. Burns, Prof. Smith, and Prof. [Louis D.] Sandlin and Rev. [H. L.] McMurray. Then walked over muddy road and hill to McMurrays' house. River still high and rafts moored to the bank. They said eleven rafts had gone through the narrows the day before, one being smashed all to pieces.

The McMurrays have a small house with a beautiful situation, and clean but primitive interior. Eight children—bright-looking ones. Mrs. M. looked like a fine, impassive pioneer with a baby in her arms. Her people were once from New England. Mr. M. took the baby while she piloted us up a hill for the view—followed by three dogs, six children, three calves (partway) and a sheep. The view down the river is beautiful, and one gets a great sweep, for Goose Creek and Redbird and Bullskin come together at Oneida. They swim, canoe, etc. in summer. Natives cannot get used to the former—especially the women going in with the men. One woman said her only objection to Mrs. Sandlin (matron) was that "she goes washing with the men."

We then went down to Mr. Burns's house for supper. It is a very simple frame affair, three–four rooms. He has five bright-looking children who delight in Kipling, Joel Chandler Harris, and fairy tales of all kinds. We had delicious fried chicken, biscuits, butter, milk, jam, etc.—all of their own making. . . .

Went to evening service, where Mr. Burns preached an impassioned sermon on God's love. Went to bed early.

[January 18] Early breakfast and a springlike day—with clear skies and warm winds. John spoke at chapel and then we visited a number of recitations [in the morning]. Eight teachers, one of whom was a woman (primary). They have 138 pupils now. Buildings three—a good brick school and a girls' dormitory and a very poor boys' dormitory (abandoned). Boys board and room in town. The grounds generally were clean. The school is on a high hill with a beautiful view, and they are trying to start grass and trees. Great desire to build up an agricultural school, for land is good, and in the end, Mr. B. says, people must come to that. Wishes, too, sloyd and domestic science. . . .

The beginnings of the school are most interesting. Mr. Burns was mountain boy and brought up in one-roomed log cabin—cooking over wood fire, etc. Said (joke!) his right shoulder was higher than left because he carried wood so much as a boy. His father was Kentucky Baptist preacher from Oneida—leaving for West Virginia because he foresaw feud beginning (Burns-Combs). Mr. Burns born there and brought up in a community practically northern in spirit and sentiment. Most of West Virginia, Mr. B. says, is a northern state, thrifty and clean. Before seventeen, Mr. B. had only seen one man who had been in penitentiary, and murders were practically unknown. Father, however, brought boys up Anti-Unionists and fiery Democrats. Mr. B. said he actually thought when a boy that a man from the South hurt in the North would perish from neglect—no one would look to him. Hated Yankees and says many, many people do now. Some of the best work northerners can do is to come down and let southern people see what they are really like. . . .

Kentucky was a revelation to him when he came back to it as a boy— feuds, killings, and all. Was pretty wild and fell in with his people's ways. Used to carry on his raft a box of weapons to be used against Combses. Used to go down river on rafts—and said they could tell, as far as a raft could be seen, from where it came, North, Middle or South Fork—such a difference in people. North Fork people most degenerate—descendants of Virginia folk who came through Big Stone, Pennington Gap, etc. Many of them were escaped, indentured servants, tenantry, etc., poorer stuff. The Middle Fork drew some of these people and some of those who settled on South Fork—that is, North Carolina people coming through Cumberland Gap and Wilderness Road. Some West Virginians later drifted down by Pennsylvania. These people were hardier, bolder, and less degenerate. Also were, and are, the most desperate of all. As an example, the big loggers have to leave detectives on North and Middle Fork to protect floating lumber, keep people from sawing off ends and rebranding it. None of these necessary on South Fork.[32]

Says feuds did not originate with war—early as 1806, and grew out of character and descent of the people. He went in for a while, but found he was getting in too deep and went back to West Virginia. Told us at another time how he was "killed" in a scrimmage, hit on the head with a gunstock and thrown over the fence into a brambly field—supposedly dead. Young fellows had been drinking moonshine. His supporters went off, and as he began to show signs of life, his enemies took him in cabin and kept him, nursed him, at night. In the morning, being not badly hurt, he walked home. Took him all day. Stole into cousin's cabin, where he was living, for the night, and before people were awake, stole out into the woods and brooded all day. Back again at night and out the same way for three days, brooding. The first two days he spent thinking over what step of redress he could take—what men he could enlist—what to do, and not possible to do—a new kind of gun to buy etc. But the process of being "killed" was not pleasant—and at the end of the third day he came back with an "iron-clad resolution" never to have any more feuds.

While in West Virginia he became converted and felt he owed something to his Kentucky people. Came back and taught summer school in mountains and winter school at Manchester. This was the time of the famous White-Garrard feud, which grew into the Baker-Howard. . . .[33]

Finally, principal of Berea told Mr. B. that he would do more good to mountaineers by teaching at Berea the young normal teachers than keeping at that work. So he went to Berea and there met McMurray (then young with only one child). They became great friends and studied together. . . . They were talking over Berea complications one night . . . and McMurray said, "Brother Burns, let's go up into the mountains and found a Baptist mountain school." Mr. B. said his heart leaped, but he hid his heart as he wanted to test McMurray, so told only difficulties in the way. But a little later, McMurray said the same thing, and then Mr. B. said, "Brother

McMurray, I'll go whenever you are ready." Mr. McMurray immediately resigned his position—and mounting his wife (baby in arms) behind him on little western pony, they set out, Mr. B. with them. The Baptist Board [would not help]—said their board's work was not secular, but spiritual. . . .[34]

Mr. B. made own tools, hewed and quarried rock in hot August sun, and began on foundation. People thought him crazy, but inside a year the school had begun with one hundred pupils. He never exploits people for money, but trusts. Speaks at churches and is now thinking of trip north. . . . Says if his work has a place, it will endure. . . . Has little use for mission boards. . . . Thinks the state has failed. Says new law will not be really effective for one hundred years. Is eager for every improvement—sanitation . . . hospitals, intensive farming. Is eager to give the people an appreciation of the beautiful. Says they haven't enough culture to see anything in the trees, woods, flowers, etc. Wishes our New England mission boards would send down a few young married couples to live in the country and show people how. . . .

. . . The school has done wonders in bringing people together. White and Baker children in school together. Frank Burns and Levi "Lee" Combs were on the first Board of Trustees, though neither knew what a board of trustees was. Wanted to back Brother Burns in his enterprise. . . .

Mr. B. is liberal-minded Baptist—would take anyone at Communion and any kind of baptism. Some of the Mission Baptists have withdrawn fellowship from him on account of missionary views of his school. So there is now the anomaly of a missionary Baptist association, Arminian in theology but antimission in practice, opposed to the association Brother B. has been compelled to form and which is in keeping with the liberal Baptists over the country. . . . Burns says there is more hope for Hardshells with new young preachers that are coming in than for many of so-called mission Baptist Churches with antimission practices. . . .[35]

We got off [from Oneida] about 1:30 [in the afternoon of January 18], Mr. Burns, John, and I, and had a beautiful ride down the river, fording at the mouth of Laurel Creek. The air was like spring—full of bird notes and red birds fluttering to and fro. There are some fine mountainsides of uncut timber and good stretches of bottomland. Elms along the river and white sycamores. . . . Got into Manchester a little before five and had supper. We three talked over the fire for awhile.

[January 19] Got up about five and were ready to start by six—saying a reluctant goodbye to Mr. B., who seems like an old friend. A beautiful morning—ground stiffened by frost which silvered the country. A little new moon shone up over the mountain, and a bright star just below. Gradually a pink glow came in the east, but the sun did not rise over the mountaintops for an hour or two. Bluebirds and yellow-hammers about. We had a splendid, invigorating ride, though the roads were hard for the horses and kept growing worse as we approached London. We fell in with two young fellows on mules. They lived in Barbourville but had been mending telephone wires and poles broken by sleet storm. We fell into companionship of the road and chatted until they swung off south. Got into London at 12:15. . . . Found the train schedule had been changed, so possessed our souls in patience, wrote, etc., and slept till ready to take the 2:00 a.m. train to Hagan.

[January 20] Got 1:48 train O.K. and slept by fits and starts all the way. Many miners and loggers on the car, freely passing around moonshine—which scared man near us very much. Got into Hagan at 6:10 a.m.—dim and misty. Got breakfast at little hotel and sat round fire while people discussed the murder at Harlan, whether Harlan people would lynch murderers, etc. A young fellow of Irish countenance but related in Harlan got off train and went along with us [a sixteen-mile trip on horseback]. My nag was stiff of knee and reared dangerously without apparent cause. I got him over one mountain—a high one (Cumberland)—and enjoyed myself in spite of feeling that I might be pitched off any moment. The road is very curving, in loops on itself, and the wood growth is heavy—not much cut. We wound up between great oaks and beeches whose trunks were outlined black against blue haze of ridges and hills beyond. Down in the valleys lay heavy clouds of mist, through which the river gleamed. As we turned [on] the top of the mountain, into shadow, we could look back and up where the sun struck across the illumined great shoulders of slanting rock. Lower down we ran into beautiful fresh rock ferns, moss, rhododendron, holly, and hemlocks.

At the second mountain, my horse balked and refused to continue. Finally I got off—and removal and exchange of saddles showed that all three had raw sores on their backs. By padding we fixed up, and although my new mount moved slowly and walked downhill sideways in evident pain, we got along. We kept meeting wagons on very narrow roads and had some difficulty in passing. Road in fearful shape, rocky or heavily rutted and still in curves and loops. The cabins were more primitive in general than any we have seen—much isolated, log and one-roomed. In one I heard a banjo going and wished I could stop off.

The rest of the way we followed creek beds and river bottom, winding along half asleep in the sun. The day was as warm as summer, birds singing and men ploughing some rich-looking bottomland. A good sixteen miles, it seemed, but we finally made Harlan near one.

We were lodged in the Teachers' Home at the Presbyterian Academy and spent the afternoon reading mail, one a letter from Mr. Glenn showing his usual interest:

[Mr. Glenn to JCC]
January 18, 1909

Your letter of the sixth was duly received. I noted with interest your point about the gas and coal mining. I will look up the article in *Everybodys* for January.

Mrs. Glenn had a very enthusiastic letter from Miss Pettit about your visit to her settlement at Hindman. They seem to have enjoyed having you and Mrs. Campbell and feel that it was very helpful to them. She also thinks that your expedition is a wise one and will be valuable.

My memories of Harlan town that January season are of unpainted gray houses along a gray river, which lent a damp chill to the whole scene.[36] One could not have guessed from any outward signs that the region was underlaid with coal—iron across the Virginia line—and that a great development would soon be under way.

We talked, as usual, with the principal of the school and teachers (seven, with also a resident preacher) and got their point of view. We went to chapel and visited classes in the good, though crowded, brick schoolhouse. One evening we met a gathering of prominent citizens at Judge Lewis's home for what my diary terms not an especially interesting discussion.

While at Harlan, we rode the eight miles to Evarts (January 21) along the beautiful valley by Clover Creek, passing a number of fine bottomland farms. Martin's Creek was said to have still more. Good farming country, our hosts at the Black Mountain Academy told us, and they were eager to buy a farm and to put industrial work into the school. Excellent vegetables were grown on a nearby hilltop farm. John spoke twice, as he did at Harlan, preached at an outlying chapel, and interviewed various people.

On our return to Harlan (January 23), we went over, briefly, to the murder trial going on at the courthouse, and heard evidence grim and sordid enough. The room was filled—some women, and a crowd of men standing down in front or sitting on windowsills or back of seats.

A steady pattering of spit on the floor. The day before, they said, everyone who came in was examined for concealed weapons. The use of brass knuckles and the general conditions surrounding the crime were new to our mountain experience, but at Evarts we heard of a number of cases in which "knucks" were used. There we were told that killings in the past year had been more numerous than usual— "eleven since August (on account of election?)." Some of these were combined with liquor stealing. The accounts sounded unusually brutal.

From Harlan, on January 25th we rode back to Hagan—a pleasant, leisurely journey—and took a 6:00 p.m. train to Hubbard Springs, where we had supper. An 8:45 p.m. train carried us to Cumberland Gap for the night; we were up at five for a 6:10 train. We arrived at Knoxville between 9:00 and 10:00 a.m. on January 26th, dead tired and sleepy.

Some places have to be sacrificed on such a schedule. We cleaned up in the morning at Knoxville, our usual resource for ablutions and good food, and went down that afternoon, still dull and inert, to Maryville College.[37] We did not take in, I am afraid, all the information furnished us so generously by President Wilson and his staff in the next two days. They were in the midst of a celebration in honor of the completion of an endowment fund. John went to the basketball game the first afternoon, and that evening I joined him for the speech-making and the great bonfire, which lighted up that gentle valley region dotted with black cedars. Another chapel talk next morning, more class visiting, and we were off on the five o'clock train, President Wilson going to the station with us. It was cold, with snow flurries. We arrived in Knoxville about six o'clock, numb with sleep.

We were still tired as, after two quiet days, we left Knoxville on February 1st for Jefferson City. There we walked up to the Baptist college, Carson and Newman, which was quite an imposing building on a hill. Dr. Jeffries, the president, showed us about [it] and talked with us, as did one of the teaching staff. They had five hundred students; four dormitories in addition to the big recitation building, all good-looking—one for boys and one for girls who were paying, boarding pupils, and two likewise for boys and girls working to cover part expense on a cooperative basis. There was no industrial training except a start in cooking for girls.[38] They were very kind and hospitable to us, asking us to dinner, but all we could think of was rest, so went down to the town to hunt up a hotel. There seemed only one near the station—most unattractive—and there we sat "before a dead fire and a dropping grate, dingy bed, and cracked bureau until . . . a fire was started in the sitting-room; then we sat there until three thirty (with an interim in the dining room over pork), writing and reading and viewing the lithographs of dead relatives."

We then left by train for Greenville, arriving between 6:00 and 7:00 p.m. Dr. Gray, the president of Greenville-Tusculum, was waiting at the station with a team to take us out to the Presbyterian college—four miles in the lovely cold moonlight. A cordial reception in Virginia Hall, where Dr. Gray and his family were living while their own house was being finished, a big open fire in the living room, a good supper, and a comfortable night's rest revived us.[39] "In the morning we went to morning chapel and heard some unusually good singing by the Boys' Glee Club. (Mrs. Gray thinks there is more musical feeling in Tennessee than in North Carolina.) John led exercises but did not give a talk. There are about 250 students— nice-looking and really picked, as they are the selected of ones who come up via day schools, Home Industrial, etc. Of course, some come from the town. All looked pretty well dressed and acted self-possessed."

The school buildings we thought good, though my diary records the boys' hall "out of shape." The campus was naturally very attractive. There was no industrial work for boys but a four-year course for girls in sewing and cooking. We sampled an excellent meal of their preparation after visiting one such class. Dr. Gray seemed eager to develop such training for both girls and boys, the latter in relation to raising of vegetables on a small farm they have bought. "Say people in immediate country are not in such poor condition as in the mountains. Country not so mountainous. Mountains near at hand, however, and looked gorgeous in the afternoon light—all purple, and snow ridges. Of course, their conditions are the same. A man who drove us to station said that Greenville-Tusculum represented to one thousand children their only chance for education."

After supper we drove, Dr. Gray accompanying us as far as Johnson City, over to Afton station—two miles. It was brilliant moonlight, and the road ran literally among the tree trunks—lovely. There was a wait at Afton, but the train got us to Johnson City about 10:00 p.m. Went at once to hotel (Dr. Gray to spend the night with a friend) and found fairly comfortable quarters. In the morning (February 3), after an early breakfast with Dr. Gray, we left by the 7:10 train for Loves, Tennessee.

> Loves is nothing but a station and couple of houses. We hung about the station and changed [into riding clothes] in the freight room, but no word from Mr. Webb [the young Presbyterian minister at Flag Pond whom we were to visit]. Finally the telephone operator said the postboy had gone by with Mr. Webb's horse and two saddles. We hung about till the fried tobacco juice was too much—then prowled outside to find the weather

had warmed up and the mountains were very lovely—higher and ridged like geography pictures, and snow lying on the shady side.

Along near ten o'clock, the postboy arrived with the horse, but had been unable to get the mule (which Mr. Webb promised in letter brought by boy) as said mule had followed someone off. So John and I mounted double and started off down the creek. All went very well till I slipped off going up a steep hill, and then John mounted me and he walked the rest of the way to Fordville. It is steep country and beautiful, with white pine, hemlock, laurel, etc. Brooks are clear and rushing. The ice had melted a good deal and roads were muddy in places, and ice cracked through in other places. Halfway over we met Fox, the lost mule, and he meekly turned in after Dale (Mr. Webb's horse), and so we drove him to Fordville. There we got him bridled and saddled with a man's saddle, which the loafers presented somewhat apologetically to me, and we were off again. Lost the mailboy after a bit and got into Flag Pond [sixteen miles] alone 2:00–3:00 p.m. Mrs. Webb had a fine steaming dinner ready—tomato bisque soup, roast possum [my first] (possum had been skinned and parboiled and wasn't greasy at all), and ice cream. Had a long talk, and tumbled into bed satisfied. . . .

Flag Pond is a little settlement where once was a flag pond, now drained. It has a pretty situation right in among the hills, which are ribbed and clustered with pine groups. The teachers have a little home in connection with the school, and the Webbs have a pretty new house nearby. [Mr. Webb is a high-colored, strong-featured young man; Mrs. Webb slight and dark.] Mr. Webb has had medical training, and she is a trained nurse. Both came originally from Ohio.

The Webbs, as my diary notes, were great observers and had various experiences of which they were ready to talk with frankness and conviction. Both were called out more or less frequently to help at operations, although he was rated as a preacher. He should really have been a doctor, or a social worker.

Nearly every day while at Flag Pond we rode somewhere—usually to some preaching point, where sometimes Mr. Webb spoke, sometimes John, and sometimes both. Mr. Webb refused to allow his wife to ride sidesaddle, which he said was very dangerous in the mountains and hard on the animals. We therefore all rode cross-saddle when horses were available, or double when they were not. Our first trip, on February 4th, mounted double on Dale and Old Fox, the mule, we rode to Rocky Fork, where there was a day school under Miss Jennie Moore. She had been there six years and had to raise the money for her own salary before the board would accept the work. She then also had to raise the salary of her assistant. She painted her house with her own hands. She and her assistant walked back with us to Devil's Fork, which is a narrow cut between the hills where a branch drops down in a tall, ice waterfall. The cleft was as green as summer, with tall wooden tramway built on trestles. The trucks are drawn by mules. All this country is full of water power, rushing streams, and a score of pretty gristmills with overshot wheels.

On February 5th, after dinner, we four, mounted on our two steeds, rode over to Falls Gap, by many waterwheels and Spivey Creek falls—a pleasant ride. Mr. Webb pointed out a number of pine trees in which knots had been tied in the branches, some grown large now. He explained that these were "lovers' knots." A girl or young man tied a knot in the end of a twig, and if it stayed and grew, all would be well; if it unknotted or died, the love affair would die too. We picked several on the way home. Before dark we crossed a deep mill-dam and came in at an old log house, where we were to spend the night.

[We] dismounted and went in. Mrs. Hensley [our hostess] proved to be a youngish woman and quite handsome, though unkempt. The kitchen was in great disorder—things lying all around. A table set in the middle. I took my seat between a cookstove and the open fire, while Mrs. H. dandled the baby—Edward Lee. . . . Mrs. H. said it seemed like he was more company than all the rest put together. Mrs. W. says she nurses him constantly. Says she can't bear to hear him cry, when he wants the breast. Finally she set him down among the wallow of ancient brown comforters in a homemade crib before the fire and set about supper. Mrs. W. inquired casually if she had been giving him his baths. Mrs. H. said not for some time as the second boy (?) had had a breaking out and she was afraid Edward Lee might catch it. Mrs. W. made a few mild suggestions, but at this point Edward Lee began to roar, having had enough of lying down., He was evidently not suffering, but in a rage, and thrashed about furiously. I couldn't help being amused by Mrs. W.'s tactful suggestions—that the baby was O.K. and should be taught that he could not have his way always, and Mrs. H.'s laconic responses, which ended in her calling to the smaller boy to come in and nurse the baby; so he soon appeared—round and red-cheeked—with round brown eyes and a round black hat on his round head. He picked up the baby, which promptly ceased its roars, and rocked it by thumping his chair back and forth, first on the front legs—then on the back. During all this time, Mrs. H. was making hoecake (baking in the spider) biscuit, frying pork, and boiling coffee—all at my left elbow and not greatly to my appetite.[40]

There were two other rooms in the house—lengthwise—the one next to the kitchen having three unmade beds in it and the front one having but one. Mrs. H. said she was keeping the sawmill hands (no one else to do it), and they made the linen so dirty. It certainly was dirty—no mistake! The sawmill hands proved to be four big young men and all very hungry; one apologized for his appearance and roughness. Said he would come to the evening meeting, however.

Before we finished supper, it had begun to pour, with a high wind, which drove the embers way out into the room. We adjourned to the front room while the family ate. Mrs. H. fished out a lamp without a chimney, which she set on the organ. Every time one of the doors was opened, out went the lamp in a rush of wind.

Finally the storm grew so heavy, thunder and lightning, that we decided not to walk one plus mile to the church house, but gather the few people into the house. So I took to the organ and we had our little congregation before the big fireplace, both John and Mr. W. speaking. The sawmill hands sat on the bed and all spat speculatively into the fire.

Mrs. W. and I slept together, cannily covering the dirty clothes with a blanket, and our pillow with towels from our saddlebags. The six men slept in the next room—all shut up tight from the night air [and expectorating freely, so John said].

We slept well, however, and next morning walked over to a nearby house, where the mother wove beautifully—linen as well as linsey. We got home about noon, February 6th. Late in the afternoon the tax assessor came in. He was collecting some data for Mr. Webb on families that have been to the mills. He was well informed along many lines and ready to answer our questions. He "said forest grew quickly in this country; all you had to do was to fence in a piece of land from the stock, and in a few years you had timber to clear." Used to be many killings about here; much illegitimacy and a great deal of venereal disease; the sturdy stock being run out. His visit started John and Mr. Webb on an exhaustive questionnaire project, designed to bring in data from "clergymen ministering in the mountain sections." They worked hard on this during all our stay in Flag Pond, and the result was forwarded to Mr. Glenn before we left.

Sunday, February 8, it started in raining early. I watched from the window the snowflakes on the top of the hills gradually creeping down till it was snowing with us. Then snow and rain alternated—fortunately the snow keeping up while we made our four-mile ride to Devil's Fork (Sweetwater Hollow as the people are trying to call it)—the mountains are very high that way, and the wood growth to the top was distinct in branch and twig snow-laden. The mist and cloud drifted low and sometimes hid the summit completely—then swept aside to show a shaft of sunlight and glint of blue sky before swallowing the peak again. The road was so uphill that I was sitting most of the way on Dale's tail (Mr. and Mrs. W. rode the somewhat cranky mule), but I had to admire the country in spite of my tired arms which clutched John's coat in frantic efforts to keep on (big saddle took up room). Much of the road lay between heavy growths of pine and hemlock laden with snow, which brushed off and fell on the poncho which I tried to hold over my skirt. The holly trees were particularly lovely, with the red berries peeping through the snow.

There was a very small congregation at the chapel, but John spoke his best and with effect. The day had partially cleared on our return and we got in about noon. . . . [In the afternoon] there was still a very small audience, and John spoke again, after which we went down to the teachers' cottage with Mrs. W. and talked with [the teachers].

The next day we visited the school, about forty pupils present, with an enrollment of under fifty. The public school was now closed; it had a six-month term and enrollment of sixty. The Webbs and the teachers had quite different ideas as to the work, and there was no real cooperation between them—partly a matter of point of view, partly temperament, and partly seeming unwisdom in the organization set up by the board. During our three weeks' stay in and around Flag Pond, we had plenty of opportunity to talk this over with the Webbs, along with a good many other things—denominational friction, health conditions, local mores, etc. For example, the teachers disapproved of the health work; they felt the Webbs gave too much time to what was outside the minister's special province and not enough to the church's real interests. Church work was made more difficult by the opposition offered by the Baptists, many of whom seemed to think the Presbyterians were a sort of political organization, trying to get possession of the whole country and centralize power. Mr. Webb thought the educated Baptists had no more prestige here than the Presbyterians. One local young Baptist preacher who had had college and seminary training had never been asked to preach here except by an old uncle whom he did not consider sufficiently influential. He told Mr. Webb that he, Baptist as he was, had no more influence than he, a Presbyterian. This attitude entered into the medical work. People were glad to use the service but did not feel gratitude or responsibility for repaying. Women were much neglected; they got little attention at childbirth. Illegitimacy was excused by the remark "He said he would marry me." Many mountain girls have been "bid off" by this proposal: "How would you like to put your shoes under my bed?"

Our various expeditions gave a still more intimate insight into local conditions, which was broadened and increased by a trip with the Webbs to the Presbyterian work around Burnsville, North Carolina. We left February 10th,

> a glorious clear morning with every creek and branch rushing full of water. Before getting up, I could hear the dam roaring down the road. Up pretty early, but had a busy time of preparation before starting off at 8:45 a.m. I rode Dale, who felt exceedingly lively and gay, and though I did not use my spur, he cut up along Higgins Creek in great shape. . . . Two mill wheels we passed, but they were quiet, with the water shooting out the flumes. . . . At the top [of Unaka, or Divide Mountain], as we turned down the North Carolina side, a cold wind struck us. The ground was frozen, and snow lay high up in the hollows of cornfield or ridge. . . . [We] swung up over Wolf-pen Gap to the waters of Big Laurel. There was laurel, sure enough, in great high masses. . . .
>
> We crossed Windy Gap . . . to Ball Creek—also heavily massed with rhododendron. . . . We stopped at the Swiss Post Office and store to buy more spurs, and the carrier went on with and took us across the bad ford on the Cane River [we zigzagging behind]. . . . Here was where we had our first really big sweep of the mountains ahead and behind. . . . Here also the wind struck us with a more biting chill and whistled around the rest of the way. It fairly cut us through, and the road grew muddier and muddier as we plodded along ankle-deep and halfway up to the knees. . . . The mountains were purple where the sun caught them, and black where night had begun to fall. Puffs of pink, windy cloud swept through the cold blue above them, and the sun sank brilliant yellow behind. We were tired and chilled when at last we drew up at the School [at Burnsville]. Mr. Hubbard ran down to meet us and took us to the manse, where Mr. Taylor came out and helped us fall off our horses. Mrs. W. and I were so stiff we could hardly stand. . . . We had a grand meal. . . . Very dead tired and came home to crawl joyfully into bed.[41]

The Burnsville school was the real center of the Presbyterian work, the smaller schools—Low Gap, Banks Creek, and Jacks Gap—being only a few miles away in different directions. The next morning, while John and Mr. Webb went over with the men to speak at chapel, Mrs. Webb and I talked with the women over the fire. Scraps of our conversation appear in my diary: "Too many women teachers. Outside Presbyterian schools ought to be centralized under this school or discontinued, and the money put here. . . . Believed in having a good public school here and the Presbyterians going into some other activity—higher education or something else. Baptists have a good opportunity here. . . ." Later, the men went over to talk with the principal of the Baptist school. He argued for church as against the public school: "The public school did not amount to anything and wasn't Christian." Mr. Taylor said the school was doing good work, and he thought there were more pupils coming to school "because of the two schools than there would be if there were only one—Baptist or Presbyterian."

The outlying schools called for more riding—a pleasant, if rather strenuous, time; muddy roads, study of the country, much discussion and gathering of information. We also gathered some mineral specimens, and Mr. Webb secured part of the worm of a moonshine still, which he planned to have a jeweler friend make into belt buckles for us, set with rough green beryl.[42] On our way out we stopped to visit Mr. Ray's Museum. "He is an old man, eighty-six, [who went] through the Civil War in a North Carolina regiment (Confederate). He owns mica mine. . . . Has made eighty thousand dollars in cash out of it. Mine is as good as ever, but needs two thousand dollars to put it in shape, and he does not bother. Some beautiful specimens in museum—aquamarines as brilliant as diamonds (five dollars a carat)—garnets. . . . Beryls, of course, and mica, smoky quartz cut and looking like cairngorms. Amethysts (from Arizona) and emeralds (from Mitchell)—and a fine collection of Indian relics."

We had planned, as a new experience, to go home across Bald Mountain and started boldly out to the top of McKinney Gap. On leaving Bucktown in the hollow below—a deserted lumber camp and a most dismal spot, where we waited for a man to replace a lost horseshoe—box shacks, hogs, children, scattering cornfields, and bare hills under a drizzling rain—we missed our way.

The trail was very rough, around stumps and over logs—now pitching down, now up. In one place where a great log was too high for the horses to cross, we had to drop down a steep place and, at the foot, pass under a fallen tree. I was the last, and calculated the height of the tree wrong— and as a result was nearly mashed and knocked off between pommel and log. Fortunately Dale stopped and at the second try I swung off the stirrup and, with John leading, got through. We . . . finally came to a place where an old logging road, choked by fallen trees, led up to the left, and a vague rough trail to the right. We decided on the right, and for about a mile struggled up the path—now on slick mud and again over the rough rocks of the creek bottom. It was raining in the meantime fitfully, and the clouds rolled down on us, so . . . we could see neither to right nor to left. . . . Mr. W. concluded that the path, a new one to him, must bring up between Big and Little Bald. As we wanted to go over Big Bald, we swung to the left and were immediately in a rough timber growth. We pushed ahead, the growth growing heavier and heavier and the little trail more and more crossed by fallen trees. The clouds clung in a thick fog about us, and the rain increased until it was a heavy downpour, driven hard by the wind. Still no Bald Mountain appeared.

We were evidently on the top of a ridge, and the trail swung up close to a high new rail fence. All along, where the trunks of the felled trees had been used for the fence, the big upper branches had been thrown all along the way, and our advance was a series of ins and outs and "surroundings." Dale, with his tender foot and new shoes, moved slowly along, a third in the file—and going around a tree, where a heavy, low twig branched out, stumbled, broke the twig, and pitched forward. I flew off and, by some instinct, loosened my feet from the stirrups and rolled to one side before Dale turned over. He was up in a minute, and before I could move, John was off his horse and by my side. I found myself okay, with the exception of a numb leg and wrenched ankle; Dale also, so we mounted again and continued. We must have gone two miles, with the rain pouring, wind howling, and clouds thick about us, before . . . we came to a split in the path—one along the ridge, one down. . . . Then someone remembered my compass, and we found our direction was just away from Flag Pond. The path down being nearer right, we turned downward, the horses slipping and sliding on the deep, soft black earth and stumbling over the fallen trees. It was growing dark, and Dale's legs trembled at the strain. At John's suggestion, I got down and fairly pulled the balking Dale over some great trees. I slipped myself and fell more than once, stepping on my dress, while the rain continued to drive in sheets. All along, Mr. W. had kept calling and whistling back to be sure we were safe, for it was too thick for him to see us. Now he shouted, and in a few minutes we could see smoke and we came out on a little shack near a sawmill and in the midst of stacks of lumber. It was a miserable shack, but we never were so glad to see any dwelling. An open fire was blazing inside, and a big group of men, women, and children gathered at the door to peep out at our bedraggled, dripping figures. The light glistened on our rubber coats. Mr. Webb's question was, "We've come to find out where we are."

It appeared that we were on Bruce's sawmill at the foot of Haw Ridge, three and a half miles from Street's Gap, which is five miles from Flag Pond, and were near three—three and a half miles from Dr. Fate English's at Faust Post Office. There was no hesitation, and we decided to strike for Dr. English's for the night. The rain still slatted down, night was already on us, and we were drenching wet. Besides that, my ankle pained me. One of the men, Frank Rich, then said he would take us across the ridge. He took a lantern and we followed along, by another shack where the blazing fire mocked at us, through some bars onto a road, and off to the left down another trail, which soon began to mount. We all stuck to our horses (except John at the end, who got off old Jo, quite fortunately, as Jo fell twice), although the hill was pretty vertical and the soil was so deep and slick that I wondered how we could do it. At the top we could see that we were in an old corn-field, high up, with a steep slope leading down, unmarked by any trail we could see. Then we began to pitch down. I must confess that I expected any moment to pitch over Dale's head, or have him fall with me under him. But down we moved, inch by inch, sidling along. I could hear the bleating of lambs about me, and as we passed a big log, could just distinguish two baby white fellows trying to seek protection below it. They were bleating in chorus, and I was glad to hear an old sheep answering not far away.

By the time we struck Puncheon Fork, it was black and we could see nothing. . . . At length we forded a creek, and Rich told us we were on the way to the main road. He went back, and we pushed on alone, single file. Our only guide was Mr. W.'s white horse, of whose back we could distinguish a patch. Every few minutes he would halloo, and we, answering, splashed on again. It was raining a little less, but black and dreary enough. The cabins we passed, distinguishable only by the flicker of the open fires, seemed as unattainable as if we were outlawed.

Suddenly we came out on the big road, and all the horses plucked up new spirit and pushed ahead. Uphill or downhill, we could not tell. We trotted swiftly ahead, hallooing back and forth, splashing over ford, splattering through mud, stumbling over rocks and stones. It was only three miles, but it seemed a good five. . . .

All was dark at Dr. English's house. Not a sign of life . . . the good doctor had gone to bed (been out the night before delivering a sixteen-year-old girl of an illegitimate child . . .) and his wife too. He rose nobly to the occasion, however, and soon came out. . . .

Mrs. English had got up and was throwing wood on the fire. . . . [She] got us hot coffee, hot biscuits, fried pork, and preserves, which we did justice to. Mrs. W. used some of our lemons bought in Burnsville for hot lemonade, which threw us into good perspiration.

We had good feather beds, and John undressed me and washed my feet. Mrs. Webb came in and massaged my ankle with liniment, and Mr. Webb put on a tight bandage. My! But we were glad to roll into that bed and to sleep!

I couldn't step on my foot without pain in the morning, but we were all cheerful. Our clothes were about dry, and the day was fair. Mrs. English had a good breakfast, and all was well. Neither the doctor nor his wife would take anything, and Mrs. English waited to do her dishes until we were off.

We were home before noon (February 16th), my foot soaked and rebandaged, and our adventure ended happily. A good grist of mail awaited us, and we plunged into it. Mr. Glenn's letter to me of February 11th was interesting to Mr. Webb as well as to John and me:

I was very glad to get your letter of February 4. I am particularly interested in what you say about consideration of the question whether life in the mill towns is better than life in the mountains for mountain children. I think that where conditions in the mountains have not been improved, the environment is worse for the children than that in the mill towns, but conditions in the mill towns are far from being what they ought to be. The hard work for the children and the lack of opportunities to go to school are very bad.

The argument that the mountain people are better off in the mills than they would be in the mountains is frequently used against good labor legislation which is meant to protect children and adults from unhealthy conditions, but the choice does not lie merely between mountains and mills. Admitting for the sake of argument that the mills are better than the mountains, it is nonetheless the duty of the mill owners and of the community to see that the conditions in the mill towns are such that they do not harm the physical and moral welfare of those who live there. This is not merely a question of the welfare of the children or of individuals, but a matter of the greatest importance to the proper development of community life.

The legislation against child labor in the mills and against too long hours is not going to prevent the mountaineers from going to the mills, nor will it close the mills. There was an interesting table shown at the child labor meeting in Chicago the other day, which showed that in three states where the requirements were high, certain manufacturers who had claimed that they were dependent on child labor had thrived much better than in several states where restrictions were low. . . .

I had a very interesting talk the other day with Dr. C. Wardwell Stiles about the hookworm disease and other diseases which he has been studying. He argued that we should not attempt to restrict child labor, because the children are better off in the mill town, where there is not so much liability to hookworm disease. But there are a good many of the mill towns where conditions are quite as bad, if not worse, than they are in the mountains. It seems to me to be as important to raise the standards in mill towns as it is to raise them in the mountains, and vice versa.[43]

This letter spurred the two men to fresh efforts on their questionnaire, but first we had another trip into the so-called Laurel Country, just over the Tennessee line in Madison County, North Carolina. It seemed best to do it at once, and we started out the next morning, February 17th. Fortunately, my foot gave me little trouble, and I was able to enjoy thoroughly the ride through mountains spangled, every twig, with frost crystals. In this region was a group of Presbyterian centers—Shelton-Laurel, Allegheny, White Rock, Allanstand, and others. Each operated a small elementary school like the centers around Burnsville, with two resident workers—teacher or teachers, doctor, minister, or nurse. As we visited about, we heard much of conditions existing, perhaps, more primitive than those around Burnsville, for the section was particularly isolated. We were especially interested to see Allanstand, the place where Miss Frances Goodrich had begun her famous handicraft revival, the Allanstand Industries. She was no longer there, and there was no activity to be seen—just a double log house with a collection of odds and ends, a few baskets, rolls of wool, etc. We did, however, see Mrs. Louise Payne weaving in a cabin about a quarter of a mile away, and heard that there were several other women here and in the adjacent county who were sending their work to Miss Goodrich—now in Asheville. Mrs. Payne told us she wove carpet at fifty cents a yard; could weave three or four yards a day, but with her house work, usually did not weave more than one. It took her some three days to set up her loom, warp, etc. before she could begin to weave at all. Miss Goodrich paid $1.50 a yard for linsey, which would bring only fifty cents at Flag Pond.[44]

We followed up the matter of weaving when we returned to Flag Pond February 19th. Four days later, Mrs. Webb and I made a special expedition, by ourselves, up Rice Creek, mounted double on Dale, I in the saddle and she behind.

Called first on Mrs. Blankenship in a small house to the right of the road. On the opposite side, lower down, an old house was evident—loom up on porch; a good sized barn, several out-buildings, a good deal of stock. The Blankenships have the reputation of being great workers. Mr. B. buys and sells stock, works on the farm, and [has] 8 children—2 [i.e., 1 each?] at Farm and Home Industrial at Asheville. Mrs. B. is great-granddaughter of John Sevier, quite a fine-looking dark woman with pleasant brown eyes and cordial manner.[45] Statistics are so:

1 pound wool	$ .25
5 pounds warp	$1.25 (weaves 30 yards)
1 pound wool? yarn (depends on waste?)	
6 pounds wool	probably enough to weave 13 yards of cloth; little over 2 pounds yarn weaves 5 yards.

Has woven 12 yards for $1.00, but thought it hardly paid, 10 yards for $1.00 fairer.

Says she is not a fast weaver, especially now with so much housework, field work, and is not well. Says a good fast weaver like Mrs. Profitt can weave 5–6 yards a day.

A woman [said Mrs. Profitt later] can hardly spin 2 yards a day except with help. (Mrs. Profitt's daughter does her carding.) Weaving is comparatively easy when wool is cleaned, walnut roots dug (one day), and wool dyed. . . .

Mrs. Blankenship told us how she used to make indigo dye—boiled it up with the madder, etc. It certainly made the finest dark blue—never faded. . . . Spoke with worth of her work. Said she was mighty fussy about having no roughness or knots in her cloth. All her girls can spin and weave.

. . .

Mrs. Profitt's house is quite picturesque. Stands back at the end of long lane. Hung on one stirrup while I unfastened and opened gate. Log house (recently sheathed) and two-roomed. Recess between two with spinning-wheel tucked in and big basket. Vines in front. In showing us some weaving slays [or sleys], she pulled them out from under roof of porch. . . .[46]

Mrs. Profitt has worn but sweet face; ten children. [She], however, is considered even over-careful with her girls. When men spend night there, her girls sleep in the kitchen and men do not go in till girls are up and dressed. . . .

Mrs. P. said she would just love to get hold of some indigo and fuss with it. It was a heap of trouble, but it certainly made a pretty color, and it never faded. She corroborated Mrs. Blankenship's statement that, to make a pretty gray, one must have good rich colors—a rich black and clear white. . . .

Mrs. Webb made good arrangements for Mr. Webb's suit, but I had to give up mine at present, as women must soon go into field and garden to work. Mrs. P. said some people did not want to pay fifty cents for linsey—she reckoned if they made it, they'd [be] willing!

Mr. Glenn's letter of February 14th, which awaited John on his return to Flag Pond from the Laurel Country, was interesting and reassuring as always but made him anxious to get to an analysis and summary of his findings; and he still had a number of places he wanted to visit first. The letter read in part:

I was very glad indeed to get your letter of February 9th. You need not be afraid of writing too much. I like to be posted on your movements and on what you learn. This letter is very suggestive. What you say about the relation of the boards and the schools does not surprise me, although I knew nothing of it before. I have had some inquiries as a result of your expedition, but not many. You need not worry about that. I can take care of all applications. The fact that I have not had more applications indicates that you have been very discreet in what you have said about the Foundation.

I shall be very glad to have you make a preliminary report in May or any other time that you think it is wise to do so. . . .

I will be very glad to see your schedule of questions when you have drawn it up, and to show it to one or two other people, especially Dr. Buttrick. He is very much interested in your study and is well posted on educational questions. . . .[47]

I am glad you think of settling down for a while to review the data you have accumulated and send out your circulars. That will be a wise move.

The men spent most of their last few days in Flag Pond on the questionnaire, and John got it off with a long, explanatory letter to Mr. Glenn. We followed, February 26th, laden with luggage—John riding the white, carrying saddlebags as usual, suitcase strapped behind. Mrs. Webb and I rode Dale, also carrying saddlebags. The creeks were much swollen, and in places water came rushing into my stirrup hoods. At Loves station we had to change our clothes and repack while waiting for the train. Mrs. Webb rode on ahead to Erwin, where we met later. The town was to have railroad shops, and all was booming. Again we heard the now old story of denominational friction and competition. Our visit there was to the Presbyterian School, but we found the Baptists were to start an opposition school, and there was already a "public school (present one very bad—no desks, no discipline, children on streets). Possibly new engineers, etc., will demand a good public school."

Mr. Glenn had asked us to look up, if we could, Lydia Holman, a nurse whom he and Mrs. Glenn had found very interesting. There were a number of schools in her neighborhood, so on February 27th we continued up along the new CC&O Railroad, built to give the coal areas of the Virginias and Kentucky an outlet to the seaboard. At the station, John was approached by two Baptist preachers who wished to secure his interest in the proposed Erwin school. It seemed that we had the reputation of millionaires who were looking for places to throw away our money. On the train, a North Carolina man regaled us with tales of shooting,

especially of the times when he was putting through the road (the old 4 C's) in 1869 (89?). Lots of whiskey and lots of shooting. It being Saturday—payday—we saw plenty of the former in express bundles at the stations. . . . Fare is four cents a mile in Tennessee and two and a half cents in North Carolina, and everyone buys a ticket to Caney [sp.?] Bottom, the border—a place of shacks, whiskey, and shootings. . . .

Ride is really beautiful—gorge very narrow in places—Nolichunky River very swift and rushing; then up along the Cane proper and North Cane Fork. If the curves had not been so sharp and my breakfast more settled, I should have delighted in every inch of the ride. As it was, we were both glad to get off at Penland. Found it a mere cluster of houses about a mica mill. Mr. Bailey, who seemed to be general manager . . . station agent and storekeeper, . . . directed us up to his house, where Miss Holman is staying at present. She was not there . . . came in about 3:00 p.m. after a night with a woman whom she delivered of [a] child (dead 6 or 8 weeks before birth). . . . Says she had had some two hundred cases of childbirth since coming (seven years). And has never lost child or mother.

. . . Men marry many times; wives simply drudges and servants of men's desires.[48]

If we had not heard about health conditions before, we certainly did now, with details harrowing and in cases horrible beyond belief. Most doctors were poor—no degree—and seemingly they were more interested in getting their pay than in relieving their patients. [Miss Holman] tried to work with them at first, but found they preferred her to take her own cases. Ethically and professionally, she said, she did not approve of herself at all for practicing, but from a practical point of view, it was the only thing she could do. Naturally she told us much of social conditions, the prevalence of tuberculosis, venereal diseases, the amount of insanity, imbecility, epilepsy; the effect of the extreme religious meetings. Jails were terrible places, she said, as the insane are shut up there as well as prisoners. She had found in jail, all together, idiots, epileptics (one raving insane), one murderer (two the next week), three moonshiners. Barred cells opened into the main hall. The murderer was in an iron cage in the middle of the room. There was also an insane girl whose cell opened into the same room above. She had torn off her shoes and burned them up on the stone floor, and had pulled off most of her clothes. The sheriff had taken her to the asylum in this condition.[49]

We continued our talk most of the next morning; then Miss Holman took us over to Ledger, where she wanted John to see some buildings which might be utilized, she thought, one as a home for herself and the others as a possible school. John rode Mr. Bailey's magnificent black, while I rode gentle Dan with a comfortable gait. We followed up the creek, which glittered with mica, three miles to Ledger. Going home a different way, we went

up a rough creek and over a mountain, taking down bars and picking our way across gullies, and down along a scratch in the mountain side. It was entirely dark except for a half moon and the most brilliant, starry sky. One great luminous star in particular hung low over the mountain tops in the east. Could just distinguish a few puffs of cloud—all that were left of the fluffy masses and detached puffs that were so beautiful against the clear, cold blue at sunset time. The air was cold—my feet got quite stiff—but the night was too wonderful to mind it. When we finally crawled down the mountain side, we found a better road and went along a ridge between black trunks and tall bushes. Long tree shadows lay across the road. Part of the time I was behind and was amused at the romantic picture presented by John and Miss Holman, who rode along side by side in the moonlight, talking. Near home we left my horse, and John put me on his big black, which bolted for home—a fine, great creature. John walked up.

On March 1, we took the train to Spruce Pine, where we got dinner and waited for our hack, a ponderous affair. We lumbered slowly over the bad roads, both of us tired and dull, reaching the Presbyterian school at Plumtree about five thirty. We found all was in confusion there due to a fire in December. Mr. Hall, the principal, was away, and his mother, quite an old lady, was the only one there. She could not tell us much about the school except that it "was for poor boys" and that "they all wanted to go into the ministry." Later we met several teachers and the doctor. They could not very well ask us to stay, so we went on about six thirty to the next house.[50]

Evidently the old man there was in a gloomy frame of mind. He was picking up wood as we came along, and as John called out cheerily, asking if he would take in some strangers, he hardly looked up, and simply answered gruffly, "No, I reckon not tonight." So we drove on. The horses were tired, and it was almost dark, the road rough, and no near houses. Finally we came to a cabin and asked where we could "get to stay." [The answer was] "West Franklin," three and a half miles from Plumtree, so we pushed on in the dark. . . . Fortunately the moon (at half) gave enough light to watch (for) bridges and bad turns.

About 8 p.m. we made Franklin's Store, and the driver, going up the lane to ask, returned with affirmative answer. We found an old two-story house and were ushered into room with big wood fire and two beds (with woven "kivers"). The old man was sitting by the fire with his two sons (one in Plumtree). Said he had raised four boys but couldn't keep them at home. All crazy for education. Barney was a nice-looking chap, and the second (helping at home) had a good face. The old man had a pleasant, ruddy face, gray eyes, and bushy beard. Finally Mrs. Franklin came to bid us to supper—a (strange-looking) little, bent, dark woman with round, too-brilliant eyes and wrinkled face. . . . I sat and talked to her after John went back with men. Room had two beds (boy of two to three asleep in one), cookstove, and open fire, table in the middle. Around the fire sat three little girls—the oldest fifteen (Ina), dark and bent like the mother. Mrs. Franklin informed me that "Iney' had the most terrible cough, had had it since one year old and coughed up pure corruption that smelled the most awful you ever smelled; that the doctors couldn't do anything for her, but said she would outgrow it. She reckoned, however, that they only said that to encourage her. . . . The second child had had a stroke of paralysis but was well now, though she couldn't use her right hand much. The youngest, "Americy," was a pretty, shy little thing. Mrs. Franklin had had twelve children, three dead.

Seeing Americy yawn, I suggested that she looked sleepy, whereupon the mother said it was past their bedtime. "Pull off your stockings, children, and jump into bed." This being literally obeyed, we adjourned to the front room for bed. Mrs. Franklin appointed our bed, and got off the cover to the other, evidently preparatory for Mr. Ray, our driver, but was circumvented by Barney, the schoolboy, who said he would take Mr. Ray upstairs.

I asked Mrs. Franklin if she had heard of Miss Holman, and she said she had, that she was the one who rode round just like a man. Evidently the report was good, for at our solicitation, she reckoned she would take Iney over to Spruce Pine to see her.

I couldn't much enjoy my breakfast with Iney coughing at the door and reports of typhoid near at hand, but we did eat something. Barney was off to school on horseback at seven, and we were off by seven thirty.

The morning, after a rainy night, was damp and chill. I was much distressed all the way to Montezuma by the deadenings [trees killed by girdling the trunks to prepare a clearing for a crop with the least trouble and delay]. Such a wasteful, unsystematic scheme, killing shade trees by the road, which did not interfere at all with the clearings. [Apparently no one had any thought of what erosion would do to the soil]. . . .

We made Montezuma near ten—a scattered group of buildings through which the narrow-gauge puffed, laden with timber, at the rate of eight miles in two hours. We drove up to the Methodist preacher's house to ask about the school, and found him a new young Alabaman . . . [who] didn't know much about the school. A good building from outside. Poor teachers had brought about small attendance, but church was planning to build it up. . . . We got new directions and started on to Linville.

The country grew steadily more beautiful—trees preserved, great hemlocks banked with rhododendron. The Linville (Creek) proved to be a charming, rushing creek, clear and sparkling (and full, we were told, everywhere with fish).

I shall never forget our ride, twenty miles along the Yonahlassee Road around Grandfather Mountain, to Blowing Rock. At the highest point, five thousand feet, we stopped at the Alexander McRaes's, an old Scottish couple who were delighted, in this cold winter season, to have company—especially company of Scottish descent. We joyfully piled in before the open fire while Mrs. McRae made us Scottish oatcake, and the old man told us how he happened to come to this country from the Inverness region, where he was born.[51]

> After [eating] it seemed so warm and lovely that Mr. McRae took us up on the Grandfather. A well-graded road runs up some one and a half miles beyond the house—beautiful all the way, but with a superb view at top, where a group of boulders juts out some; above rose two great crags, six hundred to seven hundred feet above us, their bases swathed in a thick growth of fir balsam. Below lay blue swales of woodland and distant rugged peaks outlined against the sky; now masses of cloud swept over them, changing them to purple or hiding them in mist—and, against the sun, glittered over them. We stood fastened to the rock, till old Alexander declared we should catch cold. Reluctantly we turned away, the enchanted Mr. Ray [our driver], who had never seen such a sight before, dug up some little balsam trees to take home. We found later that he had likewise cut some sticks of mountain birch . . . "toothbrushes for my wife." . . . The wind was rising higher as we went down, and light showers began to fall. We had a good dinner and in the evening sang to the old people and played on the piano, while Alexander regaled us with the bagpipe and talked more Scotland. They were exceedingly loath to let us go off to bed, but we tumbled in near ten o'clock.
>
> We awoke to a blinding snowstorm, which, however, after we had unharnessed and prepared to wait, fell off about ten, and we started out. The first few miles were truly wonderful, with every twig snow-laden and outlined against blue distances. To our left, the side of old Grandfather was hung with constant drifting masses of cloud from the blue; and, sadly enough, as we got out of the shelter, these began to descend on us with a heavy cold wind, which pursued us all the seventeen miles to Blowing Rock. The blue clouded over, driving snow flurries overtook us, and the drive was raw and bitter, although views were continually wonderful with mountains and drifting cloud and storm.

We had intended to spend the night at the Watauga Inn in Blowing Rock, but the teachers of a small Congregational school at Skyland, three quarters of a mile away, wrote that they would be much disappointed if we did not go there. Our

driver added his opinion that "it was powerful cold, and if we were going, we'd better go early." So, go we did.[52]

> Two sisters were running [the school] on trial, with a young girl as assis-
> tant. . . . It seems there is a seven-month good public school there, as well
> as one for Mr. Cone's tenants and nearby children. [Mr. Cone, a big mill-
> owner, had an estate on the edge of the town.][53] Although feeling is good,
> there seems to be considerable doubt as to advisability and necessity for
> keeping up the school. [One of the] sisters had been at Saluda and one
> at Joppa, Alabama. (Latter said everyone still spoke of John there as the
> only real thing.) Were new to Blowing Rock. . . . Did not know a great
> deal about conditions. We had a good time talking, however, until almost
> 11:00 p.m.
>
> The wind blew tremendously all night, and we awoke to sunny skies
> but a drifting world. Mr. Ray walked out and said that all said . . . it would
> be impossible to make Valle Crucis till the wind went down. Narrow cuts
> would be drifted ten feet deep (not much snow, but all there is, drifts) and
> wagon would blow over. . . . In p.m. John and I wrapped up and struggled
> down to the town to call on the Episcopal minister. . . . Said mountaineers
> thought the Episcopalians were Catholics, so got few converts.

Journeying down (March 5th) to the Episcopal school at Valle Crucis was not
exactly pleasant. It was cold, roads drifted, and mountains covered with snow. Most
of our conversation there had to do with the amount of illegitimacy and drunkenness, the latter, they said, having greatly improved since prohibition. There was illegitimacy in almost every family. While I talked with the teachers, John visited the
plant, including blacksmith shop, wagon factory, chicken houses. It was very pleasant sitting around the fire in the evening, talking.[54]

We awoke next morning to a pouring rain. John did his usual speaking at chapel, then the faithful Mr. Ray appeared with the hack, and behind closed curtains—
a chilly, dark arrangement—we rattled on to Banners Elk, Southern Presbyterian
work. Dr. and Mrs. Reed, the heads, were most alert and pleasant. They have been
there only a year and were obliged to speak guardedly, though in much the same
vein as Miss Holman. The doctor has no salary but supports the family—four children—as well as he can on what he collects.

> Mrs. Reed said she hoped they could stay, but work precarious. Some-
> times [Mr. Reed] did not see five dollars in a month. She herself had to do

own washing and housekeeping. Could get no help. Was ready, however, and eager to teach in school next year, a class in invalid cookery. . . . One thing of value he has instituted. Found boys had nothing to do for amusement, so sat every night in store and chewed and swapped bad stories. He set aside Thursday evening, got out all sorts of games, and put out papers and magazines, and invited boys in. Told them to bring pipes and tobacco and, when in, told them to light up, or, if they chewed, to use the fireplace. Now you cannot keep them away Thursdays, and girls are interested. . . .

We got off about three. Rain had stopped, so we viewed landscape. Snow still on mountains behind us, but it disappeared as we descended to Cranberry. Much mud! . . . [At Cranberry] John went out to interview the mine superintendent. . . . He said mountaineers made good miners, though hampered by lack of education. When he first came, mines did not pay, but now paid and man earned three dollars a day. Had difficulty in finding men well enough educated and trustworthy to keep time. Had worked men up to subscribing for pay school.

The town was simply a group of mill shacks—many neatly painted and heaps and heaps of lumber piled about the terminus of the narrow-gauge to Johnson City.

We got back to Spruce Pine the next day, Sunday, March 7th, about 4:30 p.m., and parted with our happy, homesick driver. Miss Holman was waiting and, on our urging, stayed over and took the train with us to Marion next day, "a wonderful looping road around a shoulder of the Blue Ridge. The best scenery we have had, truly beautiful in its mountain sweep and marvelous in engineering." We left Miss Holman at Marion and hastened on to the station to catch the train to Asheville, which fortunately was late and had much baggage to load. We threw ourselves out of the surrey and tumbled aboard to the cry of "All Aboard!" Our winter rambling was coming to an end and we were not sorry.

Asheville, like Knoxville, meant a great cleaning up, some new clothes, and letters, *letters,* waiting, coming, and going. One from Fred Webb in Scottish style took us back again to life in the Flag Pond field:

My dear Campbell:

Sabbath though it is, I'm sair tempit to try my new paper on you. It's a grand day, the day, and I have enjoyed every moment. Went to Rocky Fork this morn and had a good meeting and all very enthusiastic about Mr. Campbell's sermon. "He's a good old man." At 3:00 p.m. I saddled and started for the Spivey. Arrived at "Little Cornelius's" place at a wee before six. Found them in joyful expectation of my coming, and cared for man and beast very well. At nine that evening Dr. [T. C.] Hensley, who had made sundry calls that p.m., came in and we bunked together. Had a long talk about spinning and weaving, and Little Cornelius told me how they "warp up a loom." I'd have given half my night's rest if you could have heard it. The first thing a woman does when she a-fixes to weave is to send on and git her a whole ramption of bale thread, etc. I have Mrs. Cornelius under promise to weave our flax cloth, and she will soon begin on it. I've sent for the "ramption of bale-thread"—warp.

Dr. Hensley and I started early on our trip, left the waters of Spivey, turned down the waters of Big Creek. Had a fine view of the Green and Black Mountains. We passed a few houses of the one-room log type, a few two-room frame, and a couple of fair quality two-story frame houses. Four mills in a half-mile made us smile. . . . Where we operated is one-fourth mile from Cane River. . . . House was clean, spick and span. Nice old hand-woven "kiverlids" on the beds, indigo and madder, and indigo and rosene—one of the old dyes. Got in touch with a woman who had sixteen of them, though all but two were dyed with "dimont" dyes—"much purtier." . . .

Well, we operated. Splendid piece of work. Made many friends. Practically a miracle. A country practitioner was the "a naesthetist." I wish you could have seen him. Long and lank, short trousers which did not come quite to his brass-eyeleted brogans tied with groundhog-hide strings. We watched him like a hawk as we worked, for we couldn't tell what he might do with the chloroform. . . . I got in about eight calls along in the two days, which wasn't so bad for one who was neglecting his work. We will operate on another man for a bad hernia Thursday. Dr. Bissell will come over (from Shelton-Laurel), and I'll neglect my parish work again as we—Madam and I—do nearly a day each of hospital work gratis for the good of the cause. . . .

Write us when you can. Lang as we're here, the latch-string is in easy reach of you.

A few days later, he forwarded notice of the exhibit at the usual Presbyterian Conference at Maryville College, June 22–27. Last year, the notice explained, there were maps, drawings, and herbariums, specimens of handicraft such as basketry, chair-caning, needlework, sloyd work, and wood carving, weaving, and the like. The same kind of exhibits were to be repeated this year—including weaving, basketry, straw and shuck weaving, needlework, etc., "from the schools and communities that are grouped around Burnsville under Mitchell Peak to those at Marshall on the French Broad, through all the closely federated fields of the famous Laurel Country on by the way of the Flag Pond country to the Nolichucky, and on across the Cumberlands."

Mr. Glenn wrote, March 4, 1909:

"I have gone over your schedules pretty carefully. They seem to be admirably prepared and to be very comprehensive.

I am sorry, however, that I have very serious doubts as to the advisability of circulating them. The fact that they are so comprehensive means that it will take a good deal of time to fill them up. The people to whom you want to send them are not used to making records. Most of them will probably balk at the job. Many of them, if not most of them, will be unable to give answers that you can depend on for practical use. They are not equipped for making accurate answers to such questions as you propose. It must be remembered that while many of the questions are simple, some of them involve very important problems of school and economic organization.

Before I have the circulars printed, I would like to confer with Dr. Buttrick and Dr. Frissell. . . . Meantime, will you kindly let me know what you think of the difficulties which I suggest?

A week later, March 11th, he wrote again:

I enclose a copy of a letter that I have received from Dr. Frissell. Dr. Buttrick's experience confirms my feeling that you would get very little information by sending out your proposed schedules. I also feel that unless it is possible for you to coach beforehand the people who are to fill in the answers, the information sent in on such schedules would be of very little value.

If you succeeded in getting in a sufficiently large number of schedules giving you reliable information, you would have to give a great deal of time to going over them and tabulating them. Will it be worthwhile to give that much of your time to tabulating answers of doubtful value? Is it not better to put down your own individual observations and experiences into a report and let us then consider whether it will be advisable for us to go further and in more detail into the study of the mountain problem?

I will be glad to have your very frank expression of opinion. You may feel that we are looking for much more minute and detailed information than we really expect. I feel that you must have already gotten so much important information that it will take you quite a while to make up a report on it.

An answer to this last reached Mr. Glenn before we received it. Writing March 10, John summed up the experiences of the past week and told of his feeling about the schedules:

We have had the most strenuous week in all of our experiences. . . . I had known something of blizzards in the west, but I never encountered such a one as that which held us stormbound at Blowing Rock for two days. North Carolina has given us a very clear idea of mountain storms. This blizzard experience is the last of a series of somewhat thrilling experiences. . . .

I have read with interest Mr. Neve's letter to Professor Payne. I feel that both the state and the church are working toward the same end—true citizenship. Each has its difficulties, its weaknesses, and its strengths; and I am hoping very much that a way may be found through this investigation whereby the church's work in the mountains may supplement the state's work in these regions and that many causes of misunderstanding may be removed.[55]

I was much impressed by the work that is under way at Valle Crucis under Bishop Horner's direction and by his evident grasp of the mountain situation. He is trying to demonstrate what I think can be demonstrated, that the mountains can be made to yield a fair living to the mountain people if they are intelligently directed. . . .[56]

I thank you for your review of the schedules and for your frank statement of your doubt as to the advisability of circulating them. I do not at all regard your suggestions as an interference with my plans. The highest wisdom is necessary in getting at the facts, and I welcome your suggestions and shall be very glad indeed to have those of Dr. Buttrick and Dr. Frissell. There are, I think, some few men in the work who could answer the questions and who would take time to do so; others who could answer some and would fail entirely on the rest. I have been so handicapped in getting authoritative statements on matters that are important that I knew of no other way to test my growing convictions. There seem to be no state or county reports from the mountain sections that bear on vital questions, and the time is too short to make personal research along these various lines. The charge is likely to be made, if my report is made public, that it is a general, surface report—as it must be in part—and that I have not taken available means to prove or disprove my own opinions. There ought to be official records along health lines, birth and death; and I am in possession of confidential information, which of course I cannot use, that some of those in charge of such departments know there are such lacks and have urged, for the sake of the state and for the sake of the districts, that these facts be hidden. There seemed to me to be no other way for me to do than to write to the state authorities; failing there, to write to the county authorities; failing there, to write to the physicians. Having done that, I would have some right to claim that I had done all I could and must rely upon my own deduction. I did not expect to get definite information from many of the county superintendents.

The difficulties you have mentioned are real difficulties. Personally, should I return to the mountains, as I hope to, I would prefer that the schedules should not be sent out; and the more I have thought the matter over, I have wondered if, after all, it would not be better to have those inquiries go out somewhat in the nature of personal letters to men who I know are to some extent qualified to answer them. The letters to the church workers and ministers are to prove or disprove the verbal complaint that has been made to me everywhere of poor management on the part of directing officials. The general questions on all of the papers were for the purpose of checking. The difficulties are real, and the test is a poor one, but it is the only test that has presented itself to me as feasible.

After the first few days at a hotel, we moved over to the Home Industrial School, a most pleasant and comfortable place, presided over by Miss Florence Stephenson, one of the best known of the Presbyterian mountain workers. Miss Johns, second in command, was also a very able woman. The two reminded me of Miss Pettit and Miss Stone—not that they actually resembled each other, but one had a strong personality and much charm, while the other was the careful, detail woman. All the staff were most helpful, showing me about the school and making all sorts of valuable connections. Among other things, Miss Stephenson got us a good stenographer, Ada Bagwell, one of their old students, who made it possible for us to catch up on our letter-writing. While John departed (March 11th) on a three-day trip to the Laurel Country to meet with board officials, I was taken on an inspection tour of work at the Normal and Collegiate Institute, the Pease House, and the Home Industrial itself.[57] Miss Stephenson took me to call on Dr. (Chase) Ambler, a prominent physician, and Dr. Fletcher, whose father had doctored in the mountains for years around Waynesville. We talked with Mrs. Horner, wife of Bishop Horner, under whose general authority the Valle Crucis School was conducted; and interviewed Dr. Swope, rector of the Episcopal Church at Biltmore.[58] We drove out to Farm School and spent most of a day looking over the plant and discussing with Dr. [J. P.] Roger, the head—an interesting man, a Canadian who was brought up on a farm, had college and medical training, also industrial, and had practiced a number of years. Our talk was of problems of education and agriculture, also the character of his student body. Many of his boys have worked in the mills, which he thinks are bad for them physically and morally. He said his baseball, football, and tennis have been a great help in doing away with disciplinary problems.

When John came back—on Saturday afternoon, the 13th—I could report a very busy and profitable time, although I must admit that my strongest impressions were of Miss Stephenson, her keen mind, executive ability, and power of organization—not to mention her social gift. John, too, was pleased with his adventures. He had met and discussed with a number of Presbyterian officials and had been able to get over to the Baptist School at Mars Hill.[59] And he still had time the next day for a number of interviews which Miss Stephenson, thoughtfully arranged by inviting people he wished to meet to dinner and tea: Dr. Roger; Dr. [Thomas] Lawrence, retired head of the Normal School; Dr. George T. Winston, formerly president of the North Carolina Agricultural and Mechanical; and Dr. and Mrs. H. H. Briggs, he an able eye specialist and brother of the wife of Dr. Hensley, whom we had met at Flag Pond. We even ran down to Brevard for the night to see Mr. [C. H.] Trowbridge, head of a Southern Methodist school. Full of information, we got off on Monday, March 15th, with the affectionate farewells of all the household, the girls waving from the windows. Even at the station, John had a hasty last interview with the superintendent of Southern Presbyterian work, Mr. P. S. Smith. Then Dr. Winston joined us just in time to catch the 3:35 p.m. train to Waynesville, where, talking interestingly all the way, he drove us up to see the magnificent view at Eagles' Nest. We parted with him at Dillsboro, he returning to Asheville, we continuing by buggy—John driving, and the driver following us on horseback—to Franklin, the northern terminus of the little railroad which passed through Demorest. At the Demorest station, Miss Sheak, Miss Rawn, and Jessie were awaiting us with a joyful welcome. The house was ready; supper was all but on the table. And so we returned from our wanderings—as my Line-a-Day put it, "a jolly homecoming."

5

Report and First Conference, 1909–1913

Back in Demorest, the Campbells began catching up on work at Pleasant Hill and local problems. Visitors came by to discuss education for the mountains, and plans were made to attend the Southern Education Conference at Atlanta in April 1909. Campbell and John Glenn of the Russell Sage Foundation planned to meet there, and Mr. Glenn suggested that letters of invitation be written to others who were interested in and supportive of the investigation and the mountain study.

The Foundation was pleased with the survey and the work that Campbell was doing and authorized the continuation of it for another year. After months of deliberation, he was awarded a salary of $2,500 to continue the study of mountain conditions. Letters of support came from many who read parts of the report, such as Dr. Wallace Buttrick, secretary of the General Education Board in New York, and Dr. Wickliffe Rose of the Peabody Education Fund in Nashville.

Embarking on further investigation, Campbell often found it difficult to gather statistical evidence. Board policies were liable to change, and schools might be shifted around or discontinued. He found that those trying to establish industrial schools, in which children learned occupations as well as reading and writing, were "nothing doing." They cited the need for better teachers, graded schools, and higher ideals. Campbell was becoming an authority on mountain matters, and his "engaging personality and generous interest in other people not only built enduring friendships but laid a foundation for cooperation with boards, agencies, and individuals."

There are letters to the Russell Sage Foundation extolling Campbell and his study. Many letters, too, asking for advice on setting up new schools and on the comparative advantages of mill life for mountain people against rural life. Correspondence covered conditions of health, diet, infant mortality, hookworm, child labor, education, wages, morals, and living conditions.

By May 1910, the rough draft of the study was submitted, but John Glenn suggested that releasing the report might be premature, as it would be beneficial for Campbell to work in proximity with Dr. George A. Buttrick, to have access to the records of the General Education Board in New York. Work continued on the report, with attendant correspondence and conversations, culminating with the Mountain Conference in Atlanta—a representative group, thirty or so, of those working in the mountains. Camp-

bell wrote that he was pleased with the lack of denominationalism and the common accord shown by the group.

How good it was to stay in one place a little while and not be on schedule, catching trains, meeting new people, drawing new conclusions. The little house was a haven where we could put away our clothes and papers, or spread them out when needed; we could relax and eat what and when we wanted. Outside in the yard, March flowers were blooming, and violets of many kinds. Mockingbirds sang in the budding hollies, where a few red berries still lingered. The entries in my Line-a-Day from March 15, 1919—when we arrived back at Demorest—to June 2—when we set forth again—do not make the period sound exactly restful, but in my memory it was a time of peace, sunshine, and accomplishment. Plenty of work to be done, but it was work in which we were vitally interested, and we were eager to be at it.

John was besieged by old friends and old students, eager to shake his hand and tell him how glad they were to see him—perhaps to tell him some of their troubles, too, if he had a moment to listen. College problems were brought to him from the day of our arrival to the day we left. Mr. [Henry Clinton] Newell, now president, was away when we first returned; but Dr. [Charles Flint] Allen, who was left in charge, came in to talk over things almost daily. Mr. [W. E.] Wheeler of Pleasant Hill, on a three-day visit, wanted to talk over many things. Commissioner [Jerry] Pound, up from Atlanta to lead an educational meeting, was interested to have a talk on education for the mountains. Then local problems such as the future of the Fletcher Home—an institution under the general care of the school trustees—called for long afternoons of discussion. In such ways went the first week.

Miss [Ada] Bagwell (John's secretary)'s arrival in the midst of all this was a great help. We drove over to Mt. Airy to meet her train, and thereafter the mornings, at least, were usually given over to writing, the report taking precedence over everything else.[1] The mound of letters awaiting us was only the beginning of a steadily increasing flow of correspondence: queries to be sent out; answers, made to those already sent, to be digested and acknowledged, with their sometime voluminous data; requests for special information; suggestions as to new contacts and possibilities. Mr. Glenn had written that he thought it very advisable for John to attend the Southern Education Conference at Atlanta, April 14–16. "There will be gathered there a number of the best men who are interested in southern educational work, including that in the mountains. It will give you a chance to see more people whom you want to meet than in any other way. Mrs. Glenn and I hope to be there."

He wrote again on March 15th:

Mrs. Glenn has just suggested the possibility of getting together there a few of the people who are especially important in mountain work. What do you think about this? Whom would you like to have?

As to schedules, I feel that they would better wait until we meet in Atlanta. It may or may not be wise to publish your report. I think the best thing to do would be first to prepare a confidential report for the Foundation and then to determine what, if any, part of it should be published. If you could have an outline of your report and the general conclusions shortly before the Atlanta Conference, so that I could look it over before seeing you, it would be a great help in determining our future course. I realize that publishing a report such as you would make would be a very delicate question. Everybody connected with mountain work and the people themselves seems to be sensitive about it. If we are going to accomplish anything, it will have to be done in a very careful and tactful way. I would rather go a little too slow than a little too fast. We need not close up our work at the end of the year if we find there is reason for giving more time to it. That is a matter which we can talk over when we meet, unless it is necessary for you to have the question settled sooner. I am sure that several weeks put in at Demorest in digesting your information will be time well spent.

John was delighted. Mrs. Glenn's suggestion of getting to the conference in Atlanta a few of the people who were especially interested in mountain work appealed to him strongly, and so he wrote to Mr. Glenn, sending him a list of people who might be invited. Mr. Glenn's answer was characteristic:

I have gone over the list carefully and have been thinking about the advisability of inviting a number of people. I have also talked it over with Mrs. Glenn. I am inclined to change my mind.

I feel pretty sure that we would get more out of an intimate meeting of six or eight people who are specially well qualified to speak with authority on our subject than if we have a larger gathering. This small number would talk very freely to each other.

I hesitate very much, as director of the Russell Sage Foundation, to invite anyone to the conference in Atlanta. Your investigation has already stirred up the hope that we are going to give aid to some of the schools and colleges. I enclose a letter which gives clear evidence of this. . . . If I were to send but a number of invitations to workers in the mountain field, it would undoubtedly excite their hopes. They would come to Atlanta with possibilities of grants on their minds. This would affect their method of looking at things and interfere with their value as advisers. It would not be unnatural for them to feel that if the Russell Sage Foundation wants their advice, it ought to pay their expenses.

I would rather, therefore, that you should do the inviting of a few people at your own discretion, both as to choice and as to numbers. They have either met you personally or know about your investigation and would be likely to come if they really feel seriously interested in the proposition. I think it will be important to give a pretty clear intimation that there is no probability of grants.

John followed the advice and wrote personal letters of invitation to Dr. White, Miss Berry, Professor Bruce Payne, Miss Pettit, Principal Burns, President Murdoch, Dr. Duncan, and Bishop Horner, all with "a slight personal reference to the formation of our acquaintance."

Probably he was, on the whole, rather relieved to let the schedules go for the moment, although he knew Mr. [Frederic] Webb would be disappointed. Mr. Webb was finishing up some of the schedules for the Department of Labor, and in his impetuous, whole-hearted fashion had become convinced of the benefits of mill experience. "And so they put our pet schedules in cold storage," he wrote. "Well, do tell! Who cares—we made 'em, didn't we? And they can't be improved." And again, on April 9th, "If you can, without exciting suspicion, secure from your informant, who said 'at least 25 from my immediate environment who had gone to the mills had been morally and financially injured,' the names of some of these people, I will be very much pleased and would like to investigate the cases thoroughly. Personally, I do not believe that many can be found."

What pleased John, and relieved him most, was the hint in Mr. Glenn's letter that the investigation might be continued. He could now go ahead, knowing that what he said at this time was not, probably, his last word on the subject; that he might be able to amplify or modify his statements later on. He would have time to finish, on the basis of the information he had in hand, several days before the Atlanta meeting. He worked, as was his wont, with nervous intensity.

Entries in my Line-a-Day read:

J. busy on report.
J. and Miss Bagwell busy on letters.

We worked all day on report.

The girls (Miss Sheak and Miss Rawn) here in the evening helping; and after they left, J. and I worked past twelve midnight.

Worked all day on report. To bed at twelve.

It was not all work, of course. There were many chances to relax:

March 25. At 4:00 p.m. went walking with Mary Sheak and Isabel Rawn. Got apples at Free's and picked arbutus and galax.

March 28. Had early and pleasant tea with two of the teachers.

March 29. J. and I called on the Butlers, talked to Miss King, then went walking up the Mr. Airy road.

April 2. Late in p.m., J. and I took a little stroll around the lake.

April 5. Sat on the porch for a while in full moon after working in the eve. Miss S. dropped by, and we walked home with her round the lake.

One had to get out! It was something just to be alive with all that breathtaking succession of arbutus, blossoming shad, forsythia, japonica, peach bloom, azalea, dogwood, wild crab apple, and laurel, which make spring in the mountains such a season of unbelievable beauty. Our upper porch was wreathed in purple wisteria, and the two great rose vines of red and yellow, climbing to the second story, made a glory of the simple little house.

It was almost impossible, too, for John to refuse a request to speak to some group, to preach at the Union Church [there in Demorest], to say he could not come to dinner or supper, or play tennis down in the park (his reputation being still high), or take part in an expedition to catch some of the giant bullfrogs whose sepulchral chorus filled the night hours.

In spite of interruptions and diversions, however, the report continued to progress steadily. It was a happy day (April 9, 1909) when he was able to write Mr. Glenn:

I am sending you by registered mail our preliminary report, in sectional form. I include a number of pictures from my personal collection which may help to illustrate some of the conditions touched upon in the report. . . .

I shall bring a copy of this report with me to Atlanta, in case the original arrives too late for your perusal. An accident prevented my mailing this report to you yesterday.

We ourselves followed the report to Atlanta on the 13th, carrying high hopes and several copies of the great work. Mr. and Mrs. Glenn were already there, and conferences between them and John began that very evening. After breakfast together, all four of us went to the main conference session; but I am afraid my own attention, at least, was centered on what Mr. Glenn had said and would say, and what kind of a meeting of mountain workers we would have in the afternoon.

I cannot remember today just who was at that parlor conference; there seems to be no official record. Mr. Burns wrote, regretfully, that he would be in the North; and Miss Pettit, I think, could not come; but the majority of those invited responded—an interesting and interested group. They were pleased to have been asked, pleased to meet each other, and, after the first awkwardness, ready to discuss quite freely. John was very happy; the meeting had gone off even better than he could have hoped—a forerunner, it might well be said, of the Conference of Southern Mountain Workers, which did not actually materialize, however, until four years later.[2]

We went home in high spirits. Nothing was finally settled and could not be until the trustees of the Foundation had had time to consider and vote on it; but Mr. Glenn had indicated that he personally was in favor of another year of investigation. Mrs. Glenn had been more than kind and encouraging, and both were pleased with the gathering of mountain workers. Mr. Glenn sent me a beautiful bunch of roses; we breakfasted and dined together and attended the night sessions of the conference at the auditorium; there was opportunity for several long talks. Altogether, from our point of view, the occasion had been a great success, and we were excited and hopeful.

We were not left long in doubt about the coming year. On April 27th, Mr. Glenn wrote to John:

> I am glad to say our board of trustees yesterday authorized me to ask you to continue on with this work for another year.
>
> I should like to talk over with you, when we meet, the question of salary and expenses. If you have considered what would be a suitable arrangement since I saw you, I should be very glad of any suggestions.
>
> I repeat what I said to you personally in Atlanta, that the Foundation expects to pay the living and traveling expenses of Mrs. Campbell and yourself while you are engaged in this study, wherever you may be. This is to continue until we have a chance to make the new arrangement. Your expenses up to date have certainly not been high.
>
> I feel that if possible we ought to compensate the people with whom

you have stayed from time to time for your board. Please feel at liberty to do whatever you think wise in this connection.

Mrs. Glenn and I both enjoyed being with your wife and you in Atlanta, and we feel that your work has been more than satisfactory. You have gotten more information and gotten it in better shape than could reasonably have been expected.

To which heartwarming communication John answered on April 29th:

I count it a privilege to be permitted to continue the work in which we have become so deeply interested.

We are much gratified that our work is satisfactory. That result has not been reached by our efforts alone, but has been fostered by the intelligent direction and sympathetic interest which have been manifested by you and Mrs. Glenn.

And he meant it. It was not just a polite acknowledgment. No one could have been more considerate or have contributed more than Mr. and Mrs. Glenn to making the study thorough and broad in scope.

The matter of compensation took some time to work out. John was still carrying debts incurred during his illness. Securities, because of the times, were paying little or nothing; and he had not been able to pay off much of what he owed. On May 7th he wrote Mr. Glenn very frankly as to how he stood; it was not a large debt, but debt it was:

I should like, of course, to have a salary large enough to pay my living expenses and to decrease my indebtedness as rapidly as possible. I do not expect Mrs. Campbell will travel with me this next year as much as in the past year, though there are places to which I should like to take her as she would be helpful. Traveling and living will probably be higher unless my work and residence are confined to the mountain sections as in the past; and out of my salary I suppose there would come, properly, the cost of maintaining my home. . . .

As I stated before, I have never made the money side a consideration; the work is first; and in this opinion Mrs. Campbell coincides. I do not, of course, know what my work in this field would seem to you to be worth to the Foundation; and I know that you will not believe that my reluctance to mention a figure is due to any other reason. I am quite willing to leave the matter in your hands, and shall be satisfied with whatever arrangement you may make. Should I find myself unable to meet my obligations on the basis of remuneration you suggest, I will tell you so frankly. I have enjoyed my work greatly and know that I shall enjoy it more during the coming year and feel that I can be of service, which brings its own peculiar compensation.

It was two months before the matter was finally settled.

[Mr. Glenn to JCC]
July 12, 1909

This is to confirm our conversation held early in June with reference to your engagement with the Sage Foundation for another year. I have been away so much that I have been unable to write to you sooner.

We would like you to continue your study of mountain conditions. You will receive a salary of $2,500 a year, beginning May 1, 1909. Your expenses will be paid whenever you are away from your home on business of the Foundation. Whenever you think it important for your study that Mrs. Campbell should accompany you, we will pay her expenses also when away from home.

We had not waited for this assurance to go on with plans and work, nor had Mr. Glenn expected us to do so. He had spoken and written with sufficient definiteness; and as for us, only a major calamity could have turned us from our undertaking. It goes without saying that we were cheered, and encouraged too, by the copies of letters from Dr. Wallace Buttrick and Dr. Wickliffe Rose which Mr. Glenn sent on in his usual thoughtful fashion. Dr. Buttrick, then secretary of the General Education Board in New York City, wrote Mr. Glenn on April 25, 1909:

I have been reading Mr. Campbell's report with very great interest. It is so interesting that I read it through at a sitting and have promised myself the pleasure and profit of reading it again. He is doing a fine piece of work. In particular would I commend his modesty, his open-mindedness, his fine power of distinguishing between things which differ, the way he shies at humbugs and cheap appeal to the emotions, his orderly classification, his appreciation of the value of things fundamental, and his all-around sanity. Wherever he comes up against things that I know about, I feel myself agreeing with him, and so I am disposed to believe what he says and to follow his conclusions when he opens up new things to me. Sometime I want to have a long visit with him.

Dr. Rose of the Peabody Education Fund in Nashville, wrote on May 16:

I have gone over Mr. Campbell's report very carefully. I am impressed with his good judgment at every point. His recommendations appeal to me as being in the right direction.

With reference to the continuation of his work, which seems to me to be eminently wise, I think he would do well to make a thoroughgoing study of the public school, its past history, its present condition, possibilities for its improvement. He will have at this point opportunity for a bit of constructive work. I hope he will also continue his study of the economic basis of this mountain life. This, as it seems to me, is the root of the whole matter. If this mountain life can be organized upon an effective economic basis, the other things which make for civilization will come. Without the economic basis, we may only hope, thorough education, to draw the people away from the mountains into larger lines of opportunity. It seems to me that continued effort in these two lines will accomplish great good.

I am favorably impressed with his suggestion of looking toward the establishment of some organizing agency which could serve to bring together the various agencies which are now at work in this mountain region. I am convinced that much harm has resulted from lack of mutual understanding on the part of these various agencies. Once more I wish to express my appreciation of the temper and the wisdom of this preliminary report.

John had already, when the famous schedules were discarded, put into effect his idea of sending out inquiries, somewhat in the nature of a personal letter, to men who he thought were to some extent qualified to answer them. Here is one, addressed primarily to the heads of denominational boards:

Dear Sir:

For some months I have been visiting the mountain schools of the South in the interest of the Russell Sage Foundation and have been interested deeply in the efforts put forth by the church schools. Wishing to bring before the Foundation in my final report the extent of the mountain school work of the different denominations, I write to ask you if you will kindly fill out the statistical table sent herewith and return it as soon as convenient.

Thanking you for your kindness in this regard, I am

Respectfully yours,

John Campbell

Such queries brought him much information, but it did not take him long to find out that even the schools of one denomination were not always listed by the board to which they were attributed. Some were under boards of education or missions, men's or women's boards, or perhaps were only sympathetically affiliated with a certain denomination. How, for example, was one to know schools of the "Soul Winners Society," or single schools under the Women's Christian Temperance Union of Kentucky, the Federation of Women's Clubs of Georgia, the Southern Industrial Education Association, and the Daughters of the Confederacy? Truly independent or private schools were hardly to be discovered at all unless one happened to hear of their existence.

Writing later, in 1912, to his friend Rev. W. E. Hudson, of the Mountain Work of the Southern Presbyterian Church, he asks:

Please tell me what is meant by the Presbyterial Union of Holston Presbytery. Is it a union of the various branches of the Presbyterian Church jointly conducting these schools? You have set down the following schools—Appalachia School, Conasauga School, Farner School, and Wetmore School—as under the Presbyterial Union of Holston Presbytery. They are set down on the "Exhibit of the Educational Work of the Presbyterian Church in the U.S." as under the Presbytery of Knoxville.

Oh why, why, cannot our boards have one system of management! It would save some of us poor fellows a lot of brain fag. This is not directed to Presbyterians alone, but to denominational control quite generally.

My own denomination is the most remiss in sending me the data that I want.

He found, in fact, that he had embarked on a long investigation, in the course of which board policies were liable to change, individual schools might be shifted or even discontinued entirely, and new ones make their appearance.

If statistical data were often unsatisfactory, a letter like the following, in answer to a query about crime in the mountains, was a real help. It came from a judge in the Kentucky mountains who had just resigned from his office to take up private law practice and was dated April 23, 1909:

> I doubt whether I am able to answer the letter fully; on two or three questions you ask me, I have had a divided opinion, or rather, my opinion has been changing from time to time as new developments come to my knowledge. I do not think that crime is on the increase in the mountains of Kentucky—rather, I think that there has been a steady improvement throughout all of the thirty or more mountain counties in Kentucky during the last decade.
>
> The only form of crime that has been on the increase is that of corruption in elections and ordinary elections and such crimes as are closely connected therewith. I believe that corruption in the way of bribery and the use of liquor in elections has had a constant increase for the last twenty years. I know of no circuit judge in the mountains of Kentucky who has any hope of reelection except through corruption in its vilest forms. There may be exceptions to this, and I hope there are; I only say that I know of none such.
>
> The church schools have undoubtedly been a blessing to the extent that enlightenment and wholesome Christian teaching tend to lessen crime. To that extent, I think one may say that the church schools have helped to decrease crime; but the church schools are only a drop in the bucket. They do not reach the great mass of the people, and they cannot reach them. With very rare exceptions, people of the Baptist faith will not profit by the teaching of the Methodist or other denominational faiths; but the great mass of the mountain people have a great leaning to the Baptist faith. It follows, therefore, that in order to get the best measure of success through denominational schools, the Baptists should have the larger proportion of such schools when the fact is, they have the lesser proportion. I believe that the educational salvation of the mountains of Kentucky, Tennessee, North Carolina, and Georgia will come at last through the public schools—the grades and high school for such communities as can afford it and the county high school as provided now by law for Kentucky, sustained by local taxation.
>
> It seems to me that denominational schools must necessarily be limited to the few, whereas education by state and county authority, if backed up by reasonable compulsory attendance laws, would reach the great mass of the people. I do not mean by this that I am against the denominational school; rather, I realize its limitations.

Not all answers evidenced as much wisdom and education and thought as this, though some showed considerable ability to set forth conditions.

Will say, as to industrial conditions in this part of the mountain region, "There is nothing doing." A feeble effort to start an industrial school at X or other point in this county has been made, but nothing has come of it so far. Agriculture is in a very primitive state of development, while the possibilities are almost unlimited. Education is in a bad way; the state is trying to make some changes, but the progress is slow. We need better teachers. We need graded schools. We must have higher ideals stimulated. We have plenty of latent talent. Politically, we are standing off like a whipped child with our finger in our mouth, refusing to have anything done for us.

Another explained:

Well, I don't understand you very well. County is a bad Republick County, but us demacrats tries to hold them down some. Religion has gone down hear a good deal. There is a crank of religion they call sanktifacation that has heart the country a great deal. Our school is in bad shape. The whole country is taught by womens or young girls so the schools hant no count. There is a sight of tobacco rased in —— County, it is a tolable good farming country, some cole and timber yet, no tolable water corses hear. The —— R/R runs thoe the center of the county. Thare is a big saw mill at ——. They have a fine boom and cach logs that they by at the head of the River.

To a third correspondent, the "Sage Foundation" referred to in the letter of inquiry could mean but one thing—broom sage! He therefore obligingly answered that there wasn't much sage around where he lived, but he thought there was a good foundation for raising it.

At this time, too, began the long correspondence with many different people at home and abroad in regard to the Danish folk schools, first called to his attention by Dr. C. C. Claxton, then superintendent of secondary education in Tennessee. His first answer, dated April 30th, came from the American consulate general, Copenhagen:

These folk schools (Folkehøjskoler) are schools for men and women established for the special purpose of making good citizens of the pupils.

The main subjects are native language and history, world history, physics, writing, and arithmetic; gymnastics is also an important feature. Agricultural and horticulture departments are often connected with these
schools.

The Danish folk schools are established by private initiative and are
therefore owned by either private persons or stock companies, but since
1851 they have also received a yearly subsidy from the state.

It is required that the pupils stay at the school and board with the manager; the daily social intercourse between teachers and pupils is considered
of the greatest importance. . . . From 1844 to 1896 about 125,000 men
and women have frequented these folk high schools, and this figure is constantly increasing.

This rather brief and not entirely correct statement was gradually supplemented
from a number of sources, and slowly a truer picture of the folk schools began to
unfold. It was a short-term school for young adults, intended not to impart exact
knowledge for its own sake, but to *awaken, enliven, enlighten*—awaken to new
ideals; keep purposes alive and in action; and directed, with increasing percep-
tion of values, to the good of community, country, mankind. If such schools, John
thought, without academic requirements, examinations, or credits, could have had
such a profound influence in bringing about the high level of rural culture in Denmark—an intelligent and aspiring citizenry and a cooperative organization mar-
veled at by all who studied it—might they not have a suggestion for rural education
in the mountains? Just what the Danish schools were like, how they were managed
and taught, was less clear, even when explained in considerable detail by J. Christian Bay, a Danish scholar, librarian of the John Crerar Library in Chicago, and
once head of a folk school in Michigan.[3] Personality was said to play an important part in the teaching; and the spoken or "living" word—the word of an aspiring, inspiring personality—carried a power far beyond that of books or the "dead"
word. John himself could believe this; but he realized after reading all he could find
on the subject that there was a certain vagueness about it all; it would be difficult
to convince others who had not been thinking along such lines of the educational
value of such teaching, so different from the usual American idea of education. He
must see for himself before he could speak with requisite authority. "You may be
interested," he wrote Mr. Glenn on May 24th, "to know that in a letter received
today from Stockholm, Sweden, I learned that there are in Nebraska, Minnesota,
and Iowa people's high schools founded by Danish immigrants on the pattern of
such schools in Denmark.

Mr. Glenn, always open-minded about the possible value of new ways and means, agreed that it would be well to visit the folk schools in this country and learn all one could about them. He suggested also that we both visit, as interesting and suggestive places, the Ontario Agricultural College at Guelph, Canada, and MacDonald College near Montreal next fall when they would be in full session. He thought it would be wise for John to accept an invitation to deliver an address at the National Conference of Charities the last of May in Buffalo, and greatly approved his stopping off in Washington to see the commissioner of labor and to consult with Gifford Pinchot (then with the Forest Service of the US Department of Agriculture) as to the effect of the Appalachian Forest Reserve on the life of the mountain people. In due time Mr. Glenn forwarded Mr. Pinchot's comments written to him on June 15th:

> Just a word to say that I have not only read Dr. Campbell's report with very great pleasure, but have seen Doctor Campbell himself, and have established what are to me very pleasant relations. I liked the report. It is not final, as Doctor Campbell himself says, and its conclusions are, therefore, not conclusive. But there is a lot of keen observation in it, and I am sure it is valuable. The only possible criticism I could make is that the treatment is a little distant—lacks intimacy and close contact with the problem—but that is manner as much or more than matter. It is a good piece of work, I believe. In particular I was glad to read what is said about the forest problem.

Both Mr. and Mrs. Glenn had been greatly intrigued by my ballad discoveries, which continued whenever I had an opportunity to hunt for singers. I even discovered a few near Demorest, but my great ballad experience had to wait until John, who wished for a closer view of conditions in North Georgia, decided to make a trip up into Rabun County. One of the Piedmont girls, Della Moore, whose home was in Rabun, had told me of her mother's singing, and I was all agog to hear her. Mary Sheak, the youthful matron as well as domestic science teacher at Piedmont, wanted to visit her girls in their homes; and Isabel Rawn, fresh from Wellesley, was full of enthusiasm over the idea of finding really old ballads still being sung. John, Mary Sheak, and I made ready to go on horseback. Isabel took the branch railway to Franklin, which passes through both Demorest and Rabun Gap. We planned to meet at the Moores'.

Our start was hardly propitious. Not many miles from Demorest, we had to ford a small stream. Miss Sheak idly loosed her rein to let her horse drink, and he promptly lay down in the creek with her. She mounted again, and we continued on our way, though the weather had turned dark and stormy. We did not reach a stopping place till 8:30 p.m. The next day it rained again. Poured in thundershowers all the afternoon. Still we valiantly pressed on. At last the rains ceased and May 1st dawned. "A glorious, shimmering, windy morn of fresh greens and deep sky. Off early through woods and over mountain of wonderful beauty. Arrived at Della Moore's in time for dinner."

What a day that was! The Moores—widowed mother and two daughters—lived in a little log house at the foot of a mountain about two miles up the valley from Rabun Gap center. A wilderness of rhododendron and laurel almost smothered one of the two swift branches which flowed down either side of the cabin; the other branch ran open to the sun. The last thing I heard at night was the rushing of the water, and above it, in the morning, the songs of birds.

The songs of birds, yes, but no birdsong could have haunted my dreams as did those songs which Mrs. Moore sang to us. "She sings the really old ones," Isabel Rawn greeted me, "all about the little penknife ['The Cruel Mother,' Child 10], lily-white hands ['Lord Thomas and Fair Ellinor,' Child 19], and milk-white steeds and brothers all wallowing in their own blood ['Earl Brand,' Child 4]. Mrs. Moore, please sing her about the proper tall young man, who took part of my father's gold and half of my mother's fee. You know—the one that has 'Hush up, hush up, you old vilyun' ['Lady Isabel and the Elfknight,' Child 3]."[4]

And Mrs. Moore sang—not without considerable urging, for she was sensitive about the absence of her teeth. She needn't have been; her voice was sweet and true and her words distinct in spite of the fact that she covered her mouth with her hand. She told me she had never worn anything in the winter but homespun—her own weaving; the sample bits of plaid homespun she gave me were beautifully done. My Line-a-Day tells me that John made a number of visits on this trip; doubtless he gathered data of value. For me, however, there was never to be another singer quite like Mrs. Moore. Her memory had remained green through the years; her songs remain the best I have collected. "Mrs. Campbell's great singer," Cecil Sharp was to say later, explaining that while a collector might pick up isolated songs, usually there was in a neighborhood one great fountainhead from which the others drew or had drawn. This I found to be true as my experience increased.[5]

The past months of travel, study, and broader acquaintance had given John not only a far more objective and balanced point of view but a confidence and authority he had not enjoyed previously. He was becoming an authority on mountain matters, while his engaging personality and generous interest in other people not only built enduring friendships but laid a foundation for cooperation with boards, agencies, and individuals. He had never felt happy that he had not been able to finish raising the endowment at Piedmont, and now that he was not employed by the American Missionary Association but by the Russell Sage Foundation, he felt free, as he had not before, to bring Piedmont's position to the attention of the AMA. He wrote to H. Paul Douglass, DD, superintendent of education and an old Andover acquaintance, on May 7, 1909,

> I have wished very often during the past year that your work would call you to the region in which I have been carrying on my study, for I have wanted to talk over many things with you.
>
> The Sage people have asked me to continue my work with them, and I am hoping that I may have the privilege of looking into some phases of mountain life with you during the year to come.
>
> One of the particular things of which I wished to speak is the situation here at Demorest. As an old AMA worker and as a trustee of Piedmont College, I am deeply interested in the progress of the work here. I have, by reason of this year's work, a basis of comparative judgment, and I feel more strongly than ever that there is a splendid opportunity here, if rightly grasped. The thing that has been needed above everything else is a policy upon which our northern leaders and our southern leaders and the men here upon the ground could agree.

After pointing out different reasons in favor of developing Piedmont, he concludes: "What you will be able to do, of course, I do not know. I know that the demands upon the Association are great, but is there not some way by which this endowment can be secured? Newell is coming to New York, and I am sending this letter in the hope that you gentlemen in the office and he will be able, jointly, to find some way by which the deficit this year on current expenses may be lifted in part, and the endowment secured."

Douglass answered on May 20th:

> I thank you for your letter of May 7th in regard to the Piedmont situation, which, with other similar statements, was before the Executive Committee at its last meeting and also before the Finance Committee, to which the matter of immediate steps toward the solution of the difficulty was referred . . . As a result . . . the Finance Committee approved a plan for immediate relief, the details of which will be communicated to you by President Newell. . . . Let me assure you that your statement of confidence

in Piedmont and its opportunity, in view of your comparative study of mountain schools, weighs very heavily with me in favor of the institution.[6]

We spent the summer in the Kentucky mountains. John was in the saddle most of the time, crossing and recrossing that rough country which lies between the Bluegrass and the Big Sandy Valley. I stayed at Oneida for the first part of the time with Ada Bagwell, John's nephew Gavin, and my sister Daisy G. Dame, who had promised Mr. Burns that she would start a kindergarten for him. It was a pleasant spot on the South Fork of the Kentucky River, where as a young man Mr. Burns had spent those exciting days which he had described to us, running rifles down the river on a raft in behalf of his family side of a big feud. Those days were over now; his school was built, and he was looking for new and better ways of teaching—"the only way to stop feuds." He was not in Oneida for much of the summer, but with or without him, we took part in the life of the little community, fishing in Red Bird and Bullskin creeks, setting trout lines, picking blackberries and wild plums, calling on neighbors, "washing with the men,"[7] attending preachings, funerals, or picnics, as might be, and doing all the things one can do so pleasantly in the mountains in the summer. Ada Bagwell was regularly occupied with her typing, while between times I continued, with the help of my sister, gathering local history and ballads wherever we could find them.

On July 16th, John started back to London to meet Dr. Livingston Farrand, executive secretary of the National Tuberculosis Association. He had promised that he would take him on a horseback trip through the Kentucky mountains so that he could observe general conditions. The night of the 18th the two came riding into Oneida together in excellent spirits, having visited sundry physicians and teachers on the way. On the 21st, John wrote to Mr. Glenn: "We start for Hindman, via Buckhorn, with Dr. Farrand tomorrow. I met him in London last Saturday and arranged for conferences with some physicians and teachers. I think he is interested in the situation and purposes some betterment work. I shall take him out to the railroad at Beaver and return to Hindman to visit schools in that vicinity, and will work back this way."

Eager to get back to my first ballad field, I decided to go as far as Hindman with them, taking Gavin along. So, at 9:00 a.m. July 23rd, one day late, we got off, "all the crowd out snapping pictures and watching our progress. I rode the brown mule, with Gavin up behind; John on the stylish black, and Dr. F. on the old brown horse. Gavin had a hard time to keep seated at first, and clutched me about the waist frantically with many adjurations not to go fast. However, he got settled after a bit and really behaved quite heroically, considering the uncertainty and discomfort of his position.

Dr. Farrand, slim and good-looking in his khaki, proved a delightful companion. We rode along very merrily "up Bullskin, across Buffalo, over Whoop-for-Larry Hill (very steep it was, too), and down Squabble Creek twelve to fifteen miles to Buckhorn, arriving at about 1:00 p.m." Off again at 7:30 a.m., we rode "up Gay's Creek to Chavis and down to the Middle Fork through pretty country; up Grapevine twenty-four miles to Hazard; thence by Dwarf to Hindman twenty-one miles without a stop. Pretty tired. Three doctors in the evening, to meet Dr. Farrand."

A small conference ensued when Mr. and Mrs. Murdoch followed close on our heels, with Mr. [James B.] Kinnaird of Jackson. Health was the main topic of discussion, the Hindman nurse, Harriet Butler, Miss Pettit, and Miss Stone all taking part. Not until Dr. Farrand and John had ridden off on their way to the railroad at Beaver, and the Murdochs and Mr. Kinnaird on their way to Buckhorn and Jackson, could I think of ballads. Even then I could not be quite free until John returned at midnight of the next day. He had covered the last of the long miles in a faint moonlight, his nervous little wire-springed mule shying at every shadow.

Dr. Farrand wrote back with real warmth, but we heard nothing officially of his experience until Mr. Glenn sent on the letter Dr. Farrand wrote him on September 22nd. Touching John and his work, this letter reports:

In the latter state [North Carolina] the State Board of Health and State Board of Education are already planning a well thought out and interesting scheme of regular hygienic instruction in all the schools of the state, which can easily be made to include the plan suggested. Should this beginning develop successfully, we shall endeavor to inaugurate similar campaigns in the other states in question.

I have thought that you might be particularly interested in this information, since its initiation should properly be ascribed to the Sage Foundation through Mr. Campbell.

May I say just a word in closing as to my impressions of Mr. Campbell and his work, gained through very close association and observation of him in the fortnight we spent together. I regard him as a man of quite extraordinary capacity and fitness for the work he has in hand. He shows broad and unprejudiced judgment and uses at all times most remarkable tact in dealing with the somewhat peculiar characters with which he comes in contact on every hand in that region. The consequences are that he had the confidence, respect, and admiration of everyone and is obtaining a fund of information which cannot but be invaluable in all subsequent studies and investigations of the region.

The opinion I formed of him in Kentucky was confirmed by what I heard of him in North Carolina, where he had been investigating a year ago.

You are certainly to be congratulated upon having obtained so unusual a man as your representative.

As I read over the files, I realize how impossible it will be to convey the scope and growing complexity of the study as it progressed, opening up from day to day new phases, new considerations. So many details are interesting in themselves but not important except in their cumulative effect on his thinking. As it happened, the fall of 1909 is a difficult one to summarize. John made the trip to Guelph and MacDonald Colleges recommended by Mr. Glenn; to Ames, Iowa, and Tyler, Minnesota, to visit two of the folk schools started by Danish immigrants. Unfortunately, the Tyler school was not in session, so he could only talk with the principal. He stopped at a number of points in Wisconsin, and on his way south made a short detour through the Ozarks in Arkansas in order to visit a successful Italian colony at Tontitown.

Continuing his journey into Alabama, he had, as he wrote Mr. Glenn on November 30, 1909, "a helpful talk with H. D. Gunells, the state superintendent of education." He wrote further: "He appears to be a broad-minded man, and sympathetic with every effort that looks toward betterment. He seemed to think what I had come to feel was very important—that the greatest need in the mountains is a permanent effort for keeping alive a public sentiment for better things. Whirlwind campaigns are helpful, he thinks, for arousing sentiment for the enactment of legislation, but a continuous local effort, stimulated from without, is needed to make such legislation effective."

With such thoughts in mind, he crossed over to his old school on Sand Mountain at Joppa, Cullman County. Here he was greeted with touching affection, but his meditations as he looked about him were tinged with melancholy not entirely due to old memories. What had this work into which he had poured all his youthful enthusiasm accomplished? "There have been remarkable changes," he wrote Mr. Glenn in the November 30th letter, "due very largely to the introduction of soil-making crops." He makes no reference to the school, though later he spoke many times of finding one of his girls teaching "the same kind of school I had taught her to teach." Albertville, where the District Agricultural School was situated, was not far away, and he drove over for an interview with the president. His letter continues:

From there I went to Boaz, where the Methodist Episcopal Church has a school of about four hundred students. They have a forty-thousand-dollar dormitory and are doubtless doing good work. I asked the question as to whether they were needed, within six miles of such a flourishing school as Albertville, which has seven hundred students. The reply—a reply I receive often—was that the state schools exert little influence over the characters of their students, do not maintain control over the student body, and that the church schools reach a very needy class that is not reached by the state schools, and for whom the state schools have made no provisions in the way of scholarships, etc. The president of the Albertville school frankly admitted the lack implied by the criticism last mentioned above and has a plan by which the state can reach such needy students. He has promised to submit this plan to me.

I was interested to learn of your succession of visitors from the mountain schools. I have not come to a definite conclusion, as yet, as to the wisest methods of help, but they should be along lines not antagonistic to state effort but cooperative with it, and along lines of neighborhood betterment, which the state cannot as yet, and perhaps never can, foster.

Mrs. Campbell wishes me to say that she is at work upon the ballads and will endeavor to send some of them to Mrs. Glenn before the holidays.

The last comment was to indicate that I was struggling to put my tunes in some sort of form which could be read by a musician—a difficult task for me, who had had no training in such notation. I did, however, finally send to New York, after much painful effort, a bunch of manuscript, which Mr. and Mrs. Glenn passed about to a number of interested friends.

Our letters, mine as well as John's, always received most careful attention from Mr. and Mrs. Glenn. Mr. Glenn wrote John on February 8, 1910:

I read some extracts from the letters at the meeting of the Southern Education Board the other night, and they excited much interest and led to a very interesting discussion. I wish you had been there to see the interest in the mountain problem and answer some of the questions that were asked. Mr. Claxton showed special interest and seemed to know more about the situation than anyone else.

Miss Pettit, Miss Stone, Miss Holman, and Mrs. Wetmore are all here. Mrs. Glenn had them to lunch the other day, with three of our lady trustees. The latter were much interested. I shall be glad to hear what you gather in your trip through the Carolinas.

Before this could be answered, John heard from Miss Pettit. In her letter of February 21, 1910, she said:

So often lately have we wished that we could have a chance to "get some counsel" from you and Mrs. Campbell. You know by this time what has happened at Hindman. Our home and schoolhouse have been burned . . .

Miss Stone and I want you to tell us exactly what you would do in our place. I do not know of anyone whom I consider more capable of advising us. You know what we have done and the ideals that we have for the work that we have not been able to carry out. I am tired of unrealized ideals. . . . This is what you are to tell us, shall we go on with our work there. . . .

I shall be grateful for any word from you and hope that you will not hesitate to be very frank and offer any criticism that you have of our work and plans.

John replied to Miss Pettit on March 2nd:

I appreciate greatly the evidence of your confidence in my judgment but feel that you overrate it greatly. The questions you ask are very important ones and should be considered very carefully in the light of future development in the mountains. I hesitate to give you anything as final, and it is not as a full conclusion that I express my opinion. I do not, of course, know all the local conditions and influences of association and sentiment that may enter in, but when you ask me what I would do under the same circumstances, I cannot but give you some of the questions that I would consider seriously before coming to any definite decision.

I would, first of all, ask myself whether I could approach more nearly to the realization of my ideals in Hindman or elsewhere. Should I desire to stay in Hindman, I would ask myself whether my present position was strategic and hygienic; whether there was room enough or a sufficiently desirable area available and adjacent to the present site. One of the strong reasons in my judgment for going elsewhere is the one you have already advanced—that Professor Clark's school is also in Hindman and serves a certain need which you would not care to duplicate. County high schools seem to be a future possibility and, as a general thing, will probably be placed in the county seats. I should ask myself seriously whether the reestablishment of the school in Hindman proper would make for or against the growth of a county high school. Should not the people give toward the establishment of such a school as well as to the rebuilding of yours with a somewhat questionable policy of an alliance between your school as an independent or semiboard school and what would be a strictly public enterprise? If these considerations, and others that I may not have touched upon, would seem to me to be of sufficient weight to warrant removal to another section, I should expect and require the community in which the school was desired to give substantial evidence of that desire in the way of land and money.

The question of what reasonable possibility existed for a normal country life in the mountains was beginning to loom large in John's mind, stimulated by the discussion which had begun at Fred Webb's on the comparative advantages of mill life for mountain people as against rural life in the mountains. Personal investigation of the mills, for which Fred Webb had argued so earnestly, had to wait into the new year, 1910. It was a "secondary and incidental study" and at best could only be superficial, but John was observing and considering the whole matter for two or three years, in the course of which he wrote hundreds of letters, visited many mills and mill villages, and held numerous interviews with mill men, state commissioners of labor, teachers, doctors, ministers, and others. Letters to Mr. Glenn during this period contain the gist of his findings as they took form—covering conditions of health, diet, infant mortality, hookworm, child labor, education, wages, living morals, etc. In one of March 2, 1910, he said: "My feeling at present is that the situation is looked at too narrowly. . . . There are hundreds of mills; they differ in conditions in different parts of the same state. . . . There are mills where the living conditions of the people and their homes are as bad as anything I have seen in the mountains. There are others where the buildings are better and the sanitary arrangements better; but people earn more money, but they do not seem to save anything, speaking generally."

A week later, on March 9th, he wrote Mr. Glenn a detailed commentary on various factors, concluding:

I am very confident that much more can be done, agriculturally and horticulturally, in the mountains than has been thought possible heretofore. The movement to the mills will probably continue, but much can be done to help the mountain people who go to the mills by the right kind of betterment work. . . . The question of enforcing betterment is a hard one for the mill men, because the mountaineer is very independent. He is let alone to follow his own inclinations very largely in most matters, especially when the demand for labor is great. Very little, comparatively speaking, can be done with these fathers and mothers, and I find myself driven to the conclusion that this whole question between rural and mill life centers in the child. It is a many-sided question but finally resolves itself to the answers one gives to these considerations:

Whether an out-of-door life, with some approach to the normal life of the child even under depressing limitations, or an artificial life of labor indoors, with some attendant benefits, is better. I can but feel that enough of the limitations in the out-of-doors and near-normal life can be removed so as to make it more beneficial, in totality of effect, for the mountain child than the most promising artificial life.

A carefully balanced statement of his conclusions is contained in a reprint of a speech, "From Mountain Cabin to Cotton Mill," which he delivered at the Ninth National Conference on Child Labor, held at Jacksonville, Florida, March 12–17, 1913. After disposing of various angles of the question, he gives figures showing that the mountain people form a very small percentage of the total number of mill operatives. He asks, Why defend the mills by putting forth the limitation of mountain life, when

all the mills of the South, if manned entirely by mountain operatives, would affect less than one-third of all the rural mountain population in only five of the eight states, and when in point of fact only a small fraction of the total 250,000 operatives are mountain people? . . .

The real questions, therefore, are not whether the mountain fraction of operatives is better off in the mills than in the mountain environment. The questions at issue are these: Are the conditions now existing in the mills all they ought to be? Is the employment of children in gainful occupations right? Ought the unrestricted employment of women in such industries as the cotton textile industry to be allowed?

If we all will but open our eyes, we shall see that there is a nationwide rural question in this land of ours, and not one pertaining to the highland section of the South alone.

All this time we had been collecting data on the ancestry of the people now living in the mountains. John had been interested in this from his early days in Joppa, as his lists of names compiled there show. He also noted words obsolete elsewhere, or with obsolete meanings: *Hit = it; proud = glad; devil = tease; got to studying =*

thinking; aim to = intend to; right smart = very; clever = good-natured. Local and family traditions, prevailing customs and characteristics, ballads and superstitions had given him added ground for deductions. As he went more deeply into the topography of the area and its settlement, he saw that any, even tentative, speculations about the people called for more research than he had time to give. He called upon friends in the mountains for lists of surnames common in their special area, lists of pupils' names in the schools. My sister Daisy Dame, still teaching kindergarten in Oneida, Kentucky, in the spring of 1910, collected names and words, ballads and other evidence of one sort and another, and called on "Brother Burns" for help with local history.

Miss Pettit and Miss Stone at Hindman, Fred Webb at Flag Pond, Dr. R. F. Campbell, "Lawyer" Sondley and Dr. Winston at Asheville, and many others added their aid.

He then enlisted my sister Ruth Coolidge to delve into the volumes of the Boston Public Library and Athenaeum, in pursuit of the Scotch-Irish (illusive because listed usually under *English*) and German immigrants who came to this country in great numbers in the eighteenth century. It involved a long and complicated bit of research, demanding not only the consulting of Revolutionary pension lists, the census of 1790, *Century of Population Growth*, Faust's *German Element in the United States,* and other authorities, but also consultation with John at Demorest on the findings. Incidentally, she stopped in New York on her way south to see if she could secure other information he wanted. John wrote her, on March 7th, before she left:

> The data I want to cover in my report include the number of children of school age, white and black, of both sexes, in each of the mountain counties; average attendance, per capita, of appropriation for school purposes, total appropriation from district, county, and state funds. . . . Number of local tax districts in each county (this will probably be impossible to get), number of teachers, grade and pay of teachers; kind of schools; cost of buildings, equipment, library, etc.
>
> I can get all of these, Ruth, up to date, from the books that I have, so there would be no need of copying all of that stuff from records that are six or eight years old. If there is valuable information along other lines, on the county basis, I should like to have as much of it as you could get in a day or two. Get a fair estimate as to what the material is, and we can see what would be valuable, over and above what I have here, that is up to date. . . .
>
> We are looking forward with much pleasure to your visit. The peach trees and arbutus, as well as the flowering shrubs of the forest, will be in

process of blossoming while you are here, and we shall have some very pleasant outings together, as well as pleasures in work.

She arrived, in her usual radiant health, ready for work or play. My Line-a-Day, March 20–April 20, 1910, is full of "Ruth and John busy on report." When he was away on frequent trips of investigation, she labored on and checked with him on his return. It was not always easy for her, for he wanted exact statement and proof of every conclusion. He was, too, meticulous in choice of words. I can see the two halted over a disputed phrase: he with blue-gray eyes shining, wavy gray hair erect, hand emphatically gesturing as he protested that the word she had used did not exactly express the meaning he had wished to convey; she, pink-cheeked, bright-eyed, and a little on the defensive, would explain her reason for her choice and her willingness, nevertheless, to defer to his wish.

It was by no means all work, however. My Line-a-Day records some tennis almost every day with various partners (sometimes John played his old brilliant game), lovely walks for crab apple blossoms, violets, and dogwood, or wider vistas of the mountains. My mother came on the 9th, bringing a young friend, Rosamond Ritchie, as traveling companion, for a few days. Then the festivities became even more lively.

I find among Ruth's letters home one dated April 12, 1910: "Went to a church social supper, where the ladies of Demorest compete in making the most delicious cake. Afterward there was some pretty poor music until mother was asked to play. Then I sang 'Holy Night' and Olive 'O Sole Mio,' in a burst of applause; and then both of us, 'Why Adam Sinned.' People hadn't realized that Olive sang at all! Such a demure little puss as she is. John was proud as a peacock!"

John, having to go to Atlanta, accompanied Rosamond when she left, and the letter continues: "John came back last night after a gay bout in Atlanta with Rosamond. He certainly gave her a magnificent time. He is an ideal domestic man, for he brought back, besides talcum powder, [peroxide of] hydrogen, and other toilet articles, the following vegetables which cannot be bought in Demorest: cauliflower, strawberries, radishes, lettuce, green peppers, tomatoes, celery, and asparagus! We occasionally get tiny lettuce and asparagus brought in from the country, but Demorest stores carry none of these things."

No wonder we spent the rest of the evening luxuriating in the vegetable basket. Sunday following, April 17th, was apparently a great day, for I record: "Glorious, brilliant day after the rain. Sunday school, and at service, Ruth sang beautifully. Many compliments for herself and mother. Company at dinner, and later John, mother, Ruth, and I took a walk back of Safford's. Azalea lovely. Mountains clear."

Ruth had to leave on the 23rd, going home via Oneida to get more data for John and to see my sister Daisy, who was shortly to come to us and to go home with mother. From Asheville to Knoxville, Ruth traveled over one of the old pioneer routes of which she had read so much in her researches. A letter to her husband, Richard B. Coolidge, dated April 25, 1910, tells of her journey:

The train route follows exactly the winding course of the French Broad. The river, which is broad but shallow, flows along beside the railroad the entire way, and the hills slope abruptly down into the water. The railway has barely a footing along the side of the hills. Now and then the valley widens a little and a cabin catches root on the side with a few acres of scrupulously tilled ground and a little trail leading to the top of the hill. There, though the whole hillside is a mass of trees and precipitous rock, the bare top is just visible where the patient mountaineer has brought the only available land under cultivation. There are only one or two really beautiful spots, with a sheet of green grass, like the fashionable resort Hot Springs, but the rest is wilderness in most beautiful, varying curves. The foliage was so fresh and green or even a pale soft yellow that the leaves seemed blossoms and did not get many glimpses beyond the curving hills with their masses of trees and the sharp bends of the river with other new combinations of hills; but once or twice a vista opened and we saw the mountains with snow resting on their shoulders. As we came slowly out of the steeper hills, a snowstorm rolled over the mountains like a Nantucket fog, turning the hills beneath them to a deep blue almost like the ocean. It was simply beautiful. This is the same cut through the mountains that the pioneers followed from the Watauga settle-ment in Tennessee to and fro from Asheville and the North Carolina moun-tain settlements. It must have taken three hours of steady mountain twisting and turning before we came into the level country of Tennessee and saw the fields white with snow and the storm itself still driving across them. It will certainly work great havoc here among the fruit trees. It is almost ludicrous to see what an interest one gets to have in the success of the fruit down here.

A few days earlier, on April 19th, John wrote Mr. Glenn:

So much has been said of the degenerate stock from which the mountaineer is alleged to have sprung that it seemed best to give some time to an histori-cal consideration of their ancestry. Mrs. Coolidge has looked up the histori-cal data, which I have reviewed as far as I have been able. We have taken up the early settlements of the tidewater sections of the southern Appalachian states, the movement to the frontiers, and the mountain settlement proper.

I think we can substantiate the claim made in my preliminary report, that the dominant strain in the mountain section of the southern Appalachians is Scotch-Irish. There is also a large German element . . . and the English strain is, of course, strongly marked. . . . We have summed up enough evidence of a presumptive nature to warrant the conclusion that many of the people in the mountains today are descendants of this early stock. It is too generally claimed by those who argue in favor of the mill movement that all the mountain people are the offspring of degraded, indentured whites of the Colonial period.

Should you so desire, my conclusions as to the ancestry of the mountain people, together with related questions, could be submitted within a few weeks.

Although Mr. Glenn had written, on April 4th, that the Foundation "would not wish to stop until you have finished your report," it was plain to see that there was still much time-consuming work to be done on it if different phases of the study were to be covered as John felt they should. He wrote Mr. Glenn, roughly outlining his plans. It was a real relief to get word that the trustees of the Foundation had voted to renew the appropriation for the southern mountains study.

[Mr. Glenn to JCC]
April 26, 1910

This enables me to continue our arrangement with you as before, if it is agreeable to you. I think the question of your future work can be left until you have finished your report and we determine what we shall want to do about that.

I suggest that you send me sections of your report as finished. It will be easier to find time to read them carefully and make suggestions as the work proceeds. Your outline seems excellent.

[Mr. Glenn to JCC]
April 28, 1910

Dr. Buttrick and I agree that the best way for you to get the information about public schools, including high schools, is to get it directly from the state superintendents of education. . . .

This process will, of course, take time, but it seems very important to get information that is as recent as possible and be sure that what you have is accurate, even though this may delay the completion of your report. I do not want you to hurry with your report.

The ancestry chapter was not finished as quickly as John had anticipated. Some of the difficulties are suggested in the following extracts from letters he wrote to Ruth Coolidge:

May 11, 1910

I have run across some things that I should like to confer with you about. Olive is going over the card lists and says there are about ten names she cannot account for. She will write you about these.

I am up against a few figures this morning in rereading the proof for Miss Bagwell, but I think I can ferret them out. In the second part of your paper, on pages 64 and 65, you state . . .

On pages 68 and 69, in speaking of the increase of population in North Carolina, you say . . .

In the first place, what do you mean by "in that period"? Do you mean . . . ?

Olive will enclose in her letter a few cards in regard to which I am uncertain. . . .

I shall be glad to receive from you also any deductions from your conversation with Mr. Burns and others in Kentucky as to the mountain population. . . .

Would it be well, do you think, to send a very brief statement further regarding the Scotch-Irish . . . ?

May 17, 1910

I am again puzzled by some of your figures. It would be a great help to me if, at your earliest convenience, you would consult the *Century of Population Growth;* I have found what seem to me a number of mistakes, although I am not sure you took them from the same table.

The trouble is, Ruth, that I do not want to let these figures go in until I am perfectly sure of them, and I write to ask if it will be possible for you to verify all of the figures of the second part if I send you the copy. . . . I want to get this paper out of the way so that I get at my own part without the necessity of shipping all the bulky material I have north for compilation. I may get time to do this myself; still, this week is broken into, and next week I am going to Atlanta in response to a telegram from Mr. Glenn.

May 23, 1910

You are right and I am wrong, and I am mighty glad I am. I went over the figures carefully, at your suggestion, and found that my eyes had played me false, just as you suggested. I think you are very nice not to use the opportunity to give me the Merry-Ha-Ha's. . . .

I am glad, too, to have Fleming's full statement. I am going over it carefully and think perhaps I shall incorporate it all. I do not wish to seem to shut off just criticism of the mountain people, and his statement will give some idea of a certain lowland attitude toward the mountain people. I can modify its effect by a personal statement that I myself had taught in the Sand Mountain region and found many mountaineers who were in the Confederate service. These were later comers, however, and it will bring to the fore the idea that there are today in the mountain region of Alabama certain people needing help, even if we grant full credence to Fleming's estimate of the worthlessness of the Sand Mountain dwellers during the Civil War.[8]

I shall be glad to incorporate also a statement from you, made somewhat prominent, as to the character of the Scotch-Irish. I have no desire to prove any theory in regard to them. The only point I wish to make prominent, if it is a fact (and I believe it to be), is that they are good stock. . . .

If you find any other oversights, I should be glad to know of them. I am getting somewhat stale on the paper. I would have taken my oath that I had looked up those percentages so thoroughly that there could be no mistake, but yesterday, on my return, I looked them up again and found I was mistaken. Such mistakes make it essential that a certain freshness of mind be brought to bear upon all figures.

John was getting pretty tired, and probably it was fortunate that at this point Mr. Glenn wired asking if he could go down to Greensboro, North Carolina, to a health conference. Here he met a prominent speaker on health matters, Dr. Woods Hutchinson, who asked if he could take him on a horseback trip where he could observe health and general rural conditions in the mountains. John interrupted his ancestry labors to do this, enlisting as guide and leader a young Episcopal rector, Rev. Theodore Andrews, who lived at Franklin, North Carolina, and was able to outline a satisfactory four- or five-day expedition. His plans, as outlined on April 13th, still sound very attractive—through some of the loveliest parts of the mountain country:

Day 1. Franklin to Aquone on the Nantahala—22 miles.

2. Aquone to Tusquitee—climb the Bald—8 miles ride, 8 miles walk.

3. Tusquitee to Hayesville—10 miles (Perhaps the doctor could make an address at the Hayesville Courthouse).

4. Hayesville to Slagle on the Nantahala, via Shooting Creek—25 miles.

5. Slagle to Prentiss, via Skenah—16 miles (With an early start, it would be possible to catch the 3:00 p.m. train from Prentiss).

This trip takes in all classes of mountain communities untouched by the railroad. As I have traveled through this region and know many of the people, I feel more equal to conducting a trip thither and am sure the doctor will get a better idea of conditions as they are than if we went to highlands.

The trip was made according to plan. Dr. Hutchinson wrote to John on June 5, 1910:

What a fascinating trip we did have and how cleverly we—and the Clerk of the Weather—managed to compress experience of all four seasons into six days. . . .

I have never stopped talking about the charms of the Georgia mountaintops since I left them, and my memories of crossing the Nantahala Alps—à la Napoleon—and competing with freezing "shorn lambs" for a night's shelter in the Tusquitee valley grow ever more vivid and enjoyable. I have made them into an epic for my small boy, which scored quite a hit with him.

It was during this trip that the travelers came across a little girl with congenital dislocation of the hip. All three men were greatly touched, and John undertook to find out if anything could be done for her. In the file are sixteen letters having to do with the matter. The Board of Health, the specialist in Atlanta, and church philanthropy all agreed to help in her treatment; but when the parents found out the time it would take, the distance and uncertainties, they lost heart and would not let her go.

Two rather important hints as to how things were crystalizing in John's mind are found in the following two letters he wrote to Mr. Glenn:

May 5, 1910

I have just had a long talk with Dr. Douglass, who had recently been promoted to the position of secretary of the American Missionary Association. He asked for an interview some time ago, and while here yesterday on business, we went over the whole mountain situation.

I am encouraged to feel that he is beginning to view the whole mountain question in the light of today's needs. I find that the secretaries of the home missions boards of the various denominations have an interdenominational committee; and if it seems desirable sometime in the future, when matters are further under way, I believe they could be called together in conference on the mountain question.

I have kept in mind the suggestion made either by you or Mrs. Glenn that one of the most important things is to get the different church boards working together on some broad, practical basis. Until recently I have not seen just the opening or opportunity, but it now seems a possibility. When the time seems propitious, I shall bring the whole matter before you.

May 10, 1910

I am sending you also a rough draft, which indicates, in a general way, my idea for mountain betterment. The outer circle represents the object to be worked for—the general mountain welfare. The two innermost circles, the general sources of help to be drawn upon. The means by which these can be drawn upon by mountain schools, workers, etc., in the regions needing help, to be a central cooperation mountain department, with whatever field organization is necessary; these to act as a go-between, by way of advice, publication, and correspondence, and by bringing to the mountains from the outside betterment forces experts to lecture, exhibit, and demonstrate to the people generally and to the local workers the lines of effort best suited to the betterment of their particular environment.

Such extension work as Professor [James P.] Faulkner has indicated I had in mind as a possible method in field organizations to disseminate knowledge in the out-of-way places, and also to arouse and maintain the necessary local interest—the central department to keep in touch with the external and internal forces of betterment; to be the confidential adviser of individuals and schools on the field who wish to know of work in other sections of the mountains that has proved profitable; to give to the field-workers also information regarding outside forces already organized that might be of service to them; and to serve, also, perhaps through the general office of the Foundation in New York, as confidential adviser to those wishing to contribute wisely to mountain work. I feel very sure, too, that such an organization would be helpful in federating and unifying denominational work—not so much directly, perhaps, as through organizations that are now forming for that purpose.

This is, of course, but a rough draft of the kind of activity. It may be necessary, in some instances, to establish independent centers in the mountains. Personally, I feel, however, that the forces already in existence should be tried to the full through some such intermediate agency.

Mr. Glenn felt that it would be better not to undertake any active organization of mountain agencies just at this time, but as he wrote John on May 11, 1910,

I think it would be wise . . . if any special opportunities arise, to take advantage of them if delay would seem likely to prevent your having another good chance. . . .

As I think over the matter of your report, I wonder whether it would not be better if you could bring your material north and work on it either in New York or nearby, so that you could be in close touch with Dr. Buttrick and his records and so that you and I could easily confer as you progress. I put this merely as a question. I realize, of course, that it may be much more advantageous for you to be working in the atmosphere of Demorest.

Mrs. Glenn asks that you will tell Mrs. Campbell that she received letter and the ballads and that she expects to lunch tomorrow with Mrs. Rice and Miss Natalie Curtis to confer about the collection.

Mr. Glenn's suggestion that we might work on the report in the North during the summer, in or near New York, opened to us a happy alternative. We usually spent our vacation time at Nantucket and could, if agreeable, after we had done all the possible sorting of material at Demorest, establish our headquarters there, near enough to New York for John to go on for consultation when needed. Mr. Glenn was quite agreeable to the plan, and we were more than happy, especially I, for whom the island had been a second home since my birth—indeed, a summer home for my family for many years before that important event. My father had fallen in love with it in the two years he had spent there as principal of the high school shortly after his return from the Civil War. My oldest sister, Daisy, had been born there. My father was no longer living, but Mother had bought an old farmhouse, perhaps 150 years old, which stood quite by itself a mile or more out of town on the North Shore, on the edge of the Commons. Here was an ideal headquarters, with room not only for ourselves, secretary included, but for all our data accumulated and accumulating in rather overwhelming fashion. We could continue at will our sorting, studying, and getting into shape; we could bury ourselves in writing, and when we were tired we could run down the grassy lane for a swim in the nearby sea, or walk along the curving beach mile on mile. Sometimes we tramped instead over the wide open, windy moorland where sea salt mingled with the scent of grasses and flowers, bayberry, and clethra. For that matter, the house itself, like the house in the *Master of Ballantrae,* was "full of the scent of moor, song of lark, and sound of the sea in all its chambers."

Under these conditions the final sections of the ancestry chapter progressed rapidly and were duly dispatched, the last of July, to New York. Mr. Glenn, who had just retired to the mountains of Virginia for his vacation, acknowledged the receipt of the different installments but did not read them at once. He wrote me on August 25th:

> It's a wonderfully lovely country just at the foot of the eastern slope of the Blue Ridge, with spurs of the range all around us. It is warm today, but there is a delightful air stirring and everything looks fresh, and lots of birds are making themselves agreeable. This is not as bracing an atmosphere as that of the N.E. coast, but it seems to suit my southern blood better. I had a delightful day in June at Sagamore Beach. I suppose Nantucket is even more so. I hope you and Mr. Campbell are enjoying it and not working too hard. I think it would be an economy of time if you would both for-get mountains and reports and Foundation, and turn your faces entirely toward the great inspiring sea for a good month and come back to the report with a fresh full head of steam on and a change of view. Tell him there's no rush and that a month's holiday is one of the requirements of the Russell Sage Foundation.

It was good as well as kind advice. John should have followed it, for he was not strong; but he was already under full head of steam and could not stop. When his secretary became ill and had to leave in early August, he drafted me—a willing substitute—into her place and went on with his work. I was not much of a stenographer, but I could type after a fashion; and my knowledge of the area was a distinct advantage as we studied maps and folios and verified conclusions. I knew what he was after and could work without supervision, as he wrote Mr. Glenn later, leaving him free for more directly creative work; naturally he could progress more rapidly. How well I remember the piles of topographical and other maps, folios, bulletins, and publications which littered the house and which had to be painstakingly examined before the exacting investigator could be satisfied as to the accuracy of every detail. I felt like a specialist on mountain topography before the summer was over. On August 31st John wrote Mr. Glenn:

> I have under way a section on the topography of the mountain country and the distribution of population. It will not be of great length, but the facts contained therein necessitated a study of practically the entire Geographical Survey of the Southern Appalachians and of Kentucky and West Virginia. It has been a wearing task, and I am glad it is over, but it has paid. I shall be able to submit this, I think, together with distribution of population, according to the census of 1910, by the middle of September. I am receiving a few returns of the 1910 census, but so far they have not been very helpful.

Again he was disappointed. Slow census returns and aggravated hay fever delayed him longer than he had expected. Before Part II was finished, we had moved into an apartment in Boston, where we could easily consult the public library for data lacking. Not until December 20, 1910, did he write Mr. Glenn:

> I am sending you by American Express today the second section of my report. Part I, which you have, is the "Ancestry and Early Settlement of the Mountain People." Part II, which I am sending, deals with the "Topography of the Mountain Country" as it affects its settlement, and the "Distribution of Population" in the mountains today.
>
> The part of this section that deals with the "Distribution of Population" will be supplemented by data based on the 1910 census (when available), and comparisons will be drawn in order that increase or decrease of population may be shown and some conclusions reached as to the influences producing such increase or decrease.
>
> I am to follow this by a summary of the resources of the mountains and a statement of the general condition of the people. That section is to

be followed by one dealing with the remedial agencies and institutions already in the field for the development of resources and for the general betterment of social conditions. The final section will be a discussion of suggested efforts for betterment and my own conclusions, based upon my study, as to what needs to be done.

I regret that this section has taken so long, but as my work progressed, the necessity of an understanding of the resources of the mountain region became more apparent, and a division of that section into regional belts a requisite for such understanding and systematic grouping.

I expect to leave a week from today for Chattanooga. My address is to be given on the morning of the 28th (Southern Education Association meeting). I shall go direct from there to Washington but will return via New York and will stop for your advice and suggestions.

Such trips sound simple on paper. John came home afflicted with boils and exhausted with travel and interviews. On January 17, 1911, Mr. Glenn wrote to me:

I am sorry, though not surprised to hear, that Mr. Campbell has not been well. I felt when he was here that he needed either a rest or more fresh air. I hope that as long as he is not in good condition you can persuade him to take enough rest to freshen him up. It will be a great deal better for his work if he gives up for a few days, rather than if he tries to struggle on when he is not in good shape. There is nothing so detrimental to good work as too much conscience.

He did rest for several days, even did not try to answer letters. Dr. Claxton had written him on January 2, 1911:

I hoped to have an opportunity to talk at some length with you in Chattanooga about your findings in the Southern Appalachians. I was prevented from hearing your paper on the subject. If you have anything in print, I wish you would send it to me at once.

I wish that you would also write me if, after having studied the problem, you believe that my plan for schools for "grown-ups" is feasible and if you think such schools will be helpful. I should also be glad if you will make any suggestions in regard to the establishment and necessary modifications in order better to adapt them to the needs of the people.

John was not ready to pass any final judgments. Perhaps he thought he had not studied the schools carefully enough or thought through the question of adjustments. He tentatively suggested the possibility of choosing certain centers in the mountains to be operative during laying-by time and possibly during the inactive months of winter, when appointees from state universities and agricultural colleges might win the confidence of the communities and give lectures suited to the community's need. Dr. Claxton's reply was prompt and unequivocal:

January 20, 1911

Your suggestion . . . is very good, but I think the school ought to be permanent, with two sessions, very much as they have in the Scandinavian countries—the winter session chiefly for men and the summer session chiefly for women, but both sessions open, of course, to both sexes at any time. I hope to talk this matter over with you sometime soon.

Later (March 27, 1911) Dr. Claxton wrote Mr. Glenn asking if he would send Mr. John C. Campbell to the Jacksonville Conference for Education in the South, to tell the conference something about the educational needs of the mountain people and how they could be met, something John had neither the time nor the strength to do.

John had been working very hard on the "Resources" section of his report, soil being one of the moot subjects. He was enormously excited and pleased to receive from the US Geological Survey a report of the seven-year study, under government direction, of Dr. Leonidas C. Glenn, professor of geology at Vanderbilt, entitled "Denudation and Erosion in the Southern Appalachian Region." He wrote Mr. Glenn about it on February 16, 1901:

I was greatly delighted to have my own views confirmed by a man of scientific training who had studied a large part of the field. The great question that confronted me in seeking to estimate the farming possibilities was that of erosion. This is most extensive in the area studied by Dr. Glenn. He reaches this conclusion, however: "Much of the mountain area is properly agricultural land, and as the population increases, more and more of this area must be brought under cultivation. This means that steeper and steeper slopes must be cleared and that danger of erosion must increase unless improved methods of agriculture are introduced. . . ."

He confirms also a second conclusion that I had reached, that one can no more generalize about agricultural conditions in the mountains than about other conditions in the mountains.

He makes the following statement on this point as to agriculture, "It cannot profitably be a long range or general study," and concludes by saying, "The agricultural lands of the Appalachian Mountains are generally fertile and, if wisely handled, will support safely and permanently a much greater population than now inhabits the region."

It was now possible to go on and finish up the chapter on resources. It was mailed to New York on March 4th, followed March 25th by "The Mountain People and the Cotton Textile Industry of the South," section IV.

In answer to John's query as to when he wished it, Mr. Glenn answered, on March 28th:

There is no absolute date fixed to finish the report. It should be finished as soon as it can be done properly, but it is better to take a little more time in order to make it more complete, if this is necessary; but do not take time merely for the sake of making improvements which are not really essential. My feeling about all these things is that hurry is unfortunate. It not only results in a bad product, but causes more delay in the long run.

It always takes a long time to get these reports into final shape.

In spite of this reassuring letter, the next section, or chapter, no. 4, "School and Church," followed rapidly, on May 13, 1911. It was a relief to get it off. John had had an infected finger, painful and hampering, and I had had an operation for appendicitis, which delayed the coloring of the maps supposed to accompany the text showing regional belts, contour lines, railroads, water courses, county seats, location of schools, and cotton mills. Mr. Glenn had a few general criticisms on the parts already received—to be talked over later—"probably the chapter on ancestry should be condensed, and chapter on resources should be amplified. . . . 'The Mountain People' and the 'Cotton Textile Industry' is capital. I do not know that I shall have any serious comment to make on it. . . . It is better to reserve fuller comment until I see you—probably at the Conference of Charities in Boston."

John agreed heartily: "The chapter on ancestry is altogether too long, but I wanted all the data on record. It should be condensed for the final form." A new government publication had just been issued bringing mineral resources up to date and necessitating his going over the "Resources" section. He went on to say:

When opportunity permits, I shall be glad to have a long talk with you and to receive any suggestions that you may offer. Personally I have wondered if the results of this investigation might not be more far-reaching if the report were to be simply a confidential report to the Foundation and to those inquiring for it. It has seemed to me that there is danger of giving offense to the mountain people and to others by some of the things said that need to be said, but in all these matters your wider outlook will be able to decide what is the wisest to do.

I expect to have the last section finished by the end of this month, or very early in June, though I shall be busy for two or three weeks after that, bringing up to date the information regarding distribution of population in the mountains. I have all the data now as to numbers, rural and urban, within my field, on the basis of the 1910 census, with the exception of figures on one state. This last section need not be held back for that, however.

He continued his work in his usual intense fashion, and I worked, too, at ballads when I was not helping on the report. The ballads had taken up a good deal of my time. I had, with the aid of a musician, finally gotten the music in reasonably good shape—at least so I myself could read it—and had sent it, with the words, to Professor [George] Kittredge and Leo Lewis, professor of music at Tufts; both wrote Mr. Glenn with real enthusiasm about the collection. Under date of March 14, Professor Lewis said:

It is now nearly two years since Mrs. Campbell told me of her interesting work in gathering some of the songs of the southern mountaineers. It required no extensive examination for me to make up my mind that she was in touch with something which had not merely novelty, but great importance from the musico-historical side. It was clear, too, that whereas one might have wished to use purely scientific methods in the gathering of information, those methods were quite inapplicable to the task in hand.

Finding that the beginnings of Mrs. Campbell's records of the music were so incomplete as to make interpretation of them impossible, I made some suggestions which she had doubtless reinforced by suggestions from other quarters, by which records of the songs might be made accurate, or as accurate as they could be made without the use of a phonograph or without the assistance of an expert, whose very presence would certainly vitiate the performance and consequently vitiate the record.

Mrs. Campbell's records are now in a satisfactory state, as is proven by the mere fact that one can, from her records, play the piece in a way which she recognizes to be the correct way, and that is the only practicable test of correctness in this case. I regard it, too, as an amply satisfactory test.

It therefore appears that insofar as this work is complete, we have a substantial and unique contribution to the literature of what might be called "American Aboriginal Music." Of course, the word "aboriginal" does not absolutely apply; but it is not out of place when we consider that the beginnings of American civilization are contemporary with the bringing of these ballads to this side of the Atlantic. I judge that we are in danger of losing, by death and contact with the outside world, the persons and instrumentalities by which these songs are to the present preserved. I hope, therefore, that Mrs. Campbell will find the opportunity to give the results of her investigation to the public. I know that German scientists who have spent so much time upon Indian music would greet with delight a record of this sort. I have no hesitation in giving my professional opinion as to the general importance of the material, and am glad to give my personal opinion that anything which Mrs. Campbell would authorize as a result of her investigations would be genuine and true.

Professor Kittredge's letter bore the date of March 16th:

I have examined with great care the remarkable collection of songs and ballads which Mrs. Campbell has made in the mountains of the South.[9]

The collection is of real interest and importance. The subject of folk songs is now attracting attention among scholars and investigators both in this country and in Europe. It concerns students of literature very directly; and it is also of much consequence to those who are interested in social conditions. Harvard University has recently made two grants of money to Professor Lomax of Texas to assist him in gathering such material among the cattle men of the South and West.[10]

The collection made by Mrs. Campbell ought to be printed, so as to be made accessible to the world. The music should accompany the words. Mrs. Campbell has an unusually sympathetic attitude of mind toward these people and has had uncommon success in inducing them to sing to her. In a few years, this oral material will have perished. She has rescued a good deal of it, and the results of her efforts should be perpetuated. . . .

I should be glad to give you any further information about this aspect of the matter that you may desire. I feel that it is my duty—as a professional student of literature and as a good American—to do what I can to bring about the publication of these extraordinarily interesting songs.

Mr. Glenn was properly impressed as to what he called "the exceptional value" of the material and the importance of publishing it, but he did not feel sure as to what would be the best method of publication—through an outside publisher or through the Russell Sage Foundation. For me it was important, he said, "at the earliest possible moment" to get the music into proper form; and if it required expenditure of money, he thought the Foundation would be glad to supply the funds. I did not feel like accepting this until the question of who was to do the publishing was settled; but I did continue, as fast as I could, to work on the music and on an introduction which would give a mountain flavor to the collection.

The final chapter of John's report—"Conclusions," no. VI—was finished June 4; and John carried the whole precious package to the post office in the afternoon. Many additions and corrections would have to follow, he knew, but the big work was done and he was full of relief and joy. Now the question of publication must be settled and the bigger personal one of his future work.

It was almost the eve of the big Conference of Charities and Corrections in Boston; Mr. Glenn would be there, and he would discuss these matters. John went in to meet him with suspense and anticipation. It was a gala week, with many celebrities on the program—Jane Addams and Louis D. Brandeis among them. The Glenns were there and Carl Kelsey; Hindman, Oneida, and other friends. John was much with Mr. Glenn; and when at last the sessions were over and the lunching, the dining, and entertainments, he knew that he had a permanent place on the Foundation staff, the question of the exact character of his work to be settled in the fall. He was to go on and complete the report, and then they could talk about its publication.

We went again to Nantucket for the summer, the first part a real vacation. By the middle of July we were again at the report, which moved along rather slowly as we revised it to include data from the US Census of 1910. We did not hear from Mr. Glenn for two months. Then came his letter of September 15: "As it has been some time since I heard from you, I would like to know what you have been doing during the summer and what you are doing at present. I would also be glad to have any suggestions you have to make as to the future."

John replied, telling how with new 1910 census returns available, he had supplemented in detail—county by county—his figures for "Distribution of Population." "I have gone over the figures several times myself; and Mrs. Campbell, as well as the stenographer, has been over them all at least once. It may be best, however, to have an expert statistician go over the whole. . . ." This chapter was now done, except for copying. Chapter II, "Resources," had also been checked and was under way for amplification. The cotton-mill section was ready, with corrections on the basis of the 1910 census. "I shall be busy with the rest of the work for another month at least, as the changes in these chapters necessitate change in others. There have also taken place within the last year transfers of church-school properties from one board to another." John then went on to say:

As to the future, there are several things that I should like very much to do. In the way of investigation, I should like to inquire carefully into the effect of the opening of coal mines in West Virginia and southwest Virginia upon mountain life, and then to write a chapter which would be a sort of companion chapter to the chapter on the "Mountain People and the Cotton Textile Industry," and could be called, possibly—"The Mountain People and the Devil of Coal and Iron Mines." I have learned through acquaintances formed this summer something of the situation brought about in the mountains—West Virginia especially—by the introduction of foreign labor and Negroes, and I now have access to state officials and church leaders in West Virginia that I had not before. The study seems of especial interest and importance in its possibility of throwing some light on the coming situation in Kentucky and the Cumberland Plateau.

It seems also of vital importance, if good is to come to the mountains, that those working to solve its problems should confer one with another. I have received somewhat encouraging reports of the Maryville Conference this year and feel that it might easily be made to exert a much wider influence. The time seems somewhat propitious for endeavoring to bring it about. I have understood that the denominational note is now sounded to a much less degree in these conferences than formerly and that there is evidenced a disposition to broaden its scope. I should like to work carefully toward that end after conferring with you as to ways and means, some of which I have in mind.

The Holman Association and the Southern Industrial Education Association (with headquarters in Washington) have also asked for conferences a number of times. I should like to talk over with you, after the work immediately in hand is over, the advisability of meeting with their directors, as has been asked.

Dr. Claxton expressed a desire earlier in the summer to talk over with me matters pertaining to the mountains, and I should very much like to keep in touch with him in the hope that in his new position he may be able to further educational plans in the mountains. He is especially interested in the folk school, and there is enough in the idea, it seems to me, to warrant a careful study of it in its native environment. I should like myself to do this sometime—but not just now.

The furtherance of the suggestions I made in my concluding chapter that seem wise or in keeping with the plans of the Foundation would be other things that I should like to attempt.

It was a red-letter day when, after a morning of stiff work, we finished the report—December 9, 1911. John took it into town and got it off by American Express. He followed it with a long letter to Mr. Glenn on December 11th—largely a recapitulation of what he had written in September. The main points stressed were:

1. Whether it was wise to publish the report if the Foundation was going to undertake constructive action on the basis of the findings; and if wise, how this might be done in a way to minimize resentments.
2. Suggestions as to what form "constructive action" might take.
3. Importance of searching out ways and means by which denominational and private schools might work in greater harmony with state movements for better public schools.

Enlarging on the last point, the December 11th letter said:

Dr. Claxton [then US commissioner of education] and the state and county officials would be in the foreground in this public movement for better public schools, and the rest of us who are interested and who know more or less about the situation would only be guests helping upon request. More could be done directly through me or someone else, in bringing schools, not public, into line and in helping private and general betterment agencies not under federal or state control into touch with these more general movements, and in bringing about conferences to promote a much needed interrelation and coordination of work.

I am very glad that I have been able at last to send you the report. It has been arduous and nerve-racking at times, but I have enjoyed it thoroughly.

As I look back over the three years with their many delays incident to establishing facts and to the consequent prolongation of the study, I am reminded anew of your patience and consideration and the uniform thoughtfulness and kindness which have removed many difficulties and which have rendered the conditions under which the work was done easy and pleasant.

Permit me here to express my sincere appreciation.

As a result of John's report and of his outline of further study and services he hoped to carry on in the mountains, the Russell Sage Foundation now contemplated setting up a new department to undertake an extended program for the mountains. There was a natural delay in getting the new department under way. Mr. Glenn wanted an outline of the plan of work which John thought advisable; and John was as specific as he could be, considering that plans were necessarily of an experimental and evolutionary character, dependent on the tact and initiative of the one who was to carry them into action. Mountain problems were largely rural problems, he said; it would be valuable to study what was being attempted in this and other countries for the correction of wrong conditions in remote rural sections. Valuable, too, would be inquiry into what might be done under federal, state, private, or corporate auspices in various fields.

It would be important to attend, at least in the beginning, the various denominational summer conferences already in existence in the mountains, and to have conferences with the boards themselves, bringing to their attention new lines of work in rural communities, coordination of effort, and abandonment of work where it was no longer needed.

He would have plenty of opportunity to speak at national meetings of different boards and bring before constituents new lines of work which board officials often feel should be done—

in fact in the North and in the South and in the remote mountain field itself, the effort should be made through every proper channel to create a desire for the things needed.

As I see my work in its beginnings, it is largely that of giving information, creating public opinion, and in being a "promoter." I have heard that a "promoter" is one who promises the sea for use if others furnish the ships and men to man them. I should not care to be that kind of a promoter, but rather one who knows from experience what can be done and could through personal acquaintance lead those actively at work to see the needs and to apply to the right source for help when there are such sources. . . .

It is an attempt that will require tact, sympathy, and judgment; and if I am to try it, I should be glad to feel that I might at any time come to you and others whom you suggest who will see the relations of this work to the more extensive work carried on outside the mountains.

The next step was an invitation to a small, important dinner conference. Mr. Glenn wrote to John on January 2, 1912: "I want to get Rose, Dillard, Dr. Frissell, and one or two others to meet several members of our staff at dinner January 25. Probably I will want to make your work the foundation of a discussion of social possibilities, especially in the South. My object is to get the two sets of people mutually acquainted, and help all of us get closer cooperation and greater mutual help in the various fields. I shall, of course, want you to be there."[11]

Following this was a notice of a meeting of the members of the staff of the Russell Sage Foundation to be held on Thursday, January 18, in the Trustees' Room, 906 East 22nd Street, at 2:30 p.m. Thus was John formally recognized as a permanent member of the staff and his general program accepted and discussed. He had opportunity, too, to talk over many things personally with Mr. Glenn, such as his need for establishing a home now that we were expecting a new member in our family, and the importance of having residence in the South—a point which Mr. Glenn at first did not wish to concede because he felt that all Foundation offices should be together in New York. Later he accepted Asheville as headquarters of the Southern Highlands Division, "Division" instead of "Department" being, seemingly, a way of making clear the fact that it was different from the rest of Foundation work in being so far from central offices. Similarly, John was secretary instead of director. We could never see that there were any other differences, unless it was that because we were so seldom in New York, we received special attention and courtesies while there.

Before leaving New York, John had a conference with Mr. Mitchell, president of the University of South Carolina. He reported on it in a letter to Mr. Glenn dated January 29th:

My conference with Professor Mitchell was a very interesting one. He seemed to grasp the idea of the need of the field at once, and on his own initiative suggested practically what I have suggested as to the remedy, that is, some agency or person to act as a "social service engineer," to seek out the work to be done, local people to do it, and to bring them and the local agencies into connection with the agencies and forces outside that might cooperate. He said he was going to write you and asked if I had any objection. Of course I could offer none.[12]

He then explained that Professor Mitchell seemed to feel that this work ought to be done in some government department, financed possibly by the Sage Foundation for five or ten years until the government itself would take up the work.

It seemed to be his thought that I ought to be in Dr. Claxton's department and endeavor to do for the rural regions in social lines what Dr. Knapp did so well in agricultural lines under the Department of Agriculture. I told him, as I feel, that the ideal way would be for a government or state agency, supported by the people, to do this work, but that politics might interfere somewhat and that I knew nothing about the relation of philanthropic boards to government agencies and of the interrelation of such boards. I am not sure but that the kind of work I am doing, if it is to be nationally undertaken, awaits a new government agency, such as a permanent rural commission or a department of social services.

This question, which involved one of Foundation policy, was not answered for some time. In a letter of March 26th, Dr. Claxton took up Mr. Mitchell's thought, suggesting that John be appointed special collaborator of the Bureau of Education at a nominal salary. On April 3rd, Mr. Glenn wrote John that he felt

cooperation between such agencies as the Bureau [of Education] and the Foundation is more effective than partnership. The Foundation can back the bureau more strongly, more vigorously, and to better purpose if it is entirely independent of the bureau and can endorse its plans as an impartial critic. We can be a more helpful ally to the bureau in an independent position than if you became a member of its staff.

I will be glad if you will consider these suggestions carefully and make any others by way of adding to or differing from them. Dr. Claxton's suggestion is a very important one and ought to be considered very carefully. If it is wise to adopt it in this case, it will probably be wise to adopt a similar policy with reference to connection with government bureaus in other cases.

His position seemed well taken, and the matter was dropped.

John came home from New York satisfied and happy, but so tired that he was miserably ill with indigestion—"toxic poisoning"—for over a week, and did not start on a projected trip south until February 15. His mind, however, continued actively at work on future plans. Mrs. Glenn had earlier suggested the possible use of ballad material in connection with a mountain pageant. On July 23, 1909, she had written to John:

> Mr. [Percy] MacKaye shows the adaptability of the pageant idea and it its dramatic possibilities and power as an educational influence. It may be that in connection with some of the schools there might be developed a form of pageant that would illustrate the differences between the various mountain communities and would draw on their traditions (your old ballads, for instance) to supply dramatic incident.
>
> Of course, the pageant idea is likely to be overdone and to be created as a mere spectacle, but it can be used as a means of developing community spirit and of tying together, therefore, in a common purpose, people of a given community.

John now enlarged on this idea in a letter to Mrs. Glenn dated February 12, 1912:

> There has been in Knoxville in September, for the last two years, an Appalachian Exposition. I am of the impression it is an annual event. It has occurred to me that this exposition might present an opportunity for a pageant which would have more than local significance and, in the large, would be a pageant setting forth what has been done by the mountain people (and what, through them, has been done by the South and those who followed them) for Western, for trans-Allegheny settlement.
>
> You will pardon me for reviewing facts that are already known to you, that I may set forth the sequence in which they occur to me: William Bean, who settled in northeastern Tennessee, was the first settler of Tennessee and a pioneer of settlement west of the Alleghenies. There followed the Watauga settlement, with the notable leaders Robertson, Sevier, and Shelby. From this settlement, [James] Robertson set out with his company and founded what is now Nashville. From the same mountain settlement, Sevier and Shelby, reinforced by [Col. William] Campbell from Virginia, led their mountain riflemen to Kings Mountain, defeated the British under Ferguson, which led to the retreat of Cornwallis from Charlotte, the first move in the retreat which ended at Yorktown, the culmination of the struggle for freedom.[13]
>
> There is historical evidence, fascinating and picturesque, relating to these events that is too little known. Our school histories touch upon them lightly, or pass them by in silence.

I should like to see an impressive representation of the part these pioneers played. The reasons for my desire are various. The Civil War has been as a curtain which has shut out somewhat from the South itself and from the North, the notable achievements of the South prior to that time. A worthy pageant would serve as a beginning to national history and might tend to strengthen the growing feeling that there is still a larger part to play. If rightly staged, and rightly reported, such a pageant might serve, too, to bring to northern minds the debt of gratitude that is owed the South for her leadership in this western movement.

I am interested especially in bringing before the East and West, and the South, the part these mountain pioneers have had in taking the initiative in the advance of Western civilization. We might appropriate the title of one of [James R.] Gilmore's books and call the pageant, "The Advance Guard of Western Civilization."

Certain scenes, as they come to mind, stir one deeply in the thought of their staging: for instance, the meeting of Robertson and Bean before the latter's cabin; some of Robertson's council meetings with the Cherokees; his setting out for Nashville with his company of men by land and the embarking of the women and children under suitable guard for the long canoe journey down the Tennessee and Cumberland; the meeting of the clans at Watauga and the address and benediction of Parson [Samuel] Doak—the founder of Washington College, Tennessee, the first college west of the Alleghenies—as he blessed them and urged them on to Kings Mountain, to lift against the oppressor "the sword of the Lord and of Gideon." Numerous scenes suggest themselves to illustrate growth and development. I presume something of the founding of Knoxville could be brought in to give it a greater local interest.

Unfortunately, as he found out later, the Knoxville Exposition had been given up that year, and growing war clouds seemed to put an end permanently to the undertaking.

Miss Petit had written to me the previous year (April 21, 1911) of her decision to start a new school "over Pine Mountain way." She said in part:

For ten years I have been dreaming of getting a school started over there. There are really no plans, except that when I get one hundred thousand dollar endowment for Hindman so that Miss Stone will not have as much trouble with money and can manage this school here, then I shall go over there and find a location and start one. I dare say you think I have courage, but I want to do it bad enough too. But most of all, would I like to have you and Mr. Campbell go over the proposition with me and help find the location and help in any other way you can: give me the plans and ideals to work to.

Later she also wrote to John, and he replied from Nantucket on October 4, 1911:

I would like nothing better than to meet with you on the field, go to Pine Mountain, and in the rides and rest periods talk over the whole matter thoroughly with you. You are asking some very important questions which should be given weighty consideration. I recognize from my own experience the appeal that the independent school has for one, but there are many difficulties in the way of bringing about the ideal necessary for the carrying on of independent work. Local trustees too often do not see the work in the proper perspective. "Foreign" trustees (if I may use the term "foreign" in the mountain acceptation of the term) view the situation at long run or, coming for a hasty visit to the field, make up their minds as to what should be done from conceptions formed in their home environments, which are entirely different; and unless they are broad-minded enough to give full confidence to the person in charge to have full control, there is liability of obstruction based upon the conscientious difference of views. It is hard, too, to get trustees to do more than trust. They are willing to give the sanction that their names carry, but generally they are too busy with other interests to take any active part in the raising of funds. If one chooses trustees financially able to support the school, if such trustees have ideas and hobbies as to the running of a remote rural school, there may follow necessarily the development of a kind of school not adapted to mountain conditions. . . .

Another objection to independent work is that so much depends upon the head of the school. All would go well, I am very sure, while you live and remain at the head, but unless you were successful in training up a successor imbued with the same splendid spirit which has characterized your work and Miss Stone's, the foundation which you have laid might be overturned.

Do not take this, however, as opposition to independent work; sometimes it is necessary and there are ample returns in the intangible influences for good set in motion during the brief period of an individual life. . . .

My work is absorbingly interesting, and were I not engaged as I am, I should be tempted, and Mrs. Campbell as well, to come and throw in our lots with you.

When she wrote again how anxious she was to see him, he finally arranged to meet her on his way south at the station in Providence, where she was stopping on a money-raising tour. A long letter of February 20, 1912, to Mrs. Glenn, whose interest Miss Pettit had enlisted, gives a fuller understanding of his views on the matter:

When Miss Pettit first wrote to me in regard to the school a year or more ago, I told her that so many schools of that nature stood in danger of losing ground and influence after the dominant personality that had founded them passes away. It was, therefore, highly important to determine first of all who should be back of the school. I further suggested that it might be possible to have some connection with the state forces. If this could not be brought about so as to give the state a controlling influence, it might be that the state superintendent, or the president of the state university, could at least be ex-officio member of her board, and that the county superintendent of education be officially connected with it in the same way. The relation of the state forces should be thought over carefully, and if there is no practical or legal way in which they might have a voice, their cooperation should be ensured in some way.

It is highly important also that the establishment of this new school should not retard the common public schools in that vicinity. To avoid this, I would suggest that the branches ordinarily taught in the public school should not be taught in the Pine Mountain school; and before the school is established it be understood by the community that they were to establish and maintain to the best of their ability their own community school, which the Pine Mountain school would further in every way.

I think the best plan for consideration would be somewhat as follows: To have as part of the Pine Mountain school, work with children too young to enter the community school; that is, to have as part of her work kindergarten work. To have also manual training and domestic science, which would not be taught in the common school; such work could be after school hours and could include all community students that might be attending the community school; it might also take in the adults of the community. Furthermore, I would not take as residents in the Pine Mountain school, as enrolled students in the Pine Mountain school, any students except those older—on the basis of the Danish folk school. . . .

This is a very inadequate outline, but in some such way all legitimate community activities could be stimulated and not retarded; and in which all permanent state forces would be having a share. . . . The school must not be a substitute for anything the community itself could provide, but it should supplement and stimulate; and an adaptation of the Danish folk school idea seems to me at present the most promising way.

I pause before the volume of correspondence and the number of contacts to which the files bear witness in the following months, indeed years. The rough outline of the trip which began February 15, 1912, and continued to March 18, may serve to indicate the kind and scope of John's work as it developed.

1. Providence, Rhode Island.
A meeting with Miss Pettit to discuss the Pine Mountain School.
2. New York
Meeting with Dr. Warren Wilson of the Country Life Department of the
    Presbyterian Church (Northern) to discuss what he had discussed the
    previous week with Dr. [George F.] McAfee of the Home Mission Board
    of the same church, new standards of social work for the mountains.
    Meeting with Rev. Mr. [Harry C.] Phillips, La Grange, Georgia, mill
    welfare work.
3. Washington
Conference with Dr. Wickcliffe Rose to make important connections for
    southern trip. Advised with Mrs. [Martha] Gielow, president of the
    Southern Industrial Education Association, about the future of their
    work and need of auditing accounts.
4. Charleston, West Virginia
Conference with Mr. [L. J.] Hanifan, supervisor of rural education and
    friend, in regard to high schools.
5. Winchester, Kentucky
Conference with Rev. W. E. Hudson, in his capacity as superintendent
    of mountain work of the Southern Presbyterians, in regard to work in
    schools under the board.

Joint conference with Rev. Hudson and Prof. John F. Smith of Berea College
in regard to the public school.

Conference with Archdeacon [F. B.] Wentworth of the Episcopal Church
about his work and mountain work in general.

6. Lexington, Kentucky

Meeting with Dr. [J. A.] Stucky in regard to his eye work and general
findings in the mountains.

Meeting with Mr. [T. J.] Coates, supervisor of rural schools, Kentucky, in
regard to a new kind of mountain school and cooperation of state with
such agencies as the Russell Sage Foundation.

7. Bowling Green, Kentucky

Conference with Dr. [J. N.] McCormick, State Board of Health, and Dr.
Fred Mutcher relative to state program for general health betterment.
Also re vital statistics.

8. Nashville, Tennessee

Meeting with Dr. L. C. Glenn, professor of geology, Vanderbilt University,
to discuss findings as to soil possibilities in the mountains and ways to
bring findings to the attention of those interested in the mountains.

Conference with Governor [Ben W.] Hooper, who approved discussion
of mountain questions having a place on the program of the coming
Sociological Conference, May 7–10. He introduced J. H. DeWitt,
chairman of the Program Committee.

9. Knoxville, Tennessee

Inquiries regarding the Appalachian Exposition and a possible historical
pageant. Found it had been given up this year in order to be merged with
a conservation exposition in 1913.

10. Maryville, Tennessee

Called on President [Samuel T.] Wilson and Rev. [Hubert S.] Lyle in regard
to broadening the scope of the Maryville Mountain Conference, June
18–June 25.

11. Asheville, North Carolina

Conference with Rev. R. F. Campbell, leader in the Southern Presbyterian
Church, and Dr. George T. Winston, former president of the N.C.
Agricultural and Mechanical College. Visited Presbyterian workers.

12. Demorest, Georgia

Discussed plans for summer school at Piedmont College and rural
conference week.

13. Naccochee, Georgia

Drove fifteen miles from R.R. to meet Rev Hudson and Mr. [John Knox]
Coit, president of Southern Presbyterian School, to go over plans for
school and neighborhood work.
14. Atlanta, Georgia
Went with Rev. Hudson to a meeting of the Southern Presbyterian
Mountain Committee—convened to reorganize their mountain work.
Concerning that meeting, John reported to Mr. Glenn on March 27,
1912:

Among the prominent leaders of the church present were Dr. [R. O.]
Flinn, Dr. [S. L.] Morris, and Mr. John J. Eagan. I met with the committee and, at their request, gave my idea of what should be done in the
mountains. Later on I met with these three gentlemen at luncheon and
dwelt more in detail on matters that were of interest to them. They gave
me a very responsive hearing and cordial reception and appreciated the
readiness of the Foundation to cooperate with them. As a result of this
meeting, influences have been put in motion whereby this church and its
mountain work is to be brought in touch with state forces and national
forces that can be of assistance. A very strong desire was expressed on the
part of some of these men for cooperation with other church boards doing
work in the mountains, and they asked me to make suggestions as to how
this could be brought about.

On my return to New York, I went to Dr. [Charles S.] MacFarland
of the Federated Church Council and laid the matter before him for his
suggestion. As an outcome of this interview, Dr. MacFarland has set in
motion certain measures looking toward bringing the two branches of the
Presbyterian Church into closer union in their mountain work.

He described in detail a number of other interviews made on this same trip—
notably one with Dr. E. C. Branson at Athens and another with Dr. P. P. Claxton
en route to New York. Dr. Branson, then president of the Georgia State Normal
School and also president of the "Georgia Club," which was working on state surveys, was more than ready to help the Southern Presbyterians in their proposed survey. Dr. Claxton was interested in having John appointed one of the representatives
on rural education in his department. He also wanted his cooperation on some
questionnaires in connection with the making of uniform county surveys. Doubtless, they talked too of the folk school; they could hardly have spent three hours
together without discussing this subject of mutual interest.

A letter of March 14 from Rev. Hudson to Mr. Glenn confirmed John's letter:

We have recently had a meeting of the Home Mission Committee of the Southern Presbyterian Church in the United States at Atlanta, Georgia. Some of the most prominent elders and ministers in our church attended that meeting. One of the most important subjects that came before us was the mountain department, which has just been inaugurated in the Southern church. Mr. John C. Campbell was present, at our earnest solicitation, and gave advice and help which we consider invaluable. I happened to meet Mr. Campbell during my vacation at Nantucket last summer, and he has assisted me continually and most helpfully in getting a grip upon the mountain situation. He has opened up the subject to me and put me in touch with other persons who were able to give much help, and I cannot tell you how grateful I am for his services. I want you to know that Mr. Campbell has had nothing to do with my writing this letter. I am doing it because I felt you ought to know something of the splendid services which he is rendering to the mountain people.

John might well have been encouraged, for, though at the time he could not realize how, out of this trip, especially his meetings in Nacoochee and Atlanta, would begin one of the most important and desired accomplishments of his study—the Conference of Southern Mountain Workers. As the outline of his journey indicates, he had taken every opportunity to get in touch with people who had influence and some knowledge of his subject—especially with denominational leaders—whom he hoped, in some way at some time, to bring together to discuss mountain work. As he had written Mr. Glenn, he thought the Maryville Conference could get its scope broadened and could include other denominations and so gradually might develop into a meeting ground for all denominations. And this might have developed, given time, had not his own stimulating personality and advice, combined with the course of events, brought about a different and more rapid outcome.

He came back to West Medford, Massachusetts, my old home, in time to greet our little daughter Jane, who appeared on the scene April 1, 1912. John was enormously excited and happy. He couldn't do enough for mother, baby nurse, doctor, and everyone concerned with the event; and his joy expanded into all his correspondence, business or personal. He did not have to start out on a long trip until May, so had time to enjoy his daughter and to incorporate new material into the report. The Foundation editors had suggestions for revision, and he also went down to New York to consult with them.

He had promised Miss Pettit that he would try, after the Nashville Sociological Conference May 7–10, to go with her and her party to help locate the Pine Mountain school. It proved to be a strenuous trip, though he always enjoyed horseback, and the country was beautiful with spring bloom. Measles, a serious matter in the mountains, had descended on the Creech family, who were to furnish lodging and guides. Only one son, Columbus, was able to help. Miss Pettit, however, got the school located and had a satisfactory meeting with men of a timber and lumber company who had promised to help. She wrote John on May 22:

I hope you are safe at home with Mrs. Campbell and Jane, and that you found them well. . . .

After you left us that morning we found plenty of purple rhododendron (red laurel, Uncle William called it), and a rattlesnake. . . .

The journey down Line Fork was almost impossible for a wagon. I just wonder and wonder how we did it. I don't believe you would have enjoyed it except the scores of bright-eyed boys and girls that we met in the road. . . .

I wish I could tell you how grateful we are to you for coming. It has helped tremendously, and I am sure that I must call on you many times.

To Mr. Glenn John wrote on May 31, 1912:

I met a number of people I wanted to see at Nashville during the Sociological Conference; while there, I had opportunity to confer with Dr. [Hubert S.] Lyle, chairman of the Maryville Conference program, with a number of state health officers in regard to their work, and with those interested in combating tuberculosis. I am trying to interest them all in carrying their campaigns into the mountains. One of the things I am called upon to do increasingly is to suggest to those doing mountain work the names of others who are doing work and who might desire to become associated with the questioners—in fact, a part of my work seems to be an exchange for mountain social workers. . . .

I am planning one or two mountain conferences for the fall. It seems best to get the workers themselves to realize the necessity of this and do as much of the planning as possible.

The time to turn south came all too soon; it was hard to tear himself away. The baby was having a struggle with the food problem, and we could not but be worried about her. Such difficulties are long-winding, however; his plans were laid, and he felt he could not wait longer. He left June 11. In Washington he had a long interview with Chief Forester Graves, whom he had known years before as a schoolmate. Mr. Graves offered him every assistance that his department could give—reports, data, and numerous illustrations of Southern Appalachian resources. He stopped at Altapass to see Miss [Lillian] Holman and found Dr. [Joseph Hyde] Pratt, state geologist of North Carolina, who happened to be there and who went over and approved his statement on the geology and topography of North Carolina.

At Asheville he lunched with Bishop [Junius M.] Horner and met the newly appointed superintendent of the mountain work for the Home Mission department of the Northern Presbyterian Church, Mr. Marshall C. Allaben. Dr. [A. E.] Brown, superintendent of the Baptist work, was away. He then joined a party of Presbyterian mountain workers en route to Maryville, where he found that the chairman of the program committee had faithfully carried out some of his suggestions made in a previous visit and at the Sociological Conference in Nashville. Rev. W. E. Hudson was there, the [Isaac] Messlers, representatives of the Dutch Reform Church, and Professor John F. Smith of the Christian Church. There were addresses and sermons by state officers and workers from state institutions, and by United and Southern Presbyterian pastors. John was able, in his own talks, to present his new ideas on mountain work to teachers from the whole region, and the recreation plan for afternoons brought him many friendships in an easy, natural fashion. He became well acquainted with Marshall Allaben and talked over many aspects of mountain work with him. Some of the things they talked about appear in a letter Mr. Allaben wrote to John on July 3, 1912:

I find, on my return from Kentucky and Tennessee, that I failed to return to you the copy of your plan for folk schools, and am enclosing it herewith. I am also sending, by Adams Express prepaid, the coat which you so kindly loaned me. I assure you it was of great service to me on my trip to Manchester.

We found an interesting situation at Manchester. I made the proposal which I outlined to you, but Mr. Walker, whom you will remember as one of the influential members of the community, seemed to think that they could do about as well by hitching up with the county high school. The county superintendent, Mr. Hatton, however, seemed to feel that our proposal would be the best one in the long run. I hope we shall be able to do something for Manchester and Harlan along the line that you have indicated in this paper.

On my return I reported the Maryville Conference to our officers, and they seemed very much interested in your work and accepted with avidity the suggestion that you come here and talk to our officers first, and then to our Women's Board; so you may look for an engagement sometime in September with us, if that will be convenient for you.

He closed with a most appreciative statement of what their acquaintance had meant to him: "The need and opportunities of that field loom large on my horizon today, and I am hoping that I shall be able to communicate to some of our people a share of this enlarged vision that I have as a result of my conference with you and the others."

John's report to Mr. Glenn written July 3, was jubilant:

Mr. Allaben has said that he would see to it that most of the mountain workers of the Northern Presbyterian church should attend the Maryville Conference next year, and Mr. Hudson, the superintendent of the Southern Presbyterian Mountain Work, has said that his workers would attend and that he would see to it that a travel fund be raised to pay the expenses of those who could not otherwise afford it. I think there is great promise of this conference growing into something that has been very much needed to promote comity among the denominations.

The superintendent of the Congregational Board has assured me that he would attend next year, and the program committee of the conference have asked me to secure him, if possible, as a speaker. He has consented to speak.

I shall try to get Dr. [Charles S.] MacFarland as a speaker and some of the YMCA and YWCA people, Dr. [E. C.] Branson and others. The committee has asked me to do what I could to make it a success, and they have been over-generous in the estimate of my services this year.

I came from the conference with a feeling of elation and with the conviction that the Foundation would be of great service in bringing together the forces working for betterment. They seemed to need only someone to point the way and to join their hands. . . .

I have a suspicion, which I do not voice much, that the recent appointment of the field superintendent of the Southern Presbyterian mountain work and the appointment to the Northern Presbyterian mountain work (offices not in existence before) are a direct outgrowth of the need made apparent in the investigation undertaken by the Foundation.

Again we spent the summer at Nantucket. John, radiant over his new daughter and enthusiastic over the progress of his work, felt that indeed his dearest wishes were coming true. He was deep in revision of the "Ancestry" chapter, which he felt still needed further condensation and clearer statement of conclusions. I could not help him very much; little Jane was still having trouble in getting the right food and occupied most of my time. Fragments from Mr. Glenn's correspondence with John indicate the general progress:

July 22, 1912

I think your suggestion to put the "Ancestry" chapter into the appendix is probably a good one. I am not sure. I think we can tell better when we get it in final shape. . . .

Please understand that I agree with you that it is important to have in the book a clear discussion of the original sources from which the mountaineers came. It is important that readers should know what the ancestry of the mountaineers was. The two questions are how far they should go into detail, and whether it is better to put the story at the beginning or in the appendix.

August 6, 1912

I have your favor of August 3 with reference to your chapter on ancestry. All the suggestions that have been sent you . . . have been sent merely as suggestions. There has been no intention to require their adoption. The chapter is in your hands to put it in what seems to you the best possible shape. . . .

I especially, however, do not want you to give up your judgment because of suggestions that you receive from me, or anyone else. All I want is to get your point of view clearly before the reader. This is not an easy task for anyone who knows as much about the whole intricate subject as you do.

[JCC to Mr. Glenn]
August 29, 1912

My work is getting on fairly well, although I am sorry to say that I appear to have worn out the climate and my hay fever has come back with renewed vigor. I think I have the substance of the chapter on ancestry disposed of all right now.

And again, on the same day:

Rev. W. E. Hudson . . . is here and I have had a number of interviews with him. . . .

Mr. Hudson is very desirous of making surveys in his field and also wishes to know how to arrange for exhibits. . . .

The Northern Presbyterian Church, the Southern Presbyterian Church, the United Presbyterian, and the Associated Reform Presbyterian, I believe, are to hold their national assemblies in Atlanta in May, a beginning, we hope, of efforts for a union of these Presbyterian bodies.

I am giving Mr. Hudson a letter of introduction to you, and I would be grateful if you could make an appointment, if you are to be away, with the director of the Foundation's Department of Surveys and Exhibits.

If it should come about naturally, I would be glad if you would suggest and could arrange for Mr. Hudson's meeting Dr. MacFarland. Doctor MacFarland has written me a number of times in regard to the bringing together of the church agencies working for the mountaineer. He has been desirous especially to get in touch with the Southern Presbyterians. I do not feel that it would be wise for me at the time to appear anxious that Mr. Hudson should meet Dr. MacFarland, but I hope that he may. Dr. [Alexander] McKelway of the National Child Labor Committee is also summering here. I have met him once and plan to have an interview with him later.

From Boston John wrote Mr. Glenn on October 5 that Rev. Hudson had asked him to go with him

to a few of their more important mountain schools in Kentucky to speak to their faculties about the new kind of work to be done. He wants me late in October or early in November. There are also avenues opening to the Baptist mountain work—work that I want very much to get in touch with, for the Baptist church and Baptist mountain school are the "native" organizations of the mountains. Someone in the Southern Baptist Theological School at Louisville [who] is making a study has written to me a number of times for information, and I have told this Mr. Brown, I think that is his name, that when I come south I will come by Louisville. He has been referred to me by Dr. [A. E.] Brown, who is the superintendent of Baptist mountain work, with headquarters at Asheville, North Carolina.

I have also received an urgent invitation, which I have accepted, to deliver an address in New York on the 19th of November before a meeting of the Women's Board of Home Missions of the Presbyterian Church (North). They want me to tell them of the new work to be done. This is the board under which most of the mountain work of that denomination is being done. I am very pleased to have all of these opportunities. I am to give an address on mountain subjects before the Men's Club of one of the Congregational churches in Boston on Tuesday night.

At this point another Mr. Brown is heard from—Dr. William Adams Brown of Union Theological Seminary. His letter of October 7, 1912, was exciting in the extreme, indicating as it did that John's efforts to bring together denominational leaders in mountain work were definitely bearing fruit:

Mr. Glenn tells me he has referred to you a letter which I wrote him bearing upon your work in connection with the problem of the southern whites. He suggests to me that I write you directly about the plans for our proposed conference, and I shall be most glad to do so as soon as they have taken more definite shape. The whole matter is still very tentative, a suggestion having come to me from some friends among the Southern Presbyterians that a conference called by some of us in the North to consider the whole problem might do much good and bring about results which the southern churches themselves, working independently, could not attain. Any light which you may have to shed upon this problem, or any suggestion as to the best way to set about such a conference, would be much appreciated.

Perhaps John saw him in New York when he was on the point of leaving for the South, but there is no letter in the file. Another letter from Dr. Brown, however, dated November 8, must have reached him at Winchester, Kentucky, where he was preparing to take his mountain trip with Rev. Hudson:

It looks now as though the plan for our conference was going through and that the Southern Baptists and Southern Presbyterians would officially unite in an invitation to a preliminary conference to be held in Atlanta. This conference would also include those of us from the North who are interested in the matter, and Mr. Flinn has written me asking for the names and addresses of those whom we think should be invited. May I ask you for your counsel in this matter? I have written Mr. Flinn that I thought by all means you should be invited to be present and take part, if your engagements permitted your coming. . . .

P.S. If it is not troubling you too much, I should greatly appreciate your sending me a transcript of that portion of your report which summarizes the statistics as to the bodies working in the mountain field.

Further details as to the projected meeting had to wait until John returned to New York. He was traveling and busy with interviews. A letter he wrote on November 5 to Mr. Glenn from Asheville reports:

Since writing you last, I had a conference with Dr. Claxton (now US commissioner of education) relative to his plan of sending someone to Denmark to study the Danish folk schools. He asked me if I could go now, and I told him that there were certain matters in my line of work, as well as family reasons, that would make it inadvisable for me to consider going abroad before fall. He said that fall and winter were really the best time to study folk schools, and that if he did not find just the man before June, he might want me to go in September. I told him that in that event, if it were agreeable to the Foundation, I would consider it, as I thought it a very vital matter for the mountain work that such schools be considered as possibilities for the mountains.

He wants someone who knows the mountains sympathetically, who has a salary so that the government would only have to pay expenses, who could present the work personally by speech and pen, and someone who understands and speaks German. I have the qualifications so far as German is concerned, and he seemed to feel that I had the other qualifications and could be borrowed from the Foundation. . . .

I am to furnish Mr. Claxton the names of representative mountain leaders and church board officials, whom he is to call into conference at Washington relative to matters pertaining to mountain education.

I am going this afternoon to Knoxville to see Mr. Goodman, and shall probably go to Emery, southwestern Virginia, to see Professor [J. R.] Hunter of Emory and Henry College, which is doing Appalachian school extension work. I have written Dr. [William S.] Claiborne of the University of the South, asking if he can meet me in Knoxville to talk over their proposed folk school. I shall leave Knoxville probably Saturday or Sun-

day for Winchester, Kentucky, and if time allows I shall go to one or two
mountain schools to further the conference idea.

Another letter must have reached him before he reached Asheville—an official
announcement from Mr. Glenn that the trustees of the Foundation had voted an
appropriation for his department and had raised his salary. Acknowledging this, in
the same letter of November 5, from Asheville, he suggests, in his usual cautious
fashion, that he come very quietly into [i.e., settle in] Asheville without any publicity as to his heading a new department of the Sage Foundation. Mr. Glenn's answer,
November 9, was short and to the point: "I think it will be a waste of time for you
to try to get people to think that the Sage Foundation is not established wherever
you are settled. The fact that you are working as a member of the staff of the Foundation and living in Asheville will be accepted by most people as clear evidence that
your office is there. You may do what you please in this connection, but there does
not seem to be any possibility of hiding the Sage Foundation under a bushel. Everybody knows that you are a representative of the Sage Foundation."

On November 11, John reported to Mr. Glenn from Winchester:

I shall be in the mountains with Mr. Hudson until Friday morning and
then go to Louisville, and I expect to be in New York Monday night.
. . . I hope to be able to attend one of the Rockefeller Hook Worm Clinics
tomorrow in one of the mountain counties. . . .

I want to see Mr. [Lee F.] Hanmer and Mr. [William C.] Langdon on
my return and if possible to see you on the 19th or 20th. I hope to spend
a few days with Mrs. Campbell, to finish up some work before going to
Chicago for the Rural Social Service meetings prior to the meeting of the
Federated Council of Churches on December 3 and 4.

I have not received very good reports about our little daughter and we
are somewhat anxious about her.

After his New York stay, John wrote to Dr. Claxton:

I found on my return to New York that plans for a conference among
church boards doing school work in the mountains were well under way,
and I am taking the liberty of suggesting that some federal and state
authorities be called into conference, unless it is intended that this be but
a preliminary meeting for better acquaintance. . . .

It would seem to me that some such preliminary meeting on the part of the church people feeling the need of cooperation would be an admirable forerunner to a more definite conference called by you with discussions of specific things you might suggest.

I do not know yet when it will be called, but I shall keep in mind your request that I send you the names of persons in authority particularly interested [in] further cooperation. This meeting is likely to indicate who they are.

The trip to Chicago was made according to plan, John returning to West Medford, Massachusetts. From there he sent Mr. Glenn a letter, December 21, 1912:

I have not written you much about my own plans since I came from Chicago because it seems impossible to decide from day to day what to do.

Our baby has been in a very precarious condition and practically all of the family, except Mrs. Campbell, had given her up the Monday I was in Chicago. . . . The prospect is now brighter, and I hope to be able to go south soon after Christmas or about the New Year.

I am kept rather busy answering inquiries that keep coming from people interested in the mountains, getting my material sorted for Asheville—material that has been accumulating for four years. In addition there are some matters with reference to the report suggested by Miss [Helen] Moore [Foundation editor] that I am busy on.

I do not like to think of that Christmas—and the days that followed, when we alternated between hope and despair. In the middle of January, John wrote Mr. Glenn:

Unless there is some sudden change for the worse in the condition of our baby, I shall be in New York, en route south, Monday night or Tuesday morning.

The baby is a little more than holding her own, and if progress is to continue, it will probably be months before Mrs. Campbell can come south.

It seems to me that the time has come for me to go south, inasmuch as there are many things waiting attention. Mr. [Owen R.] Lovejoy [National Child Labor Committee] wants me for an address in New Orleans in March. I have just received a request to be present at the Sociological Congress in Atlanta from April 25 to April 29. Mr. James E. McCullough wants me for some preliminary work, I believe, and I understand I am on the program for the interdenominational meeting of mountain workers, to be called by the Southern Baptists or Southern Presbyterians in Atlanta at some date not yet fixed. I also want to be at the inter-Presbyterian meeting in Atlanta in May, and there is much planning with others and for the Mountain Conference . . . in June.

The start was made as planned; although the baby's condition was not too encouraging, it seemed as if we had at last found the right food for her, and John left full of hope. He had begun to get his office organized in Asheville and had engaged a secretary, Elva Dickey, when word came that Jane's heart had suddenly failed, and she was gone. He took the first train home. It is hard to put into words just what this loss meant to him. A tiny creature, full of personality and intelligence, she had been to him the hope and center of a new life, of the new home to be established in Asheville. He had been very much alone since the many deaths in his own family, and while he had warmly adopted my people, little Jane was his own blood and bone. She was everything he wanted her to be, except strong. It seemed as if she could not die. For a while he bent beneath the blow. Very sorrowfully we turned our faces southward toward the mountains. He wrote to Mr. Glenn on February 22, 1913:

We arrived here Wednesday and are beginning to get located. We had a most profitable visit with Miss Delano and Miss Clement [head of the rural nursing service of the Red Cross] in Washington, and they are both coming down the second week in April to look into the possibilities of the National Red Cross doing work in the mountain country. Mrs. Campbell and I have agreed to go with them into the Kentucky mountains. . . . I regard their coming as most important and am delighted that they have finally found time for such a trip.

I shall be able to get the rooms for the office I want, I think, by the first of March. I can get temporary rooms in the same building until that time. I go to Jacksonville to attend the National Child Labor Committee Conference March 13 to March 15.

Both Mrs. Campbell and I appreciate greatly the kindness shown by you and Mrs. Glenn.

Indeed, they could not have been more thoughtful.

To Carl Kelsey, who wrote him in regard to the mountain mill controversy, he answered on February; 27: "Olive and I came south a week or ten days ago, and we had not the heart to stop anywhere. We lost our little girl very suddenly, and somewhat unexpectedly, three weeks ago last Sunday. . . . She passed quickly and painlessly from heart failure. I cannot trust myself yet to write more."

Fortunately we had plenty to occupy us from the first, in setting up the office and hunting for a home; conferences and mountain trips lay just ahead. We were more than busy with preparations. Mr. Lovejoy, general secretary of the National Child Labor Committee, had asked that John, in his address, give special attention to what Mr. [Thomas Robinson] Dawley, who had been making attacks on the committee, discussed. "I think you are," he said, "of all men who will be at the Conference, the one to answer him in a comprehensive and dignified way." John did not wish to disappoint him and worked hard on the speech, to which I have already referred in the earlier part of this chapter—"From Mountain Cabin to Cotton Mill."[14]

Mountain trips always called for a great amount of advance correspondence. On February 26 John wrote to President W. G. Frost of Berea College:

> In all probability Mrs. Campbell and I will be in Kentucky on or about the 7th of April to accompany representatives of the American Red Cross Association throughout the Kentucky mountains. They now include in their plans—a recent departure, I think—rural nursing, and I am extremely anxious, as are they, to become familiar with the mountain country, its needs, and the possibilities of their undertaking some work in the country in which you and I are so deeply interested.
>
> It occurs to me it would be a distinct advantage to them if I could bring them to Berea for a day to talk over matters with you and Mrs. Frost and with the directors of your medical and hospital work, and to start with horses from Berea to McKee, to Oneida and Buckhorn. From there to go to Hazard, to Whitesburg and to Jenkins, and then on to the Hindman region and possibly also to Pine Mountain and to the vicinity of Jackson. I should value your suggestions in this matter. Will it be possible for your Professor Smith, who has an intimate knowledge of the section from McKee to the vicinity of Oneida, to accompany us that far? I do not know how much of publicity the ladies of the Red Cross would wish to have given to this trip—at least until it is under way. I will therefore ask that it be kept somewhat confidential until they arrive and I may learn more of their wishes.
>
> You may be interested to know that I am to open a department at Asheville for the Sage Foundation, and I hope to keep in touch with all

workers and with all forces in the mountains that are working for the betterment of conditions and the right development of the country.

Professor Smith promised to get the horses and, with President Frost's permission, to go on the trip. He wrote John on March 3rd:

I cannot tell you how much I sympathize with you and Mrs. Campbell because of the death of your child. I am very sorry that misfortunes like this must come to anyone, but I am especially sorry that such a misfortune should come to you.

I feel a personal loss, for I put such a high value on the friendship of you and Mrs. Campbell that I share in no small degree your joys and your misfortunes.

Before leaving for the Jacksonville conference of the National Child Labor Committee, John wrote to Mr. Glenn, March 8, reporting changes in plans for the Mountain Workers' Conference:

I shall probably return from Jacksonville via Demorest, Georgia, to make arrangements for the shipping of our household effects. We have secured a house that we have wanted, and we are delighted at the prospect of having our own home once more.

The Conference of Officials of Mountain Work scheduled for Knoxville March 25–26 has been postponed to the 24th of April, and the place of meeting changed to Atlanta. I am enclosing a copy of the letter of call and the program.

The announcement of the change in plans had been made in a form letter signed by Dr. R. O. Flinn of the North Avenue Presbyterian Church in Atlanta, and dated March 5, 2013:

My Dear Sir:

You have doubtless received a letter from Dr. John E. White inviting you to attend a Conference on Mountain Work in Knoxville, Tennessee, March 25–26.

Since this call was issued, circumstances have arisen which make it advisable that the place and date of this conference be changed to Atlanta, Georgia, April 24th.

I am therefore writing to ask if we may hope to have you with us at that time.

Beginning April 25th, the Southern Sociological Congress will convene in Atlanta and will hold daily sessions through Tuesday, the 29th. A number of those who will attend the Conference on Mountain Work will be in attendance upon the Sociological Congress also, and by this change of date, all those who come to the one meeting may arrange to attend the second if they see fit.

The plan of the meeting for the Conference of Mountain Workers is the same as that proposed before—namely, that each board or committee working in the mountains be asked to send as many representatives as it can, and that each take care of the expenses of its own representatives.

In issuing this call, I wish to state, as in the first instance, the call is sent in the names of the Southern Baptist Home Mission Board, the Home Mission Board of the Presbyterian Church, USA, and the Executive Committee of Home Missions of the Presbyterian Church, U.S. Moreover, in this call the following named persons heartily concur: Bishop Junius M. Horner, Asheville, North Carolina; Rev. J. R. Hunter, Emory, Virginia; Dr. H. P. Douglass, New York, New York; Dr. William Adams Brown, New York, New York; and H. J. Derthick, Livingston, Tennessee. Through an oversight, the names were omitted when the first call was issued.

Please notify Dr. John E. White of Atlanta, or myself, as quickly as possible whether we may expect you to be present.

Enclosed with this letter was the following memorandum on the proposed Conference:

1. Place—Atlanta, Georgia, North Avenue Presbyterian Church, corner Peachtree and North Avenue.
2. Time—April 24, 10:00 a.m.
3. One presiding officer to be elected at first session.
4. Two addresses in opening by Rev. W. E. Hudson on "Geography and the Extent of the Mountain Problem," and by Mr. John C. Campbell on "Survey of Facts, Forces, Workers, and Institutions."
5. Main topics of discussion:
   The Church in the Mountains.
   Day Schools, extent of such, teaching and future.
   Normal Schools, the extent and future.
   Industrial Teaching, extent, future.

The Exceptional Mountain Boy and Girl; their training for teaching or
the ministry.

Education for citizenship in Mountain Communities: as Christians,
farmers, artisans, and merchants.

6. The conference to be self-entertaining

Submitted by

Dr. Warren H. Wilson, Superintendent of the Department of Church and
Country Life of the Presbyterian Church, USA.

Dr. John E. White, DD, Chairman of the Department of Mountain Work
of the Southern Baptist Home Mission Board.

Rev. R. O. Flinn, DD, Chairman of the Sub-Committee on Mountain, Mill
and City Mission Work of Assembly's Committee of Home Missions of
Presbyterian Church, U.S.

The following concurring:

Bishop Junius M. Horner, Asheville, North Carolina

Rev. J. R. Hunter, Emory, Virginia

Dr. H. P. Douglass, New York, New York

Rev. H. J. Derthick, Livingston, Tennessee

For further information address Rev. Richard Orme Flinn, care of North
Avenue Presbyterian Church, Atlanta, Georgia.[15]

John was scheduled to speak at Atlanta, as a letter of March 14 from Dr. Flinn's
secretary made clear: "Mr. Flinn asked me to write to you in his behalf and tell you
that he wanted you to make an address on 'Survey of Facts, Forces, and Institutions'
at the Conference on Mountain Work to be held in the North Avenue Presbyterian
Church, Atlanta, Georgia, on the 24th of April."

While the conference was thus brewing, preparations continued for the Kentucky mountain trip with Miss [Fannie] Clement and Miss [Jane] Delano. John
wrote Mr. Glenn March 11, this time on a matter of accounting:

What voucher shall I return for postage and for meals at restaurants, and
other places not hotels where I am staying? I shall be at a loss oftentimes
in the mountains in the matter of securing vouchers. Many of the people
that I deal with in hiring horses or paying for entertainment are people
who cannot read or write and are ashamed to make their mark. Other
times suspicion will be aroused by signing a Russell Sage voucher. They
will regard me as someone trying to get them to sign away something or

I will give the impression of spying out something. At other times, when entertained at a school, remuneration is refused, but I know that they cannot afford to keep my horse, or our horses if others are traveling with us, for nothing; feed is very high. In such cases I cannot ask them to sign a receipt for the money that I give them under the pretext of using it in some way for their work but [that] in reality is given to meet expenditures that they have actually made out of their small funds to entertain us. I shall be glad of any suggestions, and hope that now I have a permanent office with a permanent secretary, my department can be brought in line with the others, but I fear by reason of conditions existing at times and in places, it will be difficult.

On March 17, 1913, President Frost answered his letter in regard to the Red Cross visitors and Professor Smith's company most cordially as follows:

Now we want to know, at the earliest possible moment, just when you will come and how long you will stay, in order that we may get the largest possible benefit from the visit.

On Tuesday night, the 8th, one of our ladies' literary societies holds an anniversary. We hope you can be here the night of the 9th to speak to our faculty and workers, and perhaps sometime during that day, or the next, speak to our class in rural sociology.

I am hoping to attend the Mountain Conference recently shifted from Knoxville to Atlanta, though the latest date is an inconvenient one for me.

How is it that you and the others did not give Berea a chance to join in the call for that meeting?

"Brother Burns" was equally cordial. In his letter of March 7, he says: "Now won't I be glad to see you and Mrs. Campbell again? The weeks of April will be fine for fishing, and there will be some tennis too. Don't let the plan fail. And you must make us a speech or preach a sermon. We all remember you and will take the best care of you we can, and give all possible aid to your friends. Our work has grown wonderfully; you will hardly know it.

"I am here, as usual, trying to get these Yankees interested in men as well as money, with varying degrees of success."

Rev. A. G. Smith, from Smithboro, Kentucky, not so far from the Hindman region, explained about the horses John wanted, in a letter dated March 21:

Now as to horses at Mouth of Carr, I cannot say positive. There is no station to speak of as yet—absolutely no accommodations—along that line. There are no horses around me here at all. There are a few mules, only three that are safe for women, but they will not promise this, for it is a busy season now. The only thing I can say is "come to Hazard and telephone from Hazard, at Robert Cornett's, Smithboro." It is nearer than George Kelly, although either will reach me. I will keep touch on the mules, and if I can get them will tell you and you can come on to the Mouth of Carr. If not, they can procure horses at Hazard and go to Hindman. There are three very good stables there, and horses are fairly reasonable.

We would love to have them come by to visit us if possible, and I will try to arrange this.

Think I can accompany you as far as Whitesburg alright.

President Frost's courtesy—and question—were acknowledged by John on March 26th:

I have just returned to my office after an absence of two weeks. . . .

I have not had my usual strength for the last month or so, and I am "saving it up." I am forgoing public speaking as much as possible. I shall be very glad indeed to meet with the class in rural sociology for a sort of roundtable conference. I fear I shall have to deny myself the pleasure of addressing the student body.

I am very glad indeed that you are planning to attend the conference in Atlanta. . . . In the call issued to me, those listed as concurring are representatives of different denominations, but I presume invitations have been sent to officials and workers in independent schools such as Berea.

Accomplishment was the burden of his letter to Mr. Glenn, also dated March 25th from Asheville. He had been to Jacksonville, Florida, where Mr. [Owen] Lovejoy and Dr. [A. J.] McKelway appeared pleased with his address at the Child Labor Conference and thought they could make extensive use of it. He had stopped at Raleigh and talked with Dr. [W. S.] Rankin of the North Carolina State Board of Health and to Dr. [J. Y.] Joyner, state superintendent of education, about the coming new interdenominational conference and about ways in which private organizations doing educational work in the mountains might be helpful to state educational forces. He also stopped in Atlanta for suggestions from Mr. [L. C.]

Brogdon, state superintendent of rural education, and saw Dr. Flinn, who wanted the names of proper persons to speak at the meeting.

He continued:

> The work here opened well. I think much more so than would have been possible had my report been published. I am coming to feel more than ever that parts of my report which describe the social and religious phases of mountain life should be kept as confidential, and perhaps the whole report delayed in publication until the work here is well established.
>
> We have found a very comfortable home and hope to be settled in it about the middle of May. . . .
>
> We have had no severe storms here in Asheville, but we had difficulty in getting from Jacksonville to Atlanta. Fifteen to twenty miles of the track were under water for long stretches. In several places the water came over the first step of the Pullman. Our train was the last one through for twenty-four hours.

The storm had not touched Asheville, but it did touch the Red Cross. Miss [Jane A.] Delano, called to the Ohio flood district, was not able to make the Kentucky mountain trip. Miss [Fannie C.] Clement, however, wired that she would meet us at Winchester, Kentucky, if traveling was possible. We picked her up at Winchester on April 4th, and with the advice of Rev. Hudson and the help of Mrs. Hudson made our final preparations for a start the next day. Miss Clement was full of eager curiosity and entered into every phase of the trip, from interviews with doctors, nurses, mountain workers, and local people at every stop, to all the vicissitudes incident to a horseback expedition in the mountains. We started in bright sunshine; redbud and peach were in full bloom; flowers starred the hillsides and fringed the woods. Then it rained on us; we lost a horseshoe; one horse gave out; twice we had to ride double, Flag Pond fashion, for considerable distances. Roads were exceedingly bad much of the way, banks slipped in places, and mud was deep. At Buckhorn we were delayed several days by high water but managed finally to get out by ferrying horses, mules, baggage, and ourselves over the Middle Fork. Near the new railroad to Hazard, we had to ferry again. Taking to wagon at Hazard, we found rivers and creeks overflowing. At one place we got out and picked our uncertain way along broken banks while the driver put team and wagon into the swift rushing water to test out the road. Miss Clement was an undaunted and cheerful traveler—quite a fitting representative of the Red Cross. She had nothing but enthusiasm for all her experiences when John and I had to say farewell to her at

Hindman, where she delayed to see through a clinic. We, too, had enjoyed our days together, but the important conference was near at hand, and if we were to attend it, we had to move on.

We made quite a party as we started off: Miss [Ruth] Huntington, one of the heads of the Hindman School, on her way to the conference; Mrs. Fisher, whose husband was an independent mountain worker, with her three small children and a neighbor boy, bound to Lexington; John and I, loaded with saddlebags and luggage. We parted, except for Miss Huntington, at Winchester but soon picked up new conference recruits: Rev. Hudson at Winchester; Miss Pettit, coming from Pine Mountain; Mr. Messler from McKee, and Mr. Worthington from another Dutch Reform school at Annville; President and Mrs. Frost from Berea; President Wilson from Maryville. The train became a veritable house party on wheels! John, who had a remarkable faculty for remembering faces even when he had seen them only once, kept watch at every station and hailed in newcomers. He would have made a good detective, he used to say, and no one made a better liaison man. He moved about, up and down the aisle, his face shining with pleasure, introducing one traveler to another, adding a word of explanation, suggesting a topic in which he knew both were interested. His natural desire to have people relaxed and comfortable soon resulted in a general atmosphere of comradeship and well-being. Here sat a couple in deep conversation; there a group, in the process of becoming acquainted, opened up to receive a newcomer, or broke into smaller units in order to talk more intimately. Long before Atlanta was reached, the conference had begun, and one of its greatest objectives, mutual acquaintance, was well on the way to being realized. To become acquainted with the rest of the assembled thirty-five was not hard after this beginning. Indeed, the atmosphere of friendliness and mutual confidence which pervaded that first meeting was carried on into those that followed it and still today, years later, characterizes the sessions of the conference—now for the first time called the Council of Southern Mountain Workers.

John wrote to Mr. Glenn twice—once from Atlanta and again several days later from Asheville:

April 26, 1913

We emerged from the Kentucky mountains three days ago and since have been in the Mountain Conference here. The conference had the pick of mountain workers and leaders. Miss Berry and Bishop Horner were not here—to my sorrow. I do not know why. Perhaps they are in the North. Will write details of Kentucky trip and conference a little later.

A unanimous vote was given to send you a note of thanks for what the Russell Sage Foundation was doing for mountain work. One enthusiastic Baptist brother said, "Even if the Foundation has not done or should not do anything else, the work it was doing to help mountain work to a better basis justified its existence."

If the chairman doesn't forget, you will probably get the note of thanks.

May 8, 1913

The Mountain Conference was a great success—it far surpassed my expectations. There were thirty or thirty-five in attendance—a very representative group of mountain workers.

The Virginia people were not there. Dr. [George P.] Mayo was coming, but the change from Knoxville to Atlanta probably necessitated other arrangements; Bishop [Junius] Horner was not there, and Archdeacon [Frank] Wentworth. The Episcopal work was therefore not represented, and Miss [Martha] Berry did not have a representative there; but practically all other important work was represented.

There were no discordant notes save one, and that was sounded by a little Congregational man who could not rise above a local disagreement with the Baptists. The Baptist people displayed a splendid spirit. The meeting is to be an annual affair. I was chosen president of the Executive Committee to arrange for the next meeting. I am enclosing a list of those who would be regarded as official delegates, although there were others in attendance. The secretary and I are entrusted with the responsibility of securing the substance of the impromptu speeches given. I am sending also a list of those who are on the Executive Committee for next year. Representatives are to be chosen from the Episcopal Church and from the Northern Methodists, and two women are still to be chosen to be added with these to the Executive Committee for next year. It was a splendid meeting as all testify, and good feeling prevailed throughout.

The Sage Foundation was thanked repeatedly. Aside from the desire to say a pleasant thing, the thanks were prompted, I think, by a real feeling of gratitude that some independent organization had been instrumental in quietly bringing various boards together in such a conference.

A final report summarizes what John felt was one of the most important aspects of the meeting:

Denominational interests were eliminated, and all the time and energy were devoted to the common cause—the spiritual and material uplift of the Appalachian section. The conference proved to be exceptionally free from any selfish propaganda. Those who had made careful surveys presented the facts ascertained. The problems involved and the results to be attained were discussed. The individual methods of dealing with the various phases of the work were presented, so that we had not only the theoretical but also the practical viewpoint. . . .

This is the first general conference on mountain work, and it promises to be fruitful of much good.

6

The Southern Highland Division

Beginnings, 1913–1914

Returning from the first Conference of Southern Mountain Workers to a new house in Asheville, the Campbells settled in just in time for a stream of visitors. John hired a secretary to help with the compilation of data and with the bookkeeping, as a strict detailed account of funds spent was needed for the Russell Sage Foundation.

Campbell went with Miss Fannie F. Clement, a nurse, who was keeping account of funds expended, to Berea, where they were cordially received. They then proceeded to McKee to talk with Rev. Isaac Messler, in charge of the center for the mountain work of the Dutch Reformed Church, with out-stations at Grayhawk and Annville, five or six miles away. Continuing their journey, they interviewed some doctors in Clay County, then went on to J. A. Burns's school at Oneida. This expedition, conducted by the mountain people themselves, Campbell considered the best example of mountain work. After several days at Oneida, they visited the Harvey Murdochs in Buckhorn, Perry County. Then, ferrying their horses across the Kentucky River, they proceeded to Hazard, the county seat of Perry County, to interview doctors there. To get to Hindman, they jiggled in a "jolt-wagon" for twenty-five miles.

The office had to be set up for carrying on the work of the new Conference of Southern Mountains. John Campbell was the appointed chairman of the Executive Committee, and the secretary was Isaac Messler. The nominations for the committee included Dr. John E. White, ex-officio, William Goodell Frost of Berea, the Rev. Henry J. Derthick, and Dr. Warren Wilson, who was superintendent of the Country Life Department of the Presbyterian Church. They wanted nominations from the Northern Methodist Board, the Congregational Board, and the Episcopalian Board and wrote to Rev. A. E. Brown, superintendent of the Mountain Schools of the Baptist Mission Board as well. The Nominating Committee was anxious to be all-inclusive, or "liberal," to have all denominations and interested parties represented.

The chapter continues with all the activities that preceded the conference. Campbell was torn between the concerns of the office and the editing of his report about mountain conditions for the Foundation. The correspondence included confidential facts, and it was difficult to publicize many of the concerns without violating a code of ethics. Letters indicated frustration over trying to find data about the public schools, when the state superintendents of education confided that data derived from the counties were "value-less." Other correspondence indicated a desire for the YMCA to extend its work into the Southern Highlands and a hope that women's projects could be encouraged.

In this chapter Campbell outlines his ideas about what the work of the Southern Highlands Division should be and describes the struggle between the denominations and also between the northern and southern schools and the organizations that supported them. A map of the Southern Highland region was created, with locations of the mountain schools classified denominationally. The finished map was seven and a half feet wide and six feet long.

We came back from the first Conference of Southern Mountain Workers May 3, 1913, directly to the new house in Asheville. "Blythewood," it was called—a low, rambling, brown house which we rented from a family who had moved to California. It stood far back from St. Dunstans Road, to which the land in front sloped gently down, opening pleasant glimpses of "Kenilworth," Busbee, and Cedar Cliff. The other three sides were set in woodland, where hermit thrush and ovenbird sang by day and the little screech owl and whippoorwills mourned on a summer night. Yellow-hammers chattered noisily on the outskirts; bluebirds and Carolina wrens darted in and out of the wide porches. In the big oaks at the entrance, the spring song of the brown thrasher fluted in joyous variety. A few lingering daffodils were still in bloom; and the caretaker of the neighboring place welcomed us with a great bunch of narcissus poeticus.

The house was much too large for two people, and inside it was coated—furniture and walls—with the penetrating soot which a soft-coal city dispenses lavishly even to its rural environs. It took us several days, with several extra hands, to get it clean; not a cheering start, but we loved the place and soon contrived to get it washed up. From the beginning, it overflowed with guests, a large number of them mountain workers who came to regard it as a haven and source of fresh inspiration. We had no car, but there was a trolley to town. John often walked the mile or more to his office, and I walked with him whenever I could. If he rode home, the screaming halt of the trolley car on the way downhill to Biltmore heralded his coming. He usually got off at our neighbor's stop, and it was a few minutes before his figure, often accompanied by other, perhaps unfamiliar, figures, came in view walking up the winding road and passing between the great oaks which marked the boundary of our domain.

This period was perhaps the most idyllic of our lives—beautiful surroundings, good neighbors, and absorbing work, in which we both found satisfaction and variety. John seemed well and full of energy, and there was always something in which I could share, though I soon found I could not manage the big house, dispense constant hospitality, and be of much value in the office. We partially solved this problem by securing, from time to time, one of the many young girls who had attended the Presbyterian Home School nearby and who was glad to be back near the city for a while, with a regular, modest income under pleasant conditions. We made each girl a part of the family and took her out on many a pleasant jaunt. Thus I was able to entertain semiofficial guests, help out when needed in the office, and even accompany John on some of his trips.

Miss [Elva] Dickey, John's secretary, proved an efficient and interested helper—well equipped, with her special Census Bureau training, to compile and edit bulletin material and data for the report. She had a keen and orderly mind, which she exercised in many directions; and she was clever with her hands, too.

Typing (and hers was beautiful) and bookkeeping were primary needed accomplishments in the office. Every trip John took called for accounting; and mountain trips in particular, while they did not deal with large sums, were what one might dub "fussy" in variety and detail. Take, for example, the trip in Kentucky with Miss Clement, made just before the Atlanta conference of 1913. John had advanced money for the arrangements for this trip to Professor Smith of Berea College. Here is Professor Smith's statement to John, written May 5th, which had to be combined with other expenditures:

I should have sent you a statement of your account days ago, but I have neglected it in the pressure of duties. A trip to Barboursville and an address, a trip to Mt. Vernon and an address, an address before the Mountain Band, a trip to Louisville, and other numerous things have caused me to delay this till I could have the health reports copied and ready. They are not yet quite ready, but I am sending itemized statement with check for balance.

To Manchester	$ 8.50
For DeYoung's horse	5.00
For Livery horses	16.00
For Joe	5.60
Expenses at McKee	2.50
	37.70
Check	2.30
40.00	$40.00

I shall be glad to learn of the conference when I see you.

By the way, I have been offered a position at Oneida again. It looks like a good opportunity. What would you do about it?

With cordial wishes to you and Mrs. Campbell, . . .

This was followed by an explanatory letter from John, May 10th, to Miss Clement, and more accounts:

I have received recently from Mr. Smith a statement of our accounts summarized as follows:

General expenses to Oneida	$8.60
For livery horses, including his own	
(for which, of course, we pay)	26.60
Mr. Smith's expenses at McKee	2.50
A total of	37.70

I have entered against the account you owe me, one-third of this, or $12.56, which I have itemized as follows:

General expenses Berea to Oneida	3.70
Cost of livery horses, keep and return	8.86
	12.56

a total, as you will note, of $12.56, given before as your share. The other items on the bill I am rendering will explain themselves, I think; they are your share of the expenses incurred from Oneida to the time we left you at Hindman.

During my absence, a check for $13.00 was received from Mr. Taylor, the business manager of Berea College. He expressed his own regret and President Frost's that the assistant clerk at the hotel did not understand that we were the guests of the college. I should much prefer to have paid our bills, but inasmuch as they have been insistent in their courtesy, I have accepted the refund with our thanks. I have credited your account with a third of the thirteen dollars.

Send me the check at your convenience; I am receipting the bill in advances you requested. If there are any questions about it, do not hesitate to ask me.

Sent to Miss Clement as an enclosure was the following:

Statement of expenditures by John C. Campbell for Miss Fannie F. Clement on trip from Berea, Kentucky, to Hindman, Kentucky, April 7–21, 1913.

General expenses from Berea to Oneida	$3.70
Livery horses from Berea and return and their keep	8.86
Horses and keep from Oneida to Buckhorn and return	2.33
Incidentals (loss of saddle pocket and reward	.67
Meals (Bill Bishop's)	.50
Paid Mr. Murdoch in lieu of hotel bills	5.00
Ferrying horses across river and return	.42
Paid livery boy for taking back horses	.25
Meal at Altro	.50
Railroad fare from Altro to Hazard	.73
Hotel bill at Hazard	1.50
Meals and incidentals en route to Hindman	.50
Team—"jolt wagon"—Hazard to Hindman and return with keep of mules and driver	3.34
Paid Miss Stone in lieu of hotel bills	<u>5.00</u>
	$33.30
Refund of the Berea Hotel bill	4.33
	$28.97

Received payment:
[signed] John C. Campbell
May 10, 1913.

Another letter went from John to Professor Smith on May 12th:

Thank you for your letter just received. I hope I did not seem insistent about the account—I merely wanted to get it into my April report so as not to raise any possible question with our accountant. I know well that you were very busy.

We had a splendid conference, and it promises to be a permanent thing. I think there were some thirty representative mountain workers assembled. They honored me by selecting me as chairman of the Executive Committee. This committee is to have in charge matters pertaining to a meeting probably in April of next year.

I should like to know more about your Oneida offer. It seems to me you could be of great service there. The work looks promising, and money is probably coming in. Oneida has a distinct advantage in being a work for mountain people managed very largely by mountain people. If the workers on the field keep broad-minded, and in touch with all outside forces as well as forces on the field, it is a unique opportunity. If you could be given a broad field to carry out some of the ideas that we have talked over so often, it would seem to offer opportunity for the accomplishment of certain ideals that would prove of great help to the mountain country. Mr. Burns and Oneida are coming into prominence—a prominence that is both promising and fraught with some risks. I think you could be of great help. Were I in your place, I should think the matter over very carefully before turning it down; at the same time, I should want to know quite distinctly what my field was to be and how much freedom I was to have in carrying out some of the ideas that seem to be essential.

Please keep me in touch, for I am deeply interested both personally and officially.

Let me thank you again for all of your helpfulness. The latchstring is out for you whenever you come this way. Mrs. Campbell unites with me in cordial greeting and sincere thanks.

The full account of the trip with Miss Clement was sent to Mr. Glenn earlier—on May 8th:

Mrs. Campbell and I met Miss Clement at Winchester, Kentucky, on the morning of April 4th. On that same day we had interviews by appointment at Winchester with Miss Pettit, Miss Linda Neville, and Rev. W. E. Hudson . . . with Mr. French of the Kentucky State Tuberculosis Commission, and a visiting nurse from Lexington, who came with Miss Neville and Miss Pettit.

On the following day, April 5th, we went to Berea and were met at the station by President Frost's secretary. In the afternoon President Frost himself took us to see whatever we wanted to see in connection with their work. In the evening we were invited to dinner by the business manager of the college, Mr. Taylor, after which we went to the president's home for a roundtable conference with about eighty of the faculty. I was asked to speak of the new needs of the mountains, and many interesting points were brought out by questions. On the following day, Sunday, President Frost took Miss Clement to one of the boarding halls for lunch and for conference. In the afternoon we all went to the president's home again for a meeting with some of the faculty and for dinner. On Monday morning, April 7th, the president came to the hotel early to bid us good-bye, as we were taking horses for a cross-country ride to McKee, twenty-five miles away.

President Frost was most cordial. . . . I found on my return here a check covering the amount of my hotel bills which I had paid while there. Of course I could do nothing but accept.

We arrived at McKee in the afternoon of April 7th. McKee is the center for the mountain work of the Dutch Reformed Church, with out-stations at Grayhawk and Annville, five and six miles away, respectively. The work is in charge of Rev. Isaac Messler—a very strong man. We were at these stations parts of two days and met, while there, a Mrs. Ralston from New York, one of the temporary field secretaries. At Grayhawk a hospital is being erected, and the work is to be along medical lines largely; at Annville the work is to be industrial, with emphasis upon agricultural effort. The work at McKee, the center, is the ordinary academic work and the usual church work.

From Annville we continued our trip to Manchester, the county seat of Clay County, to interview some of the doctors; and the day following we went to Burns's school at Oneida. Opportunity was given Miss Clement while there to confer with the nurse, and we all visited some of the outlying country. Burns was very busy most of the time we were there. His work needs many things, but there are great possibilities in it. It is the best example I know of mountain work for the mountain people conducted very largely by mountain people. In consequence, it has its strength and weaknesses. At Oneida we parted with Professor John F. Smith, of Berea, who had accompanied us thus far.

After several days' stay at Oneida, we took horses and mules to Buckhorn in Perry County to see Mr. and Mrs. Murdoch in their work. They have a hospital and a nurse and hold clinics in the spring and fall, and are branching out in agricultural lines. We were there from Saturday until Wednesday morning, April 16th, because of high water. On Wednesday we succeeded in ferrying our horses and mules across the Kentucky River on flatboats, got to the railroad, and went to Hazard, the county seat of Perry County, and interviewed some of the doctors there.

On the following day, April 17th, we took a joltwagon for a twenty-five-mile ride to Hindman and arrived in time for one of Dr. [James A.] Stucky's clinics. Mrs. Campbell and I had to hurry back because of the

Mountain Conference in Atlanta, but we were able to see some of the work of the clinic of the first day. Hindman has improved greatly in general appearances. There are many new buildings, and I am happy to say that Miss Pettit's departure to Pine Mountain is regarded simply as a necessary move because of the growth of the school; the Pine Mountain School is looked upon as a child of the Hindman School. I was very anxious to have that go out as a correct impression and wrote Miss Pettit about it several years ago. Miss Stone was ill at the time of our visit, and we saw comparatively little of her, but all of the faculty spoke very kindly of Miss Pettit and her new work. Miss Pettit spoke very frankly and cordially of Hindman and Miss Stone. Miss [Ruth] Huntington, a Smith College girl whom I know quite well, succeeds Miss Pettit at Hindman. She is very efficient, has a clear mind, and is a real asset for Hindman.[1]

The clinics have done good work. There is much hostility to Dr. Stucky because of the newspaper publicity, for which they hold him responsible. Miss [Linda] Neville, they tell me, is especially hard to control. The workers on the field, and Miss Pettit also, have a very kindly and appreciative regard for both her and Dr. Stucky, but they do not feel that their visits to them are an unmixed blessing. They are more or less outsiders and view the mountain people as "other kind of folk," and like to give their own work for the mountain people publicity without regard to the effect of such publicity upon the permanent workers on the field and the station long established. For this reason Miss Pettit insists that she will not have them at her new school at Pine Mountain, although they are personal friends of hers.[2]

It is the old question again. There is a kind of publicity that helps, and a kind that hinders; and the kind that helps does not generally come from those who do not understand the mountain people. The Bluegrass people seem to know the mountain people as little as do the people from the North.

We left Miss Clement at Hindman. On our way to Atlanta, we met on the train Mr. Messler, Mr. Hudson, President [Samuel T.] Wilson of Maryville College, Miss Pettit, Mr. [William A.] Worthington of Annville, and several others en route to the Mountain Conference at Atlanta.

I hope Miss Clement will have opportunity to give you her impression of the possibilities of the Red Cross work in the mountains. She seemed to be impressed with the magnitude of the work as well as with its possibilities. I believe she can work it out. In places the nurses will be self-sustaining; in other places there will be needed funds to sustain the nurses until they shall have won a place in the confidence of the people.[3]

I was impressed anew with the need of the Kentucky field. There are so many people in great need, despite much advancement in industrial development. I had opportunity while in Demorest for a trip into the country. If I may judge of improvement in northern Georgia from what I saw from Demorest as a center, there is considerable hope, agriculturally, for northern Georgia.

This is a very inadequate statement of our trip. We enjoyed it thoroughly. Miss Clement is a good campaigner and a charming traveling companion. I was sorry Miss Delano could not come, but hope she may have opportunity some time in the future to become personally acquainted with the mountain situation.

Another letter to Mr. Glenn, written the same day, concerned Miss [Lydia] Holman, the nurse we had visited, at the suggestion of the Glenns, when our 1908–1909 study trip took us to Penland, North Carolina:

I had an interview with Miss Holman while in Atlanta and asked her directly if she would care to go into the mountain section of some other state under the direction of the Red Cross. She said she would. Her only hesitancy in enlisting under the Red Cross seemed to arise from the thought that she might be called into rural nursing outside of the mountain country. She felt that her training and experience fitted her especially for the mountain field.

I told her that I thought it was too bad for her to carry the burden of local or state resentments or misunderstandings, if another mountain field, equally needy, should open to her. She expressed herself as entirely willing to enlist under the Red Cross for mountain service or to enter some hospital work in the mountains under some church or independent school.

It seems to me this is a way out of the dilemma. Of course, I did not commit the Red Cross or imply that I had been talking over the situation with its representatives.

Mr. Glenn replied to John's "interesting" letters on May 13th. Three days later he wrote again:

Checks are being prepared for the petty cash and other statements enclosed in your letter of the 13th. I agree [with] you that it was desirable to have Mrs. Campbell accompany you on your Kentucky trip. I should think it proper for the Foundation to pay her expenses from Asheville to Winchester and return as well as from Winchester to Hindman. You may charge them accordingly.

You need not trouble about vouchers where it is inconvenient to secure them. Vouchers are not necessary for expenditures for railway tickets, which need only be entered in the traveling expense books.

Other important first business of the office was to complete machinery for carrying on the new Conference of Southern Mountain Workers—a long correspondence, for John was concerned that the newly appointed Executive Committee, of which he had been appointed chairman in Atlanta, should share in every decision. He was anxious, too, that a liberal policy be followed from the first, which involved another sheaf of inquiries. He was greatly gratified that the answers, cordial and inclusive, indicated a temper which augured well for the character of the organization. The first letter, May 10th, was to Rev. W. E. Hudson of Winchester, Kentucky, who had been chairman of the Nominating Committee in Atlanta:

This is just a note to express our appreciation of the kindness of you and Mrs. Hudson in our recent visit. It is a great help as well as pleasure to me to feel all the official relations reinforced by such kindness and friendship as you have always shown.

In the list of members of the Executive Committee sent me by Mr. Messler, there appears to be one person lacking. Dr. John E. White was, as I recall it, elected ex-officio member of the Executive Committee by the conference after you had reported a committee of seven, with three appointments to be made—namely, from the Northern Methodist Board, the Congregational Board, and the Episcopalian Board, and two appointments at large, to be filled by women. On Mr. Messler's list there seem to be only six in addition to Dr. White, ex-officio member. The names of the six are as follows: Campbell, chairman; Frost; Flinn; Childs—substitute for Dr. Warren Wilson; Derthick; and Hunter. My impression is that you were also a member. I did not get to the meeting until after the Nominating Committee brought in its report; and Mr. Messler, the secretary, was not there until after. You were on the Nominating Committee, I believe. Can you tell me whether you were placed upon the Executive Committee, as I hope? If you were not, who is the stray one?

In filling the denominational vacancies, it seems best to write to the mission boards for their nominations. As to the two women members, we must, I suppose, confer with one another. Several of us have thought that Miss Stephenson, who has been in mountain work for twenty-five years, and Miss Pettit, who has been in the work almost that long, I believe—both of whom were present at the conference—would be admirable selections. If you are a member of the Executive Committee, will you please write me your view? If you wish to concur in the selection of these ladies, will you please do so officially in your letter, or if you have other selections to make, please do so.

The "stray one" was not Rev. Hudson, but Rev. A. E. Brown, superintendent of the Mountain Schools of the Baptist Mission Board. On May 24, 1913, John sent him and the other members of the Executive Committee the following letter:

It was suggested by various members of the conference at Atlanta that I, as chairman of the newly appointed Executive Committee, write to the members of that committee for their choices for the two places on the committee to be filled by women.

Acting upon that suggestion, I write you and for your information send you a list of the ladies present at the conference, with such information as I have regarding them. There may have been other ladies present, but these are the only ones recorded on the secretary's list as having registered:

Miss Florence Stephenson, principal of the Horne Industrial School, Asheville, N.C. Miss Stephenson has been connected with this school for twenty-five years and is one of the oldest workers under the Women's Board of Home Missions of the Presbyterian Church, USA.

Miss Katherine Pettit of the Pine Mountain School, Pine Mountain, Kentucky. Miss Pettit was one of the founders of the WCTU Settlement School at Hindman, Kentucky, and was associated with Miss May Stone in the conduct of that school for ten or twelve years. This year she has gone to Pine Mountain to carry out a long-cherished idea of establishing a work on a new basis. This is now possible because the work at Hindman, with which she has been so intimately associated, is on a sound basis.

Miss Ruth Huntington has been in mountain work for three years and is the successor of Miss Pettit at Hindman.

Miss Lydia Holman has been a visiting nurse at Altapass, North Carolina, and vicinity, for the past six or seven years.

Miss Frances L. Goodrich is a community worker, connected with Presbyterian work in the mountains of North Carolina for some years.

Miss Mabel Moore, Wearwood Academy, Sevierville, Tennessee. I am not acquainted with Miss Moore's work.

Miss Mabel Drake Gill, Sewanee, Tennessee, is connected with the University of the South at Sewanee and is endeavoring to build up an institution similar to the Teachers' College at Columbia University. I think I am right in this impression.

Miss C. S. Parrish is connected with the Department of Education at Atlanta, Georgia.

Mrs. W. G. Frost, of Berea, Kentucky, and

Mrs. John C. Campbell of Asheville, North Carolina, were also registered as in attendance at the conference.

May I hope for an early reply as to your two choices? I do not know that one is limited in his choice by this list; I have sent it merely that you may know who were present.

President Frost answered on May 27th, and Rev. Flinn on May 28th, both men indicating a different selection from the one suggested by John. Rev. Flinn added:

May I ask in this connection that you send me the names of the members of the Executive Committee, together with the officers of the association? I would like also to have you secure for me from the secretary the names of all those who were in attendance upon our conference in Atlanta, with their addresses.

If the minutes of our meeting are typewritten or printed, I would be glad to get a copy of these. As host of our little gathering, I was often interrupted and thus unable to attend all of its sessions, and thus am in the more need of full minutes of the same. When are we to meet again, and where, and what are we to do in the meantime? It was the closing sessions especially, when such matters were being considered, that I was unable to attend.

Before these letters were received, John sent another letter, May 28th, to all members of the Executive Committee:

At the Mountain Conference held in Atlanta recently, the chairman of the newly appointed Executive Committee was instructed to write to the Methodist Episcopal, Episcopal, and Congregational mountain boards to ask that they name their representatives for the Executive Committee.

As I recall this suggestion, it was made to invite boards doing work in the mountains who were not represented in the conference. It occurs to me that there are two other denominations—the United Presbyterians and the Associated Reformed Presbyterians—who are also doing mountain work and were not represented in the conference.

Is it your wish that these boards should also be invited to name representatives for the Executive Committee, or shall the call be issued simply to the three named, which were assumed to be, I suppose, the only boards not officially represented?

Prompt responses were received from three members of the committee. Rev. Brown wrote, on May 29th:

The spirit of the motion referred to in your letter must have been to invite each denomination doing work in the mountains to name a representative on the Executive or Central Committee, and that being true, I would suggest that you invite each denominational board doing work in the mountains to name a member of our committee.

We would have no right to go into the excluding business even if such a spirit existed, and I am sure it does not exist, and therefore I am sure you will be within the limits of our authority to invite each denomination doing business in the mountains to name a representative.

On the same day, Rev. Flinn wrote:

I would suggest by all means that you invite the United Presbyterians and the Associated Reformed Presbyterians to appoint representatives for our Executive Committee. It seems to me that what you are trying to do is to enlist all who are interested in this work in a cordial and concerted effort to cooperate in the accomplishment of our common task.

President Frost wrote, on May 30th: "Your considerate thought expressed in your letter of May 28th to invite representatives of all the religious organizations which are working in the mountains meets my most hearty approval."

To Rev. Flinn went a letter, on May 30th, giving the lists for which he had asked, and adding:

Mr. Messler is to send me the minutes, resolutions, etc. in a week or two, copies of which I shall send you. The time and place of our future meeting is left to the Executive Committee. When the membership of this committee is completed, I will, as instructed, take up the matter of time and place with them. It was suggested tentatively that a good place to meet next year would be Knoxville, and the time, April.

No action was taken as to what should be done in the interim, but I shall be happy to receive any suggestions looking to an even more successful meeting than this past year's, a meeting which it will be difficult to surpass, and for the success of which we all feel deeply grateful to you.

A long letter from Professor J. R. Hunter of Emory and Henry College, Emory, Virginia, Methodist Episcopal, suggests the possibility of another choice in the selection of women members of the Executive Committee: "Allow me to say in conclusion, however, that experience has taught me that we need working members more than any other kind." He then invites John to become a "working member" of a special group of their college (Methodist), if he can spare time twice a year to plan with the group for "evangelistic and social betterment in an area around White Top Mountain." John replied on June 5th:

Your letter of June 2nd is received, and I thank you for the suggestions contained therein. From letters received from the various members of the Exccutive Committee, I think we are agreed that the denominations doing work in the mountains should have representation on the Executive Committee. We feel, too, the difficulties arising from too large an Executive Committee. This is a matter that I think, however, can be adjusted at our next meeting after we have all gotten together and know each other.

As to the matter of my becoming officially connected with your board, I will say that it appears to me unwise at present to have official connection with any institution. When I took up this work, I severed all connection with institutions in my field—even with the college with which I was so closely identified for a number of years. I thank you, however, for your kind thought in the matter and would say that I should be happy at any time to meet with your board and to cooperate in any way in my power for the development of the work you have been doing.

When are you going to Georgia? Are we to have the pleasure of seeing you in Asheville on your way? Please let me know whenever you come.

These and many other active concerns of the office seem to have completely submerged the editing of his report on the mountains and the filling in and correcting of details, but as letters and new data indicate, this was far from the case.

For months Miss [Helen] Moore, editor of the Foundation in New York, had been going over chapters of the original report, with a view to making the whole ready for publication. She presented suggestions at various times, some of which seemed to indicate a desire for more picturesque and extreme, if not sensational, treatment of his theme. John's point of view appears rather fully in a letter he wrote her on June 24, 1913:

> I thank you most sincerely for the material sent me. I have been much interested in it, both in the outlines and in your correspondence, and now I am going to try your patience and soul once more.
>
> There are certain things that I must not do and other things that I cannot do. It is necessary for me to keep always before me the fact that my work is now to be of a constructive kind. If the Sage Foundation should wish a very frank and full statement of social and [words missing] matters. Often they have said: "You sure did hit us where we needed it and all them things you said was so." I have had men walk out into the dark, take my hand, and with sobs tell me they were guilty of all these things, and that for the sake of their children, if for no other reason, they were going to give them up. They thought more of me for facing them and telling the things they knew and I knew were true. They welcome me back always, but if I should go out of the mountains and publish those things, I could never work again with them—and I ought not to be allowed to, for in my judgment and in their judgment, I should have violated a code of ethics such as physicians or nurses would violate if they should tell the intimate things learned in the families, homes, or regions to which they were seeking to minister.
>
> I know that there are those working for the mountain people who think it is all right to do these things, and who hold that publicity is necessary to correction, but publicity of these intimate things must not come from the forces seeking to remedy. So much for the moral and social phases—I can touch upon some such matters lightly; I must be silent on many.
>
> As to the matter of the public schools, I have, I suppose, the latest records of the eight mountain states as to schools, etc. I know that I may seem very egotistical and very stubborn in my persistence in their nonuse. They are valuable as showing tendencies, but as a basis for computing statistics, most of them are utterly worthless. State superintendents of edu-

cation have said to me, in confidence, that the data derived from county sources from which state reports are made are valueless. I will not take your time to enter into all of the whys and wherefores, but will indicate just a few points. In the past, the amounts of money appropriated to the counties by the state were based upon the number of students of school age, enrollment, etc., and from my personal knowledge, as well as statements of state superintendents, these county reports have been padded. One will often find in this year's report a lower enrollment or a smaller number of children of school age in a county than in the past. This is not due to a decrease in population, but to the fact that reports have been padded in the past—and, in these instances, detected. There is also a lack of machinery for collecting data; lack of funds; lack of uniformity in blanks; lack of help in state offices to compile statistics when gathered. We have detected in our office here, in several reports, numerous errors in cross-addition, and totals forced. It seems worse than useless to draw any conclusions from inaccurate data inaccurately handled. . . .

I have Professor [William] Gillette's book and think it valuable. When he speaks of the "mountain whites," I find myself somewhat perplexed. He generalizes, I feel, from local conditions or from conditions in one section of the mountains only. For instance, on page 29 of his book, he says: "As before noted, the mountain whites (I do wish he would not call them that. There are practically no Negroes in the regions of which he writes, so why not say *mountaineers* simply?) occupy the adjacent portion of eight states, embracing a region of some two or three million acres." If one takes his maximum—3 million acres—there will be less than five thousand miles in "Appalachian America." The mountain counties of western North Carolina alone embrace an area of ten thousand square miles, not to speak of the thirteen thousand square miles within the thirty-six mountain counties of Kentucky, and there are six other Southern Appalachian states— not including Maryland. It seems to me that he is generalizing from observations in a limited area of the Alleghenies and Cumberlands where Kentucky, Virginia, North Carolina, and Tennessee meet, and with observations drawn presumably from a small section of the Kentucky mountains, for he speaks of the Big Sandy, Licking, and the Cumberland rising there. These rivers are Kentucky rivers in the main.

I think his arguments, based on the persistence of old English words and phrases, to sustain his position that the people are the descendants of the redemptioners of Colonial times, [are] open to question. He loses sight of the fact that many of the Scottish and Scotch-Irish were from the lowlands of Scotland and that the North-of-Ireland Scottish, or Scotch-Irish, prior to their migration to Ireland, were a mingling of Scottish and North-of-England folk, who would naturally have in their vocabulary many purely English words and phrases.

He is not altogether correct in his deductions as to moonshining. He writes as if the people generally had a strong taste for intoxicants. As a matter of fact, most of the mountain counties of Kentucky, even, are dry. He seems to be writing from conditions that prevailed long ago, or from local or regional conditions that do not obtain generally. There is, too, much about feuds that he appears to have overlooked.

As to the kinship between mountaineers east of the Mississippi with those of the Ozarks, it is probably true that there is kinship. I saw, years ago, occasionally, wagon trains of mountaineers going to the Ozarks, and I sometimes saw them coming from there to this section. It is an open question as to whether they were the more adventurous ones who went from here or whether they were the shifting, shiftless class who could not make good here. Some of the church boards, I am told, have recently given up stations in the Southern Appalachians to transfer their work to the Ozarks. I should like to make a study sometime of this trans-Mississippi mountain section. My impression at present is that educational facilities are not better there than here and that much less has been attempted.

You will not think me a carping critic, will you? I admit I am jealous of whatever good reputation the Southern Highlander may have, and when practically all those who know the mountain country and the mountain people from years of acquaintance hesitate, I fret a bit when others decide so many things about them. Only recently, a gentleman to whom I look with greatest respect and gratitude for his knowledge of southern questions, and for his helpfulness to me in my work, caused me to feel that he was making very favorable generalizations for the whole mountain region from his observations in a county in which conditions had improved greatly in the last ten years through the influence of several church schools whose usefulness he has questioned. A few days since, I learned from a state official in charge of one of the state institutions that there were more deaf and dumb from that county than from any county in the state, and one naturally asks himself, "Is this condition which exists in one of the oldest mountain counties due to decadence in population from intermarriage, or is the county so up-to-date in its handling of its helpless ones that it sends them to the state institutions rather than keep them at home?"

Dr. Gillette's book has helped me in its classifications of communities, etc.—and all with whom I have come in contact in my work have been of help to me—but underneath all is the feeling that no one of us yet has the truth of the matter. I think the highway of social progress through the mountains must be built by specialists in the various phases of social life coming into the mountains to study and to study long, and who feel some things that cannot be expressed altogether. My work, as I see it, is to act as a guide to those individuals and agencies and to put them in touch with those on the field, working with problems at first hand, but with a deep love and responsibility with and for those with whom they are working. I want to be just as helpful as I can be, and I know that my department may be very helpful if I view my work aright. The agencies that come in to study, I hope somewhat under the direction of this department, are the ones, I think, to give the publicity, and I ought to just keep still and "saw wood." Part of the wood to be sawed is a report, eventually, which shall call attention to possible lines of development and to certain needs which can be published only in outline, but talked over with investigators very intimately. Some things can be published fully.

I can, however, see the other point of view—the need of making very clear to the public some things that I ought not to make clear. The engineer must not create prejudices or animosities among the mountain people, who really have to be relied upon, after all, to furnish the most labor. They need outside help, and outside help needs them. You see, Miss Moore, I am try-ing to be two things: a sort of engineer who is surveying and a consulting physician who has diagnosed and hopes to help in the healing process. The mountain people are the patients with whom I do not always come into direct contact, but the officials of some of the boards and agencies—who are to be the active physicians—will not consult me if I give away publicly the diagnosis or violate what they might consider "professional ethics."

When and where the next conference should be held, and what topics should be discussed—topics which would "appeal to you," be of particular interest and importance to mountain workers—called for still more correspondence. Knoxville was the unanimous choice for the meeting place, as the most central and conve-nient spot for most people, and so it continued for many years: "We went to the Knoxville conference."

When the correspondence was finally completed, seven denominations, two independent schools, and, through the chairman, the Russell Sage Foundation were represented on the Executive Committee, which had as women members Miss Pettit and Miss Stephenson.

John did not count on correspondence alone to bring together the different denominational elements and private and public agencies working in the mountains. Conferences or meetings were another avenue of contact. He mentions many in his letters to Mr. Glenn, some of which he had addressed and others merely attended.

Mr. Glenn, a veteran conference-goer himself, usually had the same dry response when asked what he thought about the advisability of going to this or that meeting: "It might be a good thing for you to go if you haven't too much important work to do. Ordinarily, except for one or two special addresses, one gets most from meeting and talking with certain people who know something bearing on one's particular interests."

"There will presumably be a large number to whom it might be worthwhile to talk about the Southern Highlands," he wrote in relation to one large conference in Memphis. "To most of the general membership, however, your subject will merely be one that is interesting. You could probably get publicity in the southern papers if you want it. You will undoubtedly also derive benefit from being in touch with the membership of the conference, and with hearing a number of papers. The question is one entirely for your own judgment. Above all things, though, keep within the limitations of your strength, at least until you get entirely well."

The advice was sound, and John, having been ill for several weeks, tried to follow it. He made every effort to limit his schedule to the occasions when he could perhaps be of some help or could hold discussion with individuals or groups he especially wished to meet. When Dr. Brown asked him to take a trip of two or three days to speak to his mountain teachers and prospective mountain teachers on the needs of the mountain schools, he promised to go. On his return, he wrote to Mr. Glenn, June 24, 1913, that at Ridgecrest, the Baptist summer campground,

they received me very graciously and passed a resolution of thanks, despite the fact that I spoke plainly in some matters with reference to overlapping of schools, etc., which went a little counter to some of their practices. I also went to the YMCA Conference at Black Mountain, on request, to meet Professor Smith of Berea and Mr. [Henry] Israel, secretary of the International Committee of the YMCA. It has long seemed to me that in Mr. Israel's department—the County Work Department—lies one of the solutions of mountain questions. There is needed some county organization on a Christian but nondenominational basis, which shall be a leader in all things that lead to what may be termed, perhaps, productive Christianity. Such an organization would serve as a point of contact for the many movements in which local leadership is necessary to ensure success. I have been after Mr. Israel for two years in the hope that his department will begin work in one or two typical mountain counties.

He attended the Maryville Conference, Presbyterian, USA, again on June 26, 1913. "John had a good conference," says my diary, but "Hot, hot, hot!" it continues the next two days. "Hot ride home, but Asheville comfortable and house lovely." He reported to Mr. Glenn:

I expected to have only a minor part this year, and was scheduled for only one morning conference. However, the interest was so general that I was asked to lead roundtable conferences each day during the period not occupied by the regular program. These roundtable conferences were attended by most of the workers and gave evidence of the desire to learn all they could about existing conditions. This sounds to me a bit like "self-advertising on the part of the Southern Highland Division," but I feel sure you will want to know just what is being accomplished. There seems to be a disposition now to regard this department as an adviser, counselor, and friend and, for less than in the past, as an avenue for securing funds to further private plans.

He would have liked to go to the 1913 reunion of his Class of 1892 at Williams College, but this hardly came under Mr. Glenn's category above. Besides, he had no time. To Reunion Chairman (Haskell) he wrote:

Your "Last Call" for the twenty-fifth reunion of our class has just reached me. I regret more than I can tell you the necessity of my saying that I cannot be present. I am just opening a department here for the Russell Sage Foundation, and in consequence, it does not seem best for me to leave. Give my love to all the fellows, and express to them my sincere regrets, and my hearty good wishes for them personally.

You were so kind as to think that I was good enough to be a minister. I went through the Seminary but concluded that I was not the right kind of man to make the right kind of minister, so I never became ordained and am therefore not entitled to the "Reverend." I have been a teacher instead until the last six years, five of which I have been engaged in a comprehensive study of the southern mountain country, out of which study has grown this department.

I had the great pleasure of meeting your brother on the train to Washington some months ago. I think I recall a statement of your brother's to the effect that you are a practicing physician. If you are a lawyer instead, please regard the "Doctor" as prophetic of the LLD which someone, some day, will grant you.

Correspondence with Mr. Henry Israel, research and editorial secretary of the International Committee of Young Men's Christian Associations, County Work Department, New York City, opened up some new avenues for possible help in the mountains. Mr. Israel wrote John on August 7, 1913, a month or so after they met at Black Mountain:

This is the first opportunity I have had to give any attention at all to the accumulated mail. I have just returned from our Estes Park, Colorado, Summer School, where we had a most profitable time and some interesting conferences, particularly with reference to the Mormon menace in those states as Utah, Nevada, Wyoming, Idaho, etc.[4]

Let me give you some definite assurance that the text on Grundtvig and the Danish folk schools is under way of translation. I cannot see how we can promise much before January first of next year, but you may rest assured that we shall push this matter along just as speedily as it is consistent.

Now let me tell you that we have discovered two good friends. A prominent business man and his wife of Boston . . . were not unknown friends to us from previous contact with them. But we had an opportunity to discuss thoroughly the whole program of the mountaineer problem, and I will not tell you in detail in this letter what we did, but we got them interested to see the possibilities of investing time and money over a period of ten years for some constructive work in putting a man on the job in that section. Let me say that they are vitally interested and very open. They have it, without doubt, in their own possibility as well as in their influence, to do no small thing for the mountaineers of the Appalachian region.

Now, I am very anxious to know whether you can provide us with a copy or two of the county map on the mountaineer problem as it presents itself to you, out of your investigation. We would welcome such a map. This map is the first thing. In the next place we are wondering whether it would be possible for you to the accompany us some time this fall to Boston to open up the whole detail of the problem in the mountaineer section, and then lay before them a five- or ten-year policy, which I am sure they are ready to listen to. Let me say furthermore that I have indicated to them that they ought to pay the mountains a visit and which has also been most favorably received. I am sure when they once take hold of this matter, it will be done thoroughly.

Now this is merely a preliminary effort on our part, but it indicates to you that we are at least considering this whole matter, and you will also know that when we once get at the job we will give it the best that we can afford.

I wish you would formulate a letter in which your conviction is expressed regarding the need of our department taking a hand in the solution of the problem, as I have indicated in a previous letter. We want to do all we possibly can, but we do not want to impose ourselves or our program on any situation without having the consummate endorsement and call of the folks who are already on the field.

I am also wondering whether the report which the Russell Sage Foundation has in hand might be made available for private study on the part of certain persons as I have alluded to above.

I am sending you in a roll two outline county maps on which you can indicate the counties that are included in the mountaineer problem. I wish you might also suggest some simple text that would give us some light on this feature of the work in which you are so much interested. I have been talking so much about it with such a small asset of information that I may be going far asea in my enthusiasm.

John replied to Mr. Israel on August 13th:

Since our first interview in New York, some time ago, when I had the pleasure of talking over with you the possibilities of the County Work Department of the YMCA undertaking work in the Southern Highlands, the idea has come to seem very practicable to me.

The great thing needed in the Southern Highlands is local leadership and initiative, which will serve also as a bond of connection with "foreign and nonmountainous activities" for the furtherance of rural welfare in that region. The mountain people are predisposed to religious activities. Unfortunately some of the religious work attempted in the past has been too much upon a denominational basis. I would not be understood as saying that all of the denominations working in the Southern Highlands have been governed by denominational interests, but the mountaineer, because of his own denominational leanings, has viewed too much the efforts of religious bodies as the effort of a denomination to propagate itself. The YMCA, which is Christian without being further classified, would, in my judgment, meet a need which no one church can meet.

For years, I have felt that an effort should be made to hold the strong young leaders to whom the former method of presenting Christianity no longer appeals. It must be presented as something virile and productive—productive of the best things of this life, not merely of a hope for the future. Your organization can do it, I believe; at least it is worth trying as an experiment, an experiment which should cover a period of years.

Because of the remarkable urban growth in sections of our country in past decades, stress has been placed upon urban leadership; and in our missionary effort, while too great stress has not been placed upon the need of the highest type of leaders for the foreign field, too little emphasis has been put, perhaps of necessity, upon the need of statesmanlike leadership in the rural sections of the home field. If anywhere statesmanship in Christian leadership is needed today, it is needed in the rural sections of our own land. The Southern Highlanders are, perhaps, the most intensely rural section of our country, and the native leaders in the highlands are men of keen minds. Most of the leaders are men of legal training, and they will come to follow Christian leadership when there is a more general presentation of Christian claims by men of virility, spirituality, power, and vision.

The trouble will be to find the men to lead this work, but wherever there is a great need, men will be found to meet it—and surely this is a need, and one which calls for the best that is in a man.

Cannot you take two or three or more counties, study them somewhat yourself by traveling through them, take a number of men who know mountain life, train them for your country work in some of your summer schools, and grapple with this situation? I know of no work more worth doing, and no work which will call for such diplomacy and such initiative as this work, which I trust most sincerely you can undertake. From this field, with an area of over a hundred thousand square miles, with over five millions of people—practically all rural—there is a call which ought not to be unheeded longer by you.

I should be very glad indeed to cooperate in any way in my power. It seems to me that your department is peculiarly adapted for leadership in an intelligent, productive Christianity in the Southern Highlands. I have a hope, which is somewhat more than a hope, that some financial support for this work can be found within the mountains. Eventually, if your men "make good," there will be little doubt of such support being gained, for sections of the mountains are developing rapidly, and more money will be available in the mountain country than at present. For some years there will be need of much of the support being guaranteed from without. The coming development of the mountains is not only an assurance of future financial support, but an imperative call for immediate Christian effort such as you can render, that a society emerging from a somewhat pioneer condition may not be overwhelmed by the evils which often precede and generally accompany the opening up of a section hitherto shut off.

The following letters of August and September 1913 throw light on some of the concerns of the Asheville office:

[JCC to Mr. Glenn]
August 14, 1913

A short time ago, I went to Black Mountain, North Carolina, in response to a call from Professor [Jerome] Dowd of the Department of Economics and Sociology of the University of Oklahoma. Professor Dowd is a native North Carolinian who spends his summers at Black Mountain. Black Mountain is a station on the Southern road a half-hour ride from Asheville. It is a section in which the Southern Presbyterians, Southern Baptists, and Southern Methodists have summer colonies and Chautauquas; and I think the Episcopalians are also developing a colony there; and that plans are under way to establish a Roman Catholic colony.

The Southern Baptists have not been willing to enter the Federal Council, and at the recent General Assembly in Atlanta, there was some pulling away from the council on the part of the Southern Presbyterians. It was Professor Dowd's idea that these various denominations might be willing to set aside as "interdenominational days" three or four days during their summer Chautauquas that the various bodies might meet together for study and discussion of the larger things of interest to all.

At his request, I went with him to confer with the managers of the Southern Presbyterian and Southern Baptist Chautauquas, who are quite willing to appoint committees for the furtherance of the plan. They expressed themselves hopeful of its success, providing none of the things for which their denominations stood would be jeopardized. I hope that the plan will carry, for it may be through the acquaintance and confidence established in this way that some things very much needed and desired may be accomplished that cannot be accomplished, seemingly, by the Federal Council.

[JCC to Miss Pettit]
August 20, 1913

It occurs to me that I did not answer the question you asked in a recent letter, with reference to scholarships, etc.

My experience leads me to think that the best way of handling scholarships is to have them entirely on a work basis—that is, to have certain "jobs" that pay so much; the scholarship to sustain the "job" and the student assigned to the "job" rather than to have the scholarship money assigned to a particular pupil. It saves complications with donors and causes the pupil to feel that the benefit derived by him depends upon efficiency rather than upon the kindness of some individual. I feel quite certain that this is the better way. Of course, some of these "jobs" would not pay the full way and could be supplemented by payment on the part of the pupil or parent.

I would, by all means, have all the boys and all the girls do a certain amount of work, so as to put them all on the same basis. I would not allow a pupil in the school who was simply a pay pupil.[5] Announcement could be made, if necessary, that in order to keep the expenses of the school down, and to enable all to come at a moderate tuition, the cooperation of all must be enlisted. Care of one's own room, waiting on the table, and similar duties for boys and girls should be regarded as a part of the regular work of the day, for which no allowance is made in scholarships and in which all must participate. The "jobs" should then be assigned on the basis of individual needs, and as far as possible, the number of hours put in at a fair price per hour (which should not be too much in advance of mountain prices to raise false wage standards) should pay for the scholarship.

On any other basis, the pupil is brought to feel that partial work, or work indifferently done, is paid for at a rate even higher than he could obtain when he goes back to his own community. I am quite sure that much harm has been done by a careless use of scholarships. Education should be regarded as something worthwhile—worth working for, and working for thoroughly.

Eventually, I think thoughtful givers will endow grades of work as well as individual pupils. You will run less risk of losing interest in endowing "jobs" than you will by securing a scholarship for a pupil and having to ask the donor for permission to reassign the scholarship every time the former recipient leaves school.

I hope these suggestions may be of some value. They have grown out of hard experience and are matters of quite deep conviction with me. . . .

P.S. If it is ever necessary in special cases to grant money payment without a recompense in work, I would suggest, by all means, that the student receiving such payment should give their personal notes, bearing interest from the date of graduation to the time of payment; and if the student be a minor, to have the note endorsed by some responsible kinsman or friend.

[Mr. Glenn to JCC]
August 22, 1913

Thank you for your interesting batch of letters under date of August 14th. I am very glad to get such good accounts of your summer's work.

Both Mrs. McCormick's interest and that of Mr. Israel's friends open up possibilities of substantial contributions toward the increase of work in the mountains. It will be well worth while to keep in close touch with both of them and influence them as far as possible.

I am sorry that I cannot see the way to authorizing a trip to Denmark. We must keep our expenditure down as much as possible for the next year, because our income will be decidedly limited for the time being. A direct study of Denmark's schools would be useful, but I do not believe it is necessary in order to start some such schools here. There is sufficient information available in this country to make the foundation for starting one or two of these schools experimentally and developing them along lines that will fit in with local conditions. Such a course would result probably in a few more mistakes than would be made if a direct investigation of Denmark's schools were made first by the person who is going to direct the school; but I feel sure that a little ingenuity and study will produce practically as good results as will be found in Denmark, and schools which will be more suited to our particular conditions. It seems to me that the thing now is to find someone who will bear the expense of at least one school and be bold enough to establish it and trust to native good sense to develop it on sound and practical lines. Your particular function is to find, if possible, a financier and a superintendent; and when that is done to let them launch the school with your advice and that of other people like Dr. Claxton. I would have no doubt about its being thoroughly successful under these conditions.

What do you understand is Mr. Israel's particular function in the Country [*sic*] Work Department? I was favorably impressed with him when I saw him last year, and I would like to get in touch with him again soon. His letter is very interesting, though it would be better if he had taken some lessons in English. I think it very desirable that you should go to see his backers whenever opportunity offers. Their interest is very promising.

I am sorry that the Maryville Conference was not better attended. Please let me know more in detail about your "roundtable conference." Please do not have the question of "self-advertising" on your mind. It is necessary that you should report the facts—whether they are favorable or unfavorable.

I am glad to hear that Prof. [Charles] Kent has been in touch with you. He is a fine man and probably successful in getting things done. I shall probably go to Virginia next week, and if I get a chance, I will try to see him and have a talk with him. Miss Clement paid me a short visit the other day. She was still enthusiastic about her mountain trip. We did not have time to go into details.

I can see no objection to your suggestion about the "interdenominational days" at the Chautauquas of the Southern Presbyterians and Baptists—quite the contrary. According to the reports of the Synod of the Southern Presbyterians and Baptists, there was less pulling away and more sympathy than was expected. I should like, however, to get the opinion of Dr. MacFarland on this question. He will not be here until Monday. If I get anything out of him, I will let you know. The standing of the Federal Council with the southern churches has proved to be stronger than we had anticipated. . . .

P.S. If Danish schools are to be started, it would seem important for the person who is to organize and direct them to go to Denmark, rather than someone who would not have the direction of them.

[Mr. Glenn to ODC]
August 22, 1913

I have before me your two interesting letters of May 30th and July 25th. I have not had a good opportunity to write you since my return from the Pacific

Coast. I have, however, been thinking about the ballad situation, and have had a talk with Mr. Rogers, the secretary of the Schirmer Company. I am puzzled to know just what is the best thing to do, but there are several things that I am clear about.

First—from what Mr. Rogers says, I am sure that they would not publish the report. They might, however, have the printing done for us entirely at our expense and in our name.

Second—I am quite sure that the book would have a comparatively small circulation, and its sale would not pay for the cost of publication. Its publication would be expensive. It is really a highly technical product and will be sought only by those people who are interested in studying ballads as folklore and from an historical point of view. The number of such people is necessarily quite limited. I would be convinced that I am wrong only by actual evidence of other similar publications which have paid for themselves.

It is invariably true that professional people that want something published will assert that it will have a large circulation. They believe they are right, but I have been caught a number of times in just that trap. When I see the limited circulation of the R.S.F. publications, some of which appeal to a rather large number of readers, I am very skeptical of anything that is as technical as your book. The fact that its matter is very interesting does not affect the argument.

The question of cooperation with other people is certainly a puzzling one. You have what apparently no one else has, the music. Few people could correctly get this music; even if they had the right kind of an ear, they would not be able to give the time to it that you have given. I would think it was unwise to surrender your material entirely to the tender mercies of any specialist or specialists unless you knew them very well and were sure that they would give your collection its full due. . . . If I see Prof. Kent in Charlottesville, I will talk to him about the whole question.

[JCC to Mr. Glenn]
September 3, 1913

Enclosed herewith is a clipping from yesterday's *Asheville Citizen* which bears upon the subject of the interdenominational plans of which I wrote you. I shall try to keep in touch with Professor Dowd and others, and hope I may be of service.

Yesterday I attended some rallies in this vicinity with Dr. [W. S.] Rankin, secretary of the State Board of Health; Mr. [Elliott B.] Millsaps, who has charge of the farm demonstration work of western North Carolina; Mr. [David S.] Weaver, who is special agent of the demonstration work in this district; Dr. [D. E.] Sevier, county physician; and Mr. [William H.] Hipps, county superintendent of education. I spoke briefly of the interrelation of school, farm, and health work. I had planned to go to four or five other rallies with them this week, in different parts of the county. My hay fever, however, seized hold of me unexpectedly and forcibly yesterday, on my return; and if it keeps its present grip, I shall not only have to give up attendance at these rallies but may have to seek higher altitude for several weeks. I do not want to take a vacation at this time.

With reference to the inquiry in your letter of August 22nd as to Mr. Israel's particular function in the County Work Department, I would say that he is intimately connected with county work and general rural work, both in this country and in foreign countries, being, I believe, the research and editorial secretary, County Work Department, of the International Committee of the Young Men's Christian Associations.

The roundtable conferences to which I referred in a recent letter had to do with the various phases of mountain life—topography, resources, etc., and remedial measures.

[Rev. Brown to JCC]
September 16, 1913

Yours, concerning the resignation of Dr. [Richard O.] Flinn from the Executive Committee of the interdenominational conference on mountain work received. I regret very much that Dr. Flinn's other duties compel him to resign. It will be a distinct loss to our committee, but I have no doubt Dr. [D. H.] Ogden is in every way fitted for membership on the committee and that it will be a pleasure to be associated with him. It is especially fitting that he should be on the Executive Committee since he is chairman of the Presbyterian Committee on Mountain Work.

P.S. I beg to acknowledge the receipt of the magazine *World's Work*. I have not yet felt equal to the task of reading the article on education but have no doubt I shall enjoy it to the fullest. Thank you very much.

From one of John's old students in Joppa and in Pleasant Hill came the following:

[Fred Donaldson to JCC]
September 28, 1913

Your letter came yesterday, and I was mighty glad to get it. I have been reproaching myself for some time for not dropping you a line as I promised I would soon after getting here, but now you have given me a grand opportunity to talk with you, and I am going to avail myself of it to the uttermost. Therefore and hence, do not be surprised to get a young book from me. There will not be a great deal, if any, that will be of interest to the public at large, I trow, but there may be enough interesting spots in it to repay you for wading through the mess. Perhaps it would be well to have your eyes in good condition, and see to it that the light bulbs are giving normal amount of light. Stenographers are not growing on every tree around here, but thanks to the fact that I have a machine of my own, the trouble of deciphering my script will be spared you.

This is a great country down here [Florida], and I am enjoying life very much, altho as yet I have not even begun to nibble at the corners of coupons. It has been nip and tuck to make ends meet with me this summer, but now the world looks much more hopeful, and it will be but a matter of time until I am on my feet financially, I think. The first thing that fell to my lot on coming down here was the erection of a nice stone wall covering the fronts of two five-acre tracts. As the pay was by the rod instead of by the day, and the wages I would receive had been computed on the basis that I should lay three or four rods a day, I found that actually my intake was less by several cents than I had been told it would be. You see they had neglected to advise beforehand that their system of wages was by the piece. Well, I managed to scrape along, and the more rock I handled, the faster I did it, so that by the time I was through I could earn a very fair wage.

There has been something for me to do ever since coming down, and this winter promises to furnish more, as it is the busy season. I never have felt better than I am feeling now, and have never been so tanned. It is simply impossible for me to escape from my cooking, however, for there is another old bachelor here (thirty-four) who has to live somewhere and has difficulty in finding a place that is suitable, so we have gone into cahoots and rented a very comfortable cottage for the year and are keeping house. It has its great advantages, but sometimes after a day of it in the field, I wish that he knew more about cooking than he does and that I did not have to think what we will have to eat and how to get it in the shortest time allowable. On the whole, we enjoy it immensely. I think that I shall tell you more about it at the end of my next, for it comes in under the head of means to attain unto the hopes now held.

Elaine is all right—she is even better than ever, and that is going some. I do not see any chance of our wanting work among the mountains this year, either of us, but it would not surprise me a bit if another year I should like very much to get a start in that work. I am not rushing the China idea for myself, and she had told me that it will make no difference to her or with her if I do not come. I should have gone this spring if I could have felt that it was the ethical thing for me to do under the circumstances, but I did not.

The problem of the life work is certainly a problem when one has to choose something that will not only benefit humanity, but at the same time be sufficiently appreciated by the same to furnish a respectable living for himself and family. There seem to be good prospects here—shall know more about them in the spring, but I am not sure in my own mind that the work will really satisfy me, even with the dough attachment. I must consider the latter for a little while, until I have cleared up what I owe for my college to Mark and the institution.

Now I am going to stop this, so as not to tire you before the real article comes your way. It will be sent along as promptly as possible, which may be the latter part of next week. Remember me to Mrs. Campbell and to Gavin.

It was a great disappointment to John when an interdenominational conference which was to have taken place at Highland College, Breathitt County, Kentucky, October 30, 1913, had to be canceled because of an epidemic of smallpox in that vicinity. It had been called by Miss Pettit of the Pine Mountain School and Rev. W. E. Hudson, superintendent of the Mountain Work of the Southern Presbyterian Church, but John had been influential in bringing it about and had helped in all the planning. As he had written Mr. Glenn on September 26th: "It promises to be a very representative gathering, and I am now trying to get some of the government experts who have been sent to Hindman to attend the conference. I am hoping that ultimately arrangements will be made for conferences in the mountain sections of all the Appalachian states, inasmuch as many of the workers cannot afford to attend the interdenominational mountain conferences, the first of which was held in April this year."

He was, however, able to attend another meeting of rural mountain workers in the laurel country of North Carolina, under Northern Presbyterian auspices.

John's active contact with the mountain work of this Northern Presbyterian Mission Board had begun in 1908, as it had with the fieldwork of many other denominations. He came to know gradually during that time principals, ministers, and teachers and saw and discussed the conditions under which they were working. Governing boards of most denominations, usually far removed from individual pieces of work, were hard to reach. Their headquarters and membership were widely scattered, and officers were not familiar with actual conditions existing, as were the field superintendents, who could not always convince them that changes were necessary.

In addition, some denominations had several boards dealing with mountain work. As a previous official of the Woman's Board of the Presbyterian Board of Home Missions of the Presbyterian Church, USA, explained:

Up to 1897, the Board of Home Missions of the Presbyterian Church, USA, had a "Woman's Executive Committee," which, while under the direction of the board, raised its own quota of funds and had a large say in the administration and support of educational and medical work. In 1897 the name of the women's group was changed to that of "The Women's Board of National Missions of the Presbyterian Church," but the same relationship with the "Home" or "Men's" board (as it was usually called) remained.

The "squabbling" you were aware of was, as you say, not confined to the Presbyterians, but was apparent wherever the women of a denomination had become successful enough in raising funds to demand the right to say how those funds should be used. With greater resources, often, for their projects, they could build new buildings, pay better salaries, serve better food, and keep properties in better repair. And since their projects were often units within larger projects operated by the "men's boards," there was ill feeling and jealousy over the differences, which were obvious. I remember even . . . visiting school campuses, under our Board of Home Missions, in the midst of which were attractive, new girls' dormitories, well furnished, well staffed, serving excellent food, etc., in great contrast to the rest of the campus, the girls' dormitory being a "women's' project."

Around 1910–1911, a Country Life Department of the board was set up, with Dr. Warren H. Wilson as superintendent. He was an able and energetic head, as well as a man of warm heart, strong convictions, and quick tongue, which sometimes led him into friction. John found him a cordial friend and, although they differed on some points, worked with him wherever he had opportunity. Dr. Wilson's letter of September 23rd was therefore very welcome:

We are clearing up the program of our Country Life Camp (October 20–24) at Big Laurel, North Carolina. I have a very hopeful promise from you that you will be present on those dates and take charge of one hour, with the cooperation, so far as you desire it, of Dr. O. F. Wisner, now making a survey in the southern mountains, at present in Owsley County, Kentucky. I hope you can confirm this promise and use one hour each day in a description of mountain conditions as you have explored them and a description of four topics such as shall seem good to you in the way of constructive work in a mountain community.

You know about what our workers are, and you know the needs which confront them better than anyone else. We hope to make this meeting of lasting value. If you have any suggestions as to the use of it for other persons than those for whom it is planned, I will be very glad to extend the advantages of the meeting to them. Our present plan is to invite to it only our workers, about thirty-seven in number.

John replied on September 29th:

Your letter of September 23rd is at hand. I am planning to attend the conference at Big Laurel for at least a part of the time, from the 20th to the 24th of October. Possibly Mrs. Campbell will go with me. I trust most sincerely that nothing may prevent my attendance.

With regard to your question, I will say that I shall be very glad indeed to cooperate with Dr. Wisner. May I suggest that instead of my giving a set address on mountain conditions for an hour each day, that those hours be used as roundtable conferences. I shall be glad to lead off and to call upon others to speak on topics that may be brought up and which may be of peculiar interest in view of papers that have been read.

With reference to your inquiry as to persons other than those of your immediate workers to whom the conference may be helpful, I would say that I feel that we who are working in a sense independently, as church workers or as workers under philanthropic boards, need to touch elbows with those who are working as public officials in communities, county or state. I would therefore suggest inviting the county superintendent of education and the county health officer—if there is one—and if not, one or two of the leading county physicians.

Dr. L. B. McBrayer, of Asheville, a mountain man, is much interested in the kind of work you plan to do and has recently been furthering county conferences in Buncombe County, looking toward local support for the election of a permanent county health officer.

I have wondered, also, whether it would be possible to secure the attendance of some of the Presbyterian teachers in your larger schools in this section—schools that are preparing, in a somewhat direct way, students for rural teachers or as rural workers. President [Edward P.] Childs, however, would know more about the feasibility of this than I.

I look forward with much pleasure to meeting you and other co-workers in the promising field of rural service.

Correspondence of this sort could hardly fail to bring John, if he were able to go at all, and in this case it brought me too. It was bitter weather, spitting snow—one of those early mountain cold snaps. The steep hill slopes were a brilliant tapestry of color. My eyes wandered out to the glowing landscape while we huddled, in deep discussion, over the fire. John was at his best on an occasion like this—alive, vivid, full of humor—the center and life of the group. We had some fine walks, too, and a long horseback ride with Dr. George Packard, who was studying the situation as a possible place to work under the Country Life Department. I heard some ballad singing—in this, Cecil Sharp's first and later hunting place—and at Dr. Wilson's request explained its significance. Altogether it was a very satisfactory occasion for us all. John wrote Mr. Glenn on October 28th:

I have just returned from a Country Life Conference in the laurel region of Madison County, North Carolina. The conference was under the auspices of the Country Life Department of the Presbyterian Church, USA, of which Dr. Warren H. Wilson is superintendent. To me it had in it more of promise for the mountain country than any mountain conference I have attended hitherto. It is the augury, I hope, of what will take place in other sections when the work of the mission schools, as schools, is over.

The Women's Board has been doing most of the mountain school work of the Northern Presbyterian Church. In the French Broad Presbytery, which covers the territory in question, the community school work is over. There are fifteen or more teachers' homes and schoolhouses which are now being converted into community centers, reached from a central station at which are located a skilled farmer and women versed in domestic science and household arts. They have a circuit which takes in regularly these fifteen stations. Three or four days in every six weeks they devote to instruction at each station in farming, household activities, and in social entertainment of some sort—especially music for the neighbors. They are also desirous of undertaking medical work. I was able to find them a physician and his wife of the kind wanted, who spent a week on the field and are now at my home for a day or two. They have told me, confidentially, that a proposition had been made them by which they will be able to take up the medical work of that district in the spring.

It is a country entirely unreached in a medical way. We know this physician very well. He used to have a hospital in the East, which he has given up, and his two leading nurses are now taking courses in district nursing through scholarships which we were able to secure for them through Miss Clement's department of the Red Cross. I am hoping that with this beginning that is likely to be made, there will be an opening in a year or so for the Red Cross.

The discussions at the conference were of a high grade. The workers impressed me very favorably. The point of meeting was twelve or fifteen miles from the railroad, over a very rough road, but there were fifty-six in attendance—all eager to learn, and all contributing something of help that had come from their own experience.

Dr. [Harold W.] Foght, of the US Bureau of Education, came from Washington and gave some very forceful and inspiring addresses. He had just returned from Denmark and is enthusiastic over the promise in the Danish folk school for the mountain country.

Dr. Wilson was especially happy in his attitude and in his addresses. I have noticed a jarring note in many of his public addresses in the past, but there was an entire absence of this throughout this conference and a very evident desire on his part to learn as well as to impart.

There are some points of friction still existing between the Women's Board and the Country Life Department. Possibly the Women's Board regrets somewhat that it has given over this promising field. Possibly the officials of the several boards have not been tactful in their dealings with each other. I feel that my close personal acquaintance with these officials helps out the situation considerably.

I had three set addresses: one on the "Economic Situation in the Mountains," another on "The School and the Need of Readjustment," and the third on "Denominational Distribution in the Mountains, together with the Readjustment Necessary to Bring Denominations More Closely in Touch." I was called on to participate in the discussions at every session, and Dr. Wilson and other officials seemed to appreciate very much the fact that I had come to cooperate with them. I hope that nothing may occur between boards to set back the work that is so well begun.

Dr. Wilson also wrote Mr. Glenn, on October 31st:

We have just held in North Carolina a training school attended by fifty-six workers, men and women, in mountain communities and boarding schools. Mr. John C. Campbell of the Russell Sage Foundation was with us throughout the five days of our meeting, and I write to express to you our indebtedness to the Foundation for his services.

Not only were Mr. and Mrs. Campbell personally of the greatest help in the meeting on account of their experience as mountain workers themselves, but especially helpful to us in the present juncture in our work was the extra knowledge possessed by Mr. Campbell and the authority he has through the investigation he has made. I know that you are aware of our appreciation in this board of the value of Mr. Campbell's investigation, but I wish to assure you anew of its practical use to us at a particular time.

Mr. Glenn replied to Dr. Wilson on November 1st: "Thank you very much for your kind note about Mr. Campbell. I am very glad to get your opinion of his work. I had already heard from him about the conference. He spoke especially of the value of your presence there. I hope to have the pleasure of seeing you at the Rural Life Conference on November 6th."

Mr. Glenn also had some correspondence relating to the October conference with a well-known minister and writer (Presbyterian) of that time, Rev. William Adams Brown. He wrote Mr. Glenn on November 19th: "I understand that the Sage Foundation has recently been cooperating with our Department of Church and Country Life in a conference dealing with the work in the southern mountains. As the department has been subject to some criticism by those who do not understand its purpose and aims, I should appreciate it if you would write me your own judgment of the value of the work that we have been doing along these lines, and the wisdom with which it has been conducted."

In replying to Rev. Brown, November 26th, Mr. Glenn used some of John's letter:

The following quotation will interest you in view of your inquiry about the rural life department:

I have just returned from a Country Life Conference in the Laurel region of Madison County, North Carolina. The conference was under the auspices of the Country Life Department of the Presbyterian Church, USA, of which Dr. Warren H. Wilson is superintendent. To me it had in it more of promise for the mountain country than any mountain conference I have attended hitherto. It is the augury, I hope, of what will take place in other sections when the work of the mission schools, as schools, is over. . . .

Dr. Wilson was especially happy in his attitude and in his addresses.

My impression is that on the whole it has done good work; its rural surveys have, I think, been as good as anyone could do in such pioneer work. I should, however, like very much to have a talk with you about the department and will try to call you up early next week in the hope that we may lunch together at the Century or make some other arrangement. It is just possible, however, that I shall not be able to call you until after December 10th. I am going away for the rest of this week and have to be in Baltimore for the Federal Council of Churches Executive Committee meetings for three days next week.

Our Mr. John C. Campbell expects to be here on Monday of next week. If he is here, would you like to talk with him, and if so, would you lunch with us? I shall not be able to tell you definitely until Monday morning.

The files do not reveal whether the Monday meeting took place when John and I were in New York. In Washington, December 6th, on the way home, he wrote Mr. Glenn:

President Wilson of Maryville College met me here this morning, and we spent part of the day going over the manuscript of his book. Meet with the trustees of the Southern Industrial Educational Association at the home of Judge [Seth] Shephard tomorrow afternoon to suggest a possible policy.

I have several appointments for Monday on matters pertaining to my proposed bulletins. We shall leave for Asheville in all probability Monday night. We both thank you, Mrs. Glenn, and the Misses Brown for the delightful and restful visit in your home.

On returning home, one of his first letters was to Rev. W. E. Hudson, December 12th:

I am very, very sorry to tell you that the Southern Presbyterian data on mountain schools has not yet been received. You do not mean to give me to understand that you are going to allow the "Northern" Presbyterians to get ahead of you in this respect. If you will answer soon, they will not. Seriously, I know how busy you are, but I am being pressed for religious statistics, and I cannot get them out until I have heard from the various superintendents.

One more thing. I wrote to Mr. Ogden for suggestions as to the interdenominational conference, speakers, etc. In view of his recent appointment, he preferred to have me direct my inquiries in those respects to you. I should appreciate your suggestions in these matters also.

I have just returned to Asheville after an absence of a month. We were at West Medford several weeks and found Mother Dame much better than we had anticipated. She is gaining steadily, and if all goes well, we hope to have her with us in a month or two. I trust that both you and Mrs. Hudson are getting some rest, and that Mrs. Hudson is again in her accustomed health. With very kindest regards to you both from Mrs. Campbell and myself.

John also wrote on December 13th to Mr. Glenn, reporting more in detail as to his visit in Washington, with reference to the problems of the Southern Industrial Educational Association:

We arrived home Wednesday. Our stay in Washington was most satisfactory. The US Geological Survey people were most cordial and are to furnish me with estimates for illustrations I might want to use. If it can be done consistently, the work that I desire to have done for the bulletin will be undertaken by some of the experts of the survey. Mr. Graves and his colleagues in the Forest Service were most kind. I am to be furnished with a traveling exhibit on "Mountain Land and Forest—Their Use and Abuse," which I can take to the conferences and loan to mountain workers.

On Sunday afternoon I met with the directors of the Southern Industrial Educational Association, at the home of Judge Shephard. All the directors were there, with the exception of two. Dr. Claxton attended, which I am told was an unusual thing for him to do. We discussed the whole situation very thoroughly, and I outlined various activities that might be undertaken.

One of the directors told me confidentially the next day that what I had said made an impression and that as a result some of the "progressives" had discussed a plan to invite Dr. Claxton and myself to act as a committee to outline their work, pick out a man who might be sent abroad to study the rural situation, and to pick out a field of activity in the Southern Highlands. My informant was so kind as to say that they had more confidence in my knowledge and judgment of the mountain situation than in Dr. Claxton's, but I urged the desirability of placing Dr. Claxton at the head of this movement—both because of his position, and because of the fact that he is one of their trustees. In addition, he has a real interest in the mountain people and the mountain country. I urged further that another one of their trustees be appointed to the committee and that I act as an adviser rather than as a member of the committee. This, I think, will be done if the project contemplated is furthered. I am very hopeful that something is to be done.

Mrs. [Martha] Gielow was present, and at her request I had a private conference with her the next day. I think there is a disposition to treat her fairly, as the originator of the association, but she does not see the situation at all as it is. I think she has some very good ideas. Her inclination toward the dramatic handicaps the association in various ways, I am inclined to think.

[Mr. Glenn to JCC]
December 15, 1913

I am very glad to hear about your meeting with the Southern Industrial Educational Association and that the result was so satisfactory. I agree with you that it is much better to act as an adviser than as a member of the committee of the association. They should appoint a committee of their own membership, authorized to bring in suggestions for reorganization, and those on the committee should confer with you insofar as they choose. If you become a member of the committee or of their board, you become to a certain extent responsible for their official action. I think it important to avoid getting in this position.

On the other hand, it might be that if they decide on a plan which is really valuable for the mountains and will be consequently carried out, it would not be objectionable for you to be a member of their board, or of any special committee they may appoint—just as Mr. Hanmer is a member of the board of Boy Scouts, and other members of the staff have taken positions on boards where they could be useful. Such membership, however, is personal, and not official.

I write this merely that you may know what I think. Please use your own judgment in deciding what to do.

Here was the SIEA, made of up prominent Washington citizens who felt a desire to help mountain people, influenced, many of them, by highly colored stories of poverty, ignorance, worth, and need. Approached by its president in February of the previous year (1912), Mr. Glenn had referred the matter to John, as he did all mountain—indeed all southern—matters. John was not especially impressed by their published material, nor by his first interview with the president, Mrs. Gielow, which he had described in a letter to Mr. Glenn as early as March 27, 1912:

> The impression I gained was that it [the SIEA] was not altogether fitted to do the work that it hoped to do. . . . Possibly the overemphasis on the picturesque side of the work and the dramatic presentation, together with the personal sacrifice made, which is emphasized, influenced me adversely. . . . I stated that it would be well, as in other philanthropic work, to have the books gone over and audited by some banking house or auditing firm that had standing in business circles and had no connection whatever with a particular association or school.

And on another Washington visit he had written Mr. Glenn (January 31, 1913):

> In Washington, I was called into conference with the secretary, a Mrs. [C. David] White, and the president, Mrs. Gielow, of the Southern Industrial Educational Association. Mrs. White and her husband, who is connected with the United States Geological Survey, were especially desirous of having their appeal made less dramatic, and along the lines of practical efficiency. . . .
>
> In all probability I shall go to Raleigh on February 11th to attend a Social Service Conference called by Dr. [Watson S.] Rankin of the State Board of Health. I want to see him and also Superintendent [James Y.] Joyner, who has always been a great help to me. I want particularly to learn from him just how organizations such as the Southern Industrial Educational Association can be serviceable to the educational forces in the rural section of the mountains.

The report on John's meeting nearly a year later with the directors of the SIEA, as given in his letter of December 13, 1913, above, was followed by another letter that he wrote to Mr. Glenn on January 3, 1914:

Yesterday Professor Frank Waldo, of Cambridge, Massachusetts, called upon me, and I had a most interesting visit with him. Mr. Waldo was formerly professor of astronomy in Harvard University and was also connected with Columbia and Princeton.

It appears that he has known the mountain people of western North Carolina more or less intimately for eighteen years, having come here and lived here for some time to further matters connected with titles of mountain lands purchased by his father prior to the Civil War. Apparently he has a genuine interest in the mountain people and has some very sane ideas as to the kind of schools that should be started in the mountain country.

It would seem that he is intimately acquainted with President Wilson and was a member of the same church in Princeton. It came out casually in our conversation that Mr. Waldo saw Dr. Claxton for a few moments in Washington. He called on me seemingly to ask if there might not be an opening for a man of his training for work in the mountain country. I could not but wonder if possibly he was prompted to his inquiries by some knowledge of Mrs. Wilson's interest in the mountain people and of the reorganization of the work of the Southern Industrial Educational Association. I wanted him to be in touch with you if there was anything of the sort in his mind, so I suggested, as an answer to his inquiries as to whether there might be an opening, his writing to you and telling of his work, his interest, and his connection with the mountain people. He did not make his desire a matter of much conversation. I felt that possibly it was brought forward in the hope that I might suggest an opening through the Southern Industrial Educational Association. . . .

I received yesterday from my friend Rev. William E. Hudson, superintendent of the Mountain Work of the Southern Presbyterian Church, a letter saying that he had received a letter from a Dr. Taylor of Washington, D.C., who, I infer, is Mrs. Wilson's pastor. Dr. Taylor had asked Mr. Hudson for a list of the mountain schools. Hudson can give only those of the Southern Presbyterian Church, and he asked me to send a list of the others to Dr. Taylor. I agreed to do so if Dr. Taylor wanted me to.

Mr. Waldo has also asked me for a list of the schools, which I am to furnish him, and for a map upon which he can locate the schools.

I am delighted with these evidences of Mrs. Wilson's interest (I cannot escape the conviction that Mr. Waldo's interest is in some way connected with hers, or at least that he knows of it), and I am very hopeful that the Southern Industrial Educational Association is to be a real help in the furtherance of the right kind of schools in the Southern Highlands.

Additional information reaching him the next week, John sent Mr. Glenn another letter about the SIEA on January 10, 1914:

I have just learned that the Mr. Taylor of Washington, D.C., to whom I referred in a recent letter, is, as I thought, Mrs. Woodrow Wilson's pastor. It would appear that he was recommended recently by Mrs. Wilson as a trustee of the Southern Industrial Educational Association and that Mrs. Wilson suggested his availability for consultation as to the work, if not for utilization in a more important capacity. I wonder if this does not mean that he is a possible candidate for the office of managing secretary or supervising field secretary that the board seems likely to appoint eventually.

I know nothing about Mr. Taylor, and he may be just the man for the place, but it seems to me all-important that the right man should be selected. If the person in charge of this new work is to promote rural education and possibly to become director of a model rural school, it is highly important that such a person should have an intimate knowledge of the mountains, and should know something of industrial education, and make some study in this country and abroad of the kind of work to be promoted.

The association in the past has been giving sums, generally comparatively small, to different schools for so-called domestic science, manual, and industrial training. Usually the persons on the field who have administered the funds have not been people trained especially for those kinds of work. I am a little fearful that the same kind of work will go on. . . .

There would be less objection to this policy if in these schools there were teachers able to use the fund for the kind of work that is supposed to be done by it. I feel very sure, however, that under existing circumstances it would be a much wiser expenditure of money to concentrate upon one or two schools and to place in them teachers of the right training, or to establish a new kind of work entirely as an example for existing schools. The danger is that the present policy of the association will be continued and that a field secretary not acquainted with the people, country, or kind of work to be done will visit the schools and approve the work done on the basis of the self-denial and noble spirit of those engaged in it, or measure it by standards not adapted to the mountains. I fear, too, it will continue to be looked upon as "missionary work," for which many subconscious excuses will be made because of the devotion of those engaged in it, rather than as a kind of work which is to set ideals for rural education in the mountains and elsewhere.

You will not misunderstand me, I am sure, or feel that I minimize the devotion of the workers on the field, or that I discount the spiritual aspects of the work. I do feel, however, that it is of the utmost importance that a kind of work be promoted in the mountains which shall lift the mountain country out of the "field of missions" as that phrase is generally used. The work must be of a kind that emphasizes as its aim self-support on the part of the mountain people, to enable them to maintain their own churches and other institutions. This cannot be done without emphasis, and strong emphasis, upon the proper kind of school.

I deal with many men of purely academic training who minimize this kind of work, and I am perhaps overanxious when new enterprises arise that the proper kind of men be chosen, who believe fully in the right kind of education for the mountains. There is danger, too, that in this new enterprise not only money but time will be wasted in securing facts already gathered by others. There is needed an expert (or one who is ready to become one) in matters that pertain to rural life.

There is a real desire on the part of individual members of the association to help the mountain people, and I have written as I have in the hope that the Foundation may avail itself of this genuine interest to advance what is so much needed.

It is difficult to explain all the contacts through which John hoped that something might be accomplished for the mountains. Most of them are described in his voluminous correspondence with Mr. Glenn, but many come through other letters and personal interviews. Many activities took place at the same time, with sometimes interruption of weeks in individual projects. I have tried in this record to pick passages which show the variety of his interests: the educational problem—improvement of the public school and the establishment of a different kind of independent school by denominational and private agencies, which would not compete with the public school, such as the Danish folk school adapted to mountain conditions. He emphasized constantly the cooperation of agencies with each other, with the state, the Red Cross Nursing Service, the Young Men's Christian Association, and with such agencies as George Peabody College, the Southern Industrial Educational Association, and others. Sometimes a possible plan can be followed quickly and easily through his general correspondence; sometimes an idea appears and reappears through the months.

The following inquiry from Atlanta, for example, was sent on January 5, 1914, by Agnes Raoul (Mrs. T. K.) Glenn first to the Russell Sage Foundation in New York and then to the Asheville office:

I have lately been appointed one of the eleven directors of the Tate School, near Tate, Georgia. The buildings are not yet constructed, and I want to find out what school in the South, what school in the East, and what school in the United States is the most perfect example of a country industrial school. I want to visit some of the schools already established in order to be better informed as to what is most desirable.

Mr. Sam Tate of Tate, Georgia, has given five thousand acres of land and a small sum of money to the school. A landscape architect has been employed to make the plan of the place, and the first building has been begun, but very little else has been done yet. There is no city or town in that district. The place is sixty miles from Atlanta, in the mountains of north Georgia.

There are very few Negroes in that district, and the plan is to establish an undenominational school for white boys and girls to teach them how to live in that country and to emphasize technical education without omitting grammar-school work. The idea is not to bring the children to town but to teach them how to live in the country. The ignorance of the people is almost inconceivable, and the unhygienic conditions of life in that healthy climate are appalling.

While I think I understand the end toward which we are working, I do not know by what means to acquire it, and I would be most obliged if you would direct me to the best sources of information on the subject.

Mr. Glenn answered this letter on January 13th:

I am glad to hear of a school which wishes to train children for country life. Two schools that come to my mind first as having the best theories and best equipment are Miss Berry's school at Rome, Georgia, and

Hampton Institute at Hampton, Virginia. Although Hampton is a school for Negroes, its equipment and methods would be valuable in any industrial school. I should also refer especially to the Orphan Asylum Society in the State of New York, Mr. R. R. Reeder, superintendent, Hastings-on-Hudson, New York. The superintendents of all these schools are people of exceptional experience and wisdom.

Allow me to emphasize this one point very strongly. The most important thing to do is to employ a high-grade, first-rate superintendent before any laying out of grounds or building is begun. This is the only way to avoid serious mistakes which later on will have to be corrected or will seriously hamper the work of the school. The theory on which the school is working, and the methods by which the theory is to be carried out, should be determined before any progress is made on the physical side and before children are taken in.

Your superintendent should devote several months to the study of existing schools in different parts of the country. We should be glad at any time to direct him to the best schools, and possibly some of our staff could make some visits with him.

The special purpose of the Child-Helping Department of this Foundation is to advise as to the conduct of institutions of various sorts for children. Our Division of Education, of which Dr. Leonard P. Ayres is director, will advise as to educational matters.

The headquarters of our Southern Highland Division is Room 412 Legal Building, Asheville, North Carolina, and in charge is Mr. John C. Campbell. Mr. Campbell is well acquainted with the schools for mountain boys and girls, as well as with others in different parts of the country.

I am sending your letter to each of the directors of these departments, and they will be glad to give you any advice or information which you may wish. Dr. Hart can probably help you in finding a superintendent.

I suggest also that you write to Hon. P. P. Claxton, commissioner, US Bureau of Education. Mr. Claxton is thoroughly familiar with the educational problems of the South. Also Mr. Wickliffe Rose, Southern Education Board, Washington, D.C., who can give you some help.

I shall be very happy if you will let us give you any further information or advice.

John's reply to Mrs. Glenn's letter was dated January 20, 1914:

I am much interested in your letter of January 19th. The questions you ask are of vital importance, and I wish very much that we might confer over this matter.

Some of the best schools for mountain children are here in Asheville, and some of the prominent officials supervising work in the mountains are here in Asheville. Superintendent Brown of the Baptist Mountain Work; Superintendent Childs of the Northern Presbyterian Mountain Work; Bishop Horner of the Mountain Work of the Protestant Episcopal Church; and Dr. [Robert] Campbell and Rev. R. P. Smith of the Southern Presbyterian Church—men who know the mountains and mountain work intimately—are all here. It would seem wise for you, or representatives of the proposed school, to come here and view the work that is being done about Asheville and to meet these people. I can arrange meetings for you with them. If this plan seems practicable to you, and possible of execution, please write me as to when you could be here, and I will arrange matters for you.

There is to be an interdenominational Conference of Mountain Workers (which includes also those doing independent work in the mountains) which is to meet—probably in Knoxville—sometime in April. It might be of interest to you to attend that conference.

There are schools in Kentucky that it would pay you to visit.

It will give me much pleasure to be of any assistance to you in my power.

The importance John gave to agricultural training and medical services for the mountain people comes out strongly in a letter he wrote to Mrs. Anna B. Taft of the Department of Church and Country Life, Presbyterian Church, USA, who had sent him an extract from a letter from Mr. [A. L.] Lawsing, a church extension worker in Laurel Country. John's letter, characterized as wise and significant of his work and methods by Mr. Glenn, was dated January 7, 1914:

I thank you very much for sending me the extract from Mr. Lawsing's letter of December 25th to Dr. Wilson. The sound hard sense of the letter adds to my personal estimate of the man formed while at the conference on Big Laurel. So many plans for the upbuilding of mountain farms take no account of the fact that the average mountain farmer cannot afford to experiment with crops suitable to soil, etc., which, like the apple crop, for instance, take some years to bring returns. He must content himself with a crop which, though meager, brings support for himself, family, and stock, even though he knows that the fertility of the soil is being impaired by the succession of the same crop.

It requires a trained mind to give proper direction and demonstration in such matters to secure the necessary yearly support and the larger future returns which will arise from the wise selection of seed, and succession of varied crops adapted to soil, elevation, and slope.

A number of mountain schools committed to industrial and agricultural education are making the sad mistake of training boys to farm bottomland merely. Such land is scarce in the mountains, is worth one hundred dollars or more an acre generally, and with the increase of population is increasing in price. As the population increases, there will be the necessity of farming steeper slopes than those that are now being farmed. I have a testimonial of government experts who know the mountain country to substantiate the claim that the soil of these mountainsides is fertile and that they can be retained by proper terracing and ploughing and made to yield much more abundantly. I am impressed with Mr. Lawsing's plea for instruction to till *typical mountain lands* at a small outlay and with implements possible of ownership by the mountain farmer. By "typical" I mean typical for the local environment. I am convinced that the agricultural education of the future must take account of the prevalent local and regional types. The United States Government will, I am sure, cooperate in such an effort.

If it should seem wise for you to lease a farm for a number of years, with ultimate purchase in mind, it would be eminently wise to have the purchase price fixed. Otherwise there is likely to be misunderstanding as to price, so apparent will be the increased value of the land due to its wise cultivation. I know from years of personal experience on the field that it is a difficult matter to convince persons not in intimate touch with the field to view this kind of work favorably. Some boards have sustained heavy losses in their attempts to further agricultural education in the mountains. I am very sure, however, that most of the losses have arisen from not having trained and adaptable people in charge of such work. You are very fortunate in having a man who is not lacking in these qualities so essential to success.

I am deeply interested in this attempt you are making in the Big Laurel region, and it is possible that at some time I may be able to suggest to persons in your church—friends of mine—the wisdom of furthering this kind of work through their contributions.

I am even more interested in the medical possibilities of mountain work. To me it seems the quickest and surest means of gaining the confidence of the mountain people, without which no permanent work can be done. I hope most earnestly that the prospect of having a physician in the Laurel field is to become a reality. How much it is needed only those of us know who have lived for years in isolated mountain regions. It seems to me that it is a statesmanlike, may I not say prophetic, vision that Miss [Frances] Goodrich has of this work. As I understand it, the plan is not to endow permanently a so-called medical missionary, but to subsidize for a limited number of years a physician of ability and character in order to give him an opportunity to gain the confidence of the mountain people. After a few years he will probably have a self-sustaining practice.

I am sometimes misunderstood when I emphasize the industrial and medical side of mountain work. They are in my judgment the most promising means of evangelism in the mountains for the next generation. The church that first catches this vision and makes it a reality will be the leader in constructive rural Christianity.

I trust you will pardon this long, earnest, and somewhat intimate letter. You know that for twenty years I have been in the mountain field. Discouragement has weighed heavily at times, but the things that are being attempted in the Laurel field are to me the most promising that I know for the mountain country and for rural sections of our country generally. There must be not less emphasis upon the spiritual than in the past, but there must be more emphasis upon the industrial and on the health sides of our work. Development of such Christian activities would rest fittingly upon the splendid foundation laid by the Women's Board and Miss Goodrich. You Presbyterians have been leaders in mountain work in the past, and the opportunity is now yours to be pioneers in a much greater work than ever done before—a work which through the wisdom of those who direct it will enable the mountain people to contribute more and more to the spiritual means of life, without which all else is of little importance. I wish I were able personally to finance this much-needed medical work.

You are fortunate again in having in mind for this work people of training and character. Did you know that the doctor you have in mind intended going to the foreign field but was prevented from so doing by the illness of his father, and that his wife was in China for ten years and went through the Boxer uprising? I know them both personally. They are strong Christian characters, and the doctor's skill as a physician is unquestioned.

Added to my personal interest in this field and in this proposed work is my strong desire to have in the mountains a demonstration of what can be done, to which I can refer other church boards when they ask me as to what the future work in the mountain country is to be.

I fear I have wearied you with this long letter, but I ask that my deep interest in your plans plead my pardon.

The doctor John knew and had proposed was appointed, as appears from his letter of January 17, 1914, to Mr. Glenn:

Mr. Waldo, of whom I wrote in my letter of January 3rd, called upon me again yesterday. He told me he had not written you inasmuch as he expected to come north soon and preferred to see you in person rather than to write a long letter giving his ideas.

I was up in the mountains day before yesterday in the so-called Laurel country where the Country Life Department of the Presbyterian Church, USA, is carrying on work. I gave a very brief talk. They are carrying on extension work, holding a two-weeks school in agriculture, domestic science, and singing. I was pleased with what I saw.

You will be interested to know that the matter in which I have been much interested, the placing of a physician in the field, was decided upon favorably day before yesterday. They have appointed Dr. [George] Packard and his wife from Massachusetts, people whom I recommended. They are to come to the field about the first of April. The doctor's salary is guaranteed by individuals for three years—he, however, is to get as much as possible from the field—after that time his full support is to come from the field. There is in mind, I believe, a hospital within the next few years. I was much pleased this morning to get a very ready response from one of the leading physicians here to my inquiry as to whether some of the specialists here would be willing to cooperate in clinical work in the Laurel country. I expect some of them will go up into the region with me sometime this spring.

I received the other day a copy of the minutes of the Southern Industrial Educational Association's meeting of December 27th, 1913—the meeting in which the future policy of the association was discussed. I presume you have a copy of the minutes. If you have not, I shall be glad to send you mine should you care to see them.

So often and warmly had John expressed his feeling about lurid publicity and misrepresentation of the mountain people in print, that the following comments written to Mr. Glenn on January 23rd seem mild indeed:

Thank you for the clippings referring to the book *A Son of the Hills* and criticisms of the review. I think it were well to have in the library most of the books that are issued on the Southern Highlands, and if it meets with your approval, I should like to have the books here. I am asked continually—personally and by correspondence—my opinion of various books that have been issued on mountain subjects.

I have not read *A Son of the Hills,* but if Mrs. [Harriet T.] Comstock's story treats of the mountaineer in the way the review suggests, the criticism is well deserved. The term "mountain whites" is an abominable term and entirely unnecessary inasmuch as the upland population of the mountain country has comparatively few Negroes. The mountaineers are an entirely distinct class from the so-called poor white trash—the latter being generally the "down and out" groups in the valley, the lowlands, and cities, without ambition to go elsewhere and without the ability, seemingly, to compete with Negro labor.

What the critic says of the missionaries to the mountains is true to a certain extent, but it leaves a wrong impression when he says that Baptist elders and Methodist circuit riders had threaded every trail and preached in every cove and settlement for generations before the "self-constituted missionaries" discovered this country. The statement is true, but it is a truth that grossly misrepresents facts. Many of these "self-constituted missionaries" have done splendid work in shaping the life of the sections in which they labored, despite the mistakes that many of them made.

I am sending you two poems which I am sometime going to use in an article on "moonshining." The first represents the general impression that people have of the mountain country; the second is much more nearly the fact. Of nearly 250 mountain counties, about nine-tenths are dry, if my memory serves me rightly, and long before the prohibition wave swept over the South, a large percentage of mountain counties were dry.

There is so much misrepresentation that I am tempted time and time again to write articles for the press, but I feel very sure the best way for this division to be helpful is not to get into the papers, nor to print anything except facts which have been carefully sifted, the sources weighed, and information gleaned with the help and cooperation of the agencies whom the facts themselves may criticize.

Enclosures:

1. KENTUCKY'S HILLS
Kentucky's hills are full of rills
And all the rills are lined with stills,
And all the stills are full of gills
And all the gills are full of thrills
And all the thrills are full of kills.

You see the feudists dot the hills
And camp along the little rills
Convenient to the busy stills
And thirsting for the brimming gills
And when the juice his system fills
Each feudist whoops around and kills.

Now if they'd only stop the stills
They'd cure Kentucky's many ills;
Men would be left to climb the hills
And operate the busy stills,
But that, of course, would mean more gills,
And that, of course, would mean more thrills,
Resulting in the same old kills.

But all the hills and rills and stills
And all the gills and thrills and kills
Are splendid for the coffin mills
And make more undertaker's bills.

2. THE SOUTH IS GOING DRY
Lay the jest about the julep in the camphor balls at last,
For a miracle has happened and the olden days are past;
That which makes Milwaukee famous does not foam in Tennessee,
And the lid in old Missouri is tight locked as it can be;

Oh, the comic paper colonel and his cronies well may sigh,
For the mint is waving gaily, and the South is going dry.

By the stillside, on the hillside, in Kentucky all is still,
For the only damp refreshment must be dipped up from the rill;
No'th Ca'lina's stately ruler gives the soda glass a shove,
And discusses local option with the South Ca'lina "Gov."
It is useless at the fountain to be winkful of the eye,
For the cocktail glass is dusty, and the South is going dry.

It is water, water everywhere, and not a "drop" to drink,
We no longer hear the music of the mellow crystal clink,
When the colonel and the major and the general and the jedge
Meet to have a little nip to give their appetites an edge,
For the eggnog now is nogless and the rye has gone awry
And the punch bowl holds carnations, and the South is going dry.

All the nightcaps now have tassels and are worn upon the head,
Not the "nightcaps" that were taken when nobody went to bed;
And the breeze above the bluegrass is as solemn as is death,
For it bears no pungent clove-tang on its odorific breath;
And each man can walk a chalk line when the stars are in the sky,
For the fizz-glass now is fizzless, and the South is going dry.

Lay the jest about the julep 'neath the chestnut tree at last,
For there's but one kind of moonshine, and the olden days are past,
For the water-wagon rumbles though the Southland on its trip,
And it helps no one to drop off to pick up the driver's whip;
For the mint bed makes a pasture, and the corkscrew hangeth high,
All is still along the stillside, and the South is going dry.

Cal Snodden.

Plans and programs for mountain schools continued to flow into John's office. On January 29, 1914, he forwarded one to Mr. Glenn:

I enclose herewith a copy of a letter received from Mr. [R. W.] Selvidge of
the George Peabody College for Teachers, Nashville, Tennessee. . . . [His]

plan strikes me as possible of good results if the persons directing it can connect properly with the mountaineer.

I like the idea of "protracted meetings" for a gospel of education. The mountain people are familiar with the method in religious activity, and if the idea can be developed properly by people who do not make it apparent that they have come to the mountains to uplift the people, it ought to bring good results.

Mr. Selvidge's letter, dated January 24th, went as follows:

Many things have intervened to delay my letter to you concerning our plans for mountain work.

As we see the situation, there appear to be at least four distinct lines which should be developed, and in our opinion they must be developed together. It appears that any successful attempt to improve conditions must be directed toward—

1. Improvement of economic conditions;
2. Sanitation and health;
3. Improvement in educational facilities and practices;
4. Improvement in the religious life.

I simply mention these as the lines along which we wish to direct our activities. Our plan for carrying out this work, insofar as we have developed a plan, is somewhat as follows:

Select some point where conditions appear favorable for the development of our plan, and establish there a "center," and place in charge of this the very best man we can get. We want this to be a school of the people in the very highest sense of the word. We want to teach there the things the people need to know, without respect to traditional curriculum or activities of school. We want to teach them how to refine, organize, and use in a profitable way the handcrafts which they now practice. We believe that if the production and distribution of these things are properly organized, they can be made an important source of income to the community. This simply means to take advantage of existing knowledge and practices in the community to bring into it a new life and new interest. In addition to this, through the Knapp School of Country Life we hope to improve methods in agriculture, fruit growing, and animal husbandry. In fact, we expect to study carefully the local situation and do anything we can to improve economic conditions.

Through our Department of Health and Hygiene, by precept and example, we believe we can greatly improve conditions with respect to health and sanitation.

In the matter of education, in a somewhat narrower sense, we hope to maintain a school which will teach all who come the things they need to know. In this school we shall place no limitations on the curriculum, nor restrictions as to intellectual attainments of the students. Our purpose shall be to give instruction and service in any direction opportunity may offer. We expect this school to touch in some vital way the life of every member of the community.

In this work we hope to secure, and we believe we can secure, the cooperation of local authorities interested in public education. We expect to enter this undertaking, not with the attitude of one stooping down to lift somebody up, but rather the attitude of men who are attacking special problems which have not been very successfully handled. The geographic and economic conditions make some special treatment necessary.

We believe that such a "center" should offer a great opportunity for the development of the religious and moral elements in the community. It seems to us that it should be possible to develop within the community a spirit of cooperation and assistance which will supersede the petty feuds and neighborhood quarrels which so often exist.

It is our plan to make this center a training school for people who wish to engage in this special line of educational work. Students who are interested in taking up such a line of work will go to this center for practical training. In this way we hope to prepare men for the work in other centers which we wish to establish. From time to time during the year, we expect to have large gatherings, and once during the year we expect to have a "protracted meeting," or "educational revival" for four or five weeks. At this "big meeting" we expect to have all of the teachers of the community and all of the neighborhood round about, and we expect to stir up so much enthusiasm for the various lines of social activity that the regular organization which remains in charge of the center will be able to maintain interest and carry on the work during the remainder of the year.

This may appear to be relying to too great an extent on the emotional life of the people for it to be of any considerable educational value. However, I am personally of the opinion that the first step toward the improvement of conditions is through the emotional life of the people.

The plans as thus roughly sketched are some of the things we have been thinking of in connection with this work. Of course it will be necessary to modify them in many instances. Just what modifications will be necessary can be determined only when we are on the ground.

At present we have no fund available for this work, but the work as outlined is about what we hope to establish and carry on.

We shall be very much interested to have your criticisms, suggestions, and advice on this matter.

Invitations also continued to flow in, among them one from Mr. W. D. Weatherford, who wanted John to come to his summer school. Mr. Glenn wrote John on this question, February 2, 1914:

This is in reply to your letter about Mr. Weatherford's invitation to take part in his summer school. I have no doubt that this summer school is an excellent thing to carry on. Apparently, however, Mr. Weatherford has not realized what real training in social work involves. No "thorough-going" courses in anything can be given in so short a time. Nevertheless, it is possible during the short period of a summer school to get some new facts into the listeners' minds.[6]

There seem to be several good reasons for going to the summer school. It will get you in touch with people whom you may not see otherwise, and will make you and your facts and your plans better known, and will give you, probably, more of a standing. If it does not interfere with any other important work, or with your holiday, and you think you can lecture without making trouble for yourself in the mountains, I should be inclined to advise you to go. Can you not talk "cooperation" and the importance of utilizing all outside sources without running much risk? These ideas will be new to most of your hearers, and valuable to them.

All this is by way of suggestion. You will have to use your own judgment and decide according to your better knowledge of the situation. I should be satisfied with your decision, whatever it may be. If you decide not to lecture, would it not be advantageous to be present at the summer school in order to meet the people?

When this letter arrived, John was ill. On January 31st he had had what was described as a "*minor* operation on the nose," a measure which the specialist thought "might relieve colds and help prevent hay fever, which every autumn grew more troublesome." The operation proved long and tedious and was followed by persistent bleeding, aggravated by high blood pressure. Four nights later, after the second nose plug had been removed, he fainted away on the floor, to my consternation and that of Miss Dickey, who had come up to be with me. John always referred to this harrowing occasion as one of the most restful and delightful experiences of his life, but Miss Dickey and I could not see it quite in that light. Nor could my mother and sister Daisy, who came speeding down from Boston on February 18th to help. It was several weeks before he gathered strength enough to go back regularly to the office. Miss Dickey came up to the house more or less regularly for dictation in this interim.

Mr. Glenn wrote John on February 7th:

I am very sorry to hear that you have had to have even a minor operation. I hope the trouble will soon be over. Until it is over, let your work take a backseat. You will save time by getting fully recovered before you resume steady work. What Mrs. Campbell says about your high blood pressure causes me a little anxiety. It ought to be possible to relieve this condition. If you have not done so, I hope you will have yourself thoroughly examined by some very competent physician. The observance of proper regulations as to diet, exercise, etc., ought to be effective in relieving it. It does not indicate anything serious at present, but high blood pressure is a thing that may increase steadily unless it is very carefully looked after.

Please give my kindest regards to Mrs. Campbell. We are still enjoying some of your Christmas foliage.

John did not get entirely rid of his trouble, and too frequently my Line-a-Day notes that "John not feeling very well," "tired," "shaky and tired," "rather tired, and stayed abed." In general, however, as soon as he began to get about, he paid little attention to his blood pressure, for which the doctors seemed unable to find any cause except "history and worry." "*Concerned,*" not "worried," he would always say when I saw him growing tense over some situation or question which he was trying to help solve. The following five letters show some of the work of the office during these weeks of convalescence while John was also making plans for the April conference in Knoxville:

[Rev. Franklin J. Clark to JCC]
February 5, 1914

I had the pleasure of bringing to the attention of the Council of Advice that paragraph of your letter of January 23rd in which you suggest that a member of our board be nominated to represent it on your Executive Committee. The Council of Advice thought that I should be that representative, but before actually electing me thought that they would like to know a bit more in detail just what would be involved in such an election.

I suppose the meetings of the conference are held in the South. May I ask just what the purpose of the interdenominational Conference of Mountain Workers is, and what our board would be expected to do in case they should elect me as its representative? Is there any financial responsibility involved in such representation, and is there a particular object or set of principles to which we should subscribe if we enter the conference? I am sure our board would want to know all the details, and if you could find it convenient to let me have a statement at your leisure, I shall be glad to bring it to the attention of the other officers.

May I say personally that as it has fallen to my lot to have the oversight of the departments in which the mountain work lies, it would be a great pleasure to me to be associated with those men who are engaged in the same work. I feel that I know very little about the mountain work, and I know there is much to learn.

[JCC to Rev. Clark]
March 3, 1914

I regret exceedingly that I have been unable before to answer your inquiries of February 5th. Because of illness I have been absent from the office for over a month.

I am happy in knowing that there is a possibility of your being appointed as one of our Executive Committee. I hope to issue this week the call for the second meeting, which is to be held April 22nd and 23rd at Knoxville. If your council should choose you as their representative within a few days, would you be so kind as to telegraph to me to that effect, at my expense, so that I may have your name listed with the others of the Executive Committee before the call leaves the office?

There are no financial obligations that you incur so far as I know, other than meeting your own expense at the conference and to and from the conference. There are no fixed charges of which I know. The only expense incident to the last meeting was the cost of publishing the minutes and addresses—which probably are not to be published, because so few copies of the impromptu addresses were furnished. Contributions were received at the last meeting for this purpose, but these were the contributions of individuals. As I recall the circumstances, twenty-five dollars were received in dollar contributions.

The only particular objects of which I know are the furtherance of acquaintance among those doing work in the mountains and those administering work of the mountain mission boards, in the hope that such efforts may lead to more effective work. To my knowledge, there are no set principles to which one subscribes if he enters the conference.

I hope very much you may be present at the meeting in Knoxville, even if your council should not think it advisable at this time to appoint a representative. The churches represented on the Executive Committee up to date are the Southern Baptist Convention, Christian, Congregational, Methodist Episcopal South, Presbyterian USA, Presbyterian US, Reformed Church in America, and the United Presbyterian. There are representatives also from a few of the leading independent mountain schools, that is, schools not under any board. A part of the Executive Committee were chosen at the meeting in Atlanta, and some churches not represented at that meeting were asked to appoint representatives on the Executive Committee of the present year.

I trust that we may have you as one of our Executive Committee and also have the pleasure of seeing you at Knoxville.

[Dr. Claxton to JCC]
February 13, 1914

I saw Mr. Childs at Raleigh last night.[7] I was very sorry you could not come down. I sincerely hope that you may be out again soon.

I wanted your assistance in finding a man to serve as secretary and field agent for the Southern Industrial Educational Association for the next three years at a salary of $3,500 a year with $1,500 a year traveling expenses. This money is given for this purpose by Mr. Cleveland H. Dodge of New York.

This man should be one who can very quickly sense the situation through information already collected by you, by this bureau, and by other individuals and agencies, verify this information by visiting some of the typical schools, and together with all those who are engaged in the problem, work out a definite, constructive policy and obtain the hearty cooperation of all the agencies working toward the improvement of school conditions in this section. Do you know a good man? He should be a southern man who can sympathize with the mountain people and gain their confidence; also a man who can gain the confidence of those with whom he must work on the outside. He should not be a minister of any church. The best man I can think of is Professor J. J. Doster, professor of education at the University of Alabama. Do you know him? If so, what do you think of him? Have you any good man to suggest?

I also wanted to talk with you about a man for the principalship of a folk high school. Our committee here will employ such a man as soon as we can find him, and put him to work at the job of finding the best place for such a school, working out the plans for it, gaining the cooperation of the community, and getting together a faculty with the hope that the school may be able to begin work next fall.

Do you know a good man for this work? When are you coming to Washington? Will you attend the Richmond meeting of the Department of Superintendence of the NEA?

[JCC to Mr. Glenn]
February 23, 1914

I had hoped to be in the office today, but my strength and the weather prevent. I am getting along very well, however, and hope to be at my desk early this week. I am taking up the letters from you that have accumulated during my absence, and would thank you for the suggestions made therein. I am especially glad to know your decision about the books.

Professor Waldo called on me again yesterday. Sometime at your convenience, I should be glad to know what your Boston friends think about him. I probably shall see him from time to time, and it would be a help to have an estimate of him from an authentic source.

I am writing to Mr. Weatherford that I shall be glad to have some share in the Black Mountain meetings and that I shall write him a little later as to the line of discussion that I shall be free to follow.

Mr. [Eugene T.] Lies, general superintendent of the United Charities of Chicago, called to see me the other day to ask if I would speak on the social needs of the Southern Highlanders at the National Charities meeting in Memphis, beginning May 8th. I agreed to do so if it should meet your approval and time permits. I asked him to change the subject to one that would call attention to the strength rather than the weakness of the mountaineer. The subject we agreed upon tentatively was as follows: "Releasing the Potentiality of the Southern Highlander." I could say the things I want to say under either subject, but the latter would be less likely to offend.

The time for the interdenominational Conference of Southern Mountain Workers is decided, practically, for April 22nd and 23rd at Knoxville. The place of meeting will probably be the Imperial Hotel, with one of the churches open for a general public meeting on one of the evenings. I shall be kept quite busy getting ready for this meeting as most of the details are left in my hands.

Mrs. Thomas K. Glenn (of Atlanta) and Mrs. Hodgson came from Atlanta to see me some days ago. Fortunately, it was in the interim of a day or two when I was not under the doctor's thumb. Mrs. Campbell, Miss Dickey, and some of my friends were good enough to see that they reached the people and places I wanted them to see, and when they left I think they were both weary in mind and body but very grateful. I think the superintendent that they have picked will come to see me also, and possibly I may be able to take him to one or two schools.

I am enclosing a copy of a letter from Dr. Claxton. Unfortunately, I do not know, at this writing, of any man suitable to serve as secretary and field agent for the Southern Industrial Educational Association. Professor ———, now in tuberculosis work in Kentucky, might do. He is a southerner, a mountain man, formerly president of Union College, Barbourville, Kentucky, and later at ——— College. He and President ——— did not agree, and if the reports that have come to me from various members of the faculty of the college are true, he was placed in such a position by the president that he could not remain and retain his self-respect—in fact, he indicated as much to me himself. I think ——— is a Harvard man or took postgraduate work at Harvard. My impression is that he was at one time a minister in the Methodist Episcopal Church South, but of this I am not at all certain. Possibly Professor E. C. Branson of the State Normal School at Athens, Georgia, might consider this work. He is doing a splendid work where he is, however, and might not wish to leave. I do not know Professor Doster, of whom Dr. Claxton writes.

I may be of some help in assisting Dr. Claxton [to] find the principal for the folk high school. The man who suggests himself at present is Professor [John E.] Calfee of Berea College, who has done extensive work in the mountains, has done extension work, and was principal of a Presbyterian school at Hyden in the mountains of Kentucky before he went to Berea. I think he would not be averse to severing his connection with Berea. The General Education Board people would, I think, be especially helpful through their knowledge of the various men in the field. For the principalship I would urge looking up Calfee. I shall give more thought later to the question of a secretary and field agent. If you know anything of Professor Doster, or could find out anything, I should be glad to learn about him.

[JCC to Mr. Glenn]
March 3, 1914

I am enclosing herewith a copy of a letter to Mr. [Karl] deSchweinitz of the Charity Organization Society, which may perhaps serve to answer also your inquiry of December 15th with reference to the school at Penland, North Carolina. I have been unable to go into the matter further, personally. I had hoped before this to be in that section to see for myself, but I am sorely disappointed in being unable, as yet, even to go to the office for any work.

I am sorry that I cannot give a more encouraging report. I am perplexed about the situation and about Bishop Horner's work. Rev. Mr. F. J. Clark of the Domestic Mission Board has done his best to give me information about the Episcopal mountain schools, but there are no returns on his list for schools under Bishop Horner's jurisdiction, and there are other mountain schools not included. I do not wish to do injury to the splendid work that is being done in certain localities by able and consecrated men, by issuing a report on mountain schools which should omit their fields because someone has neglected to report. I am therefore holding back the bulletin material on mountain schools until I am able to get in touch with these men themselves.

I neglected in my last letter to you to thank you for your inquiry regarding *Our Southern Highlanders* by [Horace] Kephart. I have it in my library and find it of interest. I regard it as authentic in certain chapters, such as the chapter on the ancestry of the mountain people. There are some errors, I believe, in topography, and he does, consciously or unconsciously, what so many writers do, picks out the interesting, picturesque, and unusual, and through lack of qualification leaves the impression that what he depicts is general. He also quotes as peculiar to the region phrases and expressions that I am quite sure are found elsewhere. On the whole, however, I regard it as one of the best of the popular books written on the subject.

Probably after Mr. Glenn received the copy of Dr. Claxton's letter—the record is not clear—he raised the question as to whether John was interested in the position offered by the Southern Industrial Educational Association. Perhaps Mr. Glenn thought that John would himself be a good choice for the position, or he may have thought that additional opportunity and salary would be a welcome advancement to the secretary of the Southern Highland Division of the Russell Sage Foundation, who, after all, was not largely reimbursed. At any rate, he inquired frankly if John would like to consider the position for himself.

On March 5th, John wrote his rather full reply to Mr. Glenn's direct query:

In order that I may answer fully the two queries growing out of what is hoped will be a wider participation of the SIEA in mountain work, may I lay aside for a moment the thought of myself in connection with the Southern Highland Division, and tell you what I conceive its work to be, although I realize that this work is inseparably bound up with the personality of the secretary.

The work of the division has to do, according to my view, with all phases of rural life in the mountains and not merely with those that have to do with the educational work of schools. Sanitation, medical service, various phases of agriculture and industrial work, the homeless child, the cultivation of a proper home life, the fostering of friendship between religious leaders and ultimate federation or cooperation in religious work, in fact, all that is embraced under rural social service is properly within the scope of this division. The Southern Highland Division is a forerunner in the mountains for many agencies that are operative in urban and more settled rural communities but which have not yet touched the rural life of the Southern Highlands. If I may say so without irreverence, I have regarded myself, in my capacity as secretary, as a sort of "voice crying in the wilderness 'Prepare ye the way,'" and when the way is prepared for any of these aforesaid agencies through the aroused interest of the mountain people themselves and intelligent direction by those now leaders (some of them blind leaders at present), the activity of the division should cease in the line of the newly introduced agency as soon as that agency has established proper connections in the mountains.

If the SIEA does its educational work properly in the mountains, I should regard that eventuality as the direct result of the efforts of the Southern Highland Division. The reorganization of the SIEA is due in no small degree to the efforts of this division, and the appointment of Dr. Claxton as chairman may possibly be due to my insistence that he above all men should be chosen. I do not regard their new plans as reason for the

Russell Sage Foundation withdrawing; it is simply the first decisive battle won by the Southern Highland Division of the Russell Sage Foundation. They will need every atom of influence that this division of the Foundation can exert to make their work successful.

In reply to your question as to whether I would like to be secretary of the SIEA, I would say that while I am not at all indifferent to the thought of an increase of salary in the near future, I could not at this time consider the position—and the reasons are not alone personal. You, who know my real feeling of sympathy and affection for the South and its peoples, will not misunderstand the statements following.

A broad-gauged southern man who knows the lowland and knows the highland South should if possible be appointed secretary. The lowland South, wherein is most of the wealth and influence, needs to be reminded again and again of the fact that, although the highlander, by reason of his geographical environment, has been made somewhat akin to the North politically, he is, notwithstanding, a southerner, and as a southerner in need of what the South can give him, he should look first to the South for aid—and not look in vain. Such reminders to the lowland South would be accepted more graciously if coming from a native southerner. Although both of my parents were from abroad, and my sympathies are largely with the South, the mere fact that I was born and educated in the North makes me a northerner in the eyes of the average southerner. Had I chanced to have been born in the South and moved north during my childhood, receiving exactly the same training, and living in the North as long as I have in the South, I should be regarded as a southerner. For a long while in the work of the SIEA, emphasis must be placed upon the adjective "southern." The chief task of its secretary, for some years to come, will be the task of raising money in the South in order to establish one or two model schools, or to convert one or two existing schools into schools of the right kind. The minds of the people in Washington with whom I discussed this question privately inclined to a secretary of this sort, who should, perhaps, first go abroad for a year to study rural education and then return to raise money to establish the right kind of school in the mountains.

While I would suggest the beginning of this sort of work in the mountains, the SIEA, if it rises to its possibilities, should include in its activities the *whole* rural South, and not the highlands merely. Were I able or inclined to do this work at present, I should hesitate because I am not a native-born southerner.

I think, perhaps, it is in the minds of some of the trustees that this secretary is eventually to become an adviser of all mountain schools. Ultimately that may come to pass, but there must be some years of tactful management before a southern secretary, who necessarily has to emphasize the word "southern" to raise money in the lowland South, can hope to exert a directing influence over the work of a hundred or more distinctly northern schools manned (or rather womaned) by northerners and supervised by northern field agents or by secretaries in northern offices who are somewhat jealous of their prerogatives.

The forty Southern Baptist schools would have little if anything to do with such a southerner unless he were a Baptist; and not only that, the Baptists need conversion to the idea of a public school not dominated by church influences. The fourteen independent schools are about evenly divided between the North and South, and the southern schools of the independents are generally southern merely in having the head of the school and the majority of the trustees southern. The money for running these schools, and the teaching corps, are largely from the North. I am afraid that human nature would not step aside readily for Christianity even in Christian mission schools. I find in my work that human nature is human nature whether it is northern or southern. There are seventy-five or more other schools with various church affiliations, which, though not proselyting for their own church, have not yet learned the lesson of decreasing that others may increase.

Just as the northern schools in the mountains have been handicapped in their beginnings (and some still are) by the differences between northern and mountain traditions, so the SIEA will have an initial handicap in the overcoming of the differences between the traditions of the lowland and upland South.

The Southern Highland Division has had its work greatly facilitated by the prestige of the Russell Sage Foundation, which does not seek to advertise itself, has no axe to grind, and is national and not sectional in its scope and outlook. I cannot but feel that the Southern Highland Division, aided by the prestige of the Russell Sage Foundation, can be instrumental in furthering the purposes of the SIEA in the mountain schools.

It is a difficult matter to present on the written page the great need of this field, the conflicting interests of the various agencies that are honestly aiming to work toward the same goal, and the extreme delicacy of the task of reconciling them. Many of the workers are extremely isolated, know little of each other's work or of new and better methods, and they are looking to this division for vision and for practical direction to realize the vision when it appears. It would be easier to explain this by word of mouth, but one must necessarily pause when he realizes he would have to speak of his own training, temperament, and personality as the chief factors in bringing about the harmony desired.

I hope the trustees will feel that the possibilities of service in this field are sufficient to justify the continuance of this division until it has met the needs which called it into existence. The success of this first year of constructive effort justifies, from my point of view, all the expenditures for investigation during the five years preceding. My wish is to see this work finished and then to be free to do what I should like most of all to do—to go back into the mountains again and, in some rural social settlement, to carry out through connection with national and state agencies brought into the field, some of the things that I am constantly urging others to do. If the Russell Sage Foundation should feel the work of the Southern Highland Division of sufficient importance to justify its continuance for some years, I should regard it as a betrayal of trust to take any other position even at a considerable increase of salary, unless family reasons demanded it, but if the Foundation should feel otherwise, I should be unhappy to continue the work, even were my salary much larger than it is.

I appreciate greatly your thought of me in connection with the secretaryship of the association. If I am giving satisfaction to the trustees, I should prefer to carry out under the direction of the Russell Sage Foundation some of the purposes I have in mind. I cannot but feel a bit disappointed that the prospect is that the money for the mountain work is to be limited, but if the work we are doing is giving satisfaction, I should like to continue it longer—even with limited means. We are making steady gains, and I think we are coming to be a real influence in promoting a better understanding among those who are working in and for the mountains and in bringing to them helpful suggestions for their work.

I have realized from the beginning that the life of the division was to be comparatively brief—not more than ten years at the limit. As soon as the health, agricultural, educational, social, and religious forces of nation and state are actively at work in the mountains, the work of this division is over. The success of the division will be achieved when it is no longer necessary. I do not think that the time for withdrawal has come as yet, and the Southern Industrial Educational Association cannot enter into the heritage of the Southern Highland Division of the Russell Sage Foundation.

I believe I am looking at this question disinterestedly. I appreciate, more than I can tell you, your expressions of confidence in me, your appreciation of my work, and your belief in its ultimate effect. It has been a great pleasure to be connected with an organization such as the Foundation.

I regret that I have not been able to express fully to the trustees my idea of the work and to give my reasons for working as quietly as I have tried to work. I am confident that this is the only way in which the work can be done. I was at work on a report of the first year's activities of the division when I was taken ill. In that report, I was entering somewhat minutely into the reasons for the existence of this division, its field, the importance of the work it is accomplishing, and the need, from my point of view, of carrying on the work as it has been carried on.

I have written fully and frankly, as you have requested, and I am grateful to you for having given me this opportunity to express some of the things that have been in my mind for a long while. I shall be quite frank in telling you when I believe the work of the division is done. You, I am sure, will believe that at any time I will accept a decision of the trustees that might be counter to my own convictions or wishes. Whenever the work is done, I shall regret more than I can express the severing of a relation which has made all of my work under the Foundation so pleasant.

On the same day this letter was written, Mr. Glenn sent one to John about attending the National Conference of Charities and Correction:

I see no reason why you should not go to the NCCC at Memphis in May if you think it wise to do so. The question is one entirely for your own judgment. There will presumably be a larger number of southerners to whom it might be worthwhile to talk about the Southern Highland work. To most of the general membership, however, your subject will merely be one that is interesting. You could probably get considerable publicity in the southern paper if you want it. You will undoubtedly also derive benefit from being in touch with the membership of the conference and with hearing a number of the papers.

Above all things, though, keep within the limitations of your strength, at least until you get entirely well.

John replied to Mr. Glenn on March 7, 1914:

Your letter of March 5th is at hand, and I am glad to have your views as to my attending the NCCC to strengthen somewhat my growing conviction that I ought not to attempt it. Work has accumulated during my illness, and I as chairman of the Executive Committee of the Conference of Mountain Workers, which is to meet in Knoxville on April 22nd and 23rd, have about all I want to do in addition to my regular work. I have therefore written Mr. Lies that I shall be unable to accept the invitation to speak at the meeting in Memphis. . . .

I thank you for the clipping from the *New York Post* signed by Dr. Dillard. I agree with him in his position that most of the lowlanders, the so-called poor whites, are "worse off" than most of the highlanders, and I should be very glad indeed to see some association formed to assist them. I am glad to have his opinion that the mountain people are "as a whole, freer, happier, healthier, and more thrifty," which substantiates my own views of the mountain people and causes me to feel that the people with such native advantages should be given the educational advantages that the poor whites of the lowlands have but which they do not accept—perhaps because the common public school would not help them much. I wonder if the SIEA ought not properly to consider the suggestion contained in this article by Dr. Dillard?

A few days later, he received the response to his long letter of March 5th. Mr. Glenn wrote on March 9th: "Thank you very much for your full, interesting and enlightening letter. I have had nothing from you in writing which puts the whole situation quite so clearly as this does. I would like to think over what you say about the association, and if I have any comments will write you a little later."

On March 12th, Mr. Glenn sent John another letter:

The question of the function of the SIEA depends largely on what they are aiming at. It seems to me that they are at liberty to decide whether they want to help mountaineers only, or whether they want to spread themselves out and help the lowland people as well. I imagine that in the near future they will not have funds for a very large work, and they will probably do better to confine themselves to a small field. However, it may be well for you to call their attention to Dr. Dillard's suggestion; it will probably be a surprise to them. Maybe it would be better if they would devote their entire attention to the lowlanders and let the mountain field alone.

The idea of a promising new experiment appeared in correspondence with Dr. Warren H. Wilson, superintendent of the Department of Church and Country Life of the Board of Home Missions, Presbyterian Church, USA. The letters are given in full:

[Dr. Wilson to JCC]
March 9, 1914

Our Mr. Lawsing, extension worker in Madison County, living at Big Laurel, has been offered a place as farm demonstrator for Madison County. The United States Government offers to pay $300.00 toward his salary. Dr. [W. E.] Finley approves, with the understanding that we would pay $900.00, and so give Lawsing a total salary of $1,200.00. I write to ask what you think of this proposition.

We have a strict rule against any alliance in our educational work with the government, and unless this case comes under another head, our board would probably not consent to it. There is a disadvantage in that Mr. Lawsing's time would in greater degree be taken away from our work, and he would be named as a government demonstrator.

On the other hand, he would secure prestige in this manner. He would accomplish just as well the purpose for which we put him there. There would be an advantage in our saving so much money. Furthermore, if the government is to put a farm demonstrator in Madison County, we would not desire to duplicate their work.

Do you think that this would be an advisable arrangement, and in particular, do you think that it would be objectionable as an alliance between religious and governmental work?

The matter has to be settled by the 15th of the month, I suppose, so that I would be glad to hear from you soon.

[JCC to Dr. Wilson]
March 11, 1914

I am deeply interested in your letter of March 9th, which has just reached me. In a recent issue of the *Asheville Gazette News,* I read a notice of the action of Madison County with reference to the matter of a farm demonstrator, and I wondered then if Mr. Lawsing might not be asked to take the place. I had sent Mr. Lawsing letters of introduction to Mr. Hern, the newly appointed government agent in this line, and to state officers, and had written to Mr. Hern telling of the work Mr. Lawsing was doing. I wanted Mr. Lawsing to get in touch with the state and federal agencies that would help him in his work.

In reply to your question, I would say that as a general rule, I do not believe in any other agency doing the work that a county, state or federal agency could and should do for all the people. All the work that our various church boards are doing in the mountains, except [that] which is commonly regarded as strictly church work, is justified only so long as public agencies are unable to do it.

May I suggest your asking Mr. Allaben and other members of your board whether there is not some precedent for the making over of board funds to county, state, or federal agencies? My impression is that you have given, or offered to give, the salaries of teachers in some common or high schools in the mountains, provided teachers of a certain preparation were employed. It would appear to me that the question you raise is the same question.

At this writing, I can see no objection to a church board supplementing the salary of a public agent, providing the absolute control and direction of that agent is in the hands of officials chosen by the public, or by representatives of the public properly appointed. There are decided objections, on the contrary, to county, state, or government funds being made over to supplement the salaries of persons engaged in denominational work, with the control of the work subsidized in the hands of denominational authorities. If, therefore, you make over to the government this fund and make over the control with no restraining strings, it would not appear to me at all as an alliance of church and state.

Before coming to any definite conclusion on this matter, however, may I suggest your seeking the advice of men who have a broader practical knowledge of this matter than I have. I would suggest your getting in touch with Mr. Glenn of the Foundation, and, through him, with Dr. Buttrick of the General Education Board.

If the plan under consideration should carry, it would add not only to the prestige of Mr. Lawsing's work, but would help all of your work in the French Broad Presbytery, because of the very apparent disinterestedness of your effort. Mr. Lawsing could do you just as much good, if not more, as a government agent, and the stations that he now reaches could be reached just as well by him under other auspices.

I do not quite know how the $300.00 paid by the government is secured. If it is from a fund given by the government, without any of it coming from Madison County, it seems a little unfair that Madison County should receive for a farm demonstrator $300.00 from the United States Government and $900.00 from the Department of Church and Country Life of the Presbyterian Church, without the county itself contributing anything toward the salary of an agent whose work is to be for that particular county. Would it not be advisable to say to the county authorities that your department would provide half of the balance, that is, $450.00 (or possibly $600.00), leaving the county to pay in the latter case $300.00—as much as the government offers.

In order to stimulate the county to its fullest activity, the arrangement, if made, should be for a limited time. Perhaps it would be well to have it run for a period of three years, with reconsideration at the end of that time, or with some understanding that the amount paid by your department should decrease from year to year, and at the end of some stated period, the county assume all financial obligation not met by the United States Government.

If it should come about that Mr. Lawsing should leave you in this way, the Country Life Department might well congratulate itself on having brought about in a very short time one of the things the need of which justified its entrance into the field.

If arrangements cannot be made, it does not necessarily follow that Mr. Lawsing's work is finished. He may well be used for several years of intensive work on the circuit he now covers, aiding the work of the demonstrator who may be appointed, and when his work in Madison County is done, you will need him in new fields in the mountains which will open to you, I am very sure, when it is known what the Department of Church and Country Life is accomplishing and is planning to accomplish.

Please be so kind as to let me know what you have decided.

[Dr. Wilson to JCC]
March 16, 1914

We received your valued letter this morning, and we are indebted to you for your careful thought upon the question of our relation through Mr. Lawsing to the government farm demonstration enterprise.

Our board is very strict about such matters as bring us into an alliance with the government, and I have been unable to present this matter in such way as to avoid the objection that it is an alliance with the government. I fear it will be impossible to carry it through on that basis. This reduces us to the alternative you mention, that Mr. Lawsing, in case the government places a farm demonstrator in Madison County, must transfer his work to another county and thus prepare the work for the farm demonstrator.

It is just possible that if Dr. [W. E.] Finley urges the matter in a new form, there may be some reopening of it, but at present it appears to be adversely settled.

The preparation for the Second Conference of Southern Mountain Workers was now going forward urgently. In planning the program, John wrote to Miss Fannie F. Clement (superintendent of rural nurses, American Red Cross), who, as already related, had traveled with us to study mountain conditions in Kentucky and North Carolina; his letter of March 11th to her asks:

Would it be possible for you to come to Knoxville for April 22nd and 23rd to attend a Conference of Southern Mountain Workers? I am chairman of the Executive Committee and have considerable to do with shaping the program.

We are planning to give one session up to rural health matters, and I want very much to have you come, for a talk on the rural work of the Red Cross.

After the conference, I wish you might be free for perhaps a week to go with Mrs. Campbell and me, if we can arrange it, on a mountain trip in North Carolina, of as long or short duration as you have time for. I should like especially to have you go with us up into Madison County to see Dr. Packard and his wife—people who are coming into this region at our suggestion. It is possible, through acquaintance established, that there may be an opening in that field for some of your nurses. Do try to come, if possible, if only for the conference.

Please let me know as soon as possible. I should have written you much earlier, but have been shut in because of illness for six weeks, and I only came to my office again the other day, for a few hours' work each day. I would not give the impression that I am or have been seriously ill, but I have been under the doctor's thumb, and he seemed to indicate that I would be seriously ill if I did not remain under his thumb for some time.

Doctors and nurses seem to get hold of one somehow, and it is because of the hold that you have on Mrs. Campbell and me that we want you to come again and to get a hold upon others in the mountain country who need the many things that you and the Red Cross can give them. Now, after that, which is a statement of truth, can you hesitate a moment to come to the conference?

The call to the conference went out on March 14th. Eight denominations, two independent schools, and, through the chairman, the Russell Sage Foundation, were represented on the Executive Committee. The letter follows:

You are most cordially invited to attend the second annual Conference of Southern Mountain Workers, which will meet in Knoxville, Tennessee, April 22nd and 23rd, 1914.

Officials of boards, presidents of colleges, and principals of schools are requested to extend this invitation to their associates and to members of their faculties and to send the names of those likely to attend, as early as possible, to the chairman of the Executive Committee.

The purpose of the conference is to promote acquaintance among those engaged in the work in the Southern Highland region and, through exchange of ideas, to further the best methods of work.

It is purposed to make this conference a conference in fact, where questions of health, sanitation, country life, rural social service, administration, etc. may be discussed freely rather than through formal addresses. Suggestions for topics for discussions should be sent to the chairman of the Executive Committee as early as possible.

The Imperial Hotel has been chosen as the headquarters of the conference, and the various sessions will be held, with perhaps one exception, in the assembly room of the hotel—open to the conference through the courtesy of Mr. R. W. Farr, the manager.

Those attending are expected to meet their own expenses during the conference and to and from the conference, and to make their own hotel reservations. It is urged that all desiring room reservation at the headquarters hotel correspond as early as possible with Mr. Farr. The rates at the Hotel Imperial (headquarters) are enclosed, together with the rates at other Knoxville hotels.

It is especially desired that as many as possible of those who expect to attend will reach Knoxville on the night of April 21st for registration, in order to be present at the first session early on the morning of April 22nd and for an informal social gathering on the night of the 21st.

This call is issued by the Executive Committee* as authorized by the conference held in Atlanta in April of last year.

John C. Campbell, Chairman, Secretary of the Southern Highland Division of the Russell Sage Foundation, 412 Legal Building, Asheville, North Carolina

A. E. Brown, DD, Superintendent of Department of Mountain Missions and Schools, Home Mission Board of the Southern Baptist Convention, Asheville, North Carolina

Franklin J. Clark, Recording Secretary of the Domestic and Foreign Missionary Society of the Protestant Episcopal Church in the USA, New York, New York

Edward P. Childs, Field Superintendent, Mountain Division of the School Department, Woman's Board of [National] Missions, Presbyterian Church, USA, Asheville, North Carolina

H. J. Derthick, Field Superintendent, Christian Women's Board of Missions, Indianapolis, Indiana

H. Paul Douglass, DD, Corresponding Secretary of the American Missionary Association, New York, New York

William Goodell Frost, President of Berea College, Berea, Kentucky

R. A. Hutchinson, DD, Secretary of the Board of Home Missions of the United Presbyterian Church of North America, Pittsburgh, Pennsylvania

D. H. Ogden, DD, Chairman of the Committee on Mountain Work of the Presbyterian Church in the US, Atlanta, Georgia

Katherine Pettit, of the Executive Committee of the Pine Mountain Settlement School, Pine Mountain, Kentucky

Florence Stephenson, Principal of the Home Industrial School, Asheville, North Carolina

John E. White, DD, Member ex-officio, Chairman of the Department of Mountain Work of the Southern Baptist Home Mission Board, Atlanta, Georgia

Isaac Messler, Recording Secretary, Superintendent of McKee Academy, Reformed Church of America, McKee, Kentucky

*Owing to the recent death of Professor J. R. Hunter of Emory and Henry College, Emory, Virginia, the Methodist Episcopal Church South is unrepresented on the Executive Committee.

"If you can get all the churches represented to work as one team," wrote Mr. Glenn, in his own hand and in his usual laconic fashion, on March 17, 1914, when he received the call, "you will be entitled to high honor!" To which John retorted on the 19th, "I am not at all sure that I can be instrumental in having the churches represented in the conference 'pull together as one team.' I am glad, however, that they are hitched up to the mountain wagon, and though we don't know where we are going, we are on the way."

My diary, March 14th, the day the "calls" were issued, records: "Daisy, John, and I worked on invitations to the conference, Miss Sheak helping at the office. Went down again with John in the afternoon and worked until six."

Succeeding entries show some of the proceedings of the following days as they came under my eye, though I cannot try to list visitors at office and home, or "official" house guests. Nor do I remember just when the "Map of the Southern Highlands" was begun. I know that Miss Dickey and I were hard at work on it by March 20th. We pasted together the different states, and where their sizes did not agree, drew in the missing state areas. The whole grew into huge proportions, with regional divisions painted in color—the Blue Ridge, or eastern belt, in blue; the western, or Allegheny-Cumberland, in pink; and the famous "Valley" lying between, in green. We had to stretch it on the floor when at work on it and bend painfully over on knees and elbows. To locate the little stickers denoting schools, their situation, and the board under which they were working was another refinement. John was so pleased with this map that he wanted it at every one of the early meetings, and its transportation was a constant puzzle. It was hard to get it on the train, even rolled tight, and it was much too precious to be relegated to the baggage car. We usually had to slip it into the coach as unobtrusively as possible, while the conductor was looking the other way. He was not likely to disturb it, once ensconced, though he did occasionally protest mildly.

The diary entries continue:

March 20—Light snow again. Spent morning at dressmaking, map, etc. John rather tired and stayed abed.

March 22—More snow and quite cold, 44° F. at noon. Miss Dickey and I worked hard on map all the morning, while John was abed.

March 23—Dressmaking and map working.

March 25—Map and sewing.

March 26—Miss Dickey, John, and I went to meet the Packards at three. John and I got lovely arbutus. Worked on map.

A clipping from Mr. Glenn, in the midst of the activities, called for much comment in a letter John wrote to him on March 26th:

Thank you for the article received this morning with reference to the attack on the Country Life work of the Presbyterian Church. I have known something of it in the past. Personal animosities are at the bottom of it, and possibly Dr. Wilson and Mr. Stelze added fuel to the flames kindled in the last General Assembly by their fearless tactlessness. I am of the impression that there will be a struggle in the next General Assembly over the Country Life Department, but I feel that the work will go on under some jurisdiction, even if they succeed in limiting Dr. Wilson.[8]

One of the Country Life workers was in to see me this morning, at Dr. Wilson's suggestion, and we are expecting at our home today a physician and his wife from Massachusetts who are to take up work in the Laurel region where the Country Life Department is active.

My diary goes on:

March 27—Perfectly beautiful day. Spent in getting ready for tea for the Packards (the new doctor and his wife, to be on Big Laurel) and in the tea itself. About fifty here. House decorated with daffodils, arbutus, and Japanese quince.

March 30—Worked on map all afternoon.

March 31—Worked on map a good deal of the day.

April 1—Home with John at 3:00 and got after map.

April 3—Worked on map in morning, a good deal of the time on hands and knees; it was so large we had to stretch it out on the floor.

April 4—All off early for Brittans Cove. John drove Mother from Weaverville, and the rest walked. Home about seven.

April 6—Daisy and I went to the station with John to see him off for Louisville to a Conference for Education in the South, which Dr. Claxton had urged him to attend.

On the eve of his departure for Louisville, John answered at length a request from Mr. Glenn for a list of independent schools in the mountains. He had gradually discovered his hardest obstacles lay back in church organization, doctrinal prejudices, sectionalism, conflicting personalities, or jealousy, as well as in lack of understanding of local condition. Even the independent schools usually had their nonresident board of trustees who more or less ruled their actions, although resident heads of such [schools]were much freer to make their own decisions, especially if they were people of force and energy. Necessarily, John had to try to keep in touch with governing nonresident officials, as well as with field superintendents, principals, and local workers. The data he was collecting show the character of his problems. Some of these he sent to Mr. Glenn on April 6th:

In reply to your inquiry of April 4th, I would say we have listed in this office but thirteen or fourteen institutions independent of denominational organization. There are some schools that are not organically connected with denominational boards but are so strongly connected with particular denominations sympathetically that we have listed them as denominational schools. The independent schools traced to date are:

> The Berry School for Boys and
> The Martha Berry School for Girls, near Rome, Georgia
> Rabun Gap Industrial School, Rabun Gap, Georgia
> Pine Mountain Settlement School, Pine Mountain, Kentucky
> WCTU Settlement School, Hindman, Kentucky
> The Willard School, near Landrum, South Carolina
> Lincoln Memorial University, Cumberland Gap, Tennessee
> Grace Nettleton Memorial Orphanage (doing some school work)
>   situated near Lincoln Memorial University
> The Pi Beta Phi Settlement School, Gatlinburg, Tennessee

and several schools in Tennessee supported in part by the Federation of Women's Clubs. Berea College is an institution of higher learning, independent of denominational control now but in the earlier days associated with the Congregational Church. Although Berea ranks as a college and does excellent college work, by far the greater proportion of its students are not college students but enrolled in the secondary grades. This appears to be inevitable in any institution of higher learning in the mountains proper.

I regard the work at Pine Mountain under Miss Pettit and Miss de Long, and that at Hindman under the direction of Miss Stone and Miss Huntington, as among the best in the remote mountain section. The Berry schools are also very good schools. They differ from the two especially mentioned in being located in the valley section nearer railroad centers, and in bringing boys and girls from the mountain section to them, rather than being located in the immediate home environment of the students.

The Pine Mountain School differs from the Hindman School in being a little more independent. It has a permanent board of trustees, I believe. The Hindman School approaches a little more the denominational school in that it is controlled by an organization—the Women's Christian Temperance Union of Kentucky. Both are doing very good work. The school at Hindman still continues, I think, to teach the public school. The time has come, I believe, to make over the public school to the support of the community, despite the wishes of the community to the contrary. The school would then be free to develop more fully its rural social settlement features and its extension work.

We are still engaged in the work of bringing up to date our list of denominational schools. So far, we have 125. We have not complete returns from the Protestant Episcopal Board as yet, nor from the Presbyterian Board USA, or Northern Presbyterian Church, as it is more commonly called. In 1910 the Episcopal Church had about forty-eight schools. Many of these were small community schools, but some, especially in Virginia, were branching out into industrial and agricultural work. The Northern Presbyterians also had, in 1910, forty-eight stations. This church has done the most extensive educational work in the mountains. Out of its experiences have come some very promising changes. They are giving up most of their smaller community schools and are becoming pioneers in the mountains of a country life movement—the community schools developing into rural community centers.

There are, therefore, approximately 220 centers in the mountains where educational work is carried on under the auspices of the Baptist, Brethren, Christian, Congregational, Methodist Episcopal South, Presbyterian USA, Southern Presbyterian (US), United Presbyterian, Associate Reform Presbyterian, and Protestant Episcopal Churches.

As a general statement, I would say that the independent schools with strong leaders are especially worthy of support.

I would not give the impression that there is much proselyting by denominational schools. There is comparatively little of it. These schools are handicapped by management at long range and by having the final authority, often, in the hands of men who look upon the problems of the field in an academic way and from the viewpoint of financial administration.

I do not know whether any of these schools receive help from the Southern Education Fund or from the Slater Fund. My impression is that there are few such grants, if any.

The diary:

April 7—Letter from John and telegram "arrived safely in Louisville!"
Worked on map in afternoon and evening.
April 8—Got map colored and mounted in afternoon.
April 10—All day on map, completing the mounting. A successful job,
thank goodness; accomplished by Miss Dickey, Miss Sheak, Daisy, and
me.
April 11—Station at 2:00 to meet John.
April 14—Worked on map almost all day, retouching and shading. John,
Lady Sheak, and Daisy to Kenilworth for short walk to see mountains
after heavy rain.
April 15—Map, cake, arbutus. Dr. Packard came in 11:00 p.m.
April 17—Up at 5:00 to get Dr. Packard off for early train to Marshall.
Drove to Mt. Meadows—arbutus and bloodroot in quantities.
April 20—Growing cold. All went downtown on errands. John and Miss
Dickey furiously busy.

The following letter, written April 6th by Mr. Glenn to Rev. Charles L. Thompson, DD, secretary of the Board of Missions of the Presbyterian Church, USA, New York City—he sent to John with a query whether "it will be justified? I am holding it until I get your reply."

I have seen with much regret the discussions in the *Evening Post* about the administration of the affairs of your board. I sincerely hope that the Country Life work is not going to be cut off. If my evidence of the value of your work is of any use to you at any time, I shall be glad to give it. My impression is that the criticism of Mr. Weaver on the surveys is entirely unjustified and that nothing more practical has been done by any of the churches. My hope is that you will be able to make more of them.[9]

John answered Mr. Glenn on April 13th:

I have just returned from the Louisville conference and write at once in reply to your letter of April 6th with reference to the copy of the letter to Dr. Thompson that you are holding. There are so many elements entering into this attack on the Country Life Department that I hardly know what to say in reply to your inquiry.[10]

I have learned recently, in a confidential way, that Dr. Thompson has resigned his position but that it is not to be made public for a little time. I understand that Edgar P. Hill, DD, of Chicago—connected in some way with the McCormick Theological Seminar—is his probable successor and is likely to be a prominent figure on the floor of the next General Assembly, which meets in Chicago in May. He is, I infer, in favor of the Country Life work.

It has been intimated that Dr. Wilson has instigated various persons and presbyteries to write in defense of his department and that his alleged activity in this matter has aroused opposition in other presbyteries. It seems to me that a letter from you as general director of the Russell Sage Foundation cannot be criticized, as you would be writing on your own initiative and because of your belief in the kind of work that the Country Life Department is attempting. I have a very strong feeling that a letter from you would do much good and would be a great influence in securing the retention of the Country Life Department as it is, or in some other form; but whether Dr. Thompson, under existing conditions, is the right person to whom to address such a letter is an open question.

Dr. Wilson may have to go. He has aroused some antagonism by his tactlessness in utterance and his failure to consult or cooperate with leading pastors in the field surveyed, but I think that the attack on the Country Life Department is not directed at him primarily but is the result of old jealousies, perhaps of some extravagances, of too much compromise in the past; and of the honest belief on the part of many that the polity of the Presbyterian Church is being undermined or that the church ought to have nothing to do with so-called social service or economic questions. I understand that a compromise is likely to be reached whereby a clean bill of health is to be given to the board or Executive Commission, but that possibly the Department of Country Life is to be sacrificed or placed in some other department. Nothing definite probably will be known until the meeting of the General Assembly, when possibly the whole thing will be precipitated and fought out on the floor.

Fundamentally, the differences seem to arise from disagreement as to church government and administration. Philadelphia and Pittsburgh appear to want affairs managed from Pennsylvania, the stronghold of Presbyterianism, rather than from New York. Leading pastors in the large cities of the West and the superintendents of mission work in promising western fields wish more local authority. Furthermore, a large body of Presbyterians believe that the presbytery is the administrative unit. These three factions, if they may be so called, all oppose, more or less, board administration. As a matter of fact, however, weaker presbyteries, such as those in the South, where the Country Life Department is most active in actual work on the field, are so weak numerically and financially that they need help from the central Mission Board.

Dr. Weaver, who is leading the attack, is disgruntled, I understand, because of some past personal disappointments and is making use of the somewhat legitimate objections growing out of the differences mentioned above.

It is a mixed-up affair, and I am now very much afraid that fields that should be helped through a well-directed Country Life movement are to suffer in consequence of these troubles among brethren.

If you write to Dr. Thompson and he should indicate ways in which it would appear to him that the Foundation might be helpful, participation in the ways indicated by him might lead some of his rabid opponents to regard the Foundation as a defender of Dr. Thompson or Dr. Wilson rather than as an advocate of the Country Life movement in the Presbyterian Church.

Possibly you already know of the resignation of Dr. Thompson and of his possible successor. If so, it would appear to me at the present writing that a letter to his successor, or to some person less embroiled in the present strife, would result in what is hoped for.

My diary, on April 21st, says that we got "off for Knoxville on 7:00 a.m. train, John, Miss Dickey, and I, loaded with "exhibits"—including the *map*. Redbud, apple, and dogwood at various stages of bloom, lovely! Arrived something after 11:00 a.m.

This second conference, the first in Knoxville, set a pattern for many succeeding meetings. Exciting it was, and what fun! Of course, there were many preliminary preparations to attend to as soon as we were settled at the Imperial Hotel. The conference room must be put in order, a desk placed for the chairman, a table for taking registration, chairs arranged, exhibits in place, reporters interviewed. We must get a great bunch of daffodils from the outdoor market to adorn the speaker's stand, and must explore the stores for pencils, erasers, writing blocks, thumbtacks and sundry other small supplies. And all the while, every few minutes, we were greeting old friends, spotting newcomers and getting acquainted with them, answering questions, enlisting help as needed.

By seven o'clock, we were ensconced at the conference room, resplendent in our best clothes, ready to welcome and register the delegates as they drifted in. An informal reception followed, in which every effort was made to get people acquainted with each other. John, radiant with happiness, moved about, recognizing with his remembering (detective) eye, establishing connections and points of contact. If he saw some seemingly lost individual, he immediately sought him or her out for a talk, and he especially commissioned some of us to go and do likewise. Thus from the beginning the conference had a friendly, personal atmosphere quite different from the usual occasion of this sort.

Many of the addresses were perhaps not outstanding, but they were earnest and eager. John's on the mountain country was the most enlightening and valuable, as it dealt with facts obviously significant, and unknown to most of those present; and his personality warmed those facts and made them meaningful and full of interest.

A list of some of the subjects discussed, and touched upon, gives an idea of the scope of the meeting:

1. Character of the Mountain Area—complete survey of the location and extent of the problem and the various agencies at work.
2. Industrial Development through Redirected Education—failure of public school through poor and inadequate salaries; possibility of loaning money to farmers over a period of years to help them farm successfully.
3. Rural Nursing.
4. Weaving, Community Gardens, and Selling of Farm Products.
5. Cooperation between Public and Denominational Schools.
6. Mountain Resources.
7. Reports on some Individual Schools.
8. Work of Kentucky State Tuberculosis Division—need of sanitation.
9. Religion of the Mountains.
10. Health Problem.
11. Cooperation among Different Denominations.
12. Ballads and Folklore of the Mountains.
13. Homeless Children.

Probably too many of the talks centered on the speaker's own work and what had been accomplished in his field. As I wrote in the magazine *Mountain Life and Work*, July 1937, in an article entitled "Retrospect":

It is amusing now to recall how eagerly we all welcomed an opportunity to talk about ourselves! Sometimes we could hardly sit in our seats to listen to others, for wanting to talk about ourselves! How we watched the clock, and what dark looks we cast at the enthusiastic speaker who overstepped his allotted five or eight minutes!

I used to marvel at John's patience. He recognized that all this was necessary before we were ready for wider horizons. We had to express ourselves, as it were; and he tried in every way he knew to make the humblest and most remote worker feel that his or her experience was just as important as that of the most prominent in the field. He wanted all to feel welcome and at home.

When at last we adjourned in the late afternoon, it was as old friends who had come into a new life and hope: tired but full of enthusiasm, bubbling over with content. I shall never forget how a little group of us—in which I recall Mr. Messler, Mr. F. J. Clark, Mr. Israel, J. P. Faulkner, Isabel Rawn, and Miss Shea—went together to a soda fountain, and movies in the evening, sitting almost in the front row before a very second-rate picture advertised as *Mabel at the Wheel.* The humor was anything but refined, but the staid and dignified delegates laughed till the tears ran down their cheeks. Back home by the early train, John could write jubilantly to his skeptical superior, Mr. Glenn, on April 25th:

I have just returned from the Conference of Southern Mountain Workers in Knoxville, the details of which have busied our office for several months. It was a great success in and of itself, and the attitude of the Knoxville public and press was all that could be asked. I am enclosing clippings from the various papers in Knoxville. I expect to have more within a few days, but may I ask if you will be so kind as to hold these for return in the event of it being impossible for us to get more?

Dr. Claxton seemed very desirous of coming but was prevented in carrying out his purpose. He sent us a very fine letter of greeting, which will be incorporated in the report of the conference. Dr. [T. N.] Carver of the Rural Organization Service also expected to come but was detained.

The state superintendent of education gave us a fine address, and there was hearty cooperation from the county officials of education.

Twelve denominations were represented in addition to representatives from the leading independent schools, representatives of the Federation of Women's Clubs conducting schools in the mountains, and of several other organizations doing educational work in the highland section. I was very much impressed by the spirit of harmony that prevailed. It seemed almost impossible, as I looked forward to the conference, that we could have an interdenominational conference of the sort with independent workers, state officials, physicians, nurses, and others, without some jarring note. Not one was sounded.

Full recognition was given to the Foundation, the Southern Highland Division, and to the chairman for the part played by them. It was said time and time again from the floor and in private that such a conference would be impossible without the Foundation having a directing share in it. "We know that the Foundation is absolutely impartial and wants to help and not direct" was the statement made time and time again. I had a little difficulty in keeping the reporters from saying that the conference was held under the auspices of the Russell Sage Foundation, so general was the belief that the Foundation was the moving force in the whole matter. Mrs. Frost moved that the conference express its deep appreciation to its chairman for the idea of such a conference and for being the prime mover in issuing the call for the first conference last year. I expressed myself to the effect that while the Foundation had some incidental connection in a cooperative way, the call was really issued by the Southern Baptist Church and the Southern Presbyterians, with others concurring. She replied—and others so expressed themselves—by saying, "That may be true, but if it had not been for the Foundation's connection with it, we would not have responded to the call."

They know each other now, and I think it is an assured thing for some years to come. It has been quite a task. They insisted that I should be chairman again, and when I proposed that someone else should take my place, again the reply came from various persons on the floor: "You know us all, and we all know you, and no one else knows the field as you do. We must have you." Acting upon the suggestions made by Mrs. Rice and yourself when I had the privilege of meeting with you at Mrs. Rice's home, I accepted the chairmanship again, as it seemed to me one of the most important fields in which I can serve for the present.

I asked Bishop Horner to deliver an address, and he came in a very happy mood, contributing much to the interest of the conference.

Mr. Clark, secretary of the Domestic and Foreign Mission Board of the Protestant Episcopal Church, recently elected to our Executive Committee, came also, and we all lost our hearts to him. He very modestly declined to speak from the floor, saying that he came as a learner; but he is a splendid mixer, and I do not think that there was any one present at the conference who went away with so many friends as Mr. Clark.

Mr. Burkitt, the newly elected field secretary of the SIEA, was also present and made a very good impression. He is a man of charm and ability, and I think Dr. Claxton made no mistake in his selection. He was brought up on a farm and still lives on the farm out of Nashville, though closely connected officially with the public schools of Nashville. He appears to me to represent in his training the best product of vocational and cultural training. He has gone to Washington to confer with Dr. Claxton and then, in all probability, will return to Asheville for two or three days' interview with me. I shall give him all the information I can, map out an itinerary through the mountains, and get him in touch, through letters of introduction, with the best leaders, from my point of view, in the schools of the highlands.

Great interest was shown in the map that I presented. I promised the conference last year that a map would be prepared showing the various regional belts of the mountains and the location of the different mountain schools classified denominationally. Had I known how great a task it was to prepare such a map, I fear I should have faltered. Mrs. Campbell and Miss Dickey came to my rescue and have been working for months in all the spare time that they had to prepare the map. I could not anywhere—from the government or from private sources—get the kind I wanted, showing the counties, so the map had to be made from various maps brought to a uniform scale. It attracted great attention, and there were many requests for a copy reduced in size. This map was seven and a half by six feet in dimension. I think I can have it photographed and reduced at a moderate cost. I shall delay, however, until I have full data, will endeavor to find out the cost, and then present the figures to you.

Another chart that I presented, which awakened the lively interest of all present, was a diagram showing the percentage in the mountain country of church communicants and noncommunicants and the percentage of communicants in each Protestant and non-Protestant body. There is a great demand for this also. For some months I have been at work to get this in shape. There is considerably more work to be done, as I want to obtain from each denomination its own reports from the mountain country. This work has never been done before, and I am constantly receiving requests for this sort of thing.

The Baptists have about 50 percent of the communicants of the mountain country. Many of the other denominations, however, with only 2 or 3 percent of communicants, have spent as much money, if not more, for religious purposes than the Baptists; and while the number of communicants is numerically small, the area of influence of these other churches, because of their large expenditures and efficient work, is very extensive. I think if I can get to work at this and show it in graphic form, the results will be well worth while—and it may clear the air for a better understanding.

I was much gratified at the response given my request that Mr. [James P.] Faulkner, the lecturer of the Tuberculosis Commissioners of Kentucky, be sent. Mr. Faulkner knows the mountain country thoroughly, having traveled all over it with an exhibit in a wagon when he was at the head of the extension service of Berea College. It seems that the governor of Kentucky, the ex-officio member of the commission, was present at the meeting when the invitation was read. He insisted that not only Mr. Faulkner should go but also Dr. Williams, one of the commissioners, and that they should take with them their car with its exhibit. Through his interest, arrangements were made with the L&N Railroad and the Interstate Commerce Commission. Their presence, addresses, and exhibit added much to the interest and profit of the meeting.

The registration this year is more than triple of last year. Money was voted for publishing the program and list of delegates, and that matter is in our hands. Plans have been proposed whereby a regular registration fee will be paid to cover the increasing expense of the conference. As soon as the minutes are printed, I will send you copies.

I leave Monday morning for a week in the mountains of North Carolina. On my return, I go to Tryon, North Carolina, at the request of Mr. [Ralph] Erskine, to present to his trustees some ideas that we have in common for the promotion of industrial training. I shall be in Asheville thereafter until the 18th or 19th of May, when I go to Chicago for a week to the General Assembly to speak at the Women's Board meeting, as stated in another letter of this date to you.

I hope I have not wearied you with this long recital. I have felt that you would want to know all about the meeting and the attitude of the various people and agencies toward the activities of the Foundation, through this division.

I neglected to state that I went to Louisville to the Conference for Education in the South. It was helpful to me in that I met many people that I wanted to see, but the conference itself was a great disappointment to me and to others, I think, if I may judge from their statements. It was not at all up to the previous conferences that I had attended.

7

The Southern Highland Division's Widening Field, 1914–1915

After the 1914 conference, John Campbell was busy writing letters, thank you letters, and letters in response to queries posed during the time in Knoxville.

In May the Campbells traveled to Tryon, N.C., to visit a local furniture shop and for an address to the Tryon Industrial Association, which was promoting mountain crafts in answer to a growing interest outside the mountains. The Southern Industrial Education Association had opened a salesroom in Washington for "cabin crafts."

While John was trying to gather more information for the report for the Foundation, there were more addresses to board meetings all over the country and more letters to workers interested in the conference and in mountain work, such as Dr. Warren H. Wilson of the Presbyterian Church in the Highland South and Frances Goodrich, who was a Congregationalist but was working under the Presbyterian Church in the Laurel field.

Campbell proposed visiting Denmark for an investigation of Danish folk schools, an interest supported by many of the attendees at the conference and by Dr. P. P. Claxton, superintendent of the Department of Education in Tennessee. The folk schools were not to compete with public schools, but to provide another option for those who could not, for various reasons, attend public schools. John Glenn of the Foundation was supportive, but overseas travel was becoming dangerous because of the war.

The fall of 1914 was spent traveling, writing, and answering letters constantly, as well as trying to visit those interested in the work of the Southern Mountain Division; there was a constant struggle against denominationalism in education. Campbell writes of his interest in getting the Red Cross and the Country Life Department of the Presbyterian Church, USA (Northern), to cooperate regarding rural nursing. A selection of other matters required much time and effort, including an effort to pass a bill in the state legislature to secure a teachers' training school for western North Carolina, a discussion of reasonable salaries in mountain schools, and plans for the Third Annual Conference of Southern Mountain Workers in Knoxville.

Letters immediately following the 1914 Knoxville conference bring out many comments and throw light on some of its usefulness. John wrote at once to W. L. Maypother, first vice president of the Louisville and Nashville Railway:

As chairman of the Executive Committee of the Conference of Southern Mountain Workers held in Knoxville recently, I am instructed to express the sincere thanks of the conference for the courtesy shown by the L&N Railroad in bringing the car of the Kentucky Tuberculosis Commissioners to us.

As the son of a former railroad manager in the West, I take a great personal pleasure in writing this letter, for I know how unaware and unappreciative the general public may be of many unadvertised courtesies extended by railroad officials.

I have known, by reason of my work, how much you have done to assist a number of organizations in the Kentucky mountains in their efforts to better rural conditions, and I am delighted in being the means of expressing the hearty thanks of a conference made up almost entirely of the representatives of rural organizations.

He wrote in characteristic vein to Miss Ella L. Schenck, a teacher at the Berry School, who had talked with him at the conference and who was eager to start a new school in the mountains:

I regret exceedingly that the multitude of things seemingly necessary for me to attend to at the conference prevented me from having the pleasure of talking over more fully the matters you touched upon, which are of great interest to me. I hope you will let me help you in any way I can.

Possibly I seemed discouraging to you. I did not mean to be, but I have seen in my experience of twenty years so many projects go upon the rocks because people followed their feelings merely, that I am perhaps overcautious. It seems to me you have a very good idea, and the impression I meant to give was that you should seek the best advice possible from people intimately acquainted with the region in which you wish to begin your work. Should it prove to be in the highland section of the South, perhaps I could be of further help to you. Should it be in New England, I could assist, if you wish, in putting you in touch with leaders in New England acquainted with rural life, rural education, and rural needs.

I feel very strongly that the time is past for starting a new school on a purely denominational basis. No one believes more than I do that education is less and worse than worthless unless those taught are imbued through the teaching with the altruism of Christianity. If one believes so strongly in his own church as to convince him that it is right to spend time and money to bring the unchurched or those otherwise churched into his own denomination, there is some justification for denominational propaganda toward that end. I do not so believe, however. . . .

I would urge you most strongly to found your school on the fundamentals of Christianity untagged by a denominational name if you wish to be widely helpful and if you wish to succeed. I emphasize this especially if you undertake work in New England. If you wish to work under your own church, I would say it were better to join your interest with those of some school in the Southern Highlands under the church board of your preference and help them to the larger views which we in all our better moments hold.

At the end of April, an important matter arose in connection with the Country Life Department of the Northern Presbyterian Church. This followed John's letter of April 13th to Mr. Glenn (see chapter 6) regarding mounting difficulties. On April 25th he wrote again to Mr. Glenn:

I am enclosing herewith the correspondence with reference to a matter I deem of great importance.

I have accepted this invitation [to speak at the meeting of the Woman's Board of Home (or National) Missions, of the Presbyterian Church, USA] with a reservation that will make it possible for me to withdraw later should you think it inadvisable for me to attend. I want very much to be there. I may be helpful in saving the Country Life work under Dr. [Warren] Wilson, or even its continuance under the Woman's Board of Home Missions.

I should not, of course, take an attitude of partisanship in the matter, but I had hoped that there might be opportunity for me to be in Chicago on invitation during the General Assembly. I am quite sure, if I am there, I shall be asked privately by different officials of the board as to the value of the Country Life movement. I am consequently delighted to go on a Presbyterian invitation.

Mr. Glenn replied to this letter of April 30th:

I think it will be very valuable for you to go to the Presbyterian General Assembly.

Since getting your letter about Dr. Thompson, I have not taken any further steps. I thought it would be well to see Dr. William Adams Brown, but I have had no time to do so. If I get a chance, I will talk to him. Do you think of anyone else I might approach? As I am leaving on Tuesday for Memphis, I do not see how I can do anything before the meeting of the assembly.

You may feel at liberty to say that I believe strongly in the Country Life work of the Presbyterian Church and hope that it will be continued. I do not wish to endorse Wilson too strongly, but I would be perfectly willing to say that I believe on the whole he has done good work and that his point of view has been very much clarified. Please use your own judgment as to quoting me to this extent. There will be a deficit in the Presbyterian Home Mission Board this year of $138,000. I had a talk with [Charles S.] Mac-Farland today, and he felt that the best thing to do, in view of the deficit and general confusion, is to let the question of the Country Life Department alone.

In response to a letter from its chairman to members of the Southern Mountain Workers' Conference, asking for expression as to the strengths and weaknesses of the 1914 program, suggestions for the next year's program and for the conference arrangements, including date, came many comments. The following are a sampling:

From George A. Hubbell, president of Lincoln Memorial University, Cumberland Gap, Tennessee:

It is a happy thought to gather the impressions of the members of the conference at this time.

Mrs. Hubbell and I were much pleased with the general tone and feel that there was much of profit. We were particularly pleased with the evening lectures and suggest that that feature be continued, and that stress on health and housing might very well be future topics for special consideration.

We suggest that the presentation of the work which various schools are doing be substantially reduced. A fair amount of it is very interesting, but it perhaps excluded from the program some other things that would have been of greater interest and service to our workers.

For example, a good crisp discussion on the method of managing boarding halls; on the relation of the school to the surrounding community; on the method of organizing and utilizing the play spirit of a county or a certain region, and the like. In a word, we would like to know how others have best solved some of the everyday problems which press themselves upon our attention all the while.

From Rev. Benson Howard Roberts, pastor, the Union Church, Berea, Kentucky:

. . . a valuable and important meeting, both in present results, the stimulus that comes from association, the suggestions given, and the increased impression of the importance and value of the work.

I would suggest that a thorough discussion of some stated topics might prove of value. For instance, a paper on rural recreation, followed by a discussion of what is being done and what may yet be done along that line. The discussion to have at least as much time as is given to the paper. Other topics such as the development of mountain agriculture, rural nursing, if given thorough treatment, could but result in good.

The only weak feature in my mind was found in the reports of the denominations, some of which were very ordinary.

From Mary F. Hickok, principal, Normal and Collegiate Institute, Woman's Board of Home Missions, Presbyterian Church, USA, Asheville, North Carolina:

I wish to express my very great enjoyment of the conference recently held in Knoxville. It was most instructive and inspirational, and I hope I may be able to attend the conference next year.

. . . The fall or the spring would be equally convenient. . . . By waiting till spring, those present would have more to report because of a full year's work and experience.

The committee has so thorough a knowledge of the needs and conditions of the entire work that any program that they arrange will be helpful to all. (Every) feature of the past conference was both interesting and valuable to me. I was impressed with the spirit and harmony and cooperation.

From U. V. Williams, MD, Kentucky Board of Tuberculosis Commissioners, Frankfort, Kentucky:

I must say that my attendance at the Conference of the Southern Mountain Workers at Knoxville was a revelation and a benediction to me.

Not being familiar with the object or the work, I was wholly surprised at the largeness and the usefulness of the conference. I had previously no conception of the work or the character of the constituency of the mountain section and only a vague idea from missionary workers when visiting our communities in the Bluegrass. Sometimes, I am sure, greatly exaggerated . . .

I cannot close this without expressing to you the gratification that I received from the attendance on the conference, and thank you for the courtesy that was extended to us and the opportunity to present the workings of our commission. . . . In regard to the program, I think that matter should be left entirely to the Executive Committee.

From James P. Faulkner, lecturer, Kentucky Board of Tuberculosis Commissioners, Frankfort, Kentucky:

I have no adverse criticisms whatever to offer to the recent Conference of Mountain Workers. It seems to me that the conference is unique, and the program was just of the kind to be most helpful to the delegates and the movements they represent. That it will give strength to each by the discovery of a unity of purpose, I am assured, and that has been much to be desired for a long time.

From B. M. Beckham, DD, principal, Board of Missions of the Methodist Episcopal Church, South, Ferrum Training School, Ferrum Virginia:

I think we might derive some benefit from a study of the Danish folk schools, if the subject could be presented by one fully acquainted with it.

I wish we could get Dr. Warren Wilson to meet with us.

Could we not get a representative of the US Department of Agriculture to give us some information as to how best to teach that subject to mountain people?

Would it be possible to have an address on the methods of the Swiss in farming mountain land?

From Mary Pollard, Pi Beta Phi Settlement School, Gatlinburg, Tennessee:

I enjoyed the personal contact with the workers as much as any one part. The tuberculosis work was tiresome, simply because Dr. Faulkner repeated in his public address most of what he said at the car. It was the trouble of his being so full of his subject that he did not know when to stop, I suppose. That was the only thing of it that I did not enjoy. I wish we might have time for personal talks. Can't we have dinner together next year? Some way there is a chance to hear good things at a dinner that one never hears at other places.

The talk on the religion of the highlanders was worth the whole expense to me; it was so sympathetic, and I, probably as well as many of the other younger workers in the field (by which I mean newer rather than younger), needed the sympathetic touch. And I wish there could be a little discussion next time of the boy problem—what others are doing to keep the boys. And can there be something on the handwork among them, and how it has been or can be encouraged? These are some of the things that are puzzling me.

I am sending with this words of a ballad for Mrs. Campbell. I haven't the music, but will get it as soon as I can. I am no musician, and I am waiting for Miss Bishop to copy it down from the singing. I think I can get more, for these come from one girl.

From Rev. Franklin J. Clark, recording secretary, Domestic and Foreign Missionary Society of the Protestant Episcopal Church, USA, New York City:

The recent conference at Knoxville was tremendously helpful to me in many ways, and I brought home a great deal of information, not only from the addresses, but from my personal contact with the members attending the conference.

I wonder if it would not be helpful to those who are doing the work if some time were given to a discussion of problems and plans. In your addresses you gave us a great deal to think of along this line, but I thought that the principal thing that was drawn from the other workers was of a historical nature. A good bit of time was given to the history of the starting of their work, which was exceedingly helpful to me but would not be interesting again. All of those workers who attended the conference must have faced and solved problems common to the whole work. Their experience would have been more than valuable. They must be making plans ahead, and an interchange of ideas along this line might be helpful. . . .

On the whole, the conference at Knoxville was one of the most suggestive and interesting I have ever attended, and I think this is partly due to your generalship.

Characteristic is the personal interest shown in this letter of John's, written May 18th, to a mountain worker not able to come to the conference:

I was both pleased and pained to receive your letter. Pleased, because of the confidence that you show in me. I shall be most happy to do anything in my power to find a suitable location for you should you leave. . . .

I am pained because of the great loss you will be to all of that region. I am wondering if you will feel free to write me confidentially to let me know why you feel it necessary to leave. Your place cannot be filled, for the devoted service that you have put in through the years in —— County cannot be readily taken up by another. You have gained the confidence of the people, and they all love you. I do not say this to cheer you, but speak out of my knowledge. Has anything been done that I can right? What are the conditions upon which you could stay? I may be instrumental in bringing about conditions which would make it easy for you to reconsider your decision. I shall regard whatever you write as confidential if you so wish it. Please think the matter over very carefully.

Out of my years of experience in the mountains and my observations in my travels through the mountains, I regard as one of the essentials of success in any field of labor, the continuance in that field of labor by the right person. You are the right person, and I am hoping very much that any causes of friction which may have led you to reach this decision may be removed. You will pardon me, will you not, if my confidence in you, appreciation of your work, and my conviction that you of all persons are the one to lead in the health movement in your part of Kentucky, prompt me to write so freely?

I shall be most happy to help right anything that may be wrong, or to find just the right place for you should it be impossible for you to remain.

Mrs. Campbell would send her love to you did she know that I were writing. We were very sorry not to have you with us at Knoxville. I am going soon to Chicago to the meeting of the General Assembly of the Presbyterian Church, USA, but shall be back in a week or ten days.

Please write me freely and fully. You may count on my interest always, and my hearty cooperation.

Early in May, John was invited to Tryon, North Carolina, to visit the furniture shop of a Mr. [Ralph] Erskine, who had come to Asheville to talk with him about the problems of mountain industries and who had also been in touch with Mr. Glenn. He was also invited to give an address to a group of people in Tryon and thereabouts, known as the Tryon Industrial Association and working for the promotion of mountain crafts. There was growing interest in crafts native to the mountains in many centers. The Southern Industrial Educational Association maintained a salesroom for "cabin crafts" in Washington and at this time was hoping to move this project to New York City for a larger market and to broaden support. Mr. Erskine's furniture factory was already making a profit.

John went to Tryon on May 4th, and the occasion is sketchily described in my Line-a-Day, for I went with him:

May 4, 1914—Met at station by auto, entertained at hotel, dinner at invitation of Mr. and Mrs. Washburn. John made a fine speech in the evening before Tryon Industrial Association. *Great hit.*

May 5, 1914—Poured all night, but nevertheless Mrs. Washburn sent auto; cleared on way to house. Pleasant breakfast. Autoed to Mr. Erskine's shop—then to Industries. All very interesting. Train at twelve o'clock laden with baskets.

Later, on May 19th, John wrote to Mr. Glenn:

I enclose herewith a clipping sent me from Tryon with reference to the address I gave there upon the invitation of Mr. Erskine and the people interested in the mountain industries.

Mr. C. G. Burkitt, the newly appointed secretary of the Southern Industrial Educational Association, has been my guest for a week, and I have spent much time with him going over the whole mountain situation. I marked out an itinerary for him. He went from here to the Berry Schools at Rome, and will return about the 28th or 29th of the month. I am arranging to get him in touch with the people at Tryon. He may be able to be of service to them.

Mr. and Mrs. Thomas K. Glenn of Atlanta, Georgia, who have written you in the past with reference to organizing a mountain school at Tate, in Pickens County, Georgia, came to Asheville again a short time ago to see me. Mr. Burkitt was here at the time. Mr. and Mrs. Glenn are going to Washington to see Dr. Claxton, with whom they entered into correspondence at my suggestion when they were here before. He is very much interested, and the Glenns are trying to arrange a time when Dr. Claxton,

Mr. Burkitt, and I can meet them at Tate, look over the ground, and meet the trustees to outline plans. There seems to be no lack of land, and the prospect of funds is very promising, according to Mr. Glenn's statement. They are going slowly in order to be sure that the kind of school that they purpose shall be the kind that is needed.

I leave for Chicago tomorrow to speak before the Women's Board of the Presbyterian Church, under whose auspices the mountain schools of that church are conducted. I hope to be back early next week, but if it should seem advisable to remain a little longer at the General Assembly, I shall do so.

Thank you for your letter of April 30th giving me your position with reference to the Country Life Department and the liberty to quote you. I shall be careful as to how I use your name and as to what I myself say. The situation at this writing seems to be somewhat delicate.

Previously, in March, Mr. Glenn had inquired of John how much he used an adding machine. At this time a rented one was being used for getting material ready in many aspects of the study of the highland area, now, with Miss Dickey's help, well under way. In a letter of May 20th to Mr. Glenn, after explaining briefly the economy of purchase of a suitable machine, John wrote at length regarding this, and in a fashion which shows the breadth and scope of the material gathered and the need for it to be made available:

I have delayed answering your letter about the adding machine because of my absences from the office during the past six weeks, in attendance at the conference in Knoxville and elsewhere, and also because I wished to get final statements as to the best figures. . . . I enclose copies of what they offer. . . .

There are 251 mountain counties in the field of my study. These are arranged not only by states, but by the regional belts in which they lie. We have tabulated general tables which have been compiled on a county basis by state and region, as I have said, from the volumes of the Thirteenth Census. The regional arrangements are our own, and not from the census. Schools, and individuals even, wish to get data on a state basis, and they are coming to want it on a regional basis. In many such cases it is necessary for this office to select from the census what is wanted and to verify these rearranged figures before they are sent out.

The *general* tables that have gone out so far are:

Total population by nativity and race.

Number of persons and number illiterate, 10 to 20 years of age, by nativity and race.

Males of voting age by nativity and race.

Illiterate males of voting age by nativity and race.

Number of persons and number attending school, 6 to 20 years of age, by age groups.

Number of persons and number attending school, 6 to 14 years of age, by nativity and race.

Number of children under 6 years of age. Color and nativity of farmers.

Number of persons and number illiterate, 10 to 20 years of age.

Tables showing farm area and livestock.

We are working on the farm products, on the same county and regional basis, and on tenancy in the same way.

From these general tables of the US Census, we are planning to draw up text tables to bring out similarities and differences between regions and states and to emphasize points which particularly need emphasis. . . .

I do not know that the relevancy of all this will be apparent at a glance, but we are finding it more and more necessary to have these data to meet inquiries at conferences, by letter, and in office calls.

In addition to data drawn from the Thirteenth Census, we are now working on the Religious Census. There is great interest in this on the part of all denominations working in the mountains. . . . The effect of the government Religious Census is weakened somewhat by having its schedules taken at a time four or five years remote from the time at which the figures are obtained for population. We never know what percentage of the population are communicants—a question that I am often asked. We are getting from the different denominations direct their records for the areas for which data are wanted. These reports are for varying periods of time and are apparently inaccurate in the handling of figures. We are making considerable progress in getting data from denominational boards and yearbooks, but all the figures sent in need verification in this office. It is slow work, not only because the figures need verification and need to be brought to a common year, but also because ecclesiastical boundaries, for which these figures are given, do not always coincide with the boundaries of the mountain counties. It is worth doing, however, and the tentative results shown by us in the Knoxville conference awakened great interest and the desire for fuller knowledge, and the promise of full cooperation from the boards represented.

I also want this office to be able to furnish full information on the public schools. One of Dr. Frost's [of Berea] sons has been studying the public school situation in the mountain region for the Bureau of Education. I furnished the list of mountain counties to Dr. Claxton a year or more ago. Dr. Claxton told my secretary, when she called upon him for data last December, that this study included only the Blue Ridge section and that the valley section should be included in such a study, for it is a part of the mountain problem. The so-called valley section is a valley-ridge section in which there is often just as much isolation as in the two belts which are regarded in a restricted sense as the highland belts. . . . It seems to me the only true way to study the mountain situation is to take the three belts, making the necessary qualifications for each.

I want all this in the office because I have been emphasizing during these five or six years the need of just this thing, a need which seems to become apparent more and more to those who are working in the field itself.

We need a machine to do this work, and it will need to be a listing machine and not simply an adding machine which does not print.

On June 11th came Mr. Glenn's reply authorizing purchase of a fully equipped Dalton machine, which lightened the statistical work and set it forward more rapidly.

Meanwhile, on May 30th, John reported to Mr. Glenn on the Presbyterian meeting in Chicago:

I did not think it worthwhile for me to stay in Chicago until the end of the assembly. I was very much interested in the outcome of the controversy over the Board of Home Missions. . . .

Fortunately, the expected fight did not occur, but a plan of organization was presented by the Standing Committee on Home Missions which seems to meet the criticism.

The board is to be enlarged from twenty-six to thirty members, and the promise was made that the members resident in New York and the vicinity would bear only such necessary proportion to members from other parts of the country as to provide for a quorum for the transaction of the board's business. There is to be a council to meet once a year, composed of one member from each synod. Some initiative and supervision is given to presbyteries in local mission work and in the supervision of missionary workers. The names "Church and Country Life" and "Church and Labor" are dropped in the new plan, but power is given to the board to do the work itself, according to its judgment. I do not know what part, if any, Dr. Warren Wilson is to have in the work under the new arrangement.

He added in another letter of the same date:

The trip was eminently worthwhile. I received a very cordial and appreciative hearing, and at the request of the officers of the Women's Board, I met with them in a conference of two or three hours to go over all their work with them. Their superintendent, Mr. [Marshall] Allaben, is to be here the first of the week; and I am to confer further with him. I think they all feel the necessity of giving redirection to their efforts. . . .

Mr. [C. G.] Burkitt, field secretary of the Southern Industrial Educational Association, is to be here this week for further conference and in order that I may make out a new itinerary for him.

I am to go to the Maryville Conference about the middle of June.

Soon after sending this report, John received a letter, dated June 2nd, from M. Katherine (Mrs. F. S.) Bennett, acting president, Woman's Board of Home Missions, Presbyterian Church, USA:[1]

I want to take a moment of your time to express to you again the pleasure that it gave us to have you with us at the annual meeting of our board in Chicago.

Your presence and words were a great help to us, and I only trust that you did not find that the trip, with the attendant talking, was too tiring. I have felt very guilty ever since, when I recalled how late we kept you up and how much we demanded of you. I trust, however, that the return to your mountains has brought rest and recreation.

Please accept my individual as well as our individual thanks. I am hoping to be in Asheville next October for some little time and am planning to have some further insight into the tremendous constructive policies that you are developing for that highland region.

Mr. Glenn replied to these, "I am glad to hear that the Presbyterian assembly did not put the Board of Home Missions entirely out of business," and commented on his reading of a copy of John's address before the assembly, "I think it puts the case admirably."

Dr. Warren H. Wilson had written also, and John replied:

Thank you for your kind letter of appreciation received recently. I am very glad indeed if any word of mine helped out in Chicago. I am delighted to know that the work is to go on.

With reference to your inquiry as to whether I can be with you in August, I would say that it now seems unlikely. August is a month I do not enjoy. It is my hay fever time, and I am planning my vacation then, that I may be in a climate where it will not lay hold of me. . . . It will be easier to get people to Hot Springs than to Big Laurel. I like very much the idea of meeting on the frontier of your work. . . .

I think the topics that you have indicated are very good. May I suggest a number of conference hours on "The Country Church"? I am being asked more and more as to the possibilities of the church in the mountains. It seems to me that a continuance of the discussion as to the future place of the Presbyterian Church in the highland South would be profitable. It would be wise, I think, to emphasize Presbyterianism for the mountains as a unifying force, rather than a Presbyterianism which might be strong for itself, and in that strength be divisive.

You may count on my cooperation whenever and wherever you hold the camp, and my presence if possible. I shall be with you in spirit anyway.

Another letter written June 3rd, to Miss Frances L. Goodrich, a Congregationalist but a worker under the Presbyterian Church in the Laurel field, shows the interest we both felt in the developing work in that area:

In reply to your inquiry as to the Congregational school in the mountains doing the best work, I would say that Pleasant Hill Academy in Cumberland County, Tennessee, of which Rev. W. E. Wheeler is principal, is adapting its work to mountain needs more than any Congregational school in the mountains with which I am acquainted. Piedmont College at Demorest, Georgia, Dr. F. E. Jenkins, president, is greatly in need of money. Their work is for both the lowland and highland students and appears to be developing along the regular college lines. I had charge of both of these institutions at different times.

I am wondering if the Congregational Church to which your friends belong would not be willing to further the interdenominational fellowship that is under way in your Laurel field? Dr. and Mrs. [George] Packard are Congregationalists, and if my voice as a Congregationalist will help your friends to decide to help in this work and further the interdenominational cooperation so much needed everywhere, you may say that I, a Congregationalist, know of no better work to which Congregational money could go than in helping the introduction into the mountains of medical work. It might make a splendid first contribution toward a hospital.

I enclose a check for fifty dollars, first payment on a hundred dollars which Mrs. Campbell and I have promised to this work. It is a little more convenient for me to send fifty dollars this month and fifty next, and I hope the division will not inconvenience you. We both hope that you will have a very pleasant, restful, and profitable vacation.

On June 11th, Mr. Glenn forwarded to John a comment on the Danish folk schools made by Mr. Leonard P. Ayres of the Foundation Staff Division of Child Hygiene, whose school surveys and studies of public school problems in education were proving widely valuable and effective. Mr. Ayres had had the reading of John's report at the Knoxville conference. Mr. Glenn wrote:

In response to an inquiry which I made of Dr. Ayres, he sends me the following in regard to your report: "I find this very interesting. Probably the Danish folk schools are among the most efficient and hopeful educational institutions in existence. I believe some modification of them will prove most valuable in America. I doubt if the Presbyterian Board can successfully carry through the necessary experimentation and demonstration."

John was greatly heartened by this brief note. He had recommended the folk school so many times as worthy of experimentation and trial and had been asked almost as often for definite plans as to the proper folk school setup, that he needed to get a real firsthand understanding of it and be able to speak with confidence and authority. He now wrote, June 18, 1914, to put before Mr. Glenn with earnest conviction a plan for visiting Denmark, which had been maturing in his mind for some time:

Thank you for your letter giving me Dr. Ayres's view as to the possibility of some modification of the Danish folk schools for rural America.

I feel it necessary for the highest usefulness of this division during the coming year that I know something of the Danish folk school from personal study in Denmark. One of the most important things I am to do next year—if not the most important—is to give advice in the matter of readjustment of school work to board officials whom I have converted to my views.

If the Foundation approves of giving me two months, or a little more if necessary, on pay—one month being my regular vacation—and will pay my expenses while in Denmark, I will meet my own expenses to and from Denmark. The Foundation's expenditure for such purposes will come well within the balance of the budget for the present fiscal year after allowing for all office expenses, salaries, etc. to its close. From time to time I have been asked for information as to the necessary expenses of such a trip, so I wrote to one of the government commissioners to Denmark. I send his letter herewith.

Already demands are made upon me for definite plans of readjustment. I have read all I can find on the Danish folk schools and have interviewed Dr. Claxton a number of times with reference to them. Dr. Claxton shares with me the conviction that the church and private schools of the mountains should more and more leave the training of the children to the public school, and that the church and private schools, through redirected activities, should stimulate the public schools of the mountains. There are thousands of boys and girls in the mountains who are not reached to any extent by the public school or the church school. Many of these are youth of seventeen and eighteen and on, who will not go to a school where necessarily, as the situation now is, they are placed in classes with children far below them in age. It will be a long time before the public schools will be able to care for them, for the time is not yet, or in the near future, when the rural public schools of the mountains will be what they ought to be. There is need of careful, steady, and persistent effort—not merely an occasional whirlwind educational campaign—to create and strengthen public opinion for better public schools.

The church schools ought not to compete with the public schools in their curricula, but should seize the opportunity that is theirs to focus their work upon work preliminary to that of the public school, and of meeting the needs of the youths and maidens of seventeen and over who are soon to become the molders of public opinion. The church schools should also be reaching the older folks through an educational extension system which would employ not only the teachers in these schools but which would also enlist the services of state and federal experts as well as representatives of philanthropic organizations.

Denmark, with poor soil and poverty, succeeded through this kind of work in making her soil productive and her people well-to-do. I have urged upon the Presbyterian Board and upon others the advisability of availing themselves of Denmark's experience. . . .

By reason of the Foundation's connection with the mountain country for the past six years, I, as its representative, have a standing and will have a standing for a long time that no one else has or can have. Presbyterian officials and the workers on the field in various other denominations want my definite suggestions in readjustment because, as they say, I have a background of twenty years' experience in the mountains and acquaintance with the whole work and with their problems—an experience and acquaintance that others have not.

I have urged upon the Presbyterian officials the appointment of a commission consisting of their school superintendent, their field superintendent, and a few other influential members of the Women's Board, and that this commission be sent abroad to study the schools in foreign countries, especially the schools in Denmark, Norway, and Sweden. The officials agree that something decisive needs to be done. They have told me confidentially, however, that a number of their officers and many of their constituency hold to the old idea of missionary work and need to be converted to the new. They want me to lay the possibilities of this new work before their officers, and, through publication and addresses, before their constituency. . . .

Now that I have brought them to my views as to the need of redirection, I should be able to give them definite direction when they look to me for guidance. Somehow they have come to look upon me rather than upon anyone else as the person to lead them. My lack of personal knowledge of the folk school handicaps me in this leadership, and handicaps me also in my efforts to bring the church people into touch with the government men who know the folk school but not the mountains. I feel that I, at least, ought to know the Danish folk school as well as the mountains if I am to justify belief in me as a safe leader, adviser, and cooperator.

There is an element of pathos in the return to me of board officials and mountain workers after their experiences with persons to whom I have directed them. Because of lack of understanding of mountain conditions, their plans and suggested modifications often seem impracticable, and their lack of understanding and sympathy has led some of them into unguarded statements which have injured the work and the people engaged in it. I am sure you will not misunderstand me as overestimating my own importance when I say that the workers feel that I *do* understand the conditions under which they labor. Even when the persons whom I have introduced to them get them into trouble, they come back to me, feeling that I can understand even these troubles and that if I, myself, will outline the plan and present it, there will be more assurance of success. When they come back to me thus and I have nothing more definite to suggest, I feel just a bit as if I am giving them a stone when they come for bread. (At this point I was interrupted by President E. P. Childs, field superintendent of the Mountain Work of the Presbyterian Church, USA, who came to enlist my services late in October to lay before the Synod of Tennessee this whole matter of readjusting their school work.)

I do not wish to seem insistent, but I feel so keenly my need of personal knowledge of these matters, and the opportunity is so promising for the next year because of the preliminary work of this year, that I venture to run the risk of seeming insistent. I see no immediate prospect of this opportunity being seized if I do not grasp it, and now is the psychological time for me to lay hold of it. . . .

P. S. I have just read on page 159 of the *Literary Digest* of June 13th the following: "Much butter is imported from Denmark because Danish cows have greater enterprise and technical education superior to ours." I crave the same advantages for the mountains.

Mr. Glenn knew all the points made in this long letter; John had kept him well informed, as their correspondence shows. He knew Dr. Claxton's belief in the folk schools of Denmark and his wish to send John abroad to study them for the government. He had seen the various inquiries for advice and information about them which had come in from many sources, especially from the Presbyterians.

Bruce Payne, president of George Peabody College, was an old friend and decidedly interested, as was Professor Tate, and also Professor Selvidge (of his staff, School of Country Life), who had worked out interesting suggestions for the future of the Knapp School. He seems to have been a bit slow about answering the vital question; his definite answer arrived in a letter dated July 17th:

I cordially approve of your giving two months to Denmark. I also think that your budget can stand the expense of the trip on the basis suggested by Mr. Foght, namely, an expense of not over three hundred dollars. Look into cooperation in agriculture too.

If we are right in our facts about the importance of the general principles underlying the Danish folk schools, a personal inspection of them ought to give you material and suggestions that will be useful not only to the mountaineers, but to the country at large. I also believe that you know how to make the information that you already have and will acquire by your visit effectively useful. The few other men in this country who have seen the Danish schools seem not to have the kind of ability that is necessary to convince the public and officials. You also have the R.S.F. to back you.

I have asked Dr. Ayres what he knows about these schools, and he tells me that he thinks favorably of them. I also asked whether he had any suggestions as to special points for you to look into, and he said he had not. It might be well for you to write to him, telling him of some of the points that you specially want to know about, and see if he has any suggestions as to practical methods of investigating them.

If you decide to go, please let me know when you expect to leave. If this office can do anything to help you about getting a ticket or otherwise, please let us know. . . .

Can you send me some literature about the Danish folk schools? . . .

I am sending Mrs. C. a book on *Folk Ballads of Southern Europe,* which I think will interest her, together with an interesting criticism of it from the *Evening Post.* I hope Mrs. C. will enjoy reading it. When I go down to Virginia, I shall try to see Dr. Alonzo Smith and have a talk with him on the ballad question.

John replied at once (July 20th):

Thank you for your letter of July 17th and for your kind words with reference to me. I am very glad indeed that I may have the opportunity of studying the Danish folk schools for two months, and I am grateful for the appropriation of three hundred dollars for the purpose.

The delay has not seriously interfered with plans—the decision was worth waiting for. However, in order to escape my hay fever, I shall leave here early in August, attend to a few personal matters in Boston, and give Mrs. Campbell opportunity to see her mother, who is quite feeble—for Mrs. Campbell will go with me.

I hope to be able to leave by the 14th and hope that your plans are to be such that I may see you before sailing and that I may consult with Dr. Ayres, to whom I shall write on my return from Atlanta.

I should like very much to have a letter written to the Danish Embassy in Washington for their suggestions, and I should like also a letter to our minister in Denmark. I should appreciate your help in these matters.

I will write you soon as to literature about the Danish folk schools.

I leave tomorrow for Atlanta to meet Dr. Claxton and Mr. Burkitt. We are to accompany Mr. and Mrs. Thomas K. Glenn and some of the other trustees of the Tate School in Pickens County. They are to take us in automobiles to Tate, where the situation is to be looked over and plans for the school to be discussed. I will write you on my return.

With this joyous news and the confidence born of it, John set out to meet Dr. Claxton in Atlanta, preparatory to moving on to Tate.

Meanwhile, other requests had come in and were reported to the New York office. John's handling of two, revealed in the following three letters to Mr. Glenn, show some of the relationships which had grown out of the work of the Southern Highland Division and the Knoxville conference:

June 20, 1914

Enclosed herewith is a letter from Mr. [Gifford] Pinchot requesting me to serve on the Federal Council's special Committee on Church and Country Life. I am withholding my answer until I can have your views as to the wisdom of my serving. I appreciate the invitation very much, and personally should like to accept, but I feel a certain hesitancy which I cannot fully explain.

My personal relations with the Baptist leaders in the mountain work are very friendly. Many, if not most, of these men are bitter opponents of the Federal Council—they have so expressed themselves to me. I enclose a confidential letter from Dr. John E. White of their own church, which shows the Baptist missionary official attitude toward the whole matter of conference with non-Baptists. There were not as many representative Baptists at the Knoxville conference as there should have been. They promised me that they would come if possible, and I of course accepted their explanations for absence, although some of them seemed to me not sufficiently strong to keep away men who were in sympathy with conference between denominations.

There is the same division of sentiment on the Southern Presbyterian

Mountain Mission Board. In order to bring the Baptists and some of the Southern Presbyterians in, the leaders in organizing the Southern Mountain Workers' Conference gave assurance that the conference was for purposes of conference only, and that there were no plans contemplated for federation, union, or anything of the sort.

Because of my connection with the Foundation, I am viewed as impartial, and consequently have been put forward as chairman, and probably can remain chairman until I refuse absolutely to hold the office. I am a bit afraid that if I connect myself officially with the Federal Council, it may appear somewhat as violating the original agreement, in the making of which, however, I had no active part, though I regarded it as wise under the circumstances. Connection with the Federal Council by the chairman might serve, at least, as an excuse for doubting and reluctant brethren to withdraw entirely. It is desirable that I keep in touch with the Baptists especially, even if they do not come to the conference, for nearly 45 percent of the church communicants in the mountain counties are communicants of that church.

My feeling is that I would be more serviceable in the mountain field to the Federal Council by maintaining my present attitude and that I might risk success in my field by official connection with a committee whose activities are to be concentrated for two or three years upon the state of Ohio.

If you should agree in this view, would you suggest my writing as frankly to Mr. Pinchot, withholding, of course, Mr. White's statement?

July 14, 1914

I have recently returned from a conference at Montreat, North Carolina, where I was summoned by the committee in charge of the educational work of the Southern Presbyterian Church. We had a long and most interesting conference, and I received a most cordial reception.

A representative from the committee has just departed from the office, after telling me confidentially of tentative plans for the consolidation of four of their schools of higher learning in Tennessee and the possibility of some cooperation or affiliation with the United Presbyterian mountain work. This he urged me to hold in the strictest confidence. I urged strongly that the higher institution of learning that they were contemplating through the consolidation of the others should not be of the ordinary college type, inasmuch as it would be a duplication of the work done by four or five other Presbyterian colleges in Tennessee and would also be duplicating the academic work of the University of Tennessee. I suggested consideration of the folk school adapted to meet mountain conditions and the establishment of one higher institution along these lines. He was much interested and wanted me to come to a second meeting of the committee on July 23rd.

I am to be in Atlanta on that date to meet Dr. Claxton and Mr. Burkitt, to go up into the mountains of Georgia to visit the site of the proposed Tate School and to talk over plans for its curriculum.

I am to be kept in touch, however, with the plans of the Southern Presbyterian mountain educators, and I am hoping that the same relations may be established between this office and the Southern Presbyterian Board.

Dr. Allaben has just written me asking again if I could not go to the Ozarks. I have deferred writing until I shall know more definitely what my plans are to be.

July 27, 1911

I enclose herewith a letter from Dr. Tilden Scherer, who is president of King College, who is the gentleman who conferred with me about the consolidation of the Southern Presbyterian work, of which I wrote you under date of July 14th. I am much pleased to see in their resolutions that their body had decided to "confer with all agencies, religious, secular, or independent, through which helpful counsel may be secured." I have referred him to Dr. Ayres and promised him any assistance that this division may give.

On the same date, John also wrote to Mr. Glenn about the trip into Georgia to consult about the proposed Tate School:

I have just returned from a trip into Georgia. At Atlanta I met Dr. Claxton about twelve miles from Tate, Georgia. Those who went with us from Atlanta were Mr. and Mrs. Thomas K. Glenn, Mrs. Hodgson, Major Gwinn (chairman of the School Board of Atlanta and also a member of the board of the proposed Tate School), and three or four other gentlemen from Atlanta and one from Athens, Georgia, all directors of the proposed school.

We had a long conference with Mr. Tate and these directors, and the result is that they are going to start a folk school adapted to mountain conditions. Dr. Claxton is to outline plans, and I am to confer with them again on my return from Denmark. It seems likely also that they will send one of their number—probably the superintendent of the proposed school—to

Denmark while I am there in order that he might have the benefit of the observation of these schools that I purpose to visit.

Immediately following this visit came a wire to John from Major Gwinn, inviting him to become the head of the new Tate School. Although keenly aware what it would mean to be able to work out this new type of school, near, yet far enough from, his old school in Demorest, he did not delay his reply, sending it to Major Gwinn on July 29th:

> Your telegram has just reached me. I appreciate more than I can express to you the honor you and your colleagues would confer upon me in placing me at the head of your institution. It was indeed a great pleasure to meet such a group of altruistic and capable people and, did I feel free at present, I should be most happy to accept. What the Sage Foundation may have in store for the mountain work during the coming years, I do not know; but so long as I can be serviceable to them in this field, and so long as I feel that my work under their direction is still undone, I could not accept any other position, however attractive it might be to me personally.

The letter goes on at length, with recommendation of two persons for consideration for this position, both well known in the field, and ends: "It is needless, I am sure, for me to tell you at length how much interested I am in this work and how ready I shall be always to cooperate with you and your colleagues in this promising pioneer venture in rural education."

Meanwhile, the Russell Sage Foundation office in New York had booked us to sail on August 12th on the *Frederick VIII* of the Scandinavian-American Line, from New York directly to Copenhagen. The interval would give us time to visit my family for a few days in Nantucket and Boston and to see Mr. Glenn in New York. The annual report of the work of the Southern Highland Division was completed and mailed. We said our farewells to our friends in the mountains and made our journey northward on July 30th.

Alas for the best-laid plans! With all business arrangements in hand and packing complete, we were at Nantucket in process of parting with family, when a Western Union boy rode his bicycle up to the door. He carried a wire from Mr. Glenn, and this was followed by a letter Mr. Glenn wrote John on August 5th:

> I am sorry to have to say that I think it would be very unwise to go to Europe at the present time. Germany apparently has no respect for any neutral

nation. If she should be successful elsewhere, she is just as likely as not to try to capture Denmark. In the second place, the people of Denmark are probably so excited over the war that you would find nothing in normal condition and would probably have your trip for nothing. It is very unfortunate and very disappointing, but I would not be willing to have anyone connected with us go to Europe at present, unless there were very great emergency. A third reason is that as the big vessels are likely to be withdrawn for war purposes, all ships that are carrying passengers will probably be overloaded for several months to come, and you might find it very difficult to get passage back for some time.

It is, of course, possible that the war may be over shortly. I sincerely trust that this may be so. It is such a colossal catastrophe and so affects every nation in Europe, that they may be forced as a matter of preservation of national life to quit at an early date. It is hardly likely that things will settle down by next week, but it may be possible to transfer your passage engagement to a later date, so that if peace comes within a few weeks, you can still go. Meantime, you may be taking your holiday. If it seems wise to go later, this need not prevent your staying as long as you expected to. If you wish me to cancel your passage or to make arrangements for a later passage, you would better telegraph and send your tickets. Perhaps you can arrange this in Boston.

Can you come down to New York for Saturday? I think it would be better to come for a conference, as there is a possibility that you may be able to get off to Europe some time later in August, and I shall be away after this week until nearly the end of August. . . .

With much regret that I feel it necessary to interfere with your trip.

How anxiously we watched the papers may be imagined, but the clouds grew heavier and heavier and the news steadily worse. We stayed north for two or three weeks, then made plans to return to Asheville, by boat as far as Norfolk to help John continue to escape hay fever. Mr. Glenn wrote his high approval of this, adding, "It is sad that you cannot be in Denmark! May the fierce war kill itself soon!"

When we started south, we took with us my sister Mrs. Morgan Bacon and her youngest daughter, Priscilla, on their way home from Nantucket to Salt Lake City. A rough voyage and a hot, dusty train ride enhanced the charms of Blythewood when we at last arrived. Showing them the beauties of the Southern Highlands, so different from the stupendous Rockies, broke the anticlimax of our unexpected return. We slipped back into our usual life almost as if we had never thought of going away—almost, for the disappointment was a keen one, and in the quiet distance of the mountains, troubles in Europe seemed unreal indeed. When we thought of our steamer tickets in the Sage Foundation safe waiting for war clouds to fade away, we wondered if, after all, we could not have been using them. Fortunately, we did not learn until later that conditions in Denmark were fairly normal that first year of the war. We could have studied schools to our hearts' content and have had, too, the help of M. Eagan, minister to Denmark, who went over on the ship on which we were to have sailed! Disappointing, but not to be helped!

John heard from Denmark, as appears from his letter of September 11th to Mr. Glenn:

> I am receiving a few letters from Denmark in response to my inquiries. As soon as I hear from several other officials, I will send you the substance of the letters, or copies of them.
>
> Thank you for your congratulations on my freedom from hay fever. I escaped about three weeks beyond the usual time. My old enemy seemed, however, to be entrenched on the Virginia–North Carolina boundary and captured me as I crossed. I am now in irons, hoping to be paroled as the first frost arrives. Otherwise everything is going nicely.

One may imagine that Mr. Glenn was almost as disappointed as John, especially as all the activities of the Foundation had to be curtailed, at least temporarily. When John wrote him in regard to the estimated cost of printing the leaflet which was to summarize the second Conference of Southern Mountain Workers at Knoxville (thirty-six dollars for three hundred copies), he answered on September 22nd that the Foundation had to be very careful about expenses. "The Foundation's income may be seriously affected by present financial disturbances, and we may have to cut down some of our expenses. At the present moment, I would specially urge that you do not make any plans for traveling without consulting me. If there is any expenditure which does not seem necessary, please omit it. I hope the situation may clear up and improve within the next month so that we may not have to take any drastic measures. Meantime, we have got to go slow."

John reported his travel plans to Mr. Glenn in a letter of September 29, 1914:

> I shall be glad to receive the books and bulletins on cooperative credit and hope they may be serviceable through suggestion to workers in the mountains.
>
> I have your letter, also, with reference to expenses. I am now at work on a report of the past year's work and plan for the future. These plans provide for considerable traveling this fall to further some of the work under way. I

shall, however, submit all my traveling plans to you, and we shall endeavor in the office to keep our expenses down to the minimum.

There are two places to which I should go in October: one is to Lebanon, Tennessee, October 22–25th; the other to Lewisburg, West Virginia, on October 27th. Officials of the Synod of Tennessee of the Presbyterian Church, USA, have invited me to meet at Lebanon in conference with church, state, and other country life leaders, to plan for their Country Life work in the Synod of Tennessee, of which western North Carolina is a part. The Southern Presbyterian Church has also asked me to meet with them at Lewisburg. They are to establish the new Synod of West Virginia and want me to confer with their leaders there assembled on their educational work in the mountains. These meetings are so important that I think I ought not to fail to be there.

I have also written to Dr. Wallace Buttrick, as you suggested, for information on some of the work in which the General Education Board was interested in Mississippi, in the way of public school teachers getting into close touch with the home. This information was furnished, and I have established connection through correspondence with those doing this work in Mississippi, and I also found similar interesting work in Alabama.

Dr. Allaben was in Asheville recently and spoke to me again about wanting my opinion on the entrance of his board (the School Board of the Presbyterian Church, USA) into the Ozark region, after visiting the field where they have been invited to begin operation. You may recall his speaking to you about this some time ago. I told him that possibly I could go sometime early in November, and I had planned two circular trips to include these various points.

Mr. Glenn replied on October 1st: "It will be wise for you to accept the invitations from Lebanon and Lewisburg. They are both important. You can let me know when you have made plans for other work, and I will then know better what our resources are going to be."

The requested care about expense did not keep us from taking some weekend trips, mainly at our own expense, such as one in the Laurel country. John wrote Dr. [W. E.] Finley in Marshall, North Carolina, on September 30th:

If the weather promises well, Mrs. Campbell and I will come up to Marshall on the early train Friday morning, en route to see Dr. and Mrs. Packard.

Will you be so kind as to order for me, at the stable, a good, strong, automobile-proof horse and top-buggy? We should like a horse that we could use under the saddle as well as drive. In all probability we shall go to Allegheny on Friday morning and come back Monday.

My diary records the trip:

October 2, 1914—John and I sprinted to get breakfast cleared up and be off at 6:30 a.m. Dr. Finley met us at Marshall—good horse and buggy— and we had a fine drive over, making White Rock in four and a half hours, arriving Allegheny about 2:00 p.m. Rather quiet day, talking, etc. Miss Goodrich and Miss Fish over for the night.

October 3, 1914—Allegheny. Uncertain weather after rainy night. All hands cooking, etc. Up to picnic and baby show at Carmen—fairly attended on account of shower. Successful, however. Two ballad singers kept us late. Talked late in evening.

October 4, 1914 (Sunday)—Allegheny. Dr. Packard was called to White Rock, and John drove him over, Mrs. Packard and me with him. He went at once to examine his patient, and we went to church out-of-doors, then had a lovely ramble up on the mountain after nuts. [I remember today how the sun shone, and how red the little vines were.] Late in the afternoon the doctor had to operate—a serious appendectomy—primitive and unsterile surroundings, on a prominent citizen well on in years. We had serious doubts as to whether he would recover.

John and I took the buggy on the 5th and went by Carmen. There we saw "Mrs. Reuben Hensley and Mrs. ——; had a pleasant time and got ballads; then drove over the line (Tennessee–North Carolina) to see Minta Carter. Home about six thirty and early to bed. Doctor not home yet." He was still with Mr. Tweed when we left—and several days later—but his patient was improving and eventually got well, to our surprise and relief.

John returned to an office full, as usual, of letters to answer, largely inquiries for information and help. Mr. Glenn's were always first to have attention. In reply to a question he raised as to the usefulness of the *New York Times* for office purposes, John wrote on October 15th:

Our local papers are decidedly local in character, and even in some local occurrences, the *Times* has published the news two weeks in advance of our papers, which have then quoted from the *Times*.

The two papers of cosmopolitan character that give most attention to the Southern Highlands are the *New York Sun* and the *Times*. I want always to know what correspondents in the South and contributors say of the highlands in northern papers. Of the two papers mentioned, the *Times* seemed to me to be the better for our general purposes, although the *Sun* is always fair to the mountaineer.

We should have in the office not only more dailies, but the leading religious periodicals of the many denominations with whose boards I deal. Inasmuch, however, as such papers are published by the publishing department, generally of the denominations rather than by the boards with which I deal, I cannot get them free of expense, and hence we are debarred from the help that such papers would give.

I tested the *Times* a year personally before making it an office paper, but felt this year that in view of our constant use of it in the office, and of the absence of other leading papers, it was legitimately an office expenditure.

Letters showing conditions such as he had had to meet himself in earlier years always aroused John's sympathy; they were too close to his own experience to be passed over lightly.

October 15, 1914

My dear Mr. S——:

Your letter of October 13th has just come to the office, and I appreciate deeply the situation in which you are placed. I have received letters from other sections of the mountains which are almost exact duplications of yours in their appeal, and I know how true they are, for I myself have been in the same situation—even as to the furniture. My first home in the mountains, twenty miles from the railroad, was furnished with furniture which I myself made out of drygoods boxes, and fresh meat was so scarce that I could get none for the first three months, and after that at uncertain intervals—and they were generally long. I too have had teachers who have given up good salaries elsewhere and have come to the mountains to live on a mere pittance.

I cannot, however, help you to reach Mrs. Sage. I do not know her, having never had the honor to be presented. Many misunderstandings arise, through a confusion in the minds of many, of the Sage Foundation with Mrs. Sage's private beneficences. I am quite sure that some of my former trustees have misunderstood me, and perhaps still think hardly of me because I cannot bring the needs of the school of which I was president for a number of years to the attention of Mrs. Sage.

I hope this letter is not the last that I am to receive from you, for I may be able to bring your school to the attention of some donor at some time. I want to know more of it, and I want to come to see it, that I may be better prepared to give information.

I am sending you in this mail a copy of the *World's Work* for September 1913, which contains an article, on p. 549, on the activities of the Sage Foundation. You will find a very inadequate statement of the work of this division in that article.

The income of the investment is used for what are regarded as wise methods of work. I must confine myself to activities along the general lines laid down. I feel very sure that there is no surplus of funds, and I presume that philanthropic boards and foundations are having great difficulty this year, as are other institutions, in sustaining even at the minimum the activities under way.

I would assure you that your letters have not worried me, as you appear to feel they might have done. I shall be glad at any time to do anything that I can to assist you.

In the latter half of October, John went, as planned, to Tennessee. He sent a report on the meetings there to Mr. Glenn on October 31st:

I have just returned to the office after an absence of ten days, journeying to and in attendance on the meeting of the Synod of Tennessee of the Presbyterian Church, USA, at Lebanon, Tennessee, and the newly formed Southern Presbyterian Synod of West Virginia at Lewisburg, West Virginia. I delivered three addresses at Lebanon and one at Lewisburg and was called into conference by the Educational Committee of this new synod. There is a great chance of being of help to people working under the respective synods. They need, and want especially, advice along educational lines.

The Southern Presbyterians particularly have urged strongly that I return to West Virginia at their spring meeting to visit their institutions and outline definitely the work that they should be doing. I feel strongly the need of a more careful study of West Virginia, which is a mountain state in its entirety and which has conditions, because of its industrial development, that are likely to obtain in the mountains of Kentucky in the near future. I have agreed to go back in the spring if it is possible so to do;

and if it meets your approval, I should like to spend a month or six weeks in West Virginia and in the western border of "Old Virginia."

One of the most promising things I noticed at both synod meetings was a very evident desire on the part of these two branches of Presbyterianism to get together. At the first synod, a committee was appointed to look into matters of cooperation with the Presbyterian Church US in its educational work; and in the Southern Presbyterian Synod at Lewisburg, there was an official representative from the Northern Presbyterian Synod of West Virginia, and there was appointed an official representative of the southern church to meet with the northern church next year. I urged strongly the need of cooperation.

A few days later, on November 4th, John wrote Mr. Glenn another letter:

I am returning herewith the letter from Mr. [J. E.] McCulloch which you were so kind as to let me read, and which should have been returned earlier.

I do not know Mr. Cunningim, whom he mentions as dean. Dr. John E. White is an able man, much sought after in the South. He is pastor of the Second Baptist Church of Atlanta, Georgia, and has been of help to me in my work. He is a progressive Baptist, an official of the Board of Home Missions; and he has written me confidentially in the past that he is diametrically opposed by some on his board in his efforts to bring denominations together. He is a busy man, and I doubt very much whether he would be able to carry on both his pastoral work and work in connection with the American Interchurch College.

Mr. Glenn answered both of these letters on November 7, 1914:

I was much interested in your letter about your trip to the synods in Tennessee and West Virginia. Your news seems to be very significant. I will be glad to talk this over with you a little more fully when I see you.

I would also like to talk to you about McCulloch's Interchurch College. I have some interesting information about that which I would rather keep until you come. . . .

When you come north, it will be advisable to be prepared to stay here for three or four days at least, if necessary.

John replied, on November 9th:

I am glad to know that you approve of my coming to New York. It seems to me that I shall be better able to make wise suggestions after talking matters over with you and seeing the gentlemen I want to see. . . .

Today or tomorrow I shall send you an extract from an address by Dr. Robert F. Campbell with reference to the establishment of an Appalachian Synod as the administrative district for Southern Presbyterian mountain work. As Dr. Campbell so aptly says, in the past it has been "a homogeneous work under heterogeneous administration." That condition has characterized too much of mountain work. There is a stirring among many of the mountain boards—a stirring for which I think the Foundation is responsible. One of the chief things necessary now is wise direction in the shaping of plans.

The Southern Branch of the Presbyterian Church was now heard from through a letter to John from Dr. Tilden Scherer, president of King College, Bristol, Tennessee, dated November 11th:

Since writing you during the summer we have not ceased our efforts to work out a plan for better cooperation in our educational work in this section.

I wrote you concerning the organization of the Appalachian Christian Education Board. Five of our presbyteries and educational institutions are at present represented on this board, and it is likely that two others will join us in the near future.

The territory contemplated for the operations of this board includes parts of western North Carolina, eastern Tennessee, southeast Kentucky, and southwest Virginia, embracing a large proportion of the mountain country. Another movement parallel with this, and doubtless with much greater possibilities, is under way, looking to the establishment of the "Mountain Synod" of the Southern Presbyterian Church as contemplated in the scheme suggested by the map gotten out some time ago by Rev. W. E. Hudson. It is now almost certain that this new synod will be set up during the coming year. This will mean that all of the educational and home mission work of our church in this territory must be readjusted to a new basis.

Just here, in my judgment, is a place for the operation of this board which we organized last summer, for it will be several months before the new synod can be set up and then another year or two before any plans can be definitely formulated. Since this board represents practically the same interests and involves the same constituency, it seems to me that we should be investigating conditions with a view to formulating definite plans for the future. I am the more encouraged to believe that this should be done before the formal establishment of the new synod and the creation of a strictly intrachurch body, for there are phases of this work which I am sure should have the best thought of the best informed men. I am planning, therefore, to try and get the members of this board together sometime near the last of January or during the month of February, and we want to call to our assistance the leaders in various lines of educational work in the country. In other words, while it would seem necessary to make this a more or less formal meeting of this board, yet we should make it the occasion for bringing together for counsel and assistance many of those who are far more able than we to solve the considerable problems involved.

We are finding it necessary, in the organization of our forces, to coax the eastern Kentucky and southwest Virginia people a little, and I am inclined to think that Bristol, being on the border, would be the most desirable place for such a conference. Do you think we would be able to bring together here, besides our more local men, men who are interested in such educational agencies as the General Education Board, the Carnegie Foundation, the board which you represent, and perhaps the education boards of the Northern and United Presbyterian Churches, and possibly also the representatives of the national and state departments of education?

I realize that in attempting to work out the educational problems of a denomination, it will be very difficult to conserve the interests, allay the prejudices, and harmonize the plans and efforts involved when so many men of so many different opinions and viewpoints are brought into such a conference.

However, the education and civilization, not to say the evangelization, of the southern mountaineer is either a very serious matter, or there is a great deal of unnecessary talk about it. The comparatively little information I have on the subject convinces me that there is a great deal of wasted money and effort, due to conflicting agencies working without a well-devised plan. Now that our Southern Presbyterian Church is about to readjust her plans involving all of her work among these people, it seems to me that she should have all of the light on the question that can possibly be gotten. Certainly, as one of those intimately interested in her educational work, I know that I must have more light on the subject than I have at present, and I am not willing to go blindly into an undertaking fraught with so many difficulties.

As I believe I have indicated to you heretofore, I have in mind in a general way a system of preparatory schools located with special reference to the needs of destitute sections and so equipped and manned as to train the children to become useful men and women if they permanently remain in their local communities, and to fit them for work in schools of higher grade which shall offer not only the cultural but also the vocational lines, and that this whole system of schools should be "topped off" by an institution of higher learning where the most competent and promising of those from the lower schools can receive the best possible training for any given work. My judgment is that the schools for the mountain people should all be located within their own bounds so that it would not be necessary to send them away from their native hills, for if they are educated here, they are far more likely to remain here to devote their lives to the development of the wonderful resources of their own country.

From my point of view, and from the point of view of the church which I represent, all of this educational work should be so constructed and guided as to allow for the conservation and promotion of the religious as well as the intellectual nature of the people. By religious, I do not mean necessarily denominational, for I do hope that a scheme can be devised by which the Southern Presbyterian Church, while taking care of those religious interests which would be committed to it in the readjustment of their policy, can cooperate effectively with all other agencies. I am frank to say I do not know how all this can be done, but I do believe that there is a solution somewhere, and if enough of those who are interested and informed can combine their wisdom and consecration, this problem can be solved.

I have not meant to weary you with this long letter, but conditions are such here now it is impossible for me to see you personally and talk matters over with you, and I have not been able to say what I wished in as brief a compass as might have been desirable. I will certainly thank you to write me as soon as you can conveniently and give me such suggestions as you think would be helpful under the circumstances.

I have wondered how your trip to Denmark resulted. I fear it was not as pleasant and profitable to you as it might have been, in view of the miserable conditions prevailing abroad during the last few months.

John's reply to Mr. Shearer's letter is not in the records, but as appears later, they met within a few weeks to discuss the questions raised.

All during the first part of November, John was completing his annual report for the Russell Sage Foundation and preparing his proposed budget for 1915. He found time for a characteristic note to Dr. Packard, already hard at work in the Laurel field, the occasion being that Mrs. Packard was visiting us for a week. John wrote, on November 13th:

> While at synod meeting at Lebanon, I heard a fine old gentleman—a missionary from Alaska—deliver a most inspiring address. He quoted one of his own poems, which was written in response to a poem that he saw inspired by the peace one might find in a large city. This gave to him the inspiration to write on the peace he found in the wilderness.
>
> The poem appealed to me strongly, and I know it will to you, for I have heard indirectly, through Dr. Finley, that one of Mr. Tweed's sons—the one in Marshall—says "That Dr. Packard is one of the most all-round men I ever knew. He told me all about the stars, and he talks to the stars when he rides through the mountains." It appealed to me as I know it will to you, because in the work in which I have been engaged in the past, and in the work in which you are engaged on the frontier, there are not people hankering for that job, and unless we minister, probably no one else does.
>
> We are having a delightful time with Mrs. Packard, and I hope she will be able to stay for some time.
>
> I want very much to be here when you are here. Yesterday I received a telegram asking me to hold myself in readiness to come to New York tomorrow if wired for. I am awaiting another message, and if it comes, I shall go tomorrow afternoon, getting back in about a week or ten days. I may go to Boston, and if so, I shall call upon your mother. If I do not have the pleasure of seeing you when you come for Mrs. Packard, as we hope you will come, I shall endeavor to see you soon after my return, for I want very much to talk over a number of things with you.

Mr. Glenn had agreed that John had best come to New York for a series of conferences. By letter and telegraph it was planned that he leave Asheville November 18th, Wednesday, to spend some days in the city for special appointments with nine persons, talks with Mr. Glenn, and participation in a full staff conference at the Foundation. This was to be followed, for both of us, by a hurried journey to Boston to visit my mother in West Medford, who was seriously ill. John discussed the conferences he would like to have in a letter of November 16th to Mr. Glenn:

The engagements you have made with Dr. Pritchett and Dr. Buttrick for the mornings of November 20th and 21st are entirely satisfactory to me. I should like a brief conference with you, however, before seeing these gentlemen. . . .

I plan to see the following persons while in New York [positions and addresses omitted]:

Professor John E. Calfee
Dr. Warren H. Wilson
Dr. Charles S. MacFarland
Mrs. F. S. Bennett
Rev. W. E. Hudson
Mrs. John S. Allen
Rev. Franklin J. Clark
Dr. S. Hall Young
Mrs. Martha S. Gielow.

I want to see Mr. Calfee first, to talk over the many things asked in his letter [about the public schools in the mountains]. . . .

Dr. Wilson has written me recently about their Country Life work in the mountains of North Carolina. I want to talk over that matter and plans that I have formulated for centralizing their work, enlarging the medical work, relocating their agricultural expert, and talk over the possibilities of establishing a cooperative association for marketing the produce in that section. I have been instrumental in finding a small market here in Asheville for a small part of the output of the Girls' Canning Clubs, and I feel quite sure that much could be done in that line as well as in others, were a suitable plan worked out.

Dr. [W. E.] Finley of Marshall, North Carolina, field superintendent of the Country Life Department under Dr. Wilson, came in to see me Saturday, at Dr. Wilson's suggestion, to talk over a plan for the federation of the different denominations in the field of the Country Life Department. I want to see Dr. Wilson about this and to confer with Dr. MacFarland as to the feasibility of the plans submitted to me.

Mr. Hudson, former superintendent of Mountain Work of the Southern Presbyterian Church, is at Dr. White's Bible School in New York, taking a postgraduate course of some sort. There is a possible opening for him in the Country Life Department under Dr. Wilson, and I want to talk it over with him.

I want conferences with Mrs. Bennett, Mrs. Allen, and Mr. Clark with reference to the work of their boards in the mountains.

Mrs. [Martha] Gielow, of the Southern Industrial Educational Association, at the Park Avenue Hotel, wrote me a few days ago asking if I would be coming to New York soon and saying that she wanted to see me.

I should like to see Mr. Calfee on Thursday, if you do not wish to see me then. If, however, you wish to see me on Thursday, and time is limited, I shall see Mr. Calfee on Friday. Will you be so kind as to make an engagement with him for me? Possibly it would suit his convenience to take dinner with me Thursday evening at the Prince George.

I am writing Dr. Wilson for a possible engagement on Friday or Saturday afternoon. I want to see Dr. MacFarland after talking over matters with Dr. Wilson. The other engagements can be attended to after I get to New York.

I plan to be at the staff meeting on Monday, the 23rd, running over into Jersey for Sunday with friends, unless you should have some other plan for me.

Mrs. C. David White, recording secretary of the Southern Industrial Educational Association, wants to see me in Washington and has suggested a possible meeting with the trustees of the association. I do not know that this is advisable at this time, but I shall want to see her. Miss Clement and Dr. Claxton had planned for me to stop on Thursday in Washington, but I think it best to come through to see you on Thursday or early Friday, stopping at Washington on my return.

As soon as I am free in New York, I wish to run up for a day or so with Mrs. Campbell's mother. She is seriously ill, and there is a likelihood of her being taken from us at any time. . . . From Boston I plan to go right through to Washington on the Federal Express, unless you think it advisable for me to return via New York.

There were very full days in New York, November 18–24. We got away to Boston and West Medford on the 24th and remained there four days. From West Medford he wrote Mr. Glenn, on November 25th, his comments on a letter Mr. Glenn had received from Richmond, Virginia:

I enclose herewith the letter from Richmond with reference to the establishment of a training school for lay workers under the auspices of the Southern Presbyterian Church.

The purpose of the school seems admirable, but I am exceedingly doubtful of their accomplishing what they wish, unless they secure the right sort of men for teachers. Too generally the men chosen for instructors in such work are men of ministerial training who have not been or are not in active touch with the affairs of everyday life. It has been my observation also that men, after training for the ministry, regard themselves as set apart, and oftentimes, I know not why it is, the laying on of hands seems to bring about a change and aloofness which keeps them from mingling with the publicans and sinners whom they should serve. There are difficulties also that arise from grouping students for instruction in rural work or work in industrial centers in city surroundings. The assumption is, apparently, that all social groups, whether urban or rural, react alike to stimulus given. This is not so (of course I am judging from experience in my own field). The student who has trained in such surroundings takes a long while to learn that there are certain resistances to what may perhaps be termed social media that he has known nothing about and does not know how to meet.

I feel, therefore, that those who are trained for particular work should receive their training in an environment as nearly as possible like the field in which they are to labor, that they may know what the resistances above mentioned are.

I feel, too, that the instructors should be men who are constantly in touch with the conditions which they are trying to teach students to correct.

This is a very inadequate consideration of the letter in regard to which you wished my suggestions. I do not feel that there is much promise of success unless there is very careful consideration of these facts.

On November 29th, we returned to New York for John to have further talks with a number of people, including the Foundation group. We then moved on to Washington for the planned meetings there, thence returning to Asheville via Mars Hill College (Baptist). John's letter to Mr. Glenn on December 9th gives a brief and partial report, in perspective, on his many conferences:

I hoped ere this to give you an account of my doings since I saw you last in New York, but I have not had time until the present. After leaving you, I had a long and helpful conference with Dr. Ayres and Mr. Lutz, and then with Mr. Hanmer [all of the Russell Sage Foundation staff].

I telephoned Mrs. Bennett, president of the Women's Board of the Presbyterian Church, USA (Northern), that I wanted to have the opportunity to see her. She urged me to come, and by the time I reached the office, there had been assembled all the officers of the board, with whom I had a two-hour conference relative to their work.

Previous to this, I had a long interview with Mr. Bruce Payne, Mr. Calfee, and Dr. Coulter, president of Washington College. Mr. Payne and I talked over the desirability of his institution having a corps of people well trained in rural subjects, who during part of the year could act as an extension faculty in the mountains and lowlands of the South. He wanted me to come over to Nashville. . . . I suggested to Mr. Payne that it would not be necessary for him to have buildings for summer schools in the mountains, but that in all probability arrangements could be made with various church boards for the use of their buildings, dormitories, and boarding facilities. I felt that so far as possible, institutions in the mountains should be used to their full capacity.

The plan suggested appealed to Mr. Payne, and I talked over the possibility of such cooperation with the Women's Board. They fell in with the idea, and I arranged for a meeting with Mrs. Bennett and Mr. Payne.

In Washington, I had a long interview with Miss Delano and Miss Clement. For a long time I have been working to get the Red Cross and the Country Life Department of the Presbyterian Church, USA (Northern), to cooperate in the matter of rural nursing. I am happy to say that through this interview, and through preliminary work with Dr. Wilson and people on the field, a beginning is to be made in January whereby the Country Life Department is to supply four hundred or five hundred dollars toward the salary of the nurse, and the Red Cross is to furnish the nurse and to supplement the salary somewhat. I do not know, but I think that Miss Delano herself is supplying the supplementary sum.

We have invited Miss Clement to Asheville for the Christmas recess in order to take her through the section where her nurse is to begin work, that Miss Clement may have some preliminary knowledge. I was very happy to have the opportunity of seeing Miss Delano, for she had some very sound ideas, I thought, as to the beginning of work and the amount of salary to be paid the nurse. I feel, too, that Miss Clement sees the need of elasticity in methods.

The trip to Mar's Hill [North Carolina] on the invitation of the Baptist College president was a hard trip but very profitable. My reception was most cordial. I spoke twice: once to students and once to a joint meeting of students and citizens. I shall nurture the connection established, in the hope of further cooperation with the Baptists.

I [have received] a letter from President [James E.] Allen of Davis and Elkins College. . . . This is an outcome of my trip to West Virginia. I have an invitation to revisit West Virginia in the spring at the meetings of the presbyteries, and perhaps I can combine the two at the expense of Dr. Allen.

Dr. W. E. Finley, field superintendent of the Country Life work of the Northern Presbyterian Church in the French Broad Presbytery, came to Asheville to see me the other day on matters of interest to his field. After he had departed, Superintendent E. P. Childs of the Northern Presbyterian Mountain Work called at the office for data and urged my coming to New York in February, when he and the officials of their board were to get together, go over their work, and outline a policy for the various schools in their field. I told him I would write you about it and give him a definite reply later.

Hon. Charles R. Crane—the ambassador to China who did not go—called at the office Saturday with Mrs. Crane to ask questions about the mountain field. They are deeply interested in this field. Mr. Crane said that his son, and heir, was also deeply interested, having married a Virginia lady, and the intimation was that they were seeking information as to how to give money wisely. Mr. Crane is coming to Asheville again during the winter and intimated that he would like to take a trip with me into the mountains in the spring. Mrs. Campbell and I took dinner with Mrs. Crane at their hotel on Saturday evening and had opportunity to speak a little further on mountain questions. Mrs. Woodrow Wilson's name came up in our conversation, and I told him of the proposed scholarship fund, of which I spoke to you. Mr. Crane was on his way to see President Wilson and suggested that he would like to know more about the scholarship fund in order to contribute toward it.

President Scherer of King College, Bristol, Tennessee, the writer of the letter which I read, at your suggestion, at the Century Club, came from Bristol to see me, and I have spent the day with him going over his plans. In all probability I shall be wanted for a meeting with the educational leaders of the Southern Presbyterian Church at Bristol early in January. We are talking also of the advisability of a larger meeting later with representatives from the state and federal departments of education, the General Education Board, the Sage Foundation, and possibly the Carnegie Foundation. It is felt by Mr. Scherer that because of the attitude of certain denominations toward Mr. Carnegie and the [Carnegie] Foundation, it might be prudent not to have a representation from that foundation, which, in the estimation of many ecclesiastical leaders in the South, is not sympathetic toward schools with denominational affiliations. President Scherer was not at all expressing his own feeling, but was merely raising a question of prudence.

I shall write you within a few days of other interesting letters that I have received, which indicate that the seed sown has not fallen upon barren soil.

Let me, in conclusion, thank you for the kindness shown, which made my stay in New York so pleasant and helpful.

Dr. Bruce Rayburn Payne, mentioned in the foregoing letter, was one of the people John had met at the beginning of our field study in the fall of 1908. At that time he was professor of psychology and director of the Summer School at the University of Virginia, and, as I remember him, a very handsome and attractive person. In January 1911, he was elected president of George Peabody College, and from then on he and John had much discussion on how the college might serve the mountain South. Mr. Glenn had written, on June 7, 1912: "Bruce Payne is developing some important ideas about the connection of his institution with mountain work. He will have here next week Mr. Tate of South Carolina and another member of his board. He wishes to get them interested in the mountain problem and help them to understand it better." Mr. Tate later became professor of rural education at George Peabody College.

In John's correspondence with Dr. Payne, possibilities of interesting the national office of the YMCA in country work in the mountains appeared from time to time. Tentative plans for starting a folk school were considered seriously by various agencies and individuals, notably one at Tate, Georgia, as mentioned earlier in this chapter. Dr. Franklin J. Clark and Dr. Payne both were interested in this, but the main correspondence between Dr. Payne and John was in regard to the possible setting up of summer training courses for teachers in very rural sections.

Some of John's correspondence immediately after the New York visit throws light on various aspects of John's work. He promptly answered, on December 12th, a request for information from Dr. Wallace Buttrick of the General Education Board:

I enclose herewith the information that you wished regarding the religious census of the mountain country.

These figures are drawn from the last US Religious Census, taken in 1906. There are figures for the mountain counties as I formerly estimated them—from Maryland to north-central Alabama on the east, and the western escarpment of the Cumberland Plateau on the west. In all, there are 247 counties. Since compiling the data given, I have added the four counties of western Maryland and two more counties in Alabama [raising the total of mountain counties to 253]. The figures given, however, do not include data from these six [additional] counties.

The Baptist communicants constitute 42.5 percent of the communicants of all denominations and 44.2 percent of all the communicants of all Protestant bodies. I have not, as you will see, included the Conservative and Progressive Dunkers, using only those denominations going under the name of "Baptist" of one sort or another, though the Dunkers might properly be included as Baptists in fact.

From the figures of Dr. V. I. Masters, editorial secretary of the Home Mission Board of the Southern Baptist Convention, sent me some time ago, we find the Baptists to be 46.6 percent of all denominations. Dr. Masters uses the 178 mountain counties which he regards as mountain counties within the Southern Baptist Convention's field; mine is the larger field, which included the mountain counties under the Northern Baptist Convention as well. Of course there are slight differences as to what the mountain counties are; and I have found, from comparing Dr. Master's figures with the census report from which he drew them, that there were some errors made by the compiler transcribing them. Possibly there may be a few errors in our work, but I think not, as the figures have been read back and checked.

Under separate cover I am sending you the condensed report of the Southern Mountain Workers' Conference in which you expressed interest. I wish very much that we might have the privilege of hearing you at our next conference in April. I shall take the liberty of writing you of this later on.

It was a pleasure and help to me to have had the opportunity of conferring with you in New York, and I am much pleased to know of your interest in the mountain people and country.

Letters from and to Mr. Glenn included the following:

[Mr. Glenn to JCC]
December 12, 1914

I am returning Dr. R. F. Campbell's address on the Appalachian Synod. It is very interesting and makes a strong case. It raises the question in my mind as to where the support for the general expenses for which the synod would be responsible is to come from. Are there in the mountain district enough churches with money to spare to support the synod? Dr. Campbell seems to think that more money will be given in the district than is now given. Is this likely to be true?

[Mr. Glenn to JCC]
December 14, 1914

I am glad to get your interesting letter of the 9th. It shows that you have done a good deal of valuable work in a short space of time.

Will you kindly have made for me a summary covering the year ending September 30, 1914, of your visits to various places, giving in a line or two the purpose of each visit, including, as well, visits made to you? Send also a similar summary covering the period from October 1, 1914. Such summaries will show the demands made on you by schools and other agencies in a most telling form. Let your secretary make as many copies as she can make clearly. The carbons may be made on orange paper. No hurry.

I wish I could spend the Christmas recess with you and Miss Clement. It would be very interesting.

I suppose it would be advisable for you to revisit West Virginia in the spring.

It is probably also advisable for you to come to New York in February. This, however, should be dependent on what else there is to do. If you come to New York in February, arrange to be away for at least two weeks so that you can see various people more or less at leisure. Of course it is not necessary to stay two weeks unless engagements require it, but by all means ward off any other engagements that might hurry your visit here. It looks to me as if it would be important for you to pay two visits a year to New York and spend from two to four weeks each time. This seems a large hole to make in your work, but it is the only way to get in touch with the central boards.

[Mr. Glenn to JCC]
December 16, 1914

Your letter of November 25 about the training school for lay workers of the Southern Presbyterian Church was very good. I agree with your points.

I had a very satisfactory talk with Dr. Phillips when I was in Richmond. He impresses me as having very intelligent views on the subject of training and as being anxious to establish high standards. I think he is a man whom it is well worth while to get in touch with when you have a chance. You may be able to help him in getting practical training for his students, and you may find among the students some who will help you in the mountain districts.

[JCC to Mr. Glenn]
December 17, 1914

Your letter of December 12th with reference to Dr. R. F. Campbell's address on the Appalachian Synod was received some days ago. I delayed answering until we should have time to get the maps ready for you. I am sending the maps, under separate cover, in this mail.

You may be interested to know that the three presbyteries known as Kanawha, Tygarts Valley, and Greenbrier were united in the Synod of West Virginia at the meeting I attended in Lewisburg on October 27th. If the proposed Appalachian Synod is constituted, the mountain work of the Southern Presbyterian Church will be managed by the people within that region. In the Appalachian Synod there will be located the cities of Asheville, Knoxville, Bristol, and, in all probability, Abingdon. There will be, in addition, some churches in the smaller cities and richer valley sections of the mountain region thus enclosed.

There is some reason for feeling that this new synod will be able to meet its own expenses. Since Asheville became a separate mountain presbytery, it has greatly increased its local support and has grown very rapidly. From figures recently received, I learn that Asheville Presbytery, since organized separately, has increased 100 percent in church membership, 300 percent in its contributions toward the salaries of pastors, 500 percent in its contributions for beneficent causes, and 1,000 percent in its contributions for educational purposes.

[Mr. Glenn to JCC]
December 21, 1914

Thank you for the two additional maps of the mountain region, showing the Appalachian Synod divisions. Your statement about the increase in contributions, etc. in the Asheville Presbytery is very interesting and significant.

A personal letter John wrote four days before Christmas to an Asheville friend and neighbor, Mr. Rutherford P. Hayes, the former president's son, who was wintering in Florida, comments rather gaily on the condition of his own health, which was giving us increasing anxiety:

I trust that your health is not giving you much concern. I am much amused at the various reports of my own condition. The insurance people turned me down; and records that I have from different physicians rank me all the way from a normal and very good risk to an abnormal and very poor risk. Dr. Dunn carries me along the even tenor of my way, and I have somewhat of a notion that I shall live out my full measure of years—just as I would were I a Presbyterian. As I grow older, it seems to me that times are not very different from those at the opening of the Christian era, when there was, as the record says, one who suffered many things from many physicians. When doctors disagree, I suppose the best thing for us to do is to do what we want to, provided it is at all reasonable, and to go on cheerfully.

Another comment on one of his health problems came on January 7th in a response to an invitation to speak in Nashville, given by Dr. W. D. Weatherford:

Your letter of January 5th is at hand. I shall be very glad indeed to speak on the Southern Highlanders but would ask that the date assigned me be as early in August as possible—prior to the 10th if it is at all possible.

My archenemy, hay fever, always makes me a visit early in August, and I must flee before him sometime between the 10th and the 15th if I am to be of any comfort to myself or my friends.

Your invitation is one that I want much to accept.

Sending his annual report for the year ending September 30, 1914, and also, in answer to Mr. Glenn's request, a summary for the first quarter of the new year ending December 31, 1914, John explains, on January 12, 1915:

In each case I have given a travel summary as well, thinking that perhaps it would be interesting to know what has been accomplished on each trip.

It has been a little difficult to show just what has been done, because so much of my work has been in the nature of "seed-sowing." I have tried to indicate both the planting season and the harvest.

Some of the "seed-sowing" has already been mentioned in the preceding pages. "Harvest" was a bit misleading word to use, perhaps: it suggests concrete accomplishment rather than response to his suggestions, which sometimes brought definite final action, sometimes were carried out in part, but often meant long conferences and correspondence, with gradual progress over an indefinite period. The early January letters to Mr. Glenn which follow show John's method of working and something of its scope and trend:

January 13, 1914

I send herein a letter received this morning from Mr. [Harry] Howell, superintendent of City Schools, Asheville, N.C. Mr. Howell is a wide-awake North Carolinian, under whose leadership during the last year our schools have made considerable advance.

Asheville is agitating the commission form of government, and the time may be ripe for a survey.

I shall appreciate greatly your kindness in putting Mr. Harrison in touch with Mr. Howell.[2]

January 13, 1915

It seems likely that I shall go to Nashville sometime before the end of the month or early in February to spend a week, as approved by you, with Dr. Bruce Payne and the faculty of the Seaman A. Knapp School for Country Life.[3] I am extremely anxious to plan with them for the training of teachers for the mountain country and for reaching the teachers of the church schools—and the public school teachers of the mountains—through a kind of perambulating teacher's training school during the summer months. I think I touched upon this in the summary of my report for the quarter ending December 31, 1914.

Some of the church schools in the mountains could, and would I am sure, offer their buildings for the purpose. I arranged a conference between Dr. Payne and Mrs. Bennett, president of the Woman's Board of Home Missions of the Northern Presbyterian Church, for this purpose.

Perambulating schools for country life and of the folk school type have been successful in Norway, which is deeply cut up by mountain ranges and fjords into innumerable mountain districts. They have used rented quarters or large farmsteads for schools of this kind for a few weeks or months, and I see no reason why this type of school cannot be utilized for vitalizing teaching in the mountain sections.

I shall stop on the way at Maryville to arrange for plans for the Maryville Mountain Workers Conference in July. I am on their Executive Board, and they await my convenience in calling together the other members.

On the same day, he wrote also to Mr. Glenn of going to Washington for consultation with Dr. Claxton, Dr. Carver of the Rural Organization Service, and others, relative to the coming Knoxville conference.

I want to seize the opportunity offered by Dr. Claxton to talk over with him the whole mountain problem as well. I have learned that he has been—or is soon to be—in conference with the Dutch Reform Church Mountain Board, looking to the changing of one of their schools in the mountains of Kentucky to the folk school basis.

And in a fourth letter of January 13th to Mr. Glenn, he wrote:

I am enclosing a copy of a letter from Professor John F. Smith of Berea which may be of interest to you. I am also sending two clippings, one relating to the Ellen Wilson Memorial Fund and the other to a training school for teachers in western North Carolina.

Dr. Homer McMillan, secretary of the Executive Committee of Home Missions of the Southern Presbyterian Church, came to see me about this fund after my return from New York, and I made some suggestions in a letter to him, a copy of which I enclose, together with a copy of the letter to which it is the reply.

I went to Marion, North Carolina, a short time ago on invitation of the committee—consisting of educators and Board of Trade men—in order that I might know what is being done to secure a teachers' training school for western North Carolina. It is something that is very much needed but in the past has been blocked by the efforts of two small schools in western North Carolina that train teachers—for local work largely.

I do not know that the efforts to put the bill through this legislature will succeed, but it is something that will eventually come, for it is very much needed.

The Northern Presbyterian Normal and Collegiate Institute here in Asheville is supplying most of the best teachers for western North Carolina—a work which the state ought to be doing for itself and is abundantly able to do. I have been bringing the possibility of the establishment of such a state school before the authorities of the Northern Presbyterian Church to urge their redirecting their work so as not to stand in the way of or compete with the work of the state school when established.

The Northern Presbyterians have recently lost, by fire, their Farm School building nine miles west of here, which will, I feel, force a careful consideration of plans for the future. I may be called upon to confer with them in the consideration of these plans later on.

Two days later, on January 15th, John took up again with Mr. Glenn the questions raised by the loss of the Farm School:

I have received this morning, as I thought I might receive, a strictly confidential letter from Marshall C. Allaben, superintendent of the School Department of the Woman's Board of Home Missions of the Northern Presbyterian Church.

The recent loss by fire of their Farm School building near Asheville opens a way for any readjustments of their policy in the mountains which may be thought desirable. A special committee composed of the presidents and treasurers of the boards and other prominent persons in the Presbyterian Church will take up this whole question. I have been asked to give the plans careful consideration and to send a statement of my views at my earliest convenience, that the committee may be able to discuss the question in the light of suggestions made.

It is so important a matter that I thought it advisable to give Mr. Allaben opportunity to ask me to come to New York prior to, during, or subsequent to the meeting. I should rather go prior to the meeting if possible. It will be sometime, probably, before the end of the month.

The burning of their Farm School building near Asheville has hastened the discussion of plans relating to their future policy, which I thought would be discussed a little later, and of which I wrote you.

Should Mr. Allaben be inclined to ask me, and you approve of my coming, I would postpone my visit to the George Peabody College for Teachers in Nashville and could on this trip see Dr. Claxton in Washington.

I have recently been in correspondence with the secretary of the American-Scandinavian Foundation of New York City—a foundation established in 1911, I believe, and of which I have lately learned. They offer scholarships of $750 a year for persons in the north countries to come to America for study, and also to Americans who wish to study the institutions of Denmark, Norway, and Sweden. I want to talk over with the secretary the possibility of their financing jointly with some of the church boards the sending of a commission made up of prominent officials, and educators of the mountain country, to Denmark to study the folk schools, their adaptation in Sweden, and their modification in Norway to meet the mountain conditions. I should like to do this prior to the meeting of this Presbyterian Committee and also to talk over with Mr. Allaben personally several well-qualified men with whom I would like to have him in touch.

Before receiving the foregoing letter, Mr. Glenn had written expressing interest in John's going to Washington to talk with Dr. Claxton. He commented further, "With reference to folk schools, I would strongly advise not holding back until you can go to Denmark. An experiment or two and a few mistakes will help you in sizing up Denmark when you go there."

On the 18th he wrote hastily to express his interest in "Mr. Allaben's proposition" and to urge John to come to New York well ahead of the meeting on the commission, and to stay as long as desirable.

Plans were made for the New York trip. At the same time the program was being arranged and all general plans were being made for the Third Annual Conference of Southern Mountain Workers in Knoxville in April. As it turned out, John could not go to New York, for illness prevented. He was able, however, to write, on January 21st, a long letter to Mr. Allaben giving his thinking about the situation in North Carolina which was confronting the commission:

Your letter of January 11th is of the greatest interest to me as it brings up, through a concrete case, the important question of educational policy for the mountain country.

Were I in charge of the Farm School, I should undoubtedly want it rebuilt on a larger scale and with an increased appropriation to carry on plans that I might feel were of promise; and as a friend of those now in charge of the school, I could wish that they be given what I should want under similar circumstances.

You have, however, not raised the question as to what one might like to try. As I understand your letter, you have asked my opinion as to which of two plans is the more statesmanlike with a given expenditure. I must therefore try to be an impartial judge.

Nearly twenty years of experience in the mountain country as a teacher and investigator convinces me that plan "B" is the wiser. In support of this belief, I am prompted, in response to your inquiry, to make the following statements and suggestions.

If you continue the work, in a modified way, on the Farm School site (or if you decide to remove the Farm School to what you may regard as a more needy section), establish only *one* other school for the present, preferably in one of the neediest counties of Kentucky or West Virginia. Should you remove the Farm School, it might be well to reestablish it on the Cumberland Plateau of Tennessee. Try out the work of these schools for several years before establishing a third, and use the fund that may be in reserve to develop to the full the type of school begun.

Make provision for freedom in the use of this fund to ensure getting the best teachers possible and for furthering some of the educational experiments that they, after consulting with others, may feel will be of great good.

The greatest need in the mountains, educationally, is for Christian men and women, well trained and with personality. I would not imply by this statement that there are not a number of teachers now in the mountains with noble purposes and charming personality. The Women's Board has had a notable group of women teachers; we need more men teachers, however, not fewer of the women of the type named, and we need in these men and women alike a splendid blend of noble purpose, personality, and training.

I believe most sincerely that one should not make salary much of a consideration in such work. On the other hand, I know that it is practically impossible to get and to hold men of the type that is desired without a salary sufficiently large to meet the legitimate needs of themselves and their families—there should be as teachers in the mountains more men with families.

I would urge, then, that you put much of your money for these schools in men and women rather than in buildings. Pay as high salaries as you possibly can, even if thereby you limit your efforts to one or two new schools. A few such schools, efficiently manned and womaned, will do more for the mountains by example and through actual work than many schools established on the plea that such and such communities need "some sort of school."

If possible, I would pay the superintendent at least eighteen hundred dollars to begin with, if he be married—and by all means he ought to be a married man. I would start the masters of the cottages with at least nine hundred dollars if they are single and twelve hundred dollars if they are married. Furthermore, I should give to the superintendent and masters the assurance of some increase in salary at the end of a stated number of years, provided the work was satisfactory. This would tend, in time, to give you a corps of experts who have chosen rural teaching as their lifework, from which you could select workers for new fields as conditions might require.

Another reason for paying fair salaries—which is among the legitimate reasons spoken of, but which may be emphasized here—is the necessity of persons engaged in such work getting away from it regularly for vacations of investigation of institutions working along lines of rural social service which they see are needed in their own fields.

It would be a splendid thing if all the cottages occupied by the boys might have the home influences that would come from a real home. These cannot be had without a woman in the home. I realize that this may be impracticable (especially from the viewpoint of the wife of the master), but I should wish it were a possible thing to have the masters of the cottages married men. I must be frank to say, however, that I myself might be unwilling to be the master of such a cottage home if I had children, even should my wife be willing to assume the responsibilities incident to making a home for the boys of the cottage.

If the plan of having married masters in charge of the cottages should be thought impracticable, some of the home influence that is desired might come by throwing about the meal hours and other social hours the influence of woman. Possibly this could be done by having the right kind of woman in charge of the dining hall, who might have also certain supervision of the boys' rooms, and who might assist the wife of the superintendent in the social life of the school. The boys would be thus brought into touch with the niceties of life which men by themselves are prone to minimize or overlook.

We must get into this new kind of school much of the spiritual and cultural to prevent its sinking to a material and "bread-and-butter" basis. To create this spiritual and cultural atmosphere, I feel that the influence of woman must be felt to an appreciable extent. Paradoxical as it may seem in this connection, it must be said that all of the schools of all of the denominations in the mountains have been too much under the influence of women; but notwithstanding, I feel strongly that this is not to be corrected by having the schools overmanned. We must have more men, but we must not make the mistake of going to either extreme. The mountain boy and the mountain man need to see the true reciprocal and complementary relations of men and women. We have failed pretty generally in our schools to show them this because we have had too few men; we shall fail in the future if we have too few women.

Another mistake has been that too many of our men and women teachers in the mountains have had the urban viewpoint. It is a good thing to know the urban viewpoint, but we must keep teachers long enough to have them know and feel the mountain rural viewpoint in such a way as to promote the best things in rural life.

Perhaps I have said enough about the things suggested by the consideration of a fair salary.

Now, as to buildings: let your buildings and your farm equipment also be such as can be copied and owned by the people themselves with some thought and effort on their part. The buildings should be comfortable and artistic. Whether they be built of logs or lumber is a question of locality. In some places, even quite remote, it may be more expensive for a community, under changing conditions, to build substantial, comfortable, and artistic cabins of logs than to bring in a portable sawmill and have the logs cut into lumber. I would emphasize not putting a large amount into buildings. There are not a few instances in the mountains where the continuance of work is based no longer on the need but on the bare fact that there is a considerable investment in buildings. I am very sure that it is wiser to put a great deal of money in men and women of the right sort, who can be moved to the need, rather than in buildings that outlast the need.

You are sending truly the better education in your plans which contemplate bringing training near to the home and the home environment. I admit it is not well to prepare every boy or girl to live in the community in which he was born, but I am very sure that the education of a rural people should be for rural life. The exceptional student could be sent to other institutions by a wise system of scholarships, should his family's means be too limited to send him. The school of a community should be for the need of that community and to raise the general average rather than to train the exceptional few. Too much attention has been given to the "exceptional few," who, it was hoped, would go back as leaders. We ought to face the fact that the training we have given practically makes it impossible for those few to go back. Perhaps, after all, we have made the mistake of taking as potential leaders those who are ready to follow rather than the original and forceful ones who would naturally, at first, hold somewhat aloof from anything which would tend to draw them from their own. We must work *with* the people and not *for* the people.

Your plans contemplate stressing agriculture, and you are right, for despite industrial developments in the mountains, the large majority of mountain people for generations to come must live by agriculture. Population is dense in parts of the mountains, and as it grows denser, the hill slopes will need to be cultivated. Bottomland is decreasing, not only relatively with the increase of population but in actual extent as poor methods of lumbering cause to be brought down debris to cover the lower level lands. With the increase of population, together with the relative and actual decrease of bottomland, the price of this level-lying farming land will increase. As a result, many a boy in the mountains will be forced to leave the mountains, even should he wish to be a farmer, unless he is taught farming adapted to mountain topography conditions and needs. Many of our best so-called mountain schools are located in the accessible valley sections of the mountains and teach only bottomland farming. The method and equipment used are unsuited to hillside farming. Even when the tracts of these schools have hillsides available, the authorities are forced to till the bottomlands in order to supply their dormitories and cut down their current expenses. Some of those in charge of these schools know that they ought to be giving attention to terracing, the adaptation of crops to elevation soil, slope, etc. They do not, however, undertake this work, which is unremunerative in its earlier stages, because they feel that they have not a budget sufficient to allow for this pioneer type of teaching.

Our state agricultural schools, many of them, are so situated as to be of little help to the mountain boy who hopes to be a farmer. As the Women's Board and other church boards have been pioneers in the better kind of training of the old type that now exists, so must they be pioneers, in the mountains, in the newer and better kind of education.

In order to get ready money back into the mountains, our new type of school, if placed where it is most needed, must take up the question of marketing, both with its students and, through extension work, with the neighborhood. The economic questions, so fundamental, must be solved. At present many of our mountain schools teaching mountain farming are on or near railroads or in accessible valleys where the question of a market is not pressing, as roads are good and the markets near for any surplus produce. However, there is generally nothing to market, as there is no surplus, because whatever is raised is consumed at the school.

We must have, in charge of this new type of school, men who will give careful thought to these things and who will be alert to take advantage of all agencies and helps, within and without the mountain area, that may assist them in solving these questions of agricultural life in isolated rural sections, as well as alert to the many other questions of spiritual, economic, and general rural social welfare.

While our schools need not give less attention to the welfare of the individual, there is at present great need of emphasis upon community welfare, that there may be an environment in which the noble aspirations awakened in the individual may grow. Service, "beginning first at Jerusalem," should be the motto of our schools. Too often we have given the impression that the promised land for the mountain youth lies somewhere yonder where the rainbow touches the plain.

There are many other things that I would like to write concerning the new type of school, and of the interrelation of the vocational, cultural, and spiritual, but I have already written at too great length, I fear. If this be so, let my deep interest in what you propose to do, and my faith in Presbyterian administration as an agency for doing it, plead my excuse.

I shall be happy indeed if I can cooperate in any way with you in the working out of these plans of betterment.

To Mr. Glenn he wrote, on February 1st:

I had hoped to be in New York on Wednesday so as to attend the meeting on Thursday of the presidents and treasurers of the Presbyterian boards (Northern)—a meeting to which I was invited by Mr. Allaben. I have not been feeling quite like myself of late, and a week ago yesterday it seemed best to take to my bed. I am still in the house, although I am able to carry on my work through Miss Dickey, who comes to the house usually once a day.

Apparently there is nothing serious the matter. . . . I am very comfortable now and expect to be at the office tomorrow or the next day. It does not, however, seem advisable to come to New York just yet, and I am writing Mr. Allaben to that effect. I had made all plans to come and have asked a number of people to address me in your care, as has Mrs. Campbell, who had planned to accompany me in view of her anxiety over my indisposition. Will you be so kind as to have any mail for Mrs. Campbell or me sent in your care redirected to us at Asheville?

I have been much interested in the accounts that I have read of the meetings of the Committee on Industrial Relations, and thank you for the reports that have been sent. If the examinations are properly conducted, good ought to result from the clearing of the atmosphere.

Plans for the next meeting of the Southern Mountain Workers' Conference are well under way.

Just before this, he had written to my sister Mrs. Coolidge in West Medford:

I thank you for your inquiries and affectionate concern for my welfare. I am getting on very nicely. Some days I have considerable distress, but I can always find relief by going home and lying down. I have an expert doctor on my case, and I think we are going to win out.

My busy season is approaching, and I have calls from a good many sections. There is just a possibility that I may be in New York early in February, but I doubt very much my ability to get to Boston this time.

Olive is busy with her various duties, and the season is approaching when birds, buds, and her garden seeds will take precedence with her above everything except her husband, concerning whom she worries more or less. It is very pleasant to be worried over as she does it, and I therefore do not wish to dispel altogether her illusion that I am one of those spirits for whom "Earth is but a resting-place and Heaven is home"—with a likelihood of going home in a hurry. I like the resting-place too well for that, and my relatives and friends.

He had also in the meantime written to the members of the conference Executive Committee in regard to the next program:

The time has come to take up in a definite way matters relating to the third annual meeting of the Southern Mountain Workers' Conference. We were asked by the last conference, as you will recall, to name Knoxville again as the place of the meeting.

As your chairman, I wrote letters to those in attendance last year, while the conference was still fresh in their minds, inviting their suggestions as to the program, time of meeting, etc.

In order that I might have the help of other members of the Executive

Committee in the consideration of suggestions made, I called together recently the local members of the committee, namely, Miss [Florence] Stephenson, principal of the Asheville Home School; Dr. A. E. Brown, superintendent of the Department of Mountain Missions and Schools of the Home Mission Board of the Southern Baptist Convention; and Mr. Edward P. Childs, field superintendent of the Mountain Division of the School Department, Woman's Board of Home Missions of the Presbyterian Church, USA.

We felt, after careful consideration of the suggestions, that it would meet with the wish of the large majority if more opportunity be given for the discussion of matters with which those on the field have to deal, and if the time be set as near as possible to that of last year. We suggest, therefore, that the time be Wednesday and Thursday, April 21st and 22nd.

Please write me at once any suggestions that you may have, in order that the call may be issued as soon as possible. May I, without seeming too urgent, ask again that you give this your immediate attention, as I myself must be away from the office for longer or shorter intervals between now and the first of May, and it is not an easy matter to find a time when the local members are all in Asheville.

Mr. Glenn expressed concern over John's illness, along with regret that he could not come to New York. He wrote further, "Your letter to him [Mr. Allaben] is admirable and convincing. I hope that he will succeed in getting his directors to accept your point of view." And again, "Your suggestion to Mr. Allaben of the Social Center Worker is very interesting. I am sorry that his letter to you does not indicate that his board took some action along the lines you had previously suggested." However, on February 13th John was able to write, "They have modified their plans for the Farm School, and I hope that they will put into effect later on plans for a new school, modified still more to meet the suggestions that I made."

On the same day came a hurried request from Mr. Glenn for information about the Patterson School (Episcopal) in Legerwood, North Carolina.[4] John's reply, also written on February 13th, shows the breadth of his acquaintance with and real knowledge of situations:

The Patterson School at Legerwood, North Carolina . . . is one of a group of schools in western North Carolina under the supervision of Rt. Rev. Junius M. Horner, bishop of the Missionary District of Asheville.

From information in the office, I learn that the school has a limited equipment, a house not well adapted to the purposes of the school, twelve hundred acres of land—three hundred of which are good for farming. The school is land-poor. The place is regarded as strategic, and the people greatly need the example of a well-managed farm school. Unless there are resources adequate for immediate annual needs, the school must set an example of an ineffective struggle for existence.

The information above given is from a confidential report from Mr. Charles O. Burkitt, secretary of the Southern Industrial Education Association, who has just come from the Patterson School. Mr. Burkitt was so kind as to leave me a copy of this confidential report, the original of which was sent to Dr. Claxton, who is chairman of the Board of Trustees of the Southern Industrial Education Association.

This bears out my own impression of the school. My impression of Mr. [Hugh A.] Dobbin (the principal and director) was very favorable. Mr. Burkitt and others who have visited the Patterson School have also been favorably impressed with him.

My feeling is, and it is the feeling of others also, that this work, and the work of some of the other Episcopalian schools in that section, is perhaps not receiving the attention that it should receive, because of the somewhat ambitious and radical plans of the bishop for the Valle Crucis School in Watauga County, North Carolina. The bishop has, for some years, been working on a plan whereby he hoped to support this institution by its orchards.

From information I recently received, I learned that there are 280 trees bearing apples and 2,800 trees from three to five years old. Four thousand bushels complicate the problem of this enterprise: care of trees, care of crops, storing of picked fruit, transportation of fruit to the railroad—sixteen miles away—shipment, finding the best market, and keeping down expenses. It appears, on the whole, that a strict accounting would show little net profit for an extraordinarily fine yield of fruit. Yet this plan is a pet plan of the bishop's, and it is said in some quarters and felt in others that this plan and this school are receiving attention to the great detriment of others—among which is the Patterson School. I could wish that Mr. Dobbin might receive funds and be given the freedom to put into operation land that he, as a practical man, might feel had promise of returns.

During this same month came a letter from Dr. Claxton bringing word of a prospective meeting of state superintendents of education, together with secretaries of church boards doing work in the mountains, a step which John had been urging. Dr. Claxton was scheduled to be one of the speakers at the coming Knoxville conference in Asheville. Even more immediately, he was concerned about the Southern Industrial Educational Association. He asked John to come to Washington to confer about these and other matters.

After reporting to Mr. Glenn, John wrote on March 4th:

There are matters having to do with the Knoxville conference that make it necessary for me to go to Washington within the next few weeks. I have written to Mrs. White [of the SIEA] to this effect. There are also questions bearing upon the mountain work of some church boards that may make it desirable for me to be in New York sometime soon, and if I go to Washington, I may decide to come on to New York at this time—especially if there be questions raised about which I wish your advice and suggestion.

Mr. Allaben, superintendent of the School Work of the Woman's Board of the Northern Presbyterian Church, returned from Cuba recently via Asheville, and we had a long conference. He expressed the wish to see me again in New York. He has a real desire to further some of the things in mountain work that I have advocated, but I judge that he has to proceed toward them by way of compromise, because of the sentiment naturally felt by donors and other supporters for localities in which well-established and successful work has been done for years by persons of dominant personality.

I have also had several long interviews with a Presbyterian pastor from the North who came to Asheville to confer with me among others. He is endowed for life and apparently has the promise from one of his former parishioners of a hundred thousand dollars or more for mountain work, if he can find something that will develop into a permanent work under his direction. I am trying to help him, but it is quite a proposition to direct a man in middle life, thus equipped financially and unequipped personally, for the field he purposes to enter. He realizes now, I judge, that he has made his choice influenced by a concept of mountain people and mountain conditions drawn largely from what he had heard and read about them and that perhaps, in fact, conditions are not altogether what they had seemed to him to be. He apparently has felt that all of the mountain boys were Abraham Lincolns in embryo.

Fortunately, I think he feels the danger in his financial equipment of growing so lazy as not to do any work worthwhile, or becoming so insufferably independent as not to be able to work with anyone.

Mr. Glenn replied on March 6th that if John thought it advisable, he himself would be glad to go to Washington, too, to meet with the SIEA. He added: "The story about the Presbyterian pastor is interesting. It seems a pity to lose such a good sum for mountain work, but it would be worse to have it misdirected."

Mr. Glenn's letter arrived March 8th. The same day John wrote to him again:

I have just received your letter of March 6th. Tomorrow morning I leave, to be absent in the mountains northeast of here for a few days, to talk over some plans that some of the people are considering there as to possible mountain industries. I want to find out definitely what they purpose before I go to Washington, so that I may get the opinions, in Washington, of experts as to the feasibility of their ideas. . . .

Would you think it advisable for me to state while there, or to write prior to my going, that you or I, or both of us, could meet with the [SIEA] trustees at a date fixed to fall within the period of time that I should be in Washington on my return? If they have in mind any reorganization, I hope very much you can be there, for I am sure you would be very helpful to them and could speak definitely on points that might be raised, in regard to which I would have no information.

John planned to get off on his mountain trip on the morning of the 9th, but as my Line-a-Day records, "big snow" prevented, holding him at home for a week. The trip was important to him, for he felt the development of mountain industries valuable both economically and culturally and was eager to foster the beginnings of handicraft at Allanstand and Tryon, as well as at many other points in the mountains. The postponement of a week gave time for necessary conference planning and correspondence. The "call" was mailed.

Asheville, North Carolina
March 1, 1915

My dear ———:
    You are most cordially invited to attend our third annual conference, at the Imperial Hotel, Knoxville, Tennessee, April 21st and 22nd, and to participate in its proceedings.

We would urge that you plan to reach Knoxville in time to attend an informal social gathering in the assembly room of the Imperial Hotel on the evening of April 20th. This feature of our last conference was especially pleasant and helpful in promoting acquaintance.

Although the conference will partake more than ever of the nature of a conference, with free discussion by persons meeting at first hand the many questions of rural welfare, there will yet be opportunity to hear several persons of national reputation who know the mountains and who are engaged in work that may be helpful to the mountains through adaptation.

We are already assured of the presence of Hon. Philander P. Claxton, US commissioner of education.

The American Red Cross will send an exhibit of its rural work, and it is likely that its moving-picture exhibit will also be available.

Those who wish to know more fully the character and aims of the conference may obtain a booklet of the proceedings of the last conference by sending, in the enclosed envelope, addressed to the chairman of the Executive Committee, stamps to the value of twenty-six cents.

Please send also any suggestions that you may have for the conference, and state whether or not you will be present. Your suggestions are sought even if it is impossible for you to attend.

Very truly yours,

THE EXECUTIVE COMMITTEE

By John C. Campbell, Chairman

With the "call," this enclosure was sent to the new names on the conference mailing list: "For the benefit of those who have not hitherto attended the conferences, it ought perhaps to be stated that this conference is the outgrowth of efforts to bring together, for acquaintance and consultation, officials and teachers of schools engaged in work for the white boys and girls in the highland section of the South. It would be a real help if we might have you present with us."

The mountain trip was finally made. Back in Asheville, John wrote Mr. Glenn on March 17th: "I have just returned to the office after a trip of three or four days into the mountains and am awaiting word from Washington as to whether the people whom I wish to see are likely to be there the latter part of this week or the first of next. In the event of their being there, I shall go to Washington and will phone you as you suggest when I learn what the situation is."

To Miss Katherine Pettit, who, jointly with Miss Ethel de Long, was director of the Pine Mountain Settlement School in eastern Kentucky, the two being titled its Executive Committee, he wrote on the same date, urging her to come to Knoxville:

> On my return from a brief visit in the mountains, I found on my desk a letter from Miss Newman. Miss Newman writes that you have decided not to come, but that she hopes the school will be represented by some of the workers. We have received from Miss de Long also a statement that she cannot come.
>
> I am writing to ask, with all the earnestness in my power, that you both come, and if that is not possible, that you at least will come. You and Miss de Long are among the pioneers in new methods whom I am counting upon to help those of us who believe in new methods to persuade to the newer and better things those who are pursuing the old.
>
> Miss Berry is coming, Dr. Claxton, and quite a representation of agencies and schools that have not met with us before. I know it is hard to get away, but this conference is the first getting together of the various agencies doing work in the mountain country. I ought not to get away and am very sure that I ought not to be running the affair so much as I am forced to do. I shall feel very much as if I had lost one of the mainstays if you are not there.
>
> You may recall our first meeting in Baltimore, when you and I were called into conference before I undertook my work with the Sage Foundation. Ever since then I have felt that you understood the need of some of the things that I was driving at so insistently.
>
> While I know of your reluctance to speak in public, yet I feel that your presence and your mingling with those attending the conference is of the greatest help. Whether you like it or not, or whether you feel you deserve it, you are looked up to as one of the leaders in mountain work. You and Miss de Long have seen the wisdom of having work elastic enough to meet new conditions, and it will be a distinct loss to the conference if you are not present. I hope you will come.
>
> Please do not say again that you cannot come, but that you will bring Miss de Long and others of your workers with you. I urge this especially in these initial meetings until some policy can be wrought out. I trust that by return mail you will relieve my anxiety by saying that you will come. Your last letter got my hopes up, and this letter of Miss Newman's is a distinct jolt, from which I shall not revive until I hear definitely that you are coming. This is not a fairy tale. If these conferences are to prove of any value,

they must be made valuable by having in attendance those who are meeting successfully the problems that we are discussing.

Later in March, John went north. On April 1st he wrote Mr. Glenn about his
visit to Washington:

I returned yesterday after a very interesting and I hope ultimately successful meeting with the trustees of the SIEA. As soon as I've caught up with
the correspondence needing prompt attention, I will write you a letter giving full details of this meeting and other meetings and interviews held during the recent trip north.

At the request of the SIEA trustees, I shall write out my views as to
the work best suited to their organization. They were unable to get certain
people that they wanted, so did not write you to attend the meeting; but
their purpose is to have a full meeting in the near future, which they hope
that you and I and others may be free to attend. It will be a real help to
them then, I am sure, if you can be present.

I had, as you suggested, an interview with Mrs. Beale, and we talked
over some plans that may lead to closer connection between the Red Cross
work and the mountain country. . . .

I enclose a clipping from the *Progressive Farmer*—Mr. [Clarence] Poe's
paper. A number of inquiries are coming in, and I suppose they are due to
this notice. I do not know how they got it, but I suppose it is from some
of the invitations we sent out. I do not know how long we can continue to
hide our light under a bushel, and perhaps it may not be desirable.

I am grateful to you for the suggestions made for this conference in
Knoxville and your careful consideration and advice as to the plans I
talked over with you. The real problem now before me in the management
of this conference is not as to how to make it grow, but how to restrict it
to those who are vitally interested in the work to be done.

Further correspondence before and about the conference and about postconference plans include the following two letters from John to Mr. Glenn:

April 7, 1915

I enclose herewith . . . requisition for fifty dollars in addition to petty cash
reimbursement. This is to meet traveling expenses of Miss Dickenson and pos-

sibly of others to the Knoxville conference. There are one or two other public school teachers that I may want to get.

From Knoxville I shall go to Nashville for three days to confer with Dr. Bruce Payne and his faculty relative to the possible extension of their work into the mountain country, and from Nashville I go to Chattanooga to attend the Conference for Education and Industry in the South. I am to have a number of interesting conferences at Chattanooga with people who are coming, and I have agreed to put Mrs. [Edward] Beale in touch there with persons to whom I think she could be helpful.

April 19, 1915

We have been having busy days with visitors of late. As an outgrowth of Mr. and Mrs. [Charles R.] Crane's interest in our work, Mr. and Mrs. Frank Scott of Chicago called upon us. Mr. Scott, I infer, had some legal connection with Mr. Crane. Mr. Scott gave letters of introduction to Mr. and Mrs. Julius Rosenwald of Chicago, who presented them. Mrs. Campbell and I have had several very pleasant visits with them, and on Saturday we went with them on a day's mountain trip. They all give evidence of considerable interest in the work we are attempting. I wish very much that these wealthy gentlemen with interest in the mountain field might make over to the Foundation, in trust, certain sums to carry on, under the Foundation's direction, work for the mountain people. I think many of the boards could be brought into closer cooperation through something of this sort.

I leave in the morning for Knoxville. Mrs. Crane goes with us; Mr. Crane is obliged to go back to New York. Mr. and Mrs. Rosenwald expressed a desire to go to Knoxville also, but their plans include a visit to Hampton Institute, and they leave for that point tomorrow. I will write you fully of the conference on my return. I expect to get back to the office the first week in May.

The conference, April 21st and 22nd, proved a successful one. After it was over, John went directly to George Peabody College in Nashville, where he spent three days in conference with Dr. Bruce Payne, moving on to Chattanooga for another two days of interviews. Thence he proceeded to the Berry School in Mount Berry, Georgia, where he was scheduled to speak, then went on to Demorest for a brief visit to Piedmont College. From Nashville, on April 24th, he sent his first report of the conference to Mr. Glenn:

I am on my way to Nashville to confer with Dr. Bruce Payne and some members of his faculty relative to extension of their work into the mountains. This will be the only opportunity for some days to write you, in all probability.

I wish there were time now to give you in detail a report of our conference in Knoxville. There was a notable group present, in number a little larger than last year, but much more representative in that there were only eight or nine chance visitors from Knoxville, the others being connected with some church organization or state agency.

Dr. Claxton attended all sessions both days and was very helpful to all.

Bishop Horner was there with a fine group of young rectors from his diocese. Mr. [George P.] Mayo of Virginia was a most helpful member of the conference, and Rev. Franklin J. Clark of the Episcopal Church Mission Board in New York was, last year and this year, one of the most helpful men in the conference. He is a very good mixer and a very lovable man. We think there is no one who attends our conference more generally liked than Mr. Clark. It is due to his untiring efforts, I feel, that Bishop Horner and others of the Episcopal Church interested in mountain work were persuaded to attend and bring others.

I should value very much your strengthening my own expression of thanks to Mr. Clark. Miss Dickey, my secretary, will send you the clippings from the papers. She has had to carry a great burden of detail for the conference, so I have sent her up into the mountains with my friend Dr. Packard for a much needed rest. You will undoubtedly hear from her within a day or two. However, on my return I will give you a full account.

I am much encouraged, by reason of the spirit evidenced by these conferences, to feel that the things on which all agree are going to be emphasized, and the things on which there is disagreement are relegated to the background, and that there may be established between the church and the state agencies a close bond of sympathy.

Bishop Horner, at my request, put in form a motion which was carried unanimously, that the conference publish as a conference some statement as to what the mountain work is, and its requirements for those proposing to enter it. I was very desirous of having this go through, as it will be the first example to the public of united effort. Dr. Brown of the Baptist Church concurred in this action.

I am reelected chairman and am appointed to take the initiative in correspondence with the various church boards in issuing this publication. Between fifty and sixty dollars was raised toward this work.

Mrs. Crane was a most enthusiastic listener in the conference and on her own initiative has volunteered to pay half of the expenses of the next conference.

There were many expressions of appreciation to the Sage Foundation for having so generously allowed me to carry the expense for necessary things not provided for. My division is to be reimbursed for some of these expenditures. I told them, as a member of the conference, that the expenses should be paid just as far as possible by the conference. They agreed very heartily to this opinion. . . .

Prospects for the future of the conference seem very bright, and I want very much an opportunity to talk over with you many things that I have thought over in connection with it.

On his return to Asheville, John reported on his visit with President Payne at George Peabody College to Mr. Glenn, on May 8th:

I had a most interesting time in Nashville at the George Peabody College for Teachers. I met at luncheon a goodly representation from the faculty and had opportunity to set forth my ideas as to how they might connect with mountain work.

The Seaman A. Knapp School of Country Life of the George Peabody College ought to become, I feel, a leader in the solution of mountain problems. This is a permanent institution and a southern institution, and not bound or limited as are so many of the state institutions. It would be much easier for this school to cooperate and give direction to the work of the church schools, inasmuch as the church school authorities and boards would not feel that there was the danger present in union between church educational work and state educational work.

The Northern Presbyterians feel a hesitancy in cooperating with state agencies for education. This is due not to any real spirit of antagonism toward the state schools, but because they have made some former protest against a certain kind of cooperation in Indian work between the government and the Roman Catholic teachers in the Indian schools; and the Presbyterians, wanting to be free from any countercharge that they themselves were doing something of the sort, have been very reluctant to enter into any sort of scheme for cooperation which might give a semblance of truth to such charges. It would be much easier, I think, to persuade them and others to follow the lead of a school which is avowedly for the promotion of country life and rural education, and which is a southern school but broad in its sympathies and affiliations.

I understand that the Seaman A. Knapp School of Country Life is a development of the idea of Dr. Buttrick. My impression is that he, with Dr. Walter Page and others, were discussing a suitable memorial to Dr. Knapp, and when others had mentioned various kinds of tablets, etc., Dr. Buttrick gave expression to the thought that the most suitable memorial to Dr. Knapp would be a school for the promotion of country life.

A year or more ago I broached the idea to Dr. Payne in New York that the Knapp School should extend its work into the mountains, and he gave very ready assent to it. I went to the Women's Board of the Northern Presbyterian Church and put before them a plan by which they could furnish their buildings at different places in the mountains for summer schools for the use of an extension faculty from the Seaman A. Knapp School of Country Life.

I feel that in the mountains we must adapt some of the methods that are used in some of the foreign countries, of sending trained teachers to train local teachers and to give right direction to local educational efforts. It is almost impossible to get the teachers from remote rural sections to the Normal Schools in distant centers, and the teachers in the distant centers often know very little of the conditions under which the remote rural teachers of the mountains are obliged to impart instruction. This plan would be mutually helpful to the teaching force and to the local teachers taught. A real need will be met in the mountains by some such arrangement. From year to year, different parts of the mountain section would be reached.

There would be need of one permanent man in the mountains to take charge of the preliminaries, to follow up results, and to keep work in the mountains in touch with the Seaman A. Knapp School in Nashville. If there could be brought about a cooperative effort between the Seaman A. Knapp School and the Southern Industrial Educational Association, the expert in rural pedagogy whom I suggested to the Southern Industrial Educational Association would be the type of man needed. It might be well in the beginning, and eventually would be necessary, possibly, to have a demonstration school in the mountains from which, as a mountain center, this work could be directed. This demonstration school might possibly be a mountain annex of the Seaman A. Knapp School. It should not be a large institution, but should be just what the people themselves could make it under the right leadership, and the people of the community should get much of the education that they need in cooperating with this rural pedagogue in building the school and in furnishing the material for it. The domestic science expert and the weaving expert and later experts in manual training, etc., suggested to the Southern Industrial Educational Association, might possibly be connected with this school and do their extension work in the other schools from this school as the original center.

The Seaman A. Knapp School is a school that is going on for years. The Southern Industrial Educational Association has not the equipment or the personnel to give permanent direction, but they could help to begin a work that would be larger than any which they themselves could possibly further separately, by cooperating in some such way with the Seaman A. Knapp School of Country Life.

I thank you for sending me Dr. Dodge's letter. He is right in his statement that the work in the mountains must necessarily be slow, and it will be difficult to find and keep the right kind of experts unless there is some permanency and future in the work that they undertake. I feel that this idea of cooperation that I suggest, and which I have had in mind for a long while, will be very helpful in securing the right kind of people. This plan would link up rural work in the lowlands with rural work in the highlands, and the mountain side of things could be well guarded by a contract to the effect that certain people should do all of their work in the mountains, and the extension faculty of the Seaman A. Knapp School should spend a certain part of the year in mountain work.

I am confident that what is needed for the mountains is a natural leadership that is permanent and broad. Temporary agencies in education, such as the church schools, should cooperate wherever possible with the state and national agencies and be pioneers in new methods. Under all the circumstances, it seems to me that the Knapp School is the logical leader for a number of years to come, for it is, as I have said, for the whole South and is not likely to have the hindrances, real or fancied, that might come up in connection with other institutions.

I feel, too, that the health work should, if possible, be under the real, or at least under the inspirational, leadership of the state and national agencies.

On the same day he sent a second letter to Mr. Glenn with a further account of the Conference of Southern Mountain Workers in Knoxville:

I am sending under separate cover several copies of the list of organizations represented and persons in attendance at our conference in Knoxville. It was a much more representative group than last year. All of those listed as visitors, with the exception of one or two, came to Knoxville purposely to attend the conference and were not casual visitors. Our enrollment exceeded by eight or nine the enrollment of last year and really is more significant than it seems, for quite a number of those in attendance last year were casual visitors. Undoubtedly there would have been more from Knoxville had not one of the papers made an error in the date of the opening of the conference.

The Southern Methodists expected fully to be represented, but the prolongation of their conference in Nashville, on the same date as our conference, prevented their coming and prevented some of their speakers from being present. The Associate Presbyterian denomination, represented last year, sent letters of regret that they could not be represented this year inasmuch as other engagements prevented. We had this year a new denomination in the Seventh-Day Advent[ist] Church.

There was also one Negro in attendance from southern Alabama. He had heard of the conference and came to the door and sent in word to me as chairman asking if he might not come in to listen. I felt that it would be wise to admit him, and so expressed myself to Bishop Horner, Dr. Brown, and Dr. McBrayer—representative southerners in the conference. They agreed heartily, and inasmuch as the conference is self-directing and all matters not provided for must be settled by vote of the conference, it was necessary to put the matter before the conference. These gentlemen heartily seconded the suggestions made, and the colored school teacher had the benefit of whatever good came from the conference. I think this teacher was simply someone who had heard of the conference and strayed in.

The conference reached a higher level than ever before. The first year in Atlanta, the time was given up very largely to getting acquainted; last year emphasis was placed upon the work of the church schools and the need of readapting their work to changing conditions; this year we endeavored to show what could be done through the little public schools, how state agencies for education might help, how cooperation might be carried on between church schools and the public agencies for education, and much emphasis was placed upon health work. We touched also upon stimulating industries in the mountains, and methods of cooperation to further this. I have had already some very appreciative letters. Mrs. Crane expressed herself as greatly pleased and interested and said it was the best indoor conference she had ever attended. She was so much pleased that she purposed sending Miss Margaret Wilson a night telegram telling her of the conference. I think she carried out her purpose in this respect.

As soon as I have the resolutions and minutes in form, I will send you copies. I will also send you an outline of the program.

You may be interested to know that among the prominent speakers and persons present, the following were native to the mountains so far as I know:

President Sidney G. Gilbreath
Hon. Samuel H. Thompson
President Bruce R. Payne
Professor R. W. Selvidge (Ozark Mountains of Missouri)
Rev. A. E. Brown, DC
Rev. Hubert S. Lyle
Rev. Hugh A. Dobbin
Rev. A. Rufus Morgan
L. B. McBrayer, MD
George W. Booker, MD
Dr. James P. Faulkner

I thank you for the *Outlook* containing the article "The Church of the Lean Land." Among the gentlemen pictured on page 989 is Mr. Mayo, who attended the conference; Mr. Ellis, Mr. Mason, and Archdeacon Neve, who were unable to attend but from whom we had very cordial letters of regret.

One of the interesting outcomes of this conference is an unconscious getting together evidenced in a motion fathered by Bishop Horner. The conference as a conference is to issue a booklet setting forth the needs of the mountain field and the qualifications desired in those entering mountain work. The matter is left in my hands, but the church boards have promised cooperation through their representatives. It is agreed that if any church desires special qualifications in the work rather than those published in the composite draft, that such qualifications will also be printed over the signature of the secretary or proper authority of the church in question. I think this is one of the best things that has come out of the conference. It grew out of what may have been, on the part of the bishop, a chance remark some months ago, which we fostered and which Mr. Clark, I think, helped me to get before the conference through strengthening the bishop's chance remark into a resolve and motion. The only objection made to it was in the form of a question by Dr. Brown of the Baptist Board, but he acquiesced readily when provision was made for publishing, if desired, the special requirements of the several denominations.

I think this whole matter will not be altogether easy and will require delicate handling, but I am hoping very much that by another year we shall have something on record which, in a measure, commits us to joint action. I had not dared to hope for this so soon, and I would not have thought it advisable to suggest it myself. I think we are taking a long step in advance toward fellowship by this action.

The rest of John's contacts with the SIEA may be gathered from a letter of his, with the date torn off but probably written sometime after the end of April 1915, when the detailed SIEA plan was submitted. Addressed to Miss Cora Neal, new field secretary of the association, it was firm in tone and reiterated advice and some of the suggestions made before; especially, he urged that the trustees definitely decide on what they would like to do, state why they have chosen it "in preference to others, and why you believe your plan and your administration of it, if properly financed, would help the mountain people." The letter continued:

This is all-important. Of this I am confident, not only from long years of hard personal experience in the field of raising money for mountain institutions, but from a later knowledge of what donors of other than very small sums are now asking.

Therefore, to repeat, the most important thing is that you get your organization to decide on something very definite, and to be unwavering, whatever decision is reached. . . .

As I recall the suggestions made when I had the privilege of meeting in conference, in response to their generous invitation, with your officials, they are somewhat as follows:

1. A school of a new type—preferably along the lines laid down by the Danish folk schools but adapted to meet conditions in the mountains

and to general American ideals. . . . I suggested further the selection of a proper person who should, first of all, become thoroughly acquainted with the mountain field if not already so acquainted; this person to be then sent to Denmark for a study of the Danish schools, with further study in Norway, Sweden, and England and brief study of what is being done educationally in Switzerland and Germany—the whole study to cover about a year of time; then to return to this country to build up such a school in a mountain community carefully selected for the purpose.

2. Or the selection of experts to promote domestic science, weaving, etc., rather than the giving of small scholarships for that purpose. . . .

3. Or to arrange with some leading teachers' training school in the South for establishing at points in the mountains—different points perhaps from year to year—a summer school adapted especially to mountain teachers.

In another letter, written to Dr. Payne on May 14, 1915, John also followed up on his visit to Nashville, stating at some length his proposal for the extension within the mountains of the teacher training program of the country life school at George Peabody College:

I feel strongly the desirability of the Seaman A. Knapp School of Country Life's having an extension faculty to reach the remote rural sections of both lowlands and highlands, in order to give wise direction to the educational efforts of those regions from which it is unlikely that teachers would come to central Normal schools.

Interested as I am in the mountain country, and feeling that it is in large part a country with rural conditions intensified, but with a strong rural population, it is essential, from my point of view, that this extension faculty give a definite part of each year to the mountain country and that this mountain work be guarded in order that the strong pull from the lowlands, when your work is begun and its value known, may not take from the efforts for the mountains and the time needed for them.

As time goes on, this faculty would develop naturally as the needs are seen, but I would recommend that at first a teacher of rural pedagogy, one in household economics, and one in agriculture be appointed; and if you have established connection with the Red Cross or any other organization looking to the betterment of sanitary conditions in rural sections, a teacher or nurse from this department also. There might also be a teacher of fireside industries such as weaving, etc., but I regard the first four named as the more important at the beginning.

It might be advisable at first to make arrangements with the mountain department of some church board for the use of one or more of their plants in the mountains during the vacation months. There could be brought together there in a summer school of two or three months the public school teachers of the region or regions you wish to touch, as well as many of the workers in the mountain schools of the various denominational boards.

You might be able to enlist under your direction, to supplement your extension faculty, the services of some of the best teachers under these various boards and also the services of state schoolteachers and experts in various lines of rural activities under the auspices of the US Government or state departments.

Eventually, I think, you should look toward building up a demonstration school in the mountains, and it might be wise to begin in this way, beginning at the ground and having the community, under your leadership, build up a school suitable to the needs of the community. From this as a center you might branch out in your summer extension work.

Whichever of these methods you may deem wiser as a beginning, you would need as your permanent representative in the mountains some man who is a teacher and who knows the mountain country and people thoroughly. It should be his duty to arrange preliminaries for the summer work in the mountains, after consultation with you and your extension faculty, to help you in your summer work in the mountains, to follow up results, and through him there should be established a permanent connection between the mountains and the Seaman A. Knapp School of Country Life. This could be done by making it possible for him to be called to Nashville whenever you may want him, and to send to him, from time to time, members of your extension faculty to consult with him as to their work and to learn from him the conditions under which those whom they are to instruct must carry on their work.

I think I spoke to you of other agencies with whom you might connect. If I can be of assistance at any time in arranging for a meeting looking toward any cooperation between you that you may mutually deem wise, I shall be glad to be of service; and I shall be glad to render any assistance in my power in developing the plan or in helping you to put the plan into operation when it is developed. It is a work that needs to be done and a work that I believe in thoroughly. For this pioneer work the Knapp School is eminently fitted, and in the furtherance of it I believe the institution will develop itself as well as the region it seeks to help.

8

Ballads Added

Part 1, 1915–1916

The ballad search had been going on for six years, during which time three conferences had been held. William Chauncy Langdon, a specialist in pageantry, had been working with the Russell Sage Foundation, and he suggested that Olive Campbell meet with Cecil Sharp, "the great English ballad authority," who was visiting in America. In spite of the latter's painful affliction with gout, he was delighted to know about her discoveries: he previously had felt "that there must be such survivals current in America." Olive had transcribed the tunes as she played them on the piano, a rather unscientific, though practical, method. The music needed to be more technically correct, so a meeting in the spring was planned.

Much correspondence followed, with planning for trips to find the ballads again and record the tunes properly. Money would have to be found to pay travel expenses. John Campbell was also looking for funds to support summer schools for several months of the year in the mountains and for extension work by the schools that were already in existence. A lively discussion ensued about teacher training schools: they were "still dominated by the academic ideals of the past." John Campbell describes the general state of schools in the mountains and states that teachers should be familiar with the people, customs, and culture of the localities in which they are teaching.

Much of the chapter consists of a copious correspondence between Cecil Sharp and the Campbells about the proper methods of collecting ballads and how the work should be adapted to fit in with the life and habits of the singers. Olive Campbell insisted that her object had always been to help the people, who were her friends: "I would not be willing to have their confidence violated." Sharp assured her that he valued her work and that her part in the collections would be noted. Progress was slow, owing to other obligations of Cecil Sharp and to the difficulty of ocean travel during the war.

A brief account of the fourth Conference of Mountain Workers in Knoxville closes the chapter, listing the organizations represented from the government, charitable organizations, and faculties of mountain colleges. Community service was the general topic of discussion. A committee was selected to appoint a commission, representing most of the interested parties, to make a survey of the mountain field and report their findings at the next conference.

The Mountain Workers' Conference was fully organized and in the successful swing of its third year when our ballad search, pursued intermittently over six years, took a new and exciting turn. For some months there had been working with the Foundation a certain William Chauncy Langdon, a specialist in pageantry. Immediately aware of the importance of the study and the interest of the ballad angle, he most kindly put me in touch with the Fuller sisters—delightful folk-song singers from England. He then set about getting me an introduction to Cecil Sharp, the great English ballad authority, whom, of all others, I had most wished to meet. As it happened, he was in this country in 1915 for a short stay while war conditions prevented his work at home. On the chance of seeing him, I went up from Asheville in June and with Mr. Langdon's help made the long desired connection.

Mr. Sharp was out at Lincoln, Massachusetts, a guest of Mrs. J. J. Storrow, who met me at her imposing front door with what she confessed, many years later, was a definitely suspicious eye. Mr. Sharp was not well, she at once informed me; he really should not see anyone, but he was so anxious to find genuine ballads that she did not like to refuse him. Would I please watch him, and if he showed restlessness, excuse myself as soon as possible. I gathered that he was not an altogether easy guest to entertain when ill, and I could hardly blame her for hesitating to introduce somebody she did not know at all and who might turn out to be an imposter, or at best an unmitigated bore. The introduction was not exactly cordial, but after all he had wanted to interview, and this was my chance. I followed Mrs. Storrow when she opened the door and ushered me into a small room just off the hall, nearby. She then left us alone.

The object of my search was sitting before a table in a carved, high-backed chair, one foot extended on a stool. Keen gray eyes took me in swiftly, manila envelope and all, while he made his apologies for not getting up to greet me. He explained that his gout was a family inheritance, not at all due to high living, which he could ill afford on his income, had he wished it. Then after a few more general remarks, he asked to see what I had brought. I laid my humble offering on the table before him without further ado, and watched him undo the tie and lift out the precious bundle of papers. It was my time to observe.

A long, thin English face and aquiline nose bent above the manuscript. I could see that his hair was graying and high on his forehead. He was perhaps fifty-odd (later I found he was fifty-six, born November 2, 1859), with a fresh color; his movements were quick and vigorous. I waited in silence as he turned the papers. From time to time he looked up to ask "How does this go?" or "Will you please sing that?" Then abruptly, "How did you take these down?" I explained that I had to learn each song from the singer, getting him to repeat again and again until I knew the tune, and had written down the chords. I would then hunt out a piano or organ—by no means always available—and set down the tune as well as I could. I was, of course, no musician! Where I could not go back and recheck, I set it down to the best of my ability from my notes and memory. "Don't you know that that is very unscientific?" was the uncompromising comment. I admitted that I knew it was not scientific, but it was the only way I could get the tunes, as I could not get the singer to the piano, or a piano to the singer. Whereupon he went back to examining the pages, asking me to interpret here and there. Before he realized it, we were deep in the pile of songs, and there Mrs. Storrow found us, when rather apprehensively she at last peeped in on us. Two excited faces looked up to greet her! "I had felt sure," Mr. Sharp explained, "that there must be such survivals current in America." People had brought songs to him, but only now he found any trace of what seemed genuine. A careful study and recording should be made as soon as possible. We began at once to discuss a feasible meeting in the spring, when he hoped to come back from England.

On the wings of the wind I hurried back to John. He was as excited as I, and so was my sister Daisy, who had helped me hunt for these songs. So indeed were Mr. and Mrs. Glenn, and all my friends who had followed sympathetically the fortunes of the ballads from the beginning. The next step, in the form of a letter, was not long in coming. On June 24th he wrote me:

Dear Mrs. Campbell:

I am still at Lincoln, but I move on to Eliot tomorrow, where the above address [Dr. Moore's Camp, Eliot, Maine] will find me for the next three weeks. I have been thinking a great deal about your ballads and of the necessity of completing the work which you have so ably initiated. Mr. Richard Aldrich, the musical critic of the *N.Y. Times,* has been staying here, and I have had many conversations with him upon the subject. He agrees with me that something ought to be done to ensure the preservation of all these ballads before it is too late, and also to discover whether there are not other folk survivals in the district besides ballads, and of equal value, such as singing games, dances, carols, etc.

I feel too that the investigation would be peculiarly congenial to me to undertake because it would in a sense complete the work upon which I have been engaged so long in England. But as you know, I am a very busy man and it would be extremely difficult for me to give up the necessary time; and moreover, as you may not perhaps know, I am a very poor man, so that there would be financial difficulties to overcome in addition. In these circumstances it has occurred to me that it might be possible to get some university or public body in America to help in the matter by making a subsidy. Mr. Aldrich agrees to this and has promised tentatively to make some enquiries.

But please understand that I do not wish for the world to queer your pitch, so that I shall not move in the matter any further except with your complete concurrence. Indeed, it would be quite impossible for me or anyone else to do the work without your good help. So I am writing this in order that I may discover how you think and feel with regard to this scheme. It would be very kind of you, therefore, if you would write me a line or two and frankly tell me whether you would like me to cooperate with you in the way above suggested, in the event of my scheme materializing.

Forgive this long letter.

I answered almost immediately, trying to explain how pleased I would be to have him carry through his suggestion:

If it could be arranged, I could not think of anything more fortunate. There is a vast amount of material untouched here—"ballets," as they call them, of all sorts, new and old; singing games, of which I have collected very few as they came along; and some carols. There are also old-fashioned dances, much frowned upon by the people because of their strict religious ideas concerning such amusements. Possibly these are folk dances, though I am doubtful as to that.

There has been some collecting done—notably in Kentucky, Virginia, and North Carolina—the latter two folklore societies making an attempt to secure music. But the upland region of the South contains over one hundred thousand square miles, and you can readily see that very little, comparatively, has been done—almost nothing with the music. Personally, from now on, I shall have little opportunity to do any work, but I think I might put you in touch with people who could be very helpful to you.

The chief difficulty in the way, as I see it, is whether you would not find the rough travel, the inconvenient—often primitive—quarters, and poor food too great a strain on your health. When I was traveling with Mr. Campbell in his study of the whole region—social, economic, educational, etc.—we generally tried to stay, when we could so arrange, at one of the mission schools in the mountains—at least to make one a center. I could probably arrange for you to stay at one of these, although most of them are not in session until September. Would it be practicable for you to undertake a preliminary trip before planning a definite investigation, in order that you might see the possibilities and difficulties?

Mr. and Mrs. Glenn had been interested in the ballad collecting for several years and had helped me to meet people who might further both the collecting and publication. He now wrote to John:

I am delighted to hear that Mr. Sharp is so enthusiastic about Mrs. Campbell's ballads. I do not see right at present where there is any money in the R.S.F. treasury to pay the expenses of this trip, unless it comes out of your budget. If we take it from that, it will probably mean cutting off some other things that are more directly in line with your work. I will, however, be glad to consider the question if you will tell me how long Mr. Sharp would probably be in the mountains and what the expense would amount to.

Do you think Mr. Sharp would get much by his visit to the mountains unless he stayed a number of months and made careful investigations through the whole mountain country? Of course, it would be a good thing for him to see even a part of the mountains, so as to understand the background of the ballad.

Of course, it would give me great pleasure to do anything I can to further such an investigation, but I do not think it comes directly in our field. I think it would be better to get the money from some other source, if possible. Some of the artistic and literary group may have access to people who would give money to this, who are not giving anything materially to philanthropic matters or for social betterment.

And again: "I have told Mrs. Campbell to charge the expense of her trip [to Massachusetts to see Mr. Sharp] to your budget if you have no objection. It is a very proper charge against the Foundation."

Mr. Sharp answered July 15th that he wished he might come down before returning to England, but that he had his own summer school of folk song and folk dance at Stratford to direct, and was sailing for England on the following Saturday in order to be there for the opening on the 27th, closing with, "Well, good bye for the present. I hope it will not be long before I return once again to this country, but I have no plans at present."

John commented to Mr. Glenn in reply, "I am not sure how valuable such a study by Mr. Sharp would be; it would depend largely upon his temperament and the time given. It seems to me more and more the temperament—or personality, perhaps, is a better word—is essential in any phase of this mountain work. If scholarship can be coupled with the right personality, then one has the ideal."

Meanwhile, John had received from Dr. Payne, during the busy July days of summer school at George Peabody College, a long letter in which he said that he and his faculty were ready to commit themselves to the extension plan for teacher training which they had discussed together during John's visit to the college and which John had described fully in his letter of May 14th. [See chapter 7.] The opening and closing sections of this letter, dated July 17th, show Dr. Payne's strong feeling about this plan for their Seaman Knapp School of Country Life:

> Since you were here some months ago presenting to us the needs of an extension faculty to carry the various helpful departments of George Peabody College for Teachers to the mountain districts of the South, our faculty have continued their discussions and interest in that matter. Your letter of May 14th has put the matter in still more concrete and precise form.
>
> Although I have been thinking over the matter for several years and have had several discussions with you and others concerning it, it has always seemed wise to me to thrash a thing of this sort out in all of its details so as to convince myself and all of my colleagues that the thing is absolutely right, proper, and helpful for the entire clientele involved. . . . If we do not so work it out until we believe in it with our whole hearts, souls, and minds, we cannot get up enough courage and power with which to carry it forward. We have reached the point that we have faith enough in this enterprise, if we can obtain the resources, to make it go.

The letter goes on to concur specifically in John's suggestion as to the desirability of plans for four faculty experts who would conduct summer schools of four weeks each in three selected places, hopefully located at existing mountain schools which would be strategically located and which would contribute buildings for school sessions and for teachers' residence. Money would have to be found for salaries and maintenance. In regard to a demonstration or model school, he wrote:

> It seems to me that the demonstration or model school in the mountains that we would want to find would be one that is already operating there,

which we would hope to make better. I do not at this time feel that the erection of our own demonstration school up there under artificial conditions is really what we want, because it seems to me that a demonstration school must be conducted under the same practical conditions that the mountain worker has to work under.

For this very reason we should need a permanent mountain worker who would stay in the mountains about nine months in the year, and who would stay with us about three months in the year. We must not forget that it is as important to keep our own faculty's sympathies and intellects educated toward this great group of people as it is for us to render services up there. Even the faculty that goes up there must not he continually emptying its mind without any possibility of renewing it from time to time. It will therefore be necessary for them to come back to the college for three or four months in the year.

It will be necessary for them to gather information from other parts of the world for about two months in the year. It would be very important that they do rural work in other parts of the country than the mountains for some period in the year, in order that they may absorb practical working plans and ideas in other rural sections and be able to translate them in terms of the needs of the mountains. I fancy that there are enough methods and ideas in the world to revolutionize and to greatly advance the interest and life of the people in the mountains if we could find those ideas and methods and sift them out before taking them to the mountaineers. . . .

I do hope that something can come of this, for I have all my life hoped to reach a point in my own thinking where I was as sure of my plans for the people in the mountains as I am of these plans which you have suggested. Now that those ideas are there, I shall never rest satisfied until the money can be procured for this faculty and they shall be put to work. You understand, perhaps better than others, how near my heart all this work is, for I was born and reared in pretty close contact with the mountain people of western North Carolina. I have lived and worked in Virginia, North Carolina, and Maryland, so that in many ways the whole enterprise is very near to my mind and to my heart. If this plan that you have suggested does not work, therefore, I shall suffer more intense pain than comes to a man who has merely an academic and a professional interest in the cause. But some plan will work, and we shall find it, if this is not the right one.

I do thank you for your continued interest and abiding goodwill to our cause here, and the cause of the people of the South as you have shown it in so many years. It is one of those things which keeps a man's heart up when the dark hours come, and strengthens him for the heavy tasks that must come in our generation to those who labor in the heart of the South.

This letter John forwarded to Mr. Glenn, as he previously had forwarded his own to Dr. Payne. In turn, Mr. Glenn sent these two letters to Mr. Wallace Buttrick, general secretary of the General Education Board, who replied immediately on the day he received them:

Thank you for your letter of the 19th with the enclosures from Mr. Campbell. I at once read them through and handed them to Dr. [Simon] Flexner, who also read them through. They are very interesting and confirm our conviction of the great strength of Mr. Campbell. He is a very valuable man, and you are to be congratulated on having him as your associate.

I noted with particular interest what he says about the Seaman A. Knapp School and the possibility of its doing extension work in the mountains. The principal difficulty is that Payne has no money for extension work. Furthermore, the Knapp School has not yet found itself. Flexner and I have a notion that it will be necessary for Dr. Payne and his associates first to establish their school at Nashville before they extend themselves very much. Mr. Campbell's idea is valuable, and very likely points the way for an extension of the influence of the George Peabody College in the course of two or three or more years, but just now Dr. Payne ought not to spread out. Mr. Rockefeller sometimes speaks of things as "too scopy." That is the peril in the first instance at the Peabody College. Intensive work at home should be Dr. Payne's great task.

I thank you very much for sending me those letters, and I have a strong notion that one of these days Mr. Campbell's fine idea will point the way to useful service.

A trip to Atlanta about this time, at the end of July, to talk with representatives of the Ellen Wilson Memorial at the beginning of their work, resulted in John's being invited to meet with the directors later in the year. The extreme heat and pressures around the journey brought on what was called an attack of acute indigestion, which incapacitated him for a number of days. He managed a long letter to Mr. Glenn on July 26, touched off by the letter from Mr. Buttrick:

I enclose also an extract from the address of Dr. Claxton, who spoke before the mountain workers of Knoxville on the subject "Some Suggestions for the Better Adaptation of Education in the Upland South." It is a great satisfaction to me to feel that the US commissioner of education thinks, with me, that while the educational problems of the mountains are problems of rural education, they yet require intelligence of a high order for their solution. In fact, they need specialization in effort to solve them.

Dr. Buttrick was so good as to consent, when I last saw him, to my submitting to him later some plan for bettering mountain schools. With your approval, I should like very much to come to New York this fall—possibly in September—to talk it over with Dr. Buttrick. I wish that President Payne could be there also. Even if the General Education Board should not feel justified in granting money for the carrying out of this plan, with their approval of the plan as a plan, it would be easier to secure support from one or two people that I have in mind.

I have thought long on the matter, and to me the plan suggested offers great promise. We can do nothing without the right kind of teachers; we cannot get the right kind of teachers without the right kind of training; we cannot get the right kind of training without the right kind of trainers. . . .

Most of our teacher training schools are still dominated by the academic ideals of the past. The pedagogy of these schools exercises itself in presenting subjects by methods developed, through a long series of years, by minds academically trained. The subject and the method are prominent, and there is an unconscious presupposition that the processes will appear as logical to the untrained mind as to the trained minds which developed or present them. I am extremely desirous that the plan I have suggested be put into effect before the Knapp School takes on the mold of the past and that it finds itself by finding the right methods, through knowing the psychology of untrained minds and by knowing the environment which has helped to produce that psychology. The danger that I see is that teachers will come to the Knapp School who will be taught by old processes, upon which there has been grafted something of the so-called rural pedagogy.

Peabody, if it ministers to Tennessee alone, should minister to the whole state and not merely to the urban or bluegrass sections of the state. Tennessee is admittedly two states in one; practically, it is three states in one: East Tennessee, Middle Tennessee, and West Tennessee.

I have been looking over this morning the teacher situation in that state and have had made some computations from the data in the office. These figures are taken from the 1912 report of the Tennessee state superintendent of public instruction, and while I feel very sure that some of the data on which these findings are based are open to question, they yet indicate marked tendencies.

Of the 3,570 *white* teachers in the mountainous section of Tennessee, 61.7% have had training below high school training; 22.2% have had training equivalent to high school training; 5.8% have had Normal training; 4.8% college training; 5.5% training unknown. (The terms *Normal* and *college* are not always used descriptively; the former has for its justification, often, a short course of coaching to enable teachers to pass examinations; and the latter is not infrequently a euphemism for a secondary school with a few fancy extras.)

These teachers are scattered at the rate of one for every 5.0 square miles. In the nonmountainous area, which is a third larger than the mountainous, . . . there are 4,174 *white* teachers, 63.8% having had less than high school training; 20.5% having the equivalent of high school training; 8.1% having had Normal training; 5.6 having had college training (2.0% training unknown). There is one teacher to every 5.7 square miles.

According to the 1910 census, 79.8% of the population of Tennessee is rural. Some very definite and large work for the rural schools should be done through the Seaman A. Knapp School.

The mountain section of East Tennessee is divided by the rich East Tennessee Valley, which is a part of the mountain section. This valley section of the mountains is one of the richest sections of Tennessee, and, of course, data from this section included in the total of the mountains makes the data for the mountains in their entirety more nearly those of the lowlands. But even in the East Tennessee Valley section of the mountains, rich as parts of it are, 55.2% of the *white* teachers have had training under high school training; 28.4% training equivalent to high school; 6.9% Normal training; and 6.1% college training (3.4% training unknown), with one teacher to 3.9 square miles.

The George Peabody College for Teachers is likely, as I have stated above, to draw from the high school, Normal, and college trained teachers, but something very wise must be done for the high percentage of teachers with training under high school training who go out into the public schools.

President [Sidney G.] Gilbreath of the East Tennessee Normal School (a school that is doing splendid work), when questioned after his address at the Knoxville conference as to how many teachers they were turning out, said he did not think there had been over 200 in three years; and in reply to the question as to how many teachers were needed, he said that in East Tennessee alone, 1,000 new teachers were needed each year. Dr. Claxton interjected, "3,000 new teachers needed, and turning out 200!" President Gilbreath in reply said: "We have a number of excellent schools in Tennessee—but if every institution, every college, every university, and every high school should engage in training teachers, and if every graduate of every institution should go into public school work, they could not supply the demand."

In my letter of May 8 to you I gave reasons as to why Peabody should be a pioneer. The church schools, which are as yet the best in the remote mountains, would cooperate with Peabody as they would not so readily do with state institutions. I do hope that some constructive plan will soon be put into operation for grappling, at least in its beginnings, with these great problems. The Knapp School will become the kind of school it ought to become through its faculty learning in the doing, in the different rural environments of the state.

I am deeply concerned that this plan be given careful consideration, for I am reminded constantly, "What you advocate is all right, but where are the agencies to lead constructively in this work?" The teachers of teachers must know the rural environment and rural psychology, or they will bring discouragement, as some of the government men have done in farm demonstration work, who, with lowland training, good of its kind, go into the mountains and put a wet blanket on efforts because they are not the same as those to which they have been accustomed. The secret of success is in finding people who know not only principles, but how to adapt and apply those principles under varying conditions. It seems to me often that in this matter of rural reconstruction, we are permitting the blind to lead the blind; and in many of our efforts for betterment, beginning at the top, we are attempting the impossible task of putting on the cornice of the edifice before we have laid the foundation stone.

President Payne, too, wrote to Mr. Glenn and also to Wickliffe Rose, a Tennessean, former faculty member and dean at George Peabody College, now in New York and a member of the General Education Board of the Rockefeller Foundation, the Sanitary Commission, and the Southern Education Board as well. John counted on help from him, indeed soon learned that he warmly favored the plan. Mr. Glenn wrote, on August 2nd, that he himself was intensely interested and "encouraged," but that Dr. Buttrick had just left the country to spend six months in China to look over the work of the Rockefeller-China Medical Education Board. Dr. Rose's reply to President Payne stated:

My observation of the farm demonstration work in the South during the last few years, and our own experience of five years in conducting a system of education for the masses of the people, confirm an opinion which has been growing with me for a number of years, namely: that the traditional belief that you cannot educate grown people, even very mature people, is erroneous. I am a thorough believer in the German system of extension teaching. Our educational system must be organized with a view to teaching the whole community, regardless of age. The field of work for the Peabody College suggested by this correspondence which you send to me is a practically unoccupied field of enormous proportions and with enormous possibilities for usefulness. The college should by all means undertake to occupy it.

President Payne made some further interesting comments:

One point I wish to make very plain. It requires more training, greater diversity of experience, more power and leadership, more tact, more consecration than any other sort of work I know of. A mediocre or average man will fail in it more quickly and more completely than in any other phase of educational work, so that the usual advice about taking young people and letting them grow up in the work does not appeal to me at all in connection with this mountain work. If we can't get money enough to buy some full-grown people at once, then let us wait. For we are making a terrible draft upon the lives of those messengers of good sense. We are asking them to give up their family life and home life for many years. We are asking them to sacrifice their opportunities for financial remuneration and for professional advancement. We are asking them to isolate themselves from the companionship of their intellectual and social peers. We must pay them for all this. They will have the missionary spirit, but we should not take a dishonest advantage of that rare spiritual possession. We ought to pay more rather than less for it.

John was disappointed that Dr. Buttrick would not be available until January but decided to make a trip to New York in September nevertheless. He wanted to confer with Red Cross officials and with Presbyterians, at their headquarters. Also he wanted to see several people about ways and means of setting up motion pictures in remote mountain areas. As he wrote Mr. Glenn: "For some years I have been studying on a plan of bringing educational motion pictures into the mountains on such a financial basis as to make possible the establishment of circuits in the remote mountain schools and communities." He had found that this had been successfully done in the North and wanted to enlist both Mr. [Lee F.] Hanmer's interest through the Department of Recreation at the Russell Sage Foundation, and an experienced person who might come to Kentucky or North Carolina for an experiment of this sort.

John's illness kept him at home and quiet during August, with time for much consideration of the Peabody College project and plans for seeing various people on his trip north. He got off about the first of September. Just after he left, a letter arrived for me from Mr. Sharp, dated August 15, at Dragonfield, Uxbridge, Kent:

Your letter of July 29 has just reached me together with another very important one on the same subject—as to which more later on. I will do what I can to harmonize the six tunes that you are going to send me, but domestic matters will claim almost my complete attention for the next few weeks, and I may not therefore be able to do them all at once. I am glad you like the books I sent you. Apparently I did not send you my book *English Folk Song: Some Conclusions,* which discusses the whole matter scientifically. If you have not got it, let me know and I will send you a copy.

The letter above referred to was one from Mr. Aldrich telling me that there is every possibility of my obtaining financial assistance in my proposed scheme of collecting in your district. You know how I want to do this if I can spare the time and can summon the physical strength. You know also what I feel about the part you have played in the matter, because I discussed this in my letter to you of June 24th. In case you have lost my letter I quote the following sentence from it: "Please understand that I do not wish for the world to queer your pitch, so that I shall not move in the matter any further except with your complete concurrence. Indeed, it would be quite impossible for me or anyone else to do the work without your good help. So I am writing this in order that I may discover how you think and feel with regard to the scheme. It would be very kind of you therefore if you would write me a line or two and frankly tell me whether you would like me to cooperate with you in the way above suggested in the event of my scheme materializing."

Unhappily, I have mislaid your reply—at any rate I have not got it with me—but I am pretty sure that you did not make any comment upon that part of my letter to you. I still feel with regard to this point exactly as I did when I wrote to you, and I do not wish to commit myself and undertake to explore your district for ballads, etc., until I know whether I have your approval and possibly—indeed I should hope for it—your personal cooperation. I should like, for instance, wherever possible, to hear sung the tunes which you have already noted, because I am sure I should be able to note variations of rendering of many of them made by the singers in the different verses of their songs. In some cases I might wish to take phonographic records. In other words, if I am to undertake this job at all, I should wish to do it as thoroughly as possible, and this would be impossible if I were to omit all the work which you have already done. With regard to the publications that would eventually follow, both scientific and popular, I should be perfectly willing to stand in with you or come to some arrangement. The simplest scheme would be for us to form a partnership and the results of our work to be published under both our names. You would bring to the pot an intimate local knowledge of the district and of the people and a certain amount of material that you have already collected, and I should supply experience in this particular kind of work and a certain amount of musical and scientific knowledge. It would [be] very nice if you could spare the time to accompany me when I am collecting, but if not, you could direct me whither to go, and I could bring the results of my work back to you for examination by both of us. It seems to me that without some arrangement of this kind, it would be impossible to do the work completely and thoroughly, and I am not at all anxious to embark upon the project unless I am assured that this can be done. It would be a thousand pities if any personal considerations of this sort were to prevent such important work as we are discussing from being done, and I feel sure that in this you will agree with me. Will you therefore think the matter over—I should suggest your discussing this with your husband—and let me know what conclusions you come to? In the meanwhile, please regard what I have told you of Mr. Aldrich's letter as confidential.

Perhaps you will also tell me whether it would be feasible to explore the district in the late autumn and winter. In England I have always found that period of the year most profitable because it is easier in the evenings to catch people at home. I should like also to know whether the expense would be great and something about the amounts of the gratuities, if any, which you are accustomed to give to the singers.

If the partnership suggestion does not appeal to you, please do not hesitate to make any alternative proposal. With regard to the rights of publication, for instance, it might be a good plan for you to take the American rights and me the English.

Forgive this long letter, give it your careful consideration, and reply as fully as you can and as expeditiously as possible!

P.S. This is a duplicate of a letter written to you ten days ago, now reposing at the bottom of the sea off the coast of Ireland in *SS Arabic*!!

Immediately, September 4th, I acknowledged the letter, pending detailed reply, and sending along the six ballads which he was expecting. To John in New York, I also wrote at length on September 4th, sending along Mr. Sharp's letter for him to share and enclosing my own long letter in answer to Mr. Sharp for him to read and forward if he approved. I suggested that he write Mr. Sharp himself. This he did at once, apparently with pleasure that matched mine, and sent mine along too. They are, I think, of interest in the light of later developments:

[ODC to Mr. Sharp]
September 4, 1915

By now, I trust you have received a letter sent you September 4th, acknowledging your letter of August 25th and enclosing six ballads for which you were so kind as to offer to write the accompaniments. In these days one feels very doubtful about the mails.

No, I did not receive the book on English folk song to which you refer, and I should like very much indeed to have it, for I know nothing of the scientific side of the matter. It was very kind of you to think of it. The other books are of an increasing source of pleasure and satisfaction to me, and I do not see how I could have gotten on without them. The introduction of the first folio is of special interest to me, and, save a few minor details, might be written about these people here.

I am indeed delighted to hear of the probability of your coming to this district. As I said in my other letter, the only real objection that I could see would be in the matter of your health, for the country is very rough, distances are great, and living conditions often hard. I think, however, that Mr. Campbell and I could be of real help to you in alleviating the last situation. There is one other point to consider—the very democratic spirit of the people, which is, I imagine, rather more independent than that of English people of the same class—although, frankly, I know little of the English people. The mountain people are sensitive, proud, and shy, but will do things for you if they like you and feel that you like them. I have never paid them gratuities of any kind, although I can imagine under certain circumstances that it might bring results. Yet, on the whole, I should say that you would have to feel your way very carefully.

I write these difficulties—for I cannot call them objections—in the beginning, for I do not want you to be overpersuaded, by my eagerness to have you come, into situations you did not understand. Except for these points, I should say that you might find the people much like the people among whom you have done your own collecting. Of course a great many of them will have no conception of what England is or of their relationship to her.

Now in the first place, I want to make it clear to you that I in no way have a special right in collecting material from this region. I believe that I was about the first to begin it—at least the first to do anything with the music—but there are a number of other collectors, and the state folklore societies are doing their best to gather up material. I do not need to tell you, I am sure, that all this is being done in a very scattered and unscientific fashion. The collections are usually made without the music, and the folklore societies are generally headed by college professors who depend upon their students to gather and bring to them material from districts where they are teaching or living. Sometimes the music is brought, but more often the words merely. Some of the states have no folklore societies, but you will probably find that here and there people have been gathering up fragments of verse or song that interested them. I think there has been but one effort made to gather any of the singing games of this section, and I am sure that there has been no attempt to preserve the dances. Dancing, indeed, is looked at somewhat askance in the mountains, and to see it done, one must get the confidence of the people and be invited to "frolics," "log rollings," "corn huskings," " 'lasses bilings," "watermelon cuts," and so on, all of which may be accompanied by excessive drinking and even less desirable features. The "furriner," that is, the man from outside the mountains, whether he is from the North or South or from across the water, generally falls in the class of missionary, who necessarily has nothing to do with the occasions I have just mentioned; the commercial traveler; and the revenue officer, any one of whom is regarded with some suspicion. I might say here that most of these festivities take place in the fall and winter; for other reasons, too, the fall and winter are especially good times to get at the people. The roads are good in the fall, but while they are very poor in the winter, and traveling for the investigator is correspondingly hard, for this very reason the people stay more at home and, once harvest is over, are much more ready to give time to singing and storytelling.

Now as to my own part in this matter. As I have written before, I shall be only too happy to cooperate, but when I said that for this coming year and possibly for some years succeeding, I would not be able to do much active work, I was absolutely sincere. Conditions are such that I cannot go into the field for some time, but that would not prevent me from putting you in touch with localities, some of the singers whom I found especially satisfactory, and people living in the mountains who might be able to help you. Indeed it is possible that Mr. Campbell might be able to personally take you to some of these places or introduce you to people who could do this. I have always found it a very great advantage to be introduced—or, as it were, vouched for—by someone known to the people of that locality, preferably by some native of the district.

I want you to understand that I would not for a moment think of your plan as interfering with anything that I may have done in the past, even supposing that sometime in the future I might want to do more collecting; indeed, it would be a distinct advantage to me to work with you. In collecting the songs, I was not considering any possible financial gain or literary prestige. I liked them, knew they were valuable from a scientific point of view, and I hoped that if I could get them published, they would be a real contribution to folklore and that through them attention might be drawn to the mountain situation in such a way as to help the mountain people. One cannot help these people by exploiting their peculiarities and weaknesses, but this would be a legitimate and unobjectionable method of directing attention to them, provided it were done without too minute explanation and description of existing conditions. In other words, my object has been twofold: to preserve the ballads and to help the people. I have always felt that these people were my friends, and I believe that the ballad singers from whom I have gathered material have always felt that I was their friend. I should not be willing to have their confidence violated.

I have never expected to make anything from it in a financial way (and the publishers have seemed to feel this more strongly even than I have). All I have hoped for was to get the songs published in a scientific and attractive manner and to recover eventually any expense to which I had been put in getting the notation corrected and the harmonizing done. Please do not infer from this statement that I absolutely disregard the financial end of matters, for Mr. Campbell and I have to consider this very carefully.

I admit frankly that I should like to have such work as I have done receive what credit may be considered due it, but so little have I considered this matter that I have tried to get together the various collectors throughout this region in order that we might all contribute our work to a common volume, which should be the authority to which all collectors in this section might refer, at least until more collecting was done. In sounding one or two of the people, I met with just the point of which you speak in your letter; the whole matter could not be brought about because of personal and financial considerations and sectional jealousies. I certainly do not mean to let such considerations govern any decision I may make. I want the collecting done, and done by the person most competent to do it; and if I could have wished for a definite result from my work, it would have been to attract to this region just such a person as yourself. Such a study as you would make would be invaluable.

Now as to the work I have done. I may as well explain the whole situation, if you are not already wearied with this long letter. While in the North, I saw Mr. [William Arms] Fisher of Oliver Ditson. He looked over some of my material and professed to be very much interested; asked me to make a selection of from twenty to thirty ballads, have them corrected and harmonized *well,* if possible, and returned to him in the fall, when he would seriously consider them for publication. At this time he told me that you were the only one qualified to write the accompaniments, but asked me not to mention to you what he had said to me. I only do so now that you may not misunderstand my position in the matter. In the short time that I saw you, and under all the circumstances, I did not feel that I had any right to ask you to write those accompaniments, nor to discuss any financial arrangements, especially as you had had no opportunity to look over the material carefully and to decide as to its real worth. Moreover, Mr. Fisher had made no promise of taking the songs, and I realized that it would involve a great deal of expense for me, which I could not afford unless assured of publication. Of course, this matter had nothing to do with the six ballads which were to go to the Fuller sisters, although it would be desirable that they should be included in such a selection.

Now that is just where the situation stands; I have not seen Mr. Fisher again nor had any correspondence with him, nor do I feel in any way bound by any understanding or agreement with him. I feel reasonably sure, however, that he would publish a collection of twenty or more of my ballads if you should write the accompaniments, and if you would care to consider this, I should be glad to make any financial adjustment that would seem fair to you. If, on the other hand, you would prefer not to do this now, but to wait until you have done some collecting yourself here and were able to recheck some of my melodies, I would be glad to delay the matter until we can discuss it more fully. I would say here, too, that I have sent Mr. [Frank] Rabold, at his suggestion, three or four of the melodies to see whether he can do anything in the way of accompaniments.

I will say frankly that it would be a matter of pride to me to have my name linked in partnership with yours, and I appreciate fully the scientific value such a union would place on my contribution. At the same time I should not wish to presume on your generous offer, and I should be glad, while accepting a partnership, to leave any details to what may be determined as fair after you have gauged the value of the work I have done and the assistance given to you by Mr. Campbell and myself in your proposed search and collection of ballads in our southern mountains.

[JCC to Mr. Sharp]
September 15, 1915

A letter from Mrs. Campbell has just brought the good news of the possibility of your return to this country soon to study the ballads of our Southern Highlands. I write at once to assure you of a very warm welcome from both of us and from others interested in the mountain field who, I know, will do everything in their power to further your studies.

I have lived in the mountain country for twenty years and for the past eight years have done much traveling in research work in that section. I feel that it may be possible for me to open many doors to you by accompanying you, should you wish, to certain centers, and at other times by introducing you in other ways to mountain friends.

Mrs. Campbell has an extensive acquaintance in the mountains and with people in and out of the mountains interested in ballads. She has a peculiar genius for making friends, and I feel very sure that her introductions will be of the greatest value.

We are very happy in the prospect of having a little one come to our home in January or February. We are the more happy in that there will thus be filled to some degree a place left vacant by the loss of a little daughter. Though Mrs. Campbell will, therefore, be unable to accompany you, she can give valuable assistance, and I shall be glad, because of her interest and your interest and my own interest in the mountain people, to put myself as far as possible at your service in reaching the best centers and the people best able to further your research.

Mrs. Campbell has asked me to give you some idea as to the expense of such a study as you purpose to make.

In my first year of field service, Mrs. Campbell traveled with me. We spent approximately twenty-five hundred dollars. This, however, was for a whole year's work and included expenditures for long trips into Canada and to sections of our own country far removed from the mountains.

The actual traveling and living expenses in the mountains proper are very low. Away from railroads, one has to travel on horseback or in vehicles. If one hires a horse, the cost will vary from $1.25 to $1.50 a day, depending upon the length of time one wishes to keep the horse. Your own living expenses in some sections would not be over $1.50 a day. The best way in my judgment would be to spend as long as necessary at the best centers. I mean by centers, places in the remote mountain country where church mission boards or other philanthropic organizations have established schools for mountain boys and girls. From such centers the more isolated valleys are accessible. A number of the students at these schools would know some ballads, and their parents many more. Usually the teachers of these schools have the confidence of the whole countryside and could get you into the homes as no one else could. I have a somewhat intimate acquaintance with the teachers at a hundred or more of such centers, and from this number we could make the best selections for your purpose. The living expense at these schools is often as low as three dollars a week. At many of these schools, you would be entertained gladly without cost, although you probably would wish to make some little donation toward the work of the school amounting to what your living expenses would be for the time you were there. It might not be necessary to keep a horse all the time you were at one of these places, inasmuch as you would be able to rent one by the day to reach places not easily accessible on foot. It is a little difficult to estimate the expenses definitely, but I should say that three dollars a day would be a very generous allowance for your expenses while in the more remote part of the mountain country, and five dollars a day a very generous allowance for hotel bills and train travel in those parts of the mountain country covered by railroads.

If you are asked to submit an estimate of the cost, may I suggest your reckoning on a longer time than you may now be contemplating. I feel very sure that after you begin, the field will offer such prospects as to invite a much longer investigation than you may now be contemplating. Possibly, too, you may wish to see some of our college and university professors and presidents and secretaries of folklore societies who have been interested more or less in a study of mountain ballads from a literary or other point of view. Such persons would be located for the most part within the confines, or near the borders, of the highland country. If you should think best to do this, five dollars a day allowance would probably be ample for this purpose. After having made a generous estimate of expenses on this basis, I have generally found it wise to allow a considerable sum in addition for possible deviations from the original plan. I am estimating merely on the basis of expenditures in the mountain country and am not taking into account your expenditures from England and in the cities of America which you may wish to visit in the interests of the study. These expenses, I feel, you will know better than I.

It would give us much pleasure to have you come directly to Asheville; in fact, this would be by all means the best thing to do in order to plan the campaign. Asheville, North Carolina, is in the Southern Highland region and is a strategical mountain point. My office is located there because of this fact. Thirty dollars would be ample allowance for railroad travel, including sleeping car and dining car rates, from New York City to Asheville. You could get a sleeping car at New York which would take you right through.

Of course, we are regarding this whole matter as confidential and shall so regard it until it is fully determined that you are to come.

I trust that you will call upon me for any service that I can render. It would give me much pleasure to send you a letter of introduction to my superior officer, Mr. John M. Glenn of New York City, general manager of the Russell Sage Foundation, and letters to other friends in New York who might be of some assistance to you.

In closing, I would express my appreciation of your generous offer to Mrs. Campbell. She has done a good bit of work—in fact, she has been a pioneer in this country in this work—and I naturally would be much pleased to have her work receive the recognition it would receive were she associated with you. As to the business details, they will not stand in the way. We are, first of all, interested in this work, and we are very happy in the thought that there soon will be enlisted in the field that has claimed so many of the best years of our lives, your interest and ability.

We hope to hear soon of a definite decision and, soon after, to see you in person.

The trip north proved satisfactory on all counts. John had a series of conferences in New York and in Boston which were worthwhile and helpful. His Asheville doctor had wanted a consultation with a physician in New York in regard to his frequent attacks of "acute indigestion," and this he was able to accomplish. Thereafter, instead of going on to Rochester, New York, with Mr. Glenn to attend a meeting of the American Public Health Association, where he had planned talks with Red Cross officials and others about the need of nursing in rural mountain areas, he decided to heed medical advice and relax for a few days. A visit to his dear and old friend of college days, Professor Carl Kelsey of Wharton School, University of Pennsylvania, on his farm in Mendenhall, seems to have brought both much pleasure in talk of old times and discussion of present farm problems. The two continued with spicy correspondence about John's attempt to meet Carl's need of farm help by getting an unemployed former student of his from the Georgia mountains to try a Pennsylvania farm. This proved brief because of the lad's overpowering homesickness.

John returned to Asheville on September 23rd, feeling rested and reassured, though realistic about his condition and limitations. Mr. Glenn had written to ask, and on September 29th he reported the specialist's opinion as given to him:

I have delayed writing you more in detail about the conference with Dr. J—— until his report to Dr. D—— should be received—to check my recollection of what he told me personally. I had a long interview with Dr. D—— yesterday.

"Dr. D—— had received from Dr. J—— a lengthy letter and a minute report of the examination. My blood pressure is high, but my organs seem to be in good condition. Dr. D—— said that while Dr. J—— did not say so, my case appeared to be one of the somewhat rare cases of individuals who have a high blood pressure without an apparent definite cause and with a hardening of the blood vessels. Dr. D—— was much pleased to find that Dr. J——'s diagnosis confirmed his own in all particulars. It was in large part because Dr. D—— found me so normal in other regards but with a high blood pressure, that he wished to have Dr. J's expert opinion. Dr. D—— had been giving me an iodide of some sort as a precautionary measure, which Dr. J—— thought it unnecessary to give, at least for the present.

They both felt that my present line of work was beneficial; advised not staying at the desk too long and not getting overtired. Dr. J—— said that altitude—except very high altitude—did not affect blood pressure, so that it would not be necessary for me to leave the mountains. They both felt that a little more care needed to be taken in high altitudes in the matter of exercise, and that I would be a bit more comfortable at sea level. While holding this view as to altitude, they both felt that it would be wise to take a vacation of a month or two each year at sea level, preferably at the shore. I told Dr. J—— that I had been accustomed to go to Nantucket in past years, and he thought that was a very suitable place for me.

I put the question directly to Dr. D—— as to the possibility of my engaging in work actively for the future, and both Dr. D—— and Dr. J—— feel that with care I can go on for a number of years. I asked Dr. D—— if I might count on ten years more of activity, and he said that I could count on that and then we could take account of stock for the future. I am to continue to go to Dr. D—— once or twice a month to have him keep a general oversight and to observe any possible changes.

Both Mrs. Campbell and I are much encouraged and pleased over the results. I have not been accustomed to guard myself, and watchfulness on my part will probably be hard at first, and irksome. I had thought that possibly it might be necessary to give up my work and to leave the mountain country, and I shall be very glad indeed to try to accommodate myself to conditions in order to remain where my chief interests are.

Now came two letters from Mr. Sharp in England, the first answering mine and the second replying to John's written to him from New York:

[Mr. Sharp to ODC]
September 27, 1915

Your two letters have now reached me, together with the six ballads. I am moving house this week, so please address me in the future to 27 Church Row, Hampstead, London, N.W. I may have told you this before, but I am not sure.

I have read your long letter very carefully, and I think I understand how the matter stands. I should probably find your singers a little different from the peasants in this country, but even so, I do not think that I should find much difficulty in getting on with them and persuading them to sing. Our peasants are by no means all of one type in this country; for instance, in those parts where they are not wage earners but are their own masters, they display a much more independent spirit. I expect that the people in your part are more like these than the normal agricultural laborer who has worked all his days for hire.

I feel sure, too, that were I to see you and have an hour's talk with you, we should very soon come to a working arrangement, probably on the partnership line which I suggested when I last wrote. Otherwise I should not presume to recheck your work or to ravage your preserves. The ballads that you have sent me are most tantalizing; and I'm sure that if you could sing them to me, I should understand at once how they go and how they should be written down—I am referring to the tunes only, of course. But as they stand, they are incomprehensible to me. I hate to have to say this, for it sounds very presumptuous and I do not want to dampen your enthusiasm nor to discourage you in any way from continuing the work. But from experience I know the extreme difficulty of noting correctly these very difficult tunes irregular in time, curious in rhythm, and cast in unusual modes. In many cases, I can make a shrewd guess of the way in which certain phrases should be sung because I know the kind of mistakes which novices usually make; but in other cases, although I am practically certain that there is some error in your notation, I cannot be sure of its precise nature. In the circumstances, therefore, I hesitate to harmonize any one of them, for there is not a single one without some difficult point of the nature above mentioned. What a pity it is that we live so far away from each other!

All of this makes me keener than ever to come out and put to good use my knowledge and experience. Like you, my enthusiasm is wholly for the subject itself. I am not out to make money, although, like you, I cannot afford to neglect that side of the question altogether. I have a wife and a family of four children dependent upon me, and I am a poor man, although I have been writing, publishing, and selling a vast number of books during the last fifteen years. Pioneers rarely become rich men, but then they have many compensations; for it is no small pleasure to have taken a hand in preserving such a fine peasant art as folksinging or folk dancing. I look upon it as a great privilege to have been able to do work of this kind, because I feel that posterity will need the primitive songs and ballads to keep their two arts of music and dance real, sincere, and pure. And I also realize that this is one of the most important duties of the present generation; for if the work is not to be done now, it can never be done at all. I have only published a very small percentage of the songs, dances, etc. that I have recovered, so that the greater part of the work of my collection will have to be done by those who come after me. I have not assimilated a twentieth part of the tunes written down in my manuscripts, all of which I have bequeathed in my will, at their request, to the authorities of my college, Clare College, Cambridge. I have to be content, therefore, with a very modest income; but I must have something to live upon, so that it will be impossible for me to come out and work with you unless I can get substantial help from the Carnegie Trust or some other public authority. In confidence I may tell you that I think it is very possible that the Carnegie Committee will view my application favorably—

Mr. Richard Aldrich (musical critic of the *New York Times*), who is placing my application before the trust, having written very encouragingly to me last mail.

I think I told you that my wife has recently had a very serious attack of illness and that she must be an invalid for some time to come. I could not possibly leave England while she lies as she does now, but if things go as I have every reason to believe they will, I think I ought to be able to get away in January next. I mentioned to Mr. Aldrich the great part that you had played in this matter, and I told him that I could not undertake the work except with your ungrudging approval. I am now writing to him by this mail to say that I am pretty sure that I can come to some satisfactory arrangement with you and that he may therefore regard that difficulty as good as removed. I feel that your letter justifies me in saying this much, but if you think I am overly sanguine in my interpretation of your wishes, please let me know at once.

I am sending you by this mail my book on English folk song. It was written several years ago, but the theories that I then enunciated are the theories which further experience has only served to strengthen—in the main at any rate.

If you can find among your collection any tunes which you feel pretty certain are noted quite clearly, please send them to me, for I should very much like to harmonize some of them for you. I know Mr. Fisher of Oliver Ditson's, and I am quite sure there would not be the slightest difficulty in getting that firm to publish a selection of ballads collected by you and me. As a matter of fact, I am now doing a volume of English folk songs for them.

[Mr. Sharp to JCC]
Hampstead, London
September 29, 1915

Your long and extremely interesting letter of the 15th inst. reached me yesterday, a few minutes after I had mailed a letter to Mrs. Campbell in reply to one which I had just received from her. Your letter and that of your wife place me in possession of all the facts that I wanted. It is clear to me that your point of view with regard to the collection of these ballads is identical with mine. I need not expand this point, for I have written very freely and fully to Mrs. Campbell in my last letter, which no doubt you will see. Your estimate of the probable expense is very clear and concise in the circumstances and tells me just what I wanted to know. Whether the Carnegie Trust is able, and will prove willing, to make me an adequate grant remains to be seen. Mr. Richard Aldrich, musical critic of the *New York Times,* who is very keen about the matter, has approached the trust on my behalf. He tells me that Dr. [Henry S.] Pritchett, the chairman of the committee, views the question very favorably; the matter has not yet been placed before his committee but will be put before them at their first meeting, which I understand is to take place early next month. Mr. Aldrich knows the position very well—he happened to be in the house when Mrs. Campbell called upon me at Lincoln. I cannot help thinking that it would be a very good thing if you and he could meet and exchange views. I do not know if you would care to do this, but I am writing by this mail to Mr. Aldrich and making the suggestion.

Will you allow me in conclusion to thank you most cordially for the expressions of goodwill and kindness and promise of help which you and Mrs. Campbell have so freely and generously made? Whatever may be the outcome of this particular business, I hope, on my return to America, to thank you and Mrs. Campbell personally for all the trouble that you have taken on my behalf.

After this, we could do nothing on the ballad matter but await next developments. John had written Mr. Sharp that fall was usually the favorable season for taking mountain trips, especially trips in which connections could be made with various institutions and people, and work forwarded in which he was interested. Early in October, Dr. [W. E.] Finley, supervisor of the country church work of the Presbyterian Church, USA, in the French Broad Presbytery, invited [John] to make visits to a number of stations in the Allanstand, North Carolina, area, where meetings would be arranged, beginning with a community fair. John arranged that Mr. and Mrs. Rutherford P. Hayes of Asheville and Mrs. Louise Perry, a physician on the North Carolina Committee for the Prevention of Blindness, should go along with him, hoping to increase the interest of all three in the farming and health problems in the mountain region of their state. Farming experts from the state and the county demonstrator were to meet them on the circuit planned by Dr. Finley: Allanstand, Cedar Creek, Greenville, by wagon and horseback. This proved a well-carried-out and wellreceived program, all of the invited guests having taken active part in it.

A visit to a Seventh-Day Adventist School followed, with an invitation to address their conference at Hickory, North Carolina, in December. On the 22nd of October, there was a journey to Knoxville, where John spoke at the meeting of the Tennessee Synod of the Presbyterian Church. In the same month he made two more visits, writing Mr. Glenn:

I am going away tomorrow (October 27th) or the next day to Burnsville, North Carolina, to visit one of Mrs. Cyrus McCormack's mountain schools, and next week I shall probably take another trip for a few days into western North Carolina. Then we are going to settle down and compile the rich material we have gathered, following out the instructions given me at the Southern Mountain Workers' Conference, namely, to issue a booklet setting forth the needs of the mountain country and the qualifications for mountain workers and leaders as viewed by the various denominational officials and leaders on the field.

We are receiving a splendid response, and some letters are most inspiring. I have been especially pleased with the letters received from Mr. [George P.] Mayo and Archdeacon [Frank B.] Wentworth of Winchester, Kentucky. They are most liberal in their view and comprehensive in their grasp of the needs.

In his acknowledgment of receipt of John's annual report to the Foundation, and of the foregoing letter, Mr. Glenn commented: "If you succeed in getting the pamphlets which you think of written, I will try to take care of them out of the publications budget. I am satisfied, however, that if you wish to get any pamphlets written, you have got to make up your mind to devote yourself to them for a given time, and not let visitors or trips interfere. This requires much resolution, but I think in the long run it will pay both for you and for your clients."

From a new quarter came a request to John, this time to make an address at the meeting of the Southern Conference for Education and Industry early in 1916. Mr. A. P. Bourland, the executive secretary, wrote enclosing a copy of a letter he had written to ask Mr. William Chauncy Langdon to speak on pageantry as a possibility for recreation and education in the mountains and inviting John to speak on ballads. This seemed timely to both of us. John wrote Mr. Glenn:

I send herein a copy of a letter of Dr. Bourland's to Mr. Langdon and also a copy of Dr. Bourland's letter to me. At present writing, I think it may be wise for me to attend this meeting and speak as Dr. Bourland wishes, for I feel the pageant and ballad will be splendid things for mountain communities if a systematic effort is made to conserve the old and stimulate the new through them. I shall accept tentatively; at any rate, I can give them assistance in framing a program. If Mr. Sharp should be here at that time, it would be a fine thing to get him. I am sending also a letter I recently received from Mr. Sharp. I hope very much that the plan will go through. If you should feel free to further the matter by your own approval expressed to Mr. Aldrich or Dr. Pritchett, it would be appreciated.

The reply came at once:

With reference to the invitation from Mr. Bourland to attend the Southern Conference next year and speak on ballads, I think it is well, as you say, to accept tentatively and give them all the assistance you can in forming a program. If you could get someone like Mr. Sharp or Professor Kittredge who is thoroughly posted on this kind of literature and the benefits of publishing it to address the conference, it would probably be better than attempting to do it yourself.

I will try to get in touch with Mr. Aldrich next week and find out just what he has done.

Trips and visitors were not the real obstacles to pamphlet writing, of course. John's eager, restless mind lighting on new, unexplored avenues of help for the mountains drove him ever onward to new fields. Among other tentative plans he had been considering was that of possible cooperation between the new Town and Country Nursing Service of the Red Cross, of which Miss Fannie F. Clement was superintendent, and the Country Life Department of the Presbyterian Church, USA, headed by Dr. Warren H. Wilson, by which trained public health nurses might be made available to certain remote areas. The Presbyterians had been getting interested, and a nurse was now working in the Laurel field. The difficulties following were of many sorts, which brought harried visitors to John's office for help and sent him out to the field to try to reconcile elements in the situation. Miss [Fannie] Clement, with whom he felt well acquainted through our recent journeys together through mountains, wrote frankly of the rising problems. He replied to her on November 12th:

I have just received your letter of November 9th and am much concerned over it. A great deal of the trouble arises from differences in personality, I think, and probably there is much to be said on both sides. Recently, at the Presbyterian Synod Meeting in Knoxville, I had an interview with Dr. Wilson, Miss Taft, Miss Goodrich, and Dr. Finley. I pointed out some of the large rural movements in which they might become leaders through a full cooperation with the Town and Country Nursing Service. Having in mind my last interview with you, I assured them that the Town and Country Nursing Service could provide a Red Cross Nurse fitted to meet any need peculiar to their field, but that it was absolutely essential at the beginning to have a very clear and definite understanding on both sides. I suggested to them, as you once suggested to me . . . that they find the nurse who would fit into their field—a nurse whose qualifications would be those required by the Red Cross, and that she then become a Red Cross nurse.

I realize somewhat the difficult task you are undertaking, of placing nurses of high character and high grade in the mountain field when there is so great a demand for them elsewhere at much better pay, and I do hope you will not grow discouraged. I do not know of a task more disheartening than to give of one's best to meet a very apparent need of helping a people who themselves do not seem to appreciate the need or the efforts made to meet it. . . . You and I are engaged in a very difficult kind of pioneer work—the work of removing obstacles in order to promote cooperation. The greatest need that I see in all social work is this need of cooperation between social agencies, and a requisite for success in cooperation is understanding and acquaintance.

I have to whistle pretty resolutely sometimes to keep up my own courage. One of my greatest tasks is to endeavor to convince really good Christian people that the only things for which their agencies ought to work in the mountains—and elsewhere—are the very broad Christian principles that apply to all humanity and that increase in church membership, and denominational recognition for work done, are legitimate as "by-products" only. But these "by-products" do loom large sometimes in the eyes of those furthering denominational and institutional work. . . .

There are large possibilities before the Town and Country Nursing Service that I long to have realized for the sake of the mountain people, as well as for the sake of isolated people everywhere. . . . I do hope, Miss Clement, that you can come down and hold a conference with all concerned, that a sound basis may be reached for a new attempt in the light of this first experience. The possibilities are so great that they must not be wrecked by friction growing out of jarring personalities on the field, misfits, initial mistakes, or lack of clear understanding. Do come this way. Mrs. Campbell joins me most earnestly in this wish.

Kindest regards and best wishes, with the deepest sympathy for you in your perplexities—a sympathy which grows out of many similar experiences.

Apparently he followed this up with a visit to the Presbyterian work in Burnsville, North Carolina, for he writes a letter of thanks to Mrs. T. U. Chesebrough, at the Stanley McCormick School, December 8, 1915:

I arrived home last night at midnight after quite an adventurous trip. We killed a calf and our train was wrecked. Fortunately the brakeman, whom we dug out from under the car of lumber, did not seem to be seriously hurt. We missed connections for Marion, so I came by way of Johnson City.

It was all an adventure, and I had a very pleasant time in Burnsville. Mrs. Campbell would express with me her sincere thanks for the courtesy and kindness which made my visit with you and Mr. Chesebrough so pleasant.

In the intervals between trips, John had been studying the returns from his inquiry as to the needs of the mountain area which had come in over the past months. Of this collection he wrote Mr. Glenn:

We have been working somewhat strenuously in securing and compiling information from persons acquainted with mountain conditions and needs, for publication in a booklet to be issued under the auspices of the Southern Mountain Workers' Conference. You may recall that I, as chairman of the Executive Committee, was empowered by the conference to collect such data. I have now a mass of splendid material from the leaders in the mountain schools, bishops and superintendents of denominational boards, and field supervisors, and am now receiving some excellent letters from state superintendents of education, superintendents of secondary education, presidents of Normal schools, and from other secular educational institutions in or near the mountains. I am also securing information from officials of the state boards of health and from county physicians or health officers in the mountains.

We shall have a publication, therefore, eminently worthwhile. Thinking you may be interested in some of these letters, I am sending you copies of some from Virginia, namely, one from Mr. [R. C.] Stearnes, state superintendent of education, another from Mr. [John P.] McConnell of the State Normal School for Women at East Radford—a man who knows the mountains thoroughly—and letters from President J. G. Eggleston of the Virginia Polytechnic Institute, Archdeacon [F. W.] Neve, and Mr. Mayo. I have a fine letter also from Kentucky from Archdeacon [F. B.]Wentworth. I am much pleased that my request is receiving such generous and helpful response. A book such as we purpose to issue should become a guide, inasmuch as so many southern leaders have expressed themselves so freely and fully. I feel that much good will be done and very little harm.

The preparation of this material for publication will take some time, as well as preparation of other material from this division itself for submission to you for publication as soon as the conference booklet is well advanced. I shall be very busy thereafter in getting ready for our next conference in March or April and in helping with the program for the Southern Conference for Education and Industry in New Orleans, so I shall not wish to take other than necessary journeys.

At this time came two invitations to speak. The first was from Dr. Warren H. Wilson, who came to Asheville following his letter to urge John to address the Interdenominational Home Missions Council of Church Board Secretaries meeting on January 13th in New York, "having the disposition, I am told, of some thirty millions for missionary work." The other was from Miss Belle H. Bennett of Richmond, Kentucky, asking that he speak before the joint Council of Northern and Southern Presbyterian Women's Boards, to be held the week before in Atlanta. Both John and Mr. Glenn felt these important to undertake. As John wrote, "should I accept the invitation to speak to the Men's Council a week later, I shall have touched practically all the denominations and boards doing work among the mountaineers."

A cause for which John never failed to speak whenever an opportunity presented itself was that of a broad Christianity as against a narrow denominationalism. Dr. Warren Wilson had sent him a copy of his pamphlet *Second Missionary Adventure,* which he acknowledged, on December 11th, with real enthusiasm:

I have read with deepest interest *The Second Missionary Adventure,* which you were so kind as to send me and for which I thank you most sincerely. I found it so gripping and stimulating that I put other things aside and read it at the office.

You have struck the right note, and I feel that those who control our missionary enterprises, as well as those upon the field, will be greatly helped by this book. I am happy in the thought that I may be classed as one of the later missionary adventurers and am grateful to you for helping me to classify myself. "They are not sure they are in the right" covers my case, but there are some things that I feel so sure about that I cannot let go of them until otherwise convinced. I am counting on you as one of the men to bring about what I feel must come if Protestantism is not to fail— a much closer approach to union among Protestant bodies than now exists and much less emphasis upon denominational names. I sometimes fear that some of our Protestant denominations are Protestant in theory only and anti-Protestant in practice. For myself, I much prefer the authority of the pope and of the Roman Catholic Church, which has some historical continuity and consistency, rather than the popery of some Protestantism.

Warren Wilson replied, December 13th, by return mail:

Thank you very much for *those kind words* about my Oberlin address. It has been a curious adventure itself. I wrote it on a train traveling between Montana and Chicago in a hurry, being asked at the last minute to speak in Oberlin when a man I had recommended could not do so. I think it fell perfectly flat when it was read at the college commencement, but it has been so interesting to some persons that they got it published, and it was sent to you by Miss Taft. I feel very deeply the things that I said in that address, and think that the principles there stated are vital.

I do not know what to say about denominationalism as you speak of it. I agree with your point of view in your letter. I am inclined to think that in French Broad Presbytery, however, we ought to build Presbyterian churches; that is, I think we need to work for our own denomination as the organized vehicle of the spirit that you express in your letter. There is no alternative except to organize union or independent churches; and these do not succeed. Furthermore, I think they would be less acceptable to the mountain people than any one of the chief denominational names.

As I have gone over our work, I believe we have made a mistake in saying all the time, "We are not working for the Presbyterian Church," partly because nobody believes that such is the case—such a statement is not taken sincerely by the hearers—and partly because it ought not to be true. We ought to make that organization a vehicle of the whole Christian, educational, and humanitarian message. If we have an organization at all, it must have its particular leaders, meeting places, collection of funds and expenditure of funds, and responsible, clearly defined way of working. I believe we have not worked down there in a sufficient degree for the Presbyterian organization, and this would mean, of course, the Presbyterian tradition. There is danger in doing so, but there seems to be a greater danger in denominational self-effacement. The thing I want to do is to enlarge the denomination until it shall be as big as the service of Christ would be if he were there to render it. What do you think about this? I would be glad to have you write me frankly, chiefly because I think you are the very man who must guide us doing such a thing as this and keep us both from narrowness on the one side, and from a dough-faced, meaningless neutrality on the other.

I am sending you a copy of the report of the Home Missions Council of last year. I have just received word this morning to the following effect:

"The three sub-topics are:

1. Mountain and Rural Fields of the South.
2. Village and Open Country Fields of the East and Middle West.
3. Rural Work in Village and Open Country of the Far West.

You will be the speaker on "Mountain and Rural Fields of the South." As we have two hours for the treatment of these three themes and a report, I think that you ought to speak between twenty and thirty minutes. Do not hesitate to use thirty if you think best. Your presence in this annual meeting will be of great help, because there will be many phases of this work in which you can take part. The secretaries usually sit right through the three days with surprising solidity and take in everything that comes along, and we want you to sit with us just as many hours as you can give.

John could not let this pass. On December 21st he wrote to Dr. Wilson:

I am much interested in your letter of December 13th and hope we may have a long conference at some time over the questions raised. There are so many considerations forming the background that time forbids a full discussion, but, in reply to your inquiry, the following considerations suggest themselves at random.

Ignore it if we will, the fact remains that in the mountains, both from preventable and nonpreventable causes, many of the agencies now working there are still regarded as "foreign," and yet despite this, and the additional fact that the South is somewhat strong on denominationalism, there is yet a broad Christian influence apparent at times that tends to minimize denominationalism and sectionalism.

From my present light, I think it would be a serious mistake for you to emphasize in any marked way the building up of the Presbyterian Church in the French Broad Presbytery. All the work of Packard and LeFevre would then be lowered in the minds of the people to a Presbyterian mission basis—if I may use "lowered" in this connection without being misunderstood—instead of kept up to a broad humanitarian basis.

The mistakes that many of the churches have made in the mountains and in other rural sections have come through sending too many cheap men to the country and in not maintaining the too few good men who have gone. Furthermore, these men have been forced to seek as much of self-support on the field as possible, even before they were well acquainted, bringing to the minds of the mountain people—naturally suspicious of outside influences and unaccustomed to a salaried ministry—the thought that a "foreign" denomination was trying to push itself into a field naturally belonging to the so-called native denominations, in an effort to displace them. If you will place in the mountain field more well-trained, whole-souled, broad-minded ministers, who show they are Christians first and Presbyterians only secondarily, and keep them there, the Presbyterian Church will grow.

If you can teach your constituency in the North not to try to measure spiritual results by means of missionary statistics setting forth how much money we raised on the field (much of it from nonnative sources, i.e., from teachers and workers) or how many were added to the church (regardless of the fact that some ought not to have been added) and to be willing first of all to get people into the Kingdom, even though that may mean making them better Baptists or Methodists rather than joining the Presbyterian Church, your church will grow greatly in influence, though at first it may grow slowly in numbers.

The Baptist and Methodist Churches in the mountains met a real spiritual need in earlier days, when some other denominations preferred to centralize their work in what seemed to be strategic centers. The denominations first mentioned—especially the Baptist—continuing to try to meet the urgent spiritual needs of frontier folk, and their successors—outlying rural people—have reaped their just reward. This reward is evidenced in numbers and in a loyal allegiance, which still claims some unnecessary things which sprang from pioneer and extreme democratic conditions and from a ministry, full of zeal, interpreting the scriptures literally and unaided by the training of schools.

Through long association, many of the unnecessary things have grown very precious to those belonging to these "native" churches. There is need there, as in other churches, of continued instruction to impress the fact that Christianity, if it is to be spiritual, must be ethical. There is there, just as elsewhere, too much emphasis upon the ecclesiastical, the ceremonial, and the dogmatic.

The South has not had the educational advantages of the North; this is especially true in rural sections. The South is, and will be for many years to come, distinctly rural, and the denominations that succeeded so well in pioneer days must await the laying of certain educational foundations before they can make themselves strong in numbers. These denominations that I have called "pioneer" are now recognizing the need of a broader education for their people, and if the so-called broadly educated denominations that lost out in pioneer days are not broad and liberal in educational, ecclesiastical, and spiritual matters, they will lose out again, and the broadened "pioneer" churches of the old days will, with others who rise to the occasion, be the pioneers of the better day ahead. Spiritualized democracy in church matters is going to win the South, not selective and exclusive aristocracy.

We Presbyterians and Congregationalists, not to mention others, tend to be just a little too exclusive. Your exclusiveness appears to me to come from an overemphasis of Presbyterian traditions; our exclusiveness—democrats as we claim to be—from too much pride in a so-called broad education which tends to welcome any straying heresy as a long-lost truth, if its phraseology sounds philosophical, and consequently learned. We have got to unbend. There is in the South an increasing number of people—many of them unlettered—coming to feel that emphasis on denominational ways and means, traditions, and history, is not essential to spiritual welfare. These and other literate and illiterate thinkers may be gathered into the church that emphasizes the things of common agreement and minimizes the denominational unessentials, not merely in word but in act. Your church will fail of winning these influential ones if you emphasize the unessential, namely, traditions that are peculiarly Presbyterian, and Presbyterian ways and means of doing things.

There ought to be, and is, some way of making Christians through organizations without having the organization, polity, etc., stumbling stones. The Presbyterian Church has been a leader during the last three decades in educational work for the mountaineer. Had it been more concerned to keep strong ministers in the field, and to prevent the friction between principals of schools and pastors on the field, your churches would have been more numerous and influential. I would not have the statement given too wide application, but I feel that if I tell you what you want to know, I must say that if some of the influential workers on the field—and I mean influential—had been less provincial religiously, the church as a church would be stronger today in the mountains. It is too great a church to be provincial. If the attitude of the few should come to be the policy of the organization, you may as well go out of business so far as your church work is concerned, for the work that you are doing, or propose to do, would then be regarded by the people for whom you are working as a bait merely, sprinkled along the way to "toll" them into the Presbyterian trap.

What I have said of denominations would apply equally to union churches. Our workers from the North, whoever they be, must not let their loyalty to the ecclesiastical company in which they are enlisted stand in the way of their full allegiance to the Captain of the Host, and they must be big enough and wise enough to take the ways by which the native people express themselves religiously, even if these be very different from their own, and beautify them and make them deeply significant rather than displace them by ways foreign, or seek to have the people themselves displace them, through argument or discussion in the guise of sermons tending to show that "foreign" ways are better than "native" ways. Too many of us in the past have come south with the intention, subconsciously held, of northernizing the southerner and of Presbyterianizing or Congregationalizing or otherwise-izing those naturally Baptists and Methodists. Our business should be to Christianize and Americanize, and I feel strongly that we ourselves are not Christianized and Americanized if we cannot get rid of a number of sectional and denominational things that have been fastened upon us by a former environment and take on ourselves some of the good things of the environment in which we work. I admit that this is not easy, and the way is not altogether clear, but I know it can be done, and I know there is a way.

I do not know that the union church is a solution; my impression is, however, that the union church movement is growing. If my memory serves me aright, Mr. [Henry] Israel of the YMCA International Committee told me a few years ago that there was an increasing demand upon his organization to supply ministers for union churches. The demand is significant even if the churches fail. Any evangelical or union church would succeed, at least locally, I feel, if properly manned and sustained, but the church with an organization back of it has many distinct advantages, and if "our way" is not too evident, and "your way" more often welcomed; and denominational names and traditions, which in and of themselves necessarily express the divisive things, are relegated more to the background, "foreign" denominations in the mountains will succeed more than they have, because they are getting away from denominational bypaths into the highway of universal Christianity.

It is "up to" Protestantism to "make through some union in diversity," or to acknowledge defeat; then the only hope will be through an enlightened Catholicism or a new "Reformation" with Christian service more clearly defined.

There is no need for me to tell you how genuinely I value the work of the Presbyterian Church in the mountains; I value it because of the splendid educational work it has done and is doing, under the Women's Board, and the new promise through the work of your department. It is dear to me as the church of my childhood and early youth. Some of my most tender memories and many of the most helpful influences of my life today have come from association with it. Whatever it does in the mountains or elsewhere is of concern to me, and I view with a feeling akin to sorrow any tendency on its part to emphasize denominational and divisive things, especially in the mountains, where such things have been, and still are, too much emphasized by some who have not the educational background of the Presbyterians. Your church knows, or should know, better. If we are to have provincialism, let us have a native and not an imported variety.

I hope to see the dawn of that day when there will be no Northern nor Southern Presbyterian churches, and when influential members of the church of my childhood will never again raise the question whether one who leans forward toward Calvinism can possibly fall backward and slide like a Methodist if he wants to, and when the efficacy of baptism will be measured not by the amount of water or method of application, but by the Spirit.

There is some argument of "foreign" ways and means, perhaps, on the basis of having things done in decency and in order, but decency and order may spell disaster to spontaneity and noble impulse. I have gone into some houses very orderly and decent, without a speck of dust visible and not a thing out of place, which were not homes; I have been in other houses where dust and cobwebs were evident, and the many babies on the floor and chairs upturned and toys scattered everywhere made walking precarious, but which were homes because love abounded. I could cite cases somewhat similar of churches in the mountains.

Let me say in conclusion what I have said earlier: find the right man and then sustain him. By "sustaining" I not mean merely financial support, important as that is, but sustain him by letting him feel that he has a man's job, recognized as a man's job by those supporting him and giving him [the feeling] that he is an ambassador of the Most High, not merely an agent of a church whose officers and constituency would measure success by petty standards. I know some would regard me as advocating impractical views, but they are not impractical. Such views are made to appear so only by the arguments used by a constituency fed on missionary thrills, unconsciously demanding more thrills, even at the cost of truth, who demand some evidence, even if it be poor, of how much good they are doing, despite their Master's command not to let the left hand know what the right hand is doing.

Some, too, would probably think me harsh in these statements, but I feel that I can write you freely some convictions that have grown out of long years of experience in the mountains—an experience which causes me to feel that the chief obstacles to Christian progress in the mountains are not so much on the field itself, but are laid by those who support missionary work and who are unable to put themselves, in imagination, in the place of those for whom the work is being done. Lacking this sympathetic understanding, they cannot allow things to be done for others as they would have others do for them, were conditions reversed. It is human, perhaps, to want to say "Lo here" and "Lo there," and to be doubtful of the invisible, intangible things of the Spirit, but if large things are ever to be done for the Kingdom, we must get rid of this human frailty.

I hope, more than I can tell you, that you will be allowed to develop your mountain and rural work on a broad religious basis, supported by a constituency willing to give all the glory to the One to whom it properly belongs; and if, as is perhaps natural and unavoidable, they want some evidence of influence and growth, that they will be willing to rely upon the statement of a trustworthy representative whom they might send to the field to investigate, rather than on printed statistics which belittle the work and injure the influence of the worker on the field. If this can be done, and I believe it can, your work in example and influence will be a stirring promise of spiritual redemption for the rural highlands and rural America.

I have written you from my heart, and I hope that I have not wearied you by the length of this letter.

Word from Mr. Sharp, sent December 20th from London, did not come until after Christmas, and then it brought both disappointing and encouraging news:

I have just heard from Mr. Aldrich that the Committee of the Carnegie Trust have definitely decided *not* to give me any assistance in the matter of the ballad collecting in your neighborhood. This is, of course, a surprise as well as a disappointment to me and also to Mr. Aldrich. But there it is, and one must make the best of it. I do not feel at all inclined to drop the matter on this account if I can possibly help it; for I feel that the work must be done somehow or other at all hazards.

My friend Mrs. Storrow wrote to me the other day and advised me very strongly to come out and continue the work which I started last spring, and she seems to think that I might be able to make it profitable. I think it is very likely that I shall take her advice and come out in the course of the next few weeks. If I do this, and am at all successful, I could probably afford to spend a month or two prospecting in your district toward the end of my stay. In any case, I could meet you and discuss the matter much more closely than we have been able to do by letter. As soon as my plans mature, I will let you know. There is practically nothing of a profitable nature for me to do here.

I dispatched a week ago the MS. of the book of one hundred ballads which I think I told you I was doing for Oliver Ditson's. This book will, I think, interest you very much, for it contains a good many songs and ballads which I have already published, revised, and collated with material which I have collected since their original publication, together with several that have not yet been published. The volume is to form one of the Musician's Series.

With kind regards to you and Mr. Campbell and with best wishes for the New Year.

Mr. Aldrich had written to Mr. Glenn of his regret at this decision of the Carnegie Trust. Together John and he were already trying to interest three other persons in Mr. Sharp's research in the ballad field when the above letter arrived. This proved of no immediate avail, but we all three looked forward expectantly to his coming, nevertheless.

The two addresses John had been asked to give took him first south and then north: "The Future of the Church School in the Southern Highlands," for the Council of Women for Home Missions to Atlanta, Georgia, January 6, 1916; and "Rural Mountain Fields in the South" for the Home Missions Council to New York City, January 13, 1916. Both Mrs. F. S. Bennett and Dr. Wilson acknowledged the second. Mrs. Bennett wrote John:

You hurried away so on last Tuesday that it was not possible for me to find an opportunity to express to you my appreciation of your coming to us, and of the words that you spoke at that time.

It certainly means a tremendous forward step in missions when we all get together in this way, and that it is not only an interdenominational mingling, but a mingling of undenominational bodies with denominational. We not only appreciated your coming, but it meant much to us to have the appreciation of the work of the past years expressed by you and to feel that your guidance in new movements for the future was an aid that could be called upon at any time.

Dr. Wilson wrote Mr. Glenn on January 18th:

The address of Mr. John Campbell at the Home Missions Council was deeply appreciated, and I wish to thank you on behalf of our committee for lending us his services and his expert knowledge.

The report of the Home Missions Council publishes brief outlines of the addresses, and they have asked Mr. Campbell for a part of his address. I wonder if it would be possible for the Russell Sage Foundation to publish Mr. Campbell's address in a pamphlet which could be distributed. I would be glad to aid in its distribution, and I think it would be of great value. The things he said were very carefully weighed, and they are the result of years of study and experience. They were enjoyed at the time, but their value will depend upon careful reflection and study by the secretaries present. It would seem to me that this address, therefore, might well be published as a separate pamphlet in order that it may be distributed and used in a way commensurate with its value.

Mr. Glenn replied to Dr. Wilson the next day:

Thank you very much for your kind note about Mr. Campbell's paper. I am hoping that both the paper read at the Home Missions Council and the one read before the Women's Council may soon be put into pamphlet form. You will of course receive some copies as soon as they are printed, and we shall be very happy to have your cooperation in making them as widely useful as possible.

I was glad to hear your paper on the Home Missions Council. It was very interesting and practical.

John made some revisions in his addresses before releasing them for publication. On January 28th, Mr. Glenn wrote him: "Please do not give too much time to polishing up your address. When you get one ready, send it along without waiting for the other. I can have them polished up here if there seems any necessity for it, but your paper on the church school was in such good shape that I doubt whether polishing will be good for it."

Both manuscripts were sent off to New York on January 31st.

It was good to hear again from Mr. Sharp, who wrote January 18th:

I have just received your letter of January 4th, and it is nice to know that you want me to come out and tackle the ballads with you. You will, therefore, be glad to hear that I have practically decided to leave for America very shortly—probably on the *Nieuw Amsterdam,* which sails on February 7th.

My primary object is to get some shekels together, with which to support myself and my family, as my income has practically disappeared owing to the war. But I have every intention of following up your ballads, and as soon as I have succeeded in my chief object, I shall turn my attention to Asheville. I will let you and Mr. Campbell know directly when I arrive in America and will keep you informed of my movements. From what Mr. Campbell told me, I gather that it would be more convenient to you—as it will also be to me—to pay my first visit to you a little later on, say, March or April.

In many ways, of course, it will be an advantage to both of us to be unhampered by the Carnegie people, for it will give us a free hand and allow us to make our plans as we think best, untroubled by other considerations. I am looking forward very eagerly to seeing you again and talking over the matter very fully with you, and also, I may add, to making the acquaintance of Mr. Campbell. Perhaps I may be able to see Mr. Campbell in New York. Will you tell him that I shall be staying at the Hotel Algonquin on my arrival?

Many thanks for your New Year's wishes, which we in England appreciate very much just now.

John forwarded a copy of this to Mr. Glenn at once, saying, "We are delighted to know that he is coming, and I admire his pluck. Would it be agreeable to you to have me send him, at the Hotel Algonquin, to await his arrival, a letter of introduction to you? I should like to have him know of your interest." This was done, with a welcoming letter to the hotel, but there was no word of Mr. Sharp's arrival for some weeks.

On February 5th an exciting event interrupted the office. John sent a letter off to Mr. Glenn:

> I am very happy to write you that our longed-for little daughter arrived this morning at two o'clock.
>
> All is well with her and with Mrs. Campbell. We shall probably name her Barbara, after my mother.

Barbara certainly did complicate office operations, but she could not put off the conference. Letters were already under way to the scattered members of the Executive Committee, and answers were coming in as to the time of the meeting and subjects of discussion. On February 4th John's old friend Dr. A. E. Brown, superintendent of the Southern Baptist Mountain Missions and Schools, responded in characteristic fashion to his "Brother," "Professor Campbell":

> Being a Baptist, I am free from the influence of the moon, except in the planting of my potatoes, and so I give my preference to March the 29th and 30th. April is not a good month for me, especially the latter part of it, as I am closing up the year's work then.
>
> I think your suggestion as to discussing the work of the teachers in the local community is splendid. We discussed that pretty well at my teachers' conference at Ridgecrest last spring, and I am going to have it again this spring.
>
> Since you so courteously insist on suggestions from the members of your Executive Committee, let me venture this suggestion: that we confine our discussions to our work.

The Executive Committee agreed on these dates, and the full two-day program John labored to build on schools—new aspects of work and adaptation to mountain needs; extension and community work; health and nursing services; and cooperation among Christians of different denominations in a rural community. With representatives of all church boards maintaining work in the mountains; with President [W. G.] Frost and Professor John E. Calfee of Berea College; Dr. [George A.] Hubbell of Lincoln Memorial University; Miss Martha Berry, of the Berry Schools in Georgia; Miss Ruth Huntington, of Hindman; Miss [Frances] Pettit and Miss [Celia] Cathcart, of Pine Mountain; Miss [Josephine] Bundy, from Asheville School; Mrs. Wells, of Highland School; Mr. [Isaac] Messler, of McKee Academy; Mr. [J. T.] McGarvery, of Hazel Green; Dr. [Robert L.] Moore, of Mars Hill College; Mr. [Harvey] Murdoch, of Witherspoon; Dr. [E. A.] Sutherland, of the Nashville Agricultural and Normal Institute; Dr. [Samuel] Wilson, of Maryville College; with Miss Emma Wilson, of Town and Country Service, Red Cross; and Miss Grace Meigs, of the United States Children's Bureau; and with Dr. E. C. Branson, of the University of North Carolina; Hon. S. W. Sherrill, superintendent of public instruction, Tennessee; and Dr. [R. Q.] Lillard, of the Tennessee State Board of Health, the conference promised well. In a letter of March 1st to Mr. Glenn, John wrote:

> I wish very much that Mr. Hanmer could come to this conference; he is a good mixer, and I should like to have him meet these rural leaders and to talk to them for a short time on ways and means of promoting recreation in remote rural communities.
>
> The prospect for the conference seems very bright. . . . I think it is going to be difficult to keep some away; some state officials who have not responded to invitations in past years, this year have written urging me to write to their superior officers to ask that they be sent. . . .
>
> As time goes on, it becomes more and more evident that this division is becoming a real force for unifying mountain interests and has found for itself a real place of influence. It also seems to me that Asheville has been well chosen as a center for this work.

His wish was granted. Mr. Glenn must himself have been intrigued, for he wrote John on March 16th that possibly he might be able to attend the conference, if he could be of real use:

> I would, of course, like to do so very much, and have a feeling that I ought to take this opportunity of getting a little closer view of your work. On the other hand, as I have so much to do here, and as I have several other conferences later on which I must attend, I feel that I should not go unless my being there will be of real use to you and, in a less degree, to the conference. Please let me know at once how much advantage you think will accrue from my being there. You would better wire.

John wired promptly and also wrote a letter, March 20th, expressing his pleasure that there was a possibility of your coming to the conference. It would be a real help to the workers on the field to feel that you regard the mountain field of enough importance to come all the way from New York to this conference. Your presence and your mingling with the workers will help to strengthen the bond of fellowship that I feel is beginning to exist between the Foundation and the church and social agencies in the mountain field. I feel, too, that the fact that you have regarded a mountain conference of enough importance to come will tend to bring the mountain country and mountain needs more prominently to the attention of persons of importance and church officials not directly connected with mountain boards.

Meanwhile, John was continuing his efforts to promote the cooperation of the Town and Country Nursing Service of the Red Cross and the Country Life Department of the Presbyterian Church, and of other such cooperative ventures. As already indicated, Miss Clement had shown interest in a number of ways since her mountain trip with us in 1914. John's talk with Mrs. [Harriet Blaine] Beale, her superior officer, in Washington recently had showed him that her interest, at least, was secure.

With a plan for furthering this cooperation, John had invited Miss Emma Wilson of the Red Cross to speak at the coming Conference of Southern Mountain Workers, and she had accepted. However, it was not easy to win the support of all members of the Committee of the Town and Country Nursing Service, as appears from the following letter John wrote Mr. Glenn on February 9th:

I do not know that I told you of my telephone conversation with Mrs. Beale in Washington. Through some oversight on the part of the hotel people, we failed to meet. However, Mrs. Beale is most cordial in inviting me to come to Washington sometime in March before the next meeting of the Town and Country Nursing Service, so that I may go over very carefully with her the matter of a sustentation fund for nurses in remote rural communities unable to support them. I shall endeavor to go to Washington and talk things over with her.

I had a few moments with Miss [Lillian] Wald here. Miss Wald is on the committee of the Town and Country Nursing Service but did not impress me as being particularly interested in this matter of a sustentation fund. I suppose I ought not to expect a full appreciation of this great rural need by even so notable a social worker, from a congested urban enter. So many of such workers do not seem to sense at all the need as it exists in remote rural regions or to be sympathetic toward efforts outside their own fields. They meet me time and time again with the statement that the state ought to do this work. The state is unable to at present. The southern states are doing a great many things along rural lines—or attempting them—and they could not do some things far back in the mountains, even had they the money, until public opinion will recognize the need and support service to meet it. It is to create a recognition of the need, and a public demand for remedies that I ask for beginnings through national or philanthropic organizations.

Miss Wald suggested at once that the Sage Foundation ought to furnish this money. I replied that I was not asking for money, but merely asking that the Town and Country Nursing Service pass upon the desirability and feasibility of the plan if money were forthcoming. It is unfair to Miss Wald to stress too much her seeming lack of sympathy.

It seems to me that the Town and Country Nursing Service must be ready, in sympathy at least, to meet this great need in remote rural sections, and if it is not, local organizations will spring up, and the Town and Country Nursing Service lose its national character. So far as I know, it is the only organization national in character suited to meet the dire need, and it could make splendid beginnings in educational and preventive measures by stationing pioneer nurses on the rural frontier.

Miss Pettit has just written for a nurse; I have been instrumental in holding the Presbyterians in line for a new nurse from the Red Cross, and Miss Clement has written me that there are three or four other nurses ready for work the first of April. They could be placed in remote regions, in all probability, if there were a sustentation fund to supplement the local support or the support given by other organizations.

I have just received a letter from Massachusetts with reference to a well-qualified nurse who wishes to enter the mountain work, and I so much want the Town and Country Nursing Service to pass upon the matter, to prevent local societies from being organized, or institutions using their nurses primarily for other services rather than for the special service for which they have received training.

There is great need for the kind of work that the Town and Country Nursing Service of the Red Cross could render.

Requests for help in setting up medical and nursing care in remote areas were coming from new places. Not only Miss Pettit of Pine Mountain wanted such service, but President J. A. Burns of Oneida Institute, Kentucky, hoped for a hospital or at least a nursing station near his institute. A woman physician in New York had been in touch with Mr. Glenn and with John, seeking advice and help. She had raised a considerable sum of money for the project and urgently wanted guidance in planning and in securing staff. She, too, believed that a sustentation fund for partial assistance would be welcome, but even more the standards, experience, and practical wisdom of the Red Cross Nursing Service. John wrote again, "I very much wish that a supervisory relation to the nursing and medical work of remote rural regions could be maintained by some organization of standing, and I hope the Red Cross may carefully consider as to whether this is not a field that they ought to enter."

During the weeks of planning details of the conference program, John and Mr. Glenn wrote constantly about the publication of "The Future of the Church School in the Southern Highlands" and "Mountain and Rural Fields in the South," the addresses John had sent to the Foundation on January 31st, after editing them with considerable care. Mr. Glenn had had copies made to get reactions in several quarters which he thought would be important and helpful. Dr. Wallace Buttrick of the General Education Board wrote: "I have read Mr. Campbell's papers with very great interest and satisfaction. I am convinced that through him your board has been doing a work of incalculable value, and work that will bc helpful to all serious people who arc interested in the people of the mountains. I find myself approving all that Mr. Campbell has said. . . . The papers are excellent and I could not wish to have them changed."

Another response came from Rev. Franklin J. Clark of the Mission Board of the Episcopal Church:

I have delayed replying to your very courteous letter of the 4th instant, with which you sent me copies of the two addresses given by Mr. Campbell on the mountain work, until I had an opportunity to read them. I finished them Thursday night and am very glad to say that they have been most helpful and informing to me. I was not surprised to find them so, for in all my contact with Mr. Campbell I have found his work very thorough and of great value. I had the pleasure of hearing his address before the Home Missions Council and appreciated greatly the way in which he treated his subject. As you are expecting to print these addresses soon, I should like very much to be allowed to keep these copies, if you have no further need of them. Thank you for the trouble you have taken to send them to me.

With these in mind, and a third (not available) from Dr. Gardner, to which Mr. Glenn in forwarding it had referred as "quite unsatisfactory," John wrote on February 17th:

I thank you for the letters of Dr. Buttrick and Mr. Gardner; I was much interested in both.[1]

I was deeply interested in what Dr. Gardner had to say. I cannot, of course, agree with him that my suggestions are utopian, for some of them are actually operative, which emboldened me to ask for further extension; others have been attempted and failed of success by so slight a margin as to warrant continued effort; still other of my suggestions—among them the training for "spiritual engineers"—have been talked over with various persons, including some denominational leaders in mountain work, and such interest has been evidenced as to give hope of the their personal support, even should full official support be denied because of the attitude of mind of ultraconservative members of boards represented by them, who might agree with Dr. Gardner in his conclusions. From my point of view, the only thing lacking to make an early beginning are funds, and a change in the attitude of mind of some administrative officials who might regard these suggestions of mine for getting together in Christian service as utopian.

I find that the best workers on the field—of whatever denomination— are men and women whom it would be possible to get together in matters of practice, and nearer together in faith, if their superior officers would be sympathetic. I quote from a confidential letter I have received from one of the leaders of the work of the Protestant Episcopal Church in the mountains:

Now with respect to the Church's services. If they are to effectively reach the mountaineer, they must be shorter, more flexible and adaptable. He (the mountaineer) needs and wants more preaching than our services, under modern conditions, social and domestic, now permit. Its character must be evangelistic, but not revivalism. The chief message must be the essential truth of Christ, not mere echoes of the early church, or quotations from the creeds of yesterday—though these have their place, a minor one. It must be as Christian as its message. It must manifest the fruit of the Spirit. It must have the positiveness, yet the charity, of true humility. Intellectual moonshine along psychological lines will not avail. Ecclesiastical censoriousness, sectarian bitterness, and bigoted dogmatism are repugnant to your mountaineer. Then again, the preacher must be a teacher, opening out the truth in the symbols of divine revelation and in the mode of thought and in the language of the day.

Dr. Gardner is right in saying that the real task with reference to "spiritual engineers" is "how to make them." My thought is that a good beginning would be made if Christian workers on the frontier—or officials in intimate touch with the frontier, through personal contact—should have a larger voice in the councils of the church; that they be invited to go to our theological seminaries to give full and free expression to their convictions to the young men training for the ministry; and that young men who feel called to the mountain ministry shall then have a way opened for them to spend some months at such a mountain center as I have advocated—sustained in part by contributions from denominational and philanthropic boards. My suggestion as to "spiritual engineers" in my paper was in the nature of a plea to officials of boards represented in the council, that they give to the promising youth who is deliberating as to what his life calling is to be, a right view of the minister's work, as being that of a spiritual engineer. Vitalizing training for the ministry and making such training fully effective on the frontier through denominational cooperation is not a daydream. It is an early possibility if the administrative officers of our church boards will remove the obstacles—and I admit there are now obstacles, but they are not obstacles that needs must exist always—by giving expression by voice and pen to the unifying tendencies emanating from the men at the front, who are facing *conditions,* not *theories.*

The General Board of Religious Education of the Protestant Episcopal Church would do a splendid thing, and play a trump card, by voting one thousand dollars for such a center and putting it up to the Woman's Board of the Presbyterian Church, USA, the American Missionary Association (the Congregational Board under which mountain work is carried on), and others, who, by all the laws of the game, would have to follow suit. I should then be encouraged to work very hard to secure similar appropriations from the Russell Sage Foundation and from the General Education Board, and the thing would be started.

In all seriousness, I should appreciate deeply a specific and minute criticism of my suggestions. I do not wish to be an advocate of visionary schemes, and I cannot agree with Dr. Gardner that the point of view is very much needed if the suggestions growing inevitably from this point of view are utopian.

On March 6th, Mr. Glenn wrote John:

I am enclosing in duplicate a revised copy of your paper on the mountain churches. I am somewhat in doubt whether it is wise to publish it at present. I have raised the question and give my reasons for your consideration. If you think there is no danger in publishing it, I shall have nothing more to say.

The paper is a fine one, and I am thoroughly in sympathy with your point of view. I feel keenly that nothing is more important for the churches and for our country than the bringing into the ministry of intelligent, sensible, vigorous young men and giving them the most difficult field to work.

I am quite sure that it was advisable for you to read the paper before the Home Missions Council, and I am sure that it will have good results. On the other hand, it must be remembered that a great many of the people whom you wish to read the paper are small-minded and timid and want to interpret the word "religious" in the very limited sense. Even in the central church boards, there are some such men. They may interpret your paper as an attack on fundamental things.

There is another set of people who must be considered; namely, Protestant Episcopal ministers who do not want to be called Protestants. Perhaps there are very few of these in the mountains, but there are some of them on our central boards who are influential. Your paper speaks, for instance, of the "oneness of Protestantism." This feature, however, can be eliminated by omitting the use of the term "Protestantism" and using broader terms.

Will the Southern Baptists and Southern Presbyterians think that you are aiming at federation and wiping out denominational distinction? If they do, will your work have a setback?

Your appeal and recommendations are indefinite. Your chief point is the securing and commissioning of strong men for the mountains. Necessarily you cannot be very concrete. In this respect the paper differs materially from your paper on the school.

Is there the same danger of irritating ministers and members of boards as is true in the case of mountaineers? Is it or is it not necessary to be as careful in the one case as you have been in the other? I am not at all sure that it is. Possibly some sharp criticism of church methods is altogether desirable.

All that you say in your paper about the local churches and the relations of local conditions to them is certainly very significant and valuable and ought to be made public. It is chiefly the latter part of your paper (say, after page 16) that raises my questions.

I think these are all the questions that I have to raise. I am putting them entirely as questions and not by way of argument. I want you to make the final decision, entirely in accordance with your own judgment.

John replied on March 11th. He began by saying: "I should be very glad indeed to postpone further consideration of the publication of my two addresses until after the Knoxville conference. We are being pushed hard with conference matters and with the publication of the booklet on *Mountain Needs and Qualification of Mountain Workers*—a booklet authorized for publication under my supervision by the last conference."

After then considering in some detail the points raised and the question of giving offense to mountain as well as church people, he went on to add:

People are wanting these papers, and while I feel very reluctant to publish them if there is any hesitancy in your mind whatsoever, and while there is any doubt in my own mind, I must yet have a good excuse for not publishing them.

I do not know yet what is wise, and therefore want to take some time to go over the whole question very carefully. My personal convictions on some points discussed in my papers are strong; in my judgment there is no question so important in the mountain field, or in the country generally, as the getting together of the non–Roman Catholic divisions of the church. I do not want to have my personal convictions, on these points or any others, do harm; nor do I wish my official influence injured, nor the Foundation embarrassed, if that is possible, by a too free expression of personal convictions. But church leaders must come to realize, more than they do, that some barriers must be let down if Christian brotherhood is to be promoted.

I look at these questions from the need of this field, and my sympathies are largely with the South, and naturally with the mountain South. If there is danger of giving offense to any group, I should prefer to risk giving offense to leaders in the North—many of them are just as limited and as provincial as any southerner or mountaineer that I have met. After all, the problems of the mountains are to be solved by the mountaineer and the southerner, and not by foreign agencies or unassimilated northerners. They can only help, and they can help much more than they are now doing, by being broader in their spirit. I must confess to more tolerance for the native mountaineer who holds to certain doctrines and practices of his church as essential than I have for those supposed to be well-informed and broad-minded, who admit that certain church views of practices are nonessential but will not yield them—even for Christian brotherhood. I want them broadened, and I want to be broad enough to be tolerant of intolerance and to keep still, if need be, for the good of the field. I hope whatever I do or say may tend to unify church bodies and to help interpret the North to the South and the South to the North, as well as the mountain country to both sections.

I should like to think the whole thing over, and not to risk, through hasty action, loss of what has been gained. Perhaps the wise course should be to do what you originally suggested my doing: to write a book on the mountain field; its topography; population, with its urban and rural classifications and its social groupings; resources of the country; church and school; and the agencies of cooperation for betterment. In that way, the approach to the whole discussion will be secured through an initial chapter of introduction, which is not secured in shorter form, and I might avoid possible misunderstandings that would arise through publishing condensed reports of the addresses, without the approach necessary, and with some things left out that some feel should be said for the good of their work, and which I myself think should be said.

John had written that a condensation of his address before the Home Missions Council was wanted for publication in the full report of the meeting. In response, Mr. Glenn wrote on March 18th:

Yesterday I forgot to say that it seems to me advisable not to let an abstract of your address be published in the report of Home Missions Council until you have gone over it carefully. A four-thousand-word abstract will, of course, condense you very greatly. I do not see why you cannot all the same get an outline of your main thoughts into that space. But I would not like to trust the condensing to anyone else—certainly not to Bro. ———.

If possible, I would like to see it, too. Your letter has suggested some new thoughts about a discussion of churches as it relates itself to the R.S.F. as a whole, which I would like to talk with you about. Indeed it has raised some questions about my own activities in church work which had never occurred to me before. If I get to Knoxville, I hope we can have a chance to confer after the conference adjourns. I would like also to go to Peabody College for a day—I must, if possible.

I shall not bother you about your papers until after the conference. . . . No one can object to your revising your papers. That is common practice and considered desirable.

In the meantime it was a great satisfaction to learn of the safe arrival of Mr. Sharp in New York. He wrote John on February 25th:

It was with great pleasure that I found a letter from you awaiting me on my arrival from the ship yesterday afternoon, and to hear the good news that you had to tell me. I hope that both you and Mrs. Campbell will accept my sincerest congratulations. I am the father of four children myself, so I can understand your feelings in the matter!

I had a pleasant though protracted voyage, arriving ten days later than schedule. But traveling in wartime is a hazardous business, and I am thankful to be here safe and sound.

Many thanks for the letter to Mr. Glenn with which you so thoughtfully furnished me. I am going away to Boston for a day or two tomorrow to see Mrs. Storrow, but on my return I will present it. My plans are at present in the air, but I have a lot of work to do here, and this will occupy me for a fortnight at least. After that I hope to have some engagements fixed up further afield. As soon as I can see my way to do so, I shall try to come to Asheville, but exactly when this will be I cannot at present say. If by any chance you will be in New York between now and March 11th, I hope you will let me know, for I should dearly love to have a talk with you.

It is nice to be over here again, though at the moment I am missing my wife and family very badly. Still, I like this country immensely and find it very stimulating to a staid Englishman like myself! Kind regards to you both.

A week later came letters from both Mr. Sharp and Mr. Glenn to John, written on the same day, March 3rd. Mr. Sharp said:

I have just returned from a lunch at Mr. Aldrich's office, where I met Mr. Glenn. I had missed the latter when I called at his office earlier in the week and presented the letter you were kind enough to give me. So it was arranged that we should meet today at luncheon. I found him a most agreeable, helpful, and stimulating person, and I discussed at considerable length with him the question of the collection of the Carolina ballads. I told him that before I can do anything in this direction, I must get through as many business engagements as I can secure, but he pointed out that it would be well, even so, to see you and Mrs. Campbell as soon as possible to discuss plans for the future when I find myself at liberty.

I think I ought to have a free week sometime this month which would allow me to pay . . . a visit to Asheville. I have to go to St. Louis for a week sometime this month. Probably either beginning on March 19 or 26. If the former, I could come to you during the latter week, or vice versa. In all probability all or the greater part of April I shall have to spend at Pittsburgh. It is just possible that all of my time this month may get filled up with business work, but there are no signs at present, so that I think I can be pretty certain of being able to devote one week in the way above mentioned. I am just aching to go through all the ballads Mrs. Campbell has collected and to hear her sing some of them and to talk over our future campaign. And I find it very difficult to keep my nose to the grindstone and stick to my work in the meanwhile. However, the ballads can wait, I suppose, for a few weeks, while the other work is really urgent and must be done. I hope Mrs. Campbell is gaining her strength rapidly. Please remember me to her.

Mr. Glenn wrote:

I have just come from lunching with Mr. Sharp at Mr. Aldrich's house. He impresses me as being a man of exceptional intelligence, not only in his own subject, but about affairs generally. He is very anxious to go to Asheville to see you and Mrs. Campbell when he can get time for it. Unfortunately, he will be busy here in New York for ten days and will then have to go to Boston and then to St. Louis. In April he has engagement in Chicago, Indianapolis, and Pittsburgh. He has also been asked to do some work for the Shakespearean pageant, which is to be held here in May. Evidently he has succeeded in getting a number of engagements before his arrival. I suggested that he try as soon as possible to pay you and Mrs.

Campbell a visit in Asheville of two or three days, so that you might talk this over together and plan for his going into the mountains later on. Please send him at the Algonquin Hotel, 59 West 44th Street, New York City, schedules of trains showing him how to get to Asheville from here, from Pittsburgh, from St. Louis, and from Indianapolis. Let him know, also, what the expense of traveling will be. Send me a copy of the letter. I told him that the Foundation would be glad to pay the expense of such a trip. I think I can squeeze it out here without charging your budget with it.

Mr. Sharp said that Mrs. Storrow of Boston was interested and had told him that she could get him some money if it was a matter of hundreds of dollars, though she could not get thousands. So it is possible that she might provide the cost of a trip through the mountains when he is ready to take it. He thinks he could get the English Folk Song Society to publish a report. I have no doubt that with the help of his name we could find a publisher when he gets something worthwhile.

He is equally interested in the ballad words and in the music, and looks upon both as a necessary part of the complete whole.

It might be possible for you to arrange to meet him somewhere in the mountains that would be nearer his route than Asheville, but of course it would be unfortunate for him not to see Mrs. Campbell. He felt that possibly he might get some of the music by hearing her sing it. He also feels that he would rather see you at Asheville so as to get a good idea of the mountain country from a good center.

Don't hesitate to urge Sharp to come to you.

This last suggestion was promptly followed. On March 6th, John sent Mr. Sharp the following letter:

Mrs. Campbell and I were much pleased the other day to receive your letter and to know that you had met Mr. Glenn and that there is a prospect of seeing you in Asheville in the near future.

We shall be happy to see you at any time convenient for you, and we both hope that you will come to our home and remain with us while in Asheville. Having children of your own, you will not, I am sure, be too much disturbed if our little Barbara should strike up some ballad which might not harmonize with the one that you and Mrs. Campbell would be considering at the time. We have a large, rambling old house, and there is plenty of room in it, so you will be able to steal away for any particular work you may desire to do. However, if it would be more convenient for you to go to one of the hotels, please do not hesitate, in view of our invitation, to follow what you regard as the more convenient course.

I think the idea of coming to Asheville first is ideal. You and Mrs. Campbell could go over her ballads together, and we could outline for your consideration some tentative plans for a ballad-collecting trip when you are free to undertake it.

After learning from one of your recent letters that it was quite likely you would come to the South, I made some confidential inquiries from persons in the mountains, and they have all been most cordial in urging your coming to them. They are persons who would be able to put you in touch with mountain people who sing ballads. I conclude from a letter that I have received lately, that you would be able, at least in one or two places, to get some of the old mountain dances, which are rather hard for an outsider to get.

For your information I am sending you schedules of the best trains from New York, Chicago, Pittsburgh, St. Louis, and Indianapolis to Asheville. . . .

We are relieved that you got to our country safely, and of course are much pleased to know that you like this land of ours.

Mr. Sharp acknowledged promptly receipt of train schedules and the invitation to stay with us in Asheville, writing on March 10th:

Many thanks for your letter of the 6th and the clear and carefully compiled list of trains. If I take a wrong turning it will not be your fault!

My plans are not yet fixed up, but I am pretty sure to be able to come to you sometime during the week March 19–25. . . . It is most kind and friendly of you and Mrs. Campbell—especially in the existing circumstances—to ask me to stay with you at your house. I shall have the greatest pleasure in doing so. I have only two vices: (1) I do not eat any animal food but live mainly on cheese, milk, eggs, etc. This may sound rather frightening to Mrs. Campbell, but my requirements are really very easily and simply satisfied in ways which I can explain in detail after my arrival. (2) I am rather a heavy smoker! I hope that neither of these will induce you to vary the terms of your invitation to me!

By the way, I assume Mrs. Campbell has a copy of Child's ballads, either the original or the digest, edited by Professor Kittredge. I usually carry the latter about with me, but in some way or other it got left out of my box on this trip. But if Mrs. Campbell has a copy, I will not buy one now but have mine sent to me from England.

I am very busy here holding innumerable classes and making preparations for the Percy Mackaye Masque, for the English Interlude of which I am to be responsible. . . .

I am looking forward tremendously to my visit to you and to seeing Mrs. Campbell's collection.

I am not likely to forget Mr. Sharp's arrival in Asheville, nor our first hours together over my ballad collection. If he still had doubts when he started, these were certainly dispelled when he looked into the material and talked to John of the background. His enthusiasm grew by the hour. John, on his side, made no pretense to any great knowledge of the subject, but he could and did answer all kinds of questions on ancestry, history, characteristics, topography, and ways and means of securing material.

John wrote Mr. Glenn:

We are enjoying Mr. Sharp to the full. He regards Mrs. Campbell's ballads as real finds, the music as well as the words. . . . He leaves tomorrow, the 24th. Last night he gave a most delightful talk to the girls of the mountain school (Presbyterian) here and taught them several folk dances, which captivated all of them. He hopes to be able to make a trip to the mountains in August and September. He is a very democratic sort of man, and I am sure he will mix well with the mountain people. He and Mrs. Campbell have completed their labors, and they are coming to the office this morning so that we may map out his August–September mountain itinerary. He feels that the trip to Asheville has been most profitable and that there is a wealth of material in the mountains, of high grade. There are a number of Mrs. Campbell's ballads that he has not found in England, and his enthusiasm over them is really contagious.

We were interrupted in this congenial pursuit by word that the Imperial Hotel in Knoxville, where the conference was scheduled to be held March 28–30, was struck by lightning on the 21st and burned to the ground. John sent his secretary, Miss Dickey, to Knoxville at once to make arrangements to provide use of a large assembly room and make reservations for most of those who were to attend. John himself went to Knoxville with a full and promising program, in spite of necessary last-minute changes.

On the day he left, March 26th, came a letter from Mr. Sharp, now in St. Louis:

I had rather a fearsome journey here, arriving near upon midnight, between four and five hours late. We got into difficulties on Friday night, and despite much whistling and shunting, in the course of which I was nearly thrown out of my bed several times, we made no progress for about five and a half hours! However, although tired, I arrived here last night none the worse.

I went through all the ballads once and many of them twice during the journey and begin to feel that I am now getting hold of them. I am really amazed at the richness of the material that you have so painstakingly won from the mountains and feel assured that the mine you have tapped will yield us a great deal more—perhaps even richer stuff—if we work it systematically. I am longing to get at it and make a start. However, August will soon be here, and I shall then have the satisfaction of feeling that I have earned a couple of months' idleness!

My baggage is just now arriving and relieves me of much anxiety. I am quite comfortable here, and it is nice and quiet. The first part of the journey to Knoxville was very wonderful. I can understand what a fascination the mountains must have for you and Mr. Campbell and expect that when I have made closer acquaintance with them, I shall be under the same spell also. I thoroughly enjoyed my visit. I knew I was going to, but did not just how much. You and I have got a jolly patch of work ahead to do, and I fancy we are going to get a lot of pleasure out of it. I shall not feel satisfied until I have personally made some contribution to the stock which at present is all yours. My experience in England has been that the longer one works at it, the more wonderful the results seem to be, and I have no doubt that is what we shall find in this case—the best is often to be found deepest.

I am afraid Little Barbara's nose has been rather dislocated these last few days, but I am sure she is now receiving her full share of attention and that she will soon forget last week. Perhaps when she is old enough to understand, you will explain everything to her and she won't mind!

I find a series of appointments already booked for me today, so I am not going to have the quiet day I looked forward to. So I must bring this to a stop. Please remember me to Mr. Campbell, and with many, many thanks for the innumerable kindnesses you both showed me last week.

Naturally I did not go to this Conference of Southern Mountain Workers, but letters and comments from many sources reinforced John's own enthusiastic reports. Apparently Mr. Glenn and Mr. Hanmer, both of whom stayed throughout the meeting and addressed the conference, had a very good time, as well as helped to make the occasion a great success. John wrote April 1st to Mr. Glenn:

I am enclosing five clippings which you wanted Miss Dickey to get for you. Miss Sarah Rogers, Miss Sheak, and Miss Brown wish me to put in their applications for positions in the school of which you are the head— according to this paper. They say salary is no consideration, inasmuch as they will be able to get a living off your farm.

Your presence was a genuine help to the conference and will have a very marked effect on my work, I am very sure. Your address, showing so clearly the sympathetic attitude of the Foundation toward church work and all social service work, will bring this division even more closely into touch with such agencies. I have heard a number of people express their appreciation of your presence and of the presence of Mr. Hanmer; they have said that all of the Foundation people seem to be very good mixers and to be chosen comrades in work. Personally, I deeply appreciate your help and Mr. Hanmer's.

I have wondered if anywhere else there could be just such a conference, beginning with an address by the superintendent of education of a "dry" state, profusely sprinkled—or immersed—with convivial illustrations, and closing with a prayer-meeting song started up—much to my surprise—by Brother Wheeler. I tried to get a glimpse of your face. Mr. Hanmer joined lustily in the song. This somewhat unexpected closing of the conference will really do a great deal of good, for last year one or two thought that we were not quite religious enough, and Mr. Ellis of Archdeacon Neve's section, not getting in at the beginning of the conference, thought that we ought to have begun with prayer. When I assured him that we opened and closed with prayer and asked him to make the closing prayer of the afternoon session, he was satisfied, and I am sure that some of these unexpected things will work together for good.

A week later he forwarded a brief writeup of the conference he had been asked to prepare for the survey, which gives the only available account of the meetings:

A meeting characterized by a spirit of friendliness, interest in the other fellow's work, breadth of vision, and cooperation, was the fourth annual

Conference of Southern Mountain Workers, held in Knoxville, Tennessee, March 28–30.

This conference is the outgrowth of an effort on the part of officials of the Southern Baptist, Southern Presbyterian, and Northern Presbyterian mission boards and the Southern Highland Division of the Russell Sage Foundation to bring together in annual conference the various denominational boards and other agencies doing work in the southern mountains and to enlist, in cooperation for mountain rural welfare, agencies of government, state, and philanthropy. Concurring heartily in the original call were representatives of the Christian, Congregational, Southern Methodist, and Protestant Episcopal Churches.

The conference has grown steadily in numbers and in influence, and at the fourth annual meeting were delegates and representatives of fourteen denominational boards, the Rural Organization Service of the US Department of Agriculture, the US Bureau of Education, Departments of Education and Health of Tennessee, the Town and Country Nursing Service of the American Red Cross, the Southern Industrial Educational Association, YMCA, and the Russell Sage Foundation. In addition to church board officials were many teachers from the church and independent schools of the mountains, and the faculties of the mountain colleges—Berea of Kentucky, Maryville, Carson and Newman and Lincoln Memorial of Tennessee, and Mars Hill of North Carolina—were well represented. Dr. Brown Ayres, president of the University of Tennessee, presided at the general evening session of the conference, which was addressed by Mrs. Cora Wilson Stewart, founder of the Moonlight Schools and president of the Kentucky Illiteracy Commission, and Dr. E. C. Branson, professor of rural sociology, University of North Carolina. The address of welcome was given by Hon. S. W. Sherrill, superintendent of public instruction of Tennessee, who, with Dr. R. Q. Lillard of the State Board of Health, represented not only their respective departments, but the state of Tennessee, having been sent as state delegates by Governor T. C. Rye.

Community service was the general topic of discussion. Space forbids comment on the many able addresses by church officials and church workers and others. The purpose and spirit of the conference—namely, cooperative action to meet recognized needs, without the sacrifice of anything that the various denominations and agencies deem essential—were well reflected by the address of Dr. William Goodell Frost of Berea College:

"In What Ways May Christians of Different Denominations Cooperate in a Rural Community?"

Acting upon the suggestion made at the third annual conference by the Rt. Rev. Junius M. Horner, bishop of the Missionary District of Asheville, there has been issued a booklet: *The Southern Highlands: An Inquiry into Their Needs, and Qualifications Desired in Church, Educational and Social Service Workers in the Mountain Country.*

In view of the rapid growth of the conference, it has been deemed necessary to change the basis of representation upon the Executive Committee. For this purpose the following committee, instructed to report back to the conference, has been appointed:

Rev. Franklin J. Clark, Recording Secretary of the Domestic and Foreign Missionary Society of the Protestant Episcopal Church.

Marshall C. Allaben, Superintendent of the School Department of the Woman's Board of Home Missions, Presbyterian Church, USA.

A. E. Brown, DD, Superintendent of the Department of Mountain Missions and Schools, Southern Baptist Convention.

William Goodell Frost, LLD, President of Berea College.

Samuel T. Wilson, DD, President of Maryville College.

This committee is empowered by the conference to appoint a commission to make a survey of the mountain field and to report its findings at the next annual meeting.

John C. Campbell, Secretary of the Southern Highland Division of the Russell Sage Foundation, Asheville, North Carolina, is chairman of the Executive Committee and presiding officer of the conference.

A more personal note to Mr. Glenn, on April 6th, finished off the conference obligations in lighter vein and with a flavor of the mountains:

I have just succeeded in getting back from the photographer the films that you desire.

The gathering of the Christmas greens was in Knott County, Kentucky, near Hindman. The lady in the wagon is Miss Stone of the Settlement School; I am handing her the greens and Mrs. Campbell took the snapshot, unbeknown to us.

The pictures of the ford are in Madison County, North Carolina. The ford is on the Shelton Laurel, in the so-called Laurel country. The Shelton Laurel is a branch of the Big Laurel, which unites with the Little Laurel to form the Laurel River, which flows into the French Broad at Runion, North Carolina. It is called the Shelton Laurel from the number of Sheltons who live on it. The ford pictures are really pictures on one ford; Mrs. Campbell and I are just a little lower downstream from where Dr. Packard and I, in the other picture, enter the ford.

It may be of interest to know that one of the chief tributaries of the Big Laurel Branch is Spillcorn Creek and that the chief tributary of Spillcorn is Calvin Creek—a not-at-all inappropriate name for a creek in the Laurel country, in which the Presbyterians have done such good work.

9

Ballads Added

Part 2, 1916

After a series of false starts, Cecil Sharp's approaching ballad-collecting visit, with his secretary, Maud Karpeles, was set for the end of July. John Campbell was planning to guide them along the collecting trips, but on July 16 one of the worst storms in local history flooded the valley, knocking out electricity, train service, and many roads. Sharp and Karpeles finally arrived by way of Knoxville, Blue Ridge, and Murphy and soon wrote jubilant letters, Sharp enumerating which ballads he found and expounding on his pleasure in meeting the people: "just English peasant folk, they do not seem to me to have taken on any distinctive American traits." From Asheville to Hot Springs, to Madison County and the Laurel Country they traveled.

Sharp wrote in September that he had collected 387 tunes, and with those of Olive's, they would have about 450 to choose from when they published "our book." Before he sailed for England in December, Sharp had acquired Putnam as a publisher. He planned to leave his notebooks in America, owing to the dangers on the seas. When discussing the introduction to the ballad book, Olive Campbell assured Sharp that the publishing of the ballads was part and parcel of what John and the foundation were trying to accomplish: they were greatly interested in furthering the folk movement in the mountain.

John Campbell was still trying to raise money for mountain schools and for their extension work. His hope was that the mountain field could be regarded as a "super-rural field" rather than a "distinctive mission field." His correspondence with Dr. John E. Calfee of the Berea faculty contained a lot of ideas under discussion, including more men teachers, training for boys in both teaching and farming, and school training for boys at the Farm School. Dr. Calfee was coming to Asheville as president of the Normal and Collegiate Institute but also with full charge of the Farm School and the Dorland School of Girls.

With the comparative relaxation of postconference days, John and I settled down in that spring of 1916 to some early correspondence to open the way for Mr. Sharp's mountain trip for ballad collecting in the late summer. It was pleasant, and encouraging too, to have Mr. Glenn share with us the letter Mr. Sharp had written him after his Asheville visit in March:

It goes without saying—at any rate to you who know the Campbells—that I received the warmest welcome, and that after the first night we were getting on together just as though we had known each other for a long time.

Mrs. Campbell and I spent many long but pleasant hours poring over her manuscripts, and I found that the value of the material she has already harvested is even higher than I had estimated. To me it is quite wonderful that anyone so far away from, and so little in touch with, any work of the kind that has been done elsewhere should have set herself such a high standard, and in effect reached it. She has just the combination of scientific and artistic spirit which work of this kind needs if it is to be of any use to posterity. Handicapped she is, no doubt, and avowedly, so far as musical technicalities go, but nevertheless, owing to a very retentive memory and a natural gift for music—particularly for melody—even where she has been unable to write the tunes down correctly, she has been able to sing them to me—I am sure with great accuracy. I have been at great pains not only to test this, but also to rewrite those tunes which needed it so that the work she has already done is now scientifically correct.

What she has so far accomplished is of great value, but I gather that is after all only the beginning. The field that has yielded what she has harvested must be a very rich one, and its exploration must be thoroughly done as soon as possible, for I gather from her that present conditions are rapidly undermining and destroying the traditions. The extent of the field is enormous, and it will take a very long time thoroughly to investigate it.

So far as I can see, I shall have finished the work upon which I am now engaged somewhere about the end of July, which will leave me free to give the following two months—August and September—to the work. Between now and then, Mr. and Mrs. Campbell are going to map out my work for me, and with this done I shall be able to make the best use of my time. When I have finished this preliminary campaign, I shall be in a better position to estimate the extent and value of the work than I am now, but I have no doubt in my mind what conclusion I shall reach.

Altogether I have had a very delightful week and a very exciting one, and I am looking forward with eagerness to August. I do not forget the valuable help that you have given me; indeed, I am very grateful to you.

Prompt and cordial responses came from mountain workers about the possibility of a visit from Mr. Sharp. Miss Pettit wrote from the Pine Mountain Settlement

School, "Of course, ballads can be found in any locality when you are willing to go up the little creeks and stop in forlorn little houses, or listen to the plowboy singing. . . . If Mr. Sharp comes to us, we shall do all we can to help him get the material he wants." Miss Huntington let us know that Hindman folk were very much interested in his coming and that board would be available there and at Pine Mountain at the rate of three dollars per week per person. Dr. Packard, at White Rock in the Laurel country, reminded us that he had a medical circuit of about twenty-five to thirty miles and urged us to bring Mr. Sharp there, where he and his wife would see to it that he got in touch with the people who sang ballads.

President Burns of Oneida, himself born in the mountains, wrote characteristically,

It has been a long time since I have heard from you, but absence and silence have only served to make the heart grow fonder. And now let me make an acknowledgment: I was never quite as good to you as I really wanted to be, just because I feared that you might think I was bidding for favor with the Sages. When I see you again I am going to forget them entirely.

I will certainly be glad to have Mr. Sharp visit our place, and delighted beyond expression if you find yourself able to accompany him. It will not be possible for me to be here during August and September, and I regret this very much. By all means bring Mr. Sharp, and if you can't bring him, then send him.

Give my best regards to Mrs. Campbell and Miss Barbara.

Such friendships in the mountain field were a constant joy to John, and Mr. Sharp could not know how they would help him, too. As other answers, and inquiries as well, came in, we forwarded reports of them to Mr. Sharp, that he might have some idea of regions and personalities. He never minced words in his comments, as evidenced by a paragraph in his letter of May 7th to me referring to a question raised by one of the "talking machine" companies about recordings:

Glad to hear from you again. The Mrs. —— of the —— Corp. is a most egregious person, with whom I have found it practically impossible to work. She has a sloppy, untidy mind and simply no artistic conscience and therefore from our point of view is a very dangerous person. I am now opening negotiation with the —— people, having decided to break with the former.

I have been working very hard, and I am feeling very fagged and looking forward wistfully to the end of July and the mountains and songs which loom then before me! . . . How lovely the spring must be at Asheville and in that lovely wood around you. Barbara ought to be impressed. Give her my love! This is permissible in springtime, considering our respective ages. I have all but finished revising your songs but have been stuck up for two or more weeks with no spare time whatever.

In mid-April John, as invited in the previous October, went to New Orleans to address the conference called by the Southern Education Board and to act as a member of its Committee for Education and Industry. His paper, "From Mountain Cabin to Cotton Mill," issued by the National Child Labor Committee in 1913, was still in demand and would be discussed. En route he talked with Alabama officials in regard to their problems in the mountain counties and stopped for a visit at Tuskegee Institute.

A few weeks later he made an equally fruitful visit to the Laurel country with Mr. and Mrs. Crane, to introduce them to the mountains and to local problems at close range. Dr. Payne of Peabody College had interested them in his plans for extension work, and they were considering a substantial gift to guarantee its beginning. Beautiful weather and pleasant hospitality at the various stations of the Presbyterian work there favored the adventure. John returned much pleased by the response of these guests. So was Dr. Finley, local supervisor of the work, who wrote at once, "I want to thank you for bringing the Cranes out here. It did all of us a world of good. I hope that my making a night owl of you here did not have any evil effect. One doesn't often get ahold of anyone to commit such a crime." Mr. Glenn was "delighted that Mr. Crane's interest had been so much developed. I hope it can be nursed up to the point of doing something really important."

Another event of May, the culmination of months of talks and of correspondence with Mr. Allaben of the Presbyterian Board, was the decision of Dr. John E. Calfee of the Berea faculty to come to Asheville as head of the several private schools maintained by that church. He was to be president of the Normal and Collegiate Institute but also to have full charge of the Farm School and of the Dorland School of Girls. A young man, well equipped and eager to be of service in the mountains, he had all along shown understanding of John's ideas and enthusiasm for Dr. Payne's plan for extension teaching. He had stipulated freedom in the adaptation and development of these schools, which the Presbyterian Church Board was prepared to give. At the Knoxville conference he had given what John called "a splendid paper" on education in the mountains from the point of view of a teacher. His numerous letters through the spring had been full of pointed questions looking forward to new emphasis in the teaching and new curriculum. A postscript in one of John's letters to Dr. Calfee shows the variety of ideas they were discussing:

> With Dr. Claxton advocating more men teachers as the heads of rural schools, to be permanent teachers, married, with a home and with a farm, ought it not to be a part of the new plans of the Normal to train boys, both in teaching and farming, and ought not some provision to be made for school training for the boys at Farm School? You could arrange it in some way without duplicating your faculty. The faculty could go out on the trains or by auto, and doubtless soon we will have a trolley system from here to Black Mountain. The Dorland School might possibly be developed along the folk school lines and for illiterate grownups or grownups who have not had school privileges.
>
> There are fascinating possibilities in this whole thing under one management, with extension possibilities through close connection with all the teachers from the central schools after they have been placed in the mountains. Keep me in mind for a job in this extension and folk school side of things when the Sage people are through with me, and let us plan to go to Denmark, Norway, Sweden, and Switzerland after a bit for a summer's study and observation.

Again, on May 23rd, he wrote Dr. Calfee:

> I am delighted to know you are to be here on or about the 8th of June. I . . . hope to be here when you come, for discussion of the very important points you raised in your letters. . . .
>
> For a long while I have hoped that the Normal people would find it desirable to make more of their library by appointing a really capable librarian, who, in cooperation with the head of the school and its faculty, should make it her aim to gather all the government, state, and other bulletins that deal with any phase of education or the betterment of rural life in general. Furthermore, to make the library a real workshop, not only for the girls while they are in the school, but for the mountain teachers as well who have no libraries of any sort at their command, it should be the further duty of the librarian to correspond regularly with the Normal girls who are teaching in the mountains, to learn their school and community needs and, in cooperation with the head of the school, to serve as an intermediary to bring to the community where the Normal girl is teach-

ing, government and state officials—and freelances like me—if it should seem likely that they could be of help. The head of the Normal school, the domestic science teacher, the music teacher, head of farm work of the Farm School should be among those who go on such occasions to these school centers to help out. It would be possible from the Normal faculty, from the residents in Asheville, and from the important visitors who come to Asheville occasionally to arrange a lyceum course of some sort; that would be wonderfully helpful.

As an illustration, let me cite what I mean. I have just taken Mr. and Mrs. Crane on a two-day trip into the mountains. They are deeply interested in the mountains; Mr. Crane has been all over the world and has had an intimate touch with Russian life and with its wonderful cooperative spirit. It would be quite easy to enlist a man like him in giving a course of lectures of wonderful awakening power. He is a gentleman of means and in touch with influential people throughout the United States. I would not myself do it, nor urge others to seek the services of such persons, for the sake of the money that might flow in, but to develop the spirit of true American camaraderie in social service. . . .

I had in mind two years ago a woman of independent means, trained in library work, who has traveled much and was at one time a YWCA secretary in a large eastern city, and who during the past years has developed a really wonderful library in a school with which I was formerly connected. I brought her to the attention of Mr. X at the Normal school in the hope that this thing might be begun a few years ago, but I have heard no more about it. I think she could still be secured for a few hundred dollars—for she takes the position, rightly I think, that all workers in an institution should be on the payroll. I should be happy, later, if you and Mr. Allaben should regard an effort in this direction as worthwhile, to put you in touch with her.

There are vast possibilities. I do not think that these things can be done at once. Changes will necessarily have to be made slowly; cooperation between the Woman's Board and other Presbyterian boards will have to be brought about tactfully, for I find that many good Christian people are very human after all and are heartily willing to cooperate if the other fellow will cooperate on their basis.

Mr. Allaben came from New York to join Dr. Calfee in going over plans for the reorganization with John, who felt that the prospect was "bright for their entering a larger field of service."

At the same time, Mr. Allaben talked with John at length about the proposed survey of the mountain field voted by the Knoxville conference. Since both were to be in Knoxville the next week en route to a conference at Maryville College, they asked Rev. Franklin J. Clark of the Episcopal Church to join them there to discuss it in more detail. John wrote Mr. Glenn:

> I am deeply interested in the prospect of this survey, in which all agencies working for the mountains may cooperate, and toward the expenses of which some of the boards may contribute funds. I infer that it is desired that I should be secretary of this commission, and I have been asked to submit to the Nominating Committee the names of officials who should constitute the commission. It would be a splendid achievement to make the Knoxville conference instrumental in securing such a survey and the publication of its findings. This division has been the prime mover in bringing it about and in all probability will be the directing agency in the survey, but it will yet be a cooperative effort with a diffused responsibility—and much more influential in consequence.

Both John and I had been thinking that Mr. Sharp would do well to come to Asheville for a visit in June if possible, in order that John should take him on an introductory trip into the nearby mountains. I had written him and he replied:

> I was glad to get your letter and delighted to read that you think it will be well worth my while to come for ten days or so next month. . . . I hope that nothing will interfere with this exciting little plan! It will be so nice to see you all again. I want to try and see that man in Washington sometime if I can and take down his tune.
>
> The pageant did not begin last night owing to the rain, and it does not look as though it could begin tonight either. I shall be glad of some warmth. It has been dreadfully cold and wet since we came here, and I have been rheumatic. The fear came on me that unless I got into the mountains pretty soon, my old-age ailments might put a stopper on the whole business—dreadful thought!

Alas for the plan! On June 6th, just before he was to arrive, came a telegram from Cincinnati: "Accident not serious prohibits visit to Asheville. So sorry. Writing. Sharp Hotel Gibson." This proved to be an accident while motoring, which injured a finger of his right hand. To a musician this was crippling to an unpleasant degree, and it was some weeks before he was able to use the hand normally. John wrote his sympathy from his own experience of the frustration of the "minor" accident. We looked forward now to his arrival in July to begin his extended collecting journeys.

John settled to the revision of his papers awaiting publication by the foundation, with a fairly uninterrupted month in prospect. Two other proposed publications claimed his thought. The first was a decennial volume containing statements from all departments, John's among them, that covered the work done and some of the results secured since the Russell Sage Foundation was organized. The second John mentioned in a letter to Mr. Glenn on June 27th:

Yesterday Professor R—— came to see me with reference to a "mission study" book on the mountaineers which the YMCA people want him to write. They have a series of books, which they write in a certain form—eight chapters to each book—in which the different groups, the objects of missionary effort, are studied. I pointed out to Professor R—— the risk of setting forth the mountain people as a distinct missionary group in the South, especially when the other distinct group in the South is the Negro. He had written me a very courteous letter previously, asking for an interview and asking, furthermore, if I intended to write a book of such a nature.

I told him of the proposed survey and said that, from my point of view, having the cooperation and welfare of the mountaineer in view, it would be better to wait until the survey (to be made by all agencies—denominational agencies included) had been made, and that a digest of such a book could be used for study; but I think the YMCA people will want him to go on with the work according to their own ideas. He asked if he might submit the manuscript to me for revision and to call his attention to the things that I thought might do harm. I agreed to do this.

My hope has been that the mountain field may be regarded in the light of a super-rural field rather than as a distinctive mission field, but with so many church boards working directly for the mountaineer, I am quite sure that my hope is not going to be realized just yet. However, if I can guide some of the efforts away from the more dangerous rocks, perhaps I am accomplishing something.

This particularly touched Mr. Glenn, who, a southerner himself, shared John's reaction. He replied:

> Concerning Professor R——'s study, it seems worth making a special effort to check the YMCA from doing something that is not going to be beneficial for the mountain work. A formal statement on missionary lines would be unfortunate. Would it be well for me to take up the matter with the Rural Department here; to write to Weatherford; to try to see John R. Mott, or somebody else high up; or to do anything else that seems wise to you? I think likely that Mr. Mott is still in Europe.

To this, John wrote:

> I hardly know what to say in regard to your inquiry of July 1st. I should very much prefer myself not to have the YMCA issue a special mission book relating to the mountain folks. The question came up, of course, in a personal inquiry from Professor R——, and I have given him my very frank opinion. I do not know that Professor R—— has been definitely engaged to write the book; I have a vague impression that the plan is for him to write a book to be submitted to them, and if he cannot meet their requirements or bring the book into the form, method, or system that they want, it could be rejected. I do not know that it would be advisable just now to take up the matter in correspondence with Mr. Weatherford, but if you should meet Mr. Weatherford at some time when you would have opportunity to present the situation fully, it would be well to do it. Naturally, it will be much better coming from you, under all the circumstances.

An earnest of interesting days ahead came in the suggestion by Mr. Glenn that John secure through the foundation office, for the Southern Highland Division library, Mr. Sharp's publications. He was sure they would be "serviceable to a number of people reached through the office—the more so, I think, after he visits the mountains." So it was that the fascinating books of his Folk songs and Country, Sword, and Morris dances, with their tunes, collected in England, came to us. These were a delightful addition to John's growing collection of material on all that pertained to mountain life.[1]

Mr. Sharp's arrival in Asheville was set for July 24th. With him was to come his secretary and assistant, Miss Maud Karpeles, who would work with him on the collecting trips. We made plans for them to visit first of all the Laurel country. John would accompany them to White Rock and, after a day or so, leave them with the Packards, who, with other workers, would guide them from that point. John wrote Mr. Sharp:

> Miss [Edith] Fish, one of the teachers on whom I am relying, is reserving the week for you, to introduce the people she knows. She has made quite a collection of ballads herself and is one of the people we shall have to count on for introductions in a certain section—to Granny Banks and a few others who sing "ballets." I think you will find a good bit of ballad material in this first section, as also in Kentucky when the time comes to go there. We are looking forward with much pleasure to your coming and shall do all we can to make you and Miss Karpeles fall in love with our mountain country.[2]

A last note from Mr. Sharp, written with difficulty, confirmed the day and added, "It is just possible I may break the journey at Washington and try to get ahold of Mr. Spiller and get that song from him. . . . It is rather hot here, and I have much hay fever and asthma, which I hope your mountains will cure. My finger is all right for ordinary purposes. It is healed but still much swollen and very insensitive."

His journey to Asheville was to prove a trying and uncertain one. A tremendous storm almost prevented realization of our carefully laid plans. When we woke the morning of July 16th, we could hear the river roaring below. One of the worst cloudbursts in local history had flooded the valley; lights, electric cars, train service, all were out of commission; milk and ice were very scarce. On the 18th John sent an account to Mr. Glenn:

> We have one wire with the outside world via Atlanta, and one rail connection—at least by this afternoon—by way of Murphy, North Carolina, and Knoxville. The Swannanoa Valley and the French Broad have been hit very hard; the Swannanoa enters the French Broad a mile below my home, so Asheville got the force of floods from both rivers. What the mountaineers call a "cloudbust" occurred in the vicinity of Black Mountain on the Swannanoa, and something of the same sort carried out three dams above us on the French Broad. The property damage has been heavy, but fortunately word was received in time for most people to get out of the path of the flood in the immediate valleys. For lack of communication, we do not know yet what happened back in the mountains on the headwaters of these streams. Marshall, one of my points of departure for the mountain country, has been wiped out—so far as rumors go—although the people

could get to the hills. Our best train, the *Carolina Special,* is marooned somewhere beyond Marshall with about three hundred passengers, and the Southern is now assembling a flock of Fords to bring them over the hills.

The citizens of Asheville have responded very generously according to their means, and I think the local refugees will be kept from dire distress; there are three hundred now in the high school building, and others are being cared for elsewhere. These are mostly mountain folks from the mill and factory district, who have lost everything. We have offered our office to the Relief Committee for any help that can be given in the way of office work, etc.

Mr. Sharp, I think, might just as well come; we can take care of him all right, and if there should be delay of two or three days getting into the mountains, he could get a good rest. I have made arrangements for his secretary here, and if he should ask if it is advisable for her to come, she can be taken care of, but if she should wish to wait a week and come later, she can be arranged for then. He and I might have to go by horseback into the mountains from another point than Marshall, but in that event the young lady could wait in Asheville.

It would be a little longer coming from Murphy, but he would get a very good idea of western North Carolina, coming by way of Knoxville and Murphy. It is a mountain road and very pretty scenery. I think he is a good sport and would not mind very much the inconvenience of local trains from Knoxville to Asheville. He might even fall in with some mountaineers—on the train from Murphy, at least—who would be able to give him some very choice old ballad.

We are all right at home, living in a primitive way with candles and cherishing the precious gallon of oil, which is dwindling. I think we shall have more, however, from Atlanta or Knoxville by tomorrow night. Mrs. Campbell's sister is here, with her little one, and we are counting on getting ice for the babies through our physician's certificate.

How well I remember the arrival of the travelers—for Mr. Sharp brought with him his secretary and faithful assistant, Maud Karpeles—on the circuitous route, via Knoxville, Blue Ridge, and Murphy. Due at 1:00 p.m. July 25th, they did not get in finally until 11:00 p.m. We met them and brought them home to bed in Blythewood.

Morning put a different face on the world. The sun shone. We talked and talked, then had tea and more talk in the afternoon. At night Mr. Sharp played delightful harmonizations of many ballads, after which packing was the order until late, for Mr. Sharp and Miss Karpeles were to be up for a start with John at 5:30. As they rolled off in the early morning light—by automobile to Weaverville, and thence by "rig" to White Rock—I tried to realize what this all must mean to the ballad hunters and almost envied John the experience of being with them. I knew something of what they would find; *they* could only wonder, and hope!

Letters came soon; excited, triumphant ones from John, and then a jubilant and more detailed one from Mr. Sharp, hastily written in pencil, on August 1st from Allanstand, North Carolina:

I am having a wonderful time, as I believe Mr. Campbell has told you. So far I have taken down twenty-five tunes, including variants. The average quality is very high, both in tunes and words. Nearly all of the tunes are modal. I want to send all of them to you. Maud has been busy all day typing the words and will probably finish them tomorrow, when your copies shall be sent off. I have just written Miss Dickey to send me some music paper, so that I may send you some of the best of the tunes.

The singers I have heard here are Mrs. [Mary] Sands, who has given me twelve splendid songs, and Mr. Frankland B. Shelton, who sang me four rather poor ones. This afternoon I tackled Mrs. Dora Shelton, got a little from her, and hope for more tomorrow.

The best ones I have got so far are two "Lord Bateman"; three "Earl Brands"; "Don't You Remember Last Friday Night"—a splendid Dorian one from Mrs. Noah Shelton; two "The Wife of Usher's Well"; "Bruton Town"—rather a rare find; "Silk Merchant's Daughter"—a very fine Aeolian air; "The 'Purbadus' Lady"—one of the most curious and wonderful tunes I have ever heard; two "Lady Margaret and Sweet William"; "Awake, Awake"—a version of my "Arise, Arise"; "Little Soldier Boy," which had affinities with "The Dragon and the Lady," a very ancient ballad; two "Daemon Lover"; "Pretty Polly"; a version of the "Broken Token." Not a bad list for a beginning—my first four days.

I find the singers very easy to handle; indeed they are just English peasant folk, they do not seem to me to have taken on any distinctive American traits. They talk English, sing English, and behave English! This surprised me not a little, but I suppose if it were not so, the ballads would not have survived. I am very excited, as you may imagine. Your absence is the fly in the ointment. It seems such hard lines that you of all people should not be sharing the delight. However, our book is assured—there is already more than enough to make an unusually interesting collection.

I cannot hope to go on like this, of course, but must be prepared for some dull patches; but I have seen enough to realize what a wealth of song it is that you have introduced me to. I don't know what I should have done without Mr. Campbell, nor how I shall get on without him when he returns to Asheville. I find the weather very hot and the traveling rather trying, but I am very well notwithstanding, and so long as there are songs to be got I shan't go under!

It was good to find Mr. Sharp was very well. He was not strong, and a victim of hay fever and asthma. He could not ride horseback, and the only way to reach many of the singers had to be by foot, often over high rail-less foot logs which were a real problem to navigate. How he managed to do so much, under all his handicaps, is still a marvel to me.

Mr. Glenn had wished for some time to see something of the mountain country with John but had been unable to plan it. Now Mr. Sharp's reports to him from the Laurel country, added to our standing invitation, often repeated, brought word from him, "I hope to get away from here [New York] about the middle of August. If so, I may be able to spend a week or ten days in your mountains. What inducements have you to offer? I would like if possible to get into the higher mountains and woods. I shall have to be at Afton, Virginia, by August 31st." John replied on August 5th:

I was much pleased on my return from the mountains last night to find your letter of July 31st and to learn of the prospect of your coming to Asheville for a mountain trip. I hope very much that nothing will interfere; it will give both Mrs. Campbell and me much pleasure to have you come directly to our home, and then, should you wish, for me to act as your guide on any of the trips that you might wish to take.

I would suggest, among others, taking the railroad trip to the top of Mount Mitchell, the highest point east of the Rockies—6,711 feet. We can go up in the morning and get back at night by the Mount Mitchell Railway, or one could spend any length of time there in a log-cabin hotel, or could have a tent with floor and stove; accommodations for $2.50 per day. Several days could be spent in this way if one should wish. I should also suggest the one-day trip to Mount Pisgah, which lies in the new forest reservation recently purchased by the government from Mrs. Vanderbilt; we could go by auto in the morning and return at night; and a more extended trip to the Laurel country in Madison County, where Mr. Sharp is now gathering ballads—where there are good accommodations to be had at some of the church centers with which I am well acquainted; going across country from there to the CC&O Railway and to the Grandfather region, or from the Laurel country returning to Marshall, going by rail to Johnson City, Tennessee, and then taking the narrow-gauge up into North Carolina to Cranberry, from which point we could reach Grandfather Mountain, thence to Blowing Rock, and return to Asheville. All of this could be done in ten days or two weeks of not-too-strenuous traveling, or a halt could be made at any one of the places, should you so wish.

My brother-in-law may be here about the same time for a long-hoped-for mountain trip, and I know that he would be very glad to climb with you to any point beyond my limit. I am delighted with the thought of your coming into my field and shall be very glad indeed to do anything I can to have you see the best of it in this general region—and this is about the best, all things considered, of the southern mountain country with which I am acquainted. . . .

Mr. Sharp will probably be in the Laurel country until September. He is finding it a very rich field and is getting material that has been lost in England. He says the mountain folks are now singing what was sung in England a hundred years ago. The ballads that he has secured in England are comparatively modern. He is very enthusiastic; in the four days I was with him, he gathered thirty ballads that he considered choice and some remarkable melodies. Our good friends at the four or five stations which he makes headquarters for different areas are most kind, and are doing everything to make him comfortable and happy, and are furthering his work, which he appreciates greatly. He will be down for a weekend on the 19th, and should you wish, we could return to the Laurel country with him, after having previously taken the trips to Mount Mitchell and Mount Pisgah.

Mrs. Campbell wishes me to say for her that she hopes you will find it convenient to make our home your starting point, returning to it as often as will suit your convenience. May we not also hope to see Mrs. Glenn? Should you wish to steal away by yourself, I shall be glad to indicate points where you could be comfortable, and I shall be glad to accompany you a part or all of the way, if that should seem best. I hope that I am not going to get a letter from you bringing the unwelcome news that business pressure necessitates your foregoing this trip.

The local trains between here and Knoxville began running yesterday, and probably the best route for the next weeks would be to take the through train from New York to Knoxville, coming then by the Southern to Asheville.

To our regret, family illness, a threatened railroad strike, and business at the foundation office prevented Mr. Glenn from making the trip, although until August 22nd he had expected to come.

Notes from John's letters, with reports from Mr. Sharp and Miss Karpeles, tell something of the experience of the August weeks in the mountains. On August 7th John wrote to Miss Frances Goodrich:

I have just returned from a trip introducing Mr. Sharp and his secretary, Miss Karpeles, to the Laurel country. . . . He spent last week at Allanstand, and today I believe he goes to Allegheny for a week, working Carmen from Allegheny. . . . Next week he goes to Big Laurel and the Spillcorn region. He is very anxious to meet William Riley Shelton (alias "Singing" or "Frizzley" Bill). Mr. Sol and others urged him by all means to see Bill. . . . He will return to Asheville for a weekend and then probably go to the Flag Pond country and perhaps to Revere, where I got track of a number of singers. Miss Shafer has sent word for him to come to Hot Springs to see a Mrs. [Jane] Gentry. He is very happy and enthusiastic, and the people themselves are taking pride in having conserved something that he thinks eminently worthwhile.

He wrote also to Miss Jennie Moore of Flag Pond on August 11th:

The last time I saw you, you were so proud of your new bathtub, and so urgent that I should come over to see it, that I am tempted to come and bring an Englishman to try it out.

Mr. Cecil Sharp, the authority on English ballads, is now in the Laurel country, the way to which was opened to him through Mrs. Campbell, Miss [Frances] Goodrich, and Miss Fish. He has found it a most wonderful field and has been staying with Dr. Packard, Miss Fish, and with the Hamiltons at Allegheny. On Monday he is going over to be with Miss Henricks and work the Big Laurel and Spillcorn country. He then returns to our house for a weekend and may run up to Hot Springs, where Miss Shafer says she has some people for him to see. Thereafter, sometime probably about the middle or end of the week beginning August 20th, I am planning to bring him over to the Flag Pond country, and I should like very much, if it suits your convenience, to have him make Rocky Fork or Devil's Fork a center, that he may have your assistance and direction in meeting the people. Miss Karpeles, his secretary, will be with him.

He has a fund especially for these ballads, and I have persuaded the others who have entertained him and his party to entertain him on the basis of paying guest. While all were so good as to want to entertain him, because of his quest, and because of his being my friend, as a guest in their home, yet Mr. Sharp wishes it otherwise, and he insists that what we do for him, getting him to and fro, shall be paid out of his fund. If it should be convenient for you, of course I shall be most happy to have him with you, and to be in your home the few days that I am to be there, but if it is inconvenient in the least, will you be so good as to make arrangements in the best place possible?

. . . Minta Carter has some people in mind who sing ballads, and I should be glad to have you list any that you may know prior to our coming.

And on August 14th to Mr. Glenn:

Thank you for the copy of Mr. Sharp's letter, which I received this morning. We look for him for a weekend Friday or Saturday. Miss Dickey had a letter from him yesterday, through which we learn that he has found more than a dozen tunes—other than these mentioned in your letter—in one of the homes to which Mrs. Campbell had directed him. I feel very confident that he could spend a year or more in different sections of the mountains, finding many ballads in one place and perhaps few in another. I should like to have him get to other sections of the mountains later. The section he is visiting at present is probably more English than many others.

One day earlier, on August 13th, Mr. Sharp had written to me:

I am sending you under separate cover more words, i.e., up to date, but only a few tunes. I have so much writing to do, what with letters and my own tune book, that I have really not had the time to do more. The sad part is that I have come to the end of my tune books, and as Miss Dickey has not sent me more, I am afraid that they are not procurable in Asheville, which is rather a serious business.

We start early tomorrow with a pack mule and a boy to guide up for Big Laurel. We return here on Friday and hope to catch the noonday train at Marshall on Saturday for Asheville, so this day week I shall be able to tell you what I have done. I think the number of tunes is now ninety-one. Of course a good many are variants, and all are not of the highest quality, but the average is high, and every one has something about it that made me want to note it. I think the finest song, i.e., both words and tune, is Mrs. Hensley's version of "The Cruel Mother." I enclose tune. That alone would have paid me for my three weeks' work.

I like the people very much indeed and find them readier to sing to me even than the English singers. No doubt this is largely owing to the planning credentials which you and your husband have furnished me.

I came across "Frizzley" Bill yesterday at Allegheny and have an appointment with him on Tuesday morning. Alas! He sang me one song very badly, and I am afraid he may be a thoroughly bad singer. Mrs. Hensley and someone else told me this. Still I hope for the best!

To which John replied on August 15th:

The ballad material which you mailed August 14th from White Rock, Mrs. Campbell received this morning. Miss Dickey has sent music blanks to both White Rock and to Big Laurel. We are delighted at your continued success and are pleased to know that you liked the Reuben Hensleys; they were very nice to us. I hope "Frizzley" Bill will turn out to be a good singer after all. . . .

We are looking forward with much eagerness to your return. All goes well at home. All send greetings and best wishes to you and Miss Karpeles. I wish I could have been there to have guided you by bypaths to Carmen, but perhaps you have found them ere this. I wonder if you got in touch with William Lamb on the Mill Branch of Upper Shelton Laurel, near Carmen, and whether you found Lizzie Shelton at Carmen, and also whether you got any word of Mrs. Sutherland—Mr. Reuben Hensley's sister? There are a thousand and one questions we want to ask, but they can be deferred till you come.

We heard further of Mr. Sharp in a letter he sent to Miss Dickey on August 16th:

The MS paper today is not nearly so good nor so suitable for my purpose as the paper you sent me to write my tunes on for Mrs. Campbell. I think that might do very nicely if cut and bound to the measurements I sent you, and in accordance with the instructions penciled on enclosed sample. Do you think you could get me a single volume bound for me at once so that I could begin on it soon after I reach Asheville on Sunday? I have already come to the end of my last blank book and am now writing my tunes on the loose sheets I have by me—temporarily.

We were in despair this morning as after two days' work here we had practically got nothing. Frizzley" Bill has failed to turn up, alas! And we meditated returning to Allanstand and Allegheny for the rest of the week. But by chance, hearing that a daughter of Granny Banks was living here, Mrs. Rice, I called on her and found she knew a lot of her mother's songs, so we shall be fully occupied for the rest of the week, I expect. I took eight off her this morning, and eight very interesting ones.

I am looking forward to my short breather at Asheville on Saturday, and to the pleasure of showing my notebooks to Mrs. Campbell.

Mr. Sharp came to Asheville as planned on Saturday, the 19th, and remained through Tuesday, the 22nd, when Mr. Glenn sent the telegram canceling his trip. John wrote Mr. Glenn on August 23rd:

We are sorry to learn from your telegram of your decision not to come, but undoubtedly in view of the railroad strike situation, it is the wiser decision at this time. We hope very much you will be free to come to see us sometime during the year.

I go to Hot Springs today with Mr. Sharp, returning tonight, and then leave for Madison County and over the line into Tennessee, where I have made arrangements for him. He gets a little better results, I think, in collecting ballads if this personal introduction is given and I can get hold of some of the people for him whom it would be difficult for him to get in touch with otherwise.

He has been most successful. I think he has collected over 130 ballads with the tunes, which, with Mrs. Campbell's, makes a total of over 200 already. There are many more sources he has not touched. The effect upon the people is what I hoped it would be; they are proud of the fact that they have retained something so worthwhile; and when his findings are published, I feel sure it will be helpful to the whole mountain country, placing the mountains in a somewhat different light before the country than that in which they have been too often viewed.

Mr. Sharp continued his success in Hot Springs, as appears from a letter to Mr. Glenn, written by John on August 26th, before he left with Mr. Sharp for Madison County and the Laurel country:

I am leaving with Mr. Sharp today for Madison County, going across the border into Tennessee. He has just returned from Hot Springs, North Carolina, where we got him in touch with an old ballad singer, and he has returned highly elated, having secured 30 from her—all of them very valuable, some of them very rare.[3] He never had an experience of this sort; I think the largest harvest he ever reaped before in England is 300 in a year's time. In less than a month, in a very limited area of the mountains, he has secured over 160. With those that Mrs. Campbell has, the total is carried well over 200.

I am very sorry indeed that we must start off without you, for we all wanted very much to have you with us on this trip. If I go with Mr. Sharp to Oneida, Kentucky, about the 15th of September, could you not join us somewhere, and after I have introduced Mr. Sharp at Oneida, you and I could continue our trip, going to Hindman, Buckhorn, and Pine Mountain. It would be a splendid trip, at a good time of the year, and the Madison County trip can easily be taken at any time. If this proposed trip would come too soon after your vacation, I shall hope for your coming for the Madison County trip sometime in October; this is a glorious month in the mountains.

My paper is well under way; it was interrupted by the flood and by Mr. Sharp's coming. I hope to have it finished soon after my return; I am now awaiting some information from state superintendents and others before completing it.

News of the travelers came soon in a letter of Miss Karpeles to Miss Dickey:

I think you will soon be sorry that you let us know how kind and good-natured you are, because now I am really going to impose upon you.

Let me explain—I think you know the Reuben Hensleys, and you may have heard that Mr. Sharp is helping to send Emma, their youngest daughter, aged thirteen, to school at Hot Springs. Everything has been satisfactorily arranged, and she is to go on September 12th. But the great difficulty is getting the outfit. As you know, it is impossible to get things here, and I was in despair until I thought of you. I am afraid the list of necessary things is a very long one, and if I am asking too much of you, you must let me know. But if you can and will get the things, I can only say that you will be doing a very real kindness to Mrs. Hensley—also to Mr. Sharp and myself.

Will you send the goods to Mrs. Reuben Hensley, Carmen, N.C., and the account to Mr. Sharp? I will leave it entirely in your hands to get suitable things, as you will know the sort of thing that is required. . . . I need hardly tell you how very grateful I shall be if you can purchase these things.

Frizzly Bill has been captured by Mr. Campbell, and he has been brought here, so we shall probably remain here until Wednesday, then go to Rocky Fork. . . . Mr. Campbell says will you please phone Mrs. Campbell on receipt of this letter and ask her to write to him at Rocky Fork. He will probably leave there for the Packards on Thursday or Friday.

Mr. Sharp took the greatest pleasure in relating the outcome of this generous plan: how Emma, fitted out, repaired to school, and how soon—"cabined, cribbed, confined"—she took steps to regain her freedom. Happening to be in Hot Springs, Mr. Sharp and Miss Karpeles spied her, with a friend, boarding a ferry across the river. When they called her, she returned and explained in a dignified manner that she was "running away home." Withal, she did not forget to thank her friends for their consideration, and the things they had given her.

And then he would laugh heartily, and approve her conduct. A scion of such a natural singing family could not be expected to fit into any Presbyterian mold; better that she kept her liberty.

On September 1st, he wrote to me reporting further progress:

We are just back after a very fierce day in which we tramped up Higgins' Creek, a matter of twelve or fourteen miles there and back, mostly over stones and boulders! However, we have brought home something for our trouble—a fine version of "The False Knight," Child, No. 3, and of "The Gypsie Laddie." Also a lovely Dorian tune to "The False True-Lover [*sic*]"! Yesterday I got a very fine tune to another love song, of a type I have never met with before. In drawing [?] Mrs. Tony Selton up Higgins' Creek yesterday, I found a Mrs. Crane, a very pretty little woman who married four years ago a man two months younger than herself, and she was only seventeen. She sang me several moderately good songs besides the splendid air already mentioned and then proposed that she should take us up the creek to see her father, a Mr. Blankenship, this morning. So we started off from here at 7:00 a.m., called for her, and toiled three and a half miles with her up the creek until at last we reached her father's house, just ready to drop. There was a house full of people, mostly relatives, of three or four generations, and there we stayed until three o'clock.

Then coming home, at their suggestion, we called on a Mr. and Mrs. [T. G.] Coates, who, I was told, might know "Dives and Lazarus." She did sing me a Lazarus song, and not a bad one, but not the Child ballad; and then it was we tackled her about others, and we got "The False Knight" and "Black David." We are too tired tonight—or rather, Maud is—to type out the words of "The False Knight," but we shall probably catch up arrears on Sunday and send it off to you. You will be delighted with it, as it is a very much older and, I think, more effective form than the Motherwell version which Child gives. I am going to cultivate Mr. Coates, of course, and go there tomorrow morning early by appointment.

In the evening I am to see Mr. Crane, whom I have not yet met, and I hope to get "The Wife Wrapt in a Wether's Skin" from him. I have heard of "Dives and the Golden Vanity" but have not yet got either.

Weather very hot, but fine in the day, cold at night. Quite comfortable here. Hope John C. got home all right yesterday.

Blythewood was a refuge to the weary travelers between spurts of collecting. Here they had always an enthusiastic welcome, a chance to clean up and eat well-cooked food, and usually a bunch of home letters waiting for them. How often I have seen them open those letters and then silently slip down into the woods behind the house to walk up and down, and up and down, talking in low voices of those young Englishmen who would no more help in the folk song and dance revival in England. Then at night Mr. Sharp would sit down at the piano and play and play; he was working on his collection for Ditson—and I loved particularly his "Queen Jane" and "Brisk Young Sailor." But many were very lovely. They mingled with my dreams.

My diary reads:

September 7—C# and K. blew in about 4:00 p.m., tired but successful.
September 9—C# and K. started for P—— but came back, took machine to Swannanoa, where we got several songs from Mr. Wells.

September 11—Off to Hot Springs for a week (C# and K).
September 16—Back in Asheville (C# and K).

Mr. Sharp wrote to John from Hot Springs on September 12th:

We did a lot of prospecting this morning, calling on the Garretts, etc., and this afternoon had a nearly three-hour séance with Mrs. Gentry. Tell Mrs. Campbell the tune to the "Gold Vanity" is a beautiful one, Dorian. Then we got from Mrs. Gentry a version of "Long Lamekin" (No. 93) and a second variant of the "The False Knight." So, with the "Two Sisters," which she gave us last night, we have now three new "Children" to go on our list. Others that we got from her were "The Green Bed," "The Tree in the Wood," two other cumulative ones, a good variant of "The House Carpenter," and several nursery ones and one or two scraps of good songs with nice tunes—altogether about fourteen from her, and I dare say I shall get a few more.

No one else has sung to us here as yet, but we have a few cues, some of which may turn up trumps. Spiny [?] Creek is evidently the place to go to, but the settlement is a long way off and it would be difficult to manage and very rough at that. We are at present basking in an exotic luxury, to which I feel we have no right! But it is rather nice all the same! It looks as if we had better stay here through the week and give up Georgia. With three Child ballads already bagged, we have done excellently well. . . . Maud will send Mrs. Campbell words as soon as she can find time to type them.

Such times have to come to a close some day. They returned again to Blythewood for the last farewell, and on September 18th finally left for Black Mountain and Charlottesville, Virginia.

The next news from Mr. Sharp came ten days later, when he wrote John, on September 20th:

The hotel at [Black Mountain] was pretty bad, but the people were kind and did all they could to make us comfortable. . . . However, it was all right and we got a fine lot of songs—twenty-six in number, including versions of "Golden Trinity" (a very fine set of words), "Geordie Mathie Graus," "Cruel Ship's Carpenter," "Swannanoah Town," "The Ten Commandments," etc. There were heaps of songs to be got there, a holiness cobbler—diseased in body, poor chap, and being afflicted with holiness,

I presume, in mind also—who had plenty to sing if you could prevail on him to disgorge! But we felt we had better get on, so left by the 5:00 train.

The scenery till it got dark was the finest, by far, that we have seen in the mountains. We have a famous singer marked down at Marion. Our Salisbury train was late, so we had to wait there till 2:00 a.m., and then had great difficulty in getting our sleeping berths. However, we triumphantly reached Charlottesville at 10:30 this morning, pretty well tired out.

I got my books written up by 4:00 p.m., when we sallied forth to Alphonso Smith.[4] He received us most friendly and was nice as we could wish. . . . He is going to send someone—a school inspector, Mr. McManaway—sounds Scotch, which is a good omen!—to see and advise us tomorrow at 10:00 a.m., and on the results of this interview much will depend. But I fancy that it doesn't much matter where we go so long as we get into the simple parts of the country, for I argue that the tradition is so alive that we shall find it pretty nearly everywhere. Certainly it has been so thus far, but of course we may be about to receive a check.

We are quite comfortable here . . . so we have pretty well decided to remain here till we move on to Chicago—perhaps via Washington. We are both feeling rather blue at turning our backs upon Asheville. It will be long before I forget the great and continuous kindnesses that we have received from you and Mrs. Campbell. You anticipated our every want even to the provision of a guest on the premises for me to argue with!

Tonight we are indexing and getting our books into shape so that we can use the material we have gathered. If we find we get no songs here, I do not think I shall try anywhere else, but get to work and prepare for the writing of our book.

The next from Mr. Sharp brought the war very close to us all, with the news that his son Charles had been wounded. On September 24th he wrote John:

Many thanks for sending me the cables from England, which have of course caused me a great deal of anxiety while supplying me with a certain amount of relief also. I had seen in the papers that the Guards had been in the thick of it, and I had been anticipating trouble for some days. I can only hope that Charlie will get through his time at the hospital all right and that then he will be sent back to England to convalesce, which I trust will occupy a good long time. Many thanks for your sympathy.

We have done quite well here, and this last week I have taken down forty-seven tunes. The country is much more sophisticated than is your part of the world, but I fancy that it would be just as easy to get good things here as anywhere else in the Appalachian district. It seems to me that the songs are to be found everywhere, and at every new place we go to, we find a large number of those that we have already collected elsewhere, together with a few new ones. We have got nothing absolutely new this week except at Black Mountain, but I have secured two very beautiful versions of the "Two Sisters," another variant of "The Farmer's Curst Wife," and a good version of the "Wether's Skin," which I had not found in America before. Some of the tunes I have taken down are fully equal to anything that I have got elsewhere. . . . We hope to move on to Washington on Thursday and get to Chicago on Friday or Saturday. . . .

Alphonso Smith has been exceedingly courteous and kind to us and is, I feel sure, genuinely interested in the subject. He is modest, too, about his own attainments and seems very ready to get what information he can out of me. Altogether I like him very much, and he is certainly a good man to have as an ally. This is really not a very good center to work from, as we are too far away from the best districts. We find it necessary to hire a motor to take us out seven or eight miles in the morning and then leave us to prospect and make our way back as well as we can—sometimes a pretty tiring proceeding. On the whole I am glad we came here.

It had proved desirable to Mr. Sharp to have in hand a full set of the *English and Scottish Popular Ballads,* by Francis James Child, the authoritative and comprehensive collection, for use in preparing for publication the ballads collected here in America. John enlisted through Mr. Glenn the Russell Sage Foundation Library to secure this if possible, writing on September 11th:

From data contained in an old letter from Professor Kittredge to Mrs. Campbell, it would appear that this set was published by Houghton Mifflin Company in 1882 and succeeding years. It was issued in ten parts, making five volumes. One thousand copies were printed at a subscription price of fifty dollars per set. Dr. Kittredge did not know whether the publishers had any unsold copies in stock but thought a few might be left. . . . Mr. Sharp will be willing to pay as high as one hundred dollars for the set. If there should be a second set, I should be glad to know of it. Mr. Sharp wants them for working purposes, and if they are in substantial form for use, he would not mind at all about the binding.

On the 27th, Mr. Glenn telegraphed, "Can get Child's Ballads in sheets unbound for seventy-five dollars. Price is low. Shall we buy. Have option until Saturday." This was relayed to Mr. Sharp in Charlottesville the same day. He wrote me the next day:

Your husband's telegram about the sheet edition of Child has just reached me. I have written and posted a letter to Mr. Glenn accepting the offer, asking him to procure the book for me and to get it bound in time for me to use it when I get to New York the middle of next month. It seems a great opportunity and one which I ought not to lose.

. . . We are very sad to think that our hunting has now to be suspended indefinitely. We have done very well here, and this is just as good a ground for collecting as any other that we have been to. We have got some wonderful versions of "The Two Sisters" and "The Two Brothers," another variant of "Sir Lionel," and I think before I leave I shall get a version, more or less complete, of the "Three Ravens." This latter is the only new Child ballad I have come across since we left Black Mountain, but of course it gets increasingly difficult to add to the large number that we have already found.

It has been a good business to make the acquaintance of Professor Alphonso Smith. He is now our strong ally and will do everything he can to help us. Yesterday he came with us collecting at Woodridge, which was a very good experience for him, although, between ourselves, rather a trying one for us. He treated the singers just as a university professor is accustomed to treat his students, and it was amusing to see the faces of blank amazement that his questions and talk produced. He is not what you would call a "born collector," but all the same he has been most courteous and kind to us. Last evening I addressed, at his request, a meeting of the faculty at their private club at the university.

The number of tunes I have collected is now at 387, so that between us we shall have about 450 to choose from for our book. I am quite sure that the important thing now is for us to get our book out as quickly as possible, and I am trying to alter my plans between now and Christmas so as to get two or three weeks free of engagements. If I can get that much, I can do enough to enable me to send the greater part of the MS to the press and to do the rest while the book is being printed. I believe I have collected about 130 versions of the Child ballads, which is quite a good number and will make a fine show for the first part of the book. I probably shall work at New York, because I know I can get a quiet and suitable room at the Algonquin, and I shall be near the public library, which is a very good one.

By the way, I am going to add to the many things that I have asked you to do for me during these holidays. I left two pairs of boots in the upper room, and I want these done up and sent to Mr. Reuben Hensley, Carmen. They are just his size and they are good boots, although they do not do for me. I had a nice letter from Mrs. Hensley the other day, in which she said that she intended keeping Emma at home until Christmas at any rate. Perhaps she may then return to school, if she is still unmarried, which is scarcely probable. Maud is writing to you and sending you, I believe, the balance of the words this afternoon.

The weather has been perfectly lovely since we came here, and it continues, making it harder than ever to give up this delightful work and plunge into teaching and lecturing again.

I have had no further news from my wife about Charlie and shall not hear details before next week at the earliest. Love to you all.

Miss Karpeles also wrote to me on September 28th:

I have been "aiming" to write to you every day for the last week, but these grandchildren of yours are the cause of my not having done so. They require a great deal of time and attention. But alas, it will now be some time before there is an increase in the family. I am just heartbroken at the thought that our collecting days are over for some months, and I don't want to go to Chicago at all, although it is not quite so hard to go to Chicago from here as it would have been from North Carolina.

I am sending you the copies of the songs. Some of the words of "The Two Brothers" are rather nice, aren't they? Professor Alphonso Smith has really been very nice. I like his modesty. He is very keen for Mr. Sharp to come to Virginia again and do some more collecting. I think he is very jealous of North Carolina. I am sure there is a lot to be found here, but of course Charlottesville is not a good center to work from.

I have never thanked you properly for having been so awfully good to me in putting me up at all sorts of inconvenient times, but I am sure you know how much I have appreciated it. Love to you and all the family.

So ended the collecting in Virginia. The next letter, from Chicago, brought the war still closer to us. On October 9th Mr. Sharp wrote John:

I found three cables awaiting me here last Friday week to the effect that Charlie was dangerously ill in the French hospital and that my wife had gone to him. The cables reach me very erratically, but although a slight improvement was recorded last Friday, I am afraid it is a case of touch and go with him. It is the wound in the shoulder which is causing the trouble, and I expect it is probably a case of pneumonia. The anxiety is terrible, and I do not know how I have got through the last week. My classes ended on Saturday, and this week I am lecturing every day till Friday afternoon. That evening I leave for New York, whither I hope to get on Saturday night. Con sent me a copy of Charlie's first letter after the catastrophe, which is so interesting that I have got Maud to make a copy for you—also a copy of the letter to me of his C.O.

We are less occupied this week, and so we are beginning the book—I must keep working or I should go off my head. If Mrs. Campbell can let me have the words at New York, I shall be glad.

Had a nice letter from Prof. [Alphonso Smith] this morning. By the way, "Alphy" is a great rival to you with Maud! My lecturette there seems to have set them thinking!

Soon Miss Karpeles reported better news, and John wrote Mr. Sharp on the 19th:

Mrs. Campbell received Miss Karpeles's letter this morning, and we are very happy over the news that the cables bring you word that your son seems to be slowly improving. We are hoping that this means for him a return to England for a long period of rest and that the dreadful conflict may be over before he is fully able to rejoin his regiment.

I am glad you had a good fortnight at Chicago. In all probability I shall see you in New York within a few weeks, as I now plan to come on about the first of November.

I am pained to know that Alphonso has become a rival of mine: is not there some ballad that you know about the fickleness of a maiden?

Barbara keeps gaining. Mrs. Coolidge is still with us; the paralysis plague, while decreasing in New York, seems to be increasing in Boston, and the doctors have advised her to remain until cool weather.

All join with me in sending love to you both.

Mr. Sharp in the meantime had reached New York, where he was to give an account of his findings on October 28th. As early as October 23rd, John had to write Mr. Sharp:

> I am sorry it does not seem likely that I can be in New York for the 28th. If some unforeseen good fortune should bring me there at the last moment, I shall appear. In any event, I shall be in New York soon thereafter and shall hope to hear all about it from you.
>
> You are most generous in the recognition you gave to the part Mrs. Campbell has played, and we both appreciate it.
>
> I hope very much you are beginning to hear favorable news from your son. My sympathy and admiration have gone out to you during all these trying weeks of suspense. When you write Mrs. Sharp, please express our sympathy and our hopes.

On the day of the lecture, Mr. Glenn wrote to John of Mr. Sharp: "Mrs. Glenn and I are looking forward with pleasure to hearing Mr. Sharp on ballads tonight. I am glad that he included Mrs. Campbell's name as a co-worker in the invitation which he sent out. It shows his good feeling. I have been very much impressed with his lack of desire to absorb everything for himself. He seems to be unusually fair and sympathetic."

A somewhat detailed account came from Mr. Sharp himself, in a letter of October 31st to me:

> I think the lecture went very nicely, and there is no doubt but that people were greatly interested. I was very tired when I began, as things had crowded thick upon me in the preceding days, but Maud said I was up to average, and I expect I was. There is no doubt that it makes a very pleasant sort of entertainment. I sang "The Knight upon the Road" and then, with Maud, "The Wife of Usher's Well" and "Cruel Mother"; while Rabold sang to my accompaniment "The Dear Companion," "Rejected Lover" (Virginia version), "Berkshire Tragedy" ("Cruel Ship's Carpenter"), and "Gipsy Laddie."
>
> Scribner's have refused mainly on score of expense. Schirmer's are biting now, and I shall probably make them an offer, as well, perhaps, as Holt and Putnam. But I am sure we shall get the book printed somehow or other, even if we have it done at our own risk by your Tufts printer. There will be no difficulty whatever in getting financial support if we need it. Everyone realized on Saturday night the urgent need of printing as soon as

possible. But the arrangements take time—that is the worst of it all—and of course we could not have a worse time in which to print a book, with paper etc. doubled in cost.

I have taken a provisional passage in the *Ryndam,* which sails for England November 30. I cannot leave my wife alone any longer, and I feel I must see my children again, if only for a few weeks. I am now trying to arrange dates for several engagements in the West, beginning about February 25 to the end of March. If I can pull this off, I shall come out again from England in time to do these, and then on their completion begin to collect again until the summer school in June–July, and perhaps go on again through August and September. But with affairs in England as they are at present, and with every possibility of their becoming infinitely worse next year, arrangements may have to be modified or given up. I am afraid to take my MS books over the ocean, and I think I shall deposit my small note books in your care, for you have copies of the words, so that if the worst comes to the worst it would be possible to reproduce them all again.

I am feeling rather the worse for wear. I found my work in New York very wearying. I suppose the strain I have been sustaining for so long is beginning to tell upon me. My boy is just about the same. The doctors are doing all they can to avert amputation, which would be a very dangerous operation. Anyhow the boy will always have a stiff shoulder, although he will have the use of his forearm and hand, if they can save the arm. I have frequent cables, and of course letters every mail. My wife assures me that anything that can be done is being done. He has the best of doctors and the best of nurses, Con says, but he looks terribly worn and haggard and bloodless, poor boy.

Sorry I shall miss your husband. I am here—Holyoke College—till Saturday night or Sunday morning, when I pass through New York en route to Pittsburgh, where I lecture on Monday afternoon—and perhaps evening also. Then back again to New York till Thursday morning, when I go to Philadelphia, and on Sunday to Toronto for ten days. Professor Gummere wants me to lecture to his students at Haverford when I am in Philadelphia, and I hope this may be arranged. I hope to be in Boston and to lecture there on my return from Toronto, November 22, 23 or 24!

Is Mrs. Coolidge still with you? I am so sorry for her. She must miss her home and husband terribly. American wives *do* miss their husbands sometimes, don't they?

John did meet the travelers once more in New York, and before they sailed was able to acknowledge (November 29th) the joyful news from them that Putnam was publishing the book:

> Hurrah! We are greatly delighted over the news. The Putnams will not, I am sure, regret having decided to publish the book.
>
> I am so glad of your genuine appreciation of the mountain people, for I grow very weary of the many who come to the mountains simply to exploit the mountaineer. Miss Wyman and Mr. Brockway are unfortunate in the persons who write up their work in the mountains and are even more unfortunate if the newspaper accounts at all represent their attitude to the mountain people.
>
> Mrs. Campbell is very happy over the news your letter brings, and Barbara too is hilarious today—probably reflecting the atmosphere of the household.
>
> With love to you and Miss Karpeles . . .

The sailing for England had to be postponed until December 8th, but, hearing no more, we assumed they got off on that day. We then studied the papers, hoping and fearing for news. On December 20th, I wrote to Mr. Sharp:

> We have been watching the papers very carefully and are hoping by this time that you have escaped the submarines and torpedoes and are safely in port. Even with the hard part of returning to England now, you must be happy to be with your people, and I hope that your son will be so well that he can join with you in whatever Christmas festivities you may feel like celebrating. It cannot be a very bright Christmas for England, yet with the late victories at the front, there is some cause for rejoicing and the hope that the war is at least nearer to an end.
>
> We are feeling saddened at this Christmastime ourselves, for this last week I lost my mother, and in spite of the fact that she had not really been herself for the last two years, one never realizes until the final break comes how hard it can be.
>
> Your registered package of notebooks arrived safely, and we have put it in safety deposit to ensure its preservation. I want to look over the tunes myself when the Christmas rush is over. I do hope that the censor will not

be too cruel and that he will allow you to send the *Folk-Song Journal;* however, I shall be more than happy to have it at any time.

Yesterday the Ditson volume came, and I am delighted with it. It really is a wonderful collection, and I should think that Ditson ought to be more than satisfied. I am beginning the sale by ordering two copies for Christmas presents for my sisters—West and East—for I feel they must become acquainted with the songs. You can imagine how promptly I sat down to play "Queen Jane" and the "Brisk Young Sailor," and they are lovelier than ever. Thank you so much.

Speaking of the censor, I have a clipping about you by Mr. Aldrich from the *New York Times* of two weeks ago. I do not much like the clipping, and I do not really think that Mr. Aldrich is as intelligent about your work as he ought to be; however, I thought you might be interested to see it. I will not send it with this, as I suspect the censors regard all newspapers with suspicion.

Now as to the introduction: I quite agree that you should write the introduction and be responsible for it. In the first place, I am very much the silent partner in this matter, and anything that is worthwhile will be said by you. In the second place, you will, of course, wish to write freely. My feeling in this matter is that you should go ahead and say just what you wish—no matter how desperate and heterodox your notions may be; get it "all off your chest." When you have said all you wish, if you will send me a draft, I will go over it carefully with Mr. Campbell and let you know very frankly and plainly anything that seems to us inadvisable, with reasons specified.

May I say here that one thing of which I have been a little afraid is that perhaps you might make some rather sweeping generalizations on the people and the mountain work which would not be true of *all* the people and *all* the mountain work. It is a fault into which almost everybody who visits any section of the mountains falls, including even people who have lived in one section or one state. One is apt to forget the great size of the southern mountain country (as large as England, Scotland, Wales, and more than two-thirds of Ireland, combined), the millions of mountain people, and the great variety of mountain work. It is true that many things which you might say of the people might be true of them all, yet the people vary tremendously in this whole area. Neither can you judge all mountain work by the few places which you visited. Any generalizations along this line would be manifestly unfair.

There is one thing, however, which I am anxious you should understand. You have suggested that some of the things you may say might be considered by us as detrimental to Mr. Campbell's work. One of the things which he has been greatly interested in furthering is the folk movement in the mountains—a movement which seeks the recognition and preservation of all that is native and fine. Take the folk song in particular. We would like to have the people recognize the worth and beauty of their songs; we would like to have the singing of these songs encouraged in all the mountain schools and centers; we would like to have them gradually displace the inferior music that is now being sung there. These things will be accomplished much more rapidly, I am sure, if there is secured the cordial, enthusiastic cooperation of workers on the field. If you should antagonize workers and board officials, you might easily retard or even seriously cripple the movement. The people have already begun to be somewhat ashamed of their songs; they need to have them appreciated by outsiders, and it is the "mission workers" in the field who constitute the most far-reaching, abiding, and influential body of outsiders. That is why one wonders sometimes if it always pays to say everything one thinks, when there is a possibility that it may hinder what one desires to accomplish. However this may be, I hope that you will believe that in whatever criticisms Mr. Campbell and I make, we are using our best judgment in furthering what seems to us the biggest end, and are not being influenced by petty considerations of what might possibly affect ourselves. I promise you that we will try to be as unbiased and unexacting as possible.

But perhaps I had better stop until I have before me what you have said: it is a little bit too much like arguing in the dark, and I might turn out almost as heterodox as yourself.

I will show Mr. Campbell this letter when he returns from the country today.

Will you please extend my Christmas greetings to your family, and the hope that the coming year may be a brighter one for you all and for England. Will you also give my love and greetings to Miss Karpeles; I do not know where to reach her except through you.

Before my letter reached him, Mr. Sharp wrote me from London, on January 8, 1917:

I have been so terribly busy since I arrived three weeks ago today, that I have been unable to find time to write to you.

The day after we arrived, I set to work on the book, and Maud and I have since then done very little else than stew away at it day by day. However, I am glad to say that we are beginning to see the end of our work, and I hope this week to hand over to Putnam's the rest of the songs, the notes, index, contents, etc., i.e., all except the introduction, which I hope to get at as soon as possible. The number of songs that I have decided to include in the book runs to 123, together with 300–350 tunes, so that it will be a book of a goodly size. I think I have included all that was really worth publishing.

I have omitted about sixteen tunes of yours for various reasons, and I am sorry to say I have been compelled to cut out the two hymn tunes. Personally I am rather weak on hymnology, and I did not feel over sure about the authenticity of the two numbers in question; so I sent them to Miss Gilchrist, who is one of the greatest authorities on the subject in England. Her pronouncement is that they are both Negro "spirituals." "Guide Me" is very closely allied to the Negro pilgrim's song in Coleridge-Taylor's *Twenty-Four Negro Melodies,* while the other one has much in common with "O'er the Crossing" and "Round the Mountain" in Krehbiel's book. "Lay this body down" is a favorite burden of negro "spirituals," as is also "been a long time traveling" and "I'm a'traveling to the grave for to lay this body down." From this it is quite clear that the hymns were not brought out from England, at any rate in the form in which they are now sung, but that they have somehow or other trickled in to the mountains from outside Negro-Methodist sources. In the circumstances I am sure you will agree that it is better to omit them, although I know you will be very sorry, as indeed I am. Perhaps it will be possible to publish them somewhere else.

In the notes I have confined myself to references to other published versions, of which I have given a large number culled from between sixty and seventy books, all of which I had in my own library except the *American Folk-Lore Journal,* which I consulted at the British Museum.

I have spent a great deal of time in the endeavor to analyze the modal gapped tunes and have made valiant attempt to apply the system adopted by the *Folk-Song Journal* in volume 4. But their system breaks down under the test, and my belief is that gapped modes have as yet been understood properly by no one. If I had time, I should like very much to see if I could not see through the mystery and devise some scheme which would really explain existing examples, including our own. But as I cannot possibly get the leisure to do this, I am afraid I shall have to confine myself in the book to generalizations.

I found all the members of my family, including my wife, extremely well and looking far better than when I left them last February. Maud is living with us, much to the delight of all my children (and mine also). We both feel the damp cold very much indeed, and at times we have very nearly sighed for the steam heater!

You have not yet sent me a reply to my suggestions about the introduction. I shall not in any case send this to Putnam's before I return to America, nor before you have seen it. My present intention is to leave England in about a month's time, so as to arrive in New York in the week beginning February 18th. I hope it will not be long after that before we are all together again in Asheville.

10

Fifth Conference and Ballads, 1916–1917

With Cecil Sharp safely at home across the sea in England, the Campbells concentrated on their own affairs. Chief among them were plans for the next conference, the comprehensive report of the work of the conference by the denominations represented there, and the proposed work of the Asheville Normal and Collegiate Institute to train rural teachers.

Of real concern to Campbell was the proposed publication by the YMCA of books about the mountain missions. He had been asked to write one and had refused, saying he was producing some bulletins that might help, but he thought it inadvisable for the mountain people to be featured in a mission textbook. He believed that the best way to help them was to send them trained workers who recognized their finer qualities instead of concentrating on their poverty and "superficial peculiarities."

By December the 1917 conference to be held in April was taking shape, and Campbell was pleased over the news that Dr. P. P. Claxton was coming, along with Harold W. Foght, specialist in rural school practice in the US Bureau of Education. In January Campbell completed his pamphlet The Future of the Church and Independent Schools in our Southern Highlands, *to be published by the Russell Sage Foundation in time for the conference.*

A draft of Cecil Sharp's introduction to the book of collected ballads arrived in February to great excitement. A long letter from Sharp came shortly thereafter, describing his recent trips in the United States. He was unable to come to Asheville to visit the Campbells but did get to the conference. A letter dated April 17 gave a "lively, detailed picture" of the conference to John Glenn, describing Dr. Claxton's opening address and other notable presentations, including the one by himself, which included a performance of some of the ballads. Cecil Sharp continued with accounts of his ballad-hunting trips with Maud Karpeles. His health was not good, but the doctors could not find the problem, finally deciding it was some sort of influenza. He wrote copiously about the kind treatment he had received throughout the mountains.

After June meetings in New York and at the Massachusetts Agricultural College Summer School, Campbell received a long letter from an Andover acquaintance, Dr. H. P. Douglass of the American Missionary Association, about the mountain work. He maintained that the AMA found it difficult to interest their donors in the small number

of mountain institutions that they already had, so he regretted that they were not pro-
ceeding very well in the direction of programs for mountain education. In a long answer,
Campbell replied that he regretted their position.

August occasioned another onslaught of letters from the ballad collectors about their
experiences: "We had a horrid journey last Monday from Pineville to Lexington. . . . The
day coaches on this line are as dirty and uncomfortable as they can be made!" Dances
were another research interest, and Sharp was excited about the "running sets" he saw at
Pine Mountain. He hoped to gather more on traditional dancing and on the children's
games that were new to him.

The first exciting period of ballad hunting was now over, and our friends were safely
across the treacherous seas in England. War was almost upon our shores, but for the
moment we could turn our attention fully to our own personal affairs. On October
5th, John had written to Mr. Glenn:

Some time ago I stated in a letter that I would write you with reference to
the outlook for work for the new year. . . .

The three things that loom largest at present are

Plans for the Knoxville conference. I should be glad of any suggestions
from you that come from your observations at Knoxville and from your
general experience for making the conference better.

The second plan, which, if wisely handled, promises much, is the proposed joint effort on the part of the denominations represented in the
conference for issuing a *comprehensive report* of their work. This office will
have much to do with that work. It is with reference to this matter in
particular that I want to come to New York. Mr. [Franklin J.] Clark of
the Board of Foreign and Domestic Missions of the Protestant Episcopal
Church is chairman of the appointing committee, and Mr. [Marshall C.]
Allaben, the author of the motion, is also a member of the committee.
There are a number of matters relating to the smooth ongoing of plans—
especially in their inception—that would better be matters of conference
than of correspondence.

Third, under the leadership of the new president of the Normal
School here, Prof. [John] Calfee, the Normal is entering upon a work
more adapted to the *training of rural teachers* and preparation for rural life
than has hitherto been true of the work of the school. I have been invited
to deliver before the faculty and the seniors—who become teachers next
year—a series of lectures on what they are pleased to term "rural sociol-

ogy." As a matter of fact, they will be conferences on mountain life. This is the beginning of what I hope may be a close touch with other institutions preparing pupils for rural teaching, ministry, and other rural activities.

This work will keep us very busy until May at least.

There are a number of other matters of interest, which I will not now take up. There is just one—that may result in much or little.

The letter continued with an account of being called in for consultation by the executors of a woman who had a private nondenominational school in the South Carolina mountains and who had consulted him in 1915 in the hope that the Sage Foundation would carry on her work. This was, of course, not within the province of the Foundation. Now, a national women's organization, with an active branch in North Carolina and disposed to start a school in the mountains, had become interested in taking over this work. John went on to say that

Calfee, the president of the Normal here, would cooperate with them in furnishing extension teachers to help out during the year and for carrying on the work during the summer months. It is all in the air at present, and they are looking for me to bring the different elements together. I do not know whether I can do it, but as soon as possible I shall make the effort. The trouble always is that most of the organizations wanting to do work want to hold the property, manage affairs, and have the name of their organization stamped on the enterprise—the willingness to cooperate being generally a willingness to have other people follow their lead and furnish a good share of the funds. I can find many opportunities for cooperation for the Sage Foundation on such a basis. However, something may come of this. . . .

I hesitate to speak of another work for the year, for it is one that I have long said I was going to do, and I intend to be a man of my word: that is, the matter of publishing bulletins. I have not yet been able to complete some that are under way. The flood, Mr. Sharp, and hay fever are the most available scapegoats. However, I am hoping that I am going to have a clearer mind and more uninterrupted leisure hereafter. The preparations of bulletins and lectures are not disassociated, one from the other, and much of the work for the Knoxville conference and the joint publication proposed can be directed by Miss Dickey under my general oversight.

In all John's planning, the spring conference, as usual, held first consideration, but so many things were linked to it or had some bearing on it that it was hard to distinguish conference work from his other activities. These continued to range widely, in the effort to promote mountain interests on all fronts.

The publication of serious books on the mountains, for example, was of real concern to John. This concern, expressed many times, and most recently to Professor R—— and Mr. Glenn in connection with the YMCA plan to prepare such a book (see chapter 9, above), appeared again in a letter of November 10th that John wrote Mr. Glenn about the same YMCA plan:

> I was much interested in the letter of Dr. Weatherford's which you were so kind as to send me. Professor R—— called upon me this summer on his return from the YMCA Summer School at Black Mountain, North Carolina. He came to ask if I purposed writing a book. I told him I had not thought it best as yet to write any book but that I was hoping to set forth, in the nature of bulletins, some facts about the mountains that might be of help.
>
> I also told Professor R—— that I thought it inadvisable for the mountain people and the mountain country to be set forth in the mission textbook. The mountaineers are extremely sensitive because of being regarded as objects of missionary effort. The term "missionary" is, in their mind, associated with work for non-Christian people, and they regard themselves as churchmen and Christian. They have not been without the ministration of the church, though they have not had church advantages to the same extent or of the same kind as people in more accessible rural regions have. It would be a mistake, in my judgment, to publish such a book.
>
> It would be a mistake, in my judgment, also, having in view the future work of the YMCA in the mountains. For a number of years past I have been working with the Country Life Department of the YMCA to get them to enter the mountain field. They should enter it, I think, as a rural field whose conditions have been made more intense because of topography. It would be more successful from my point of view if their work should be regarded merely as an extension of their rural county work.
>
> These opinions are based, of course, on my own preferences and experience for the past twenty years in the mountains.

In replying to Mr. Weatherford on November 12, Mr. Glenn enclosed a copy of John's letter and added:

> I am inclined to think that too much has already been written about the mountaineers. I do not think that literature about the mountaineers for

the general public does much good. The only sure way to help them is by sending among them high-grade workers who can see their virtues more clearly than their weaknesses. Any change in the mountaineer that will be for his permanent good must be based on his finer qualities. These, however, are little told of in books about the mountaineer. The temptation to emphasize his poverty and superficial peculiarities seems to be too great for writers to resist. I do not wonder that the mountaineers resent the way in which they are presented to the public. Nor do I see any reason why they should be selected out as a group which needs special missionary treatment.

We all know plenty of rural districts which are no better spiritually and intellectually than the mountains. I do not see that the mountaineer needs much different treatment from some of the rural folk that I know in New York and Maryland. When we know that most of the mountaineers belong already to some church denomination, it is not surprising that they do not like to be classed with non-Christians, such as the African Negroes and South Sea Islanders. I am inclined to think that as far as a book is concerned, this is a case where "silence is golden."

By December, specific plans for the 1917 conference began to occupy much time: there were the conference dates to settle and suggestions of various sorts to consider in regard to the program. April 11–13, 1917, met the approval of the Executive Committee. As to program, the first good news was that Dr. Claxton, US commissioner of education, would come. In accepting, he confirmed the date, writing further on December 19th:

I am hoping that by the time of your meeting we may have worked out fully the results of studies which have been made of conditions and needs in the southern Appalachian Mountains. If so, I should like to present our findings and have a good part of the discussions of the meeting center around them. It has been my purpose to begin a campaign for constructive work in this section as soon as our bulletin on this subject is ready for distribution.

I wish to make this bulletin as complete, as comprehensive, and as reliable as possible. It should be something that can serve as a basis for constructive work and as a source of information for all people who want to know about any phase of educational work now done in this section, of the needs, and of the best means of supplying these needs. You have a large fund of information on this subject. I am wondering if you cannot cooperate with us in the preparation of this bulletin and let us use any information which you may have and which we have not. Kindly let me know what you think of this.

Early in January, John completed the revision of his paper on the mountain schools and sent it to New York for publication by the Foundation. With the title *The Future of the Church and Independent Schools in our Southern Highlands,* the pamphlet was to be ready at the time of the conference. He wrote in his accompanying letter to Mr. Glenn the request that if there "are any changes whatsoever made—even in a phrase—will you be so good as to let me see the manuscript again just as it is to appear in print, and later the proof. There have been some recent tempests in a teapot in the local papers, stirred up by writings on mountain subjects. This paper is likely to be scrutinized carefully by certain persons who will read it. I think it is safe as it is." There were numerous exchanges between John and the Foundation editor through Mr. Glenn, but he was able to get it through galley and page proof under his own eye, and to the printer in time.

Also during the same month John managed two other papers—one, read before the Asheville Pen and Plate Club (nearly all clergymen, judges, and professionals in the law), entitled "Our Attitude toward Authority: An Inquiry"; the other, given at the North Carolina Conference for Social Service at Raleigh, "Progress in Community Activities in our Mountains."

For the Knoxville conference program, John wanted Professor J. Russell Smith and consulted his old friend Carl Kelsey at the University of Pennsylvania, who responded at once: "Though he carries a different title, J. Russell Smith is really our professor of economic geography. He is of Quaker stock, born in Virginia. He has lived on the farm much of his life and now owns and operates a place on the Blue Ridge in Virginia. He started to grow chestnuts, but the blight has stopped that. His chief crop is apples. He has studied conditions in this country, in Europe, and in North Africa. You would find him an excellent man for your conference and you could be sure of his own interest in advance." Professor Smith proved interested, and would come.

It was settled that not only Dr. Claxton but also Mr. Harold W. Foght, specialist in rural school practice, US Bureau of Education, would be there. To have both there, Mr. Glenn wrote, would be "a great thing, making the year's conference more important than any you have yet had." Dr. B. D. Gray of the Home Mission Board of the Southern Baptists and Dr. John M. Moore of the Southern Methodist Board agreed to address the conference on "The Country Church in the Mountains." Mrs.

F. S. Bennett, president of the Woman's Board of Home Missions of the Presbyterian Church, USA, accepted the invitation to be present and give a talk.

For a brief time, until it was found that his health would not permit, it was hoped that Sir Horace Plunkett, from Ireland, then visiting the United States, would also come. His books *Ireland in the New Century* and *The Rural Life Problem in the United States* had greatly interested John, and he had quoted from the former in the pamphlet on mountain schools now to be issued.[1]

The call to the coming Conference of Southern Mountain Workers at Knoxville on April 11–13 was sent out on March 1st. Ten days later John wrote at the end of a letter to Mr. Glenn, "We are quite overwhelmed with the number of letters and cards coming in, bringing assurance that the writers are coming to our Knoxville conference. If they continue to come at this rate, we shall be crowded out of doors."

Mr. Glenn responded on March 15, congratulating John on the program announced and sending a generous allowance from the Foundation toward conference expenses but expressing regret that a heavy schedule in New York would prevent him from coming himself. He wrote separately on the same date a letter of counsel, which bespoke the warmth of his interest as well as the director's viewpoint:

Mr. Clark has referred to me your inquiry about the decennial report. We ought to have your material as soon as we can get it, but the Knoxville conference has to take precedence. Please put in whatever time you can on the report before the conference without overdriving yourself or Miss Dickey, and finish it after the conference. But please make your arrangements very definitely so that you can shut yourself up with the report immediately after the conference until you get it finished. It should take precedence of everything except the conference.

I think, too, that you ought every year to give yourself at least a week of free time after the conference before you do any other work. This will probably seem to involve a sacrifice of something of importance, but undoubtedly it will enable you to do a great deal more than if you attempt to keep up your pace when you are very tired. Two things that are essential to your writing a good decennial report: that you should rest your brain a few days after the strain of the conference, and that you should give up several days or a week to it without interruption. I hope you will not mind my speaking so positively, but I think you need help in resisting appeals of people who are anxious to get your advice and help. Nothing is more fatal to work such as the staff of the Foundation ought to do than undertaking to carry the burdens of too many people. It means scatteration of thought and energy instead of concentration on a few of the major problems. When I say major I mean such things as the Knoxville conference and your pamphlet on schools. Please be very firm with yourself!

John replied on March 20th, doing his best to convey his own point of view and quandary:

I appreciate greatly your letter of the 15th and thank you for your considerate thought of my personal as well as official well-being. I do not at all mind your speaking so positively, and I know that Mrs. Campbell will be thankful for the emphasis that your injunction gives to her own repeated injunctions that I ought not to carry the burdens of so many people.

It has been exceedingly difficult this year to do promptly a number of things of importance because of any interruptions. Among the important things delayed is the decennial report, although I have given much time and thought to it and put much work upon it. I got along fairly well until I came to write of the organization of the Southern Mountain Workers' Conference and of what the conference is and does.

The conference is one of the best things—if not the best thing—that I have brought to pass. I should like for many reasons to dwell upon it at length, and incidentally to show what the Foundation, this division, and its secretary were accomplishing. When I came to this point, however, I knew that any assumption that it had been initiated by an outside agency, an assumption of official credit, or suggestion of the wide influences emanating from it for interdenominational activity or for uniting in cooperation the different agencies at work in the mountains, would probably be attended with much risk. It is not easy to restrain myself, but when I see the Southern Baptists beginning to come in most cordially, as are the Southern Presbyterians, and the Methodists, North and South, growing more responsive than in the past, great care, brevity, and silence seem to be the part of wisdom.

For there are on some of these boards (especially the Southern Baptist and Southern Presbyterian) some influential conservatives, strongly opposed to interdenominational cooperation and specially opposed to participation in social service, which is a bête noire to so many.

It was only by taking advantage five years ago of a fortunate opportunity that it was possible for me to initiate the movement by working through two progressive leaders on the Southern Presbyterian Board and one such leader on the Baptist Board. This opportunity came through a personal friendship with a very conservative Southern Presbyterian official, who countenanced much of what I think he regarded as somewhat dangerous innovations suggested by me, because he believed from his personal acquaintance with me that after all, I was sound at the Foundation. Several of these officials are no longer on the boards, and one apparently does not hold the same important position as in the past.

Reactionary influences might be set in motion if it were felt that the conference were tending to become more than a mere conference. I am now receiving some wholehearted letters from some of the Baptist leaders. If I do not wish to abandon hope of the native people themselves doing what is needed for themselves, I must hold them in line, for theirs is the native denomination of the mountains, and they are the most important numerically and influentially in the highlands. Were the division offering money for work done in certain ways, there might not be so much need of caution, for some—though not all, by any means—might, for the sake of it, work in certain ways; but where advice is the only thing given, I have the additional task of making them want to take it. I therefore spend much time with these brethren and others in this field who have the same psychological and sociological outlook, in giving them advice that they want in minor things, which to them seem important, in order to have them follow in the larger things.

The dominant denomination of the highlands is peculiarly individualistic, as are all the mountaineers, and the isolation which has produced this individualism in the native produces extreme loneliness in many "foreign" workers. Their administrative officers see them infrequently and administer at long range. Many of them come to Asheville more frequently than to any other place, and they come to the office or seek me out at my home, and they are held to the larger things by friendliness and sympathy, oftentimes, more than by assent to the wisdom of them. They come, also, to the conference and will read my bulletins, because they feel that I am their friend, but if I did not seem to them to be that in the minor things, which loom so large to them, my bulletins will go unread into the fireplace; and cooperative social service in their fields will go by the board, and they will continue to rely on prayer and faith "without works."

I have reason to know that many who come to the conference come because they feel they have a personal claim upon its chairman, who is, after all, their personal friend, of whose understanding of their own peculiar needs, given in confidence, they feel sure. For the sake of the larger things, to which I wish them to come, I do not wish to fail them in the smaller things for which they come to me. I must admit, however, that the often enforced position of counsellor, guide, friend, and father-confessor results in heavy strain. It would be unfair to intimate that this attitude of mine is one of diplomacy or strategy; it is spontaneous, and I yield instinctively and too often. But, though the strain is sometimes very heavy, the full knowledge that comes of local needs, and of the undercurrents and cross-currents of administration, enables me to give more intelligent advice when it is sought by administrative officials higher up.

There is a real native antagonism toward "foreign" agencies, including philanthropic boards, but I feel that "native" and "foreign" alike, as well as their administrative officials, are coming to regard us as a division of a foundation not seeking its own, but which is rather a friend "by the side of the road."

I had not meant to write so long a letter. I have just been resisting the blandishments of a dear friend—a noted magazine writer—who feels that I am hiding my light under a bushel and has sought earnestly for my consent to let him, in his own way, write up the work of my division in order to show what we have done for the mountain folks.[2] His arguments have been reinforced by those of one of my good friends here, engaged in mountain work. It has been difficult for me to resist the temptation, and it has been a temptation, for I am no stranger to the human desire to have my friends in the North really know what I am doing and what I have accomplished, nor am I at all averse to having the general public know what success the division has attained officially, but I am confident it would be unwise. I hope you will pardon my using the opportunity offered by your letter to "unbottle" to someone who will understand what my writer friend and mountain school friend appear not to grasp.

I shall try to be firm with myself, and shall hope for your forgiveness, as well as Mrs. Campbell's, for occasional lapses.

We are going to make a change in our residence in May, and we shall not then be quite so accessible. I hope then to be able to shut myself off at home for writing and the consideration of important things which need concentration and freedom from interruption.

The Seventh-day Adventists were brought into our conference for the first time last year. I have long promised to visit their headquarters near Nashville. They have a special meeting right after our conference: Claxton is to be there, and Foght, one of his rural specialists. I have promised to come if possible, but I shall cancel other tentative engagements. I had, prior to your letter, declined an invitation I really wanted to accept, to speak in the place of Mr. Taft at the nurses meeting in Philadelphia. It was so large a place to fill that I knew I should not be equal to it so soon after the conference, were I to do justice to matters awaiting attention.

With renewed assurance of my appreciation of your kind interest and advice.

About the middle of February, a draft of Mr. Sharp's proposed introduction to the book of collected ballads, escaping the submarines, had arrived in our eager hands. I acknowledged it February 20th, as soon as John had read it, with a few minor suggestions:

The introduction is splendid. Mr. Campbell and I have read it over carefully a number of times and are delighted with it. I think it will interest all sorts of people, for it has the picturesque as well as the scientific, and it is all very clear and straightforward. The musical explanations especially are very clear, but throughout I think no one can misunderstand either your attitude in general or your explanations in particular.

I cannot see where it would give occasion for offense, except in a very few instances to the mountain people themselves. These are where you touch upon some of their practices which have been shown up in such high lights by those who do not take the same appreciative attitude as you do. These, with a few minor suggestions or corrections, I am setting down in detail.

On a final rereading, I feel that I should like, after Mr. Campbell's name on page two, "of the Southern Highland Division of the Russell Sage Foundation," if this is agreeable to you. In a way, I have always felt like making some acknowledgment to the Foundation, for it was while they were financing our first field survey of the mountain country that I began to be interested in and to collect ballads. I have a feeling, too, that Mr. Campbell would like it, for he regards this ballad movement undoubtedly as one of the best things that has come through the Foundation to the mountains, and it is the kind of thing he always wishes to further officially as well as personally. . . .

I am really greatly pleased with the whole introduction, and my mood is by no means critical.

We have been wondering how your course of action has been affected by all the developments of the last few weeks, and I am at a loss whether to picture you in England, France, Spain, New York, or on the high seas.

We fervently hope, however, that you make your journey safely and that we shall soon have a message that you have arrived without inconvenience.

Before he had received this of mine, we had a letter from Mr. Sharp in New York, dated March 8th:

Here we are again safe, I am glad to say, but after a very perilous journey over the seas. The risk was a very real one, and the strain so great that I do not think we shall tempt fate again and return to England before the seas are once again safe.

I was very glad to get your husband's reply to my telegram announcing our arrival. My plans are rather vague at present, but I shall be running about the country doing work in various places between now and Easter. After then I shall move heaven and earth to get once again into the mountains and to continue the collecting there.

I called at Putnam's yesterday to tell them of my arrival and also with the intention of hurrying them up with the proofs, which have been coming in at a snail's pace. I found them exercised in their mind over the length of the book and the expense of printing which this involved, but, as I explained to them, I have not in any way exceeded the estimate which I originally placed before them, so that their calculations, if correctly made at the beginning, needed no revision now. Nevertheless, I am seriously disquieted by their attitude in the matter, for it is clear to me that there is a certain element in the firm, consisting of underlings who hold, however, an important position in the firm, who are doing their best to crab the book, probably because they see that commercially it is unlikely to be very successful. The head of the firm is a fine old man in his way and has ideals, which are evidently not shared by the younger and subordinate members of the firm, and it is just a question who will get the better of the tussle. In the meanwhile the book is being delayed, which is exactly the thing that I did not want. However, while I am in New York, I shall do my best to straighten out the mess if I can, and I will report to you the result later on.

I saw Mr. Glenn yesterday for a few minutes, and am gradually getting in touch with my other friends here. . . .

Maud joins me in love to you all including, of course, the miniature family.

He also wrote John, who answered on March 15th:

Your letter of the 10th has just reached me, and I should like to sit down and have a chat with you, but time forbids.

The books came yesterday, which Mrs. Campbell herself will acknowledge, but I wish to thank you for my share in the pleasure they are already giving.

Putnam will probably come round all right: it is annoying to have to help educate supposedly educated people. I am glad they had the good sense to allow you to write the announcement. Your suggestion as to Mrs. Campbell's name is all right; it will be seen from your kind introduction that I "own" her, and I shall be able to bask in reflected glory.

Yes, Mr. Glenn sent me the *Nation.* I read it with much interest and some amusement, but it was not bad, I can well understand your feeling about publicity, but I suppose it is a necessary evil.

Now as to your plans. . . . Mrs. Campbell and I have talked the matter over, and from our point of view, it seems wisest for you to come directly to Asheville instead of first to Knoxville. We could talk over many things to better advantage at that time, because after the conference we shall be breaking up for a move of household effects, and we want you and Miss Karpeles to come to our home again.

Unless you have to stop too long a time in New York after you have finished at Pittsburgh, you might be able to see Mr. S—— in Washington and to get in a few days at Charlottesville, if that is enough, coming on to arrive here the 8th or 9th at the latest. I leave for Knoxville on the 10th of April, but it would not be necessary for you to come to Knoxville for another day or possibly two days. I think it eminently desirable for you to come to Knoxville, however. You would be able to meet some Berea people, Oneida people, those from Hindman, and other folks from the Kentucky field who will be at the conference in all probability. You would become acquainted with a goodly group of workers in the mountains, not all straitlaced—though some of them are—and I could put you onto men in the Kentucky mountains in mountain work who would really enjoy a good smoke with you.

Dr. Claxton, US commissioner of education, who has done something to further ballad collecting through his department, and Dr. Alphonso Smith will be there and will speak on the night of the 11th, and I should like to have him meet you. I am expecting President Frost of Berea, and I already know that Berea will send a good group even if Frost does not come.

If you will permit, I will slip you in as a speaker some time during the conference to call attention to what you have found in the mountains, and this may tap resources of which Mrs. Campbell and I do not know. It also will give me opportunity during the conference, sometime after you have spoken, to call attention to your forthcoming book. Of course I shall do nothing of this sort if you prefer not.

I should like, however, to have you and Miss Karpeles become acquainted with these different people, for living conditions will be much easier for you if you have access to their homes and the benefit of their advice as to other homes.

We are eager to see you both, to plan with you for a continuation of the ballad campaign, to hear the latest from your own home in England, of the general situation in England, and of your thrilling trip.

You could, of course, go to Harrisonburg after the Knoxville conference, but my thought is that it might be better to accompany some of the Berea, or preferably Oneida, people from the Knoxville conference direct, and work the Kentucky field for as long a time as it seems profitable. Harrisonburg could be reached easily from New York at some future time. At any rate, we can talk the whole thing over when you come.

There were more exchanges, but Mr. Sharp was unable to come to Asheville to visit us. He did get to the conference.

John left for Knoxville on April 10th. His usual long letter reporting the conference to Mr. Glenn has a lively, detailed picture of the meeting: Dr. Claxton's opening address, Bishop Horner's claim that his school apple orchard would soon pay school expenses—and the shrewd challenges of this claim—J. Russell Smith's sound economic policies, Mr. Sharp's address, and so on. This letter, dated April 17th, is given in full:

The conference is over, and a most successful conference it was—a conference in the true sense of the word.

We enrolled the first night more delegates than we enrolled at the whole conference last year; we had in all 150 registered delegates, and I am quite sure there were 8 or 10 in addition who did not register. Last year we had 108 in all. Our audiences were from 200 to 250—so large that we had to use the Board of Commerce auditorium instead of the assembly hall at the Atkin for all of our meetings save two group conferences.

Dr. Claxton opened the Wednesday night meeting with a very good address. On Thursday morning, after the business session, Bishop Horner and Dr. J. Russell Smith of the chair of industries, University of Pennsylvania, followed. Bishop Horner's address was on "Industrial Training in Elementary Schools." It was a very good address, but when the bishop digressed a bit from his topic in answer to certain questions, he got into deep water. He asserted that his apple orchard at the Valle Crucis School was practically paying expenses and in a year or so would carry the school. There were some very shrewd mountain workers and men well up in farm bookkeeping who asked him some direct and very searching questions as to his methods of bookkeeping and as to what he was charging up against the orchard. The weakness of his position was soon revealed, but the spirit was fine, and I think the bishop as well as all of the rest of us will be helped by the suggestions and criticisms of his address.

Dr. J. Russell Smith . . . was a real find and justified the Foundation's expenditure necessary to bring him. He showed what could be done by taking the mountain man right where he is financially, without outside capital and with what he could find about him, and on such beginnings to lay a sound economic basis. He has traveled all over the world specializing in mountain farming. His topic was "Tree Crops: A Kind of Farming that Fits the Mountains," illustrated with slides. It is not mere theory with him; he is running successfully a commercial tree orchard in the Blue Ridge section of Virginia, near Harper's Ferry, I believe.

In the afternoon of Thursday, Mr. Sharp spoke, and captured the conference. His spirit was fine—not at all antagonistic or harshly critical. The criticisms he made were well made and kindly. I was interested in watching his audience. He held the undivided attention of those with college training and academic cultural background, as well as the rapt attention of the mountain teacher from remote regions with limited training. He is off now in Sevier County, Tennessee, at Baptist, Methodist, and independent schools, and then goes to Lincoln Memorial University at Cumberland Gap and on into Kentucky. We have arranged his schedule for him. I also put him in touch with some Episcopalian workers through whom connection will be established with the University of the South at Sewanee, Tennessee. The professor of English literature at Sewanee is said to have a large collection of ballads without the tunes, but he knows the men with the tunes and will direct Mr. Sharp to them. Mr. Sharp and Miss Karpeles sang a number of ballads very effectively, and the conference invited him to give another hour to the ballads on Friday morning, which he did, with as much acceptance as his first. It was a good stroke to get him to the conference. I was interested to see his somewhat changed attitude; like most of those who know the mountain people, he instinctively came to draw his illustrations from scripture.

There was at Knoxville an Old Fiddlers' Convention, which he attended, and I have a letter from him this morning saying that he got [two] nice tunes from the old fiddler who won the contest. He has this to say concerning the conference in this letter: "I quite enjoyed the conference and think it was quite the best thing to do, and I am very glad I have done it. The people were all very nice, quiet, and friendly and humble, so that one couldn't help liking them very much, even if one did not always agree. But agreement is a small matter after all. As long as people stand for something, I can always get on with them and like them, even when in opinion we may be as the poles apart."

It was very inspiring to all at the conference to have him with us. His address was couched in the choicest English, and his spirit was very fine.

After Mr. Sharp's address on Thursday afternoon, there was a very helpful roundtable conference on the best methods of giving scholarships and financial aid to students. This was led by Registrar Marsh of Berea College and participated in by a number of the leading mountain schools.

In the evening, Dr. Foght, specialist of the Bureau of Education, gave a most helpful illustrated lecture on the Danish folk school, which held the audience for several hours.

On Friday morning we had one of the best addresses of the whole conference. I never heard an address that carried so much inspiration from the mere statement of hard facts and things accomplished. Mr. C. F. Doane, dairy manufacturing specialist, Dairy Division, US Department of Agriculture, followed by Mr. J. H. McLain, another specialist from the Dairy Division, sent by Secretary Houston, told us of the government's propaganda to establish small cheese factories in the mountains of the South. It was not theory; they told us what had already been accomplished, how much money had been made, and how much of it got back to the mountain folks. Very little capital is required—perhaps five or six hundred dollars. Both of these gentlemen asserted confidently that with our mountain climate and cool mountain water and air, we were able to compete on advantageous terms with the dairy interests of Wisconsin in cheese-making and that we were just as able as Switzerland to produce cheese of a high grade. Both of these men were plain, matter-of-fact men who stirred the conference deeply because, I think, we all instinctively linked their addresses with Dr. Smith's, which pointed out the way to realize the ultimate economic independence of the mountain people.

Dr. [W. E.] Finley, field superintendent of the Laurel country, under the Department of Country Church Work of the Presbyterian Church, USA, told us of the success of the Rural Credit Union inaugurated in his field last year. Then came the second address by Mr. Sharp, with ballads by Mr. Sharp and Miss Karpeles.

The Country Church conference, scheduled to be led by Dr. [B. D.] Gray of the Baptist Board and Dr. [John M.] Moore of the Methodist Board on the afternoon of Friday, was given up because of the necessary change of plans on the part of these gentlemen, so we devoted the whole of the afternoon to the other part of the scheduled program—health and sanitation.

Mrs. Lena A. Warner, a Red Cross nurse in charge of the health campaign under the direction of the Extension Department of the University of Tennessee, told us of her work. She was followed by Miss Jackson, a Red Cross nurse under the Town and Country Nursing Service, who has been very successful in the Kentucky mountains, both at Hazard and in the mining section about Jenkins. Miss Jackson's address was especially timely. She is an East Tennessean, a descendant of Andrew Jackson, and seems to have something of his ability to do things and to make people sit up and take notice. Then followed an illustrated lecture by Dr. Paul B. Johnson of Washington, D.C., showing especially the diseases peculiar to the mountains and means of prevention, combating, and cure.

We closed with a rousing chorus of "America."

There were two very helpful group conferences on fireside industries (led by Miss Frances L. Goodrich) and extension work, canning clubs, etc. (led by Mr. A. F. Corbin of the Patterson School, Episcopal, at Ledgerwood, North Carolina).

Governor Rye, whom we had expected Wednesday evening, was unable to attend on account of his duties in connection with the Patriotic Pilgrimage—a pilgrimage in a special train touring Tennessee, Georgia, and North Carolina. I am very sure we should have had at least fifty more were it not for the war. A number who were to have come—especially for the canning club group conference—were called to Nashville by the federal authorities, and a number of our board secretaries were unable to be present on account of additional duties at this time.

We are enclosing a list of the organizations represented in attendance.

The underlying ideas of the conference were noncompetition with the public schools; redirection of church and independent school work; development of sound economic basis for mountain life; cooperation of all forces for social, educational, health, economic, and spiritual betterment. These ideas were well developed.

I was reelected chairman of the Executive Committee, to which have been added Miss Fannie F. Clement, American Red Cross; President Samuel T. Wilson of Maryville College; and Dr. E. A. Sutherland of the Nashville Agricultural and Normal Institute—a very fine Seventh-Day Adventist School. My appointment as chairman of the Committee on Survey was confirmed by the conference, and I am also directed to look after the publishing of the addresses of this conference. We collected something over one hundred dollars for this purpose, which, with what I can get from Mrs. [Charles R.] Crane, will, I think, pay for the publishing of proceedings and addresses.

There were numerous inquiries for you, and I wish very much you could have been there.

The office accumulation during John's absence in Knoxville is well accounted for in the following two exchanges between John and Mr. Glenn:

[JCC to Mr. Glenn]
April 17, 1917

I enclose a letter from Dr. [George A.] Hubbell of Lincoln Memorial University, which is interesting. Dr. Hubbell called me into conference while at Knoxville. I think I can be helpful to them in getting rid of their handicap—the word "University." I want to help Hubbell win over his trustees to the idea which is incorporated in the new name which I am suggesting for the institution—"The Lincoln Memorial Folk School." I should like to go before his Board of Trustees in May, if necessary, to help him put it through, should he desire. With a million dollars for endowment, and with their present plant, they might easily become a higher institution of the sort indicated, to which other minor schools of that character might look for direction, if they themselves are properly directed and guided.

Burns of Oneida has written me asking me to deliver their commencement address the first of May, but I have declined. I have, however, consented to deliver the commencement address of a Seventh-Day Adventist mountain school which I can reach from Asheville in an hour by auto.

Mrs. [Anna R.] Atwater, president of the Christian Women's Board of Missions (Christian Church)—the board under which their mountain work is conducted, has invited me to come to Indianapolis sometime in the fall to advise with their board as to the redirection of their mountain work.

Dr. Claxton wants me to come and spend sixty days with him in Washington to prepare a report on mountain education. I told him that I should be very glad to cooperate, but I could not give the time this summer and suggested his writing to you—that I wanted to get some bulletin material in shape and the addresses of the conference which are most helpful in press as soon as possible. I have the impression, based, however, on no secure foundation, that Claxton is not fully satisfied with the work that B—— has been doing for the department and that he would like to have me get it in shape. I told him that I had not been making a very minute survey of the public school work because his department has been undertaking it; that I had confined myself more particularly to the church and independent schools, but he seemed to want me just the same. I do not know whether he suspects that the conference has voted to make its own survey of the field and wants to get it under his department. I should be very glad to do what I can to help out in the work of his bureau, if I can do it at such a time as not to conflict with other more important things. I should not want to risk losing the salutary effect upon all denominational boards of their working together in a survey of the mountain field. If he writes you, will you please ascertain as minutely as possible just what he wants me to do, if you think it advisable for me to do anything?

Within a few days I hope to be over the strain of the conference and get at my decennial report.

[Mr. Glenn to JCC]
April 19, 1917

I return herewith Dr. Hubbell's letter. The main question about him would be whether he is able to run a university or college or folk school satisfactorily. I am surprised to hear that he is able to get his million dollars. Unquestionably the word "university" should be dropped from his title. There is a question about the advisability of calling such a school a "folk school" from the financial point of view. The term is so little understood that it is doubtful whether people would want to give large sums of money to such a school.

I have not heard from Dr. Claxton about the proposed report on mountain education which he wishes you to prepare. My presumption would be against your doing so unless you consider it of very great importance. If you are going to be able to give that much time steadily to a report, you can probably get out some publication of your own that would be more valuable. However, I think we should always keep ourselves open-minded concerning cooperation with government institutions.

Thank you for your very interesting account of the conference. It is altogether an encouraging story. I am specially glad to know that Mr. Sharp made such a satisfactory impression. He writes very enthusiastically about the conference. He evidently enjoyed himself very much and appreciated his cordial reception by the members of the conference. He speaks of the admirable way in which you handled the occasion.

The decennial report for the Southern Highland Division was forwarded to the Foundation on April 30th.

Mr. Sharp and Miss Karpeles, the ballad hunters, had left the conference on April 12th with Dr. Lillian Johnson of Monteagle, Tennessee. Mr. Sharp wrote John from Sevierville the next day:

> We got down here all right yesterday afternoon, traveling with Dr. Johnson, whom we found a most pleasant companion. The country was very beautiful through which the railroad went. Dr. Bishop met us and told us to come here—a very primitive place but just bearable! I went up to the college last night to hear —— lecture—it gave me the blues!—and after it, at Bishop's request, Maud and I sang two or three songs. I dare say there is something to be got here, but it would take a good deal of routing out, and obviously the thing to do is to get up to Story's college in the mountains and prospect there. Johnson has driven up there today with messages from me to Story, and I have no doubt but that we shall have an invitation to proceed thither ourselves tomorrow. . . .
>
> I called on one of the old fiddlers who was a winner at the Fiddlers' Convention before we left Knoxville and took two rather nice tunes off him, so I have begun to gather and made some sort of a start. This is the most American place I have yet struck, and interests me greatly. It reminds me of some of Dickens's sketches of American life.

We next heard from them in Knoxville, where Mr. Sharp wrote me on April 20th:

Maud and I got back here this morning rather the worse for wear—both of us. Whether it was the great and sudden heat, the unusual amount of exercise we took, the altitude on which Mt. Smokey Academy stands—twenty-eight hundred feet—the thundery weather, or the mountain fare—or all of these combined—I don't know, but we both feel today as if we had had a very serious illness and were in the early convalescent stage! I expect, however, we shall be fit again by Monday, when we go on to Dr. Hubbell's. It certainly was not want of care on the part of the Storys, both of whom did anything they could to make us comfortable and give us a good time. I liked them both very much, especially him. He is such a humble, simple-minded man—almost a mountain product himself. We found lots of songs, as you will see when Maud sends you the words. We got no new "Child" ballads, but two or three very fine versions of "Sir Hugh," a beautiful tune to "Edward"—far better than either Mrs. Gentry's or Mrs. Hensley's—and a fine tune to "The Two Brothers." We took down a small percentage of quite new stuff, but nothing of any importance. I found the whole neighborhood far more sophisticated than Madison County, and there was a general air of superiority respecting the "love songs," especially on the part of the younger people, the absence of which struck me so forcibly in North Carolina. Indeed it was much more like collecting in England than in America. . . . Sevierville itself is the most American town I have struck yet. It didn't look at all English, nor did the people behave at all like English people; on the other hand, there was no foreign, unassimilated population, and only very few Negroes. I got a few songs there, but not many. . . .

I should very much like to come and see you at Asheville, and it is very nice of the Perrys to ask us to go there so as to be near you, but I think it best for the present to stick to the plans we have made and go north first into Kentucky before we make for your part of the country. I am very anxious to sample the songs and the singing in Kentucky, because I suspect if I am to find a different type of song from that which I have heard in North Carolina, Tennessee, and Virginia, it will be there.

I expect you were glad to get your Lord and Master safe home again after the conference none the worse for his adventure! I quite enjoyed the conference myself, much more than I had expected.

I have been treating you very badly in the way of correspondence since I returned to America, but I seem to have been in a constant whirl since I landed, and now it is hard to find time to write, especially when we stay with friends, as we did this last week. I need not say I found your comments on the introduction unexpectedly mild! At any rate I am glad you found so few errors. All the criticisms you passed were obviously quite sound, and I incorporated them into the "test" at once. I have polished it up a good deal since you saw it but have not materially changed it. This is a very dull letter, but you know the reason! I hope a quiet day tomorrow is all that is needed to restore me to health again.

The next news was not as good. Almost daily letters and telegrams followed Mr. Sharp's letter of April 24th to John, dictated to Miss Karpeles:

I have not been very well since I came back from Sevierville and was too seedy to go on to Dr. Hubbell's yesterday, but I hope to make a start this afternoon. I don't exactly know what is the matter with me, but I have a very bad headache and a nasty cough and feel very seedy. If I don't get better in the next few days, I may come down to Asheville to recuperate, but I hope this will not be necessary. In the meantime please send on letters to me at Dr. Hubbell's until I wire you to the contrary.

On April 26th Miss Karpeles wrote John from Harrogate, Tennessce:

I believe Mr. Sharp told you that he was not feeling well, and I am sorry to say he is no better; in fact he is a good deal worse than he was when he wrote. I am quite anxious about him, especially as I do not know what is the matter. I at last persuaded him to see a doctor last night, but he really did not throw much light on the matter—only told us that he was suffering from auto-poisoning and talked at great length on germs, etc., much to Mr. Sharp's annoyance! I think he must have been poisoned in some way, either by water or [food]. Last night his temperature was over 103 F. Usually he recovers pretty quickly, so I am hoping this will be the case now, and in any case I don't suppose there is any need to be alarmed. But I am afraid this illness will pull him down a lot and I feel it is very doubtful whether he will be able to stand any sort of "roughing," even of a mild kind, for some little time.

I shall try to find out what sort of places Pineville and Barbourville are, and if they seem suitable, we may go on there, but I think it is more than likely that we shall come to Asheville, stay there a few days, and then try places in North Carolina where we can stay at a comfortable hotel. . . . I will send you a telegram when we decide what to do. We shall stay here till Saturday anyhow, and possibly longer.

A good many of the students know songs, but I don't think the immediate neighborhood would be a very favorable place for collecting.

Two days later, John sent a letter to Mr. Sharp:

We have been greatly disturbed to know of your illness but are much relieved this afternoon to receive the telegram from Miss Karpeles. I am writing in great haste, with people waiting in the office, so please pardon the abruptness of my note.

If the weather is very warm and you feel the need of getting into a cooler climate, the best place for you would probably be at Pine Mountain, which you could reach easily from Pineville, letting Miss Pettit know that you are coming. Pine Mountain is in the real mountains of Kentucky—nearly as high as Asheville. Oneida and Hindman are in the dissected plateau area, and Berea is in what is called the "knob" region—the cut-up edge of the Cumberland Plateau. We have had letters from Oneida, and they are looking for you, but unless you are straightened out, you will be more comfortable at the Boone Tavern at Berea. From Berea you could take a team to Rev. Isaac Messler's place at McKee, thence, with the assistance of Mrs. Messler, to places to which she was going to take you, from which you could go to Oneida. See Worthington at Annville, six miles from McKee.

Wire me if you go to Berea, and I will write President Frost. . . . I learn from Miss Sheak, who has just been to Berea, that Miss [Helen] Child, a somewhat eccentric daughter of Child, the ballad authority, is living at Berea, in the Boone Tavern. . . . I think she would be very much interested in your quest.

Keep us informed; come to Asheville if you are not feeling well. We will make some arrangement; you could probably do well at Marion, Tryon, and other points.

Mrs. Campbell sends her love with mine to both of you; we hope that you are better, and that you are both getting on nicely.

On April 29th Miss Karpeles wrote again from Harrogate to John:

Thank you so much for your kind telegram. Mr. Sharp is decidedly better but is far from well. We have come to the conclusion that in all probability he has had a severe attack of influenza (grippe, I believe you call it). He has been subject to this all his life and has very bad attacks. He has been up yesterday and today but is very weak and tired and has a bad cough.

We decided to go to Pineville in preference to Asheville, as Mr. Sharp is very anxious to do Kentucky if possible, and it would be a long journey to come back to Kentucky from Asheville. Also I don't think he is fit to stand the journey at present. I think we ought to be fairly comfortable at Pineville, and if so we must just await events there. If all goes well, we shall move on to Barbourville, and from there either to Manchester and Oneida or Berea, according to the state of Mr. Sharp's health. Or we might possibly go to Big Stone Gap in Virginia, which seems as though it might be a profitable place. But he will not be happy or well unless he is getting songs.

From Pineville, she reported on April 30th:

Mr. Sharp seems decidedly better. He stood the journey very well. Of course he is feeling very weak and tired, but his cough seems better. We have only been here a few hours, but in that time have received a very good impression of the place. It is most beautifully situated in the heart of the mountains, and I feel very hopeful of getting songs in the immediate vicinity. The hotel, too, is quite comfortable, far better than I had dared to hope. If we find we can get songs here, we shall stay some time. . . . I will write again in a day or two and let you know how Mr. Sharp is.

The same day Mr. Sharp also wrote John:

Thanks for your sympathy. I have had rather a smasher, but tonight for the first time I begin to feel a trifle better, although it is clear that I shall have to be careful and conserve my strength for some while.

Nothing could have been kinder than the treatment I received at Cumberland Gap. Hubbell was rather the grand seigneur and played the host on capacious lines but spoke and meant well; while Miss Buffum did the human side to perfection and made things as nice and easy for us as possible. But I was glad to get away this morning, because it was not exactly the place for an invalid.

We are delighted with this very beautiful spot and quite comfortable hotel and shall probably stay several days here, the more especially as the little ground-baiting which we did this afternoon seems to promise good results. In the circumstances, I did quite well at Cumberland Gap in taking down twenty-four tunes, some of them—and the words too—being well up to the mark. I do not feel inclined at present, and until I am stronger, to go to any other institution, so if I move on from here, it will be to Barbourville or some place with a comfortable hostelry.

Maud wrote to you this morning to ask you to send me some money, and now I want you to send me something else of prime necessity—tobacco. I want Capstan Navycut, *Mild,* i.e., red labels, of the domestic variety. It is to be got. . . . Could you send me eight of these? You see I am presuming that Miss Dickey has my name chalked up on the door and is keeping an account against me as heretofore.

Miss Karpeles had written of Mr. Sharp's illness to Mr. Glenn as well as to John. Mr. Glenn wired John to "do anything possible for him" and also wrote a letter on April 30th:

I enclose a letter received this morning from Miss Karpeles. I wired you to get in touch with Mr. Sharp to see if you could do anything for him. If you find that he is really ill and needs looking after, do not hesitate at expense in order to get him to Asheville or some other place where he could go to a hospital. I will be glad to stand behind any necessary expense. I will be glad to know anything that you hear about him.

Sir Horace Plunkett sails tomorrow for Europe. I had a short talk with him by 'phone this morning, and he told me that his operation in Chicago was very successful and he is now all right again.

On May 2nd, John wired Mr. Glenn: "Sharp better. Continuing his researches. At Continental Hotel, Pineville, Kentucky for few days. Am keeping close touch." Mr. Glenn sent him another letter on May 3rd:

I enclose a copy of a call which has been issued for a meeting of the Federal Council of Churches to be held next week at Washington. I think it will be of decided value to you as well as the council if you can be there, and hope you can come. If you cannot come for both days, come for one and be prepared to stay for the 10th. Guild wants very much to have a talk with you about the whole southern situation. The Rev. Guy Talbot has just been traveling through the South, and you can throw a good deal of light on the situation. . . .

This will be one of the most important meetings ever held in this country.

Thank you for your telegram about Sharp. I am much relieved to know that he is getting along all right.

Mr. Sharp's improvement did not last. He was able to go from Pineville to Barbourville. From there Miss Karpeles wired John on May 10th: "Sharp has relapse hope not severe temperature rather high upsets plans"; on May 12th, "Better but not well enough to get up hope to go Pineville Monday or Tuesday"; and on May 14th: "Is having very bad attack but now on the mend impossible travel before end of week at earliest." John reported further exchanges to Mr. Glenn in a letter of May 16th:

I left Washington Friday night. On Friday morning I had a telegram from Miss Karpeles, forwarded by Mrs. Campbell, which disturbed me: Mr. Sharp seemed worse, and I got in touch with Miss Karpeles at once, offering to return via Barbourville. She replied that I was not needed just then but that she would telegraph me later.

Yesterday morning I received another telegram from her saying that Mr. Sharp's case had taken a very serious turn that the doctor feared typhoid, and unless there was a marked change for the better, they would consider taking Mr. Sharp to the hospital at Lexington. I immediately wired that I would leave on the night train. Before train time I received the following telegram: "Rather better. Doctors think bad attack of grippe, not typhoid. Hope tomorrow will show decided improvement. Suggest you postpone visit till you hear from me tomorrow morning."

I am expecting a telegram sometime today. I hope it will confirm the promise of improvement; if it does not, I shall go on and get him established either at Lexington or one of the hospitals in Berea, or, better still, bring him to Asheville if he can travel that far. I hope it is not typhoid: I have felt that it might be a recurrence of malaria, from which Mr. Sharp has suffered much in the past.

P.S. Since writing the above, the following telegram has come:

Should both be glad of your help if you could come without too great personal inconvenience. A little better. Diagnosis still uncertain.
Karpeles.

I shall therefore go sometime today: will wire you from Barbourville, Kentucky.

He took Dr. Packard with him to Barbourville and on May 21st wrote Mr. Glenn about the trip:

I returned yesterday afternoon with Dr. Packard from Berea after a rather strenuous time. Tomorrow, I go out in the country about ten miles to deliver a commencement address at a Seventh-Day Adventist mountain school.

We found Mr. Sharp in bed at Barbourville. The surroundings were far from what they should be, and the physician there, while very kind, had not the facilities and I think not the training to make the examination necessary—should Mr. Sharp consent to such an examination. Sharp knew Dr. Packard, having spent four weeks at his home in the Laurel country, and the result was as I hoped it would be: he got a rather ready assent from Mr. Sharp to go to Berea—the more ready in that the interior of the [Barbourville] hotel was being repaired and painted and there was a little lull in ballad singing. . . .

The second day after we were there, it seemed advisable to move Mr. Sharp, as he was somewhat better. I had made arrangements at the Boone Tavern, Berea, previously . . . and we were met at the station by some of the college authorities in an auto. . . . There is a college hospital there, and a private hospital with good physicians. [Dr. Robert H.] Cowley, the college physician, has had good training, and I have known him personally. Both Dr. Packard and Dr. Cowley have suggested a thorough examination. . . . I urged Miss Karpeles to urge Mr. Sharp to submit to a thorough examination. . . . Within the last hour, I have received a letter from Miss Karpeles saying that she has not called the doctor in yet and has decided to wait and see if he improves without any medical assistance, inasmuch as he is so averse to seeing the doctor and has it firmly fixed in his mind that he will never get well while he is under a doctor's care.

He is up and down mentally; I never met anyone who was so utterly hopeless when he is down. It was a real help to both of them, I think, to have Dr. Packard and me with them. . . . We have them now at the best point for them in the mountains, in his present condition. There are three skilled doctors and two hospitals, one of them with graduate nurses, and President Frost and the professors will do anything that they can. While I was there, Mr. Sharp received a telegram from Mrs. J. J. Storrow, of 471 Beacon St., Boston. She has invited him to come on to spend the summer at Lincoln, Massachusetts, at her summer home. He, of course, wants to

stay in the mountains as long as possible and do what he can in the ballad line. . . .

He is finding Kentucky a wonderfully rich field—the music is better,
but the singers he has interviewed so far, he thinks are not of the same
intelligence as the North Carolina singers; their words and their conception of the story are not so good, but the music is more instinctive. He
told me that "they are instinctive musical animals," doing some wonderful
things in music that he had not dreamed of. No one can ever do the work
so well as he, and we are all hoping that his recovery will be rapid and that
the way will open for him to finish the work he so much desires to do.

I hope he will stay at Berea for the present and that Miss Karpeles will
be able to manage it. When he is feeling better, however, he dominates her
and does what he wants to—oftentimes the thing that is worst for him—
and when he is down, he is so depressed and pathetic that the best thing
for her to do, seemingly, is to let him have his own way. All this, together
with his extreme dietary views, makes it rather hard for her and for those
who would really want to help him. He behaved very well for the doctor
and me, but I do not believe I could have gotten him to Berea so easily
without the doctor's help. Dr. Packard knew how to handle him. I do not
know what sudden impulse he may follow, but I hope he will "stay put"
for a while, or go north when he is able to travel, to accept Mrs. Storrow's
invitation—but I hope he will "stay put" if he does not recover rapidly.

Mr. Sharp recovered sufficiently to give a very favorably received lecture to the
Berea faculty before leaving May 29th for Pineville and then Asheville, where he
put up for a week at the Grove Park Inn. John reported to Mr. Glenn on June 13th
that "He is decidedly improved—quite like his old self; he is not able to walk as
well as formerly, but his strength is coming back rapidly." Several days later, Mr.
Sharp left for the North and some teaching and lecture engagements there. On its
completion, he wrote John from New York on July 23rd: "Back here again in simply awful weather—Had it been feasible, we should have left for the South tomorrow (Tuesday), but there are several small jobs to be done, so we must stick it out
till Wednesday. . . . The school ended brilliantly, and I never had a pleasanter experience than that of the last three weeks. You will be glad to hear that the end of the
book is in sight, and two or three weeks ought to see my part of it completed."

John also had journeyed north in late June, for a week at the Massachusetts
Agricultural College Summer School of Rural Life and then for conferences in New
York, a journey which he found "helpful to me, both personally and officially," as he

wrote to Mr. Glenn on July 23rd, following his return home. Soon after, he received a long letter from his acquaintance of Andover Seminary days, Dr. H. P. Douglass of the American Missionary Association, written on July 30th, about the mountains and the work there:

I am sorry I could not have seen and discussed with you the matter of missionary policy in the mountains, but will read your pamphlet with great interest and appreciation.

As to Saluda, I should like to have no misunderstanding as to the position of this association, which is that it will drop the elementary grades as soon as the town provides them. So far as this office is concerned, we are anxious to have the town do this and have used all the influences we can control to secure and indeed compel it. The boarding department and the upper grades we do not feel pertain primarily to the town of Saluda.

As to the concentration of funds on a single school, it is not probable that our constituency will stand for it, and is it not clear that we could not establish such a school in a scale of salary payment and support different to that pertaining throughout our system of schools? It is extremely difficult already to keep interest in our donors in the small number of mountain institutions which we have. They want a varied and considerable number of schools which appeal by reason of their poverty and individual needs. One might say that they want schools not to be too good in the sense that they are too big or too well supported.

If someone would give us a large fund for mountain work, as we have for Negro work, we could administer in some degree of independence of the prejudices of our constituency. It might then be possible to do something of the sort.

I share the regrets of a good many people that we do not seem to be getting along very fast in the direction of a generally accepted program for mountain education. We have been looking for your report and the authority it would carry, but it does not appeal. Let me be frank in saying that in your stress on the Danish folk school type it seems to me that you have gone somewhat off on a tangent; at least, so far as I know you have failed to carry the conviction of other educational experts. I have never seen an exposition of the grounds of your judgment which was complete, or which enabled me fairly to reach an attitude toward it. The conferences have not gripped my imagination nor struck me as very profitable. Probably I have not the necessary patience to sit through that sort of thing and to take the time to make personal acquaintances which make it really profitable. I am frankly without any hope of getting any effective cooperation from the denominationally minded mission agencies. All told, I am afraid I am not a very good cooperator.

We have known each other so long, and I respect your judgment in the situation so highly, that I regret this, and wish somehow that the forces might be gotten into effective action. Is not the time for investigation now over and the time for a program at hand? If so, why not give us the result of the investigation in order to help us make a program?

John took advantage of this opening to give his views at some length in a reply dated August 11th:

I have your letter of July 30th and have read it with deep interest and would thank you for your frankness. I value your friendship and judgment so highly, and I desire so much your full cooperation, both as a friend and as a directing official of mountain work, that I venture to write at some length in the hope of clearing up any misapprehensions that may exist.

First, as to my work. It is natural for those unacquainted with its development to assume that I am still engaged in investigation, which was so large a part of my first two years under the Foundation, or to assume that I am specializing particularly along one or two lines. My field is really not a subject field but a geographical field. I endeavor to touch different phases of rural social activity within the boundaries of that field, bringing to such activities what may be of possible help from the outside. I am therefore dealing not alone with schools, but with health, agricultural, recreational, and other agencies. Naturally, schools have occupied much of my time and attention. Until there are concrete examples of what I advocate, I must continue to try to persuade leaders that something of the sort that I advocate is at least worthy of a trial. If I may say so without seeming irreverence, I am but a voice in the wilderness of ideas for mountain welfare, calling to men like yourself, "Prepare ye the way; cast up the highway; gather out the stones; lift up a standard for the people." Where I am able, or think myself able, I give advice and criticism when asked—and sometimes when not.

I could not be an expert in all these various phases of rural activity; in the common acceptation of the term, I am not even an educational expert. I have no hope of persuading the majority of educational experts to my views as to the folk school, for so many of them are wedded to the academic idols of old or to new idols of their own making—usually fashioned in urban surroundings. No one that I know has yet solved the problem of rural education; something is wrong in the schools of our mountains, and in our rural schools generally. The greatest defects arise, I think, from attention being concentrated upon the individual rather than the community. I would not be understood as implying that they have not done great good, but the day has come for a facing-about. Most of us recognize that. Some would stress still more the old academic courses; others would relegate the mountain youth to the ranks of hewers of wood and drawers of water, through the establishment of schools in which vocational courses are overemphasized, thinking thereby to solve mountain problems. What is needed is a school for the mountains and not for picked and choice individuals in the mountains. I have been drawn to the ideals of the Danish folk school because somehow the Danes have found a school for the peasant youth—a school resting on a cultural basis but sending forth students with such altruism and such practical knowledge of affairs as to have remade Denmark economically, socially, and spiritually.

Probably I have not, as you suggest, done much to convince many educational experts, but you are mistaken in assuming that those most intimately acquainted with the mountain country or with the Danish folk school are not in agreement with me. My attention was first directed to these schools some ten years ago by Dr. Claxton, our US commissioner of education, who at that time was superintendent of secondary education in the University of Tennessee and a prominent adviser in all southern educational affairs. I have studied them more or less since. His belief in the Danish folk school was so deep as to procure an appropriation from the government for a commission; and a selected group of men who know southern conditions, and are really educational experts in a sense that I never could hope to be, went to Denmark and reported favorably upon the schools. Dr. Foght, who knew the schools intimately in his native land, a professor in one of our best teachers' training schools and an educational expert in the employ of the government, was one of the commission. In a US bulletin, "The Danish Folk High Schools," on page 84, and in one of his books (*Rural Denmark and Its Schools*—pp. 303–322) he has come out squarely for the Danish folk school as especially suited to the mountain country. The late W. K. Tate of George Peabody College for Teachers—also one of that commission—in conversation with me also expressed his conviction of their great possibilities for the mountains, and he knew the mountains intimately, for he was a mountaineer. I could mention other educators of prominence who are just as certain as these that some adaptation of these schools is desirable for our Southern Highland region.

Several months ago the Foundation issued a bulletin of mine on *The Future of the Church and Independent Schools in Our Southern Highlands,* largely in response to requests for its publication by members of the Council of Women for Home Missions, and some further requests for it by individuals in the Home Missions Council, who had heard me speak on this subject in their annual meetings. I sent you one of the first numbers issued, several months ago.

I could not entertain the suggestion made by Dr. Claxton some years ago that I be one of those to go to Denmark to study these schools for the government so as to create public opinion in this country for their introduction into rural fields. My little daughter was seriously ill at that time. I took the matter up with the Sage Foundation later, however, when I was free to go, and the Foundation thought it worthwhile to send me to Denmark to study these schools. Through our State Department and the Bureau of Education, and our minister to Denmark, the proper connections were established in Denmark; an itinerary was drawn up for me by leading Danes in this country and in Denmark, some of whom had conducted folk schools in this country. Mrs. Campbell and I were in the North, with tickets purchased and about to sail for Denmark, when the war broke out. It was felt best to wait until more normal times should be reestablished.

Inasmuch as I could not report upon these schools from personal observation, I have, whenever possible, called upon men such as yourself controlling the educational policies of mountain boards to study carefully the methods of such schools for the mountain country; and for laymen and officials alike I have, in my pamphlet, by word of mouth, and by correspondence, called to their attention the four or five valuable bulletins that the US Bureau of Education has issued relating to these schools. In mountain conferences of certain denominations and in our interdenominational conference at Knoxville, there have been experts, brought by me, to discuss these schools and to answer objections to them that might be raised. At our last Knoxville conference—which was the largest and best attended that we have ever had, in spite of the war—among the notable speakers sent by the government departments was Dr. Foght, who gave us an illustrated lecture on the folk school. I am sorry you were not there to hear it, to set forth your objections, and to discuss with us the pros and cons, so that there might have been precipitated the ideas relating to these schools which are probably in a more or less nascent state in the minds of most of us.

I am sorry you do not find the conference helpful to you; it must be helpful to some, or they would not come in increasing numbers. It would, perhaps, be out of place for me to enter into an extended argument as to the value of something with which I have had so much to do, but frankness, Paul, prompts me to say that I do not think you know enough about the conference from personal attendance and observation to pass any valid judgment upon it, and hearsay evidence is not valid in any court. It has been a disappointment to me that the Congregationalists have not cooperated more in this conference. Dr. Berckman has added to its value by his suggestions and frank criticisms. It was he, I think, who, in expressing his appreciation of the conference, told me of a most encouraging conversation he had with two Catholic priests from near Corbin, Kentucky, who wondered if it would be proper for them to attend. The denominations which we Congregationalists have been prone to regard as exclusive and hard to work with have sent the largest delegations; whereas we, who are supposed not to emphasize denominationalism, but to be leaders in denominational cooperation, have been conspicuous by our absence—and it is not from lack of invitation. Only one discordant denominational note has been sounded in the five years of the conference's existence, and that, to my sorrow, by a Congregationalist—one of our supposedly representative men.

The statement made in your letter that the constituency of the American Missionary Association wants schools that "are not too well supported," schools that "appeal by reason of their poverty and individual need," comes somewhat as a shock when one reads it. I recognize from my own past experience that that has been true of a certain percentage, at least, of the constituency of our own as well as of other mission boards. It seems to me however, that the percentage, small or large as it now may be, is not altogether to blame for it, for they have acquired an appetite for the food upon which they have been fed. The personal, the individual, the appeal to mere sentiment has been overdone, and the editors of some of our papers and missionary journals have too long fed a constituency on that sort of thing. In their need for money to carry on work, so much concern has been given to further stimulation of what was already overstimulated, that the success of the work on the field has been jeopardized by giving too little heed to the dignity of the mountaineer and the self-respect of the South.

It seems to me also, however, that an increasingly large percentage of those who were once supporters of mission boards, and those who might become so (I know it is true of our own thinking laymen that I meet from time to time in New England and the North) are eager for something else, something constructive, something that does not offend any section of the country, something that will make us all feel that we are working toward a better future, away from the limitations of our common inheritance for which our forefathers were alike responsible to a greater or less degree. The Layman's Missionary movement, interdenominational movements, the Women's Club movement, the movements among our young people that stress social service or the study of economics and sociology, etc. are building up a large group that cannot be held by the old plea but can be enlisted for a large work on a larger plea.

I deplore, therefore, in mountain work, the continuance of running up "Old Glory" every time reference is made to the mountaineer and begging money for him because he helped to save the Union. Politicians have long since ceased to wave the "bloody shirt"; why should we continue it ecclesiastically? It serves to keep alive the old, and tells only a half truth, which is more dangerous than a lie. The mountaineer is really a southerner, even if a Republican. His physiographic environment made slave labor unprofitable, yet his attitude to the Negro is often less friendly than is that of the lowland southerner. There are mountain counties that I might name where until recently it was difficult to get a Negro driver to take one, yet we are led to suppose, by inference at least, and by the accidental juxtaposition of ideas, that the mountaineer is the friend of the Negro and that the only reason for his migrating into the mountains was because he did not want to be a slave owner. There is just enough of truth in it to make it dangerous as used. There is a new day about to dawn in missions. The mountain boards of some other denominations are making strenuous efforts to lay truer and deeper foundations in their work, and perhaps it is only fair for me, as a man, to say that many of the most statesmanlike plans are laid by boards administered by farsighted women.

I came to New York recently largely to discuss with certain church secretaries their cooperation in a program under way by the conference. I was unfortunate in finding that you were on your vacation. The plan, in brief, is this: to secure a statement from each board doing mountain work relating to their work, criticisms, suggestions etc. A committee was continued at the last conference, of which I was recently appointed chairman. The purpose of this committee is to secure information and suggestions from officials in charge of mountain boards and from others acquainted with the mountain field, in the hope that there may be issued later by the conference a publication setting forth the activities of various organizations in this field. I shall write you of this later.

To me, the mere fact that leading representatives of denominations—in all, fourteen—are willing to meet in ever-increasing numbers from year to year is a source of real encouragement. Furthermore, it is cheering to see southern and northern denominational representatives meeting together for conference with government, state, and other experts to talk over not only school work but agriculture, health, sanitation, etc. without considering it out of place for church boards to discuss such subjects. Knowing the mountain field as I do, I believe that the solution of mountain problems will not come from logical, rational programs alone, but will come from such programs backed by the personality necessary to make them work out. The combination of head, heart, and intimate acquaintance with the field is a combination hard to find in one person. The conference, however, gives us the benefit of such combination. The head men, if they can be patient enough to sit through a lot of discussion that seems unimportant to them, do, after all, come to understand better the viewpoint of the heart men; and the heart men, if the head men will come and be with them long enough, will take them into their hearts and keep them there, having come to know what really fine fellows they are. We need you, whether you feel you need us or not. Come down and give us the benefit of your presence and your views, and let us get at this question of mountain life by close contact with those who have to live it or direct it on the field and who want the views of those whose business it is to concentrate upon certain phases of mountain life.

In the meantime if I can be of service, I shall be most happy to serve; and if you think, feeling as I do, that I could help the constituency of our board to support something new upon which we might agree, I should be very ready—should you wish, and Mr. Glenn approve—to go before some of the leading Congregational Churches that you might mention and set forth as forcibly, convincingly, and tactfully as I could the newer things for mountain work.

Of this he sent a copy to Mr. Glenn, writing on August 13th:

I am sending you a letter recently received from my friend Dr. Douglass, corresponding secretary of the American Missionary Association, and a copy of my reply. I do not want to burden you with our correspondence, but if Douglass takes up with you the suggestion I have made, as I hope he will, you may want to know what has passed between us.

While in New York recently, I received a letter from Miss [Lura] Beam, Dr. Douglass's assistant, asking me for information relative to certain Congregational mountain schools. I called at the office and had a long interview with her. Our conversation branched off onto general mountain topics. She was apparently much interested in what I had to say and wrote after I got back to Asheville asking me to set down some of the suggestions I had made for mountain work. My reply to that letter reached the American Missionary Association office during her absence, and Douglass has answered it without having in mind clearly, I think, the occasion or background of our conversation. . . .

Douglass and I were in the seminary together, and knowing him so well as I do, it did not seem best to appear to ignore parts of his letter; the more so in that they have given me opportunity to say some things that I have not had opportunity to say before and could not say without an opening. Our long friendship may lead him to try the experiment that I suggest. If, perchance, he should come to see you or write to you, taking up the suggestion in the last paragraph of my letter to him, please grant the request if it is possible to do so. I know our Congregational constituency in New England fairly well, and I think I could say some forceful things, if I could get before the leading churches, without giving offense and without getting embroiled in the discussion of Negro problems. I should confine myself to a consideration of the mountain field and to an endeavor to say what might be helpful to mountain work generally.

Mr. Glenn warmed immediately to John's letter, which, he wrote, could hardly have given "a better idea of what you are trying to do." He suggested that John come to New York when he could "get at several important members of the board as well as the secretaries" of the American Missionary Association and added that he would be very glad to talk with Douglass himself. During this summer in Asheville, John could put in much time assembling material and preparing the study for publication. He also mulled over the plan of Professor R—— for the "book on the mountaineer."

On August 25th he wrote to Mr. Glenn:

I should like your opinion upon a matter that I have in mind. Professor R——, as you know, has in preparation a mission textbook on the mountaineer, to be issued by the YMCA. Professor R—— called the second time to see me about it, but I was in New York when he was here. It occurred to me that something of wider scope ought to be issued—what might be called a symposium on the Southern Highlands. There have been a few outstanding addresses delivered at the Knoxville conference of which I have some copies, others of which I could get copies; and there are other articles that I could get contributed. I am jotting down a rough outline of what I have in mind:

1. The Mountain Country and Its People
   by John C. Campbell
2. Resources of the Mountain Country and Possibilities of Their Development
   by Leonidas C. Glenn, Vanderbilt University
3. Forests, Water Power, and Reservations in Southern Appalachians
   by Gifford Pinchot or Henry S. Graves, chief forester of the US
4. Influences of Physiography on Social and Industrial Development
   by Willard Hayes
5 and 6. Papers on Education in the Southern Highland
   by Hon. P. P. Claxton and by E. C. Branson of the University of North Carolina
7. Danish Folk School Type for the Southern Highlands
   by Harold W. Foght, US Bureau of Education
8. Papers on Agriculture in the Southern Highlands
   by Hon. David Houston, US secretary of agriculture, and by J. Russell Smith, University of Pennsylvania
9. Progress of Road Building in the Southern Highlands
   by Joseph Hyde Pratt, state geologist of North Carolina
10. Denominational Affiliations
    by Samuel T. Wilson, president of Maryville College
11. Cooperation of Church and School
    by J. McG. Burnett, president of Carson and Newman College
12. Ways in Which the Churches May Cooperate
    by William G. Frost, president of Berea College

13. Music and Songs of the Mountains
   by Cecil J. Sharp, Esq., director, Stratford-on-Avon School of Folksong and Folkdance
14. A chapter on Health, Sanitation, Nursing, etc. (if possible)

Dr. Glenn studied the mountains for seven or eight years and has the human point of view always in mind.

The US Department of Agriculture is furthering a propaganda for the establishment of cheese factories in the southern mountains. Should Secretary Houston not care to write a paper, he would doubtless delegate someone; I have a fine paper on cheese factories from the man whom Secretary Houston sent to our Knoxville conference this year, but I should like to get the secretary's name, if possible, on our list of contributors.

J. Russell Smith is a University of Pennsylvania man who spoke at our last conference; a southerner, professor of industrial economics in the Wharton School, who has studied mountain agriculture in Corsica, Sardinia, Sicily, Italy, and our southern mountains—has, in fact, a commercial orchard in the Blue Ridge Mountains of Virginia.

C. Willard Hayes was with the Geological Survey. I think he is a North Carolinian, but I am not sure. He wrote an article on the Southern Appalachians (one of ten monographs in *The Physiography of the United States,* a book published by the American Book Company in 1896). I should like to get him to rewrite a part of the article which is printed, under the subhead indicated above, and get the permission of the American Book Company to publish it; it is very good indeed, for it sets forth very clearly the reasons why the Southern Appalachians were not opened up earlier.

Pratt is state geologist for North Carolina, secretary of State Highway Commission, state representative at National Conference of Defense, the moving spirit in good roads construction in the mountains, and a very fine fellow generally.

Burnett is president of the Baptist College—Carson and Newman. He read a very fine paper under the title "Cooperation of Church and School"—it was at the conference which you attended, and my recollection is that you were very much pleased with this paper. It is especially valuable coming from a Baptist and mountaineer and setting forth the psychological influences affecting the mountaineer religiously and otherwise.

A book of this sort, issued under the imprint of the Highland Division of the Foundation, would carry great weight, I think, much more than a book written by me alone. It would be of very general interest, and a book which I could supplement by my own writings later, and to which the attention of churches and young people's societies could be called.

We are working on plans for setting forth the work of the various agencies in the mountain field. You will recall that I came north recently particularly to consult Mr. Allaben and Mr. Clark about this matter. I shall probably be able to report at the next conference. Undoubtedly there will not be enough money forthcoming from the conference to publish the book in the form in which it ought to be published; and it might be well, if the Foundation feels able to do so, to meet at least part of the expenses of such a publication. With that publication, and the one of which I have just written, there would be two splendid books, written by southerners and northerners alike, and showing the cooperative principles of the Knoxville conference and the Russell Sage Foundation—books of value to all interested in the mountains, whether they be supporters of church boards or not. Likewise, they would furnish a splendid background for the other publications I might get ready later.

In addition to publications, his mind at this time was dwelling on the possibility of regional as well as all-mountain conferences. In answer to a letter of Miss Ruth Huntington of the Hindman Settlement School, welcoming Mr. Sharp and Miss Karpeles to Hindman and inviting John to join them, John wrote, September 7th, that he could not come until later, and then went on to say:

I could wish that more of the really good suggestions that I have made in my lifetime had been acted upon: this is one of them, namely, that the mountain agencies of each state—or of contiguous regions—would constitute themselves into a state mountain council, to discuss and thrash out in their councils all that pertains peculiarly to their region. I am a great believer in face-to-face conferences across a council table. All fair-minded persons who work fairly and fight fairly would ultimately come into such a council; understandings would be promoted through the elimination of misunderstandings, and if there is aught that is unfair, such council, knowing intimately the conditions, would be able to eliminate ultimately whatever is working against the common good. Reports of such a state council could be brought to the Knoxville conference, which has come to be looked upon, I am glad to say, with favor. Reports of this character could be carefully considered, and I am sure the findings of the committee of such a body would carry weight.

Would it be impossible, in your judgment, to have such an Eastern Kentucky gathering in October or early November? I should endeavor to get there if I could be of help. Let Hindman call it, or the schools jointly; invite authorized delegates from the mountain schools and agencies of Eastern Kentucky, including, of course, Ives. If you have not a complete list, I should be glad to send you what we have. Berea, through Mr. Vaughn, should have special interest.[3]

Knowing my personal and official interest, you will let me say, I am sure, without misunderstanding, that I believe you will always be more or less vulnerable—open to unfair attacks as well as to fair criticism—so long as you continue (if you still do) the taking of public funds for the public school, no matter what the wish of the immediate community may be. It will always be said, and with some truth, that the continuance of such a practice retards the growth of a healthy public opinion for self-directed public schools, and while there would be some mitigation through the fact that you are not a denominational school, you will yet not reach the highest to which I believe you may climb while you are thus retarded. When I come, as I hope I may, let us talk the matter over fully before the fireplace and go to the bottom of the pros and cons.

I thank you for the renewed evidence of your confidence in my judgment. I should be glad to be of service, and if any of the schools are "acting up as they hadn't oughter," perhaps they can be brought into the circle through seeing what real fun the rest are having by joining hands together.

Mrs. Campbell would join me in best wishes to you and Miss Stone and our other friends at Hindman.

Meantime, Mr. Sharp and Miss Karpeles, back in the mountains by late July, were again on the hunt for ballads in Kentucky. Letters reached us from Barbourville, Manchester, Pineville, Jackson, and Hindman. The heat of midsummer and the problems of diet and of mountain living conditions for travelers made strenuous going for them, but they were determined to pursue their collecting and to make it really comprehensive.

From Manchester, on August 15th, Mr. Sharp wrote that after three weeks they had only fifty tunes, "the average none too high," and continued:

I confess I am a little disappointed. We have been into scores of cabins, many of them looking exactly the right sort, only to be told that they used to sing them but no one had done so for twenty-five years or more. Obviously folksinging is not nearly so vital here as it was in the Laurel section, and it is difficult to explain why, unless it is the influence of the county seat—it cannot be the railroad, for that is too recent. . . . Collecting is therefore rather a slow process, as one has to wait until singers have studied and recalled what they used to sing in days gone by. We have opened up a good deal of ground round about here and have by no means yet reaped a harvest, but it will wait until our return from Oneida and will have all the meantime to ripen. . . .

I got one very interesting song from some delightful "holiness" people. I heard a woman singing and tracked her by the sound and found it was a holiness hymn—

O Sinnerman, O Sinnerman where are you going to run to (three times)
All on that day.

He says he will hide behind the [man?]. The Lord says the [man?] is bleeding; behind the rocks—they are rolling; behind the stars—they are falling; and so on, the Sinnerman verse alternating between each. Finally he says he will hide behind Hell, whereupon Satan says, Step right in! Its form is that of the ballad and the tune is a very beautiful one. The singer said it didn't come from a book, but I am wondering if it is one of the modern "revivalist" hymns, of folk origin as so many of them are. Have you heard it? The tune is a variant of "What Shall We Do with the Drunken Sailor?" The woman who sang it, Mrs. Samples, is such a nice woman, and she calls me the Sinnerman and has a fine sense of humor. Her mother sings and also her grandmother, not by any means an old woman. They said yesterday they would like us to come out and spend a whole day with them. They are all holiness people, but the grandmother doesn't mind singing love songs. She has known "Lamkin" and "The Drowned Sailor," if she could but recall them.

The travelers moved on to Oneida, returned to Manchester again, and thence made their way to Pineville, Pine Mountain, Jackson, and Hindman. Their progress was recorded in frequent letters. From Oneida [Mr. Sharp] wrote John on August 20th:

We have got practically nothing here. It is as sophisticated as Balsam!—a very keen disappointment to us and, I am sure, to Mrs. Campbell. I expect things have altered considerably since you were here. The only singer we have found here of anything like first-rate value is Mrs. Sophie Nensley, who sang "Johnnie Scot" to us on Friday but has been too ill to sing again. Mrs. Dan Bishop has probably got something, and we trudged over to her yesterday, only to find she is away. She may return today, so we are going over to her again tomorrow. For the rest, everyone frankly says that their parents used to sing them but that they have long since given up such things. We have been miles up Redbird, Crane, Doyle, as well as Tejus creeks and found the same attitude everywhere. We have still some work unfinished at Manchester, so we shall go back there for a few days and after then will let you know our plans. The weather has been hot but not unbearable. We have very comfortable rooms here, but the feeding is pretty sparse!

And from Pineville he wrote me on August 27th:

You will have heard of our little disappointment in drawing practically a blank at Oneida. I cannot think why you thought it such a good place, unless it is that it has altered a great deal of late. There are very few log cabins about—frame houses and pretty large ones are the rule; probably because the land is rich, the valleys wide, and farming a prosperous business. The whole neighborhood gave one the impression of being a prosperous, money-making community, quite above the singing of those lusty old love songs.

Manchester was better but suffered in much the same way as Oneida, but rather less. Money-making, as at Oneida, is the prevailing passion, and the desire to be genteel and behave like city people, pretty general among all classes. . . . I fancy that the sophisticating agent is money-making ever so much more than roads and facile communication. And the things that make for money-hunting are rich land for farming and coal or oil—the former more than the latter, because it is outsiders who exploit and benefit from the coal, while it is the native who benefit from the rich land. We watched the country very carefully between Manchester and Barbourville on the return journey last Saturday, and it was manifest that there were nothing but frame houses of a goodly size in the broad valleys and cabins in the narrow.

However, we have to take the thick and the thin as it comes, and I mean to test Kentucky thoroughly before we have done. We go to Pine

Mountain tomorrow and then return here again, after which we shall go up to Winchester and come down to Beattyville and Booneville, and so on, and test several counties, Leslie Ansley, Letcher, etc.—it will take us, I expect, another month at least to do this. Whether we can stand the racket of it or not remains to be seen. Maud is not very well today, but I am all right so far, and now that the weather has taken a decided turn for the better, we may get on all right. This last month has undoubtedly been a very great strain, and I couldn't stand much more of that kind.

By the way I got that version of "Lamkin" all right, and it is an uncommonly fine one that compares very well with the English form. The same woman gave me a fine version of "Little Musgrave," with quite a new and good tune to it—also a new Child, No. 2, bringing up our number of Children to sixty-one. I very nearly got "Jock of Hazelgreen" from Mrs. Dan Bishop, but she failed to remember it. For the rest we are doing quite well, if not brilliantly. I have scored 125 this trip so far. Love to you all from both of us.

From Pineville, he wrote another letter, September 2nd, this time to John about Pine Mountain:

We got back yesterday evening (Saturday), and I sent you a wire to send letters to Gen. Delivery, Beattyville, whither we hope to go tomorrow (Monday). We are both a pair of crocks. Maud started a sort of dysentery at Oneida a fortnight ago next Tuesday, and I followed suit at Pine Mountain last Thursday. Hers refuses to cease and mine ditto, so we have seen a doctor here, and he says it is a case of infection—probably from bad water. There is nothing serious about it so long as we are careful in diet, etc. and avoid complications, and he says it lasts a fortnight and is quite a common disease in these parts at this time of year. Really one runs many risks in this sort of job! Neither of us feels particularly ill, but it is of course an uncomfortable sort of thing, and we shall be glad when it is over.

Pine Mountain proved a most pleasant business. There is a mountain school—if you can call it a school—after my heart! I never met more delightful children. They behave just like the well-brought-up children of gentle folk, quiet, well mannered, very free, not the least bit assertive, and evidently thoroughly happy. Their good manners and general bearing are of course in their blood. What Pine Mountain has done for them is to teach them an added ideal, e.g., cleanliness, how to eat and behave at table, to be useful and work, as well, no doubt, as a certain amount of schooling. Miss Pettit and Miss DeLong, who are both of them wise and nice-minded, quite realize the type they are dealing with and see what they can give them and what is already theirs by inheritance. Everything is beautiful. The houses are well built, commodious, and nice to look upon. The food is first-rate and very plentiful. The dining hall with round tables is a beautiful room, and the meals are served and eaten as they would be in the houses of gentlefolk, except of course that the children wait upon themselves and there are no hired servants. The crumbs, for instance, are all swept away before dessert is served—dinner napkins are used by everyone. It was delightful to see the large cans of milk and the plentiful supply of cereals, sugar, and milk, well-cooked corn bread, vegetables, etc. that they eat. They have as many helpings as they like, and the small round tables lead to general conversation. They sing very prettily ballads and graces before meals and are singing all over the grounds and come up and speak without any shyness, just like nice children. In its way it is a model establishment without any taint of the institution, and it shows that there are some people who appreciate the qualities of mountain children and know how to handle them. I wish you could go and stay a few days there and realize all this for yourself. I expect it has much changed in the last two or three years. The staff on the whole are of the same caliber as the principals. Miss E. K. Wells (you remember her at Knoxville) is just a charming person, also Miss (Dr.) Little and pretty nearly all of them. The point is, they are all *ladies,* and that seems to me to be the solution of the problem. The schoolwork is the least of it all, and the theological side is there but kept in its proper place, so that the objectionable missionary spirit is wholly absent.

The neighborhood is a prime one for songs—a great contrast after Clay County—and singing, if not as general as in the Laurel section, is more or less universal. We hope to get back here again later on, for there is heaps to be done there. We taught the staff a few dances and the children some games, and every evening after supper we sang three or four songs and ballads. I was greatly surprised, I own, for I expected to find things very "arty and crafty," sentimental and precious. But this is not so at all. They have a strong aesthetic sense and realize the value of a beautiful environment—there are flowers everywhere, growing on the campus and bowls of them in every room. The few pictures I saw were good ones. A few schools or settlements such as this one would transform the mountains in double-quick time, but it will not be so easy to staff them—everything indeed depends on the character of those who are in power. . . .

I got some good songs—nothing new except the tunes, many of which were quite fresh to me. Our present plan is to make for Beattyville, Booneville, Jackson, Hyden, and Hazard and then perhaps Pine Mountain again from Cornetsville. But all this depends on our health and circumstances. We saw some good dancing at Pine Mountain, what they call running sets, which interested me tremendously. It is a fine form of dancing and a tradition which has lapsed in England. I want to see more of it—in its varied forms—before I publish, but they will have to be published sooner or later, because they are really fine. There are also children's games to be got, many of them quite new to me.

John sent this letter on to Mr. Glenn, on September 8th, with the following comment:

I am so glad [Mr. Sharp] appreciated Miss Pettit and her work. I think ultimately he will come to be a strong supporter of the right kind of school. He hits Burns's school—the school at Oneida—harder than any other except the mission schools, and that is the school, of all schools, that has been managed through all its existence by mountaineers. I do not think Mr. Sharp knows this. I shall be interested to hear his final verdict on the schools and mountain work. I think he will come to agree with the rest of us in the need of cleanliness, domestic science, and the niceties, as he does now to some extent in the health work—and he is quite tolerant toward the theological side of Miss Pettit's work. I am much interested in his changing view (though I do not think, perhaps, that he regards it as changing) of the mountain people and his appropriation of an ideal toward which we are all working.

To this Mr. Glenn immediately replied, enclosing a copy of one he had received from Mr. Sharp, and commenting, "The tone is very much the same as the one to you. He is evidently getting clearer views as he gets wider experience."

Mr. Sharp wrote two more letters to John, one before and one just after hearing of our plans to go away for awhile:

Jackson, Lee County, Ky.
September 9, 1917

We came on from Beattyville today, where we had a most successful week—the best we have had so far. The people are much more alive to the songs and ready to sing, and it is clear that this is going to be a rich field, probably—at least I am counting on it—getting richer as we go down the line toward the mountains. Tell Mrs. Campbell we got another Child this week, a very fine version of "The Death of Queen Jane"—some of the lines being better than the English version. The tune not so good as the English one in the Ditson book. Then we got a magnificent version of the "Two Brothers," both words and air and a very curious and new (to me) set of words to "Young Hunting." I also got another version of "The Elfin Knight."

We struck two rare good singers, one in Beattyville and the other at St. Helens. I have more or less emptied the former, but the latter seems inexhaustible. We walked to St. Helens and then two miles up a hill to her house this morning and then came on here by the three o'clock train. I can get at her by rail more easily from here. The trains suit, whereas from Beattyville it meant a six-mile walk each way, and that, in this weather (it is hotter than ever) is no small consideration. I have had an urgent letter from Miss Stone asking me not to leave Hindman out of my itinerary, so we shall try and go there from Hazard—the more especially as W. A. Bradley is staying there, and I should like to exchange notes with him. . . .

From Hazard we shall work Hindman and Hyden, then go on to Whitesburg and probably go back to Pine Mountain, chiefly to see the dancing again. After then I shall try and express my luggage to Asheville (i.e., before going to Pine Mountain) and work round by the C. and O. or some way via Ashe County, perhaps to Asheville. I cannot face the journey back via Lexington or Winchester!

I find I must be in New York on Sunday, October 28. So I shall try to get to Asheville on October 21 and have a quiet week at Grove Park Hotel, get my teeth done, and recuperate after the strain here. For it is a strain. Our dysentery is all right now but it has not increased our strength. As for myself, I eat hardly anything. That doesn't matter much as far as I am concerned, but I am a little afraid of Maud. However, we have lasted six weeks so far, so we can go another six weeks I expect, especially as the weather will soon be getting cooler and healthier.

I have taken down just over two hundred tunes this trip, and I have just passed the four thousand in my general collection. Maud wants to celebrate the occasion and is going to try to inveigle me into a drug store for a cold drink tomorrow!

Had a letter from Mrs. Storrow saying that Dr. Prichett had definitely refused to do anything to help me! Charlie has had another rather nasty operation on his arm but is getting on all right, I am glad to say.

We had a horrid journey last Monday from Pineville to Lexington, and a pretty bad one on to Beattyville the next day. The day coaches on this line are as dirty and uncomfortable as they can be made! My asthma is still pretty bad, though, on the whole, better. Hope your hay fever is holding off!

Hindman, Kentucky
September 20, 1917

Just got your letter of the 15th, and am very sorry to hear you are leaving Asheville and will not therefore be there when we repair thither next month—sorry for our sake though not for yours and Mrs. Campbell's, for I have no doubt you will both benefit greatly by the change.

I wrote you my plans so far as I can see them some ten days ago. We stay here collecting till October 21—when we go to Asheville—probably to the Grove Park Inn!—for a week to recuperate, get some decent food into our more or less emaciated bodies, and to have my teeth done by Sinclair. Hazard was what we were prepared to find it—a second Harlan—a hurly-burly of dollar-hunters, dirty, unkempt, insanitary, slipshod—I call it Hap-Hazard—and anything that I hate *except* a fairly good hotel with the use of a piano. I made good use of the latter last week and hope to do the same again next Sunday, so that if I can get on to another piano during my week in Asheville, I shall have my harmonized book ready for the press when I return to New York. Hindman is not of much use. Between Hazard and Hindman, we passed nothing but frame houses, and it is the same here. You can get things from people who live in that way, but with difficulty and not of first quality—as in Clay County. That seems to me a definite fact, the one sure point in questions surrounded with mystery and difficulty.

Yesterday we had a good day, and I must have taken down pretty nearly forty songs. The girls here are bubbling with them, and I really ought to stay here longer than I intended. However, we shall see. Today I am going to make another effort to get something outside, and believe I am on the track of something good. Remember me to Mrs. Coolidge and her husband, wild Bill [their baby son, Brad], etc. There is a chance I may be doing a week's work at Boston University in October, November, or December, in which case I shall surely see a good deal of the Coolidges and possibly you and Mrs. Campbell if you are still there.

We return to Hazard for weekend, then go to Hyden, possibly to Whitesburg, and, if I can manage it, to Pine Mountain! I saw a running set at Pine Mountain very well done, and another here the night before last very badly done. It is quite a wonderful dance, and I shall not rest till I have mastered it and got all its many technical details onto paper.

Our departure from Asheville was occasioned by the beginning of John's hay fever in early September, this time with attendant asthma. We decided to go north, all three of us, for vacation, which would enable John to escape and recover. Before we got away, he finished his editing of a revision made in the New York office of his own contribution on behalf of the Southern Highland Division to the decennial report of the Russell Sage Foundation. His letter of the 18th to Mr. Glenn reveals some of the pitfalls for the Southern Highland Division incident to such a publication:

I am returning in this mail my revision of the revised report for the decennial publication.

Much time and thought have been given to it, but comparatively few changes have been made in either form or wording. Certain expressions have been omitted that were inserted, and others have been returned to their original context because, as changed, they gave expression to what I did not intend or feel.

In writing, I am constrained always by the knowledge that this division is the only southern division of the Foundation and by the fact that its field is a geographical field, whose people have been made supersensitive by efforts to work *for* them—efforts always having their inception in a real desire to be of service but attended too often by a selfconcealed consciousness of working *for* a people and section who have not had "our advantages," rather than working *with* them and learning from them. Very possibly I share this oversensitiveness and go to the extreme in avoiding in my papers certain expressions which to many would seem necessary and entirely harmless.

Feeling as I do, however, I have avoided such otherwise innocent expressions as:

"The Southern Highland Division of Russell Sage Foundation

was created in October 1912 for the *improvement of social conditions in the mountainous districts of the southern states.*

"describing some *depressing rural social conditions in certain sections of our Southern states.*

"doing the best they could under the *prevailing educational system of their states."*

(My reference was to the type of training that prevailed in our public schools nationally, not to alleged poorer educational systems in our Southern States. The type of school is the same, North and South.)

"*remote sections where there is much illness and low standards of hygiene, where local funds or local intelligence and initiative on the subject are lacking."*

The revised form and condensation of material were so good that it has taken much time to adapt such changes as have been necessary without doing injury to the admirable form of the report.

I have endeavored, as suggested by Miss [Helen] Moore, to strengthen the conclusion. If there are corrections to be made in this revision, I shall be glad of the opportunity of going over them with Miss Moore while in New York.

We left Asheville, all three—John, little Barbara, and I—September 21st and arrived at West Medford, Massachusetts "without trouble, Barbara proving a very good traveler." John was to take a two-weeks' vacation, after which he planned to visit the Kentucky mountains and Sewanee and Madison, Tennessee, while Barbara and I remained at home. Most unhappily, Barbara's young cousin Brad, a husky little boy, had a bad cold, and as she was just as eager to be with him as he with her, we could not see to keep them apart. He was able to throw off his cold normally, but the one she caught developed into bronchial pneumonia, something in her delicate condition she was unable to combat. After about a month of specialists, fluctuating temperatures, and hard cough, she died on October 24th.

To get away, back deep into work, was our only thought, but we could not leave for several days. The United States was now plunged into war; our Asheville home was closed and our belongings in storage. We decided to keep together and follow the general travel plan outlined before, and then, perhaps, to go to Washington to work for a time on John's article on the mountain region, which had become an extended study. The plan seemed all the wiser as John was not at all well; his heart was giving him increasing pain. Miss Dickey's sister was still in Washington, and we asked her if she would not keep her eye open for good quarters for us there in January and, if possible, for her sister and her mother.

11

War Work, 1918

The fall was spent traveling in Kentucky and Tennessee, with a visit to Washington, where Campbell did additional research in the Library of Congress for his study of the mountain region, which was moving toward publication. The visits to schools at Hindman and Pine Mountain, Sewanee University, the Seventh-Day Adventist School, and the Nashville Normal and Agricultural Institute in Tennessee were arduous; most of them needed advice for the future, and the discussions were long and tiring. There were no train schedules, because the government had taken over the railroads, and trolley cars were not running. The weather was tempestuous, with blizzard conditions; it was sixteen degrees below zero in Madison. John Campbell nearly froze from being out in the weather too long.

As he continued to work on the report, he turned to Cecil Sharp for help on the origins of the mountain people as evidenced in their songs and ballads. Sharp demurred, writing that he was no expert. He concluded from his observation, though, that whatever their racial origin, their culture currently was Anglo-Saxon or Anglo-Celtic. He went on to agree with others that there were also German, French, Scandinavian, and Negro elements: "The human type represented in the mountains seems to be wonderfully homogeneous."

In February it was decided that the conference would convene as planned, in spite of the war. Campbell's health was getting increasingly worse, but he insisted on continuing to work on the book and on attending the conference in April in Knoxville. About a hundred attendees were expected, from fourteen different denominations and from independent work, public school work, and various agencies such as the Red Cross, the YMCA, and the Southern Industrial Educational Association, as well as representatives of the US Department of Agriculture. This conference was even more successful than previous ones, with themes such as agriculture and agricultural cooperation in the mountains and cooperation in other fields. Requests continued to pour in for copies of the study, even while it was still in manuscript. It was evident that there was a pressing need for a "summing up of the mountain life and mountain country, with stress upon diversities."

Afterward, the Campbells headed to Nantucket, with John Campbell's mind at rest about the ongoing work of the Southern Highland Division. Rutherford B. Hayes had volunteered to assume some of the duties of arranging speakers to talk about the work of the Food Administration, the Fuel Administration, the Red Cross, and other govern-

mental agencies that might be of help to the mountaineers. Campbell's health improved somewhat, but he and Olive remained in Massachusetts until October, because influenza was rampant in the country.

We, John and I, started south from West Medford on November 1, 1917, on what was to prove a long and arduous journey. In New York and Washington, John stopped over for a series of conferences. From Washington, we planned to visit Berea College in Kentucky, going on to Pine Mountain and Hindman, where Miss Huntington and Miss Pettit had each urged John to come to talk over future plans for school development. Thence, in late December, we would go to Sewanee and Madison, Tennessee, before returning to Washington in January. There we would remain for some weeks to make use of the Library of Congress and other sources for material needed for John's extended study of the mountain region, which was beginning to take shape for publication.

John did not forget his old friend Park Fisher from Demorest, Georgia. Park was a childhood victim of infantile paralysis but was very active on his crutches, able to drive a team, operate a stereopticon, and in general meet the emergencies and exactions of a very rough life. He was, in addition, a good speaker as well as a good photographer. John was able to answer, on the day we left, a promising inquiry in his behalf by the Bureau of War Personnel of the National War Work Council:

> Your confidential inquiry with reference to Park W. Fisher was received some days ago, but a reply has been delayed because of illness and death in my family.
>
> I cannot answer all the questions that you ask, but if I were placing men as secretaries or assistants in the work of the Army YMCA, I should readily appoint Mr. Fisher, despite the fact that he goes on crutches. He is not a college graduate but has graduated from Atlanta Theological Seminary and also from Hartford Seminary. He is a fine character and a splendid mixer, is a good musician and a general all-around handy man. I have been hunting with him many times, and while I have the use of both my hands and legs, Fisher is a quicker and much better shot than I, and I am fair. This much merely to indicate how little he is handicapped. I wish I could be more definite. He is worth looking up. He has a wife and two or three children.

In New York he [John] found that Mr. Glenn was away, but Mr. Sharp was staying at the Algonquin Hotel. While John had conferences with church board people and Foundation staff, I had good hours with Mr. Sharp and Miss Karpeles, talking of their recent experiences in the mountains, the appearance of the book, which had just been published,[1] and their plans for further collecting. Mr. Sharp was determined to finish the undertaking, to make a definitive and comprehensive collection of ballads from the southern mountains.

John did not see President Frost at Berea, but he heard from him there. Dated November 8th, the letter referred to a list of questions sent out by the committee of the Southern Mountain Workers' Conference set up to study schools in the mountains:

> Your favor of October 18th is at hand.
>
> Mrs. Frost and I suffered a simultaneous collapse nervously last spring and have been all summer at Battle Creek, with definite progress toward recovery but not yet recovered. We are stopping here [at Berea] a few days on our way south, where we shall continue to rest during the winter. This situation makes it impossible for me to give the encouragement and counsel which I desire for your important work. If it would relieve you from embarrassment for me to resign my position on this committee so that another could be appointed, I should be glad to do so. If I do come to life next spring, I shall hope to really have the opportunity to cooperate in this most important matter, but please supply my place now if you can do so to advantage.
>
> The list of questions which you submit strikes me as decidedly good. It will be profitable for every officer who fills out this blank, compelling a kind of "self-survey," and it will yield information of importance.
>
> Might it pay to insert somewhere a question or two like this: What, in brief, are the characteristics of the mountain field which should be made note of by a new worker coming into your service? What, in brief, are the distinguishing characteristics of the different parts of the mountains in which your schools are situated?
>
> Mrs. Frost joins me in most sincere friendship and regard to yourself and Mrs. Campbell. If possible, on our way north toward spring, we shall make you a visit.

From Berea John and I proceeded on our way, going to Pine Mountain after visiting Caney Creek and Hindman. A letter of November 21st from Mr. Sharp reached us at Hindman:

New York, N.Y.

Your letter of the 17th just arrived. Maud is sending out cards tonight before going to bed.

I am sorry people object to Bradley's book. It seems very harmless to me. It is not my view of the mountains, of course, but then he has avowedly written of the "transitionals." And he has a real appreciation of those with whom he has consorted. Of course it is always a dangerous thing to make a book about anyone, and I suppose any novelist has made enemies for deriving his characters and material from his friends and acquaintances. I have always been glad that I have not had to do this. But I am always fearful lest some of the stories I tell at my lectures might get back to the originals and cause offense. Luckily this has never happened—so far as I know. I like Bradley immensely, and I am sure he would not willingly hurt anyone's feelings, particularly those of his friends in the mountains, for whom he has a great affection.

Putnam's are getting out a folder, but I rather fancy they will hold it back for a day or so in order that they may add one or more quotations from reviews if there are any complimentary ones. Nothing has appeared as yet—but it is early days. Schirmer's are printing my harmonized book and are under contract to publish before May 1st!

There is quite a large scheme in the air whereby the Yale University Press may undertake to continue publication of the tunes as I collect them year by year and finally print a large volume summarizing the whole as a sort of companion and complementary volume to Child. Whether anything will come of it or not I don't know. At present it is private, so please treat this as more or less confidential. One of my men dancers has just been called up to an army camp, so at the last moment I have to take his place. I am wondering if I shall have breath enough to get through the running set! especially as I register another notch tomorrow.

It is rather late in the day to make further mention of the schools where some of the songs were collected. If I publish what I have noted this year, I shall of course make a strong point of Hindman and Pine Mountain, and I shall not forget them on Friday. Anything that I can do to help the work they are doing, I shall do with all my heart. They are just splendid places. I wrote a long letter to Miss Pettit yesterday. I am seeing Miss Stone at Boston next week. Lily Roberts tells me she has arranged a date with Mrs. Coolidge, but I don't know as yet what it is. I shall be in Boston from the 1st of December to the 15th at any rate but must in any case be back in New York for a four-day school of folk song and dance I am holding here on the four days following Xmas Day. My plans after that are vague, but I shall probably go to some quiet cheap and healthy spot near here or Boston where I can write my next book containing this year's plunder. I calculate that I can get into the mountains again soon after that.

Please remember me to Miss Huntington and my many kind friends in Hindman, and with love to you both.

It was pleasant to see old friends again at Hindman and Pine Mountain, but the trip was anything but a pure pleasure jaunt. Each school was seeking advice for the future, discussions were many and long, and at the end we had to walk over Pine Mountain, for the trail was too slippery for horseback. It was a long, hard trip for John, climbing up the steep trail in the snow and ice. We took it slowly, with frequent stops to admire the beauty of the woods, and to catch our breath. Even after we reached the top, the down trip was not easy. We slipped and slid over the uncertain footing.

I wonder sometimes why we tried to make any further studies, but we had planned to go to Sewanee for better knowledge of the Episcopal work, and go we did. It was a pleasant and profitable time in spite of John's condition (and a heavy cold I had contracted on our way in the snow). When we arrived at the Seventh-Day Adventist School, the Nashville Normal and Agricultural Institute, near Madison, Tennessee, we were able to get rest and attention—letters, too—at the rural sanitarium in connection with it.

After a bit of rest at Madison, John wrote Mr. Glenn on December 27th:

I am leaving tonight for Indianapolis and shall return again to Madison. Mrs. Campbell is under the care of a doctor here, having caught a very hard cold while crossing Pine Mountain from Miss Pettit's school to the railroad. The snow and ice prevented horses going, so we had to walk. She has added something to it since, but is getting the better of it, and the doctor feels she will be rid of it soon—at least within a week.

We had a very pleasant and profitable time in spite of it. Mr. and Mrs. [Massey Hamilton] Shepherd, who entertained us while we were at Sewanee, were most kind. There are possibilities for some good things for the mountains through the University of the South, if some of Mr. Shepherd's plans carry. They want me back there again in the spring for a conference with the whole faculty. The work at Madison, Tennessee, is also most interesting. It is the only self-supporting school that I know. They have a rural sanitarium in connection with it. Dr. and Mrs. Frost of Berea are there, and Bruce Payne phoned me this morning and wants me to meet his faculty on my return, and I feel that I shall have a profitable time while here. Dr. Sutherland seems to feel that he had found the cause for my trouble and hopes by the time he is through with Mrs. Campbell he will have gotten me well in hand. Our mails have been delayed, so I have not heard from Miss Dickey, but at last writing she was having some difficulty in finding places for herself and us in Washington. She can be relied upon, however, to find something, and I hope to be established there by the end of the first week in January.

Am doing a bit of preliminary work on the book, and all these places that I have visited—especially the one I am now visiting at Madison— tend to shed much light. I hope I shall be able to make some constructive suggestions through what I am learning on this trip.

The weather was indeed bad, with a real blizzard and temperature most unusual for that section of the South. Practically all transportation was stopped for several days and very uncertain for a week. It was almost impossible to get any definite information from railroad officials as to trains, both on account of the weather and because of the confusion incident to the government's taking over the railroads.[2]

In a letter to Mr. Sharp, written a month later, after we were comfortably established in Washington, where Miss Dickey "was fortunate enough to get a small house on short lease, just big enough, with some crowding, for herself, sister and mother, and for Mrs. Campbell and me," John gave an account of his own experience in the snowstorm:

We have had strenuous times here with snowstorms and the weather generally. We have a coal shortage here, too, but fortunately we have coal enough for another week and have paid for a ton, which will be delivered sometime. I think I have never felt the cold so much as this winter, although I was used to very low temperatures as a boy. I passed through a very trying experience in Nashville on the night of January 11th, having gone in from Madison, which is only eight miles away. I took the five o'clock interurban trolley to get back. The blizzard came on about that time, and we were over four hours getting a mile and a half; snow interfered with the wires and obstructed the track as well. After waiting in the car until sometime after nine o'clock, one of the motormen told me he did not think we could get much further that night, so I left the car and managed to find a man with an auto, who was looking for his sister lost somewhere in the storm. He took me to a telephone booth, where I managed to get word through to Madison that we could not get through that night, and he promised to take me back to the hotel. After going about a mile toward the city, he left me at a garage, half a mile or more from the hotel. I knew I was intensely cold, and very numb. When I got to the garage, both my arms were stiff to the shoulder and circulation had practically stopped in my hands and arms. I managed, however, to get some snow, and rubbed my hands, but could not do very much; a gentleman then came into the garage seeking shelter from the cold. He looked at me for a few moments and then said, "Brother, excuse me, but you need attention. I have been in the Klondike and I know the symptoms of freezing." He stripped off my coat and, with three other men in the garage, set to work upon me. After some time, the circulation was partially restored. He wanted to take me to his hotel, but no cars were running and no autos running. Eventually we started out toward the hotel, where I knew Olive would inquire for me. With his assistance I got partway and then had to give up. Just then, one lone trolley car came limping back to town, and with its assistance, I got back to the hotel.

After a hot bath, I managed to get fairly comfortable and have no ill effects except a numbness in the fingers of my right hand. The doctor says it will be all right after a month or so.

Everything was tied up the next day. I went to the railroad station, and no trains were running. Finally I induced an auto driver to take me out the eight miles. I am sure he never would have attempted it could he have imagined what the roads were like. While at the station waiting for a possible train to be made up, I saw a lady who had been on the same trolley car with me the night before. She told me they had been on the trolley until half past two the next morning, and after using all of the coal to keep warm, and getting a little more from houses nearby, one trolley car managed to get back to town, and she came upon that. It was sixteen degrees below zero in Madison that night, they told me. It was the most bitter cold I have ever experienced, and I long for spring to come.

John did not explain in the letter that he did not know what would be the effect of a hot bath on his heart. Before taking one, he wrote me a note and left it on the table beside his bed.

The weather also delayed our arrival in Washington, which we reached on Sunday morning, January 18th, some days later than we had planned. In one of his first letters from there, written to Miss Clement, John reported himself as well and sounded most cheerful. Among the many letters waiting for us were two from Miss Pettit, which called forth a long and thoughtful reply. She wrote John on January 4, 1918:

> I am anxious to know what you really thought of our school. Of course we are conscious of many blunders, but I want you to tell me if you think we are started right or not. What are our dangers? I think you were afraid we were likely to get into the conventional school rut.
>
> Most of all I want you to tell me about your plan or idea of the community work you are so interested in. Do you think our neighborhood a good one for it? If we have the faith and courage to try this new and untried work, do you think we can get the help we need? First we must have money for the salary of at least one worker, and for expenses. What agencies can we get to help us? I mean in the way of workers and lecturers. How can we get money, and how much should we have to begin? Tell me how and why we should appeal to the people to help us start a new work in this wartime. Do you believe in us enough to recommend us to the people, or to any organization that might help us? Tell me something to say to people to make them see that we are justified in starting something new and untried. Would you write an endorsement, asking anyone who may be interested but not quite sure that this is the place, or that we are the people to undertake this work, to write to you and see what you think about it?
>
> I shall be so much obliged to you, and it will be the greatest help to us in making our plans for this year and the coming years, if you will tell me in detail just what you would like to see Pine Mountain do in following out your ideas of community work in the mountains.

To me she wrote on January 10th:

> It was good to have your last two letters and to know of the things that you are doing. I am so glad to hear that Mr. Campbell has been helped. . . .
>
> Miss Canterbury and Miss Secor went to Berea for a few days of their vacation, and the rest of the time rested and read at home.[3] Miss Robbins went to Smith, Harlan County, to visit the new Presbyterian school there, and was taken sick with what has turned out to be mastoiditis. She had been sent to Louisville for an operation—eighteen men took turns in carrying her in a rocking chair across Big Black Mountain—and we do hope

she is getting along all right. Miss Shipley is ill also, in Cincinnati, so that our force of workers is somewhat depleted.

We who stayed at home stood the cold weather very well. As Miss Engberg is away, one morning when the thermometer was twenty below zero, I spent three hours at the barn! I assure you however, that the barn has not been dusted every day since she has been gone.

Miss Canterbury and Miss Secor, and everybody, were so interested in the things you said in your letter, especially about hymns and songs.

We did have such a delightful Christmas, which really lasted from Christmas Eve to Old Christmas on January 6th, when Miss Spencer and Miss Butler took a Christmas tree to the head of Little Laurel for the people down there. They said that they couldn't think of anyone who didn't come except for two people at the mouth of the creek! I wish you could have seen Miss Gaines's little girls, who sang carols from the balcony of the dining room. They sang "The Holly and the Ivy," and as they sang they hung ropes of laurel around the balcony. They wore white dresses and red ribbons, and two of the little girls carried staffs trimmed with holly and red ribbon.

Our furnace has been such a comfort this bitter weather. If you will come to Pine Mountain for next Christmas, we will let you live in a warm, furnaceheated house, if you will promise to spend all your spare time at my house.

Please you and Mr. C. and Miss Dickey look out for a good public health nurse for us. Miss Walker can only stay until we get the right one, and if we start this larger community work, we shall need another, one that has had real public health training, if we can find her.

The children were so pleased with their cards, and talk about you and Mr. Campbell. They still play fox and geese in front of my house and call it Mr. Campbell's game.

Be sure to come back with Mr. Sharp.

John wrote his reply to Miss Pettit on February 1st:

I have your letter of January 4th, and I gladly respond to your request to write you fully as to what I think of the Pine Mountain Settlement School and of the possibilities of its development.

We enjoyed to the full the three weeks that we were with you. Among the many things that stand out clearly in memory is the uniform courtesy of the children. The unconscious influence exerted upon them by your teachers must be very great to so bring out, in children so young, the innate courtesy of the mountaineer. We were much impressed, too, by their attitude toward work; there seemed to be no grumblers nor any shirkers. This too, I think, is due to the influence exerted by your faculty, from you and Miss deLong to the latest workers on your staff.

Your site and surroundings are most pleasing: your buildings charming. I was very much pleased to see the prominence given to forestry, farming, dairying, and poultry raising, to note your well-kept barn and poultry yard, and to see evidences of the enthusiasm and intelligence displayed by those in charge. It is most interesting and promising to see college graduates and girls who in other places might be regarded as society girls, taking an intelligent interest and direction in these matters, not merely in a supervisory way, but actually working side by side in the same activities with mountain boys and girls. It gives dignity to such work and a camaraderie in labor that does not exist in many places.

I was pleased, too, to note how you and Miss deLong were furthering the native culture of the mountains, reviving and keeping alive balladry, seeking to give a wholesome direction to native recreation, and that you are planning, just as you actually did when you both were at Hindman, to develop still further the fireside industries.

There are many other things which I might comment upon most favorably, but you have asked me particularly to point out some of your *dangers* and to indicate lines of future development which, in my judgment, ought to be promoted; so I pass to these at once, leaving unsaid many more things I should like to say in praise of your work but which you doubtless hear often from the many guests who are privileged to partake of your hospitality.

The great danger that I see for your school is it may crystallize into a school *organization,* inelastic and stereotyped (as so many schools have done that have started with promise), rather than continue as an educational *organism*, responding instinctively to rural needs and adapting itself to changing conditions.

Let me pause here to answer your question as to location before going further. I think you are admirably located for the type of rural work needed for the mountains of Kentucky. While you are only six miles from a railroad, Pine Mountain lies between you and the railroad, and you are shut off from many of the drawbacks of so-called rural schools located in centers coming to be urban or industrial. When your new road is open, you will have better mail and freight privileges than at present, though you may have to guard yourselves against the harmful influences of a stream of merely idle visitors of the tourist type. Pine Mountain shuts you off from much of the bustling activity attending coal-mine development, yet you are near enough to this development to know the problems affecting rural people that it brings. You are very near to one of the most intensely rural counties of the Kentucky mountains, namely, Leslie. So far as I now can see, you are not likely soon, if ever, to meet the onrush of industrialism, such as may soon engulf some good schools.

In your organization, I see certain disadvantages. Relying as you do so much upon voluntary workers, too much depends upon you and Miss deLong. If death, accident, or circumstances should remove either or both of you from the management of the school, unless other workers have been trained under you and have caught your vision, the splendid work that you have begun may fail. You should have understudies; understudies who have the sense of permanency and of security that comes from the understanding that the work may devolve upon them. They should be paid salaries.

I see, too, disadvantages lurking in the double authority under which your school is managed. Of course, at present, with the very close understanding between you and Miss Long, disagreements arising from a double authority are not so likely to occur. There should, however, in my judgment, be one head, with the members of the faculty having a voice and vote in the policy and management of the school, their action, vetoed or approved by the one head, to be brought to the attention of the trustees. The faculty should have the right to present their side of the case to the trustees in case of disagreement between the school faculty and the head of the school. Your trustees, on the other hand, should send a representative committee from year to year to look into the work of the school. I do not know who your trustees are, but in most schools that have trustees, the trustees merely "trust," and are put on the board either because of their influence or in the hope of "working" them for funds. My impression is, however, from what I have heard from time to time, that your trustees do take a vital interest in the school, are in touch with its management, and are not properly classed with the kind of trustees mentioned.

Independent schools, such as yours, have a larger freedom of action than the average school managed by church boards, but they fail too often through members of their boards of trustees not feeling their personal responsibility. In such schools, trustees leave too much to the heads of schools. There should be a great effort made to develop an esprit de corps, from the newest and youngest worker on the staff to the head of the school, shared in, too, by the trustees. With the changes made as to definite authority, and close relations with the trustees affected, this esprit de corps will tend to ensure continuity of purpose and realization of the visions of the founders of the school, even though they should fall by the way before the consummation of their hopes.

I think, too, that you, like all mountain schools, need more men on your faculty. Just how this is to be brought about, I do not know as yet: perhaps it might be brought about by getting trained men and putting them at the head of some of your departments; perhaps by having some of them live at your possible extension centers. The difficulty is not alone in finding good men who will work under women, but finding good men who have had the sense to marry the kind of wives who feel that their husbands are not belittling themselves by working under women. Those difficulties will be surmounted, I think, as your work develops.

I know that it is much easier to get buildings than to get people, but the plea is always raised that "we must get buildings first, where we can accommodate people." I would urge holding out against this temptation. Buildings too often set a work in a fixed mold, while people of the right kind will help you to shape work according to changing needs.

You have been so good as to ask me what I would do were I again to come to the mountains, as I should so much like to do. Were the opportunity mine, as it is yours, I should not, for the present, put up more buildings at the place where you are, but should try to secure the additional people and funds to do the work at Pine Mountain, and from it, as a general center, at subsidiary points at Big Laurel, Cutshin, and others that you might select as the work grows. At these stations I should place workers to do what work is needed there, a chief work of theirs being to cultivate public opinion for the meeting of general social and economic needs. Some of your workers should live at these points, to get the neighborhood touch, but should have the right to call upon your general workers at Pine Mountain, and with you at Pine Mountain and your workers at your other stations, to cooperate in bringing in of county, state, and national workers engaged in rural activities—such as education, agriculture, nursing, recreation, etc. There would be no need for buildings (of any cost at least) at these subsidiary stations: perhaps just a little cottage of the general type used by the people, but made more comfortable with the modern conveniences permissible. In most of these neighborhoods there are little school-houses available that are not in use during six or eight months of the year, and some church houses. The workers might even go far into the country, using a barn or any sort of building, or teaching in the open, just as extension workers once did in Norway, where both the isolation produced by mountains and by fjords had to be overcome.

I could write indefinitely about the kind of work you could do. There are great industries to be developed in the mountains. I speak not alone from my own knowledge, but from the knowledge of government and state experts, when I say that cattle raising, sheep raising, dairying, etc. have a great future in the mountains. Mountain public opinion must needs be cultivated, however, for their development. Some of these pursuits once existed and need only revival. The mountain dog has been the great curse of sheep raising in the mountains. The Asheville Board of Trade, instigated, I think, by the enthusiasm of a few individuals, has started propaganda against the mountain dog. My impression is, it has extended to Washington. Our Board of Trade is now getting letters from different parts of the country asking about their propaganda. You might begin the keeping of sheep at Pine Mountain. Probably, for some time, most of your sheep would be killed by the dogs, but with persistent propaganda (while it is hard on the sheep, and entails some loss) you would educate the people; dog taxes would be voted, and the sheep-killing dog would be eliminated.

I know forestry and goat raising, if the goats run loose, are not coordinate industries, for the goats will kill your trees; but a few milch goats could be kept within a goat-proof fence, and it be demonstrated by you to families far remote in the rugged parts of the mountains, where there is no pasture and perhaps no free range for the goats, that milch goats could be kept where cows cannot be.

I know there is an insistent objection that there is no pasture; but I know, too, that there are certain grasses and clovers that grow luxuriantly on the mountains; I have looked into it and could put you in touch with men who have the expert knowledge. Some of these grasses grow wild in other mountain countries; we have killed out some of our grasses by our common forest fires. It was a common practice until recent years, and is yet in parts of the North Carolina mountains, for the mountaineers to drive their cattle and herd lowland cattle on the tops of the mountains on the "balds," where grass grows luxuriantly. I know all these things are regarded as impossible by the casual observer and by him who, like the Chinaman, simply follows in the footsteps of his fathers, but it is for us in the mountain schools to show the impossible is possible, and we can prove it only by demonstrating.

You could also start a little cheese factory—a coming industry in the mountains. A number of them are now being operated very successfully in the mountains of North Carolina and southwestern Virginia under the direction of the US Department of Agriculture. Cheese factories cannot be run in all parts of the Kentucky mountains; they could not do it at Hindman—the elevation is not sufficient to ensure the temperature and moisture necessary, but in the real mountains of Kentucky, where the elevation is above two thousand feet, conditions are likely to be suitable. You might inquire of the government, and if you are too low in the valley part in which you are located, start it at one of your extension centers up on Pine Mountain itself.

There are other industries, such as the raising of seeds for large seed firms and the raising of bulbs and roots. These are occupations for women and children in Europe, carried on, generally, on small farms. I have found out recently that 75 percent of the seeds that we use commonly in America are imported from Europe—from Belgium, Germany, and other countries at war, and from Holland. Inquiry shows that most of these seeds that we have imported from abroad can be raised to great advantage in America, and our highland section is well adapted for raising bulbs and certain kinds of seeds. I know from my own experience that bulbs do well in the mountains. Why should we not now learn the lessons of the war and grasp our opportunities?

For a number of years to come, there is going to be a great dearth in some of these industries. I know some men, and could find others, who could give you direction in these matters, who could tell you where the markets are and help you do the marketing, and experts should be able to tell you the special lines of work for which your section is best fitted.

Our mountain schools must have more to do with the life of the mountain people, and economic life is a part of life. They must not be content any longer to ignore the economic side, as so many of us have done. You have not ignored it, but the danger is that you will fail, just as others have failed in their efforts, because you may not continue to find people who have the knowledge to ensure success. It is easier to find a good Greek, French, or Latin teacher than to find one who can make farming, dairying, poultry-and-other-raising pay for themselves and be cultural at the same time. Much of this work in the organizing of public opinion you could do through our main Pine Mountain center and your extension centers, and you could do it without much cost. You might, during certain seasons of the year, which might be called Chautauqua seasons, secure as members of your peripatetic faculty the best experts of the government. So few seem to avail themselves of what the government offers. There are men and women from the government who will come right to your door and stay two or three weeks if the right time is fixed for them, and tell how to take care of milk, how to make butter, and all such facts. When I tell some mountain schoolteachers of these things, they fold their hands and say, "Well, we have no grass for pasturage," and when I say, "Why do you not send to the government, then, to tell you what grasses you can raise?," they look blank, as if the thought never occurred to them.

You have been responsive and on the alert, and I am looking to you to blaze the way. I feel very sure that many of the things, cultural and eco-nomic, that I have mentioned can and will be furthered by you.

I know, too, that such a vital matter as sanitation, with all it implies, could be advanced in practically the same ways that I have indicated, by calling upon experts, without much cost to yourselves. Furthermore, there are several philanthropic boards, in addition to national organizations, that will help you in the promotion of rural recreation and general rural social welfare.

What is needed for the mountains more than anything else at present is for some institution to dare to attempt these things and to incur some risks of failure. It is easier always to keep to the beaten path, where some-one has preceded and gathered out the stumbling blocks, even if the path we are following does not lead just to the place that we want to reach. We can hardly expect the government at present to send its experts way back in the mountains to cultivate a public opinion where they have no points of contact. County farm demonstrators, too, are only human like the rest of us; they do not care to go way back in the mountains on their own ini-tiative, endure hardships, and subject themselves to inconveniences to cul-tivate public opinion, when there are people in more accessible places who need and want the things they have to give them. It is for schools like yours to be the pioneers and connecting links.

Were I a bit stronger and not engaged in the work in which I am engaged, I should like nothing better than to present the work of such a school to the general giving public. I am sure that the hearts of the American people are in the right place and that they are just as ready to give as ever. Of course there are special difficulties just now on account of the war, but the financial difficulties incurred by some schools in the past are due in no small part to questionings on the part of onetime donors as to kind of work and administration of funds, rather than to reluctance in giving.

I have not indicated any concrete ways in which the spiritual life that must permeate such work as yours is to find expression. Were I to enter upon this, my letter would extend to even greater lengths. I have some very definite views as to religious phases of work, some of which I have expressed to you; others I must leave for another time.

You know, I am very sure, how ready I am to do anything I can to further your work. You have a unique opportunity to be a pioneer school for the mountains and for rural America: you have many friends who believe in you and who are sure that you can do much to make real your ideals and ours.

A few days later, on February 4th, John wrote Mr. Glenn:

While at Pine Mountain, I made Miss Pettit a promise, in response to her urging, that I would write a lengthy letter setting forth in detail my view of the work at Pine Mountain—future promise, present dangers, etc. Enclosed is a copy of my letter. It occurred to me that in some leisure hour you and Mrs. Glenn might feel inclined to look it over because of your great interest in Miss Pettit and her work.

Miss Pettit is a wonderful woman: our stay at Pine Mountain made us more certain of that fact than ever. She has been too much inclined to keep herself in the background in past years because she feared her presence in the field would draw funds from Hindman, with which her name is so closely connected. We, with some others of her friends, feel that she now should go before the public more, that her name may be identified more and more with Pine Mountain. She is really the power there, although Miss de Long is also an able woman. Miss Pettit, however, has the larger vision of mountain needs.

Washington was a very different place from Asheville, where war seemed far away. Here we were in the midst of it, and soldiers dominated every scene: they crowded the streets and filled the buses, while officers paraded up and down "Peacock Alley" in the New Willard Hotel. "Over There—Over There" and "Tipperary" rang constantly in our ears. We could not help feeling the tense atmosphere and studying the newspapers, although our main occupation was the mild one of "researching" in the Library of Congress. There we haunted the map room hunting for old maps which showed early travel routes into the mountains and indicated somewhat vaguely the time and place of early settlements. We spent hours at this and on taking out books which bore on the question. After such work it was a relief to walk home in the winter air and enjoy the beauty of that great city.

John turned to Mr. Sharp also for help in his study of the ancestry of the mountain people. On January 29th he wrote:

> You were so good as to say that when I got ready to write my book, you would help me in any way you could. I am beginning to get things together, and I should like very much, sometime at your leisure during the next few weeks, to get your opinion, with reasons, as to the origin of the mountain people that you have met, as evidenced in their folk songs—in other words, the evidence in the folk songs you have found which leads you to believe that the mountain people are from certain sections in England, Scotland, or elsewhere.
>
> Dr. Frost was at the sanitarium in Madison, Tennessee, while we were there, and if I recall what he said, it was to the effect that his view is that many of the mountain people (probably mountain people in Kentucky) are from the South of England, their ancestors leaving after Monmouth's Rebellion. What do you think about it?
>
> I should be very glad for your suggestion or opinion on this or anything else that may occur to you relating to the mountain folk—ancestry or anything else.

The official answer to this came a few weeks later, accompanied by a personal letter from Chicago, a stop on a lecture tour that included Minneapolis, where, along with other speaking appointments, he had addressed the Women's Club on behalf of the Pine Mountain School. On the mountain people's ancestry, he had the following to say in his letter of February 18th:

> I received your letter of January 29th some time ago, but hitherto I have been too busy to attend to it. And now that I have a moment to spare, I am not at all sure that I can give you any information of value.

The racial origin of the inhabitants of the Southern Appalachians, so far as I know them, is an extremely intricate problem and one which I am quite sure is not going satisfactorily to be solved by speculative generalizations on the part of haphazard travelers like myself. The elucidation of the problem needs the assistance and careful investigation of ethnologists, anthropologists, as well as the examination of land titles and other legal documents concerning the settlement of the mountain regions. Nevertheless, for what they are worth, I will gladly give you my impressions. My first observation and, perhaps, the one upon which I feel that I can speak with some certainty, is that whatever may be the racial origin of the mountaineers, their predominant culture is overwhelmingly Anglo-Saxon, or, perhaps, to be more accurate, Anglo-Celtic. That is to say, whatever admixture of races there may be in the mountains, the Anglo-Celt has managed pretty completely to absorb them, to take them into his own orbit without himself being appreciably infected by them. I have formed this opinion from several considerations; from observing the everyday manners, habits, and customs, all of which are demonstrably Anglo-Saxon; from an analysis of their traditional songs, ballads, dances, singing games, etc.; and, finally, in a general way, from their physical characteristics. The strongest argument in favor of this view is based upon the character of the traditional songs and dances, which seem to be saturated with the Anglo-Celtic idiom to the exclusion of every other. The one dance that I have seen and collected is a very strong and concise piece of evidence, because I think there is no doubt that it represents a stage in the development of the English country dance of a very early date, certainly prior to 1650; and the fact that the mountaineers could not have left Great Britain for a century or more after that date can only be accounted for upon the supposition that they came from a part of England where the civilization was least developed—probably the North of England, or the border country between Scotland and England. The same deduction can be made with regard to the language, which, I take it, is far more archaic than the language of the South of England at the time when these people must have emigrated—but on this aspect of the subject I cannot speak with any authority. The argument with regard to the dance I have developed more fully in my introduction to the fifth country dance book, which will be published in a week or two. It is possible, of course, that the musical idiom of the songs in the mountains has become more archaic and primitive in character since the original emigrants arrived in this country, owing to the extreme isolation of the country in which they have resided; and this is a point of view which Mr. Fox Strangways has suggested in his review of our book in the *London Times* (Litt. Supplement, Jan. 17th, 1918).

All of the other observations that I have to make are much more speculative. There is, of course, the evidence of the surnames of the mountaineers, for what it is worth, and even there the names that have come under my own observation are necessarily very few in number, too few really to justify one in forming any trustworthy theory. But so far as they go, they seem to me to strengthen and bear out the theory of origin that I have already enunciated. The majority of the names of my friends in the mountains are English or Scottish; the Irish names are very few and the German names still fewer. But here again one stands on shifty ground, because the pronunciation of names is perpetually changing. I think I told you of the case of an undoubted Irish fiddler whom I met in Tennessee whose name was Julian. The very un-Irish nature of this name caused me to question him more closely with regard to it, and he said there were many of his kin in this country, some of whom pronounced the name as Julan, not Julian; and this, of course, showed me at once that the original name was Doolan, an undoubtedly Irish name. I daresay that many existing names have been corrupted in a similar manner.

In this matter, I would refer you to a very interesting article by Mr. W. A. Bradley in *The Dial* of Jan. 31st, 1918. He agrees with me in considering the culture of the mountaineer to be predominantly Anglo-Saxon, but he differs from me in his estimate of the degree of racial admixture, believing that the German, French, Scandinavian, and even Negro elements are very largely represented. I agree with him that there are those in the mountains representing each of these nationalities, but I do not think that the blood mixture resulting therefrom is large enough to have had any effect of consequence. The human type represented in the mountains seems to be wonderfully homogeneous; almost, if not quite, as homogeneous as the English peasantry.

I can give no opinion whatever with regard to Professor Frost's theory. Such a theory would need the support of actual facts, which Professor Frost has no doubt collected, but of which I personally have no knowledge whatever.

I am afraid these observations will not be of much value to you. As I have said before, the subject is an extremely difficult one, which must be investigated on a strictly scientific basis before dogmatizing with regard to it can have any real value.

Forgive a hastily written letter and do not hesitate to call upon me again if what I have above written is ambiguous or incomprehensible.

John dictated every day to Miss Dickey and tried to get down on paper some of the things he wished to say in the foreword and in the introduction to his book. There was, too, as usual, a great deal of correspondence, which called for more personal attention than he should have really given.

Inquiries came to him in regard to the attitude of the mountain people to the war, and toward the draft, food regulations, and so on. One of these from a member of the Committee on Public Information crystallized ideas already in his mind, as appears in this letter to Mr. Glenn, dated February 11th:

The enclosed letter, forwarded from Asheville, was received the other day. I called upon Mr. F—— Saturday afternoon and had a most pleasant interview with him.

I told him that there was no question as to the loyalty of the mountain people as a whole. A few counties, conspicuous among them Bloody Breathitt, have exceeded their quota of men for the army; other counties have been a bit lax, in part because of the leniency of the exemption boards. I further said that I felt very sure that the mountain people as a whole would rally to the call of the country, as they have always done, if the battles were to be fought on land, but that there was a certain holding back on the part of some because of the fear of "them great waters."

While in Kentucky, I got hold of a few rumors, from seemingly reliable sources, that one of the congressmen well acquainted in the mountains had been attempting to influence mountain people by alleging that the war is not necessary, etc. If my deductions from these rumors are correct, this man, unconsciously or consciously, has spread somewhat the same influence as Senator —— has spread. The man in question is a Republican, and it may have been biased, partisan, antiadministration criticism.

I suggested to Mr. F—— that if the Committee on Public Information should attempt to do anything, it would be wise to have a man who knew the mountains to engineer it, and that propaganda of that sort should not be started (if it were started) in such a way as to give the impression that the loyalty of the mountain people was in question. I told him that there were certain things that the mountain people could and should do: raising of more food, different kinds of crops, etc., etc. Only that would not only help the government out during the war, but would help the mountain people out long after the war, by teaching them in this emergency the things they can do. It is something that could be of great help if rightly handled; and the mountain people could be instructed on different phases of the war, of which they are now ignorant, without calling their loyalty into question, if such instruction were imparted incidentally with food and conservation propaganda, etc.

He was deeply interested, and I inferred that he is going to write you about my helping out; and I, of course, would be glad to help. My further impression is that he is going to talk it over with the Food Administration people.

I have a friend who knows the mountains, who is getting up stereopticon slides and is going, largely on his own expense, to do this very thing, but he does not know the agricultural side of things.[4] He has written for advice, and I think I could shape these various interests and give right direction to them, if I could keep my hands upon the movement. Much of it could be managed while here.

There is some question as to whether it is advisable to hold our Knoxville conference this year. In some ways it would be well so to do; in other ways, better not to. If a group could be sent, as indicated, through my instrumentality and that of other conference leaders with whom I would confer, it might be regarded as a very pleasant and helpful substitute this year for the Knoxville conference and give us wide publicity. I am sure I could get several southern boards of trade—such as those of Asheville and Knoxville—to help out in the more open country if that were desired.

I have long wanted to meet Dr. Charles McCarthy and called upon him Saturday afternoon. He became very much interested in what I had to tell him, and we conferred for about two hours. At his request, I waited in his office to meet Mr. Charles A. Lyman, general organizer of the National Agricultural Organization Society. I had called to meet Dr. McCarthy and to ask his advice particularly as to some man who had the technical knowledge necessary to help solve the problems of cooperation in the mountains. He said Lyman was the one man in the country fitted to do it. I told him of my difficulty with some government men, who had not the knowledge of mountain conditions, or who had not the sympathy with the small beginnings necessary to be made in the mountains. He said that Lyman had not only the technical knowledge, but that he had what is absolutely needed, Volspuk [*sic*] of sympathy which helps "put over" things which no amount of technical knowledge could.

We have been considering, and talking over, ways and means in the mountains, and now I should very much like to take someone, or some group of people, to show to the mountain people themselves how to do the thing. Lyman is not only a college man but a farmer and was with Sir Horace Plunkett in Ireland for a while to study his methods. We need just the same kind of thing. If the Irish cooperation plans can bring together such diametrically opposed elements as Presbyterians of the Ulster type and Roman Catholics of the South of Ireland, such methods, with the right people organizing and helping out, ought to be able to further what has already been done in getting the church agencies in our mountains to working together, as well as the people themselves. I should like very much to take a man like Mr. Lyman with me into the mountains for about a year to help organize. . . . Would it be feasible, from your point of view, if I can squeeze a part of it out of my budget, and if Lyman is free, to pay his expenses for two or three months to travel through the mountains with me, or go where I might indicate, to try to shape up in a few communities some local organization?

The farm demonstration people, with the agricultural people of the government and states, do not, after all, get way back, and the men trained in the agricultural schools somehow can't see much in farms of less than two or three hundred acres worked by modern methods. The small farmer in the mountains and the tenant farmer has to be helped.

I covet for the Foundation, and for my division, the opportunity that the war offers to help the mountains and to come, more and more, to be regarded as a vital force in constructive rural work in the highland South.

John had been in touch with the Southern Industrial Educational Association in regard to the possibility of their financing an experiment in promoting agricultural cooperation in the mountains. He wrote Mr. Glenn on March 2, 1918:

Since my last letter, I have had a meeting with Dr. Taylor and Mrs. J. Lowrie Bell at the home of Mrs. C. David White, to talk over the matter of the SIEA financing Mr. Lyman. Dr. Taylor and Mrs. White were in favor. Mrs. Bell wanted more information and is reading some literature on Sir Horace Plunkett's work in Ireland which at her request I secured for her.

The enclosed letter of Dr. Taylor's gives the present status: please be so kind as to return it. . . . In our conference, Dr. Taylor seemed to feel that the association might want to keep Mr. Lyman in some official touch with them and intimated that it might be a tacit understanding, if not an official connection. I felt that any control, open or private, would be detrimental, and I wrote him a letter after our meeting, a copy of which I enclose.

His own letter that he enclosed was addressed to James H. Taylor, DD, on February 22nd:

On thinking over the matter upon which we conferred in Washington, I am prompted to write you to express my personal appreciation of your sympathetic attitude toward the project. Aside from any action that may be taken upon it, I shall always regard our interview as one of the most helpful interviews participated in by me. It is seldom that I have the privilege of talking over matters of such deep interest to me with one who has such intimate knowledge of the highland and lowland South.

Since our meeting I have thought much of the different phases of the matter under discussion. The proposed movement has such great possibilities, if rightly launched, that I am constrained to reiterate some of the things that I have already expressed. I do so the more readily because of your appreciation of the possibilities in it.

I know something of the difficulties that may arise when you come to discuss the matter with your association. After all they are not different from difficulties which arise in most boards.

I am sure that you sounded the right note when you implied that the proper way to have it launched, for this first year at least, was as a splendid venture to ascertain, after careful investigation, what the possibilities are, whether or not participation in the venture accrued to the interest of those launching it. If your association should insist upon what we both hope they will not urge, namely, a requirement that the man going into the field should visit and report on places in which they are particularly interested, whether he is officially, semiofficially, or tacitly connected with the association, I fear what we are both so interested in will fail sooner or later.

In the first place, a man doing broad work of that sort should visit the most promising and strategic areas and cultivate them if need be. He could not be expected to dissipate his energies upon all the schools of the mountains, nor upon specified groups, inasmuch as the schools would be cooperating agencies and not the primary objects of investigation. There must ever be kept in mind, I feel, that the object of this primary service is to find whether such a project is (practical) or not, and to find a few—perhaps two or three—centers in which it could be started. But wherever such a movement is started, it is to be an organization of the *people themselves* with which the schools and all other agencies should cooperate.

Of course it might properly be expected that an investigator would be willing to give his opinion upon places in which the association is interested, should he visit them in the course of a free investigation. The high type of man needed for this work (the type to which I assume the man in question conforms) might hesitate, with the technical and agricultural knowledge that is his, and his more intimate knowledge of the movement in Ireland, to have his movements restricted in any way. He would feel, I think, that he should be free to work as he thought best, after conferring with you, myself, and others who really know the mountain field.

In the second place, knowing as I do the currents and cross-currents in agencies at work in the mountains, I am quite certain that definite connection of that sort with any one agency is fraught with danger, and the danger is more imminent if the agreement be tacit. I do not, of course, know the members of your association intimately as you do. My deep interest in the mountain folk and in this plan, pregnant with great possibilities for them, causes me to feel that if it is your feeling that the association would not enter in in the way that we both feel instinctively is best for the success of the work, it might be better not to present it to them. The whole matter could be deferred until such a time as we as individuals should be able to secure funds to launch the project in the way that we feel it should be launched. The Irish Agricultural Organization Society has always been and is still financed by public-minded individuals and organizations, willing to advance the work without getting any tangible services in return. Of course, if we could get it launched with the aid of the association and permanent support found for it later, the association could afterward become a cooperating rural agency along the lines of its special interest. It would, too, always receive credit for its disinterested participation in beginning the movement.

I cherish the hope, therefore, that the limiting requirement may not be insisted upon by the association. I so much want that we should take advantage of the splendid opportunity that is ours now during the war, to enlist all forces in this onward movement. It would be a movement which would result not only in permanent help to the mountain people, but would be a very present help to the nation in these troublous days.

It would be a great help to me to have your further thought in the matter, and I should be glad to discuss it with individuals, or with your association collectively, if you think the outlook is promising. In any case, I shall hope to have your sympathetic interest and personal cooperation in such a movement.

Many and difficult were the ways to a new kind of mountain work, and slow their realization. Cooperation among individuals, agencies, organizations, was one key, but it was a key hard to grasp and turn. Agricultural cooperation, especially, always seemed to John a grassroots step, if not through the Southern Industrial Educational Association, then through some other agency.

It was again time of preparation for the conference. John had been in touch with the members of the Executive Committee since early in January in regard to program and arrangements. By February 21st he could write Mr. Glenn that the conference would convene as usual, even in this year of war, and that the dates had been fixed as April 10–12. The program was to feature agricultural development in the mountain region. Sir Horace Plunkett could not attend, but in his stead Mr. [Charles] Lyman was to report on the Rural Movement in Ireland and his own experience there under Sir Horace, as suggestive for rural organization in America. The opening morning session was set up as a panel on "Agricultural Possibilities for the Mountain Country," with speakers experienced in mountain farming: Professor A. B. Harmon of Lincoln Memorial University; Mr. John S. LeFevre of the Presbyterian Country Church Work in Madison County, North Carolina; and Professor Floyd Bralliar, of the Seventh-Day Adventist Nashville Agricultural and Normal Institute.

The conference call went out on March 1st. John wrote to Dr. E. A. Sutherland, the fine physician at Nashville Institute, urging him to come and to bring "a goodly delegation from Madison" along with Professor Bralliar, who was to speak. In this personal letter, he reported as to himself, "I am getting on quite well, although I do not think I am gaining at all in weight—perhaps losing some. I have not suffered much of late with oppression in my chest."

In spite of this and other cheerful letters, John was not at all well, and our comparatively quiet life was broken into by an illness which greatly alarmed the household. Perhaps it was what would be called today a "thrombosis," but the doctors did not seem to know, then, the exact trouble. Flat on his bed, in pain and discomfort, he struggled to go on with his writing. Chapter 1, entitled "More or Less Personal," was done at this time and is, I still think, one of the best in *The Southern Highlander and His Homeland.*

Taxing also was a long letter to Mr. Charles Lyman, himself now convalescing from a series of operations. Mr. Lyman must understand the conference, if through his address the conference was to get a real understanding of what cooperatives were, had done in Ireland, were trying to do in America, and might do in the mountains. The letter was dated March 15, 1918:

> I am delighted to know that you are to speak at the Knoxville conference, and I hope you will be able to persuade Mrs. Lyman to come with you. In view of all the difficulties this year, it is uncertain how large a conference we will have, but enough responses are now in to indicate an attendance of from seventy-five to a hundred—possibly more. Some of the people whom I am especially anxious for you to reach will be present.
>
> Inasmuch as most of your audience will probably have a rather indefinite idea of just what Sir Horace Plunkett has done for Ireland, it might be well to explain this somewhat definitely. I want them to get an idea of the many sides of the movement; not alone the agricultural phase, rural credits, etc., but resultant social activities and, especially, possible lines of development for the women. In particular, I would like you to dwell upon the difficulties in the way of cooperation which were overcome in Ireland; the diverse elements—political, social, and religious—which were induced to work together successfully. Probably the outstanding objections in the minds of your audience to the application of such a movement to the mountains will be the difficulty in overcoming the extreme individualism of the mountaineer and in getting the different denominations (extra-mountain and mountain) to work together.
>
> You will, perhaps, understand better the latter objection if you know something of the character of our conference. Fourteen different denominations—all Protestant—are represented, as well as independent work, public school work, and various philanthropic and social agencies, such as the American Red Cross, YMCA, YWCA, Southern Industrial Educational Association, Russell Sage Foundation, etc. For the past two years, the US Department of Agriculture has sent to our meeting men who have made experiments along the lines of our agricultural need. . . .
>
> Most of these agencies, with the exception of the Baptist and Southern Methodist denominations, are "foreign" to the mountains and administered, many of them, from northern offices, but some of the people pres-

ent will be "mountaineers," with all their sensitiveness to criticism and "uplift." While these various elements are, in a way, working together, there has been from the first a tacit understanding that no definite attempt be made, through the conference, to organize them for cooperative religious work, and insofar as possible we have avoided religious, or, rather, denominational emphasis. On the one hand, this has brought upon us from some of our denominational friends the criticism that the conference is not "religious enough," while others object to the presence of "so many ministers."

With the underlying denominational and sectional divisions, the conference would be a very difficult body to address, were it not for the extreme good spirit which so far has characterized the meetings. With a little understanding of its makeup, I think you will find your audience receptive and enthusiastic, although prone to ask very practical and searching—even skeptical—questions. We have always felt that this liberty to question was one of the most valuable aspects of the conference. . . .

These various agencies represented in the conference are working *for* the mountaineer, but it is my profound conviction (shared to some extent by other workers) that all work must be done *with* the mountaineer and must be directed toward the self-support, ultimately, of mountain institutions by the mountain people. It is here that such a movement as that instituted by Sir Horace Plunkett is of vital importance to us, who, from so many angles, are really striving toward the one end of helping the mountains.

He was much concerned about Park Fisher and arrangements for him to give a series of explanatory lectures on the war in remote parts of the mountains, in line with the suggestions made in John's letter of February 11th to Mr. Glenn. Park was now writing John in more detail of his ideas. In a letter of February 24th, he said:

Thank you for your good letter just received. We read it with a great deal of interest.

Since writing you I found out about the Committee on Public Information and am in touch with them. I have a letter just ready to send to their director of pictures, Mr. Rubie. . . . I can get a great many of my slides from them at a cost of only fifteen cents each. Underwood and Underwood refused to let me copy their pictures; it may be that I will get a few slides from them after I hear from Mr. Rubie again. I will also write to Mr. Ford, as you suggest.

Thank you for your suggestions as to the material to use in my lectures. I feel that you are right that the atrocious does not want to be overdone. As I wrote Mr. Rubie, I want to have as comprehensive a set of slides and lectures as I can, and my idea is to educate the people in regard to the war and the necessity of our doing our part as individuals; in short, to educate, enthuse, and inspire the people to respond willingly and do all they can. If I get out in time, I want to work for the Third Liberty Loan, and expect to do all possible for the Red Cross.

While a good many in the mountains are lax, I know that all are not so, that we have a great many truly loyal patriots. Larue County, for instance, has, I think, about the best record for responsiveness since Registration Day, known in the whole country. I think their registration was about 132. When the call to service came, every man went, and not a single one sought exemption, a splendid record! I should not say, either, that many of those who are lax are willfully so. I feel that the occasion for so many "cold feet" is due to a great extent to their lack of a general knowledge of the "Outside" and a special lack in knowing why the war started and why we are in it. Many in those isolated places which I especially want to visit are not to blame for the way they feel, and I hope that my trip will bring a light to many that will result in a patriotic devotion to their country, and I believe it will.

I just received a letter from Miss de Long this week, and she is going ahead with raising the funds for my part of the trip, planning a five-months trip as a starter; then, she says, if it seems to justify itself, she will be glad to try for a longer time.

She said that when she was over on Wolf Creek some time ago, a man asked her for news, and she told him that things seemed to be turning a little against the Germans. "Well," he said, "I allowed things would take a turn. A feller here's got a boy in the army over in France, and he said he saw eight sun balls in the sky to once, and three moon balls, and one of the moon balls has a red and blue flag, and another of 'em had the stars and stripes. And there was eight more fellers seed hit." And he allowed things was "going to take a turn."

I am interested in what you suggest regarding war savings, and I think it a fine idea to work up in connection with the other plans for this summer.

I will see what I can do about getting Piedmont (College) interested in the conference. I think they ought to be represented.

I answered this letter on March 14th:

Mr. Campbell has not been at all well for the last two weeks, and while we are hoping that he will soon show improvement, we are trying to save him right now from extra responsibility and effort. Therefore, will you let me write a note in acknowledgement of your letter of February 24th, which was read with great interest?

I do not think Mr. Campbell misunderstood at all your desire to explain the war to the mountain people; he was anxious, merely, that such an undertaking should not go before the public in such a way that it seemed to reflect upon the loyalty of the mountain people. He did not feel that *you* thought them disloyal.

Your general scheme of action sounds good. You may be interested to know that we are making an effort to have one of the representatives of the US Food Administration present, from whom you may be able to get some valuable material that you could work into your addresses. In fact, you will probably get in touch with several people at the conference who will be useful to you in one way or another.

We are very glad that you are both coming, and shall look forward to seeing you.

About March 15th, John was willing that I should write Mr. Glenn a personal note about his illness, and I did so. A prompt letter, dated March 18th, came back to me:

I am much obliged to you for writing me about Mr. Campbell. I like always to be kept posted when there is any likelihood of his overdoing his strength. I am very glad, however, that you can write so encouragingly and hope that the present arrangement will bring him back to good condition.

I imagine that his work in Washington is less trying than what he would have to do in Asheville, because he is out of the way of visitors. On the other hand, there is danger that in working over a manuscript, one will stay indoors too much and not take proper exercise. I hope that you and he will see that there is a proper mixture of exercise and recreation with the study.

I hope that the preparations of the Knoxville conference will not burden him too much. It is of the first importance that he should get himself in good shape again.

Mr. Sharp and Miss Karpeles are here and expect to go to the mountains shortly. We are expecting to have them to dinner tonight.

On March 30th, John could write Mr. Glenn that

the doctors have promised me that I can go to the conference if I am careful. I shall go from there to Asheville, Miss Dickey to return here to close up matters. Although I have not accomplished everything I set out to by coming to Washington, we have done very well considering my handicap for the last month. I have been unable to see all the men I want to see, but meetings of that nature have been especially tabooed by the physicians, so it seems well for me to go back, and, if necessary, some time later when I am stronger, to run down, or send Miss Dickey, for anything special that needs to be attended to. I am beginning to get out again, and I think I shall get along very well now. Mrs. Campbell tells me she has written you, so I will not go into details. I suppose I shall have to settle down to the fact that I am no longer thirty and to moderate my pace accordingly.

I have been quite surprised by the responses already received and am looking forward with much interest to the outcome of the conference.

I have been unable, as yet, to have another meeting with the SIEA people but shall endeavor to see the former president, Dr. James H. Taylor, before I leave.

One letter arriving late, not long before the meeting, troubled him. It came via Marshall Allaben, of the Woman's Board of Home Missions, whom John knew well, and gives another glimpse into the conservative character of many of the group that would assemble in Knoxville. Mr. Allaben's letter of April 2nd follows:

In strict confidence I am sending you herewith an excerpt from a letter just received:

I am frank to say that the Mountain Workers Conference in Knoxville last spring did not seem to me to represent the spirit of the workers present. My companion throughout the Conference felt just as I did; that there was no inspiration for either the spiritual side or the intellectual side of the work for which we, as mission school people, must stand. Twice the sessions were opened with prayer, but this seemed foreign to the spirit of the Conference. Mr. Campbell, after making remarks that I cannot now quote exactly, apologized by saying that he was a "Church Man" even in the face of his knocks against Christian schools and Christian work. I cannot even recall the name of one speaker who most antagonized us by her wholesale denunciation of all effort for the spiritual uplift of the mountaineer, but she was a doctor who held an official position connected with the Board of Health. I can easily locate her if you wish it.

You know that we stand for the practical side of the work; perhaps even emphasize it unduly at ———. . . . No student leaves us without having been thoroughly examined and having every possible physical defect removed, and without having her ability along practical lines discovered and encouraged; but it is a case of "this ought ye to have done, and not have left the other undone." I approved of the information given concerning better methods of farming and even of the establishment of cheese factories, etc., but to rate our work on the basis of the dollars and cents that may result from it is both narrow and mercenary. I sincerely wished that you or Mrs. Bennett had been there, as I felt that your influence would be felt in raising the standard and certainly some statements would not have been made in your presence.

I had suggested to her in a previous letter that I wished her to attend the Knoxville conference, and she replied that she would be glad to go, but that she was very much dissatisfied with the proceedings last year. I wrote immediately asking for a frank statement as to her criticisms, explaining my own definite interest in the success of the conference. This is what has come. I know you are anxious to understand clearly just what the members of the conference think of the proceedings. Of course you know me well enough to understand that I have every confidence in your desire to produce just the opposite impression to the one here recorded.

I might add that Miss ——— was very much distressed by Claxton's address on that occasion. It may be that some of our workers are unduly pious, but we shall have to recognize the fact that it is these pious workers who have done the most for the mountain people and who are likely to stick the longest.

Of course, such a letter was disturbing, and John spent much time and thought on his answer before he wrote Mr. Allaben on April 4th:

I thank you for your letter of April 2nd, and there is hardly any need for me to say to you that I accept it in just the spirit in which you sent it.

It is a matter of sincere regret to me every time anyone comes to the conference and does not find the inspiration hoped for, and it is of much greater concern to me if, by any chance remark of my own (which I do not recall in this instance) I give the impression of being unsympathetic toward the church or the church schools, or what in general terms is called the spiritual side of life. If I mistake not, Miss ——— expressed to me personally at the conference much the same criticism which she has expressed to you in this letter.

I am surprised, however, to learn from her communication to you that Mrs. A———'s attitude was what Miss ——— conceived it to be. Mrs. A——— expressed to me her appreciation of the conference and invited me to Indianapolis to confer with her board. I went to Indianapolis in December, just before coming here, and had a most cordial consultation with her and the members of her board upon some of these same topics.

With so many people and so many different interests, it is difficult to keep the proper balance. Criticisms equally strong have come to me from the other side, that the church and church schools were too prominent in the conference, and again letters of commendation have come from ultraconservative church people—workers under ultraconservative boards—that the whole spirit of the conference, as well as the discussion of all subjects, was a source of inspiration to them in their work.

For the past three years, a prominent place has been given on the prepared program to the church and social religious activities, but speakers have failed us at the last moment. I do not know that I told Miss ——— that we had two prominent country church officials scheduled to speak on the last afternoon upon the church side of mountain problems, who finally did not come. I did tell Mr. [Matthew B.] McNutt of your board—or rather, of Dr. Wilson's board—that they had failed me, and I asked him as a country church specialist if he would not take the afternoon. He not only did not, but I hear criticisms emanating from him, if my informants are correct, implying that church and spiritual matters were overlooked or not provided for by the conference. Such criticisms seem a bit unfair, the more so when they come from persons who have never attended the conference before, and especially so when they come from those who, when attending, are present in sessions for only a few hours.

Distress is occasioned, I know, by speakers overemphasizing subjects of pressing importance to them. The eminent speaker to whom you refer as distressing one of our friends, in his address probably unconsciously revealed a little biting criticism toward the church schools left over from earlier struggles as a state educator, in his efforts to establish public schools in county seats where he was opposed by church people and leaders of church schools in those county seats. I have in mind one particular struggle. This does not justify showing that spirit, I admit, any more than a carping spirit in the conference toward the public school, or church organizations other than their own, is justified in some of our friends whose real Christian spirit cannot be questioned. The other speaker referred to was an impromptu speaker—a state woman with a message, who had opportunity to speak because our two church officials who were to speak did not appear. While she has a strong and somewhat striking—sometimes jarring—personality, I am quite sure that, did her critics know her personal life, the nobility of it, the hardship of it, and her pioneer struggles in the state of Tennessee for little children and other neglected ones, her peculiarities of utterance and personality would be overlooked or forgotten when one saw the splendor of the pioneer, Christian battle she has fought to arouse a state.

One cannot dictate the substance of what speakers are to say, nor control the spirit in which it is said, and inasmuch as this meeting is a conference (its chief merit), those who attend must be prepared to hear all points of view and views unduly emphasized through the enthusiasm, personality, and experience of the speakers. If it were a meeting merely for the representatives of church activities, it would be a much easier conference to arrange.

I am hoping none of the speakers on church topics who have promised to come this year will fail us. We must have the spirit of the devoted Christian workers in the mountain field, but our Christian workers in the mountain field who are under the auspices of our denominational boards that have done such splendid work ought not to judge too hastily and without full information the lone pioneers doing an equally great religious work.

This is not written in justification, apology, or defense, but by way of explanation to you, a personal friend and co-worker, whose cooperation and friendship have always been a help to me, and whose friendship and cooperation are evidenced anew by the letter which you have written me. I hope very much that you can persuade Miss ——— not to turn the conference down on one trial, but persuade her to come again to contribute to and share in the benefits which we all seek to derive from it.

With assurance of my appreciation of your kindness in writing me . . .

On hearing of John's plan to go to the conference, Mr. Glenn wrote him briefly, on April 3rd: "I received your letter telling me of your proposed movement. I hope the Knoxville conference will go satisfactorily and not be too much of a strain on you. I advise you, after it is over, to go home or somewhere else and do nothing for a week—with emphasis."

He followed this with another letter on April 6th:

I met the Rev. Franklin J. Clark on the train yesterday. I was glad to hear that he is going to the Knoxville conference. He is anxious to have you join a committee which will visit the Episcopal mountain schools in the autumn and asked whether there would be any objection to the plan. I told him there was no objection from the point of view of the Foundation but that it was a matter you would be free to determine yourself and that you would have to consider whether it was wise to undertake the trip. I do not think it is necessary for you to give a definite answer much before the time when they will be going.

If you think it is a good opportunity, I see only two reasons to prevent your accepting. First, your health; and second, your book. Both of these questions should be considered before anything else. I think that after the conference you should make your book take precedence over everything else, so as to get it done, even though it means neglecting some things that seem very important. It is still more important that you should not crowd yourself to finish your book or to do anything else until you have entirely recovered from your recent setback.

Mr. Clark said that they would pay your traveling expenses. I see no reason why they should not do it.

Please remember that in what I have said I am not trying to persuade you to accept or decline the invitation. I would like you to make your decision on the assumption that I shall be pleased with whatever you do. If there are any special circumstances that make you want my advice, I will be glad to give it to you after you have talked with Mr. Clark.

Before leaving for Knoxville, John received a reply from Mr. Allaben, who wrote on April 8th:

I have your most interesting letter of April 4th relative to Miss ——'s criticism before me. I am sorry indeed that you took this criticism so seriously as to feel it necessary to make such an extended explanation to me. I am, of course, always interested in what people say of the conference and have therefore greatly appreciated your letter, but I know how busy you are and feel very sorry indeed that we Presbyterians should thus have added to your store of difficulties. I can readily understand how in a conference like this it would be absolutely impossible to please everybody, and I have always stood strongly for your method of conducting the conference. I believe this is the first time that I have ever felt it worthwhile to send you any of the criticisms. Miss —— was so emphatic in her expression of disapproval that I sought her definite reasons, and thought you were entitled to hear them.

I believe you are on entirely the right track in your method of conducting the conference, and I wrote Miss —— that she must bear in mind that the conference was not an interdenominational one, but a meeting of all mountain agencies. We invite these mountain agencies to confer with the various denominational agencies and must be prepared to hear their frank statements of opinion. It will do our Presbyterians good to hear what the people outside the church think of us.

In spite of criticisms, the conference was very successful, even more than usually so, and the attendance of 110 persons was unexpectedly large and responsive. Agriculture in the mountains, agricultural cooperation, cooperation in many fields, with especial emphasis on the church, were main themes, developed in a fashion both practical and inspirational. The chairman, ever on the alert, was always ready to bridge over a delicate situation or to translate what seemed a threatening impasse into harmony.

On the train, on his way home April 12th, Dr. Warren Wilson, of the Country Life Department of the Presbyterian Church, USA, expressed his appreciation of the meeting and his concern about John himself, in the following letter:

My purpose in inflicting a letter upon you so soon is threefold.

First, to beg you to take some rest, and "hang the expense." Get the job out of your system, and the weariness that shows in your face.

Second, to congratulate you upon this conference, the best I have ever attended in the South, in years of attending like affairs. This was the best, solidest, most practical, technical, constructive, and I should say the "goingest" of all. You are doing a great work in holding that bunch of pietists and pedagogues to the actual job. No one else could do it.

Third, to beg you to commend me to your man Lyman from Wisconsin, Plunkett's graduate. He looks mighty good to me, and as I have waited for years for his proposal, hoping for long that I might have the training in Ireland that he has had, I want to put myself under his leadership. I am not sure I can go to Washington. I regret exceedingly that I cannot be with him on Laurel, but if I can see him afterward and get into his system of work, if especially I could supply him with a man to be trained for the organizing of communities in which we have a church and a minister fitted to carry out his plans, I would be greatly pleased. I must not ask too much, but no one can do it for me but you.

It was a lasting satisfaction to be with you and with Mrs. Campbell. You have been very much in my heart these recent months. May strength and satisfaction be yours.

The conference leader needed this letter from the most brilliant radical and yet conservative member of his group. He knew it had been a good conference. He personally was exhausted, but the effort had been worthwhile. Mr. Glenn answered my personal letter giving details, writing on April 25th:

Thank you very much for your letter of April 16. I am sorry to know that Mr. Campbell has suffered a setback on account of the conference. I am not surprised, however. It is probably very important for him to keep perfectly quiet for some while. There is nothing that he has to do that is as important as getting back to his former strength. If it is necessary to leave Asheville in order to get away from his work, I urge that he do so. Of course I cannot tell at this distance what is the wisest course for him to pursue, but I can say very positively that he ought not to let a false sense of duty get the better of his common sense and his doctor's advice. It is certainly his first duty to recuperate his strength.

Has Mr. Campbell made any definite arrangement with Mr. Lyman? I shall hope to see Mr. Lyman if he comes to New York. Where is he to be found in Washington? It is possible that I may be there at any time.

Wilson's letter is very gratifying.

Dr. Wilson, with others of the Presbyterian group in the Laurel Country, had invited Mr. Lyman to visit them for a first acquaintance with mountain conditions and a cursory survey of the farm situation in that area. Following that visit, he went to New York, and there Mr. Glenn met him. It is interesting to follow Mr. Glenn's careful thinking in response to John's previous enthusiastic letter on the possibility of securing Mr. Lyman for a few months, with the idea of advancing the cooperative movement in the mountains. This thinking appears in Mr. Glenn's letter of May 6th to John:

I had an hour's talk with Mr. Lyman a week ago. He was not as definite in his statements about agricultural cooperation as I would have liked. He gave me the impression that McCarthy's and his efforts on behalf of the N[ational] A[gricultural] O[rganization] S[ociety] had been directed more largely to getting national associations together than toward the establishment of small cooperative associations. I talked with Mr. John Graham Brooks the next day about the NAOS, and he evidently thinks they have not done effective work along the lines of real cooperation. If the NAOS had made various efforts to start cooperative agricultural societies, I think they could have gotten the necessary money from the Carnegie Corporation, but evidently they have wandered afield.

I would suggest, therefore, that before asking Lyman to do a definite piece of work for you, you give him a very definite statement of what you want done and get from him a very definite statement as to what he proposes to do. I have not a clear idea in my own mind as to just what you want done, and such a statement as I suggest from you would help me to make up my mind.

Another question that arises is whether Lyman could really accomplish anything in a visit to the mountains of a few months. Cooperative societies are of slow growth. I believe it would take a year or two at least to get a few societies started.

I am sympathetic with your idea, but I think it is important to raise these questions and to be perfectly sure what we may hope to accomplish before starting out on such a very important undertaking. The movement will not grow of itself and will probably require the attention for a long period of time of at least one person.

I agree with your opinion of the value of the cooperative movement to the mountain people. I do not believe that any material advances can be made in a short space of time. I would be delighted if we could put a good man in the field to cultivate it for several years. That, however, is not possible at present.

Last and most important. It may be a great deal better for you to stop work entirely for some weeks than to be attempting to work in what you call a "leisurely way." To keep up your work for a month or two longer as an experiment will probably result in the long run in more delay and in less accomplishment than if you took an absolute rest now. As long as one is suffering from nervous exhaustion, he cannot do first-rate work. I beg, therefore, that you will consider very carefully whether it is not wiser to suspend operations entirely for a while. I am sorry that I cannot talk the situation over with you personally. Do not let your conscience and your desire to keep going interfere with your judgment and that of your doctor.

John responded to this letter on May 11th:

I am much interested in what you write of the interview with Mr. Lyman and will write more in detail later. I do not think I ought to undertake to do any more in this matter until the question of what I am to do myself for the months following has been decided.

The crux of the situation in the mountains is how to get the mountain people to cooperate one with another. At the stage in which they are, it is not so much a question of cooperation among groups: it is a question of getting individuals to cooperate together in any group. That is what I had hoped to find in the National Agricultural Organization Society. My idea was that Mr. Lyman might, after a longer survey in the mountains, be able to make some suggestions as to how to get individuals together in a group, for that is the fundamental thing. Perhaps the NAOS has been dealing with the secondary rather than with the primary situation which is ours.

. . . The real beginning must be made, as you suggest, through a period of years and not through months, but I had hoped that the few months might give us some glimpse of possible localities for beginnings. I felt very sure of your sympathetic attitude.

The same day he wrote Mr. Glenn another letter about his health and his plans:

The wisdom of my taking an absolute rest has been apparent to me for some time, but I have been reluctant to do so at a time when, of all times, the division could be helpful to the government and to the mountain people. I have just come from a long interview with my physician, Dr. Dunn. It was most encouraging because of his reassurance that all I need is a rest and that there has been no material change in my condition since he saw me last September. He expressed the situation to my layman understanding by saying that I was like a rundown battery and that what I needed was absolute rest for a time sufficiently long until I could be "recharged." He assured me, and I put the question very definitely to him, that with rest and "recharging," I might fully expect to resume my work with renewed zest.

I had plans under way whereby I felt that this work might move forward, at least in a moderate way, through Miss Dickey under my general advisory direction, and I had hoped to gain strength enough also to go on with the book at the same time. I have made a number of attempts to continue my work on the book, but the results have been far from satisfactory, either to the book or to myself. The situation, however, has changed entirely through Miss Dickey's definite decision to enter upon government war work. I can appreciate the force of all circumstances that have brought her to this decision, and while I regret losing her very much, I cannot, under all the circumstances, but acquiesce in her decision.

The plans I had in mind were to make more effective, in the remote mountain section, food and conservation propaganda and to aid Red Cross work. I enclose a clipping from the *Asheville Citizen* which might indicate to some people that the people of the mountain section are disloyal. The other day in one of our hospitals west of here, a mountain boy (the leader of a band of deserters) died from the wounds inflicted by a posse of federal officers, and there is hiding somewhere in the mountains west of here a remnant of the band who deserted with him. To me, it seems after all but a repetition of what took place during the Civil War—the mountaineer, homesick and fretting under close restraint and discipline (to which all his life he had been a stranger), took his leave when he wished and returned at his leisure after he had made his visit. Added to this in the present war is the real fear of the unknown as represented by the expression "across them great waters." The public opinion of these mountain neighborhoods needs enlightening. Some think there is a German propaganda in sections of the mountains: possibly this is so. Whatever it is, certain mountain communities need to be enlightened about the war.

He went on to explain how he thought his office might be used while he was resting to contribute to the enlightenment about the war in remote mountain communities "which do not cooperate because they do not understand." Our friend and neighbor Rutherford P. Hayes was deeply interested in the idea and anxious to help, if he had a center to work from and a little assistance in carrying running expenses. John suggested that Mr. Hayes might be given use of the Russell Sage Foundation division office temporarily and thought that "expenses could be brought within the budget for the year." He concluded his letter by saying: "I am jealous, as you doubtless see, of the division's activities in these momentous days, and it is a source of the deepest regret to me that I cannot participate more actively. I rejoice in the assurance of my physician that I may hope to be myself again. Your kind solicitude for my health and his injunctions, together with the thought of some possible plan for the ongoing of the work, make me more reconciled to my enforced inactivity."

To Rollin Lynde Hartt, his old classmate, now on the staff of the *Chicago Tribune,* he wrote on May 16th:

It is a long time since I have heard from you or have written to you. As a matter of fact, I have been quite ill for the last three months and am dictating this letter from my bed.

There is nothing serious the matter with me, they all assure me, and I have had a number of specialists at me. I have an x-ray art gallery of my insides, and they are all right. I do not know how many specialists were at me this winter in Washington, but they could find nothing. The one who most nearly describes my feeling is my own physician here (a very good man) who, to my layman understanding, best describes my case in his statement that I am like a battery that is run down, needing recharging. When I attempt to do anything that amounts to anything, I must confess that I feel like a glass of Vichy that has stood open for some hours. In all probability, I shall go away for the rest of three or four months, if satisfactory arrangements can be made. Olive is all right.

Gavin has enlisted in the navy and has recently entered the Naval Auxiliary School at the Municipal Pier, Chicago. He is to be there for several months, I think, and my impression is that he will then be sent to Pelham Bay. Will you be so good as to look him up at your leisure, and stand somewhat in "loco avunculi" while he is in Chicago?

After Barbara's death, Olive and I went for a long trip into the mountains, and we then went to Washington (Miss Dickey coming there also) in January, where I was supposed to get my book ready. I was so much knocked out after six weeks of effort that I practically had to quit work on it. I was in bed more or less until the first of April but managed to pull myself together for our Knoxville conference April 10th–12th. We are now at Mr. Hayes's in West Asheville.

I would not give you the impression that I am on my last legs; I suppose I am suffering from nerve exhaustion and at last agree with the physicians that I need a long rest. Let me hear from you and yours at your leisure. Our greetings to you all.

Requests came repeatedly to the office for information from John's study of the southern mountain region or for the use of some part of it while still in manuscript. Some came also to Mr. Glenn in New York. He and John always responded promptly, with occasional loan of assembled material and with use of the already published *Church and Independent Schools.* One request, from J. Warren Brown of the Council of Church Boards of Education in Chicago, John answered on May 28th:

In reply to your letter of May 24th, I would say that my studies have been limited to the mountain country of the South. I have been engaged in mountain work since 1895 and, with the exception of the last ten years, during which time I have been connected with the Sage Foundation, I was under the Congregational Board (American Missionary Association) as principal of two of their academies in the mountains and president of one of their mountain colleges.

My studies have touched all phases of mountain life, but I have had most to do with educational phases, principally with the church and independent schools of the mountains.

Because of the extent of the mountain country, the great diversities in topography, and the wide range in social conditions, it would be difficult to tabulate findings as in a more limited survey. There are many things held quite commonly about the mountain country and the mountain people which are quite contrary to fact. In making this statement, there is no implication of willful misrepresentation on the part of anyone. Workers in the field, without a wide knowledge of the mountain country, have stressed local conditions and have, unconsciously, assumed and given the impression that all mountain conditions are the same as those which are true of their own locality. Writers of fiction have dwelt upon the picturesque phases of mountain life, and the newspaper headline writers have also added to the interest and misrepresentation through lack of qualification. There is great need of some summing up of the mountain life and mountain country with stress upon diversities.

I went to Washington in January to be free from office duties, in order that I might make my attempt at this task. Unfortunately, I fell ill and am convalescing so slowly that in all probability I shall be unable to go on with the work as outlined for a number of months.

It will give me much pleasure to be of any assistance to you in my power. My secretary, who has been with me since the opening of the office, is leaving to enter government war work, and I myself may be away from the office after the first of July, but under these limitations, whatever we can do to assist you will be done most gladly.

I am sending you, under separate cover, a paper of mine on the "Future of the Church and Independent School in Our Southern Highlands" which may be of interest to you. I am also sending *The Southern Highlands,* a pamphlet issued under my direction as chairman of the Executive Committee of the Conference of Southern Mountain Workers. The introduction will show its limits and limitations.

I should be glad to be put on your mailing list, and I take pleasure in placing you upon our mailing list. I hope, too, that we may have the pleasure of seeing you at our next conference.

He felt well enough to start north in early June, and a meeting was arranged with Mr. Glenn and Mr. Hayes en route, as appears from John's letter of June 4th to Mr. Glenn:

Mrs. Campbell, Mr. Hayes, and I leave for Washington Sunday, arriving Monday morning. I wired you the other day as follows: "Washington the tenth satisfactory at time and place your convenience."

I am very desirous of talking over all matters with you. It seems to me that there is a great opportunity for war leadership here in Asheville, to interrelate the various war activities. There might be given locally and regionally—I hardly know how to express it—but something of the same impetus in this large work that the Knoxville conference gives to school work, and there might grow out of it a teamwork that would hold for all social service work after the war is over. By beginning the kind of work roughly sketched in my previous letters to you, we might be instrumental in creating a spirit of cooperation, animating a sort of council of war workers.

The term "local" minimizes what I mean. Asheville is the center of influence of all this region, and practically of western North Carolina, as many of the remote counties of North Carolina have their activities listed as Buncombe County activities and are controlled from Asheville, the county seat of Buncombe.

I wish more than I can express that I were strong enough to stay here and make these very important beginnings this summer, assisted by Mr. Hayes, but I know that I would be much better able to further it and all the work of the division if I give up for a while.

The Washington meeting led to satisfactory results, which Mr. Glenn summed up in a letter he wrote John on June 21st:

I am sorry that exceptional pressure of work has prevented my writing you before this with regard to Mr. Hayes. The following is my recollection of our conclusions at our conference in Washington on June 11th. Please let me know whether this accords with your understanding. I also add a statement about expenses.

It was agreed that it was desirable for Mr. Hayes to undertake to secure and send to various mountain communities in North Carolina speakers who could talk about the work of the Food Administration, Fuel Administration, the Red Cross, and other governmental activities which bear immediately on the life of the mountain people. It is important that these speakers should be persons who understand the psychology of the mountain people and who are sympathetic with them.

It was agreed also that Mr. Hayes should have the use of your office in Asheville and that we should supply him with a stenographer and with traveling expenses. He is not, however, to carry on his work in the name of the Russell Sage Foundation, nor to give the impression that he is an agent of the Foundation. The fact that he is using your office will be sufficient to show that you and the Foundation are in sympathy with his work.

This is important because we cannot at present get authority from the trustees for this work.

It is understood that Mr. Hayes volunteers his services and that his time and work is to be regulated according to his own convenience. This arrangement is to last for such time as may be agreeable to you and is presumably only to continue while you are absent from Asheville. This will probably be until September first or October first, 1918.

This plan being carried through, John's mind was at rest about the office. He wrote Mr. Sharp on June 24th, after our arrival in West Medford:

Your note [from Natural Bridge, Virginia] was received some days ago. We had pictured you in Asheville. It was decided while in Washington that I had better take a rest until October, and within a few days we go to Nantucket. . . .

I would not give you the impression that I am seriously ill. All I need is a rest. Mrs. Coolidge will be in the house next to us at Nantucket for the month of July. Miss Daisy will be at the Medford address during July in all probability, and Mr. Coolidge can be reached through his office address.

By July we were settled quietly in Nantucket, first in a rented cottage near our old family farmhouse, and then in a little hay barn which we had long coveted and now unexpectedly were able to buy at the exorbitant price of seventy-five dollars. Raised on stilts and conveyed majestically across the field to the shelter of Hinckley Farm, this became the center of our concern and effort for the rest of the summer. Not only did the family help to pound and paint as soon as it was settled into its appointed place, but all visiting friends joined in covering the raw surfaces as fast as the carpenters provided them. Fortunately for us, it was a comparatively dull summer at Nantucket. Few people dared to face the risk of submarines, and the usual brisk building activities were at a standstill.

Like magic, partitions, windows, and doors were installed, and within a month we were able to move in under our own roof. All the neighborhood eked out the scanty furniture and general equipment, and most of what we did not so acquire we were able to buy out of an old house not far away. So began "The Cachalot," as we called it, for the barn was constructed of heavy shipwreck timber, and the old sailor who built it had sailed before the mast on the good ship *Cachalot* out of New Bedford—immortalized in Frank Bullen's *The Cruise of the "Cachalot."*

John loved every shingle. It was the first house he had ever owned, and rough as it was, and for the summer season only, it was, as the mountain preacher said, a "sweet home" to him. He used to sit and dream of the fireplace that was to be and how he could gradually add the many little comfortable touches that go to make up a real home. He was able to do some light carpentry, and his busy mind forged ahead to what he would begin on "next year."

Mr. Hayes wrote from time to time from Asheville, where he had been made chairman of the local group of heads of the various war activities, now meeting to coordinate their work. Mr. Glenn arranged that his office in New York should handle as much as possible of John's own correspondence. Evidence of the need of John's study, and direct inquiries for it, continued to come. On July 22nd he wrote to Mr. Glenn:

I enclose herewith a letter from Mr. Hayes. Please return it when you are through with it. I have had a request from him for whatever the Sage

Foundation has published in the way of war activities. Will you please send him whatever material the Foundation has?

I am returning the letter from Mr. Nearing. . . . The Methodist Episcopal people have, through our Knoxville conference and my touch with Mr. John C. Burg of their board, become interested in the reorganization of their mountain work. Mr. Burg is a friend of Mr. Shelby Harrison's, and when I saw him in New York early in the summer, he expressed his purpose to get Mr. Harrison and other men of his views on a committee for the reorganization of their educational work. Mr. Burg suggested my meeting with their committee sometime, which I promised to do. It would be well, I think, to send Mr. Nearing my pamphlet on the church and independent schools and to suggest my meeting with him and others of their board for a conference in the fall on my return. It is important that a director of publicity should get the right point of view, and a conference is much better than a letter. Just before I left Asheville, I had a letter from one of their board—I think it was from the Chicago office—with a similar request. I replied that the subject was so large that it could not be taken up by correspondence but I would be glad to answer any specific inquiries. I received a cordial reply, giving expression to the hope of a conference at some time.

There is real need for my book, and I do wish I could get at it now. Only a few days before leaving Asheville one of the Bible organization publicity men phoned me for "telling" facts about the mountaineers—size of family, number of log cabins per county, etc., an insistent chap whom it was hard to convince that log cabins and large families were not necessarily detrimental.

In early September, John had another letter from Park Fisher, written August 31st, on the job, in Leburn, Kentucky:

I was surely glad to receive your letter just the other day and have been rushing with the job that I was on so that I might answer it. When it came, I was putting a Ford brake on my buggy, expecting to have to meet a member of the National Council of Defense at Harlan most any time.

Nellie and I are both very much interested in your letter and hope that something definite will grow of it. It has been a matter of the keenest regret to me that at this time when men are so much needed at the front that I was so handicapped that I could not go. I never did want two good legs as badly as I do right now. But I am as I am and there is no use in making a bad matter worse, but if by going through the country where they have but few opportunities I can stir up interest and patriotism, where otherwise they would not be stirred, I shall feel that I am not altogether useless to my country.

My plans for this year have been long in getting something definite accomplished, but at last we succeeded in getting the State Council of Defense to back it up fifty dollars per month. Of course, with all my equipment and expenses to meet myself, that is not sufficient, but Mrs. Zande is trying to get more through friends who are interested. I have already given several lectures, both under the council and independently, and I am more impressed than ever with the great need for the lectures. I asked an audience the other night to all raise their hands who had heard one of the speakers sent out by the government in any branch, or any member of the State Council, and not a single hand was raised. I asked this question because the State Council said that my work would be duplicating what they were doing. I am sure the result would have been about the same every place I have spoken, save right around Hindman.

My audiences have averaged one hundred, which I think is very good. I was quite impressed when I finished the lecture in Buckhorn the other night. They were the first pictures most of them had ever seen (which is frequently the case), and at the close of the lecture, they voluntarily came up and contributed three dollars toward expenses! I thought that was doing fine for an out-of-the-way place like Buckhorn. This is not the school where Smith is, but over in the Ball country. Talked one day on Caney to an old Baptist preacher, and at the close of about a half hour, he said he had learned more about the war than he had ever known before. Oh I think it is a grand opportunity, and I do hope that some way will open up as you suggest so that it can be kept up next year.

I have had to furnish my own equipment so far, and this, coupled with the long delay in getting the State Council to back me up, which Mrs. [Ethel de Long] Zande and I thought had been agreed upon long ago, has put me in the hole financially. I had to buy another horse the other day, paying seventy-five dollars, which I borrowed for six months from the bank. Repairs on my buckboard cost me about twenty-five dollars, but this will all be settled some way.

Now as to my equipment: I have the buckboard, as shown in the enclosed picture; I built the bed on the rear so as to be able to keep things dry as well as safe; I have two horses which make the hills easy now; also Dr. Hillis's lecture (50 slides) on "German Atrocities"; about 160 general war slides, which I hope to add to all along, keeping up to date so far as finances will enable me to do; my Stewart Phonograph for patriotic music, which adds a great deal, as for instance in Buckhorn the other night, when I was told that a good many had never heard one before. Then of course I have my cornet, which I have carried some. I have a book giving the bugle calls but had not thought to use them especially. I have my own stereopticon equipment, with acetylene generator and a one-hundred-pound can of carbide given by the Union Carbide Company. My new double set of harness was given by Strecker Brothers Co. of Marietta, Ohio. This I believe will give you a good idea of my equipment.

My own plans for next year were rather vague, not knowing whether expenses could be provided for another year, but I have wished that arrangements might be made, for so much of this year has been lost, and yet the work needs to be done. I had hoped this year to take in the three states you mention and perhaps North Georgia, but I got too late a start so will be perfectly willing to cover all the territory possible. I don't think there is much use trying to work through the mountains in the bad winter weather, for not only is traveling so difficult, but it is hard for people to get out, and of course we want to reach as many as possible.

The terms you mention are satisfactory, though I should hope you might arrange for seventy-five dollars a month if possible, for it costs so much more to live now and, too, the schooling of the children is adding somewhat to the expense, and with my being away from home will want, if possible, to have someone with Nellie all the time. But that is a matter easily settled.

I shall be glad to cooperate with you and hope that you can arrange to be with me at least part of the time. Aunt Olive might come here and stay with Nellie. My experience so far is that I am out but very little for lodging, but of course I can't tell what it will be when I get farther from home, where I will be a perfect stranger. But I find that the phonograph and cornet are quite a help toward providing lodging, in these isolated sections!

I am to speak tonight at the lower schoolhouse if we are not rained out again, as we were last Monday night. I will soon start to Harlan County, I guess. I am using my topographical maps, having the county school superintendents locate the schools and give me a list of the teachers, with their addresses, which enables me to make my dates ahead through them.

I shall be glad to hear from you again and do hope that this will work out. Perhaps during the winter, if it seems best, I can meet you somewhere and we can talk and plan together, or perhaps you might come by here on your way south, although I don't know where I will be at that time.

Any additional information you may desire I will gladly give. I hope your summer's vacation is going to do you a lot of good. All join in love to you both.

John wrote to Mr. Glenn on September 4th, enclosing the letter from Park Fisher and returning a long letter from Mr. Sharp which recounted their activities since he and Miss Karpeles left the home of Mr. Glenn's sister, Mrs. Corbett, in Virginia. From there they were to go into North Carolina again. In his letter John said:

I have just written Mr. Sharp a long letter, giving him an itinerary in the counties of North Carolina he desires, with data as to mission schools and desirable places in which to stay. I hope very much he will go into these counties he mentions. He may find something of real value there. These counties constitute the most beautiful mountain counties of the South, and this is the best time of year to visit them.

Mrs. Zande's letter is also of great interest to me. She is touching in her inquiries relative to life in the mountains, one of the pressing problems of all of the western belt of the mountains. Mr. Hayes does not seem to have had much response from the people to whom he wrote. The work that he has been doing is more suited to him and probably more congenial. In all probability, by the first of October he will not have spent more than $150 of the $450 allowed him.

I want very much to have some very definite work done for improving public opinion relative to the war in certain areas. I have been thinking of ways in which to do this which I might direct even should I be barred physically from doing much in this way myself this fall. It occurs to me, by making certain arrangements as to a stenographer, I might save something from my budget this fall to carry on the work planned.

Mr. Glenn replied September 9th: "I like Mr. Fisher's letter very much, as well as what you say about him. Out of any balance that is left from the money allotted for Mr. Hayes's work, you may pay Mr. Fisher whatever may be necessary to carry on a campaign to interest the mountaineers in the war. This will be sufficient to make a definite arrangement with him for two months. When I see your letter, we can decide about making a longer engagement with him."

By mid-September John was really feeling better and began to make plans, including a start south in October, as he wrote Mr. Glenn on the 14th:

I am getting on very well. There has been so marked an improvement in the last three weeks that I myself notice it. It was my intention to leave here the first of October, but Mrs. Campbell wants me to stay two weeks longer to ensure the gain that I have made. I am loath to do this, for I am very eager to get back to work. However, I want to be wise. There are two weeks more of this month, and we may come to an agreement by that time.

I appreciate very much your appreciation of Mr. Fisher. He is a whole-souled fellow, and, while he has not the educational training that some men have, I am sure for the service for which we want him he will do much better work than many others with better technical training.

Mr. Glenn responded immediately to this, writing on September 18th:

I am glad to get your letter of the 14th and write hurriedly to say that I think the presumption is in favor of Mrs. Campbell's advice. It is a great deal better to make your recovery complete, so that when you go to work, you can do it with vigor, than to start two weeks too early and have a hand-icap, even though it be a slight one, all through the winter. If you are at all in doubt, follow her advice. Do not let your conscience and enthusiasm run away with your judgment.

Mr. Glenn also forwarded a letter from Mr. Hayes in which he explained what he had been doing in John's office as representative of the American Library Association, loaning books to the three large hospitals near Asheville, and his work with the Third Liberty Loan, War Savings Stamps, and the Red Cross. It was not exactly according to the previous plan, but it was satisfactory to John, and as he wrote Mr. Glenn, "probably more suited to Mr. Hayes's special experience."

He continued to be concerned about getting reliable war information to the men far back in the mountains. Having received Mr. Glenn's approval to employ Park Fisher for the purpose, John wrote him on September 14th:

Your letter of August 31st pleased me greatly, but I delayed answering it until I had opportunity to lay the matter of our correspondence before Mr. Glenn.

I have some money which will be available for us for a campaign of two months at least, ensuring for you seventy-five dollars a month and your traveling expenses. I should like very much to see you and talk over matters. Will you write me your plans as soon as you can, giving me your general routes and the approximate dates in different localities? With the money Mrs. Zande has secured for you, how long a campaign would you be able to make in her section, and when would you be free to start out elsewhere?

I do not want to take you away from Kentucky before your work is done, for that is just as important as any part of the field. There is work to be done in Tennessee, Georgia, North Carolina, and in the mountains of Alabama; also, probably, in Virginia and West Virginia, but inasmuch as we have at present in hand funds for only two or three months, it will be necessary to plan our routes to take in as much of the territory in that time as possible, and also to allow for the weather. In certain sections you ought to be able to travel until Christmastime, and possibly in others into January, depending somewhat upon the season. . . .

. . . You are having a splendid opportunity for creating mountain public opinion on the war, and a great opportunity as well for creating a wholesome public sentiment for social and civic betterment in mountain communities after the war is over.

May I urge upon you the opening of a journal at once, setting down minutely what you have already done and keeping daily track of influential people you meet in different communities that you visit, noting the special needs of these communities; also listing the good places to stay, the auditoriums (?) or public meeting houses, if any; in fact, all such data as may be helpful in campaigns of the future. I hope that you will give me the privilege of having an abstract of the journal made. Let me know also what you are short on in the way of pictures. Possibly I could do something in the way of help on my way south.

Now as to my own plans. I am eager to get back at work, a state of mind that I have not been in until lately. I suppose that is a sign of improvement. I have gained quite a bit in the last few weeks especially, and Olive is using her powers of persuasion to gain my consent to stay here until the middle of October at least. I suppose she is right, as usual, and it will be time gained in the end, but I want to leave by the first if possible. In writing to me, address me here, Box 366, if you think the letters will reach me by the first of October. . . .

It is needless for me to express at length my pleasure at the thought of our association in this much needed work. With kindest regards to Nellie from both Olive and myself . . .

Several mountain friends voiced their advice and general approval of this plan for Mr. Fisher, Dr. Brown of the Southern Baptist Convention among others to whom John had written for suggestions. He answered John on September 19th:

It surely does look good to get a letter with your name signed to it. I could not find out what had become of you. You were guilty of leaving Asheville without consulting me, and I couldn't think of anything else only that you had gone to fight the Germans. That's where you ought to be at least, and of course this new draft caught you, and I hope you fall in my company so that I can give you some drilling. But foolishness aside, I was mighty glad to hear from you.

Now as to Mr. Fisher, my suggestion is that Mr. Fisher go to the Cumberland Plateau; that he cover Fentress County, Pickett, Overton, Morgan. Perhaps some other counties there need looking after. I make this suggestion because I have just come from Fentress, Pickett, and Overton. I heard less war talk than any place I have been. To be sure, they have furnished their quota, but there is no enthusiasm over the war, and a lot of fellows ought to be investing money in War Stamps and Bonds who are not doing it. I attended the Stocton's Valley Association. I was the only man who brought in the war into his speech, and let me tell you, old fellow, I didn't fail to bring it in. You know I have one boy already in the aviation, another to go, and you know I was turned down myself on account of my age. I believe in this war, and I want your friend Fisher to make the most out of his trip.

When he gets through on the Cumberland Plateau, I do not know what he can do better than come to Cook County, Tennessee, though I know nothing personally of the sentiment there, but the border counties on both sides of the state line would be a good field for him. I want him specially to look after Mitchell County . . . it would be well for him to look after Ashe and Allegheny.

But if he is looking for just downright disloyalty, he needn't come to the mountains. We have got enough of loyalty here. Better go to Kinston and the country round about it. There is more patriotism in the mountains than outside of them.

Tell him that I will be glad to render him any assistance in my power.

On receiving John's letter with the news of the plan for him, Park wrote a reply, September 24th, from Pine Mountain:

> Looking out of my window over the beautiful landscape of the Pine Mountain School, it seems as though I ought to see you and Aunt Olive walking about the yard, for my first visit here was with you last fall. . . .
>
> I gave a lecture here Sunday night which all seemed to enjoy. Last night Miss Butler went with me to the Big Laurel schoolhouse, where we had an audience of seventy-five, gathered up as we went over in the afternoon. I plan to go to three more schools this week, then back here on Friday so as to be here for the fair on Saturday. I wish you could be here on that occasion, for I know it will be interesting.
>
> I had an awfully hard trip across the mountains. Came up Defeated [Creek] with my buckboard and it very nearly defeated me too. The roads are all washed to pieces at the top of the hill, and I succeeded in getting my buggy in a ditch, and then trouble started. The horses finally balked, and I was there for over two hours. I don't know how I should have ever gotten away, had some men not happened by who helped me out. Their team balked too, and so I helped them out. The roads are awful to drive over all the way nearly. Bull Creek was a sight. I had to go to the head of Leatherwood, then across Long Branch and up Line Fork, then across to Greasy. Well, I have decided that hereafter in this section I use a packsaddle and go horseback, leading one horse.
>
> I should like to write you more about the trip, but must get to business, as I have to leave early for Abner's (Branch) to make announcements for tonight.
>
> As there is a similarity and a connection between the work you propose and that I am doing under the State Council of Defense, I took the liberty this morning to let Mrs. Zande read your letter and talked over the situation with her, and she is very enthusiastic over it and feels it is a splendid idea.
>
> . . . My plan is to work around here for the month of October, that is, planning to stop at schools on my way to Hindman, so as to get there by the end of the month. And there a little complication sets in.

He went on to say that, feeling sure that John's plan would not materialize during the winter, he had just agreed to accept a position at Hindman Settlement School as teacher of manual training from the middle of November to the end of the first week in May. He realized that Hindman, short of teachers because of the war, needed him, but he was eager to carry on his lectures through fall and winter as the possibility of that was now opening up. His letter continues:

I have really just made a good start toward this lecturing work, and the suggestion you make in regard to working farther south this winter at this work appeals to me. While it would mean a sacrifice at the Hindman School, yet the war is causing many sacrifices, and I feel that since I cannot go across to fight, that I ought to be doing all that I possibly can here at home to help out in the war situation. Since I have the equipment pretty well in hand and the opportunity for this service, I feel I ought to go on with it. School work is, of necessity, more or less broken up these days but can be continued after the war, while this war work among the hills needs to be done right now, while the need is urgent.

It is pitiful to see the great need for simple information. I feel sure that slacking and desertions will be greatly lessened with this better understanding of the situation. Did I tell you of the instance in Knott County when a man asked me regarding the late war news. When I told him that the Hindenburg Line had been broken, he remarked, "Well, that Hindenburg has been a hard place to capture, hasn't it?"

Of course it is out of the question to do much work here in these mountains until the cold weather is over, but you are right in saying that the same work needs to be done in these other sections farther south, and it appeals to me. I feel sure that the Hindman people will release me under the circumstances, especially since I feel this my patriotic duty and since your suggestion came first. I shall write Miss Huntington at once and lay the situation before her.

We stayed on quietly in the "Cachalot" into October, after all family and nearly all neighbors had returned to the mainland. John gained slowly, and reports of influenza, becoming serious everywhere, mounted daily. John wrote to Mr. Glenn again on October 4th:

I thank you for the kind suggestions in your recent letter. . . .

In all probability we shall be here several weeks still, if the weather continues pleasant. If the grippe is still rampant in the environs of Boston, we shall probably come direct to New York. I am getting on very well and am much better, but still have to guard against getting overtired. Of late I have been very much encouraged to feel that I may be myself again. This summer I have become quite well acquainted, through a friend, with a gentleman who has been through the same experience as I, only in a more critical form. He is practically well again and has urged strongly that I see his specialist in New York on my way south. I have promised Mrs. Campbell and him that I will do so, despite the fact that I have suffered many things from many physicians.

There are a number of people in New York who want to see me, and whom I want very much to see. Among them: Dr. A. W. Harris, corresponding secretary of the Methodist Episcopal Board. He telegraphed me recently and has written me also. This word from him is doubtless due to your suggestion to his board, made sometime during the summer, that it would be advisable for their officials and me to be in conference before I should return south. . . .

I have also to meet Mr. Clark's successor of the Episcopal Board, and to see the Dutch Reform people, and the Presbyterians. I do not want to miss seeing them, even if I have to delay a bit in New York.

I have heard from Mr. Fisher, who is eager to come to me and thinks he can make arrangements to do so about the first of November. He is to write me more in detail a bit later.

Both Mrs. Campbell and I have heard from Mr. Sharp lately at Burnsville, North Carolina. He finds the vicinity a good place for work. We hope to meet in New York; if not, in Asheville.

He wrote also to Miss Huntington at Hindman, recognizing her need but raising the question whether she could defer Park Fisher's teaching appointment until Christmastime. Park was now making his way through Harlan, Leslie, and Knott counties to Hindman. As it turned out, John's request coincided with Miss Huntington's decision that the school must close for a time because of the influenza. Shortly, the lectures, too, must be given up because of the risks from assembling groups together in the schoolhouses. Park's letter of October 22nd describing the situation did not reach John until we were in New York:

I have just had a most interesting trip through Leslie and Harlan counties, portions of them, and as soon as I can get my report in shape will see that you have a copy of it. . . .

Of course the flu is going the rounds in this country as elsewhere, and I fear it is getting pretty bad too, for the people are so careless. I even found one doctor, Dr. ——, who lives on Montgomery Creek, at least if reports are true, is telling people that it is not catching. That is what the folks living at the head of Defeated told me as I came by there last Saturday. They have three cases already, and the neighbors come and go as they please. They tried to argue me down that it was not catching. One of the Slones from up on Mill Creek is just being buried.

Since I could not have public meetings with this disease going around, I decided to come home, so got here Saturday. I could have gotten here Friday, but one horse took sick as I came down Defeated; and so I had to stay over half a day and a night at Hyltons. They helped me, and we dosed the horse many times, and finally the next morning he was able to come on. I do not know yet what was the matter with him.

Along with other institutions, the Hindman School is closed. I do not, of course, know for how long. I am afraid the flu is just getting a good start here. Nearly every family on Mill Creek has it, and just Saturday a lot of Aunt Polly Pratt's folks who have been out in the mines at work came home, and doubtless have all been exposed to it; so there is no telling how much it may yet spread. Folks do not hesitate at all at coming home from "public works" after having been exposed. So far we have dodged it and will continue to be on our guard against it.

Of course this is affecting not only my services at the school for the present but the lecture business as well, for of course I cannot go on with them, even though Miss Huntington would release me, until the epidemic is over.

I still feel as I did, that the lecture work is much the broader and more important. As Mrs. Zande said when I was talking it over with her just before I left there, there are not "speakers for the war standing around on every corner" back in the hills. I have yet to find the first place outside of our county seats and railroad towns where people at large have heard a single speaker before on any form of war work, and they are so interested, and it means so much to them. I do feel as though I could not have given any service more needed at this time than what I have already given. A good many have told me that I was doing a lot more good in this way than I could have given by being in the active service.

12

The Last Year, 1918–1919

After seeing a heart specialist in New York, the Campbells headed home, knowing that there was no cure for John's condition. With the help of his new secretary, Edith Canterbury, Campbell planned to continue with his work as much as his health allowed. He corresponded with his friend Park Fisher, encouraging him about the programs he was presenting in the mountains about the war under the auspices of the Kentucky Council of Defense. A long report of Fisher's travels provides detailed accounts of where he visited, how many attendees were present, and his reception in each place. He spoke to about 5,140 people and traveled approximately six hundred miles.

Campbell kept up his correspondence, writing a long letter to May Stone about the future of Hindman, suggesting that mountain schools should not compete with public schools but continue along the line of specialization, such as schools for adults. In answer to Campbell's question about financial help for the Hindman School, Glenn advised that the Russell Sage Foundation's work was in an advisory capacity and could not assume responsibility for institutions. Work on the report continued, and plans for the 7th Conference of the Southern Mountains progressed. Campbell was present at the conference in Knoxville and reported to John Glenn that it was well attended. There were a good number of Episcopalians, Presbyterians, Seventh-Day Adventists, and Baptists, among them twelve Primitive Baptists.

As they entered Unicoi County after the conference, the Campbells were amazed at the changes they encountered. Traveling through Virginia coal country, they proceeded to Hindman, where they saw the growing effect of the mines on the surroundings, houses, and people. After speaking to the staff at Hindman about the changes to be met, they proceeded on to Washington, then boarded a train to New York. John Campbell collapsed as he reached his seat on the train.

We left the "Cachalot" about the middle of October, bound southward. John seemed to feel so much better after his summer of rest that we could face with courage an appointment with Dr. Bishop, the New York heart specialist who had been recommended to us in Nantucket. But when the recordings of the cardiograph were brought in to him, the doctor's encouraging face changed so markedly that John and I could not but know that "the findings" were bad. The tracings of the sensitive machine revealed what the human eye could not discover: the heart muscles were not functioning properly, and there was no help for them—nothing for us to do but to accept the record with what courage we could.

We talked it over and decided to continue on our way to Asheville but not to try to reestablish our home. We would stay on in the exceptionally pleasant boarding place where we had stayed the preceding spring. This would involve the least strain on John, and I would be free to help him wherever I could in his work and be with him as much as possible. No one could tell when the terrible pains would come on.

While in New York, John was even able to carry through some plans and write some letters, as this to Park Fisher on October 29th:

Your last letter was awaiting us here in New York. We got in Saturday, being held in our departure from Nantucket somewhat.

Under all the circumstances, I think you are very wise in discontinuing public meetings in the mountains. As I know the mountain people, it would be useless to attempt to gather them for lectures at a time when contagious disease is prevailing. In fact all circumstances—the present status of the war, the urgent need of Hindman—make it advisable to postpone our joint plan. I hope very much that we shall be associated in some way later. . . .

I have just written Miss [Ruth] Huntington stating that I am glad, under the circumstances, to yield any claim that I may be thought to have had upon your services. Please write me fully, at your leisure, telling me about your trips, etc. It may be the basis of future plans.

Address my next letter to Asheville, 412 Legal Building. I will write you later of my winter plans. Kindest regards to Nellie and yourself from both of us.

Park's next letter to John was written November 3rd:

I was glad to receive your letter last night. I suppose that under the circumstances that it will be best to call off our plans for the present and go ahead with the work at the school, for I guess they are in a tight place. You can guess as much from the enclosed card. Knowing that they are under quarantine for the flu, I have not been down since I got home, but Nellie was down yesterday, and they are wanting me to come down at once, as they are up against it for drinking water since their hot-air engine is dead. I guess I will go down this afternoon. . . .

Nellie has been doing a great deal around the neighborhood to help fix folks up, and they surely did need it! My! the dirt that she found, to say nothing of how they had expectorated all over the floor and walls while they had the "flu"! It gave her a mighty good opportunity to give them some straight talk about this last filthy habit. The county authorities have taken hold and are trying to break up the disease, but they should have acted long ago.

I am sending you with this letter one of my reports, which will give you a fuller account of my trip than I would have time to write at this time, with the additional interest of the pictures.

I have not given up the idea of our planned work for next spring and will keep it in mind through the winter. Even though the war closes, I still think there is a lot of that kind of work that needs to be done, and I had rather do that through the mountains at large, for I feel that someone ought to do it. If the war holds on into next year, it is much more important that it be done.

I will write you from time to time as I can, although I expect that between things here at home and the school, I will be kept very much on the go through the winter. . . .

Nellie joins me in love and best wishes to you both. I hope you will keep well through the winter.

Park's report was delayed in arrival, since, as he said in a postscript, he decided to "send this via Demorest so that my folks can read the report and then forward to you." John in turn forwarded it to Mr. Glenn. Dated October 31, 1918, and addressed to the Kentucky Council of Defense, Louisville, Kentucky, the covering letter and report went as follows:

Gentlemen:

I take pleasure in submitting herewith my report for the War Lectures given under your auspices during the past summer.

I give the report interspersed with leaves from my journal, illustrated with photographs made on the trip, and with typical incidents and quotations, that you may thus realize more keenly the condition under which they were given, and especially the utter isolation and lack of information of so many of these splendid yet neglected people of our mountains.

I trust you will permit me to say that with very few exceptions (viz: few county seats and railroad towns visited), I have reached a people who would otherwise be still unreached. Many times I have asked all in the audience who ever heard a speaker from the Council of Defense or any other war speaker who had been sent out, to raise their hands, and outside the places mentioned above and a few who had been out on "public works," I have yet to see the first hand!

One not personally and intimately familiar with these mountain people and who does not know how to get their confidence (for they are very reserved with strangers) cannot know or understand this utter isolation. Many things that are commonplace on the "outside" are absolutely unknown to them. For example—to a great many of those to whom I spoke, stereopticon pictures were unknown. More than once I was asked, when announcing pictures at the schoolhouse, if I was "going to tack them on the walls"! A phonograph had never been heard before by a great many, and I even found a few who had never seen our American Flag!

I regret very much our misunderstanding last spring (see Mr. Begley's letter of March 29th) in regard to this campaign, for it meant the loss of three months' time at least. Personally, it put me in a very hard place, for, with the continued expectation of going out soon, I could not engage in other remunerative work. This, with my equipment to provide and a family to support under the present high cost of living, is meaning considerable financial embarrassment to me. But, looking at it in a much broader and impersonal light, I regret it especially because so many communities remain yet untouched that should have been reached. So many begged me to come to their schoolhouses, and all I could do was to tell them I hoped I could come to them later.

Since I am physically handicapped for service at the Front, where I should otherwise be, it is a great deal of satisfaction to know that I have not been useless to my country; that I have taken a war message to several thousand, arousing them to greater and more willing service. In different localities they have said to me, "Mr. Fisher, you are doing a heap more good here than you could possibly do at the Front."

I realize that there are others who could have done the work much better, but the point is, they were not! I realize also that as a state organization your hands are full and that you can only reach distant communities as you are assisted by patriotic citizens in touch with them locally, and so, I wish to thank you, on behalf of these people as well as myself, for your assistance, which has very materially aided me in thus arousing, through a more thorough understanding of the situation, many of OUR REALEST AMERICANS.

Park W. Fisher

REPORT

It was my privilege to be in Hindman, Kentucky, on Registration Day, 1917, and the patriotism manifested that day was intensely interesting; but we who know the environment and isolation of this section were not surprised when the draft began to call the boys away from their homes to find a great many slackers, not only among the boys themselves, but their parents as well.

Fully realizing that something ought to be done to relieve the situation, I sent out the following appeal:

War Lectures Needed!

Back in the isolated sections of the mountains of the South are thousands of splendid citizens who at heart are true patriots, but who, due to their isolation and environment, have not the privilege which most of us enjoy, of knowing daily the progress of the War. Far from it! Many of them do not even know why there is a war nor why we are in it. They know there *is* a War because their sons have been drafted, but I leave it to you: Can we blame many of them for not being enthusiastic over enlistment, for service on a foreign shore? Would YOU want to fight without knowing WHAT you were fighting FOR? We expect our mountain people to do their duty along with the rest of the country, and they should and must, But—

I feel that WE OWE THEM an opportunity to know something definite about why this must be.

The speakers sent out by the government for War Lecturing DO NOT reach these isolated communities where there are no railroads and where often the only practical mode of travel is horseback or afoot!

I have come to this conclusion: In the present crisis our Country needs the ENTHUSIASTIC SUPPORT of all her citizens in order to keep "The Beast of Berlin" from her shores! I cannot go to the front to help, but I feel that I CAN do something here at home. My eight years experience in the Kentucky mountains enables me now to see the NEED and OPPORTUNITY of the hour and I have volunteered to do my bit by going this year to these isolated sections and giving stereopticon Lectures covering the various phases of the War.

I plan not only to encourage voluntary enlistment, but to present the Liberty Loan, War Savings, and Red Cross work as well. Starting in Eastern Kentucky I plan to speak in every schoolhouse possible, then, if time permits, to work on south through the Cumberlands, into Tennessee, North Carolina, and Georgia.

MY TRAVELING EXPENSES for several months are being arranged for by a friend, Miss Ethel de Long of the Pine Mountain Settlement School, but I need money for MY EQUIPMENT.

The Committee on Public Information has been of great assistance to me in procuring the use of some of the best copyrighted war pictures published. I will have a splendid set of slides. Strecker Brothers Co., of Marietta, have contributed a set of double harness. The Union Carbide Co., carbide for the lantern. But I need four or five hundred dollars for other equipment, including A TEAM OF HORSES.

The lectures are to be given Free so as to draw as large audiences as possible. My Phonograph, which will be the first heard by many, will furnish Patriotic Music. I hope also to be able to take one of our Mountain boys, Uins Pratt, who is completing his second year at Piedmont College this Spring, as an assistant. Our Cornets will prove an added attraction.

In asking a generous contribution toward this equipment, I feel that you are having presented to you AN OPPORTUNITY for a PATRIOTIC SERVICE that is much needed and that will bring results much in excess of the effort and money invested.

Please respond promptly for I plan to start on the trip about the middle of April. Remember—A great many of those who do know the situation have responded nobly. Will you not help others to respond?

Address—Park W. Fisher

Pastor Mill Creek Cong'l. Ch.

Leburn, Knott Co., Ky.

While responses to this appeal were not sufficient for equipment, nor had the final arrangements been completed for my expenses, yet so much of the year had already slipped away, with the importance of the work being more impressed upon me every day, I determined to borrow some money and go ahead.

Beginning in June, 1918, I gave some lectures locally, and on the 20th, acting upon request of the Chairman of the Knott County War Savings Committee, Mr. M. M. Johnson, I gave nine lectures around the County emphasizing Thrift and War Savings Stamps. By having lantern slides of these cards (with stamps attached) I was able to explain clearly to large audiences the whole idea. I found many people in the dark regarding them. One woman feared that after the War these stamps might not be worth any more than Confederate money after the Civil War! I soon explained to her that that depended altogether on who was licked—Uncle Sam or the Kaiser! My audiences during these lectures averaged 107 each night, which I consider very good, since all (save at Hindman) were given in the country. Many times has the capacity of the little school-houses been taxed to the utmost; one building, the Pinetop school-house, about 30 x 40 feet square, accommodating 225!

Our mountain people have the reputation outside of being pretty rough and given to lawlessness. This has been more or less true in the past, but I should like to say right here that during all the lectures I have given there has been intense interest and splendid attention. Only three times have there been serious disturbances—twice by boys under the influence of liquor and once by a young fellow who simply wanted to show off, but the fine which he paid later will doubtless make him less conspicuous another time.

On July 27th, Rev. W. L. Byrd of Hindman, accompanied me to the Old Carr Meetinghouse on Carr, where, preceding my lecture, he gave a good patriotic talk. Our bedroom that night contained six beds, holding 11 sleepers! We stayed over the next day for the Sacrament and Foot-Washing, conducted by the Old Regulars.

During the week following, lectures were given over in the Bail Country, followed by a night at the Charles Sturgill School on Jones' Fork, where a very enthusiastic audience insisted upon my return at some future time.

Caney Creek was next visited, the first two nights being spent at the Caney Creek Community Center. While here I received a visit from Preacher Bill Slone, who asked many questions about the War. At the close of our conversations he thanked me, saying that in that half hour he had learned more about the War than he had ever known before; that, although he sometimes saw a paper, there was so much he could not understand when he read it. Farther down Caney two nights were spent at Maryland Slone's home. Had I needed more than their cordial welcome to convince me that here was another example of genuine Southern hospitality, it was to be found as we were sitting on the front porch about three o'clock that Saturday afternoon. Some neighbors were seen returning from Meeting down the Creek. Even before they reached the house, Mrs. Slone went in and began preparing dinner for them. They stopped in Mr. Slone's store, but soon came on to the house, remarking that he would not do business with them until they had had their dinner!

As I was untying my horses at the close of the lecture in the Lower Caney schoolhouse that night, a man in his shirt sleeves was seen running wildly up the bed of the Creek, pursued by two other men who later informed me that they were trying to find out who he was as he had been shooting near some children who were returning from the picture show. When the next day the Sheriff and his posse shot down an armed deserter for resisting arrest and later jailed his brother for firing on the posse, I could not help but wonder if there was any connection between the two incidents, and to feel anew the importance of the educational War work I was doing.

A few days later, on my way down Buckhorn I passed the little log Shop of Uncle Billy Dodson, and found him repairing a muzzle-loader he had made 30 years ago, and I wished, with him, that he could try her on a Boche.

The lower Buckhorn School deserves special mention. Their appreciation of the lecture and pictures took very tangible form; as I was packing up at the close, a young woman, Nancy Noble, came up and handed me a quarter. Quite surprised, I asked her what it was for. Too full to speak, she motioned toward my outfit, and I understood—it was to help a little so that others equally neglected might have the same privilege they had just enjoyed for the first time. Following her lead, others came forward, and in a few minutes made up the sum of three dollars!

My experience in raising an audience on short notice at the John Budd Wicker School on Jones' Fork (and at several other places) can be duplicated almost anywhere in the mountains, no matter how thinly settled. With incredible swiftness news is "norated" around. On this occasion, in less than two hours notice, I spoke to an audience of 46.

In the new Church at Lackey, the first railroad town visited, the audience of 150 seemed equally interested, although they have much better opportunities for keeping posted as to the progress of the War. From Lackey to the head of Beaver my route now lay. I was quite amazed to find a new Federal Truck away up the creek where it was brought to haul lumber to the railroad. This explained the road-working I had just witnessed, as it generally takes something unusual as this, or the advent of Circuit Court, to get the roads worked!

"Big Joe Hall" soon expelled the vivid memory of the fearfully bad roads I found further up the creek, by his genial hospitality. I found them cooking with natural gas furnished by a well within sight of the house.

The community at the head of Beaver Creek turned out and filled the school house with 200 people, all very much interested.

After the lecture the next night, on the Bill D. Branch, we enjoyed an impromptu "concert" in Mr. J. G. Collins' home, consisting of the phonograph, dulcimer, and vocal selections!

While on Beaver, I followed my usual custom of stopping to talk with those I passed. While thus talking to one man, he asked me the usual question, the latest War news. I told him that the "Hindenburg Line" had been broken. "Well," he remarked, "that Hindenburg has been a hard place to capture, aint hit?"

Crossing the "gap" at the head of the Bill D. Branch, I stopped for dinner on the head of Carr, and found dinner set on an old fashioned Revolving Table!

Some fifty miles distant, the Pine Mountain Settlement School was to be my next headquarters. Leaving Hindman my route lay up Troublesome and Trace down Betty's Troublesome and Carr to our friends the Hyltons (at the mouth of Breeden's Creek) where the night was spent. The next morning as I drove through the rain up Defeated, the worse the roads became until the climax was reached just below the crest of the hill, where I was soon stalled!

Here, to make a long story short, over two hours were consumed trying to drive the last two or three hundred yards! The road had been washed away for so long that it had been forgotten! Had it not been for the timely arrival of the Agricultural Agent of Letcher County and two other men, I don't know when I should have gotten away. As it was, we had to go back down the hill, lay down a rail fence and go up through an old field, where, at the last bad place, not only did my team "take the studs" (balked) but theirs did likewise.

We were a worn out bunch by the time we arrived at the top of the hill to start down Bull to the North Fork at Cornetsville. Without special incident my trip up Leatherwood, down Long Branch, up Line Fork and across to the head of Greasy to the Pine Mountain School, was made.

Two and one-half days driving over such roads, which lie in the creek beds a great deal of the way, makes one appreciate, even more than otherwise, the quiet restfulness of the school nestling in rugged and picturesque beauty at the foot of Old Pine Mountain. Driving in between the huge gate posts, one is impressed by the fact that the days of the Genii are not past. Out of these rugged forests and moss-covered rock cliffs these "wimmin," in four short years, have fulfilled the lifelong dream of Uncle William Creech—A School for his People! And out of his people, crude and rugged though they be, they are fashioning, by influence both in school and out, a people destined for great things—a people whom our Country NEEDS, but who right now NEED OUR COUNTRY!

The great question "Why," in response to War's demands, is pathetically present in the attitude of all—men, women and little children. Whether in the cove at the head of the holler, farming the steep hillside, logging the woods, or with the children in school, news of the WAR is the thought-absorbing topic. One boy of ten years expressed popular sentiment, when going to hear the lecture for the second time, he said to me, "Give 'em a good long talk tonight on Straight! (Creek); I don't know which I like best, the talk or the pictures; I learn so much from the talk."

Excitement ran high at the Settlement School when it was announced soon after my arrival that there would be a "picture show" in the Dining-room Hall the next night, and many were the interesting remarks made about it afterward, with almost daily the question—"When will you give us another picture show?" In true mountain lingo, one of the little girls remarked, "Didn't we have the awfullest time"!

It being impossible to reach many of the school houses by driving, I left my buckboard at the School, loaded outfit on a pack-saddle and struck out horse-back.

First the schools in the vicinity were visited and I was generally accompanied by a worker from the School. Whenever possible announcements were sent out ahead by school children, but as many of the schools at this time of year were closed for "fodder-pulling" and "stir-off," word had to be sent out in different ways but always quite successfully. My plan was to reach the most isolated places and they were not hard to find!

One night at the Bledsoe school house—fifty-two were present and so quiet was the house that only once or twice a few awed whispers by some children about the German atrocities were audible. At the close I commended them for having been the most quiet audience I had spoken to. Next morning a man remarked to me that he did not go the night before, as he "did not take much to these shows" and that he looked for a pretty rough time as he saw one young man buy $2.50 worth of cartridges! After we explained to him what the "show" was, he walked several miles through the rain the next night to see it at the McKnight school house. At the close of this lecture I rode back three miles to the home of the teacher of the Bledsoe School, who, being ill, had to miss the lecture. It being then 11:30 he and his wife had retired, but I set up the phonograph and the lantern and gave them the lecture while in bed, retiring myself about 1:00 a.m. They seemed to appreciate it very much. He reads the "Pathfinder" regularly, and gives a War talk to his pupils once a week.

September 28th it was my privilege to attend the annual Fair at the Pine Mountain School, and to give a Patriotic address. A pageant, "The War in Europe," was presented by the scholars, and was not only very touching in parts but was very instructive as well. Much of it was given impromptu, and splendidly carried out by the children and young people.

We were all disappointed that Prof. C. W. Matthews, of the State University, was delayed en route, but enjoyed none the less the fine address he gave in the afternoon. A very creditable display of mountainmade and grown products was presented at the Fair.

Having filled dates during the intervening time, on October 2nd I went to Harlan to visit the War Trophy Train and to arrange future dates with the County School Superintendent. That you may know what this train meant to the people of these mountains, I feel that I must relate the experience of the Pine Mountain School.

About forty from there, including four teachers, left the school at 2:30 a.m. and walked about five miles across Pine Mountain to take the train at Dillon. They reached the railroad (about a mile above the town) just as the train blew for the station. They flagged it with their lanterns, it being still dark (between four and five o'clock) and it came so near to a stop that one partially crippled man who crossed the mountains with them swung it, and then the conductor deliberately went on and left them, and when approached on the train immediately afterward, said "No, I'll not go back for them." They showed the heroic stuff in them by walking the other ten miles into Harlan. Here they received much more courteous treatment than shown them by the railroad, the "Movie," for example, giving them a free show. Many of them also had their first automobile ride that day.

Upon having the situation explained to them, the Management of the Trophy Train, which arrived at 7:10 p.m., gave them immediate access to the train by themselves, while the speaking was going on, so that they could take the 8:00 o'clock train back to Dillon. From there they walked back the five miles to the School arriving about 11 p.m.

The following night, accompanied by a worker from the School, a lecture was given on Little Laurel. As we returned, about 10:30, we were "flashed" by a party of six horsemen, who, after enquiring who I was and where from, remarked, "Good! We are Revenue Officers." They had that day cut up a still; one of the party was apparently the "moonshiner."

Over in the Cutshin country, where I filled ten dates, I first visited Trace Fork, where I found a school election in progress. This gave me a splendid opportunity to advertise the lecture for that night. My host told me that only two people in that whole settlement had ever seen a stereoptican picture before!

Here I give a typical roadside conversation (abbreviated).

"How do you do, my name is Fisher; I am making my headquarters over at the Pine Mountain School."

"Proud to meet you; my name is Day."

"Well, we are going to have a picture show at the schoolhouse tonight and want you all to come."

"Ye say ye air?"

"Yes."

"Well, we'll be proud to see it; what does it cost?"

"Nothing at all, only to get there: be sure to bring all the folks."

"We'll sure be thar. Well, what air they doin' in the War?"

"Everything is going fine for us. The Germans . . . The Turks have even hinted at peace, and may follow the lead of Bulgaria and surrender."

"Well, God bless how soon it may come. Well, goodby. I'm proud to have met you. I may come over and visit the school some time. I'm a sort of preacher."

On the sixth I got into a big Funeral Meeting at the Maggard Branch schoolhouse (being preached for a husband and little child who had been buried some months before). After preaching was over in the schoolhouse we wended our way to the little burying ground, led by a group of singing preachers. I was quite surprised to hear a woman behind me remarking to another, "What they have to say about me when I am dead, I want them to say when I am buried! I don't think they ought to stir up the feelings all over again after folks are laid away." Finally the meeting broke up. Announcement was made for a War lecture that night in that schoolhouse and one for a later date on Wolf at the mouth of Coon. Two men then begged me to come to the head of Wolf also, one volunteering to get on his mule and "norate" it all over the settlement. Of course they got a date.

175 were present at the Maggard Branch schoolhouse that night, not counting the dogs, who soon indulged in several fights, so that I finally told the folks it seemed a choice between a picture show or a dog fight! Acting upon my suggestion, yelps from the front of the building to the door at the rear marked the exit of the canines, whereupon quiet prevailed for the lecture. That night John (the 12 year old son of my host) told me that at school they played by laying off the ground for France and Belgium; after building "towns" they would decide which to capture from the Germans and proceed to do so with the aid of home-made spring-wire guns. His father is one of the few men who has a daily paper and large War maps, so John keeps pretty well posted on the advance of the Allies. But even this family spoke of how much my pictures and lecture helped them to understand more clearly.

Next morning, I crossed to the lower Wolf school house by a "stave road," rough sawed staves being brought up one side of the mountain on a short sled and down the other side with a much larger sled.

After the lecture, that night and most of the next day was spent in a one-room log cabin, with a leanto built on for a diningroom and kitchen. The two beds and pallet on the floor show our sleeping arrangements. A warm welcome and invitation to return more than compensated for the lack of many conveniences.

From the head of Wolf the next night, I took a shortcut to Hyden where there was an attendance of 250. Although the county-seat, I was told that they had had only one outside speaker on the War. After the lecture, upon request of officials, I showed my registration card. I spent the morning around town, and went on that afternoon to the mouth of Thousand Sticks, where I spoke that night.

(Since writing the foregoing, I have had a talk with a friend from Hindman who has just been on a visit to relatives in Hyden). He verifies the reports of the suspicions regarding me, and adds a most interesting one: that while I was lecturing in the Court House I was shooting Influenze germs out into the audience from a little machine (my acetylene generator) which I had on the floor under my stereoptican table! Many of them believed this to be a fact, and quite a number were in for following me next day and arresting me, but Judge Lewis kept them from it.

Going on to speak at Hell for Certain the next night, I met a man who remarked that he started to Thousand Sticks to hear me but went back because he heard I was in jail in Hyden! From there on, including my return to the Pine Mountain School, I kept hearing reports that they had jailed me for (a) not having my registration card; (b) as a German Spy; (c) for lecturing when orders had been issued to close all public meetings. I had inquired of the Local Board doctor and other officials in Hyden, who told me there was no Flu there, and they had received no orders to close meetings, and to go ahead with my lectures. It seemed quite a disappointment to my friends at the Pine Mountain School that the facts in the case spoiled a perfectly good story!

I told a little girl at her home on "Hell for 'Sartin'" to come that night to the school house and see a picture of the Kaiser. Quick as a flash she responded, "I seed a picture of him down at grandpap's, and he had a butter-bowl on his head." On the door of their little school house was written in large letters: "PRAY FOR PEACE EVERYBODY."

From here I started back up Cutshin to fill previously made dates. Among others I found a very interesting community centering around the Wooten Settlement work, conducted by the Presbyterian Board. These workers are doing some splendid patriotic work. They not only gave me their hearty support and co-operation for the lecture that night, but an opportunity to speak at the school to the children next morning.

On the way up Paul's Creek that afternoon I met a dozen or more men who were hauling staves, hurrying home so they could get back to the show that night.

There was no night left for the little school house on Cutshin above Maggard's Branch, so I told them that if they would darken the windows with quilts we could have the pictures one morning, but upon arrival at the school house we found so many light holes between the boxing and around the windows and doors that we could not get the room sufficiently dark. We then went a little further up Cutshin to Joe Johnson's little one-room cabin, and this was one time when it was a benefit not to have a window in the house! By hanging quilts over the doors, covering a few cracks in the roof and between the logs, and placing a "gritter" over a hole in the fireplace we got the room dark. Twenty-five were present and I have had no audience that appreciated the "show" more. I stayed for dinner with them and Mrs. Johnson served dinner under the back porch roof, this, with its dirt floor, serving as kitchen and dining room. Before leaving I told Mr. Johnson that his name would be sent to the State Council of Defense because a lecture had been given in his home. "I am so glad to have my name sent there," he said. "I am poor because I have had so much bad luck because of sickness, but I wish I had thousands of dollars to help our boys. I'd give it to them if I had." And this is the splendid spirit which many of them show.

My last date was at the school house at the head of Cutshin, where the phonograph and pictures will doubtless be discussed to many a day.

I was next due in Harlan County but on my way back to headquarters for a new supply of carbide and my mail, I found they had posted notices closing all public meetings because of the epidemic of Influenze, so I started home instead. However, I hope that the opportunity may still be mine to visit the sadly neglected sections of that county.

On my way home, the first night was spent near the mouth of Leatherwood, where I gave the pictures and talk to the family who entertained me. I should have reached home the next day but one horse was taken sick soon after I crossed that bad hill at the head of Defeated and I was only able to reach friend Hylton's again, where for a half day we had to doctor the sick horse. Staying over that night I gave them the pictures and lecture, twenty-one, all members of the family, being present.

To the heroic ancestors of these mountain people our Country owes much for their part in making this great Republic what it is today. The Freedom for which they fought and sacrificed is just as dear to the present generation; and, once the issues are made clear to them, just so truly are our great President's words applicable to them—"Once more we shall make good with our lives and fortunes the great faith to which we were born, and a new glory shall shine in the faces of our people."

Summary:

Lectures given in Churches	6
Lectures given in Schoolhouses, Clubs, etc.	47
Lectures given in Private homes	4
Total lectures given	57

Counties reached:

Knott	31
Floyd	2
Leslie	13
Harlan	11
Total	57

Spoke to about	5140 people
Average attendance	97
Attendance in homes	54
Total	5194
Traveled approximately	600 miles
Raised during October for the "Y" Drive	$108.34

On reaching Asheville, November 13th, John found it necessary to make a short field trip at once, as he indicated in a letter of November 14th to Mr. Glenn:

We arrived in Asheville yesterday after a brief stay in Washington. Miss Canterbury, my new secretary, will be here December 1st. In the meantime, there are a number of things that call for attention.

In all probability, I shall go into the mountains northeast of here for a week or ten days to help adjust a situation in Dr. Warren H. Wilson's work—a situation he felt I could handle better than anyone else.

I found affairs in the office very satisfactory. Mr. Hayes had put it to good use and did, I infer, some very valuable work in war lines.

Mrs. Campbell and I appreciate greatly all of your helpfulness and the courtesies extended by you and Mrs. Glenn. I feel quite certain that I am going to get along very well now, with a little care, and that the plans outlined in the large while in New York will result in wider usefulness.

Before leaving Asheville on the 15th, he was able to answer a recent letter of Mr. Sharp's:

Thank you for your very kind letter of sympathy. I am not at all alarmed over my own condition. In fact, I feel better than I have for a long while. I now know my limitations, and if I work within them, I shall probably get along all right.

We reached Asheville day before yesterday and are going up into the Laurel country with Mr. and Mrs. Hayes, leaving this afternoon. We shall be there a week or ten days—possibly a little longer—attending to some business matters until my new secretary, Miss Canterbury, whom you met in Boston, arrives.

I hope your prospects and Miss Karpeles's for getting to England are brightened by the conclusion of the war. Upon my return and as soon as I hear from you, I shall be glad to forward the notebooks to you. I shall be on the lookout for the kind of mountain pictures you want, and when I get to my own, now packed away, I shall look over them for some that I have that may be available for your purposes.

It was a great pleasure to see you and Miss Karpeles again in New York, and I hope the day is not distant when we may see you both, either here or in England.

With love from us both . . .

In writing Mr. Sharp, John did not give the special reason for his going up into the Laurel field so soon after returning to Asheville. As has already appeared, John had long been working to bring about cooperation between the Country Life Department of the Presbyterian Church, USA, of which Dr. Warren H. Wilson was head, and the Town and County Nursing Service of the Red Cross, of which Miss Fannie M. Clement was acting director. The first effort to put a Red Cross nurse in the Laurel field had met with a number of difficulties. There was indeed a complicated and delicate situation growing out of differences in point of view between the doctor, under Dr. Wilson's Country Life Department, and the Red Cross nurse, under the same department. In a letter to Mr. Glenn on December 2nd, the day after his return to Asheville, John explained briefly:

I had been instrumental in getting the doctor to enter Wilson's work and had also introduced the Red Cross into this field on a temporary basis of cooperation between Wilson's board and the Red Cross until such a time as the situation would warrant the Red Cross nurse taking up actively public health nursing rather than bedside nursing as an assistant to the physician. Mr. Wilson heartily supports the public health work and stands back of the nurse in every respect, even paying all of her salary. The doctor and his wife are old personal friends of mine, as are some of their supporters, who have built up a splendid hospital. The doctor's view, and that of his wife, were not in accord with Wilson's, the nurse's, or with mine, but the matter is now settled. . . .

Despite the delicacy and strain of the situation in which I found myself, siding with the progressives while a guest and personal friend of the conservative, I feel very well. I am taking this as an evidence of my improvement in health.

On the same day he wrote also to Miss [Mabel] Rich, the Red Cross nurse involved. After speaking of her "admirable" attitude in the Laurel field situation and the problems of a public health nurse there and elsewhere in the mountains, he went on to say:

I should like to keep before the Red Cross the point that in remote and abnormal sections in the mountains, where little is being done, the only real agencies doing work are the denominational agencies; and if the Red Cross is going to undertake health work in such abnormal sections, it must learn to work with such agencies for the creation of public opinion for public health nursing. It would put them, I believe, in a much better light, and public health nursing would be more eagerly sought by agencies on the field if those in opposition should not have the leverage of saying that the Red Cross insisted upon standards and reports and on plans when, as a matter of fact, the support of the Red Cross nurse came entirely from the church board and that she, therefore, was equally a worker under the board, much as other workers are. I would like to have your thought along these lines, and any others. . . .

It seems to me, with all the plans formulated for the Laurel section, that there is to be a large step forward and that in health work you are going to bring the county and the state to participate. The point I hope we are always to keep in mind, however, is this: that the people who have done the most work in the remote mountain sections are church people, and that the mountain people themselves are fundamentally religious. They are apt to think, therefore, that the workers under the Red Cross and other secular organizations are not religious or animated by religious motives, unless the workers under such secular organizations participate at least by attendance in the Sabbath school and church work. In spite of what has been done in fact or imagination, do not hold aloof, even if any person, or persons, on the other side should make it uncomfortable for you.

I am striving with all my might to establish the point that religious organizations and secular organizations can work together. That is one of the reasons why I hope and pray for the successful outcome of your joint efforts in the Laurel. . . .

Mrs. Campbell joins me in every good wish for you personally and for your work.

Later, on December 2nd, John wrote another letter to Mr. Glenn:

Thank you for the statements entitled "Scour the Mountains for Flu Sufferers" and "You Ain't No Better Than We Folks Is." I read them up in the mountains, to the great interest of the doctor and his wife. Such clippings and statements relating to the larger phases of medical and nursing work in the mountains help me greatly through the broadening of the view of those shut in to whom I read them. They had their influence in the situation described in my other letter. I was very much interested in the statements contained in the letters showing the appreciation of the mountain people of medical and nursing work.

My doctor in the Laurel field had been ill for two months in Asheville, and the people missed him sorely. I made the rounds with the doctor and the nurse, and while waiting for him, one of his convalescents (a young woman by the name of Donna, a sweet unmarried mother who looked like a Madonna), said to me, "We sure did miss the Doctor— it was just like stopping running water." When one realizes what pure running water means to the mountaineer, her expression ranks almost with the scriptural expression of the shadow of a rock in a weary land. After leaving that home, our attention was attracted by a hail from a cabin on the hillside: "Hey, Doc, what shall I feed the kid?" The baby had been ill and the young father did not want to make any mistake in its diet.

A letter from President Frost of Berea, asking him [John] to come before a joint meeting of the trustees and the faculty and discuss adaptation of their work to mountain needs, pleased him very much, although he was not able to go at the time. It was followed by a long letter from Miss May Stone of the Hindman Settlement School, also asking for advice as to provision for the school's future, since both she and her associate, Miss Huntington, would soon have to give up the work there altogether. John reported this to Mr. Glenn on December 4th and outlined a plan for a new type of educational center or settlement school to be set up at Hindman:

After writing you yesterday with reference to Berea, the enclosed letter from Miss Stone of Hindman was received. It brings up in a very definite way a situation that is likely to arise in all independent work in the mountains. They have a good plant and a good clientele and are very favorably known to the giving public. It would be very difficult indeed to find successors with the vision that the founders had, and it might be almost as difficult for some of the older members of the force to strike out in new ways for the realization of a larger vision.

Hindman has kept too long the public school. I advised them ten years ago to give it up and to work along different lines. Miss Pettit, then at Hindman, inclined to my views, but Miss Stone did not. . . . It is a situation that calls for much careful thought and has in it much promise for the future of Hindman and for other schools of the mountains, if rightly solved.

As I look at the question of mountain schools, the way out for the church schools seems to be along the line for specialized schools, possibly of an adapted Danish type. The church schools have the promise of some steady income, and the plan of procedure for changes in them seems to lie in persuading those who shape the policy of those schools, both board officials and leaders in the field, of the need of changes and in showing them the goal toward which to work. I have long thought that there might be an opportunity of taking hold of some independent school, free from all denominational alliances, and developing an educational center through cooperation on the part of educational and educative forces. I feel that were I ten years younger, or even now unhandicapped in strength, that I could make some advance toward my ideal, were I to handle the situation as I should like to do. That cannot be, at least for the present; but with the Foundation back of such an enterprise, under the circumstances existing, a long step forward might be taken for education in the mountains and in other abnormal rural stations. I should so much like to develop the situation, not by being on the field regularly, but by being in New York, in touch with the agencies that I should want to have cooperate in solving it. The plan that I have had in mind is something like this, in brief:

Instead of having an educational center of ordinary type, that is, on a school basis, to have an educative center in which should cooperate agencies of various kinds, each supplying its own workers, sustaining them to cooperate with other workers sustained by other organizations at the central point; all held together by their effort for local, community, and general rural welfare work and by enough concentration in administration and direction to make the work cohesive and ongoing along some broad, definite plan. I feel very sure that I can persuade the community to take over a large part of the public school system, especially if they were promised the ongoing of the plant. I feel hopeful, too, that there could be secured the active participation of the Red Cross in public health work and in other nursing ventures in the community, those in charge of such Red Cross work to be a part of a faculty of so-called experts in a real rural educational settlement. I hope, too, through connections of long standing with the YWCA and YMCA people, to secure, possibly from each, a worker supported by them in the county seat and in county work through such a center, on lines discussed with them.

Possibly, too, the American-Scandinavian Foundation, who have given me some encouragement of future help, should a definite effort be made to introduce into this country some adaptation of the folk school, would help somewhat. The mountaineers are fundamentally religious, and if mistakes have been made in the independent school, it is because the religious phases of their life have not been given the prominence that they should. If as chaplain, in a settlement school of the sort I have in mind, could be found a married man of some maturity of thought and breadth in denominational sympathies, much could be done in bringing the churches of the mountains together. I have cherished the hope that sometime the attempt might be made in some school to find such a man, place him in charge of definite biblical instruction as a part of the regular educational work of the institution, and that without definite denominational affiliation he might become the friend and adviser of the local ministers and rural ministers of the county. Would it be possible to have a man of this sort supported not by any one church but by the Federal Council of Churches?

I feel, too, that by wise conferences and careful thought and management, a few of the church boards might make some contribution or might support someone of their own church in a center of this sort, fundamentally religious but not denominational.

It seems to me that the difficulty in bringing people together, or boards together in Christian work, arises not so much because of lack of sympathy for this kind of work, but because of the technical difficulties involved. In a school of this sort, I can see where certain of those difficulties could be overcome.

Early in December we also received a last letter from Mr. Sharp before he and Maud Karpeles left for England. Mr. Glenn had reported him in the office in late October, after the completion of his ballad collecting, "wildly enthusiastic about the gold mine he has discovered in North Carolina." His letter of December 6th to John was largely concerned with last details and plans, as far as he could see them; it concluded:

> We are rather sad now that we are leaving and saying good bye to our many friends. I wonder when I shall be back again, or indeed if I shall ever return again! The prospects of work in England are very alluring, and I have every hope of getting some very interesting jobs upon which to expend my energies. I do not look forward to our English winter, particularly in existing circumstances, but I expect my health will hold out somehow or other. . . .
>
> You and Mrs. Campbell have been very good friends to both of us, and we are very grateful to you for all the many kindnesses and courtesies you have shown us, as well as for the inestimable value of the advice you have so generously doled out to me. The mountain work has been a wonderful experience and marvelously fruitful in results. I have just received the last set of my books back from Harvard, where they have been photographed so that Harvard Library now possesses a complete copy of all that we have taken down in America.
>
> Well, good bye, my dear man. My best love to you and your wife and the wish that you may long be spared to continue the grand work which you are doing in the mountains.

John answered Mr. Sharp's letter on December 21st:

> Your letter of the sixth from the Algonquin reached me the day before you were to sail. I sent you a wire of farewell and good wishes, which I hope you received before you embarked. We are picturing you on the other side, reunited with all those from whom you have been absent so long. We feel a sense of loss in that you are no longer on this side but are confident that we shall see you both again, either here or over there. It has been a great pleasure to us to know you and to have your deep interest enlisted for the mountain folk. The work that you have done in bringing so splendidly before the American and English public the real worth of these people will be of the greatest help to all of us who are connected in any way with them.

We returned from the Laurel country recently, where you were spoken of frequently. I saw Mrs. Sands in the distance and had a long talk with "Frizzly Bill," whom I met on the road. He chuckled a great deal when I asked him if he remembered the bottle of "moonshine" he got at the still the day I got him for you. He said he certainly did remember the bottle; and then went on to explain that when he had taken one drink, it felt lonesome, so he slipped out and took another to keep it company; then they got to "quar'l'in" and he had to take another one as a peacemaker, and a number more to rejoice over the peace ensuing! He told me also that he had a son in the army on the other side and was greatly relieved when I told him that the war was really over.

Olive and I met him the following day. After he had made some complimentary remark directed to Olive, he said that his first woman was educated; but that he himself hadn't no education, but a right smart of head mother-wit; and that his first woman, and also his second woman, who was educated, used to read to him from the scriptures for him to interpret with his "head mother-wit." He said, furthermore, that both of them read to him about a "powerful sarpent" that came out of the sea, and about a woman who rode on a white horse. He said he used "ter study on it a right smart," when he was out "squir'l huntin'," and one day, eight years ago, when out "squir'l huntin' an' studyin' about the sarpent, an' the woman on the white horse," while he was "a-settin' on a log," all of a sudden it came to him "thet thot thar was all a parable; an' hit meant sin"!!

He remembered both you and Miss Karpeles and said, "Thet English feller was sure a right nice feller"! and he launched into a long dissertation on your ability in taking down the music as he sang it.

I asked him if the "likker" helped out his throat so he could sing well, and he said, "Hit sure did." This led to a long conversation with Olive and me about his moonshine days—*years ago,* according to his statement, but probably very recently, in fact.

Thank you for your good wishes for me. I think I am going to get along all right—am a full-fledged vegetarian and feel much better for it.

Let us hear from you as often as leisure permits. We both regard your visit and Miss Karpeles's as one of the pleasantest we have had, and the friendship formed as one of the choicest of our friendships. . . .

P.S. I mailed to you yesterday your notebooks, in care of Novello, London.

Meanwhile, John was able to report the entry of the YMCA into the mountain field. On December 16th he wrote Mr. Glenn:

You will be interested to know that the YWCA has at last taken up work in the mountain country, and that a secretary of a mountain county—Henderson County, North Carolina, adjoining Buncome County, in which Asheville is situated—has recently been in my office to consult me as to plans for her work. She is a Miss Rue and was at Hindman, Kentucky, several years ago.

I have also a letter received Saturday from Mr. [Henry] Israel of the Rural Department of the YMCA. He tells me that they, at last, after our joint and intermittent conferences of six years, are to take up the question of mountain counties, and that their southern secretary from Atlanta is to see me about it.

I am much pleased over the outcome of these matters, both in and of themselves and because I think it may be fairly said that their consideration and inception are due very largely to the initiative of the Foundation.

Two days later, Mr. Glenn wrote giving the Foundation's position on the expansion of Red Cross work in the mountains:

Your letters about the Red Cross nursing raise some very interesting questions. In the first place, they indicate the great need for such work. On the other hand, I think the Red Cross should give the most careful consideration to the question as to whether it will undertake any important activities beyond emergency disaster work. I was never in favor of taking the rural nursing service into the Red Cross. It is no more a Red Cross function than any other piece of social work. If the Red Cross undertakes to do social work on a large scale, it is likely to overlap and possibly stunt the work of organizations which need to be strengthened.

I have not time to elaborate my thoughts for you, but it will not do at present for the Foundation to put itself in a position of urging the expansion of Red Cross work. My present feeling is that those who are responsible for making Red Cross plans for the future should call into consultation a number of the leaders of social work, including health workers, and come to conclusions only after they have listened to discussions by people who are well acquainted with the whole field of social work and its implications and complexities. Of course if the Red Cross

is going to continue its public health nursing, I would be glad to do all I
can to see that the mountain districts are supplied with what they need
so badly.

Correspondence between John and Mr. Glenn in the first days of January refers
again to the matter of the Red Cross and YMCA:

[JCC to Mr. Glenn]
January 1, 1919

Enclosed herewith is a letter to Mr. Scott, ready for mailing, should you
approve. I should be glad of your suggestions. I hope some organization will
take up the question of rural nursing, should it be decided that such a work is
not within the province of the Red Cross.

I gave to Mr. [Howard] Hubbell of the YMCA, the other day, a letter of
introduction to you. He came from Atlanta to see me with reference to YMCA
work in the mountains.

Miss Stone is coming to see me week after next, on the Hindman
proposition.

All goes well here.

With best wishes for the New Year . . .

[Mr. Glenn to JCC]
January 4, 1919

I have your favor of January 1st enclosing letter to Mr. Scott. I send you [a]
copy of a letter which has just come to my attention this morning. It will show
you that the time is not yet ripe for making specific suggestions to the American Red Cross. I will know, from time to time, what is being done and will try
to keep you posted.

Mr. Hubbell has not yet turned up.

I am glad to know that all goes well and hope that means that you are feeling better.

I received yesterday a program of a Rural Life Conference, January 6th and
7th in Baltimore, which it might have been well for you to attend. The letter
is signed by Dwight Sanderson, who is a professor in the Department of Rural
Organization of the New York State College of Agriculture, Cornell University,
Ithaca, New York. The committee consists of the following:

Kenyon L. Butterfield, Chairman

E. C. Branson	C. W. Thompson
Mabel Carney	George E. Vincent
P. P. Claxton	Georgia L. White
A. R. Mann	Warren H. Wilson

It is a long program. I am sorry that I did not have longer notice. I am wiring you to go if you wish.

To this, John replied that he regretted that he could not attend the Rural Life Conference in Baltimore and asked for a program, for he wanted to keep in touch with this conference, adding, "It is an inopportune time for me to leave, and I fear I could not have gone even with longer notice, as my work is progressing well, and I ought to be here that there may be no further delays."

In the first part of January, John also had a letter from Miss Fannie Clement, who asked him to write the Red Cross to vouch for her loyalty, as required for overseas personnel. She had decided to leave the acting directorship of the Town and Country Nursing Service and go to France to confer with the Smith College Unit in regard to developing plans for service. On January 23rd, John enclosed the following testimonial in a letter to her: "It gives me much pleasure to testify to the high character of Miss Fannie F. Clement, to her loyalty to this country, and to her loyalty to and sympathy with the cause of the Allies. I have known Miss Clement for a number of years, in which she has served the country with single-minded devotion."

In writing to Miss Clement, he said:

Here is a letter, brief and to the point. I could throw many more bouquets, but if I should tell the director all the nice things that I could say truthfully, I fear his whole office force would be employed and other applicants would not receive the consideration that is due them.

Do let us hear from you before you sail, and occasionally from the other side. If by any chance you should go or return via Glasgow, let me know, should you wish some letters of introduction to some real Scottish cousins of mine. They would enjoy seeing you very much, give you a good time, try to kill you by overfeeding you and drinking tea, and perhaps on the Sabbath taking you, if they could, to a Presbyterian Church.

Olive is going to write soon. I am feeling fine. Nothing yet as to the mountain fund.

Please give our very kind regards to your mother, Miss Van Duzor, and for yourself accept all the good things that you must know we wish you.

On January 27th, he had bad news of Pine Mountain to report to Mr. Glenn: "We have just received word of the burning of the Pine Mountain School building, and loss of life of the bookkeeper, Miss Scott, and three of the boys. Miss Pettit wrote Miss Canterbury from Lexington. She was about to start to Asheville for a consultation before starting on an itinerary which I had made her, to visit mountain schools doing certain kinds of work of which she wished to know. On account of the fire, she has gone back to Pine Mountain, and in all probability will not come to Asheville."

Earlier the same day he had written Miss Pettit:

We have all learned with the greatest sorrow of your loss at Pine Mountain and are hoping very much that the first reports as to Miss Scott and the boys have proved to be unfounded. Let us hear from you as soon as you can conveniently.

Mrs. Campbell and Miss Canterbury join with me in sending sympathy.

At this time John could write Mr. Glenn, who had sent a personal note to inquire "just what your physical condition is." John replied, also on January 27th:

I thank you for your kind inquiry as to my physical condition. In reply I am glad to say that I am getting on very well. It is necessary for me, however, to walk a rather straight line and adhere to a strict regime. If I deviate much from the line, I am not nearly so comfortable as when I follow it. By strict attention to diet, exercise, and sleep, I am able to put in four hours of good work in the office in the morning and about two or three in the afternoon. I am really doing much better than I feared I might be able to do.

The questions that had arisen in regard to the Hindman Settlement School were very much in John's mind. Since sending Mr. Glenn his letter of December 4th about the new type of settlement school that he thought might meet the Hindman situation, he had had a long conference with Miss Stone, who came to Asheville to see him. In a letter of January 31st, he again took up the matter with Mr. Glenn, proposing committees to develop his plan and saying that, after probable preliminary and supplementary costs had been estimated and he had gone over them, he "would like to submit some such proposition as this to the Foundation, namely: that for a period of years necessary to give the plan a fair trial, the Foundation stand behind the enterprise financially for a definite sum." At the same time, he said also that, before going further, he would like to have Mr. Glenn meet Colonel Stone (Miss Stone's father) and Miss Huntington in New York toward the end of February.

Mr. Glenn answered, on February 7th, that he would be glad to talk to Colonel Stone and Miss Huntington, but, feeling that the Foundation could offer no financial help, he asked John to tell them that "they must not expect anything from me except such advice as I may be able to give them out of my experience." John responded on February 11th:

Your letter of the seventh reached me yesterday. I thank you for the careful consideration you have given my letter and the documents sent you. The wisdom of the Foundation's position in not assuming responsibility for institutions is apparent. I do not wish to advance arguments in further support of the details of the tentative plans outlined by me, but I would avail myself of the opportunity you offer to present the perplexities of a situation that is to arise with increasing frequency unless solved.

The Foundation is the only nonsectarian organization endeavoring to view impartially mountain problems in a large way and to help solve them in a way with a "mountain specialist" at its head. Both the Foundation and the division have won the confidence of the mountain agencies, denominational and secular, and of organizations interested in the mountains who look to the Foundation for leadership in the rural problems of the mountains.

Among the best agencies in the mountain field are some nondenominational independent schools, such as the one at Hindman. They have developed from small beginnings, through the ability and devotion of women such as Miss Stone and Miss Pettit. Hindman has come to the position that most of the nondenominational independent schools will reach, sooner or later; and in that sense, this situation is typical.

One or more of these independent schools may continue to live on indefinitely, at a dying rate, in their later years, through securing an endowment. It is questionable whether schools of this character should be endowed, unless it is very definitely provided for that they are to be plastic and allowed to expand with the need and not to grow fixed in a mold fashioned now. They may defer a decision through selecting successors to those now in charge. Hindman, however, whose officers have ever looked to us for guidance, because of present personal needs of its directors, and because they foresee the future, have come to us for help in the solution of this typical situation. It would be very unwise for any organization to so help Hindman as to let it be assumed that its founders were simply turning over a burden to other shoulders after they themselves had grown weary in well doing. It would be unwise, too, to grant help to carry it on in its present form merely.

There are several methods of meeting the present situation, which may be offered them: (1) to continue in the same way, (2) to seek an endowment, (3) to turn over the work to some denominational board. These are the possibilities, but they are sidesteps or backward steps.

According to my present view, the forward steps lie in the following directions: (1) county or state control, with cooperation from the government, (2) cooperative control by several denominational boards, (3) cooperation by social agencies for rural betterment. The first is premature, and practically impossible at present as regards the whole work at Hindman. The second is unlikely, though I cherish a faint hope that several boards might unite, provided a person of right personality and right standing with these boards could be found to supervise the work at Hindman. The time, however, does not seem inopportune to me for an effort to secure the cooperation of social agencies which might enlist some help from county, state, and federal government, and also some from church agencies.

If I have given you the impression that I want the Foundation to take over the school and be responsible for it, I have not altogether made clear my own view. . . .

It might be necessary, while Miss Huntington and Miss Stone are securing money to keep the school going, to secure and sustain, for a few years at least, the individual who is to work actively upon the new plan.

My thought really has been that the Foundation might act in [an] advisory way, serving on [the] several preliminary committees, with myself upon a permanent committee if it should seem best, to ensure the carrying out of our ideas; with such financial support as might be deemed necessary in conference with these committees, to make the transit from the present to some permanent basis. This financial support might be definitely limited, both in amount and in period of time in which it is to be available.

After the experiment had been made, and help granted during the transitional period, the Foundation would be free from further responsibility and all connection, if desired. . . .

The Foundation would be in the position of having stood behind an initial experiment, to demonstrate what could be done. It would have consented to make only one demonstration to point the way for all mountain schools finding themselves in the same position as Hindman.

I do hope that some path may be opened, with our help; that we may not fail in a case so typical.

Enclosed is a copy of the letter I am sending to Miss Stone. I feel sure it will be of help to both Miss Huntington and Col. Stone to have a conference with you. I want them to feel, in any event, that they have the full sympathy of the Foundation in working out a situation which must be met again and again in my field.

The conference was held in New York, as planned. It did not seem best for John to make the extra effort to go. He was suffering from attacks of intense pain, which he had not mentioned in the answer he made to Mr. Glenn's inquiry about his health, January 27th.

In spite of these attacks, his work on the study was going steadily on. John had for a long time been searching out source material on settlement and ancestry, pioneer routes of travel, land grants and boundaries, resources and development. The Southern Highland Division office now had a noteworthy collection of early and recent maps, books, and publications of all descriptions on the mountain region. In accumulating this, the New York office of the Russell Sage Foundation had been of great help through its Library Department. With material at hand, John was making good progress in formulating what was now coming to be a comprehensive report.

Plans for the Knoxville conference, too, were under way, as shown by a few of the letters of early February. On February 3rd, for example, John wrote Dr. Brown of the Southern Baptist Convention:

The time has come to plan for the annual meeting of the Southern Mountain Workers' Conference, and I write to you, as a member of the Executive Committee, for your views of the nature of the conference to be held, speakers, subjects, etc.

Would you favor our meeting without any set program, and perhaps with one opening speaker merely, devoting each session to full discussion from the floor upon subjects indicated previously? In past years some have desired this. If this should meet your views, would you please indicate the subjects you would like to have discussed?

It has also been suggested that we discuss the following program, devoting a morning session to one, an afternoon session to another, and the morning of the second day to the third, leaving the evening of the first day of the program free for groups to meet as they wish. The subjects suggested are as follows:

1. A school program for the mountains.
2. What should the church do for the mountains? What is it doing?
3. A health program for the mountains that can be put through.

A full expression of your views is desired.

From past experience we have found that early April is the most convenient time, provided we can escape dates on which various denominations have special meetings. April 1–3 has been suggested by one member of the Executive Committee, for the reason that important meetings of his denomination are to be held the following week. If this were approved, the first meeting would be the usual social gathering on the night of the 1st.

I should be very glad indeed for your full suggestions at your earliest convenience. Please make your suggestions whether you can come or not.

With assurance of my appreciation of your prompt response to this request.

In Dr. Brown's reply of February 10th, he favored discussion from the floor of the subjects John had suggested:

I have just returned from a trip through Georgia and South Carolina. I find two letters from you, one of which I will answer now, though I have not had time to thoroughly mature the matter presented.

However, I think it would be a good idea to spend more time in our conferences in a general discussion of the problems encountered in our work by the men who are doing the work. You have been bringing a lot of big "Jakes" along to give us some highbrow stuff, which we enjoyed because it was good; at the same time we had a very profound feeling that we knew more about some things than the highbrows. Now, suppose you just take off the bridle in this conference like I do in mine. I think that all three of the subjects suggested should be discussed, and if some fellows get onto the Federated Church and I explode, of course you would not be surprised. However, a little explosion now and then does the average meeting good. Let's have all three of the questions.

The first days of April will suit me, I suppose, as well as any time.

Dr. Claxton, on the other hand, proposed another set of subjects for discussion:

February 6, 1919

I am glad to know that you are planning for a meeting of the Southern Mountain Workers' Conference this spring, and I shall be very glad indeed if I find I can be present. It is getting more and more difficult, however, for me to get away from Washington. Just now we are developing quite a number of new things in the Bureau of Education, but possibly the work here will be in such a condition by the time of the conference that I can get away for a few days for this meeting.

I suggest that the conference be devoted to the discussion of three questions:

1. Adaptation of the work of the schools to the life and needs of the mountain people.
2. Promotion of the health of the people of the mountains.
3. Teaching of adult illiterates.

Just now there is pending in both houses of Congress a bill, a copy of which I am enclosing, which we hope to be able to get passed before the session closes. If this bill passes, we shall be able to undertake the work of the education of grownup illiterates and the Americanization of our foreign-born population in a far greater way than has ever yet been attempted. I cannot think of any one thing that will be more helpful to the people of the mountains than a vigorous policy of education for grownup illiterates for the next seven years. In this work the federal government and the state can be very greatly helped by the hearty cooperation of the churches and other agencies already at work.

Several days before receiving Dr. Brown's letter, John had sent one to a "big jake," Sir Horace Plunkett, asking him to speak at the conference; on February 5th he wrote:

It was with much pleasure that I learned from my friend Mr. Lyman that you were again in this country and that you were to speak in Washington at the semiannual conference of the National Board of Farm Organizations. If possible, I shall be there. I am sending this letter, however, in the event of my being detained.

You may recall my having written to you several years ago expressing our hope that we might have the pleasure and profit of having you as our speaker at the Southern Mountain Workers' Conference. You were ill at the time and could not attend. We are to hold the conference this year in Knoxville, as usual, and the tentative dates are from April first to third.

Those of us who have followed the splendid work done in Ireland long to have something of the sort done in our southern mountains if possible. It would be an inspiration to all of us to hear from you personally as to the early beginnings of the work and receive your suggestions as to how we might make beginnings here.

Mr. Lyman will be glad, I am sure, to give you at least some preliminary idea of the personnel of the conference. We number usually from 100 to 150.

It would give me much pleasure and help, personally; and I know it would please my superior officer, Mr. John M. Glenn, to feel that you were to address this conference in which he is so much interested. May we not hope to have you?

Sir Horace replied from Battle Creek Sanitarium on February 14th:

If you were at the National Board of Farm Organizations Conference, you will have heard of my disappointment. I came to the states intending to confer with many people in many places upon various subjects of importance. I knew a short rest here was indicated, and I had hoped that the insomnia I was suffering from would finally yield to treatment. I have been here ten days and am no better. I have had to cancel nearly all my engagements, and I fear it will be quite impossible for me to go down south as you kindly suggest. I must only hope for better luck next time.

John sent an answer to Sir Horace on February 24th:

I am much pained to know of your illness and trust that you may speedily recover. We wanted you very much. When I learned that you would be unable to come, I endeavored to get in touch with Mr. [Harold] Barbour through Mr. Lyman, that we might have him as a speaker; but his departure makes that impossible.

I would not impose any burden upon you, but should you recover soon, and be this way, we should be very glad to have you as our guest at the conference, even should you think it inadvisable to participate in any of the discussions.

To Mr. Lyman, John had written, "Will you not so fill Mr. Barbour with enthusiasm that no other conference compares with ours: for *you* know no other conference does!"

Most of my own days were spent at the office, where there were always ways in which I could relieve John of details, and be on hand if he felt suddenly ill. Miss Canterbury was a delightful and able secretary, and we became the best of friends. John was busy enough with preparations for the conference, correspondence, and visitors. He was working, too, as he had the strength, on his book. The basic material was in his old report to the Foundation, but there was much to add to that in statistics and new data of various kinds. He wanted, too, to rethink certain parts, especially conclusions and suggestions for the future.

On February 10th, he wrote to Dr. [E. A.] Sutherland of the Nashville Agricultural and Normal Institute, urging him to attend the conference and requesting information for use in the book:

We are counting on you to come to our Knoxville conference and to bring Dr. [Floyd] Bralliar, Mrs. [Nellie] Druillard, and as many others as possible.

In addition to the reply to the circular letter which I am enclosing, I should greatly appreciate a letter from you, also, giving me a full list of the schools in the mountains that have been established under the fostering care of the Madison institute; and, if there are such, a list of other schools in the mountains of the South affiliated sympathetically with your church or conducted under its auspices. I am endeavoring to summarize the work of the different church boards in the mountains, and I want the work that your schools have done to receive the story they merit. I should like, therefore, to have before me an historical and chronological statement of your schools, before summarizing. I do not, of course, expect to quote you. I want this for my guidance.

I am getting along very well. You will be interested to know that while in New York I called upon Dr. Bishop, who wrote the book on

"Arterio-Sclerosis" which I read while with you. I am on a vegetarian diet, not even taking eggs. He seems to feel that my trouble originated with my attack of typhoid several years ago and that one of my heart muscles is affected through being oversensitive to some constituents of some animal protein as yet unknown to him or me. I am following a rather rigid regime.

Just a word came to us on February 24 from Miss Pettit at the Pine Mountain School, where they were still struggling with the aftermath of the fire, which cost two lives as well as the complete loss of their schoolhouse.

How good it was of you to send pencils and tablets! They certainly supplied an instant need.

We are rejoicing in days when school can be held out of doors, and when we don't miss the surplus of warm clothing and bedcover we had collected. I am not really writing to you today, for I know you can appreciate how full our hands are.

A few days later we heard from Mr. Glenn, who wrote on February 26th to report on the conference with Colonel Stone and Miss Huntington about Hindman. With this letter he enclosed a copy of a personal letter written on the same date to Dr. Livingston Farrand at the headquarters of the American Red Cross:

I am enclosing a letter from Mr. John C. Campbell addressed to Mr. George E. Scott and written some time ago. Mr. Campbell sent it to me for consideration, and I felt that the time was not yet ripe for forwarding it. I send it to you now as evidence on the subject of rural nursing—not for the purpose of urging the American Red Cross to grant Mr. Campbell's request. As you know, I think the whole question of American Red Cross future program should be given a most careful and searching consideration before final conclusions as to extension of responsibility are reached, and it seems clear that you agree with this proposition.

If, however, it is decided that the American Red Cross will develop its rural nursing service, I know no section of the country where the need for such service or its educational possibilities are greater than in the southern mountains. So I hope that when you come to the consideration of this question, you will let Mr. Campbell confer with you. I think you would find no more competent adviser on the whole subject of rural nursing and its administration as well as on rural development generally.

On March 4th, John reported to Mr. Glenn:

I received a letter from Miss Stone yesterday, expressing her appreciation of your kindness and helpfulness in the conference with her father and Miss Huntington; and also her hope that the Foundation might be instrumental in finding a way out for them.

I have urged both Miss Huntington and Miss Stone to come to Knoxville. I do not suppose, however, that both can come, but I hope that Miss Stone may be there to talk over with me and one or two others who may be there, some matters that I want to know about.

Miss Stone has suggested my coming to Hindman to go over the whole thing with her and Miss Huntington on the ground, where I could also get the feel of some local people if it seemed a propitious time. I may decide to do so, especially if I decide to come to New York. I am too busy just now to do anything more than attend to the conference matters and to continue the book and my usual correspondence. I had planned to go into the mountains for a week after the conference for a semirest and consultation upon some matters; and it might be well to go to Hindman. If events so shape themselves, I should like then to come on to Washington and New York to see leaders whom I would want to consult on the Hindman matter and to talk over matters with you.

Two more letters went from John to Mr. Glenn before the conference, the first on March 20th:

Thank you for petty cash reimbursement, received, and for the $150 included in the check for conference expenses.

Miss Stone and Miss Huntington are coming to Knoxville; and it will depend upon my conference with them what my next move will be: whether to go to Hindman, New York, or to return here.

The conference promises are very good. Dr. Claxton is coming. Dr. Leonidas Glenn, professor of geology at Vanderbilt University, who has made an extensive survey of the mountain country, extending over a number of years, is also coming. He is to speak to us on the material resources of the mountains, possibilities of development, etc. He has a very human point of view as to mountain possibilities.

You may remember having sent me notice of a government publication on southern mountain farms. I wrote to Secretary [David F.] Houston, asking for a speaker, and the department is sending Mr. J. H. Arnold, the author of that paper.

Miss [Julia C.] Lathrop of the US Children's Bureau is also sending a representative, Miss Margaretta Williamson, who was associated with Dr. Frances Bradley in a health study of mountain counties. Dr. Bradley, you may recall, prepared a Foundation pamphlet under Dr. Hart's department. It was called the *Care of the Baby,* I think.

Miss Jane Van De Vrede, director of nursing service, Southern Division, American Red Cross, is to speak to us on public health.

The second letter was dated March 25th:

I thank you for your kindness in sending the checks, which were received yesterday.

I received yesterday a letter from Mr. Burg, director of Organization Matters, Savings Division, War Loan Organization, Treasury Department, Washington, D.C. One of the representatives of the War Savings Division came to see me some weeks ago on the matter of pushing a Thrift Campaign through the mountains. I thought I might put them in touch with Mr. Fisher and put it through. Mr. Burg writes me that they are going to send to our conference a representative from Washington and three other representatives, one from each of the districts in which portions of the mountain country lie.

Mr. Burg was formerly educational secretary of the Methodist Episcopal Church, with headquarters in New York. As secretary, he was at our conference last year and was greatly impressed by it. He is a very good friend of Mr. Shelby Harrison, of the Foundation.

I am still hoping to hear that you are coming.

A study of the proceedings of the Seventh Annual Conference of Mountain Workers, which took place April 1–3 in Knoxville, shows keen and good discussion on several important questions, with thirteen different denominations participating, and a number of secular organizations as well. Perhaps the greatest interest centered on the question of the relation of church and state schools, involving the future of the church and independent schools. John was at his best, as usual, as chairman, stimulating discussion and injecting brief pertinent comments. The subject was one to which he had been calling attention since the beginning of the conferences, and when asked, after much general expression of opinion, what he himself thought as to public management of public schools, his answer was unequivocal: "Merely that it *does* work. You don't need to trust your own judgment as to whether it is time for the public to assume responsibility. Don't use it; write to Dr. Claxton or to some government specialist to spend a week to three months in your county, and get his candid opinion; then abide by his opinion. My own opinion is that the time has long come for church and independent schools to stop doing public school work. They can do specialized work."

Straight, too, was his answer to the question as to whether there was any larger proportion of young people leaving their home farms in the mountains than in any other section. "The question is, Shall the schools of the mountains be based on the needs of the mountain country, or on the needs of the individual person in the mountains? Why is it necessary to keep two hundred church and independent schools for the purpose of giving to boys in the mountains training which we could give them for a very much less sum by placing them in schools already in existence outside?"

Before leaving Knoxville, John wrote Mr. Glenn, April 4th:

We have had an unusually interesting conference. I do not know the exact enrollment, but it was approximately 170. This is an increase over last year of 30 or 40. I wish very much that you could have been here yesterday morning during our discussion of church questions. A minister of the Primitive Baptist, Hard Shell, or Old Regular Baptist, as they are [variably] called, was in attendance and on our program. I did not suppose that this would ever be. He was much surprised to be welcomed and to be called a "brother." He promised me that he would come next year and that he would bring others of his church. He was from Mrs. Lloyd's region in Kentucky. Mrs. Lloyd was also here and had opportunity to speak. . . .

I am going from here to a school in the Tennessee mountains for a day or two and then on to Hindman to look into the Hindman situation more fully and then . . . Caney Creek. . . . I want very much a government specialist in education to make a survey of Knott County, that we may have a public educational expert's opinion as to the educational needs of Knott County. . . .

I plan to come on to New York to talk over with you and have your opinion on some interesting developments in denominational work. One secretary has asked me to pass upon their work; it may result in the giving up of several schools and interdenominational cooperation with one or possibly two other denominations in mountain work. I am greatly heartened over the whole situation. I have asked Miss Canterbury to prepare a little outline for you of the convention of our conference and to send a clipping, which does not at all convey the decided spirit of fellowship that pervaded. . . .

Bishop Horner was here, Mayo, Archdeacon Neve, and a goodly representation of the Episcopal Church. The Presbyterians and the Seventh-Day Adventists nearly swamped us. We had a few Southern Presbyterians, and their superintendent was here. We had a fair representation of the Baptist laity. Their superintendent was detained. The presence of the Primitive Baptists this year increased our denominational representation to twelve. Miss [Elizabeth] Fox, of the Red Cross, made a splendid impression; she is keen of mind apparently, keen for the Red Cross, but is a church woman of Episcopalian connection and has, therefore, a sympathetic attitude toward our problem. She has gone, upon my request, into the mountains for a few days. I am feeling very well. I came through much better than I had anticipated.

John also wrote a letter on April 4th to President [John E.] Calfee of the Normal and Collegiate Institute at Asheville:

I am sorry that I did not see you before you left to thank you and Mrs. Calfee for your contributions to discussion of the conference and for bringing so helpful a group of workers from the various schools under your charge. I am also deeply grateful to you for the reinforcement you brought to bear which resulted in our having with us Doctor [George] McAfee. I am going into the Tennessee mountains now for a few days and then to Hindman, Ky., and from there probably to New York. . . .

Tell Mrs. Calfee she must surely come next year. Her personal testimony as to the Hyden situation helped to precipitate the question as it ought to be precipitated.

With kindest regards from Mrs. Campbell and myself.

On the same date, President Frost of Berea wrote John:

This is, first of all, to congratulate you upon the great success of the Mountain Workers' Conference. You and Mrs. Campbell have a right to great satisfaction over the service you have rendered not only to us who were there, but to all the institutions of the mountain region.

I greatly hope you can give me a list of the entire number who were present. Possibly it has appeared in some paper, but it did not appear in any paper which I secured while in Knoxville. I wish to know whom I have met. . . .

With all the admiration and good will a letter can convey . . .

John left Knoxville for his mountain trip in high spirits by railroad to Erwin, Tennessee, and thence by car into Unicoi County, Tennessee. Changes were so marked that they could not but be constantly in our minds. Such a mixture of old and new! We saw cement bridges and foot-logs; store hats, fascinators, and sunbonnets; store coffin and the old ritual of carrying the body up through the pines to the graveyard on the hilltop; procession of people riding mules and horses, double and single; old wagon fording the creek.

He took time to write Marshall C. Allaben from Johnson City, Tennessee, on April 8th, after a visit to community work carried on under his Church Department:

Mrs. Campbell and I have just returned from Rocky Fork, where we spent Sunday with Miss [Jennie] Moore, en route to Kentucky from the conference in Knoxville. I wish you could have been with us. I drop you this line to express to you my appreciation of what Miss Moore is doing. I was especially interested in her community work and in her cooperation with the county superintendent. I called at the county superintendent's home in Erwin, and she spoke highly of the work Miss Moore is doing, in cooperation with the public school interests. I was greatly impressed, too, with the development of the whole country, from Erwin to Flagpond, and I am quite sure that it will not be many years until we shall have a system of splendid roads through the mountain country, one of which is likely to come through Flagpond, connecting at Mars Hill, North Carolina, and reaching therefrom both Asheville and Marshall.

You may be interested in knowing that we were at the Farm School recently. I was impressed there too with the beauty of your site and the fact that things seem to be growing that way. . . .

I was impressed, too, with the fact that the good road is extending on to Black Mountain, and that your school will be in touch, if you will, with the YMCA summer school at Blue Ridge, with the Southern Presbyterian summer camps at Montreat, with the Baptist work at Ridgecrest a few miles beyond. I learned some time ago that the Episcopalians had also reserved land in that region, as well as the Southern Methodists. You will not misunderstand, I am sure, when I again express my hope that the splendid work which you have done in the past at the Normal and Collegiate may be extended. With the possibilities of the southern mountain section, which is to become, at least upon the Asheville plateau, a great dairy, sheep, and cattle country, you have a wonderful opportunity for the training of rural teachers. I was talking on the way from Erwin with a specialist in poultry husbandry of the University of Tennessee extension work; he thinks there are wonderful opportunities along all these lines, but that the people must be led under competent leadership. I want so much that they should have such competent leadership that I venture again to bring before you and Mrs. Bennett the question as to whether you could not greatly extend your work along those lines. Would it be possible to utilize, both for the boys and girls, at the Farm School and Normal, your splendid property (which, to be sure, needs to be brought up somewhat) at Swannanoa? Your site is, in my judgment, equal to if not superior to the site of the Asheville school for boys. . . .

I am coming to New York in two or three weeks; and if the matter could be at all considered, I should like very much to talk it over with you and Mrs. Bennett, or with your board. I have not said anything to Mr. Calfee, because I have supposed the matter of the Normal School was more or less closed for the present. I have said, however, from time to time, I wish you could develop along rural teacher lines, with space enough in nonurban surroundings but in touch with urban surroundings, to give the benefit of both. The automobile road from the Farm School and the rail connections from Swannanoa would give easy access to Asheville; you would have space enough for development; and you are far enough away from the main line of travel to give you all the seclusion the girls will need for an indefinite period. If the matter is closed beyond recall, let my interest and conviction of the soundness of so much that you have done, plead my pardon if I venture upon a question that can no longer be considered.

We took time to go up to Cranberry by the narrow gauge, going by the site of the old Watauga settlement, then continuing along into the region of the Virginia coal country, and finally passing through the Breaks of the Sandy, towering cliffs almost unbroken from the river to the top, into Kentucky and Elkorn City. At Beaver Creek, Miss Stone and a friend joined us, and we kept on together to Lackey, where horses were waiting for us and a wagon for the others.

Eleven years before, we had come to Hindman for the first time from the opposite direction. Then it was "fortyfive miles from the road." Now it was only sixteen. That was in the late fall, wet and cold. Now, the peaches were in brilliant bloom, and plum trees were white and feathery. Redbud in masses and "sarvice" mingled with the brilliant yellowgreen of witch hazel and the red of maple.

Mining developments had not added to the beauty, but there were no large coal deposits near Hindman. One saw only the growing effect of the mines on the houses and people. We could still look down Jones Fork Mountain into the long cove below and see an old log cabin with flowering trees about, while a song with characteristic quavers and intervals floated up to us. Old and new again, and always the loveliness and the loneliness of the mountains.

It was appropriate that we should receive at Hindman word from Mr. Sharp about the next step for our ballad publication and for all the many other ballads he had collected. On April 11th he had written to me:

It was nice to see your handwriting again. The pictures arrived a couple of weeks ago and are a lovely lot. I am having some slides made, and when they are finished I will send the pictures back again. I expect you would like me to return them, wouldn't you? The music books arrived ages ago. I thought I had mentioned this in my last letter to you, but I dare say I didn't. . . .

Novello's are very anxious to do the next two volumes of the Putnam book but do not greatly relish taking on the publication of another firm. So they are approaching Putnam and offering to purchase his plates and interest in the first volume. Have you any objection to this? I shall put Maud's name on the title pages of these last volumes, as she did every bit as much work as I. I have finished harmonizing a second volume but have not sent it to press, partly because I like to keep accompaniments by me and retouch them whenever the spirit so moves me. I am never satisfied with them.

I am so rushed with work that I hardly know which way to turn. I can see no rest ahead before September. Next week I go to York for a Folk Dance School in Easter Week. Two hundred students, which means rather a big organization in a place where we have never held a school before. Eight teachers and eight accompanists, books and paraphernalia galore. Simultaneously we have a smaller school in London, eighty students. Fortunately, we have a first-rate secretary, or I don't know what would happen! You will be glad to hear that I have won my way with the education rotters and that I am now a full blown official in the board. I shall begin my inspection directly after the York business is over and pay my visits to my branches at the same time. I am lecturing on the mountain songs at Oxford University in May and later on in the month at Cambridge. I am also lecturing at several of my branches and giving one on my own account at the Aeolian Hall, Bond Street, on May 13, when we shall do the running set. The latter will create a sensation, I suspect! especially if I lead it myself. . . .

The weather has been consistently atrocious since we landed last June, up until a week or so [ago], when it got a bit better, but there is practically no sign of spring yet except the singing of the birds which I have not heard since 1916! The latest spring I ever remember. It is hard to know what to say about the Peace Conference. Wilson gets some hard knocks, of course, sometimes, but I fancy when the inward history comes to be written, it will be found that in all essential matters of first importance, Lloyd George and Wilson have stood shoulder to shoulder and combated the two Latin nations. From all accounts, human nature has had its fling in Paris, and had it not been for England and America, it would have been a shameless game of grab, leaving the world even worse than before 1916. Even now, one cannot be sure that the Right is going to win. It won't win completely in any case; there will have to be a compromise. There is this to be said, that England would have had to retire as she did a hundred years ago at the Vienna Conference, had it not been for America—at least that is how I read things. So glad John is better. Maud and I are constantly thinking of you all and the mountains—just think of this time last year!

Shortly after our arrival at Hindman, John wrote, on April 16th, to Mr. Glenn:

In the absence of Miss Canterbury and any available stenographer, I avail myself again of the services of Mrs. Campbell as an amanuensis.

There are many things regarding the marvelous development in the mountains which I have seen lately, and many things of promise here, about which I wish to tell you and in regard to which I wish to consult you, but they must wait a bit longer. I think I shall be in New York by the end of the month. It seems well worth while to wait here for ten days more.

We met Miss Stone at Beaver Creek, the appointed place, last Friday, and came in with her. You may recall that . . . Mrs. Lloyd, a freelance with many good ideas and some not so good, has also a community work in this county about ten miles from here. She, with some of her workers, came to the Knoxville conference. . . . I am going over to her place as soon as the doctor pronounces it safe for us to go. They are just getting over a small-pox epidemic. . . .

Claxton could not, at the last moment, come to the conference, being due in Alabama to confer with some Bureau of Education rural experts who are making a survey in that state. I wanted to get the leaders of this county together at Knoxville for consultation with him, but that could not be on account of his absence and the absence of some from this county who were needed. He was interested in my suggestion of a thorough educational survey of one or two typical mountain counties, to be made by some of the government rural educational experts. I have an appointment with him the last of this month or the first of next, to go into this matter. I want him to send a man to survey Knott County, to get the forces together here, and to help Hindman to make the necessary readjustments [when Miss Stone and Miss Huntington leave]. Foght is the man I want. He is now making a survey in Alabama. He not only knows American rural school situations, but is interested in the mountain situation through conferences to which I have brought him, and he knows the Danish and the Scandinavian systems thoroughly—being a Norwegian himself—and one of the commission sent by the government some years ago to the Scandinavian countries.

The letter continued with an account of a conference that brought together Miss Stone and Miss Huntington of the Hindman School, Mrs. [Alice] Lloyd and her officials, John, the county superintendent of education, and the county leader, Honorable Hilliard H. Smith, former state senator of the district and on the board of trustees of both the Hindman School and Caney Creek Settlement. John was the speaker on the possibilities of the county if there could be cooperation among all these working in the interest of the people. So well was his talk received that Hilliard Smith was asked to draw up a petition addressed to Dr. Claxton and asking that an expert in rural education be sent to help the county coordinate the educational efforts. The petition was signed by all present and was thereafter to be submitted to Dr. Duke [the county health officer], Mr. Caro Smith [cashier of the Hindman bank], Mr. Gettys, the Presbyterian worker on Carr, and Mr. Baker. "I wanted it to come as a county affair," wrote John, "and not something urged too much by myself." He added:

If this plan goes through, it may be brought about—proper corrections made and the forces pull[ed] together. If I can get Foght, he will also be able to help Hindman to a new basis.

The work at Hindman itself has grown so as to have taxed to the utmost the strength of Miss Stone and Miss Huntington. They have to struggle to keep their heads above water and are unable therefore to strike out in new ways. The first stage of their work here in the mountains is over, the interesting personal picturesque stage. The new day of countywide activity—all cooperating—is dawning. . . .

I am waiting here for a Miss [Helen] Dingman, who is doing a nondenominational community work under Allaben and Presbyterian auspices in Harlan County. . . .

Miss Dingman is now in New York, and I have asked her to call upon you, if possible. You will be interested, I am sure, in her community store and in her plans for a community church. She was formerly a teacher in Dana Hall—a preparatory school near Wellesley College—and she has a sister [Mary Dingman] whom you may know. I think she was a YWCA worker, at least during the war, of Christian Socialist tendencies. I have that impression merely.

Physically I am getting on very well.

A letter from Miss Helen Dingman, of the Harlan County Community Life School, Smith, Kentucky (under the Woman's Board of Home Missions of the Presbyterian Church, USA), of whom John writes to Mr. Glenn, had just reached us at Hindman. She had written us earlier, on April 7th:

The Knoxville conference has certainly been a stimulus to thought. My brain fairly aches with the train of problems it has stirred up in me. I am so glad I went and want to take this opportunity of telling you so again.

Mr. Mills and the Methodist doctor bombarded me at dinner that night on the train. I am afraid they gave me up as hopeless but conceded that they were interested to see how the experiment worked at Smith.

Mr. Allaben thinks we shall be able to leave the conference in New York by Monday, April 21st. I can then arrive in Hindman on the 23rd. In telling me how your plans turn out, please write direct to Hotel Arlington, 18 West 25th Street, New York City. I shall be here until April 19th.

I hope you are having restful days in the mountains after the strenuous ones in Knoxville. I cannot tell you how much I enjoyed my talks with both of you.

Please remember me to Miss Stone and Miss Huntington. As soon as my plans are a bit more definite, I shall write them when I can arrive at Ashland.

Two more letters were among those forwarded from Asheville. On April 11th, Mr. Allaben answered the one John had sent him three days earlier:

I am always interested in your letters, and particularly in the one that you have written under date of April 8th. While I doubt the feasibility of any further consideration of a transfer of the work of the Normal from Asheville, yet nothing has been done to date which would prevent that if it should be considered wise. I am accordingly sending your letter over to Mrs. Bennett, and you could see her if you were to come to New York at any time that she is at home. As for myself, I must leave for Puerto Rico on the 26th and shall not be at home again until about the middle of June.

Let me express my regret at not being able to be present at the conference, which, I understand, was an unusually well attended and exceptionally interesting occasion. I always regret missing any of these Knoxville conferences. We are just now beginning our Executive Officers' Conference here, so I have no time to write you further, but I do wish again to express my appreciation of your splendid spirit of helpful cooperation and my desire to have you continue to express your views freely on all occasions, in regard to our work.

With warmest regards to Mrs. Campbell and yourself . . .

The other letter reached us after we left Hindman. Rev. Charles L. Fisk, district education secretary, Ohio and the South-East Congregational Education Society, in Cleveland, Ohio, wrote John on April 24th to say:

I have just returned from my southern trip that made my attendance at the Southern Conference of Mountain Workers possible.

May I congratulate you on the splendid work you are doing and also on the very skillful way in which you handled the discussions, keeping things to the line and getting so much out of what might very easily get away from one. It certainly cannot but be of great benefit to the general cause of mountain work. I was more than repaid for coming.

Our departure from Hindman had been advanced by a change in Miss

[Helen] Dingman's plans, as appears from a letter John wrote Mr. Glenn on April 20th:

> A letter from Miss Dingman yesterday brings us word that she will be delayed in New York a week or ten days longer. She goes to the Roosevelt Hospital this week for a tonsil operation.
>
> We shall therefore leave here Thursday, the day we expected her, going to Caney Creek, ten miles from here, but which takes as much time from here as to go from New York to Boston.
>
> We go thence to Washington for a number of interviews which I hope will bring some good to the mountains.
>
> You will be interested, I know, to learn that there is a prospect of Mr. Park Fisher's carrying on a thrift campaign for the government in the remote mountains. He has been asked to come to Louisville for a conference, and the tone of the letter implies that they want him to go to work right away. Fisher is the man for whom the Foundation allowed by balance last year for war work in the mountains, but who was released to help at Hindman in its stress. If he gets this position, as seems almost certain, it will be due to the advice sought by those who came from the Treasury Department to our conference.
>
> Miss Canterbury writes me that I have letters from representatives of the Interior Department, calling for assistance and suggestions in the Illiteracy and Americanization campaign. This too seems to be an outcome of other connections developing through the conference.
>
> I am almost afraid that the conference is going to run away with me— it is growing so in influence, scope, and numbers.
>
> The situation here is very interesting and could be handled in such a way as to unify all interests in the county and cooperate with others off the field. They are so near their problems that they lose the vision.

We could never lose a chance to get more local history, and picked up much during our stay in Hindman. My diary is full of notes taken down from Hilliard Smith, something in this wise:

> The history of my own people would probably be the history of most of Kentucky settlement. My great-greatgrandfather, Ambrose Amburgey, came over from near Clinch River, Virginia, in 1825. They found one couple, James and Priscilla Davis, living near the mouth of Defeated Branch.

They had probably been there since 1815. He bought of them rights to over ten thousand acres of land for six hundred dollars—laid out along Carr Creek; then went back to Virginia, got his wife and two children, parents, and brother-in-law and all, quite a company with their slaves, and next year came to Kentucky. My grandmother remembered about it. They came through Pound Gap into Letcher; stopped to make a "crop" during the summer, "tented," and then came on to Carr. He settled them along different parts of his purchase. Big families—ten to fifteen children—most prolific—and in a very short time there were hundreds of them in that region.

The descendants of the slaves are still living in that section. We saw them the previous year along Defeated. His grandmother told Hilliard Smith that for awhile they didn't try to cross the hills—just went around. The region from which they came, however, was pretty rugged too.

What was to be the next step in this county? On our last evening in Hindman, John talked to the whole staff, long and thoughtfully, on what changes must be met and adjustments made, and how they must help to bring all forces together if they were to accomplish the best. It was a memorable evening, but he was very tired, too tired really, to go on to Caney Creek the next day to the meeting with Mrs. Lloyd, especially to the long discussions every evening, when, against his earnest request, she gathered in all her workers and students, old and young. Of course, she didn't really know his condition.

We left Caney Creek in the early morning to travel the four miles by wagon to the railroad. The road grew worse, and before we reached the station, we were splattered with mud, all over, and most unmercifully jolted. I remember little of the train trip to Washington, or what we accomplished there. We were eager to be on our way to New York and then move on to rest in Nantucket.

My only memory is of our hurrying down the long platform in the Washington station on May 2nd to catch an earlier delayed New York train—a sad mistake!—and John's collapse as he reached his seat. That was a long trip, and I wondered if it would ever end. I called a chair in the New York station, and we got him to the hotel, where Dr. Bishop was summoned at once. Though still suffering after the doctor left, he wanted to see Miss Dingman, to whom he had taken a great fancy. "You must pull the mountains out, for me," he told her. She stayed only a very short time, as he was obviously unequal to any effort.

Then he asked me to get paper and pencil and take down a few thoughts. I did so and read it back to him. Then he lay down to rest. Suddenly he sat up straight, and almost without warning, he was gone. This is what he dictated:

Contemplation of a Semi-Invalid

On some of the Joys of the Hereafter, if they are left to us, and our present frame of mind obtains.

After seeing my own little girls, my folks, and those especially near to me, I am going to look up Paul, if he is in the same realm or sphere, and thank him first for his change of direction when he saw the light, and then for the help and inspiration he has always been to me in getting in touch with his audiences, as in his address to King Agrippa and to the men of Athens at Mars Hill, and, having found the point of contact, his genius in departing therefrom and raising questions in the minds of his hearers as to their own errors.

I should also like to ask him as to his present attitude on the woman question. Was his alleged attitude necessary, in his view, or expedient for the time? If it were his real attitude, does he now feel that was due to the fact that he was a bachelor? Or did he qualify these statements by a phrase otherwhere used, "I speak this of *myself*," and later editors and reactors, the progenitors of the modern antis, remove this to give their own views or the views of the time the weight (of) an inspired utterance?

Have his views of the atonement changed, or has too much been read into his phraseology and parallelisms as to the "sacrificial Lamb" by the followers of Calvin especially, however they may be distributed denominationally? Did he not perhaps mean us to interpret his words in the spirit in which he said, "For we know in part and we prophesy in part, but when that which is perfect is come, then that which is in part shall be done away. When I was a child, I understood as a child, I thought as a child; but when I became a man, I put away childish things. For now we see through a glass darkly; but then face to face; now I know in part; but then I shall know even as I am known."

I should want to look up Peter and thank him for his impulsiveness. Tell him that we menfolk could understand somewhat his seeming denial of the great truth when the finger of woman was pointed at him, especially if she were young; to tell him how much his magnificent comeback—if that term can be used reverently—has meant to us, that he should go to Rome and there meet his death for his fearless utterance of the great truth.

I should like to tell him how much it meant to mortals, especially to mortals like me, who are conscious of our own frailties, when He whom we all seek to follow picked him to feed his lambs and his sheep. I should also like to ask him about the words "Thou art Peter, and upon this rock I will build my church." Did the Master mean that he was chosen in a special sense as a primate of Rome to whom we were to look as our cathedral and high church friends look, or did he mean that the church was built on the confession "Thou are the Christ," and that was the Rock? What about the keys, and his control of the hereafter?

I should like to tell him also, wrong as it was, that it has been a help to me that he was so much a man that he cut off the right ear of the high priest's servant. I have often wished that he could have amputated the right ear of the high priest himself, horizontally at the neck. We should all have forgiven him and, in our human frailty on earth, have loved him for it.

I should also like to look up John and thank him for his utterance "Now are we the Sons of God, and it doth not yet appear what we shall be. But we know that when he (or it) shall appear, we shall be like him, for we shall see him as he is."

I should like to tell him, too, how much I sympathize with him—if he is still the same John—when I contemplate the sea of trouble that misunderstandings occasion. On the lonely island of Patmos, looking upon the monotonous sea, he projects into my faith and vision the glory of the New Jerusalem when he said out of his reveries, "There shall be no more sea there."

I should like to look up Isaiah also, whether he be the first or second Isaiah, and thank him for the faith and inspiration that has come from his fortieth chapter, and the help to us invalids, especially handicapped in health, in his utterance "He giveth power to the faint; and to them that have no might he increaseth the strength. Even the youths shall faint and be weary, and the young men shall utterly fall: but they that wait upon the Lord shall renew their strength; they shall mount up with wings as eagles; they shall run and not be weary; and they shall walk and not faint."

I am not sure how early in the morning I called Mr. Glenn—it may have been midnight—but he came at once, bringing Mrs. Glenn with him. While he telephoned Richard Coolidge in Boston and made all necessary arrangements, she laid Mr. Campbell down so very gently. I shall never forget their kindness, though the rest of the night is blank to me. Richard came as fast as he could, and we all went home together.

Ruth met us at the train. She and Richard were to be my steady support during the hard years that followed, when I had to learn to find my way alone, in a new world.

Notes

Introduction

1. William A. Link, *The Paradox of Southern Progressivism, 1880* (Chapel Hill: University of North Carolina Press, 1992), 81, 89.

2. The Index to the Campbell Papers, no. 3800 in the Southern Historical Collection at the University of North Carolina at Chapel Hill, lists Campbell's birth year as 1867, so some sources have reported that date as his birth year, but Mrs. Campbell's biography plainly states the year as 1868.

3. Margaret Supplee Smith and Emily Herring Wilson, *North Carolina Women Making History* (Chapel Hill: University of North Carolina Press, 1999), 254.

4. Ruth Crocker, "From Widow's Mite to Widow's Might: The Philanthropy of Margaret Olivia Sage," *American Presbyterians* 74, no. 4 (1996): 253–55, 261. See also Ruth Crocker's biography, *Mrs. Russell Sage: Women's Activism and Philanthropy in Gilded Age and Progressive Era America* (Bloomington: Indiana University Press, 2006).

5. John M. Glenn, Lilian Brandt, and F. Emerson Andrews, *Russell Sage Foundation, 1907–1946*, 2 vols. (New York: Russell Sage Foundation, 1947), 1:13.

6. David C. Hammack and Stanton Wheeler, *Social Science in the Making: Essays on the Russell Sage Foundation, 1907–1972* (New York: Russell Sage Foundation, 1994), 12.

7. David C. Hammack, "A Center of Intelligence for the Charity Organization Movement: The Foundation's Early Years," in Hammack and Wheeler, *Social Science in the Making*, 6.

8. Glenn, Brandt, and Andrews, *Russell Sage Foundation*, 21.

9. Crocker, *Mrs. Russell Sage*, 225.

10. Judith Sealander, *Private Wealth and Public Life: Foundation Philanthropy and the Reshaping of American Social Policy from the Progressive Era to the New Deal* (Baltimore: Johns Hopkins University Press, 1997), 41.

11. Olive D. Campbell, *The Life and Work of John Charles Campbell* (Madison, WI: College Printing & Typing, 1968), 110.

12. John Charles Campbell, *The Southern Highlander and His Homeland* (New York: Russell Sage Foundation, 1921; reprint, Lexington: University Press of Kentucky, 1969), 271 (page references are to the 1969 edition).

13. Henry D. Shapiro, *Appalachia On Our Mind: The Southern Mountains and Mountaineers in the American Consciousness, 1870–1920* (Chapel Hill: University of North Carolina Press, 1978), 128.

14. Deborah Vansau McCauley, *Appalachian Mountain Religion: A History* (Urbana: University of Illinois Press, 1995), 150.

15. Shapiro, *Appalachia on Our Mind*, 123.

16. Penny Messinger, "Leading the Field of Mountain Work: The Conference of Southern Mountain Workers, 1913–1950" (PhD diss., Ohio State University, 1998), 45–49.

17. Shapiro, *Appalachia on Our Mind*, 68.

18. Campbell, *Life and Work*, 110.

19. Ibid., 278–79.

20. John C. Campbell, *The Future of Church and Independent Schools in the Southern Highland* (New York: Russell Sage Foundation, 1917); John C. Campbell, *From Mountain Cabin to Cotton Mill,* National Child Labor Committee Pamphlets, no 195 (New York: National Child Labor Committee, 1913); and John C. Campbell, *The Southern Highlands: Extracts from Letters Received from [Persons] . . . Conducting Work in the Southern Mountains* (1915), cited in Shapiro, *Appalachia on Our Mind,* 197–99.

21. Campbell, *Southern Highlander,* 208; John Alexander Williams, *Appalachia: A History* (Chapel Hill: University of North Carolina Press, 2002), 207–8.

22. Campbell, *Future of Church,* 10, 19.

23. John C. Inscoe, "A Northern Wedge Thrust into the Heart of the Confederacy: Explaining Civil War Loyalties in the Age of Appalachian Discovery, 1900–1921," in *Reconstructing Appalachia: The Civil War's Aftermath,* ed. Andrew L. Slap (Lexington: University Press of Kentucky, 2010), 340.

24. John F. Smith, "This Was a Man," *Mountain Life and Work,* April 1928, 3–4. Smith was an editor of the *Kentucky Folklore and Poetry Magazine* and published articles on aspects of mountain culture and life.

1. Family Background and Early Life

1. ODC note: Forest Grant, later of East Orange, New Jersey, for many years head of the Art Department of the Public Schools of New York City. Letters from Forest Grant to Olive Dame Campbell, July 23, 1948, in Women's Archives, Radcliffe College, Cambridge, Massachusetts.

2. ODC note: Letter from Forest Grant to Olive Dame Campbell, July 23, 1948, in Women's Archives, Radcliffe College, Cambridge, Massachusetts.

3. Ibid.

4. ODC note: Original letter missing.

5. See Appendix 1, "Lumber Rafting in the Mid-Nineteenth Century."

6. ODC note: Reported by Forest Grant from Pat Collins, writing for the *Stevens Point Journal,* December 29, 1928.

7. ODC note: Reference unknown.

8. ODC note: John C. Campbell, *The Southern Highlander and His Homeland* (Russell Sage Foundation, 1921), chap. 2, pp. 9–10.

9. Harvard College was established in 1631, the first institution of higher learning in America, to provide a liberal education for the ministry. Later, divinity students were no longer required to take classes in all subjects. This led to a growing divide in the Congregational church in Massachusetts. Harvard had become more liberal as to church theology, so Andover Seminary was founded as a separate theological seminary in 1808 with no denominational control. See Leonard Woods, *History of Andover Theological Seminary* (Boston: J. R. Osgood, 1885). Andover moved to Cambridge in 1908, and in 1922 it was affiliated with the Harvard Divinity School. See Robert L. Kelly, *Theological Education in America* (New York: George H. Doran, 1924), 290.

2. First Mountain Teaching

1. ODC note: The average elevation of this flat-topped group of the Allegheny-Cumberland Plateau Belt is about 1,800 feet above sea level, with points reaching 2,300 feet.

. . . Sand Mountain is broader and more level than the others. *Southern Highlander and His Homeland,* p. 337.

2. ODC note: John's brother, who visited them at Joppa at this time.

3. ODC note: See Appendix 2, "Letters from Joppa Pupils."

4. ODC note: John Campbell's father-in-law in Steven's Point, Wisconsin.

3. Teaching Years—Pleasant Hill and Demorest

1. Frank Edwin Jenkins, DD, was the president of the Piedmont College Board of Trustees from 1900 to 1910, when he assumed the presidency of the college. He was an active and influential Congregationalist and the author of *Anglo-Saxon Congregationalism in the South* (Atlanta: Franklin Turner, 1908). See Mary C. Lane, *History of Piedmont College, 1897–1990* (Demorest, GA: Piedmont College Press, 1993), 65–66.

2. ODC note: The general elevation of this region is from 1,600 to 1,800 feet above sea level, with mountains ranging from two hundred to three thousand feet above the general elevation. The sides of the mountains are often so steep as to be almost inaccessible. There is within the mountain section a considerable area of broken country resembling the more hilly parts of the Piedmont Plateau. *Southern Highlander and His Homeland,* p. 38.

3. Hindman Settlement School, founded in 1902, was one of the most important mountain educational institutions of the Progressive Era. Katherine Pettit and May Stone were icons of the reform movement as they worked to improve the lives of mountain people. See Jess Stoddart, *Challenge and Change in Appalachia: The Story of Hindman Settlement School* (Lexington: University Press of Kentucky, 2002); and Jess Stoddart, ed., *The Quare Women's Journals: May Stone and Katherine Pettit's Summers in the Kentucky Mountains and the Founding of Hindman Settlement School* (Ashland, KY: Jesse Stuart Foundation, 1997). For the story of the Pine Mountain school that Katherine Pettit eventually established and how it adapted its program to meet the needs of the community, see Mary Rogers's illustrated book *The Pine Mountain Story, 1913–1980* (Pine Mountain, KY: Pine Mountain Settlement School, 1980), 8: "For decades Pine Mountain provided the only medical services for an area of over three hundred square miles."

4. Fiske wrote that "the shiftless people who could not make a place for themselves in Virginia society, including many of the 'mean whites' flocked in large numbers" to North Carolina. Campbell comments thoroughly on John Fiske's theory in *The Southern Highlander and His Homeland* (New York: Russell Sage Foundation, 1921; Lexington: University Press of Kentucky, 1969), Appendix B: "A Misapplied Theory of Mountain Origin," 349–51 (page numbers in the 1969 edition). See also John Fiske, *Old Virginia and her Neighbors* (Boston: Houghton, Mifflin, 1897), 2:311.

5. The Russell Sage Foundation was founded in 1907 by the wealthy widow Olivia Sage in memory of her husband, although Mr. Sage had not shared his wife's interest in benevolent projects. See John M. Glenn, Lilian Brandt, and F. Emerson Andrews, *Russell Sage Foundation, 1907–1946* (New York: Russell Sage Foundation, 1947). Olivia Sage's story was first told in an article by Ruth Crocker: "From Widow's Mite to Widow's Might: The Philanthropy of Margaret Olivia Sage," *American Presbyterians* 74, no. 4 (1996): 253–64. The title of the biography, also written by Ruth Crocker, is *Mrs. Russell Sage: Women's Activism and Philanthropy in Gilded Age and Progressive Era America* (Bloomington: Indi-

ana University Press, 2006). Mrs. Sage herself was the author of an article that propounded her theory that the woman's talents are wasted because she "simply does not know how to . . . go out into the field of life and achieve for herself and her kind." See Mrs. Russell Sage, "Opportunities and Responsibilities of Leisured Women," *North American Review* 11 (1905): 712, http://search.proquest.com.

6. Robert W. de Forest was on the Russell Sage Foundation Board and was Margaret Sage's lawyer, friend, and adviser. Previously he was president of the Charity Organization of the City of New York and involved in many social agencies. Gertrude S. Rice (Mrs. William B.) helped incorporate the Foundation and was one of the trustees, as was Helen M. Gould, a close friend of Mrs. Sage. Glenn, Brandt, and Andrews, *Russell Sage Foundation,* 4, 9.

4. Travel in the Mountains—the Study

1. ODC note: The Anna T. Jeanes Foundation, a Negro Rural School Fund which was later (1937) combined with the John F. Slater Fund to become the Southern Educational Foundation. EMW note: For more about James Hardy Dillard, "urbane, cultivated, and charming," see Raymond B. Fosdick, *Adventure in Giving: The Story of the General Education Board* (New York: Harper & Row, 1962), 102–5. The General Education Board was influenced by Dillard's "knowledge and sympathetic understanding," and he became a trustee of the board in 1918. Dillard University, for the education of Negroes, in his native New Orleans, was named for him.

2. ODC note: There is an early dittoed version of the diary which at times differs somewhat in wording or content, though not in meaning, from the original handwritten one. Usually, but not always, the original version has been used for the extracts appearing in chapter 4. Many of these extracts have been slightly edited—for punctuation, breaking up of long paragraphs, and completion of sentences—to make reading easier.

3. Demorest, Georgia, the home of the Campbells and the location of Piedmont College, where John Campbell was president from 1904 to 1907.

4. Edwin Alderman was the president of the University of Virginia from 1904 to 1915 and was one of the most successful of the southern progressives in higher education. He was concerned about the narrow views of religious leaders in charge of church schools. See "Visions of Grandeur: Edwin Alderman and the University of Virginia, 1904–15," in Michael Dennis, *Lessons in Progress: State Universities and Progressivism in the New South, 1880–1920* (Urbana: University of Illinois Press, 2001), 217–45. The Reverend Bruce R. Payne, a professor of secondary education at the University of Virginia, wrote "Waste in Mountain Settlement Work," published in the proceedings of the National Conference of Charities and Corrections in 1908. He advocated the professionalization of social work in Appalachia and urged interagency cooperation in mountain benevolent work. See Henry D. Shapiro, *Appalachia on Our Mind: The Southern Mountains and Mountaineers in the American Consciousness, 1870–1920* (Chapel Hill: University of North Carolina Press, 1978), 192. The venerable archdeacon Frederick W. Neve was the rector of St. Paul's Episcopal Church in Ivy, Virginia. He established the Church of St. John the Baptist and its mission school in the Ragged Mountains. Neve believed that mountain people should stay in the mountains. He suggested alternatives to farming, such as planting orchards or raising stock. See Frederick W. Neve, "The Missions of the Blue Ridge, Diocese of Virginia," in *The Church's Mission*

to the Mountaineers of the South, Walter Hughson, comp. (Hartford, CT: Church Missions, 1908). In the original diary, O. D. Campbell writes more about Jerry Pound. He felt that there was little community feeling in the mountains, and there was no public law to force the creation of public high schools. He was in sympathy with church schools if they did not further denominationalism.

5. Dr. Philander Priestly Claxton was the editor of the *North Carolina Journal of Education,* which became the *Atlantic Educational Journal.* He was instrumental in the establishment of the Southern Education Board and later became the US commissioner of education. See Charles Lee Lewis, *Philander Priestley Claxton, Crusader for Public Education* (Knoxville: University of Tennessee Press, 1948).

6. The "W" Road was a reconstruction of the Anderson Pike, built in 1852 up the eastern bluff of Walden's Ridge in Tennessee. It was completed in 1893 and replaced the old "corduroy road" used by early settlers and by armies during the Civil War. See James L. Douthat, *Along the Pike: The Story of Walden's Ridge along Anderson Pike* (Signal Mountain, TN: Mountain Press, 1996), 116–17.

7. Mrs. Campbell's diary, with her harrowing accounts of their travels, is a testament to the difficulty of moving around the region in the first decades of the twentieth century. See Elizabeth M. Williams, ed., *Appalachian Travels: The Diary of Olive Dame Campbell* (Lexington: University Press of Kentucky, 2012).

8. Denominationalism was an overarching problem in mountain work. See John Charles Campbell, *The Southern Highlander and His Homeland* (New York: Russell Sage Foundation, 1921; Lexington: University Press of Kentucky, 1969), 152–75 (page numbers in 1969 edition). Another report on the serious handicap that denominationalism presented is in Elizabeth R. Hooker, *Religion in the Highlands Native Churches and Missionary Enterprises in the Southern Appalachian Area* (New York: Home Missions Council, 1933), 211–14.

9. Established in 1855, Berea College was an interracial institution that strived to meet the needs of all races. See Shannon H. Wilson, *Berea College: An Illustrated History* (Lexington: University Press of Kentucky, 2006). Mission barrels were used clothing in big round containers that missionaries collected and distributed to the "needy."

10. Rev. Isaac Messler was superintendent of Kentucky work for the Women's Board of Domestic Missions of the Reformed Church of America. See Olive Dame Campbell, *Southern Highland Schools Maintained by Denominational and Independent Agencies* (New York: Southern Highland Division, Russell Sage Foundation, 1921), 16. In 1913 Messler was appointed to be the secretary of the Executive Committee of the Conference of Southern Mountain Workers. See chapter 6.

11. S. P. Lees Collegiate Institute was established in Jackson in 1891 as a preparatory school for Central University, a predecessor to Eastern Kentucky University. See *A History of Eastern Kentucky University: The School of Opportunity,* by William E. Ellis (Lexington: University Press of Kentucky, 2005), 3.

12. An account of the origin and events of this apparently politically motivated, county-wide feud names the Hargis-Cockrell-Marcum-Callahan War "The Last and Bloodiest Feud" in *Days of Darkness: The Feuds of Eastern Kentucky,* by John Ed Pearce (Lexington: University Press of Kentucky, 1994), 31–53.

13. "Blind tigers" are bars or drinking places, usually illegal during this period.

14. A note in the diary explains that the L & E was the Lexington and Eastern line taken over by the L & N, the Louisville and Nashville, in 1915.

15. ODC note: Rev. H. J. Derthick, previously principal of, then a board member assigned to speaking and money-raising for Hazel Green Academy (Disciples of Christ), afterward principal of Livingston Academy and later still, president of Milligan College, both in Tennessee.

16. Sabbath schools were like the more familiar Sunday schools, being held on Sunday to study the Bible and give religious instruction, but many of them were much more than that. Sabbath school missionaries offered training for teachers and complete educational programs. See Fred Eastman, *Unfinished Business of the Presbyterian Church in America* (Philadelphia: Westminster Press, 1921), 165.

17. ODC note: "Miss Katherine Pettit and Miss May Stone were titled the Executive Committee of the Hindman Settlement School, actually its joint Directors." EMW note: Hindman Settlement School, founded in 1902, was one of the most important mountain educational institutions. See Jess Stoddart, *Challenge and Change in Appalachia: The Story of Hindman Settlement School* (Ashland, KY: Jesse Stuart Foundation, 1997).

18. David E. Whisnant discussed Olive Dame Campbell's ballad collecting extensively in his book *All That Is Native and Fine: The Politics of Culture in an American Region* (Chapel Hill: University of North Carolina Press, 1983). She was one of three examples he used to analyze the "cultural drama that was central" to the "multifaceted church and secular missionary enterprise in the mountains." The others were Hindman Settlement School and the White Top Folk Festival in Virginia (11).

19. Desha Breckinridge was a member of "Kentucky's premier family of Progressive reformers" and the "influential editor of the *Lexington Herald* newspaper." His wife Madeline McDowell Breckinridge, a friend of both Katherine Pettit and May Stone, used the *Herald* to publicize the activities of industrial and settlement schools in the region. See Jess Stoddart, ed., *The Quare Women's Journals: May Stone & Katherine Pettit's Summers in the Kentucky Mountains and the Founding of Hindman Settlement School* (Ashland, KY: Jesse Stuart Foundation, 1997), 32, 34.

20. The book was written by Frank E. Jenkins, DD, and is, indeed, interesting reading. There is a chapter with photographs of Piedmont College, where Campbell was president from 1904 to 1907.

21. A hackle is a large comb with sharp steel teeth for combing flax.

22. According to John Pearce's account of the French-Eversole War in Perry County, it began as a business dispute between two lawyer-merchants in 1887 in the hard-living, hard-drinking town of Hazard, Kentucky, and ended in 1913 when Fulton French tried to shake hands with Susan Eversole and was shot by her son Harry. See Pearce, *Days of Darkness*, 75.

23. This paragraph, not present in the diary (except for the quoted words), was inserted here by the author (ODC) to provide additional relevant information.

24. He is referring to the Kentucky School Law. In North Carolina parochial schools worked side by side with public schools in harmony and were considered supplemental. Some of the myriad of Presbyterian schools even received state aid. Baptists protested this practice loudly, pointing to the principle of separation of church and state. So in 1896 C. H.

Mebane, then superintendent of public instruction, ruled that "the spirit of the law seemed to be against combining Church and State in any way," thereby excluding all church schools from receiving state funds. See Luther L. Gobbel, *Church-State Relationships in Education in North Carolina since 1776* (Durham, NC: Duke University Press, 1938), 199.

25. Harvey Short Murdoch served as the field secretary of the American Inland Mission, or the Society of Soul Winners, an interdenominational organization formed by Dr. Edward O. Guerrant, a prominent and colorful figure in the Presbyterian Church. Murdoch was able to raise enough money to establish the Witherspoon Log College in Buckhorn, Kentucky, in 1903. See G. Gordon Mahy Jr., *Murdoch of Buckhorn* (Nashville, TN: Parthenon Press, 1946).

26. ODC note: Last four sentences moved up from end of entry, where they appear in the original diary.

27. Frederick Webb, minister of the Presbyterian churches at Flag Pond and Rocky Fork, in Unicoi County, Tennessee.

28. The quintessential version of this family/community feud that stretched across two states and the Tug River is told by Altina L. Waller in *Feud: Hatfields, McCoys, and Social Change in Appalachia, 1860–1900* (Chapel Hill: University of North Carolina Press, 1988).

29. Called "Bad Frank Phillips," he indeed had an unsavory reputation to say the least, but he was on the other side. He was raised by an enemy of Anse Hatfield and spent some time trying to kill the old man. Waller, *Feud*, 183–89.

30. "Burns of the Mountains" taught at Berea for a short time, where he met H. L. McMurray, a Baptist preacher from Kansas. In 1899 they decided to build a college in the middle of the mountains. Burns was from Oneida and chose his father's birthplace as the site of the school. Their first task was to get the support of feuding families in the area. James Anderson Burns wrote about his family's feud with the Combses in *The Crucible: A Tale of the Kentucky Feuds* (Oneida, KY: Oneida Institute, 1928), 45. Oneida was the center of the Baker-Howard feud as well. Burns talked the feudists into meeting in an old mill, where many of the bloody battles had been fought. In the famous meeting, Burns convinced the group of fifty enemies to settle their differences for the sake of their children, who would go to school together at Oneida Institute. See Darrell Coleman Richardson, *Mountain Rising: The Story of James Anderson Burns and Oneida* (Oneida, KY: Oneida Mountaineer Press, 1986), 136.

31. ODC note: Oneida Baptist Institute, Oneida, Clay County, Kentucky.

32. This "theory of origin" is discussed in the chapter "Ancestry" in John Campbell's *Southern Highlander*, 50–71. Appendix B of that book, "A Misapplied Theory of Mountain Origin," presents John Fiske's then widely accepted theory: that those who could not succeed in Virginia, the poor or the criminal, moved into North Carolina and from there into the Appalachians, where they were known more for their shiftlessness than their criminal nature (349–51). Also see Fiske's *Old Virginia and Her Neighbors*, vol. 2 (Boston: Houghton Mifflin, 1897).

33. Harold Wilson Coates's little book *The Great Truce of Clay: Stories of Kentucky Feuds* (Cincinnati: Holmes-Darst Coal, 1923) observed that the "deep stain upon Clay County" originated with some of its most prominent citizens. The Garrards and the Whites were salt barons, and the animosity between them probably originated as industrial competition (5).

34. ODC note: Southern Baptist Convention.

35. "Old-Time Baptists of Central Appalachia," a chapter by Howard Dorgan in Bill Leonard's book *Christianity in Appalachia: Profiles in Regional Pluralism* (Knoxville: University of Tennessee Press, 1999), 117–37, clarifies this complex issue. In a nutshell, the split derived from the fact that many Appalachian Baptists distanced themselves from the home missionary efforts of the national church in the region because they felt that their own institutions were doing just fine. The Missionary Baptists promoted evangelism, and those who opposed it were called "antimissionary" (126).

36. ODC note: Poor Fork of the Cumberland River.

37. Opened as Southern and Western Theological Seminary in 1819, Maryville College was chartered in 1842 by the Tennessee State Legislature as a Christian institution and governed by a board appointed by the Presbyterian Synod of Tennessee. See Samuel Tyndale Wilson, *A Century of Maryville College and Second Century Beginnings* (Maryville, TN: Directors of Maryville College, 1935).

38. Dr. Millard Dudley Jeffries succeeded Dr. John T. Henderson as president of Carson and Newman College in 1903. Carson College and Newman College in Tennessee were united in 1889. See Isaac Newton Carr, *History of Carson-Newman College* (Jefferson City, TN: Carson-Newman College, 1959), 63.

39. ODC note: "Tusculum College." Dr. Charles Oliver Gray served as president of Greeneville-Tusculum College from 1908 to 1931. EMW note: See Joseph T. Fuhrmann, *The Life and Times of Tusculum College* (Greenville, TN: Tusculum College, 1986), 167.

40. A spider is a long-handled cast iron pan with legs that sits above the fire.

41. Samuel T. Wilson, in *The Southern Mountaineers* (New York: Literature Dept., Presbyterian Home Missions, 1906), 131, provides excellent short paragraphs about the schools in the region. The school in Burnsville was the Stanley McCormick Academy, "ably directed in its formative years by Prof. C. R. Hubbard."

42. The worm is copper tubing shaped like a coil, the condenser used to cool the whiskey before it is bottled. The Irish and Scottish used it the same way in the fourteenth century. To learn how to make a still, see Joseph Earl Dabney, *More Mountain Spirits: The Continuing Chronicle of Moonshine Life and Corn Whiskey, Wines, Ciders and Beers in America's Appalachians* (Asheville, NC: Bright Mountain Books, 1985), 165.

43. A study of conditions in the state by the National Child Labor Board painted a grim picture of the plight of children in the Kentucky mountains. See Edward N. Clopper, *Child Welfare in Kentucky* (New York: National Child Labor Committee, 1919), 143–67.

44. Laurel Country is so named because of the huge stands of rhododendron, called "laurel" by mountain natives, that cover the mountainsides. It appears in many names of places drained by the tributaries of the Big Laurel Creek. See Margaret Warner Morley, *The Carolina Mountains* (Boston: Houghton Mifflin, 1913), 229. Morley credits Florence Stephenson of the Home Industrial School in Ashville and Frances Goodrich's Allanstand for the prosperity of the Laurel Country. The Yale-educated Miss Goodrich joined the Presbyterian Home Missions Board as a volunteer. She came to teach but ended up rediscovering the dying art of weaving, and in 1902 she helped the community revive the craft to sell items in an old log structure once known as "Allen's Old Stand," a stand being an overnight or resting place for travelers. See Katherine Caldwell, *From Mountain Hands: The Story of*

Allanstand Craft Shop's First 100 Years (Asheville, NC: Southern Highland Handicraft Guild, 1995), 2–3.

45. The French Xavier family fled France during the Huguenot persecution, moved to London, and changed their name to Sevier. In the eighteenth century, they came to the Shenandoah Valley, where John was born in 1745. A prosperous farmer, he settled his family and became one of the most prominent men in Tennessee history, elected governor of the state six times and elected four times to the US Congress. See Francis Marion Turner, *Life of General John Sevier* (Johnson City, TN: Overmountain Press, 1997).

46. "Sheathed" means covered with siding of some sort with a protective layer. Weaving sleys were then wooden pegs used to separate threads on a loom; in modern weaving, the threads are parted and arranged by reeds.

47. Dr. Wallace A. Buttrick was secretary of the Baptist Home Mission Society and helped form the Southern Education Board in 1901 to lobby for tax-supported schools. He served on the General Education Board for more than twenty years, first as a trustee and eventually as president in 1917 and chairman of the board from 1923 to 1926. He was an acknowledged expert on education and Negro schools in the South. See Fosdick, *Adventure in Giving*, 6, 180.

48. Penland is in the mountains of Mitchell County, close to Tennessee. The Appalachian Industrial School was developed by Rufus Morgan, the older brother of Lucy, who began the arts and crafts movement at Penland in the 1920s. The school was under the direction of Bishop Junius M. Horner of the Episcopal Diocese of Western North Carolina. See Philis Alvic, *Weavers of the Southern Highlands* (Lexington: University Press of Kentucky, 2003), 75.

49. Sandra Lee Barney, in her in-depth study of medicine in Appalachia during this period, discusses the role of women's clubs and settlement schools as they tried to coordinate the work of local healers and that of the scattered ranks of medical men. See *Authorized to Heal: Gender, Class, and the Transformation of Medicine in Appalachia, 1880–1930* (Chapel Hill: University of North Carolina Press, 2000), 13–15.

50. The Presbyterian School for Boys in Plumtree was established by a prominent minister and educator in the region, the Reverend Edgar A. Tufts. The Reverend J. P. Hall, brother-in-law of Tufts, was headmaster. It eventually became Lees-McRae College and Grandfather Home for Children. See *Lees-McRae College* (Banner Elk, NC: Edgar Tufts Memorial Assn., 1939–1940), 2.

51. The story of Linville, Grandfather Mountain, and the MacRae families is told in Howard E. Covington, *Linville: A Mountain Home for 100 Years* (Linville, NC: Linville Resorts, 1992). An interest in iron ore and mica mining brought Hugh MacRae as a young man to Mitchell County. William Linville and his son John had been killed by Indians in 1766 when they were camped near the "Great Falls" of the Cherokee (7).

52. Skyland Institute at Blowing Rock was a girls' school with industrial training, started in 1891 by Emily C. Prudden, who transferred it to the American Missionary Association. In 1912 it was reconveyed to Miss Prudden, then closed. See John Preston Arthur, *A History of Watauga County, North Carolina with Sketches of Prominent Families* (Richmond, VA: Everett Waddey, 1915), 253.

53. Moses Cone owned thirty-five hundred acres of land north of Blowing Rock. He

donated generously to the public schools, and his contributions to the state teacher's college, which later became Appalachian State University, were instrumental in promoting higher education in the mountains of western North Carolina. The Moses Cone Memorial Park was donated to the US Government in 1950. John Preston Arthur, *Western North Carolina: A History* (Raleigh, NC: Edwards & Broughton, 1914), 501.

54. Archdeacon Frederick Neve wrote about Valle Crucis and its Episcopal mission school in *Church's Mission to the Mountaineers.* In 1842 the Right Reverend Levi Ives, Episcopal bishop of North Carolina, gave the remote valley its name, "Vale of the Cross" in Latin. Hughson, *Church's Mission to the Mountaineers,* 92.

55. Bruce Payne was then state superintendent of rural education, and Archdeacon Neve was in charge of Episcopal missions in Virginia.

56. The Right Reverend Junius M. Horner, first Episcopal bishop of Western North Carolina. When bishop of the Missionary District of Asheville, he opened and directed the Valle Crucis school for girls in 1903; there domestic skills were taught as well as academics. Later, he bought a herd of blooded cattle and sent them to Valle Crucis along with a young agriculturist from New York, who provided the first practical instruction ever given in any school or college in North Carolina. See Arthur, *History of Watauga County,* 254.

57. The Reverend and Mrs. L. M. Pease were northerners who were involved in the early work of the Presbyterian Church in western North Carolina. On vacation there, they were struck by the need of mountain children in the Asheville area and organized the Asheville Home Industrial School for Girls in 1887, then the Normal and Collegiate Institute and the Asheville Farm School for Boys. H. Davis Yeuell claims that there was no overall design by the Presbyterian churches working in the mountains. The primary goal of northerners was generally "uplift," and education and evangelism were by-products. The southern missionaries began with evangelism, to establish churches, so that schools would likely follow. See Yeuell, *Moving Mountains: A History of Presbyterian and Reformed Faith at Work in Appalachia* (Amesville, OH: Coalition for Appalachian Ministry, 1985), 13–14.

58. George Vanderbilt of Biltmore House recruited Dr. Rodney Rush Swope to be the first rector of All Souls Church in Biltmore. Dr. Swope led the effort for prison reform when education, medical care, and welfare were the work of the church more than the government. See Isaac N. Northup and Carole H. Currie. *The Story of a Church: All Souls in Biltmore* (Biltmore, NC: All Souls Church, 1979).

59. Mars Hill, founded by pioneers, is the oldest educational institution on its original site in western North Carolina. First named the French Broad Baptist Institute, Mars Hill College was chartered by the state of North Carolina in 1859. See John Angus McLeod, *From These Stones: Mars Hill College, 1856–1968* (Mars Hill, NC: Mars Hill College, 1968), 31.

5. Report and First Conference

1. See Mary C. Lane, *History of Piedmont College, 1897–1990* (Demorest, GA: Piedmont College Press, 1993).

2. ODC note: Known to have been invited were Dr. John White, pastor of a large Baptist church in Atlanta, associated with the Baptist Mission Board; Martha Berry, founder of the Berry Schools; Principal J. A. Burns, founder of Baptist Institute, Oneida, Kentucky;

Professor Bruce Payne, from the University of Virginia; Katherine Pettit and May Stone of Hindman Settlement School, Hindman, Kentucky; Rev. Harvey S. Murdoch, head of Presbyterian College, Buckhorn, Kentucky; Rt. Rev. Junius Horner, in charge of Episcopal work in North Carolina; Dr. [Calvin A.] Duncan, synodical missionary of the Synod of Tennessee; Dr. [Charles F.] Allen, Piedmont College, Demorest, Georgia; Dr. George T. Winston, former president of A. and M. College of North Carolina.

3. ODC note: For a little while it seemed possible that Mr. Bay, on a trip home to Denmark, would gather data on the schools which might be applicable to the mountains. Unfortunately—to John's great disappointment—he was taken ill and could not finish the work.

4. "The discovery of old English ballads in Appalachia was based on the work of Francis J. Child at Harvard College. . . . The Child collection was actually based on secondary sources, rather than direct fieldwork in Britain." Arthur Krim, "Appalachian Songcatcher: Olive Dame Campbell and the Scotch-Irish Ballad," *Journal of Cultural Geography* (Fall–Winter 2006): 92. Francis James Child collected traditional ballads from England and Scotland and their American variants during the second half of the nineteenth century. See Francis James Child, ed., *The English and Scottish Popular Ballads,* 5 vols. (Boston: Houghton, 1882–1898).

5. Cecil J. Sharp, about whom there is much more in later chapters, was a distinguished scholar, a collector of English and Scottish ballads, and a collaborator with Olive Dame Campbell in the publication of *English Folk Songs from the Southern Appalachians* (New York: Putnam, 1917). "The Campbell ballad survey provides a working data base of some thirty-nine songs located by place of origin and singer to map a music geography of the Appalachian ballad in the early twentieth century." Krim, "Appalachian Songcatcher," 92.

6. Harlan Paul Douglass was a minister, a mission administrator, and a social scientist. The AMA was established by abolitionists to support schools for African Americans and "other minorities," including mountaineers. He wrote on the issue of social problems, including *The New Home Missions: An Account of Their Social Redirection* (New York: Missionary Education Movement of the United States and Canada, 1914); and, with Edmund deS. Brunner, *The Protestant Church as a Social Institution* (New York: Harper, 1935), in which they discuss religious education in mission schools (167–68) and the phases that the church goes through: "from the social gospel in 1911–13, romantic pacifism in 1914–16 . . . to a kind of apocalyptic mysticism in 1930 until now" (311).

7. ODC note: That is, swimming with the men. See chapter 4.

8. See Walter L. Fleming, *Civil War and Reconstruction in Alabama* (New York: Columbia University Press, 1905).

9. George Lyman Kittredge was a literary scholar, a graduate of Harvard University, and a professor of English literature there for many years. Though renowned for Shakespeare and English literature scholarship, he had an ongoing interest in ballads, as Francis James Child was his mentor at Harvard. Kittredge was also a dedicated folklorist and was instrumental in encouraging the collection of folk songs and folklore in America as well as England, often contributing articles to the *Journal of American Folklore.* See Clyde Kenneth Hyder, *George Lyman Kittredge: Teacher and Scholar* (Lawrence: University of Kansas Press, 1962).

10. John Avery Lomax became interested in cowboy ballads when he first heard them near the Chisholm Trail in Bosque County, Texas. He graduated from the University of Texas in 1897 and later attended Harvard University. His book *Cowboy Songs* was first published in 1910 and introduced standards such as "Home on the Range." See *Cowboy Songs and Other Frontier Ballads* (New York: Macmillan, 1922).

11. Dr. Wickliffe Rose of the Peabody Foundation, Dr. James H. Dillard, president of the Anna T. Jeanes Fund and the John F. Slater Fund, and Dr. Hollis Burke Frissell, of the Russell Sage Foundation.

12. Professor Samuel Chiles Mitchell was made president in 1909. He had "unbounded energy" and wanted South Carolina to be involved in the "full current of affairs" in the country. Edwin L. Green, *The History of the University of South Carolina* (Columbia: State, 1916), 131.

13. The Overmountain Men, a ragtag assembly of mountaineers under the leadership of John Sevier and Isaac Shelby, defeated the English at the Battle of King's Mountain. Appalachians are proud of the event, as it validates the contribution of the men of the mountains to the American Revolution. For an analysis of most of the written accounts of the battle, see Michael Lynch, "Creating Regional Heroes: Traditional Interpretations of the Battle of King's Mountain," *Tennessee Historical Quarterly* 68, no. 3 (2009).

14. Thomas Robinson Dawley was the author of a controversial book in which he proposed that the conditions for mill workers in the South were better than those of the farmworkers in the mountains. See *The Child That Toileth Not: The Story of a Government Investigation That Was Suppressed* (New York: Gracia, 1912).

15. Penny Messinger's 1998 dissertation at Ohio State University, "Leading the Field of Mountain Work: The Conference of Southern Mountain Workers, 1913–1950," describes the conception: "In 1912, John C. Campbell contacted veteran mountain workers . . . that would organize 'an interdenominational confederation of mountain workers.' . . . In their attempted reforms and in their occupations, the Appalachian reformers closely resembled Progressives in other parts of the country" (40). David E. Whisnant elaborates on the work of the CSMW in depth in the chapter "Workers in God's Grand Division: The Council of the Southern Mountains," in his *Modernizing the Mountaineer: People, Power, and Planning in Appalachia* (Knoxville: University of Tennessee Press, 1994), 3–39. See also the chapter "Southern Highlands, 1908–1917," in *Russell Sage Foundation, 1907–1946,* by John M. Glenn, Lilian Brandt, and F. Emerson Andrews (New York: Russell Sage Foundation, 1947), 2:115–24.

6. The Southern Highland Division: Beginnings

1. After the fire that destroyed the Hindman school, there was disagreement between Katherine Pettit and May Stone about how and whether the school should be rebuilt. Raising the money was problematic, and Pettit was hoping to work with children she saw more than a few hours a day, perhaps in a boarding school. Stoddart, *Challenge and Change in Appalachia,* 70–71.

2. Dr. James Stucky was a specialist in eye diseases, and trachoma was very prevalent in the mountains, owing to lack of cleanliness and lack of treatment. At the urging of Linda Neville, a local mountain worker, he held a clinic at Hindman in 1911, which received a

huge response—two days with a steady stream of local patients. Stoddart, *Challenge and Change in Appalachia*, 75–77.

3. Articles in professional journals appeared around this time regarding the extensive work of Red Cross nurses. One reported that visiting nurses in sixty-one communities reported 10,286 cases receiving care and a total of 112,836 visits. See Fannie F. Clement, RN, "The Red Cross," *American Journal of Nursing* 17, no. 6 (1917): 515.

4. Protestant missionaries could not understand why Mormons would have nothing to do with the missions they were establishing in the Southwest. "They had rejected Christian civilization for the 'dark,' 'corrupt,' and 'foreign' religion and society of their desert Zion." See Mark T. Banker, *Presbyterian Missions and Cultural Interaction in the Far Southwest, 1850–1950* (Chicago: University of Illinois Press, 1993), 35.

5. ODC note: Pupil simply paying his way, and not doing any work.

6. Willis Duke Weatherford founded the racially integrated summer school near Black Mountain, North Carolina, in an effort to improve race relations in the South. See Andrew McNeil Canady, "The Limits to Improving Race Relations in the South: The YMCA Blue Ridge Assembly at Black Mountain, North Carolina, 1906–1930," *North Carolina Historical Review* 86, no. 4 (2009): 404–36.

7. ODC note: Principal of the Presbyterian USA Normal and Collegiate Institute in Asheville, North Carolina.

8. The Progressive Era reforms, supported and promoted by presidents Theodore Roosevelt and Woodrow Wilson, included a "country life movement," promoting the application of urban social reform plans to rural regions. Such plans often involved sociological surveys such as Campbell's, to provide evidence that there was a need for change. Religious advocates of the "social gospel" came into conflict with the more traditional religious organizations, such as the Women's Board of Home Missions in the Presbyterian Church, who argued for the separation of religious concerns from those they believed belonged to government. Dr. Warren H. Wilson was superintendent of the Country Life Department of the Presbyterian Church, USA, and ran head-on into the rift. There are myriads of sources on the controversy, including Jeffrey L. Gall, "Presbyterians, Warren Wilson, and the Country Life Movement," *Journal of Presbyterian History* 76, no. 3 (1998): 215–31; Merwin Swanson, "The 'Country Life Movement' and the American Churches," *Church History* 46, no. 3 (1977): 358–73; and Warren H. Wilson, *The Evolution of the Country Community: A Study in Religious Sociology* (Boston: Pilgrim Press, 1912).

9. In the early part of the twentieth century, the survey was a relatively new technique used to attack social problems by proving that there was a need for change: hence, John Campbell's survey of the Southern Highlands. Warren Wilson and the leaders of the country life movement were an active part of this "progressive phenomenon." Wilson's dissertation at Columbia University in New York, "Quaker Hill: A Rural Sociological Study," was the "first rural community survey." Swanson, "Country Life Movement," 364.

10. In his autobiography, Dr. Thompson explained that the increase of a strong social emphasis in the home missions "awakened a good deal of criticism among men of limited vision." Opponents of the Country Life Department's concerns complained that it was "interfering with secular and political matters which must not be tolerated." Quoted in Robert T. Handy, "Charles L. Thompson: Presbyterian Architect of Cooperative Presbyteri-

anism," *Journal of the Presbyterian Historical Society* (1943–1961), 33, no. 4 (1955): 222. It should be noted that at the time of his resignation, after a lifetime of distinguished service, Dr. Thompson was seventy-five years old.

7. The Southern Highland Division's Widening Field

1. For fifty years, Katherine Bennett was at the forefront of the changing status of women in the Presbyterian Church. She became president of the Women's Board of Home Missions in 1909. By the 1920s, under her leadership, Presbyterian women were making plans to change their emphasis on mission schools as public schools became more prevalent, to broaden their forms of service, and to enlist more women in church work. See Katherine Bennett and Margaret Hodge, *Causes of Unrest among the Women of the Church* (Philadelphia: Presbyterian Church in the U.S. General Council, 1927), 19. See also Lois A. Boyd, *Presbyterian Women in America: Two Centuries of a Quest for Status* (Westport, CT: Greenwood Press, 1983), 59.

2. ODC note: Mr. Shelby M. Harrison, director of the Department of Surveys and Exhibits, Russell Sage Foundation.

3. ODC note: George Peabody College.

4. Patterson School is in Happy Valley, Caldwell County, NC, and the Reverend Hugh A. Dobbin was appointed principal of the school in 1914. See Reverend E. N. Joyner, "Down in Happy Valley," *Spirit of Missions*, February 1918, 121–23.

8. Ballads Added—Part I

1. The Rev. William E. Gardner, DD, was secretary of the General Board of Religious Education of the Protestant Episcopal Church. *Cooperation in Christian Education: Report of the Commission on Christian Education, Federal Council of Churches of Christ in America* (New York: Missionary Education Movement, 1917), 6:164.

9. Ballads Added—Part II

1. ODC note: Out of print. The Campbell collection is at the John C. Campbell Folk School, Brasstown, North Carolina, which donated it to the Southern Historical Collection at UNC.

2. Maude Karpeles, an ethnomusicologist, was Sharp's biographer and literary executor, as well as a collaborator and close friend. The entry on Cecil Sharp in the *Oxford Dictionary of National Biography* notes that she "assisted Sharp in demonstrations and accompanied him on collecting expeditions, and in 1913 became his amanuensis, effectively taking up residence in his household; she lived there for twenty years." She published *Cecil Sharp*, with A. H. Fox Strangways (London: Oxford University Press, 1933; 2nd ed., 1955); a revised edition, published in 1967, was titled *Cecil Sharp: His Life and Work*.

3. This was Jane Hicks Gentry, a well-known ballad singer and storyteller who ran a boarding house for teachers in Hot Springs so that she could send her children next door to the Dorland Institute, a Presbyterian school. A historical marker in front of her last home, Sunnybank, attests to the fact that Cecil Sharp visited her many times. See Betty N. Smith, *Jane Hicks Gentry: A Singer among Singers* (Lexington: University Press of Kentucky, 1998), 6–7.

4. Professor C. Alphonso Smith of the University of Virginia was a professor of balladry and well known as a collector. Some of his findings were published in a series of articles, "The Traditional Ballad in the South," by Reed Smith in the *Journal of the American Folklore Society,* vols. 27 and 28, 1914–1915.

10. Fifth Conference and Ballads

1. Sir Horace Plunkett was internationally famous owing to his influence on the economic development in Ireland by advocating and eventually bringing about agricultural cooperation between the Irish government and the Irish farmer. His brief biography can be found in "Sir Horace Plunkett," in *Great Irish Lives: An Era in Obituaries* (London: Collins, 2008),   http://0–0-search.credoreference.com.wncln.wncln.org.wncln.wncln.org/content/ entry/collinsglirish/ sir_horace_plunkett/0.

2. ODC note: Rollin Lynde Hartt.

3. Ives, Kentucky, is the location of Alice Lloyd College. Marshall Vaughan was secretary of Berea College.

11. War Work

1. ODC note: *English Folk Songs from the Southern Appalachians,* by Olive Dame Campbell and Cecil J. Sharp (New York: G. P. Putnam's Sons, 1917).

2. Citing the inability of the railroad system to handle the extraordinary increasing demands for war supplies, President Woodrow Wilson recommended that Congress address the problem. Under the Adamson Act, the government nationalized the nation's railroads. See Walker D. Hines, *War History of American Railroads* (New Haven, CT: Yale University Press, 1928), 5–7.

3. ODC note: Miss Canterbury is Edith R. Canterbury, later to become Mr. Campbell's secretary.

4. ODC note: Rev. Park W. Fisher, who was later secured for such service.

Index